Behavioural Finance

Behavioural Finance

William Forbes

A John Wiley and Sons, Ltd, Publication

Library of Congress Cataloging-in-Publication Data

Forbes, William, 1959–
  Behavioural finance / William Forbes.
    p. cm.
  Includes bibliographical references and index.
  ISBN 978-0-470-02804-9 (pbk.)
  1. Investments—Psychological aspects. 2. Investments—Decision making. I. Title.
  HG4515.15.F68 2009
  332.601'9—dc22

                                                                    2009009685

A catalogue record for this book is available from the British Library.

Set in 9/11pt Sabon by Integra Software Services Pvt. Ltd, Pondicherry, India
Printed in Great Britain by TJ International, Padstow, Cornwall

Contents

Preface

When I began drafting my book in the middle of 2007 I viewed it as an exercise to bring together knowledge in a field of increasing importance in the academic discipline of finance. As I finish off the manuscript in early 2009 the full magnitude of the recent financial crisis and its real economic impact is becoming woefully clear. We have been forced to ask the 'Masters of the Universe' in our major financial institutions, 'If you're so rich, why aren't you smart?' Perhaps the reason is the basic propagation mechanisms underlying the crisis are ones we all share and from which it is difficult to become immune. In his commentary on the financial crisis, *The Subprime Solution*, Robert Shiller, a towering figure in behavioural finance, writes

> The subprime crisis was essentially psychological in nature as are all bubbles.... It was caused by a failure to anticipate quite obvious risks

> (Shiller 2008, p.24).

This book examines how we might effectively model the psychological foundations of financial decision making and its impact on asset pricing and financial makers more generally. I have deliberately kept the coverage broad in order to provide an overview of the emergent field of behavioural finance. Readers eager to attain a deeper knowledge of asset pricing in particular should swiftly move on to Hersh Shefrin's book, *A Behavioral Approach to Asset Pricing* (2005). While those seeking an ever broader behavioural perspective on economic questions in general, as opposed to financial issues alone, may want to read Cass Sunstein and Richard Thaler's *Nudge* (2008).

For those of you who do bravely take the plunge into studying this book, or teaching it to your students, I hope you share my joy in discovering how a behavioural approach to financial decision making can add value to standard finance. Recently Werner De Bondt has commented that behavioural finance has now branched out far from its original founding fathers' intentions. Each of us constructs our own behavioural tradition. Researchers differ both in their research methods and the range of questions they regard worthy of study. In this book I have kept largely to modelling strategies that those trained in economics will feel comfortable with. However, outside this book's bounds lie an array of research traditions making more extensive use of psychological, sociological and anthropological research methods. This work is less frequently taught in finance classes, but the current financial crisis has exposed our ignorance and may make us humble enough to consider a broader research agenda. In this sense my book is a summary of both a rapidly growing field of research and a reflection of a discipline about to rupture as new ideas and research methods are imported from the broader social sciences.

Certainly structuring a readable book has forced me to make choices. So I privilege noise-trader models over models based on representative agents. I include a chapter on analysts' behaviour, but little on takeovers or initial public offerings, both topics of many important papers in behavioural finance. These choices reflect the author's ignorance of some areas as against others, but they also reflect a way of structuring and understanding the literature that works for me. I hope readers will find my choice and arrangement of the literature helps them understand it. If they do not I hope they will contact me and tell me how to improve my exposition. For now I return to researching financial decisions using the behavioural tradition outlined in this book.

Reference

Shefrin, H. (2005). *A Behavioral Approach to Asset Pricing*. New York: Elsevier.

Acknowledgements

When I was approached to write a book about behavioural finance for students I felt very acutely aware of my own ignorance of the area. Trying to look back on the process I am convinced of Neil Armstrong's comment on the men who first walked on the moon: 'Obviously anyone who was smart refused to do it.' The learning curve in writing this book has been very steep. I can only hope that some part of what I learned in writing the book conveys itself to the reader. In particular I hope some of my joy in writing and researching in the behavioural tradition comes over in the text.

It is traditional to thank the love of your life last in the list of helpful friends and collaborators. I hope my friends will forgive me if I first thank my wife Sue as co-conspirator and encourager of all my projects. This book has been the latest, but hopefully not the last, in the list. Amongst others who encouraged me along the way first place must go to my co-author and teacher Professor Len Skerratt. He encouraged me to write the book and was a constant source of good advice along the way.

It was in December 1995, by means of an introduction of a mutual friend, Professor John Wilde, that I first met Werner De Bondt (of De Bondt and Thaler fame). At that time I had only a vague idea of what behavioural finance was and no desire at all to write a book about it. The fact I did write the book owes much to Werner's inspiration and at many points in the book I have been conscious of making free use of his ideas in my own work. I hope he will forgive me and give me an opportunity to repay him partly.

My friends and colleagues Patricia Chelly-Steely, Jerry Coakley, Jo Danbolt, Darren Duxbury, Robert Hudson, James Montier, David Power and Andrew Woods read and commented on various drafts of the book. I thank them and hope the finished product is not too much of a disappointment. A number of excellent graduate students have suffered as I developed the ideas in the book and made them the guinea pigs for working out my ideas. I would like to thank Dina Constantinos, Ahmed El-Galfy, Mohamed Sheriff, Rexon Nting, George Yiannopoulos and Wei Kang Wang for their patience in working with me as I developed my interest in behavioural finance.

At John Wiley I would like to thank Steve Hardman for asking me to write the book and his colleagues Anneli Mockett and Nicole Burnett for their constant support. Finally, I thank my colleagues at Loughborough Business School, especially Irene Moody, for help during the writing of this book and in my work in general.

Chapter 1

Introduction

‘I doubt whether we are sufficiently attentive to the importance of elementary textbooks ’

(Lewis 1944).

This book aims to help guide advanced undergraduates and Master's degree students to an understanding of the currently topical area of 'behavioural' finance. It provides an interpretative lens on a huge and growing literature. As such it can at best be a good departure point, but never a good place of rest. As the opening quotation from Clive Staples Lewis implies, a textbook can be both helpful or even dangerous and corrupting in setting the context for future understanding and research. I hope my book helps students understand and be excited about the behavioural approach to finance.

'Behavioural finance' denotes the study of finance based on credible assumptions about how people behave, often confirmed by psychology experiments such as those by the 2002 Nobel Prize-winners Vernon Smith and Daniel Kahneman.[1] The first sentence of Shefrin's (2005) book on behavioural asset pricing states 'Behavioral finance is the study of how psychological phenomena impact financial behavior'. In reading most standard finance teaching texts one is struck by the way in which any human drama, the greed, eccentricity or caprice of market participants has been purged. As Thaler (1993, p.xv) points out, anyone reading about the tumult and avarice of financial markets, or watching it unfold on television, might be quite perplexed about how its activities could be illuminated by the neoclassical economic theory which dominates academic journals.

While the behavioural perspective was initially presented as a challenge, or an alternative to, traditional finance based in neoclassical economics, a process of assimilation into our existing corpus of theory is now well underway. Thaler (1999) has declared the 'end of behavioural finance', for as he asks 'what other sort of finance is there?'. Finance theory, like any other form of economic theory, requires some explicit assumptions about how investors' decisions are made, how they evaluate the risks facing them, etc. The only difference between behavioural and traditional approaches to finance lies in the explicit recognition of the need to ground theoretical innovations of financial decision making in an understanding of how decisions are actually made. Indeed, the attempt to decant human behaviour into the one-size-fits-all portrayal of 'economic man' may be seen as a detour from the tradition of the founding fathers of economics of whom Hayek (1946, p.14) states,

> In their view man was by nature lazy and indolent, improvident and wasteful, and it was only by the force of circumstances that he could be made to behave economically or carefully to adjust his means to his ends.

So man, far from being rational and goal orientated by nature, is only coerced into feigning to be so by the discipline of markets. Adam Smith, the founding father of modern economics, placed such emphasis on the philosophical and psychological aspects of choice that he explored them more fully in his early work *The Theory of Moral Sentiments*, prior to writing his masterpiece *The Wealth of Nations* (1776). The spurning of psychological insights by the early neoclassical economists may be seen as a consequence of the rather unscientific and speculative nature of the subject at that time. If a coherent body of experimental evidence on human choices had then existed (as later developed by Professors Plott, Kahneman, Tversky, Smith and others), the path taken by neoclassical economics and its child, traditional/neoclassical finance, might have been very different (see Camerer & Lowenstein 2004).

Recently De Bondt (2008) has contrasted 'introverted' standard finance with its focus on hypothesis generation from the logically coherent structure of neoclassical economics with its 'extrovert' behavioural alternative. In the behavioural perspective facts drive a renewal of theory or the creation of new theory. So in the behavioural approach:

> Research methods are mainly *inductive* not deductive. We collect facts based either on experiments, or questionnaires, or observation – and we organize them into a smaller number of super-facts. One might say we draw maps

> (De Bondt, 2008).

Such maps are now much needed given the 'financial tsunami' unfolding as I complete this book. In an appendix to this chapter I briefly consider how the current crisis might give us pause to reflect on the need for a modelling framework which better captures the human frailties in decision making that we are all subject to.

1.1 Illustration and Structure

To begin at the ending of this book (or at least Chapter 19) consider the collapse of Arthur Andersen the accounting firm, following it being debarred from filing accounts under the Securities and Exchange Commission's rule 2(e). Andersen's downfall contains many of the classic causes of cognitive errors that I shall be discussing in this book. I draw here on Gerstein's (2008) account of the crisis.

Andersen's started out as a prestigious, Chicago-based, audit firm led by auditors of high moral rectitude. Indeed, Leonard Spacek, who succeeded the founder Andersen as managing partner in 1947, was threatened with expulsion from the profession because of his public denouncement of declining audit standards.

With its innovative use of computers, then a novelty, in running General Electric's pay-roll system in the early 1950s, Andersen's developed an acknowledged expertise in systems audit and management information systems in general. This subset of partner expertise soon spawned the wildly popular Andersen Consulting, today called Accenture. By the recession of the early 1990s a large chunk of the partnership's total revenue came from Andersen Consulting and it was only granted independence following an agreement to pass 15% of its revenue to its poorer audit-based relations. The message was clear, an audit partner who wanted a decent salary made sure his clients were happy enough with what they were getting on the audit side to retain Andersen Consulting for other business needs, such as tax advice, corporate strategy and information systems. Rocking the boat by challenging accounting practices was not the way forward. Lowballing and cosy lunches with partners were normal.

Over the years Andersen's audit practice was challenged on a number of occasions in the courts by shareholders left penniless when their investments in Andersen audit corporations imploded without warnings from the published accounts. Such scares included Waste Management, Sunbeam and Global Crossing, but Enron was to be the hole that sunk the Andersen boat.

Enron had caused alarm by adopting a number of opaque, but possibly 'aggressive', accounting practices, including the adoption and widespread use of mark-to-market accounting to record trading profits in assets with no liquid market and consolidation of a pyramid of subsidiaries into special-purpose entities. These had not gone unchallenged or unnoticed by Andersen partners. But nothing was done because the total revenue on the Enron account was just too tempting. In fact, Carl Bass, a member of Andersen's Professional Standards Committee, was removed from their audit at Andrew Fastow's request (Fastow, now in jail, was CFO of Enron and perhaps the fall guy for many others seeking to avoid blame).

The collapse of Andersen contains three elements that are central to the discussion of financial markets in this book. These are:

- *Optimism.* Giving fee-revenue chasing priority over integrity strategy had worked so far, challenges were usually settled out of court without Andersen admitting any blame.
- *A focus on the near-term maximization of fee revenue.* Professional integrity was clearly a very important issue but by implication it was something that could be addressed later.
- *Conformity.* Whistle-blowers were not welcome and even bad practice could be justified with an 'everybody is at it' shrug.

All three elements will feature in later chapters of this book. In Section 1.2 I open the discussion of behavioural finance by emphasizing what finance theory does rather than says. That is, I focus on the use of behavioural approaches to motivate new trading strategies and seek out new arbitrage opportunities. In Section 1.3 I look at the challenge ahead for behavioural finance theorists and those who will rise to the challenge of testing those theories. I also briefly enquire whether we would be starting from here if the founding fathers of economics and finance understood what we now know about how the brain works and how it sets about deciding what to do. In Section 1.4 I return to the foundational assumptions of our subject to see how a behavioural finance research programme might steer a different, and perhaps more useful, course for finance as a subject. Finally, having looked at the challenge ahead, I turn to more immediate business and explain how I plan to cover the vast ground of behavioural finance research. Section 1.5 gives a taster of some of the areas in finance where a behavioural approach has been most fruitful, but the field is rapidly expanding to give a behavioural perspective on the whole subject of finance. Section 1.6 outlines the rest of the structure of the book and indicates how I structure the huge body of scholarship in this field.

1.2 Finance Theory as an Engine not a Camera

We can see the emergence of behavioural finance as reflecting a broader tension in economic analysis between those who regard assumptions as simply tools to generate accurate predictions and those who worry that unless our theory reflects an underlying economic and social reality it may lead us into great error (see MacKenzie, 2006 from which my discussion derives).

The definitive statement of MacKenzie's view is Milton Friedman's essay 'The Methodology of Positive Economics' in which he states,

> A hypothesis is important if it 'explains' much by little ... if it abstracts from the mass of complex and detailed circumstances and permits valid predictions on the basis of them alone. To be important, therefore, a hypothesis must be descriptively false in its assumptions

(Friedman 1953, p.14).

This has long been the orthodoxy amongst economic theorists. But from its initial proclamation there has been doubt about its validity even amongst Friedman's peers of Nobel Prize-winning economists. Thus Paul Samuelson expressed concern in his speech accepting the third Nobel Prize awarded in Economics. He argued in response to Friedman's doctrine that it was

> fundamentally wrong that unrealism in the sense of factual inaccuracy even to a tolerable degree of approximation is anything other than a demerit for a theory or a hypothesis...Some inaccuracies are worse than others, but that is only to say some sins against empirical science are worse than others, not that sin is a merit

> (Samuelson 1963, p.223).

MacKenzie (2006) points to another problem of trying to construct a theory that explains the observed stylized facts about trading in financial markets. Usually we see data taken from financial markets as a way of refuting received theory, be that behavioural or standard theory. But what if investment practice reflects a dominant or widely accepted theoretical model such that traded prices reflect that model's insights? What if traders have the Black–Scholes formula for option pricing embedded into the spreadsheets they use for issuing quotes? Then a finding that the pricing of traded option prices is consistent with the Black–Scholes equation is not surprising. Similarly the rapid growth of 'value investment' strategies and mutual funds specializing in such strategies makes evaluating 'buy losers/sell winners' (De Bondt & Thaler 1985) strategies hard to evaluate. This problem arises because finance theory is often an 'engine' for financial innovation and the refinement of new trading strategies as opposed to simply being a 'camera' which captures the complexity of real financial markets in miniature. So acceptance of behavioural perspectives on financial markets may change the data on which those models are subsequently tested.

Major apparent falsifications of existing models can lead practitioners into a search for more adequate theorizations of their trading position's value. MacKenzie (2006, p.33) discusses how the 1987 Crash resulted in a movement away from the Black–Scholes formulation of how derivatives are priced as a volatility skew or 'smile' emerged. The implosion of equity values at the start of this century may have induced such an openness to new theoretical ideas. Behavioural perspectives offer one new possible source of competitive advantage through the insights gained by a novel theorization of how markets operate.

Before rushing to compete, or replace, standard finance models based on Friedmanite unrealistic assumptions, with behavioural assumptions derived from what we know about how investors actually choose between alternatives, a word of caution is worthwhile. Hayek points out the very 'scientific' nature of our economic reasoning, based on conjectures and their potential refutability by data, may not be entirely a safe point of departure. Economics as a distinct branch of social enquiry dates back to an age when the various areas and types of study were far more loosely defined. So terms like 'moral science' and 'political economy' abounded and laying claim to a 'scientific' approach to economic problems was not seen as something to be aspired to. It is only in the nineteenth century that the idea that valuable research was 'scientific' in nature took hold. Hayek warns (1945, p.14):

> The methods which scientists or men fascinated with natural science have so often tried to force on social sciences were not necessarily those that scientists followed in their own field, but rather those that they believed they employed. This is not necessarily the same thing.

Hayek points out a very important difference between how scientific research proceeds and what we might require of a successful interpretation of economic and social phenomena, for example trading in an asset to determine its price.

The world in which Science is interested is not that of our given sensations. Its aim is to produce a new organization of all our experience of the external world, and in doing so it has not only to remodel our concepts, but also get away from the sense qualities and replace them by a different classification of events

(Hayek 1955, p.23).

For the physical sciences it is incredibly useful to detach what is happening from what we perceive or sense as happening. Hayek states the method of the physical sciences as follows (1955, p.22):

What men know or think about the external world or about themselves, their concepts and even their subjective qualities of their sense perceptions are to Science never ultimate reality, data to be accepted. Its concern is not what men think about the world, but what they ought to think.

This dismissal of the importance of the sensation of trading and interacting with others trading the same asset poses a real problem for a behavioural theory of asset pricing. But more importantly it may simply be that any coherent theory of behaviour in financial markets would face very similar problems. For Hayek the correct object of study of a 'social science' like finance is a far larger domain than most scientists show any interest in. He states (1955, p.24):

The question here is not how far man's picture of the external world fits the facts, but how by his actions, determined by his views and concepts he possesses, man builds up another world of which the individual becomes a part. And by 'the views and concepts people hold' we do not mean merely their knowledge of external nature. We mean all the knowledge and belief about themselves, about other people, and the external world, in short everything that determines their actions, including science itself.

In such a broader mission for gaining an understanding of financial markets the marriage of psychological insights and financial modelling may yet prove especially fruitful.

1.2.1 Rational Fools or Folly of Wisdom?

The very desirability of rationality as a human characteristic has not always been in doubt. Jensen (1998) contrasts what he calls the REMM (resourceful evaluative maximizing model) of human behaviour which characterizes economics at its best with the 'social victim model' of a more socio-logical tradition. The REMM model assumes humans:

- care/evaluate;
- have unlimited wants;
- maximize their well-being;
- are resourceful and creative in seeking out their best interest.

In the social victim model of human behaviour, which Jensen beliefs characterizes the approach of sociologists, actions are largely constrained/determined by social class, family background or genetic make-up.

Hayek has observed that the beauty of the price allocation mechanism lies in its ability to aggregate information about tastes and desires, which no government official could ever dream to possess. He praises the market allocation system as follows:

> The most significant fact about the market process is the economy of knowledge with which it operates, or how little the individual participants need to know in order to be able to take the right action

> (Hayek 1945, p.86).

Hence far from feeling the need to rescue investors from the rough and tumble of financial markets, we should in many ways rejoice that the market requires much less mental agility than competing allocative mechanisms.

If individual investors can fall victim to optimism how much more likely is it that politicians, basking in the glories of office, will equally be exposed to optimism if not hubris. So the behavioural approach does not give blanket support for 'big government' interventions to correct investors' mistakes, but it does suggest a role for education in reducing the worst excesses of investor bias, narrow 'framing' and speculative frenzy. It is to facilitate this learning process that the current textbook has been written. I also reflect on a form of 'liberal paternalism' which seeks to structure the way choices are made to favour some choices over others, i.e. not to smoke or to remember that even though you are young you will (hopefully) retire one day and need a pension (Sunstein 2005, Sunstein & Thaler 2003a,b).

If the liberal REMM characterization of human behaviour underpins much economic analysis it is important to be aware of its weaknesses before proceeding to exploit its strengths. A clear weakness of the REMM model is that it gives little role to the intentional or meaningful nature of conduct in many human behaviours. Action is driven by immediate perceived social gain rather than some moral or social ideal, which the person executing the action seeks to attain.

This sort of reasoning displays its most grotesque aspect in extremist sociobiologists' views of how we evolve. Elster (1984) points out that while natural selection explains the emergence of favourable mutations, via the greater progeny of those subject to a beneficial chance mutation, it cannot explain strategies based on either waiting or indirect advantage.

Since natural selection is spawning an imperfect tribe it is not clear that the correct way to develop an understanding of humanity is through a gradually refined 'scientific' understanding. As Rousseau warned back in 1754:

> The best use one can make of Philosophy is to have it destroy the evils it has given birth to . . . It is true we would not know anything then, but we would agree upon that in good faith, and in our search for truth we would have taken all the steps backwards from error to ignorance.

In this spirit, an understanding of some of the most prominent aspects of behavioural finance may make us more aware of the fragility of our understanding of financial decisions. By doing so we may hope to retrace a path backwards from arrogant errors made by earlier academics towards a more modest assessment regarding our ignorance concerning financial matters.

Any rational act reflects both the beliefs and desires of those undertaking it. Hence a judgement concerning the rationality of the act requires some consistency in the beliefs and desires it is based upon (Elster 1986). David Hume pointed out that reason is a good slave, but a poor master, and it would be a tedious individual who sought to rationalize his or her every desire. Indeed, economists have typically been very keen to draw a veil over any discussion of consumer or investor preferences (Stigler & Becker 1977). Nevertheless one may perceive that certain actions motivated by greed or spite are suggestive of irrational, or at least unattractive, desires. Further, in some situations being rational may be self-defeating. To calculate when to perform a spontaneous act of kindness or generosity for a loved one seems to be missing the point. If I concentrate on not stuttering or blushing when I meet someone I find attractive I may simply make the problem worse. The benefits of intuition cannot be reaped in a calculative manner.

Differentiating irrationality from action based on false beliefs is always difficult. Invading a hostile country in the belief that it harbours weapons of mass destruction may seem irrational after the event. But it may have seemed a quite rational act at the time given the (now proved false) intelligence regarding that hostile nation's military capability (Elster 1989).

1.3   Rebuilding on New Foundations

The construct of 'economic man' embedded in traditional finance incorporates at least (see Rabin 2002, p.600) the following assumptions:

- Investors have well-defined stable preferences, even if those preferences themselves are never explained or challenged.
- Investors base their preferences between choices on expected outcomes (not changes in expected outcomes).
- Investors maximize their own (or their families') well-being, or 'utility'.
- Investors discount expected payoffs by geometrically increasing amounts to obtain their present value. So one pound, or one euro, paid next year is worth $1/(1 + r)$, where r is the annual discount rate, and a pound or euro, in two years' time is worth $1/(1 + r)^2$ and so on.

The primary interests that motivate behavioural researchers are reflected in the structure of this book. After an initial focus on asset pricing the text moves forward to consider problems in corporate finance. In a final section, more recent applications of behavioural insights within the professional life of lawyers and accountants are considered.

The behavioural tradition enriches our understanding by incorporating at least three elements of psychological insight into financial decisions:

- The presence of biases in investors' decision making. For example, optimism, conservatism in adapting one's judgement to contradictory evidence and 'overreaction' to exciting, but rare, events.
- The use of mental 'frames' to simplify complex decisions or learning 'heuristics' to characterize and simplify data used in decision making.
- The presence of time inconsistency in choice, inducing a need to distinguish between the 'planner' and 'doer' of some proposed course of action.

In doing this finance scholars have often drawn on prior experimental evidence from the field of cognitive psychology. Only an exceptional polymath could claim understanding of both finance and cognitive psychology. So we are fortunate that many of the relevant seminal contributions of psychologists to our understanding of financial decisions are drawn together in various collected readings (Gilovich *et al.* 2002, Kahneman *et al.* 1982, Kahneman & Tversky 2000, Lichenstein & Slovic 2006, Shafir 2004, Slovic 2000). I will draw heavily on these sources below.

It is cautionary to recall that:

> The economist may attempt to ignore psychology, but it is sheer impossibility for him to ignore human nature . . . . If the economist borrows his conception of man from the psychologist, his constructive work may have some chance of remaining purely economic in character. But if he

does not, he will not thereby avoid psychology. Rather, he will force himself to make his own, and it will be bad psychology

(Clark 1918).[2]

So one objective in this text is to present behavioural finance models in the context of psychological research which supports those models' adoption in favour of the standard finance model.

1.3.1   Reasoned Emotion: The Case of Phineas Gage

Phineas Gage, a work gang supervisor on the railways in 1848, suffered a horrific injury that drove a metal bar through his brain. Miraculously Gage survived and appeared capable of movement, speech, reason, much as before. His doctor, John Harlow, was stunned that Gage had seemingly made a complete recovery. But later it was clear Gage had changed. The savage blow to his brain, which literally blew parts out, had altered him from being a natural leader of men in a hazardous environment into a foul-mouthed quarrelsome brawler. He lost his job and died of seizures at 38 years old. The awful brain injury Gage had suffered obviously left his reason intact but had fundamentally changed his emotional state and hence his personality for the worse. Could it be that the part of the brain which controls our emotions interacts in some fundamental way with that with which we reason? Therefore, impaired, or dysfunctional, emotional well-being damages our ability to reason.

This very argument is advanced by Antonio Damasio, a professor of neuroscience, in his book *Descartes' Error*, from which this horrific story is taken. Damasio and his wife and academic colleague, Hannah, suspected Gage's illness might point the way towards a neurological link between brain functions associated with reason and those usually associated with emotion. While Gage's skull had been exhumed and preserved his brain tissue was lost to his grave. And so Damasio began to look for brain-damaged patients exhibiting loss of emotional control in his practice as a neurosurgeon.

By chance a successful businessman (Damasio calls him 'Elliot'), who was having problems after having a fairly large, but non-malignant, tumour removed from the area behind the bridge of his nose, was referred to him. As with Phineas Gage, the frontal lobe of his brain was damaged by the crushing induced by the growing tumour. Elliot also had been dismissed by his employer due to his inability to focus on required tasks and function independently of others. Unlike Gage he remained well-spoken, polite and even eerily calm as he watched his personal and professional life implode. Damasio (2006, p.45) comments 'Elliot's predicament was to know but not to feel'. Trying to understand this from his professional perspective, Damasio states:

> The brain is not one big lump of neurons doing the same thing wherever they are. The structures destroyed in both Gage and Elliot happened to be those necessary for reasoning to culminate in decision making.

So both Elliot and Phineas Gage could successfully complete the calculus necessary to live a successful life, but something stopped them acting on that calculation. It appeared good reason wasn't enough to induce good, or appropriate, acts. Something else was missing.

Damasio's search to understand the dysfunctional behaviour of his patients with frontal lobe injuries led him to formulate his somatic market hypothesis. This thesis argued that emotion 'marked certain aspects of a decision context, or certain outcomes that could be envisaged as following from the decision'. He states (2006, p.xiii):

> Emotion had a role to play in intuition, the sort of rapid cognitive process in which we come to a particular conclusion without being aware of the particular cognitive steps.

Such speedy decisions may be commonplace on the trading floor or in the pressure cooker environment of negotiating a big acquisition. If this be the case then too prissy a distinction between reason and emotion in financial decisions may have little scientific support.

1.3.2   What Can Psychologists Bring to Finance?

While finance has been built out of the building blocks of neoclassical economic theory, psychology has undergone a period of tumultuous change. Ledoux (1996) describes how the post-war dominance of behaviourism and the later emergence of cognitive science tended to abstract from academic psychology's interest in why people do what they do as opposed to what they choose or how they activate the choice they make. The conscious mind and unconscious drivers or motivations or intrinsic meanings were relegated to the status of the unscientific and perhaps unknowable. At each stage psychology has been keen to differentiate mental process and neurological function. Ultimately the area of artificial intelligence has studied human cognition without recourse to the brain as an organ at all. Ledoux (1996, p.40) casts doubt on the wisdom of dividing up the process of cognition and mental and even physical responses to choices faced in this way. He states:

> Emotions do not evolve as conscious feelings. They evolve as behavioral and physiological specializations, bodily responses controlled by the brain, which allowed ancestral organisms to survive in hostile environments and procreate. If the biological machine of emotion, but not cognition, crucially includes the body, then the kind of machine needed to run emotion is different from the kind needed to run cognition.

In fast-moving financial markets, where fortunes and careers can be swiftly made or lost, such an integration of emotion cognition and physical response is likely to be key to understanding the full picture of how and why decisions are made.

1.4   Challenging the Classical Assumptions of Finance

Traditional finance models incorporate many of the standard classical assumptions of textbook economics including:

- The presence of many buyers and sellers without the ability to influence the prices of assets.
- Investors form their expectations based on full use of available information. This implies that no information currently available to investors can be used to improve their forecast of future price or valuation metrics used in implying price.
- A minimal amount of market 'frictions' distorting the message sent by price regarding the relative willingness of investors to supply or demand the asset.

The second assumption has given rise to a whole new area of research into the 'market micro-structure' of financial markets. This literature illustrates how the very process of discovering price can induce arbitrage opportunities. The field of behavioural finance largely focuses on the first two assumptions of atomistic investors and their rational expectations.

The corpus of work exploring such deviations from classical assumptions is now so voluminous that a number of books (Barberis & Thaler 2003, Shefrin 2002, Thaler 1992[3]) and several review articles (Daniel *et al*. 2002, Thaler 1999) explore various aspects of the insights it offers. A number of collections of readings by leading researchers in the field also gather together key contributions (De Bondt 2005, Thaler 1993). Other sources review the broader field of behavioural economics (Camerer, Lowenstein & Rabin 2004, Hogarth & Reder 1986, Rabin 1998, 2002). I draw extensively on these sources in writing this text. My hope is that this book will quickly lead the reader to a number of these works.

The scale and scope of contributions by those working within the behavioural field is now quite breathtaking. These contributions to our understanding of behaviour in financial markets include:

- The simultaneous presence of continuance of stock returns, or underreaction to past events, and longer term reversals of 'extreme' price movements or overreaction to extreme past events.
- The fact that equity, as a source finance, offers a rate of return to investors way above that which seems commensurate with its risk characteristics.
- The fact that, although most mergers yield a poor return to investors in the bidding firm, their popularity seems never to fade.
- The clear bias present in investment advice offered by analysts, in the form of forecasts of earnings and recommendations whether to buy/sell or hold on to a company's shares.
- The recurring pattern of the stock-market bubble/frenzy and the subsequent spectacular bust in its wake, the October 1989 crash and the late 1990s' dot.com boom in technology stocks being recent illustrations of this pattern.

In reality there can now be few areas in finance in which behavioural researchers have not been active: in the examination of share issues, initial public offerings, mutual fund performance, bond pricing and international finance and many more.

This proliferation in the application of behavioural insights is the natural result of the development of a behavioural tradition from a mode of critique into a part of 'normal science' (Rabin 2002, p.659). As this maturation occurs, it may be useful to see how fairly traditional economic modelling methods can be applied to an understanding of behavioural biases/heuristics in finance.

For this very reason the current text focuses on the presentation of formal theoretical models and emphasizes their implications for investor behaviour. Empirical papers, with all their qualifications and complex econometric methods, are treated in a more cursory manner at the end of each chapter. I also frequently cross-refer to James Montier's text *Behavioural Finance: Insights into Irrational Minds and Markets* (2006).

So this text seeks to explain the basic insights of what is now 'a moderate agnostic approach to studying financial markets' (Thaler 1999, p.12). But this approach should not be taken to imply that there are unambiguous implications of taking a behavioural approach, or a party line which pervades researchers in that field. A belief that recognizing investors 'make mistakes' could be used to justify government intervention may explain the initial aggression of traditional finance scholars to the behavioural approach to financial decision making. But this ignores the possibility that the state itself may aggregate cognitive biases to which its electorate are subject (Kuran & Sunstein 2000).

It may be a particularly apt time to learn such lessons as we gain a critical distance from the millennium boom, which saw stock-market values in the United States increase fivefold during 1996–2000, while market indices in the United Kingdom doubled (see Figure 1.2 in Shiller 2005, p.4). The subsequent halving in stock-market values around the world may give us pause for thought on the frailty of investors' judgements. More recently the 'credit crunch' and subsequent bank bailout of late 2008 reminds us that risk can be poorly assessed or simply just not heeded at all.

1.5 Modelling Behavioural Aspects of Finance

As laboured above, this text skims over a huge literature on behavioural finance. Each advance/research paper has its own peculiarities or peccadilloes, as well as drawing from and feeding into a general theme of research. As students it is useful to focus on broad themes as opposed to unique or idiosyncratic insights of particular contributions. What is quirky or offbeat now may become the orthodoxy later. But first the student needs to understand the orthodox approach, if only to be able to critique and reject it at a later date. For this reason I have made some choices regarding what to present to students reading this text. My book is largely theory driven in its approach and this has been quite a conscious strategy on my part. One reason for this is the presence of many excellent books focusing on the empirical evidence regarding decision biases and seeming deviations from rationality. One such book, mentioned above, is *Behavioural Finance: Insights into Irrational Minds and Markets* (Montier, 2006). James has been kind enough to comment and help me with my own book. So I often cross-reference his text in the 'Illustration and structure' section, at the start of each chapter, where the weakness of my own book is compensated by the strength of his.

In studying the large, complex, literature on behavioural finance at least two contrasting modelling strategies can be identified:

• *Representative agent models*. In this class of models the investment behaviour with a particular type of preference or bias is investigated sometimes under different states of the world (e.g. good and bad market outcomes). All investors are the same and their ability to learn, correct for, certain weaknesses in their decision-making process is studied.
• *Noise trader models*. In these forms of models, two types of investors, informed and uninformed, or smart and dumb traders, meet each other in financial markets. The cognitive errors/bias of the uninformed are policed by the ever-vigilant informed traders and an equilibrium price–quantity outcome results.

This text focuses, at least in its second part on asset pricing, on the latter type of models. Noise trader models follow Hayek in stressing the role of trade in propagating, punishing and hopefully correcting error and bias in asset pricing. As such they emphasize the wisdom of the market over the insight of the individual. This choice allows me to maintain a common modelling structure, which I apply repeatedly to a series of asset market anomalies in the first part. These include the phenomena of:

• optimism;
• asymmetric attitudes to gains and losses (Barberis *et al.* 2001);
• momentum (Barberis & Shleifer 2003);
• overreaction and underreaction to news, especially about company earnings (Daniel *et al.* 1998, Hong & Stein 1999);
• herding (Froot *et al.* 1992).

This limited selection of all-time great papers, which share common theoretical, noise trader, frameworks, allows me to simplify notation and more easily cross-reference or compare and contrast papers. But it is a selection and as such offers a partial, perhaps prejudiced, view to the student. To ameliorate this I try and signpost some of the most obvious gaps in the understanding offered in the main body of each chapter.

1.6   The Structure of the Book

Behavioural finance is currently in the process of rewriting pretty much all that we know about how financial markets work and how investors make decisions. So every contribution is partial and selective. This introductory text focuses on three distinct, but interrelated, areas:

- *Asset pricing*, this is the traditional core of finance and little of the rest makes much sense unless we have a coherent pricing theory for financial assets.
- *Corporate finance*, this takes place within the 'black box' of the corporation and exposes the individual actors who set outputs and subsequently prices.
- *Professional life*, where many of you are hopefully heading, or may currently be gainfully employed.

Within each subtopic too I need to limit my scope, so as not to burden the reader of an introductory text. Topics covered in the book are as follows:

- *Noise traders in financial markets*. In Chapter 6 I give some of the basic mechanics of noise trader models as a way of seeing trading, which I draw heavily upon in this book.
- *Optimism/Overconfidence*. Chapter 7 examines the impact on asset pricing of perhaps the most obvious and gross bias in human cognition. It also gives an opportunity to revisit and build upon the noise trader framework emphasized throughout the book.
- *Prospect theory in asset pricing*. Chapter 8 looks at one of the classic contributions to behavioural finance and gives a flavour of how it is being used in contemporary asset pricing modelling.
- *Overreaction*. Chapter 9 looks at one of the classic applications of behavioural finance to what we see in real markets that results from the idea that investors overweight recent information compared to long-term trends in data. A noise trader framework is once more adopted here.
- *Momentum*. Chapter 10 discusses spotting and profitably using trends in security prices. Simple versions of the efficient market hypothesis suggest such trends should simply not exist, but a behavioural perspective suggests such trends may persist and gives some guide to their possible structure.
- *Herding*. Chapter 11 examines the impact of pressures towards conformity in trading on asset pricing. Once again a noise trader framework is adopted here allowing you to gain confidence in using this approach.
- *Insider trading*. Chapter 12 recognizes that not all traders are equal. How do noise traders become subject to 'noise' while their 'smart' opponents, the informed, are not? In this chapter the noise trader framework is made endogenous and the rewards to becoming informed are characterized. The noise trader approach is further developed and motivation for its use provided.
- *The equity premium*. Chapter 13 uses the prospect theory framework developed in Chapter 8 to explain one of the classic stumbling blocks of standard theory in explaining observed asset prices. Why are equity returns so high, given that they do not seem that much more risky compared to bonds?

The corporate finance treatment of this book is narrower than that afforded the asset pricing literature. So my selection here is even more brutal and open to criticism than in the asset pricing section. So the sparse coverage includes:

- *Incorporation.* In Chapter 14 I argue that the process of incorporation masks the coalition of competing individual interests that motivate a company's decisions. Standard finance has gone within the 'black box' of the corporation using agency theory. Behavioural finance is adding new insights and generating new testable hypotheses in this area too.
- *The market for information.* Chapter 15 focuses on the flow of information between investors and managers, often via analysts employed to research companies or sectors.
- *The dividend decision.* Chapter 16 revisits the return of value to shareholders. Since the return of cash to shareholders gives shares an economic value to shareholders, how the dividend decision is made and how that decision is reflected in prices is central to both asset pricing and how the company is managed to generate shareholder value.
- *Entrepreneurship.* In Chapter 17 I ask where companies come from, who starts them and what are the personal characteristics that allow them to do so.

Omissions here are particularly easy to spot, mergers, initial public offerings, etc. In a final section I consider how you might use the material studied in this book. I give a very brief taste of the implications of a behavioural perspective on professional life for:

- *Analysts.* Chapter 18 looks at the challenges they face in doing a good job and how they should be regulated. In doing this I pass from a positive usage of the behavioural approach towards a normative usage to suggest how a market subject to 'noise' about asset value should be regulated.
- *Accounting.* Chapter 19 asks how the value and implementation of mark-to-market/'fair value' accounting might be affected by the presence of noise traders in the market. Once again I go beyond stating how behavioural bias will impact on markets towards saying how these effects should be controlled by regulatory authorities and professional bodies.

But before launching on this wide array of topics I must tell you some basic principles of the behavioural approach to finance. I do this in the remainder of this first part of the book. In doing this I revisit some of the most basic building blocks of finance. So please be patient, often the biggest problem in our thinking is what we take as given, or beyond all question. The foundational issues I discuss are:

- Expected utility as a measure of investor well-being (Chapter 2).
- Our attitude to the future, relative to present, rewards or how we discount future pay-offs arising from our investments (Chapter 3).
- How we learn to invest well and whether we manage to do so (Chapter 4).
- What we know about major disruptions in financial markets in our history and what we can learn from that history for the future (Chapter 5).

I encourage every reader and teacher to cover these chapters thoroughly, unless the reader is fairly sophisticated (in which case Shefrin (2005) may be a more attractive choice of textbook to study). For the remainder of the material, Chapters 6 to 10 give a basic coverage of the behavioural approach as it relates to asset pricing at least. In a one-semester course this might be more than enough ground to cover. But there is always more to know and often more interesting stuff than I highlight in this introductory treatment. I can only hope my book encourages readers to greater insights than I have been able to offer here.

Appendix: A Financial Tsunami

Since at least August 2007 I have been completing this book as a 'financial tsunami' (Alan Greenspan in evidence to the US Senate in October 2008) unfolds. This gives me hope that my readers may be more open to a new approach to financial modelling. In a case study on this book's webpage I consider how a behavioural perspective might help us understand the current financial (and resulting 'real' economy) crisis and how it may also give pointers towards credible policy responses.

Notes

1. Or the late great Amos Tversky, of Stanford University, whose death in 1996 was surely the only barrier to him sharing the Nobel Prize with Kahneman and Smith. See http://nobelprize.org/nobel_prizes/economics/laureates/2002/index.html.
2. Werner De Bondt, a pioneer researcher, maintains an excellent webpage that gives an introduction to such issues. Professor De Bondt has kept on pioneering and written many interesting papers since his most famous one with Richard Thaler in 1985.
3. Thaler's classic anomalies series in the *Journal of Economic Perspectives* has now run into a second series and is certainly a great starting point for those interested in the field, see http://gsbwww.uchicago.edu/fac/richard.thaler/research/Anomalies.htm.

References

Barberis, N., M. Huang *et al.* (2001). Prospect theory and asset prices. *Quarterly Journal of Economics*, 116(1): 1–53.

Barberis, N. & A. Shleifer (2003). Style investing. *Journal of Financial Economics*, 68(2): 161–99.

Barberis, N. & R. Thaler (2003). A survey of behavioral finance. In G.M. Constantinidis, M. Harris & R.M. Stulz (eds), *Handbook of the Economics of Finance*. New York: Elsevier.

Camerer, C. & G. Lowenstein (2004). Behavioural economics, past, present, future. In C. Camerer, G. Lowenstein & M. Rabin (eds), *Advances in Behavioural Finance*. New York: Russell Sage Foundation.

Camerer, C., G. Lowenstein & M. Rabin (eds) (2004). *Advances in Behavioural Economics*. New York: Russell Sage Foundation.

Clark, J. (1918). Economics and modern psychology. *Journal of Political Economy*, 26 (January): 1–30.

Damasio, A. (2006). *Descartes' Error: Emotions, Reasons and the Human Brain*. London: Vintage.

Daniel, K., D. Hirshleifer *et al.* (1998). Investor psychology and security market under- and overreaction. *Journal of Finance*, 52(3): 1–33.

Daniel, K., D. Hirshleifer *et al.* (2002). Investor psychology in capital markets: evidence and policy implications. *Journal of Monetary Economics*, 49: 139–209.

De Bondt, W. (ed.) (2005). *The Psychology of World Equity Markets*. Cheltenham: Edward Elgar.

De Bondt, W. (2008). *Behavioral Finance: Quo Vadis?* Prague: European Financial Management Association.

De Bondt, W. & R. Thaler (1985). Does the stock market overreact? *Journal of Finance*, 60(3): 793–807.

Elster, J. (1984). Perfect rationality: beyond gradient-climbing. In J. Elster (ed.), *Ulysses and the Sirens: Studies in Rationality and Irrationality*. Cambridge: Cambridge University Press.

Elster, J. (1986). Introduction. In J. Elster (ed.), *Rational Choice: Readings in Social and Political Theory*. New York: New York University Press.

Elster, J. (1989). *Nuts and Bolts for the Social Sciences*. Cambridge: Cambridge University Press.

Friedman, M. (1953). The methodology of positive economics. In M. Friedman (ed.), *Essays in Positive Economics*. Chicago: University of Chicago Press.

Froot, K., D. Scharstein *et al.* (1992). Herd on the street. Informational efficiency in a market short-term speculation. *Journal of Finance*, 47: 1451–84.

Gerstein, M. (2008). *Flirting with Disaster: Why Accidents are Rarely Accidental*. New York: Union Square.

Gilovich, T., D. Griffin *et al.* (eds) (2002). *Heuristics and Biases: The Psychology of Intuitive Judgement*. Cambridge: Cambridge University Press.

Hayek, F. (1945). The use of knowledge in society. In F. Hayek (ed.), *Individualism and Economic Order*. Chicago: University of Chicago Press.

Hayek, F. (1946). Individualism: true and false. In F. Hayek (ed.), *Individualism and Economic Order*. Chicago: University of Chicago Press.

Hayek, F. (1955). The Counter-revolution in Science: Studies on the abuse of reason. New York: Free Press Paperback.

Hogarth, R. & M. Reder (eds) (1986). *Rational Choice: The Contrast between Psychology and Economics*. Chicago: University of Chicago Press.

Hong, H. & J. Stein (1999). A unified theory of underreaction, momentum, trading and overreaction in assets markets. *Journal of Finance*, 54: 2143–84.

Jensen, M. (ed.) (1998). *The Nature of Man: Foundations of Organizational Strategy*. Cambridge, MA: Harvard University Press.

Kahneman, D., P. Slovic *et al.* (eds) (1982). *Judgement under Uncertainty: Heuristics and Biases*. Cambridge: Cambridge University Press.

Kahneman, D. & A. Tversky (eds) (2000). *Choices, Values and Frames*. Cambridge: Cambridge University Press.

Kuran, T. & C. Sunstein (2000). Controlling availability cascades. In C. Sunstein (ed.), *Behavioral Law and Economics* (pp. 374–97), Cambridge: Cambridge University Press.

Ledoux, J. (1996). *The Emotional Brain: The Mysterious Underpinnings of Emotional Life*. New York: Simon & Schuster.

Lewis, C.S. (1944). *The Abolition of Man*. New York: Touchstone.

Lichenstein, S. & P. Slovic (2006). *The Construction of Preferences*. Cambridge: Cambridge University Press.

MacKenzie, D. (2006). *An Engine, Not a Camera: How Financial Models Shape Markets*. Cambridge, MA: MIT Press.

Montier, J. (2006). *Behavioural Finance: Insights into Irrational Minds and Markets*. Chichester: John Wiley & Sons, Ltd.

Rabin, M. (1998). Psychology and economics. *Journal of Economic Literature*, 71: 11–46.

Rabin, M. (ed.) (2002). *A Perspective on Psychology and Economics*. Cambridge, MA: Harvard University Press.

Rousseau, J.-J. (1754). Luxury, commerce and the arts. In H. Clark (ed.), *Culture, Commerce and Liberty*. Indianapolis: Liberty Fund.

Samuelson, P. (1963). Contributions to problems of methodology: discussion. *American Economic Review*, 53: 231–6.

Shafir, E. (ed.) (2004). *Preference, Belief and Similarity*. Cambridge, MA: MIT Press.

Shefrin, H. (2002). *Beyond Greed and Fear: Understanding Behavioural Finance and the Psychology of Investing*. Oxford: Oxford University Press.

Shefrin, H. (2005). *A Behavioral Approach to Asset Pricing*. New York: Elsevier.

Shiller, R. (2005). *Irrational Exuberance*. Princeton, NJ: Princeton University Press.

Slovic, P. (2000). *The Perception of Risk*. London: Earthscan.

Stigler, G. & G. Becker (1977). De gustibus non est disputandum. *American Economic Review*, 67(2): 76–90.

Sunstein, C. (2005). *The Law of Fear: Beyond the Precautionary Principle*. Cambridge: Cambridge University Press.

Sunstein, C. & R. Thaler (2003a). Liberal paternalism is not an oxymoron. *University of Chicago Law Review*, 70(4): 1159–202.

Sunstein, C. & R. Thaler (2003b). Liberal paternalism. *American Economic Review*, 93(2): 175–9.

Thaler, R. (1992). *The Winner's Curse: Paradoxes and Anomalies in Economic Life*. Princetown, NJ: Princetown University Press.

Thaler, R. (ed.) (1993). *Advances in Behavioral Finance*. New York: Russell Sage Foundation.

Thaler, R. (1999). The end of behavioral finance. *Financial Analysts Journal*, 55: 12–17.

Part I
Foundations

Chapter 2

Financial Decision Making

‘ Mathematical truths make little sense to the mind, particularly when it comes to the examination of random outcomes. Most results in probability are entirely counterintuitive ,

(Taleb, 2004, p.36).

To understand developments in behavioural finance we need to be aware of failings of the prevailing orthodoxy that motivated a reassessment of how financial decisions are made under uncertainty. To do this I revisit the standard model and discuss some weaknesses in it. For it is amongst these weaknesses that the behavioural approaches to financial decisions initially flourished.

Problems raised by decision making under uncertainty are addressed by two separate branches of economics: the economics of uncertainty and the economics of information. The first sees the investor as accepting the limitations of his knowledge and getting on with making the best decision he can. The second asks what new information an investor might seek out before taking any decision at all. So the economics of uncertainty studies decisions whereas the economics of information studies the preparation for making decisions. Both areas of economics are well served by excellent textbooks such as Eeckhoudt *et al.* (2006), Hey (1979), Hirshleifer and Riley (1992) and McKenna (1986) as well as the original pioneering contribution of John von Neumann and Oskar Morgenstern (1947). I draw heavily on these sources below and indicate the sources of particular examples used as I proceed. I begin with decision making itself and subsequently ask how investors might seek to improve their decisions by becoming more informed about their consequences.

2.1 Illustration and Structure

Consider the following questions (taken from Scott Plous's 'Readers' Survey', 1993):

1. Which is more likely to kill you: being hit on the ground by a falling plane (as some residents of Lockerbie in Scotland were in 1988 by Pan Am flight 103) or being mortally savaged by a shark?
2. Including the leap year day of 29 February there are 366 possible days on which we could be born. How likely do you think you are to share a birthday with a person in your class? Or someone living on the same street as you?

These are very different contexts, but both require the evaluation of fairly subtle probabilities. I know I am unlikely to die under a plane or in a shark's mouth. But some people do tragically die that way. How likely is it to happen to me, given I am not a strong or regular swimmer, etc?

Many investment decisions involve calculations of this type. I want to invest in Bovis, a UK construction company, but it has just announced lay-offs and a weak order book. What's the chances of this being the bottom of the market and so a great time to buy into Bovis? Section 2.2 gives us a way to evaluate future outcomes by combining their possible payoffs and the probability of their occurrence into a value of each action considered, e.g. buying or selling Bovis shares. This expected utility rule is one of the basic building blocks of standard finance. Section 2.3 considers some of the concerns raised about expected utility theory by behavioural researchers and some neat counter-examples to its predictions. But the behavioural approach goes beyond finding fault with traditional structures for modelling decisions towards offering new and better ones. So in Section 2.4 I consider the role of heuristics and mental frames used to structure choice and choose final outcomes. Section 2.5 concludes and summarizes the chapter.

After reading this chapter the reader should:

- Know some of the basic mechanics of utility theory, this includes the expected utility rule for evaluating risky outcomes.
- Observe some well-known violations of the rule that question whether expected utility is quite as helpful as it at first appears.
- Understand how laboratory experiments and the study of sporting success have cast light on whether we truly choose between risk alternatives on the basis of the expected utility they seem to offer.

2.2 The Expected Utility Rule

The workhorse model of standard finance evaluates utility by asking how much would an agent/investor pay to enter a certain lottery. In an uncertain world alternative courses of actions can be seen as purchasing tickets in different lotteries. This suggests the utility of alternative actions, x, which I denote $U(x)$, can be evaluated by an investor's willingness to pay to enter a lottery with specified outcomes. For example, how much are you willing to pay to be allowed to receive a pound from me if I toss a coin and it lands on heads?[1] Such a gamble, or 'prospect', might be represented as a lottery and the utility it offers as the weighted average of the outcomes that lottery U offers $= L(\text{heads, tails}, 0.5, 0.5)$ and we might consider the general case of such prospects as taking the form

$$U(x) = L(o_i, p_i) = L(o_1, \ o_2, \ \ldots, \ o_N \ ; \ p_1, \ p_2, \ \ldots, \ p_N)$$

where o are possible outcomes which occur with probabilities p_i, $i = 1 \ldots N$. The essential insight of expected utility theory arises from the fact that the utility of any intermediate outcome, say o_6, can be expressed as being the same as a 'reference' lottery involving the best (o_N) and worst outcome (o_1).

This schema allows us to build up a cardinal ordering of anticipated outcomes by expressing a preference for outcomes as weights in the reference lottery. This little trick moves us on from considering choices with lots of different outcomes occurring with different probabilities to a simple comparison of two outcomes which occur with differing probabilities. A cardinal ordering allows us to say not just which outcome the investor would prefer but also how much he would be willing to pay to have his preferred outcome rather than his next best outcome, or his least preferred outcome. In contrast an ordinal ranking can only tell us which of the outcomes he prefers the first, second, etc., without expressing the strength of that preference. Note that the extent of willingness to pay, or the expected utility associated with an outcome, is a personal preference to each investor. So while some of us would be willing to pay 50 pence for the coin lottery above, $L(\text{heads, tails}, 0.5, 0.5)$, many would be willing to pay a lot less.

The probability weights we attach to various outcomes, heads, tails, or whatever, are simply 'statements of belief', or subjective probabilities. In some circumstances these may be very difficult to formulate, for example if I have to predict the evolution of Chino–American trade relations over the next 100 years, but I assume here I just do the best job I can. This may be difficult in a truly 'uncertain', as opposed to simply risky, choice.

Strictly speaking the expected utility hypothesis offers a theory of risk preference and not our preferences over different levels of consumption. Indeed it is a starting point for expected utility theory, as with most economics, that we prefer more than less. The attitude of the rich and poor to the same risk does appear to differ. The rich can afford to lose and so can bear more risk. So in discussing risk initially I only discuss lotteries which offer no increase in wealth on average, but just the possibility of an increase, or decrease, around the investor's current level of wealth. I do this to be clear I capture the impact of risk and not wealth on the agent's utility by keeping his level of wealth constant.

2.2.1 An Illustration of Expected Utility

Consider a proposed investment action, x, faced by an investor considering trying to 'stag' a new issue of shares (an IPO, or initial public offering, in stock-market jargon).[2] Such 'stagging' involves buying the shares cheaply at initial issue and promptly reselling them for a profit. This sort of behaviour was very popular with small investors during privatizations of government-owned enterprises during the 1980s and early 1990s. The practice regained popularity in the Internet boom of the late 1990s when the floatation of Netscape, Amazon, eBay and others appeared to offer easy money.

Assume a floatation price of 30 pence. Suppose the initial one-day price 'pop' (or mark-up of the trading price over the floatation price) can vary over three increasing levels. If the initial floatation price is set at 30 pence per share suppose that the price at the end of the day can close at either 30, 60 or 90 pence per share. Suppose, further, each outcome is equally likely. If the price closes the day at 30 pence the investor gets nothing. If the price closes the day at 60 pence the investor gets 30 pence. Finally, if the price closes the day at 90 pence the investor gets a 60 pence payoff. The outcome of this lottery can be expressed as follows:

$$L[p_i, o_i] \ i = 1 \text{ to } 3 \text{ and } \sum_i p_i = 1$$

which in this example implies

$$L(0.33, \ 0.33, \ 0.33, \ 0, \ 30, \ 60)$$

This lottery has an expected value of

$$(0.33 \times 0) + (0.33 \times 30) + (0.33 \times 60) = 0 + 10 + 20 = 30$$

Note there is no increase in expected wealth as a consequence of undertaking the investment in the IPO. The lottery is a 'fair bet' in the sense that it offers an expected value equal to its cost. While average wealth remains unaffected by the investment it does raise the variance of possible wealth outcomes. If the investor doesn't invest he keeps his 30 pence per share. If he does invest he might get nothing (if the price closes at 30), gain 30 (if shares close at 60) or gain 60 (if shares close at 90). Asking around your classmates we will soon find that each of us would be willing to invest in the IPO at different prices. Some will invest at the offer price of 30, but many will pay a lot less. This very willingness to pay then traces out the utility the gamble offers each of us in expected utility–wealth space. By doing so it renders the somewhat vague concept of utility or well-being into something measurable in cash terms. This transformation lies at the core of standard conceptions of financial decision making and hence is worth taking time to understand fully.

Figure 2.1 plots the willingness to pay of an investor faced with the reference lottery with a worst outcome a and best outcome z. A risk-averse investor would simply apply an equal probability to the two events in the reference lottery if they were both judged equally likely and mutually exclusive. So if in our example of the IPO above a gain of 0 and 60 are judged equally likely ($a = 0$ and $z = 60$, both occur with probability 0.5), the investor would be willing to pay 30 ($30 = (0.5 \times 0) + (0.5 \times 60)$).

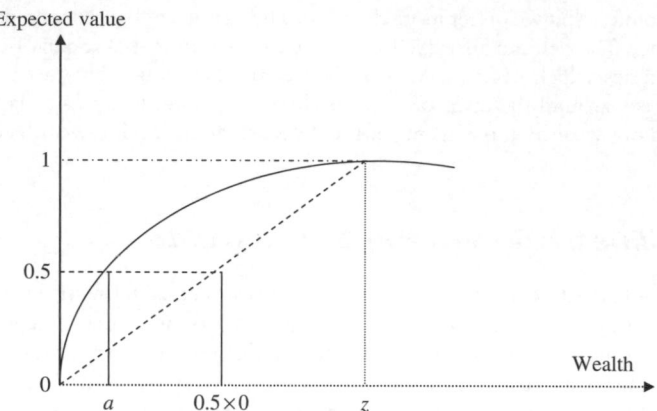

Figure 2.1   Expected utility for a risk-averse investor

Source: Based on Figure 1.1 from Hirshleifer, J. and J. Riley (1992), p.17. *The Analytics of Uncertainty and Information*. Cambridge: Cambridge University Press.

An investor who dislikes risk even for 'fair bets' like this one would be willing to pay less than 30. More generally, if we normalize potential outcomes from the lottery to lie on the line between zero and one, an investor indifferent to assuming risk (or risk neutral in the jargon) would be willing to pay one pound's expected value exactly.

2.2.2   Attitudes to Risk

The utility an investor receives from buying a ticket in a lottery of the type of the IPO discussed above depends on his particular preferences regarding risk as expressed by his utility function. Most of us dislike risk, all other things being equal (as in this 'fair bet'), and are described in the uncertainty literature as risk averse. For any given level of wealth, w, the investor prefers the least risky way of attaining it. Such preferences require the utility function, $p(w)$, used to evaluate prospect/lotteries to be concave, bowing above the 'fair-bet' probability line to imply subjective probabilities used in evaluating prospects. Along this 'fair-bet' line investors are willing to pay the expected value of risks assumed. This concavity of the implied expressed expected utility function requires the investor's utility to be increasing in wealth ($\delta p(w)/\delta W > 0$), but increasing at a decreasing rate (so $\delta p(w)/\delta W^2 < 0$). This combination of characteristics is incorporated in one common measure of risk aversion attributed to Kenneth Arrow (1970) and John Pratt (1964).

$$R_A = -w \frac{\left[\dfrac{\delta p}{\delta W} \right]}{\left[\dfrac{\delta p}{\delta W^2} \right]}$$

One function that has this combination of properties is the square-root function. Applying this we obtain the expected utility, $p(w)$, function plotted in Figure 2.2. Investors are never willing to pay the expected value of the prospect, 30, unless the maximum payoff of at least 30 is certain, i.e. there is no chance of the first-day trading price closing at 30. As long as there is some exposure to risk, even risk that preserves mean wealth, risk-averse investors undervalue the gamble. Here this results in the IPO shares being sold at a discount on their value. This discount is shown in Figure 2.3 which traces out

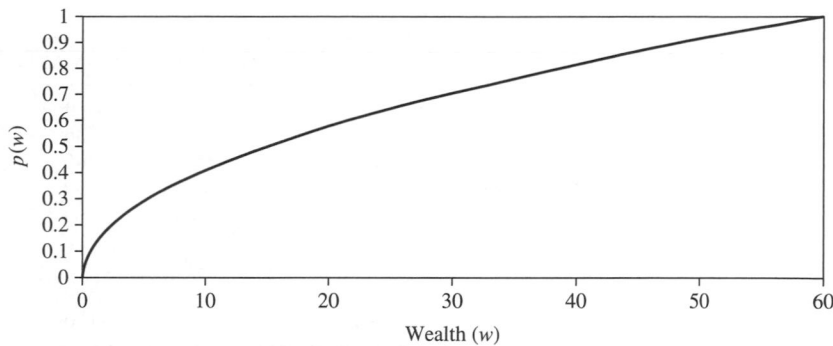

Figure 2.2 Expected value of the IPO investment

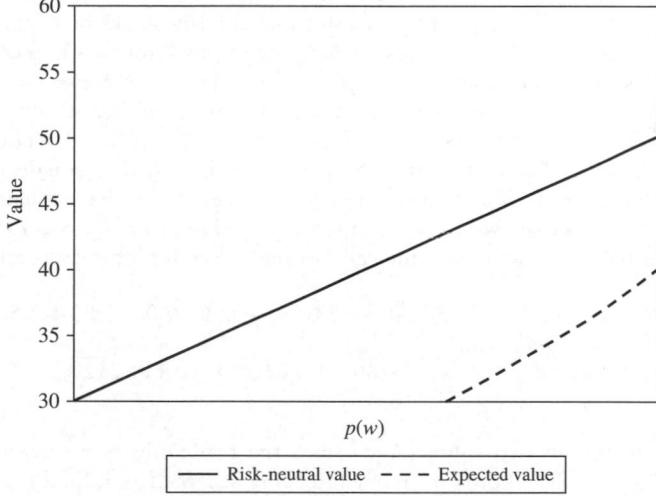

| —— Risk-neutral value | – – – Expected value |

Figure 2.3 Expected values for a risk-averse investor for the IPO valuation

the expected value to a risk-averse investor of the IPO offering discussed above relative to that resulting from a risk-neutral valuation. Because the investor is risk averse he always gives greater weight to bad outcomes relative to that implied by the probability weightings alone.

2.2.3 Diversification as Risk Reduction Strategy

A principal insight of standard finance is the injunction to hold a diversified portfolio of shares knowing some will succeed and others fail. By doing so the investor avoids bearing unnecessary risk associated with any particular security. Sufficient diversification ensures the investor bears only some base level of 'market' risk.

Table 2.1   Payoff to bidding in two IPO offerings sequentially

Payoff structure to each stage of game				Cumulative participation in both IPOs
IPO 1 payoff	0	IPO 2 payoff	0	0
			30	30
			60	60
IPO 1 payoff	30	IPO 2 payoff	0	30
			30	60
			60	90
IPO 1 payoff	60	IPO 2 payoff	0	60
			30	90
			60	120

Consider once more our IPO staging example discussed above. It is not uncommon in IPOs for high investor demand to lead to newly issued stock being allocated on a pro rata basis above some threshold minimum order.[3] Therefore if the investor bids for 100 stocks he might only be allocated 50, so that other investors can share in the issue. Suppose our investor tries to increase his chance of getting at least some shares allocated to him by splitting his bid into two. Instead of bidding for one lot of 100 shares in one company cleared at a price of 30, 60 or 90 as before, he submits two bids for 50 shares each in two different companies at the same expected range of prices in both IPOs. As before the three closing prices 30, 60 and 90 occur with equal probability. Once again the resulting reference lottery takes the form of submitting half a bid in each lottery, each of which has half a chance of being fulfilled. So we have in this case two separate lotteries played sequentially. See Table 2.1.

Calculating expected values we obtain the value of the successive lotteries as follows

$$Lottery\ for\ one\ big\ bid = 0.33\sqrt{0} + 0.33\sqrt{30} + 0.33\sqrt{60} = 1.83 + 2.58 = 4.41$$
$$Lottery\ for\ two\ smaller\ bids$$
$$= 0.111\sqrt{0} + 0.222\sqrt{30} + 0.333\sqrt{60} + 0.222\sqrt{90} + 0.111\sqrt{120}$$
$$= 1.216 + 2.581 + 2.106 + 1.216 = 7.12$$

where the lottery involving two smaller bids sums the probabilities of lucking out by getting nothing in either bid to a payoff only from one bid being accepted and, finally, coming up trumps on both bids. Note each outcome has half the chance of occurring compared to the first lottery considered. This is because each IPO bid has only half a chance of being successful. Note that the first term is simply the probability of getting nothing in both IPOs, assuming the outcome of each lottery is independent ($1/2 \times 1/3 \times 0 = 0 \times 0.166 \times 0 = 0$). By similar reasoning the last term gives the chance of all your cards coming up trumps and receiving a closing price of 90 in both IPO offering bids ($1/9 \times 10.95 = 1.217$).

2.2.4   How Best To Bear Risk

Life is risky. How can we best manage the risk? Expected utility has a very specific answer to that question. We should reallocate our exposure to risk to equate the expected marginal utility per pound/euro in each and every state. Hirshleifer and Riley (1992, p.47) call this the 'fundamental theorem of risk bearing'.[4]

Imagine an economy which pays off in two ways, either famine (state 1) or feast (state 2), depending on the 'state of the world'. Let π be some transformation of the expected payoff in each state to reflect an individual's preference across states, not captured by the expected payoff in that state. Hence the expected utility of an individual in that economy can be expressed as follows

$$U = \pi v(c_1) + \pi v(c_2)$$

where

$$\pi_1 + \pi_2 = 1$$

The marginal rate of substitution in consumption $M(c_1, c_2)$ across the famine and feast states is set to equate the utility of a final unit of consumption in that state. Of course having something left over to consume in a famine, when I might be starving, is far more valuable than preserving one final bottle of champagne and a few oysters to top off the feast. So reallocating consumption from feast to famine states (from state 2 to state 1) makes sense if I don't want to die.

Imagine an indifference curve in state consumption space (with c_1 on the vertical axis and c_2 on the other). At any point on such an iso-utility/indifference curve consumption in either state has the same value at the margin and the following condition holds:

$$0 = dU = \pi_1 v'(c_1) dc_1 + \pi_2 v'(c_2) dc_2 \tag{2.1}$$

The marginal rate of substitution in consumption $M(c_1, c_2)$ is adjusted to capture this trade-off by taking the first derivative of the slope of the indifference curve in consumption space to determine its slope:

$$M(c_1, c_2) = -\left.\frac{dc_2}{dc_1}\right|_{U=\text{Constant}} \equiv \frac{\pi_1 v'(c_1)}{\pi_2 v'(c_2)}$$

In equilibrium, prices reflect the marginal utility of consumption in each state – be it feast or famine. So prices adjust in the asset market for state contingent claims on the famine and feast state to ensure

$$\frac{\pi_1 v'(c_1)}{\pi_2 v'(c_2)} = \frac{P_1}{P_2} \tag{2.2}$$

And it is this final equality which constitutes the fundamental theorem of risk bearing. The marginal utility of a unit consumption in each state ($\pi_1 v'(c_1)$ and $\pi_2 v'(c_2)$) is equated to the relative prices of consuming in each state (P_1 and P_2).

While this is all very 'fundamental' and interesting you may wonder how it applies to trade in financial markets. Think about companies as a bundle of contingent claims on various states. So British Petroleum as claims against high oil prices, global warming, peace in the Middle East, etc. Now the relative prices of a company's equity can also be seen as reflecting some vector of underlying states. So the relative price of shares and the relative price of whole asset classes will reflect the underlying contingent claims on states those assets embed.

One particular illustration of such reasoning not working is the seemingly high return to equity which pays off highest when business is booming, there are lots of jobs and so paying bills is not a struggle for most people. Bonds conversely appreciate in value in times (or offer a higher capital gain) when interest rates fall as in recessions. The so-called 'equity premium puzzle' is such a big problem for standard theory I discuss it more fully in Chapter 13.

2.3   Expected Utility Theory: Simple But Untrue?

The extraordinary success of expected utility, especially as an underpinning to classical finance, via the development of portfolio theory and the capital asset pricing model, led most of its users to believe it was fully descriptive of how investors actually make decisions. In many situations such an assumption seems to work and we can rejoice in the inheritance of expected utility theory. But for financial decisions where expected utility theory produces counterfactual results we need to dig deeper.

Behavioural finance does this job of digging deeper to uncover why and how investors choose as they do. Sadly not all the problems of standard finance models can be solved by changing our assumptions about how investors make decisions under uncertainty. Modelling financial behaviour invokes many assumptions regarding the structure of trading, distributional properties of data, etc., which force us to look outside behavioural explanations to market microstructure or econometric estimation methods. Sometimes we need to look beyond economic reasoning to colleagues in philosophy, sociology or anthropology.

But in some cases the reason why our standard finance models seem to do us a disservice is that the reality of decision making by investors does not conform to the assumptions under which John von Neumann and Oscar Morgenstern formulated the theory (von Neumann & Morgenstern, 1947). For these pioneering authors expected utility theory constituted a normative model of how a rational person should make decisions about alternative courses of action and not a positive/descriptive rationalization about how decisions are really made. This prescription for how an investor should behave relied on a number of key assumptions including (Plous 1993, p.81):

1. An ability to rank alternatives. The investor should be able to say if he prefers one prospect/gamble to another or sees them as equally desirable.
2. An investor will prefer the dominant investment. An investment prospect may be strongly domi- nant, always offering a better payoff or weakly dominant offering a better prospect in the majority of, but not all, circumstances and no worse in any conceivable case.
3. Investors ignore irrelevant alternatives when making a decision between alternatives. So, for example, in evaluating prospects an investor should ignore outcomes that occur with equal probability under both alternative prospects under consideration.
4. Investors consistently rank outcomes. So if an investor prefers outcome A to B and outcome B to C he will also prefer A to C. This assumption is sometimes stated as implying preferences are transitive.
5. Investors' rankings of alternatives are continuous. Any one of the possible outcomes from the investor's investment decision can be expressed as a linear combination of the best and worst outcome they face. Such weighted combination of extreme outcomes is termed 'reference lottery'. If this assumption does not hold the use of 'reference gambles' in evaluating investment prospects is invalidated.
6. Investors care about outcomes/payoffs and the probability with which they will occur and not how they are presented or bundled. So breaking down a prospect into two separate prospects with the same combined expected utility cannot change their additive value to the investor.

Doubts about the validity of these assumptions have emerged from some famous paradoxes in the understanding of expected utility theory. These doubts set the background to the emergence of behavioural economics and its offspring behavioural finance. In studying these paradoxes and in building upon their meaning I shall often return to the centrality of the underlying assumptions of expected utility theory.

2.3.1 Paradoxes and Problems in Early Understanding of Expected Utility Theory

St Petersburg

Early concerns about making decisions based on expected values date back at least to the posing of the 'St Petersburg paradox' by Nicolas Bernoulli and 'solved' by his younger cousin Daniel Bernoulli 25 years later in 1738 while he was living in St Petersburg. Nicolas asked what is the value of a gamble that offers two pounds if you toss a coin and it comes up heads once, or four pounds if it lands on heads twice in a row, eight pounds if it lands on heads three times in a row etc.? The expected value is clearly

$$(1/2 \times 2) + (1/4 \times 4) + (1/8 \times 8) + \ldots = 1 + 1 + 1 + \ldots = \infty$$

Which seems a bit crazy because no one would pay that much. Daniel's suggested solution to Nicolas's paradox was simply that further increments in expected wealth don't increase utility in equal proportion beyond some point. There is diminishing marginal utility of expected wealth as with any other good. This explains the concavity of the utility function chosen in Figure 2.1. But the paradox does at least alert us to the blithe equation of expected values and expected utilities.

Ellsberg

Later Daniel Ellsberg (1961) constructed an example of choice which suggested problems with the independence of irrelevant alternatives assumption (number 3) above. This assumption has strong intuitive appeal since it simply requires us to ignore things that do not affect our maximization of expected utility. Friedman and Savage (1952) give the example of a doctor called out to diagnose a sick person. The doctor is not clear if the patient is close to a heart attack or having a nervous breakdown. Whatever the cause of the patient's distress the doctor will feel confident in advising immediate bed rest. Later the treatment required for a coronary and a psychiatric condition will no doubt differ, but the exact nature of the illness is at the moment irrelevant to the patient's need for rest.

Ellsberg asked people to choose between two types of gambles in which the outcome was determined by drawing balls from an urn containing black, red and yellow balls. The urn used for both draws contains a third set of red balls, the rest being black or yellow balls in unknown proportion. In each gamble people were asked to choose the colour of ball for which the gamble would pay off for them. In gamble 1 people were told they would be rewarded if the colour of ball they chose in advance was drawn. In the second gamble they still had to choose a colour of ball to be rewarded, but now they were told they would be rewarded regardless of their choice if they drew a yellow ball. In the case of the first gamble people mostly chose red balls in order to win. In the case of the second gamble most people chose black balls as a way to win. But the only difference between gambles 1 and 2 is that in gamble 2 yellow always pays off (whatever you choose). So you would think red and black would be equally attractive in both gambles. In gamble 2 choosing red is rewarded if you choose red, but so is black if you choose black, drawing a yellow ball is now rewarded anyway regardless of the colour of ball chosen. It seems the choices made in this context between gambling on red and black balls depend on the certain payoff available to those lucky enough to draw yellow whether you choose it or not in gamble 2. This seems to contradict the irrelevance assumption (number 3) above. How a prospect is evaluated seems to depend on how it is packaged with an irrelevant alternative.

Allais

A similar counter example to the ability of expected utility to adequately explain choice helped earn Maurice Allais the Nobel Prize in 1988. Allais observed how people made choices between two related sets of alternative gambles (see Allais 1953 or Hirshleifer & Riley 1992, pp.36–9). First people were asked if they would prefer a million pounds for sure or would they rather take a gamble offering a 10% chance of receiving £5 million, an 89% chance of receiving a million pounds and finally a 1% chance of getting nothing. Later on the people were presented with two alternative gambles offering an 11% chance of a million pounds and an 89% chance of receiving nothing or, alternatively, a gamble offering a 10% chance of £5 million and a 90% chance of receiving nothing. These alternatives can be structured as follows for the first set of gambles.

First choose between

Gamble A: receiving £1 million for sure
Gamble B: a 10% chance of getting £5 million
            an 89% chance of getting £1 million
            a 1% chance of getting nothing

Then choose in the second set of gambles between

Gamble C: an 11% chance of receiving £1 million
            an 89% chance of getting nothing.
Gamble D: a 10% chance of receiving £5 million
            a 90% chance of getting nothing.

Most people choose A rather than B in the first set of gambles. Later the same group of people mostly appear to choose D over C. This sequence of choices is hard to rationalize by expected utility theory. Consider the expected value of the gambles:

$$A: 1 \times £1m = £1m$$
$$B: (0.1 \times £5m) + (0.89 \times £1m) + (0.01 \times 0) = £1.39m$$

This suggests the group making the choice are very risk averse, leaving £390,000 of expected value unclaimed rather than face a 1% chance of getting zero. Later the same group of people make the calculation

$$C: (0.11 \times £1m) + (0.89 \times 0) = £0.11m$$
$$D: (0.10 \times £5m) + (0.90 \times 0) = £0.5m$$

and choose D. Here the increase in expected utility seems enough to compensate for the 1% increase in the probability of getting nothing.

However, note if £1 million for sure is preferred to $((0.1 \times £5m) + (0.89 \times £1m) + (0.01 \times 0))$ in the first choice we can deduct an 89% chance of winning a million in choice A above to imply $((0.11 \times £1m) + (0.89 \times 0))$. This restated version of Gamble A is preferred to $((0.1 \times £5m) + (0.90 \times 0))$ (Gamble B after the payoff, 0.89×1, as it was in A), but this is exactly the reverse of the choice people actually make in the second choice!

Once again expected utility theory seems to be struggling to explain observed choices under uncertain outcomes. This impasse encouraged the development of a more descriptive normative theory of choice, especially by Amos Tversky as well as Daniel Kahneman. Kahneman won the Nobel Prize for this work, but Tversky's tragic death from cancer in 1996 denied him that formal recognition (for a review of Tversky's work see Laibson & Zeckhauser 1998). I concentrate on just two of Tversky's contributions below. First I consider a proposed solution to the problems raised from adherents to a revised version of expected utility theory. By doing so I try to limit the scope for attacking a 'straw man' version of expected utility theory that few economists would in reality ascribe to.

2.3.2   Gambling Insurance and Aspiration

Early defence for the usefulness of expected utility as a description of risk-taking behaviour arose from misplaced criticisms of von Neumann and Morgenstern's original formalization of the theory in their book, *The Theory of Games and Economic Behavior* (1947). Specifically, reviews of the book claimed the fact that many people simultaneously buy insurance while actively gambling cast doubt over the validity of the expected utility as a rationalization of risk-bearing behaviour.

Milton Friedman in an early paper with Leonard Savage (1948) tried to clarify the scope of application of the new theory. They did so by stating four stylized facts that they believed the new expected utility theory must make sense of if it were to gain acceptance as a comprehensive explanation of risk-bearing behaviour. These were:

1. Investors prefer larger to smaller certain outcomes or more is better than less.
2. Low-income investors are willing to buy insurance.
3. Low-income investors simultaneously buy lottery tickets or gamble more generally.
4. The lotteries that low-income investors enter offer more than one prize.

Friedman and Savage pointed out that a utility function capable of both risk-averse insurance contracts and risk-loving gambles must contain both concave (risk-averse) and convex (risk-loving) segments in expected utility/wealth. Figure 2.4 illustrates what such a utility function might look like. The utility function has a 'double inflection point' as investors move from one set of preferences to another. The utility function begins with a convex/risk-loving segment where investors seek to gamble their way up to higher levels of income and wealth. The utility function has a point of inflection from risk-loving to risk-averse investment behaviour at a level of income I^*. Low-income

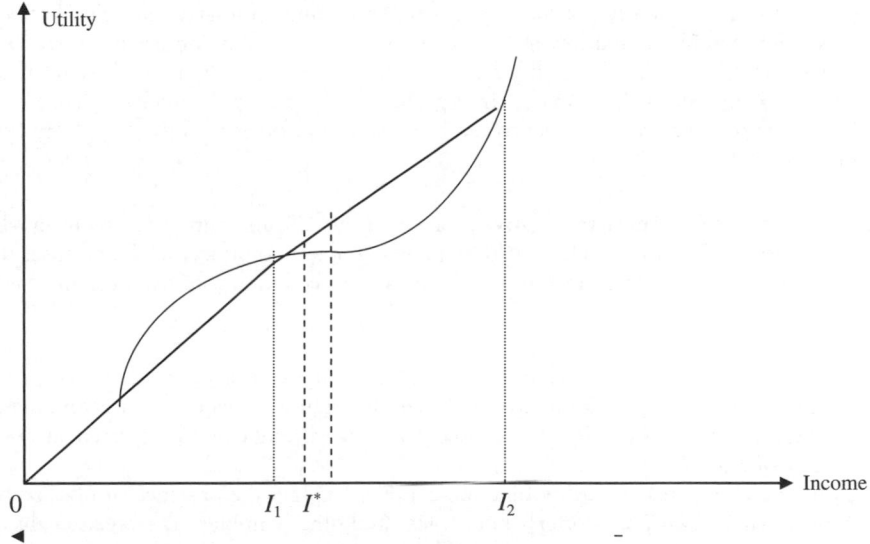

Figure 2.4   The Friedman–Savage 'double-inflection'
Source: Friedman, M. and L. Savage (1948). The utility analysis of choice involving risk. *Journal of Political Economy*, 48(August): 279–304.

investors therefore opt for either the purchase of certainty over small changes in income or a lottery ticket offering a small chance of great riches. Beyond I^* protecting current income seems worth paying an insurance premium for. Up to income I^* investors are willing to gamble to escape their becoming trapped at an income below I^*, say I_1. Near I^* low-income investors are willing to gamble a lot to raise income above I^* and higher income investors are willing to pay hefty insurance premiums to avoid their income falling further. Above some higher income I_2 investors, while keen to accept moderate gambles, are also concerned to avoid financial ruin pushing them below income I^*. This behaviour forces the mass of the distribution of investors out towards one or other of the extremes of the utility function. So the utility function of investors can be decomposed into three discrete sections:

- An opening convex arc, below some target income, where investors exhibit diminishing marginal utility of wealth (0 to I_1 in Figure 2.4).
- An interim segment where investor preferences invert and the utility function becomes increasing in the marginal utility of wealth, i.e. the next pound I earn makes me even happier than the last one did (this is the I^*–I_2 segment in Figure 2.4).
- A final convex arc, beyond I_2, above some target income, where an investor once again exhibits diminishing marginal utility of wealth.

One might think of those in the central section between the initial and final arc as the aspirant up and coming, wannabe, group who often seem quite alien to both the poorer folk from which they sprang and the truly rich set they wish to enter.

Friedman and Savage (1948) point out this interpretation of utility function accords with some of our intuition about how people's investment behaviour and self-awareness are linked. Think of I^* as some threshold point when 'lifestyles are threatened' (we need to downsize our home, or take our children out of private schools). In such a characterization I may be risk averse over gambles that simply improve my current well-being, but risk loving if I believe the gamble could 'change my life'/ 'make me rich' and permanently put me into the above I^* elite. Similarly once rich I may be risk loving over smaller gambles that allow me to move upmarket to a small house in Monaco from my current apartment, yet still reject a gamble offering me enough to buy a small island if it might impoverish me to fall below I^*. Such an interpretation accords with much evidence regarding investors' 'habit formation' with respect to levels of consumption they enjoy. To quote Friedman and Savage (1948):

> increases in income that raise the relative position of the consumer unit in its own class but do not shift the unit out of its class yield diminishing marginal utility, while increases that shift it into a new class, that give it a new social and economic status, yield increasing marginal utility.

This statement is interesting not least because of the importance attached to socially shared benchmarks about how 'people like us live' by a leading figure in neoclassical economics. Much behavioural finance and specifically the 'prospect theory' alternative to expected utility theory stresses this sort of reasoning.

Finally, this shape of expected utility function can also explain the presence of first, second and third place prizes in the National Lottery, horse races and other gambles. The precise value of I^* is likely to vary both across the population of gamblers/investors and by the original stake/investment taken by the gambler/investor. A tiered set of possible winnings allows a spectrum of gamblers/ investors to find such lotteries/investments attractive.

2.4 Frames for Actions, Contingencies and Outcomes

In a lifetime of work in experimental economics Kahneman and Tversky have constructed the building blocks of a new descriptive/positive theory of how decisions are made. The theory they advance is entitled 'prospect theory' and I discuss it in detail in a later chapter. Here I simply point out some of the counter-examples to the predictions of expected utility theory that motivated their new approach. A unifying concept behind the various contradictions of expected utility is the idea that each decision is structured within an ordered 'mental frame' and such frames can be manipulated or distorted to change an investor's decision.

Tversky and Kahneman (1981) posed simple problems like the following to their students. If the government is preparing for a deadly outbreak of Asian flu (and it is) which course of action should it take? Students were told that the government estimates 600 people will die as a result of the flu outbreak. They were then asked which course of action they would support of the two programmes suggested below:

- Programme A: a vaccine which can save 200 lives.
- Programme B: a vaccine which will stop anyone dying at all if it works, which it will do with a probability of one-third. But will cure no one it doesn't work.

Given this choice 75% of students asked chose programme A. The risk of watching all 600 victims die was too much to be compensated by the hope all would be saved. Later Kahneman and Tversky reformulated the question and posed it to another group of students. The health threat faced remained the same but now the choice offered was:

- Programme C: accepts 400 victims of the flu will die.
- Program D: offers a vaccine which has a probability of one-third of curing all victims, but if it doesn't work will result in all 600 victims dying.

Faced with this choice two-thirds of students chose programme D. The statement '400 would die' was enough to scare most students off programme C, even though it's actually the same outcome as programme A above only expressed in more dire terms. It seems clear how you ask matters, not just what you ask about, but also what the person being asked ultimately chooses.

2.4.1 The Decision Process

To address this apparent failing of expected utility theory Kahneman and Tversky suggest investors evaluate prospects in two consecutive steps:

- An *editing-framing* stage when the gamble or investment is initially structured for detailed consideration.
- A later more detailed *evaluation* of the prospect.

Consider a prospect/gamble faced by an investor. Let one possible outcome be x and its probability of occurrence p and another outcome y which occurs with probability q. Kahneman and Tversky build prospect theory on the basis that outcomes give rise to values $v(.)$ for investors, while probabilities have weights $\pi(.)$ attached to them. Values are a function of outcomes while not necessarily being equal to outcomes. Weights are a function of probabilities while not necessarily being equal to probabilities. The value of a prospect in this revised 'prospect theory' of decision making under uncertainty is

$$\pi(p).v(x) + \pi(q).v(y)$$

The first really big difference between prospect theory and expected utility theory is the fact that outcomes are now gains and losses, relative to some reference point of meaning to the investor (zero payoff, some 'normal' level of return, etc.) and not alternative terminal levels of wealth.

The second principal difference in the construction of prospect theory is that losses hurt more than gains please the investor. This seems intuitively plausible since much consumption is habit forming. It's hard to drink instant coffee once one is used to drinking ground coffee or to queue for the bus once you own a car.

Finally, the weighting function has the property that outcomes with very low opportunities of occurring are overweighted by investors, $\pi(p) > p$ if $p \approx 0$. Consequently investors underweight middling and high probability outcomes relative to the weighting attached to them by expected utility based investors, $p > \pi(p)$ if $p > 0.5$. An example of such a weighting function is given in Figure 2.5. Here at low probabilities $\pi(p)$ lies below the standard probability of expected utility theory only to switch to lie above it at higher probabilities. Obviously at some point of certainty, or impossibility, the weighting given by a prospect theory investor to an outcome and its true probability converge.

2.4.2 Inferring Big Ideas from Small Samples

Many problems in decision making under uncertainty, such as making an investment, require inferences to be made based on limited data. How many days/months of data do you need to observe before finally accepting that returns are a random unpredictable process? Eugene Fama (1970, 1991) was right, stock markets are efficient, and you can safely throw away this book.[5] A similar problem is the ordination of investment 'gurus' or 'star' analysts. How long and how bright must an analyst's star burn for him truly to be regarded as different from the swinish pack?

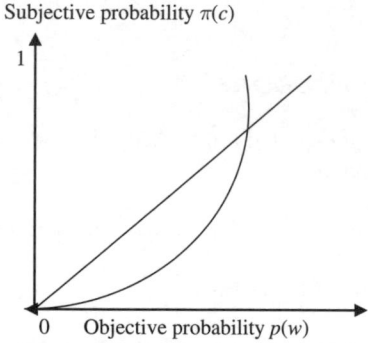

Figure 2.5   Weighting function to transform objective into subjective probabilities

Source: Based on Figure 1.2 from *Choices, Values and Frames*, edited by Tversky, A. and D. Kahneman (1981). The framing of decisions and the psychology of choice. *Science*, 211: 453–8. Cambridge University Press.

The answer to both the above questions is that we are likely to be convinced stock markets are efficient, or a particular analyst is a star, by less data/evidence than is reasonable. In a series of papers Kahneman and Tversky (Tversky & Kahneman 1971) have documented how easily we can be convinced that the world is like the sample of it we observe, or past performance can be extrapolated into the future. This 'belief in small numbers' by which large sample/population characteristics of stocks or analysts' forecasts also applies to smaller samples, motivates many applications of behavioural finance. It gives rise to a tendency to construct a distribution of expected outcomes, upon which decisions are taken, upon the basis of impressions drawn from quite limited evidence.

One easy way to discover this bias within your own thought is to try to write down a sequence of heads and tails you expect a fair coin to produce. Then toss a coin and see how close your guesses were to actual outcomes. You are likely to find your guesses implied more reversals of runs of heads or tails than one can observe in practice. This is one prediction of the well-documented 'gambler's fallacy' that bad luck cancels out. Bad luck does indeed get cancelled but this may take some time. Putting all my chips on red repeatedly can be a dumb strategy in the short to medium term, even if in the long term it has to produce equal amounts of gains and losses.

If such biases were restricted to desperate gamblers in the throes of greed and delusion they might not be so worrying. But Kahneman and Tversky document similar biases as being present amongst participants at conferences they attended as part of their academic life. They found academics with similar training (if not prestige) to themselves:

- overestimated the power of their tests despite the fact they often relied on small samples (of 10–50 in psychological studies);
- displayed undue confidence in early trends in their data and the stability of the patterns they observed;
- bore unreasonably high expectations about the ease of replicating 'true' results, i.e. they underestimated the impact of sample variability on retrieving statistically significant results;
- found spurious 'explanations' of later refutations of previous results without recognizing sample variation alone could explain the failure to verify prior results.

The authors conclude 'acquaintance with formal logic and probability theory does not extinguish erroneous intuitions' (Tversky & Kahneman 1971, p.199). This suggests these biases towards extrapolation of trends may indeed be very innate within us and not easily shaken by reasoned thought.

While we may be sceptical about research based on responses from students, or academic colleagues, with little to lose from making stupid mistakes, very similar results to those reported above have been replicated in non-experimental settings. A recent study reported an examination of 18 hours of videotaped play at a Reno casino in July 1998 (Croson & Sundali 2005). Roulette is a game of pure chance, where the ball has an equal chance of falling in any one of the 38 alternating red and white slots on the wheel.[6] After streaks of five red or black, or high or low, balls, a belief in the reversal of trend was evident. Even at the sixth red ball the probability of a red at the next spin is still 50%, but less than 10% of players bet on such an outcome (even though weirdly over 70% of the outcomes displayed a continuing pattern in the sample data).

2.4.3   Stars with Feet of Clay

This extrapolation bias is particularly marked in judging the performance of experts or those with a special talent. Sportsmen are a group which have been particularly studied in this regard. The *Wisden Almanack* gives a complete guide to cricket teams and players' performance over the years back to 1864. So sportsmen's performance records are very visible, making the observation of persistent good performance easily quantifiable. I make further use of the sporting analogy to financial performance in an appendix to Chapter 4.

Tversky and a colleague examined the belief that some basketball stars in the American National Basketball Association (NBA) league had 'hot hands', scoring with almost every basket they threw (Tversky and Gilovitch, 1989, p.313). In particular they studied the scoring record of nine players for the Philadelphia 76ers in 48 games during the 1980–1 NBA season. Despite the perception that certain players have 'hot hands' the data uncovered that for eight out of the nine players studied scoring a hit basket actually reduced their probability of scoring next time. Of course this makes sense because the defenders should be concentrating on their opponent's best scorers. For this reason the authors repeated the experiment for set plays from fixed positions (judged by the player to be where the chance of a hit was 50%). Once again they found very similar results – a hit this time did not appear to raise your chance of scoring next time you took a shot at the basket. They concluded that basketball fans and indeed players themselves perceive random sequences of successful shots to be far more structured than they are. Of course individual players and teams will score more or less than others. But, conditional on underlying performance, a 'hit' this shot is not a good predictor of a hit with your next shot, even though fans may believe it is.

The gambler's fallacy implies luck will reverse itself and reverse itself soon. A converse belief is that some gamblers are 'hot' on particular nights, seemingly not being able to lose. While the gambler's fallacy suggests the outcomes of play will reverse themselves, the 'hot hand' notion implies some players will always win against the odds.

This tension between the perception and the reality of expert performance may explain the performance of 'star' fund managers or analysts in an efficient security market. These stars understand the advice of George Soros to shout about your gains and keep quiet about your losses to gain a place in the investing public's affection.

2.4.4   Is There More to Life Than (Maximizing) Utility?

In our private life, away from academic journals, exams and the lecture hall we all clearly understand that there is more to a fulfilled life than maximizing utility. If we asked a friend 'What do you want to achieve in your life?' and he answered 'To maximize my utility', he may not be our friend for much longer. Such an objective seems shallow, hollow and slightly juvenile. Much of Adam Smith's *Theory of Moral Sentiments* (Smith 1759) was concerned with arguing that while most economic activity is driven by a desire to acquire wealth, acquiring it does not really make its recipients happy. This suggests investors may have very different objectives than those suggested in most finance texts. A wide array of phenomena, for example socially responsible investment and avoidance of 'sin' stocks, like tobacco company shares, suggests this might be a realistic depiction of investor behaviour. Karlsson *et al*. (2007) argue that we often observe choice is driven by a deeper need to achieve 'meaning' in our lives. Such meaning can come from self-discovery, a belief in some deity, or judgement in an afterlife, or the exercise of free will. None of these objectives seems at all consistent with expected utility as I have described it here.

2.4.5   Happiness, Well-Being and the Emotional Basis of Utility

Strangely the economic concept of expected utility/well-being discussed in this chapter seems to bear little resemblance to what most of us regard as the essential elements of a contented, productive life, good health, a supportive group of family and friends and satisfying work. Emotions are in many ways not only our reason for living but also the reason for feeling drawn to suicide in despair (Elster 1989, p.61). Jeremy

Bentham, the original utilitarian, sought to encourage 'the greatest happiness of the greatest number' (Bentham 1789). But happiness or sadness has largely disappeared from the finance theorist's vocabulary and openly discussing one's own or others' emotions is slightly embarrassing. Often casual remarks about 'animal spirits', 'greed and fear', or 'herding' hint at animalistic, guttural, responses to financial incentives but the usual rationalist perspective on financial decision making is maintained nonetheless.

Recently interest has resumed in the impact of 'visceral' emotions upon economic behaviour (Lowenstein 2000). Increasingly the large and predictable impact of fear, anxiety and other elative states are being recognized by researchers in economics and finance.

The behavioural approach to finance and economics has for some time recognized the impact of anticipated emotional responses, like 'regret' or 'rejoicing' (Loomes & Sugden 1982). The importance of movements relative to such reference/focal points motivates the 'prospect theory' approach which dominates behavioural finance. Of course my regret (at not getting that promotion or the death of a loved one) may promote anger or despair. So even in such models of anticipated gain and loss visceral emotions are never far from the surface.

It has been argued that emotions could be chosen or contrived. Our boss or teacher may feign anger to induce us to work hard when we are lazy. We may simply choose to avoid situations that make us anxious, like being in debt. But it is hard to see how we can programme anger, pride or shame entirely out of our lives (Elster 1989, pp.52–5).

2.5 Conclusion and Summary

This chapter has examined one of the basic building blocks of the standard model of finance and found it wanting in many ways. In response a number of alternative theorizations have been advanced to rationalize anomalous evidence within the standard expected utility framework. We explore one of these, 'prospect theory', at length in a subsequent chapter. But it is also possible that the poor quality of decision making we have uncovered simply reflects the sparse information available to investors making those decisions. To examine this possibility we study the process of learning in Chapter 4.

Questions

1. Reconsider the IPO example in Section 2.2, Table 2.1. Again the issue price is 30 pence. Suppose now that the payoffs change, say there are four possible outcomes: the price at the end of the first day could be 10, 30, 60 or 90 with each price outcome occurring with equal probability. Describe the revised prospect in the form of a lottery and calculate its expected value. Would a risk-averse investor accept such a gamble?

2. Reconsider the illustration of the benefits of diversification in Section 2.2.3. Diversification is so great! It offers greater return for less risk. So if splitting your bids into two in this lottery was such a great move, what is the effect of splitting your bids into three bids for $33^1/_3$ shares in identical IPOs? Loving the game? Now consider bidding four times for 25 shares in four identical IPOs. Comment on what this exercise tells you about the effects of diversification.

3. When Williams-Sonoma introduced bread-making machines to the United States at $275 per machine, sales were few (see Ariely 2008, p.14). The company responded with a new machine which was twice the size of the old one and nearly 50% more expensive. Soon the original model started moving off the shelves. Ariely calls the larger machine the 'decoy' product and provides numerous examples of this strategy working. Why does this 'decoy' marketing strategy work and what is strange about the fact that it does?

Notes

1. Assume I am a gentleman who plays with a fair, two sided coin with a 50/50 chance of landing on heads.
2. This example is based on one in Eeckhoudt *et al.* (2006, pp.6–8).
3. Once again this example is loosely based on Eeckhoudt *et al.* (2006, pp.6–8).
4. My discussion here follows Hirshleifer and Riley (1992, Section 2.1, pp.43–7).
5. The answer is quite a lot (see Summers 1986).
6. The figure comes from numbers 1–36 on the wheel plus the numbers 0 and 00 (or just 0 in European casinos). The house does not pay out on evens bets (red or black, high (1–18), or low (19–36)) if the balls fall on the 0 or 00 slots of the wheel.

References

Allais, M. (1953). The behaviour of rational man in risk situations – a critique of the axioms and postulates of the American school. *Econometrica*, **21**: 503–46.

Ariely, D. (2008). *Predictably Irrational: The Hidden Forces That Shape Our Decisions*. New York: HarperCollins.

Arrow, K. (1970). *Essays in the Theory of Risk Bearing*. Amsterdam: North-Holland.

Bentham, J. (1789). *The Principles and Morals of Legislation*. New York: Macmillan.

Croson, R. & J. Sundali (2005). The gambler's fallacy and the hot hand: empirical data from casinos. *Journal of Risk and Uncertainty*, **2005**(209): 195–209.

Eeckhoudt, L., C. Gollier *et al.* (2006). *Economic and Financial Decisions under Risk*. Princeton, NJ: Princeton University Press.

Ellsberg, D. (1961). Risk, ambiguity and the savage axioms. *Quarterly Journal of Economics*, **75**: 643–69.

Elster, J. (1989). *Nuts and Bolts for the Social Sciences*. Cambridge: Cambridge University Press.

Fama, E. (1970). Efficient capital markets: a review of theory and empirical work. *Journal of Finance*, **25**: 383–417.

Fama, E. (1991). Efficient capital markets II. *Journal of Finance*, **46**: 1575–617.

Friedman, M. & L. Savage (1948). The utility analysis of choice involving risk. *Journal of Political Economy*, **48**: 279–304.

Friedman, M. & L. Savage (1952). The expected utility hypothesis and the measurability of utility. *Journal of Political Economy*, **60**: 463–74.

Hey, J. (1979). *Uncertainty in Microeconomics*. Oxford: Martin Robertson.

Hirshleifer, J. & J. Riley (1992). *The Analytics of Uncertainty and Information*. Cambridge: Cambridge University Press.

Karlsson, N., G. Lowenstein, *et al.* (2007). The economics of meaning. In G. Lowenstein (ed.), *Exotic Preferences*. Oxford: Oxford University Press.

Laibson, D. & R. Zeckhauser (1998). Amos Tversky and the ascent of behavioural economics. *Journal of Risk and Uncertainty*, **16**: 7–47.

Loomes, G. & R. Sugden (1982). Regret theory: an alternative theory of rational choice. *Economic Journal*, **2**: 805–24.

Lowenstein, G. (2000). Emotions in economic theory and economic behavior. *American Economic Review*, **90**: 426–32.

McKenna, C.J. (1986). *The Economics of Uncertainty*. London: Harvester-Wheatsheaf.

Plous, S. (1993). *The Psychology of Judgement and Decision Making*. New York: McGraw-Hill.

Pratt, J. (1964). Risk aversion in the small and the large. *Econometrica*, **32**: 122–36.

Smith, A. (1759). *The Theory of Moral Sentiments*. Indianapolis: Liberty Fund.

Summers, L. (1986). Do stock market values rationally reflect fundamental values? *Journal of Finance*, **41**(3): 591–601.

Taleb, N. (2004). *Fooled by Randomness*. New York: Random House.

Tversky, A. & T. Gilovitch (1989). The cold facts about the 'hot hand' in basketball. *Chance*, **2**(1): 16–21.

Tversky, A. & D. Kahneman (1971). Belief in the law of large numbers. *Psychological Bulletin*, **76**: 105–10.

Tversky, A. & D. Kahneman (1981). The framing of decisions and the psychology of choice. *Science*, **211**: 453–8.

von Neumann, J. & O. Morgenstern (1947). *The Theory of Games and Economic Behavior*. Princeton, NJ: Princeton University Press.

Chapter 3

Discounting

‘To secure maximum benefit in life, all future pleasures or pains should act upon us with the same force as if they were present, allowance being made for their uncertainty. The factor expressing the normal effect of remoteness should, in short, always be unity, so that time should have no influence. But no human mind is constituted in this perfect way: a future feeling is always less influential than a present one’

(William Stanley Jevons, *Theory of Political Economy*, quoted in Ainslie & Haslam 1992, p.60).

Standard finance theory values assets by discounting the future payoffs that arise from holding those assets. So the Gordon growth model sees share price values as being determined by the value of the future dividend stream, for example $D/(r-g)$; or a bond that pays a perpetuity has a value given by its face value divided by the applicable discount rate (B/r).[1] In each case the discount rate captures a 'pure rate of time preference' for getting cash-flow from the asset now rather than later.

But can we safely assume that the interest rate used to discount future consumption, r, is a constant, as the discounted utility framework requires? Do we discount a dividend payment delayed from this year to next by the same amount as one paid from 20 years hence to 21 years hence? Is it even possible that I might prefer to face a dividend omission now in order to not jeopardize next year's dividend? In a review of these issues, Lowenstein, Read and Baumeister (2003, p.2) point out,

> [The] discounted utility model is a normative model because if we don't treat the future in this fashion we won't be able to make plans that we can be sure we will implement in the future. Whether discounted utility is a valid descriptive model of behavior is a matter for debate amongst economists.

If this is so we could even conceive of discount rates turning negative in the loss domain. This chapter considers some possibilities for modelling these effects of such a basic feature of standard finance.

The uniformity of approach and ubiquity of the discounted utility model is all the more surprising given the interest in the motivations for inter-temporal choice, different savings rates and capital accumulation amongst early political economists (Lowenstein 1992a). Adam Smith and his fellow Scot John Rae investigated whether cultural differences between nations could explain their propensity to make the sacrifices necessary to accumulate productive capital. Later the idea that the Reformation concept of a 'calling' by God to business life inspired Weber to attribute the rise of capitalism to the diffusion of the Protestant work ethic (Weber 1930). Consumption in this view was almost inherently morally corrupting. Nevertheless these psychological foundations of the way we choose to allocate consumption over time were soon lost once the common technology of the discounted utility model diffused through the economics profession after the Second World War. I begin by revising that model to see what aspects of inter-temporal choice it captures and which characteristics of choice it was later to suppress.[2]

3.1   Illustration and Structure

Mr Expo meets Mr Hypo going to work on a wonderful summer day. Mr Expo asks Mr Hypo about his nice winter coat, which he vividly recalls from their last meeting, and expresses an interest in buying it. Delighted Mr Hypo immediately offers to sell his winter coat to Mr Expo at an agreed price. Time moves on and winter draws near. Mr Expo meets Mr Hypo once more but this time he is shocked to see Mr Hypo shivering in his shirtsleeves. He kindly offers to sell him a winter coat commenting slyly 'I think you like the style'. Mr Hypo then resells Mr Expo's winter coat to him at a healthy profit. In fact he repeats the same trade each year and Mr Expo grows to like Mr Hypo and his generous ways very much.

How can a man as silly as Mr Hypo survive in a world of smart Mr Expos? This chapter seems to answer this question by examining an alternative to standard constant (exponential) discounting techniques. But first in Section 3.2 I try to explain the attractions of the standard constant exponential discounting model and why we see its almost universal adoption in standard finance. In Section 3.3 I briefly consider some illustrative evidence regarding why discount rates applied by investors might vary over time and more specifically decline as the investment horizon is extended. Section 3.4 presents a model of investment in an economy with declining discount rates and its economic impact devised by David Laibson at Harvard (Laibson 1997). This model allows for the presence of illiquid 'golden egg' investments that cannot be sold for immediate consumption. Section 3.5 discusses in more depth the technical modelling device used to capture a pattern of declining discount rates, that is, a hyperbolic discount rate. Mr Hypo of our illustrative example meets his maker in that section. Section 3.6 gives more detail on how future rewards and the pattern of their discounting are based on evidence from the psychologist Richard Herrnstein[3] who undertook numerous laboratory experiments into how delays in consumption/reward are valued in controlled environments. Armed with these psychological insights I return in Section 3.7 to a more detailed discussion of Laibson's model of investment under a 'golden egg' discounting regime. Finally, Section 3.8 summarizes and concludes the chapter.

After reading this chapter the reader should:

- Better understand the standard finance model of discounting the value of assets.
- Be aware of some weaknesses of that standard model.
- Be aware of evidence from laboratory experiments to support the use of time-varying, especially diminishing, discount rates.
- Understand how to incorporate falling discount rates into an asset pricing model.

3.2   The Discounted Utility Model

The appearance and almost universal acceptance of the discounted utility model advanced by Paul Samuelson (1937), while liberating to theorists in its tractability and intuitive appeal, effectively ended discussion regarding the psychological foundations of consumer/investor choice over time.

Samuelson's discounted utility model, in its most restrictive form, states that a sequence of consumption $(c_1, c_2, \ldots, c_t)$ is preferred to another $(c'_1, c'_2, \ldots, c'_t)$ if and only if

$$\sum_{t=1}^{T} U(c_t)\delta^t > \sum_{t=1}^{T} U(c'_t)\delta^t \tag{3.1}$$

where $0 < \delta < 1$ and U is a utility measure for which the first derivative with respect to consumption is positive and the second derivative with respect to consumption is negative ($\delta U/\delta c_t > 0$ and

$\delta U/\delta^2 c_t < 0$). This says utility increases in consumption at a decreasing rate, so the utility function has the standard concave shape in utility–consumption space. Here the discount rate δ captures 'the pure rate of time preference', while the two utility functions capture differences in the level of the two streams of consumption under consideration.

This type of cardinal measurement of utility that seeks to measure how much we prefer one consumption stream $(c_1, c_2, \ldots, c_t)$ to an alternative consumption stream $(c'_1, c'_2, \ldots, c'_t)$ makes (at least) two central assumptions:

- *Preference independence*. This requires that if two consumption streams share common elements, they can be distinguished from each other on the basis of their uncommon elements alone.
- *Stationarity*. This states that if the first n elements of the consumption stream to be evaluated are common then the difference in their utility can be evaluated using the remaining elements alone. It is this property that facilitates the use of a logarithmic constant discount rate, since a delay has the same impact on utility regardless at which point in the consumption stream it occurs.

3.2.1 Some Problems with the Discounted Utility Model

The reliance of the discounted utility model on these assumptions gives rise to four primary problems in explaining the evidence we have about how inter-temporal choices are actually made. These are outlined by Lowenstein and Prelec (1992) as follows:

> The common difference effect states we observe switches in expressions of preferred outcome as the time for choosing draws nearer. Consider an investor who is indifferent between a consumption stream of receiving a reward $c + x$ at time t and c alone at some later date t' and another income stream offering c alone again at t and some greater reward $c + y$ at the same later date t', $y > x$. Obviously the mark-up of y over x must be then sufficient to compensate our investor for his delay in consuming the consumption increment from t to t', where $t' > t$. If it is a sufficient reward for the delay he suffers then from standard constant discount rate discounted utility theory we have

$$u(c + x)\delta^t + u(c)\delta^{t'} = u(c)\delta^t + u(c + y)\delta^{t'} \tag{3.2}$$

Here the left-hand side of the expression captures the proposed gain in consumption, x, received with a delay until t, while the right-hand side captures the greater increase in consumption, y, offered in compensation for delaying its arrival until a later date t'. So the mark-up of y over x is a measure of the investor's impatience.

Equation (3.2) upon division by δ^t yields:

$$u(c + x) - u(c) = (u(c + y) - u(c))\delta^{t' - t} \tag{3.3}$$

Here the difference in the utility offered by the two consumption streams reflects solely the delay required of the investor in consuming the future increment. This property is denoted the stationarity property of the discounted utility function as outlined above.

- The *magnitude effect* is the observation that large prospective gains are not discounted as heavily as smaller ones in proportionate terms. Thaler's (1981) results discussed later reveal this clearly.
- The asymmetric response to losses and gains is not a contradiction to discounted utility theory, it is rather a direct implication of how that theory works. I discuss this in the next section.

3.2.2 Evaluating Reallocations of Consumption by Equivalent Gains or Compensating Losses of Present Consumption

To see this asymmetry in investor response consider two alternative ways of undertaking a comparative static exercise to evaluate the impact of an increase in consumption by an amount, x; that is an increase in the stream of future consumption by an amount x received at date t. We can consider the impact of such a variation by increasing consumption by some amount $q(x,t)$ to give

$$u(c + q) + \delta^t u(c) = u(c) + \delta^t u(c + x) \tag{3.4}$$

This is sometimes denoted an *equivalent* variation in consumption which matches an increase in consumption now by q to an increase in the discount value of future consumption of $\delta^t x$.

A very similar exercise can be undertaken by asking how much consumption would an investor be willing to give up now (call it a reduction in consumption $p(x,t)$) in order to earn an increase in the discounted value of future consumption of worth $\delta^t x$ in a comparison of the form

$$u(c - p) + \delta^t u(c + x) = u(c) + \delta^t u(c) \tag{3.5}$$

Such a comparative exercise is sometimes termed a *compensating* variation. Equivalent variations ask what sort of increase in present and future consumption makes the investor indifferent to two alternative streams of consumption. Compensating variations ask how can a reduction in current consumption be made good in the future, so as to leave the investor indifferent between two alternative consumption streams?

As in all standard finance you would not expect the form of eliciting a choice to alter the choice made. But it turns out that in this case, given discounted utility theories assumptions, it does make a difference. This is a problem for the sort of comparative static exercise we undertook to rationalize the simultaneous purchase of gambles and insurance in our analysis of the Friedman and Savage (1948) model in Chapter 2. To see how this problem arises I initially solve for q and p, given the equations for equivalent and compensating variations (i.e. Equations (3.4) and (3.5)). From Equation (3.4) an expression of the form of Equation (3.6) results

$$u(c + q) + \delta^t u(c) = u(c) + \delta^t u(c + x)$$
$$\Rightarrow u(c + q) = (1 - \delta^t)u(c) + \delta^t u(c + x)$$
$$\Rightarrow q = \frac{1}{u}[(1 - \delta^t)u(c) + \delta^t (c + x)] - c \tag{3.6}$$

Concavity of the investor's utility function $u(x)$ implies

$$q(x,t) = u^{-1}\{(1 - \delta^t)u(c) + \delta^t u(c + x)\} - c < (1 - \delta^t)c + \delta^t (c + x) - c$$
$$= \delta^t x \tag{3.7}$$

Hence for this inequality to hold $q(x,t)/x$ is less than δ^t for positive values of x and greater than δ^t for negative x and hence is consistent with the greater discounting of gains, as opposed to losses, observed in investors' choices and both experimental and market-based evidence.

The amount required to compensate the investor for the delay experienced in consuming the incremental gain in consumption, x, is simply the current present value $\delta^t x$.

It is now clear that $q(x, t) < p(x, t)$ and the compensation required to make up a loss of current consumption is greater than the compensation required to win acceptance of the delay of the equivalent gain in consumption by the investor.

If an investor's response to a proposed reallocation of consumption across time, which every investment decision necessitates, is sensitive to whether it is evaluated relative to some equivalent increase in present consumption or a compensating/offsetting reduction in present consumption, then we can imagine scaling consumption up and down by some fraction α until the investor is indifferent between the future benefit offered and its present-day cost. Here α captures relative movements in present consumption associated with equivalent increases, x, and compensating reductions, p, in present-day consumption. Setting α to zero therefore leaves no proposed reallocation of consumption to consider, while setting α equal to one allows its full impact to be felt.

To understand how the investor's utility changes on the implementation of compensating variation we can evaluate Equation (3.5) for $\alpha = 1$ when the investor experiences the full impact of the compensating loss associated with the gain in the present value of future consumption $\delta^t(c + x)$. This implies

$$\frac{\partial}{\partial \alpha}|_{\alpha=1} \{u(c - \alpha p) + \delta^t u(c + \alpha x) - (u(c) + \delta^t u(c))\}$$
$$= -pu'(c - p) + \delta^t u'(c + x) > 0 \qquad (3.8)$$

Expression (3.8) holds as long as the magnitude effect reduces the discounting, δ, applied to the gain sufficiently to allow a gain of x to offset the proposed reduction in current consumption of p.

At this point the marginal utility of consumption is still increasing, even as the full impact of the compensating loss in current consumption is borne by the investor. If it was not, the reallocation would not be accepted of course.

Returning to Equation (3.5) to solve for the discount rate applied to future consumption δ^t we obtain

$$u(c - p) + \delta^t u(c + x) = u(c) + \delta^t u(c)$$
$$u(c - p) - u(c) + \delta^t u(c + x) = \delta^t u(c)$$
$$u(c - p) - u(c) = \delta^t (u(c) - u(c + x))$$
$$\delta^t = \frac{u(c - p) - u(c)}{u(c) - u(c + x)}$$
$$\Rightarrow \delta^t = \frac{u(-p)}{u((c - x) - c)} = \frac{-u(p)}{-u(x)} = \frac{u(p)}{u(x)} \qquad (3.9)$$

Which upon substitution back into the differential in Equation (3.8) finally produces the following inequality

$$-pu'(c - p) - \left[\frac{u(p)}{u(x)}\right] xu'(c + x)$$
$$-pu'(c - p)u(c + x) + \frac{u(p)}{-u(x)} xu'(c + x)$$
$$-pu'(c - p)u(x) + u(p)xu'(c + x)$$
$$-pu'(c - p)u(c + x) - u(c) = -u(p)xu'(c + x)u(-c)$$
$$pu'(c - p)[u(c + x) - u(c)] < xu'(c + x)(u(c) - u(c - p)) \qquad (3.10)$$

Given that $u(c)$ is concave (so the investor experiences declining utility with each equivalent increase in his wealth) we also know

$$u(c + x) - u(c) > xu'(c + x)$$
$$\text{and}$$
$$u(c) - u(c - p) < pu'(c - p)$$

where the first inequality holds because concavity of $u(c)$ in consumption requires $du/dc = u'(c)$ to be negative (because the marginal value of consumption falls as its absolute level rises). In the second expression the very same property of concavity of $u(c)$ ensures $du/d(c - p)$ is positive (the marginal value of consumption rises as its level falls) and so the second inequality holds also because the left-hand side of that expression must be negative.

This is all well and good so far. The problem being that for investors to discount large gains less than small ones in proportional terms, the much documented magnitude effect, we require

$$pu'(c - p)(u(c + x) - u(c)) < xu'(c + x)(u(c) - u(c - p)) \qquad (3.11)$$

in Equation (3.10) above. This is because large gains are discounted more heavily than small ones and $p < x$ under any positive discount rate, i.e. the investor will be willing to give up less consumption than he gains in the future in any voluntary exchange of a loss of present consumption for a raise in the present value of future consumption. This implies $u(c + x)$ is a bigger increment in consumption in absolute terms than $u(c - p)$ and hence the implied inequality in Equation (3.11) holds.

3.2.3   Delays and Speed-Ups of Utility

An asymmetry exists in response to delays and speed-ups when the amount of compensation required to gain acceptance of delays massively exceeds anything an investor would be willing to pay to speed up delivery of the consumption stream.

Lowenstein (1988) has pointed out that the requirement of standard finance theory, that the means of eliciting choices should not affect the choices actually made (which rely solely on the payoffs and their probability or timing), implies equality of a premium paid to avoid a delay and premium paid to receive the same good early. That is, the 'delay premium' and the 'speed-up cost' should be the same. But in numerous experiments he found large differences between the two payments. In general we are willing to pay more to avoid the loss of a perceived delay than we are willing to pay to obtain an analogous speed-up in our consumption of equivalent goods. In short we tend to 'live in the moment'. Lowenstein (1988) interprets this apparent inconsistency in observed choice as the outcome of a 'framing' effect in inter-temporal choice, which is discussed further below.

3.3   How and Why Discount Rates Vary

That discount rates are not constant over time can be inferred from the following exercise in introspection. Consider two choices:

A

(i) Receive one apple today
(ii) Receive two apples tomorrow

B

(i) Receive one apple in one year's time
(ii) Receive two apples in one year and a day's time.

Most people choose (i) in Choice A, but (ii) in Choice B. They have a much higher discount rate when considering outcomes in the near future compared to choices involving distant choices. To some degree this is simply because the future, like the past, is another country. Who knows what will be happening in a year's time and how the number of apples we have will affect our fate?

Table 3.1   Results of Thaler's experiments to elicit personal discount rate used in evaluating prizes

Prize ($)	Value of prize deferred by ($)			Implied discount rate (%)		
	3 months	1 year	3 years	3 months	1 year	3 years
15	30	60	100	277	139	63
250	300	350	500	73	34	23
3000	3500	4000	6000	62	29	23

Source: Reproduced with permission from Table 2 from Thaler, R. (1981). Some empirical evidence on dynamic inconsistency. *Economic Letters*, 8: 204.

Motivated by this sort of introspection Thaler (1981) surveyed some undergraduate students to get an idea of the sort of discount rates they applied in making inter-temporal choices over varying time horizons for the delay experienced. So he asked the students how much they would be willing to pay for a prize in three months', a year's and three years' time. Further he varied the amount of the prize to see if the discount rate applied by the student subjects varied with the amount of the prize offered (see Table 3.1).

The most striking thing about the results is the amazingly high discount rates used at short horizons, which seem to bear no comparison to observed market rates of interest. To some extent this must reflect the impatience of youth amongst students, but it may also reflect the fact that they are subject to capital constraints preventing them from accessing further loans. At longer horizons the discount rate applied begins to look more sensible, especially for larger amounts of money. It seems safe to assume, at least amongst the student body, that discount rates fall with the horizon considered and the amount of money invested/delayed in receipt.

The decline in discount rates at longer horizons can be explained by the lack of engagement we feel with our future selves. We can 'cross that bridge when we come to it' and regard the future delay as being less disturbing than an immediate one. But why would discount rates applied in evaluating future outcomes decline as the size of those outcomes grows? At a surface level this seems counter-intuitive. If the stakes have grown should we not be more careful to make sure our choices are consistent over time (i.e. that we apply a constant discount rate)? Two possible outcomes have been advanced for why discount rates fall in the amount of future consumption at stake in the inter-temporal choice made (see Lowenstein 1992a), these are:

- Investors are *sensitive to absolute differences* in payoffs received, not just relative differences. So the perceived difference between £100 now and £150 in a year's time may be greater than between £10 now and £15 in a year's time (see the discussion of Lowenstein & Prelec 1992 later in the chapter).
- Investors may put *small differences in different mental accounts* to large differences. Small differences are marked for spending and so heavily discounted while large differences are earmarked for saving and so less heavily discounted (see Thaler & Shefrin 1981).

Thaler (1981) asked a very similar set of questions of the same students about how much they would pay to delay paying a parking fine, or a prospective loss. Again students were asked to consider their attitude to gradually increasing fines to capture the effect to different scales of prospective loss (see Table 3.2).

Students, like many others, seem to exhibit 'debt aversion', a desire to get unpleasant duties out of the way. In the limit this desire can push discount rates negative as investors seek to clear the decks of financial burdens. This sort of reasoning makes sense in a world where real options to expand current

Table 3.2   Results of Thaler's experiments to elicit personal discount rate used in evaluating prizes (continued)

Fine ($)	Value of prize deferred by ($)			Implied discount rate (%)		
	3 months	1 year	3 years	3 months	1 year	3 years
−15	16	20	28	26	29	20
−100	102	118	155	6	16	15
−250	251	270	310	1	8	7

Source: Table 2 from Thaler, R. (1981). Some empirical evidence on dynamic inconsistency. *Economic Letters*, 8: 204.

projects, or fund new ones, are valued by investors. Our attitude to inter-temporal choice may seem to reflect two emotions that we all recognize but find no place in the constant discount rate utility model. These are (see Lowenstein 1992a, p.103):

- *Savouring*, the smug knowledge of some joy to come (e.g. Cinderella shall go the ball).
- *Dread*, trepidation of some looming disaster (that oncoming dental appointment or appraisal with our boss).

In the domain of losses the students applied far lower discount rates and even these low rates fell sharply once the amount of loss being faced increased. I conclude that there is at least casual evidence to imply discount rates decline as the investment horizon recedes and the amount invested grows. For large future losses discount rates are very low indeed and possibly even negative.

3.3.1   Discounting Single Outcomes Compared to Sequences of Outcomes

A key factor determining the discount rate applicable to a given choice is whether the choice is seen to be a one-off outcome or one outcome in a series which has to be evaluated as a bundle, for example games in a football fixture, or topics in a given course (e.g. should you revise for a cash-flow or a financial ratios question in your accountancy exam?). Lowenstein and Prelec (1993), based on experimental evidence concerning choice, state:

> Any factor whether personal or situational, that causes inter-temporal choices to fragment and to be perceived as a series of individual decisions will tend to induce high positive time discounting. Likewise, factors that cause such decisions to be internally 'framed' as sequences will promote low and even negative time discounting

(1993, p.108).

This conclusion was based on a number of experiments with subjects drawn from visitors to the Museum of Science and Technology in Chicago and (those long-suffering) undergraduate students. In one such experiment 95 students were asked:

Which do you prefer? (95 respondents)
Dinner in a fancy French restaurant (86%)
Dinner at a local Greek restaurant (14%)

For those who prefer a French meal: (82 students of original 95)

C: Dinner at the French restaurant on Friday in one month's time (80%)
D: Dinner at the French restaurant on Friday in two months' time (20%)

Or in a separate choice

E: Dinner at the French restaurant on Friday in one month's time and dinner at the Greek restaurant on Friday in two months' time (43%)
F: Dinner at the Greek restaurant on Friday in one month's time and dinner at the French restaurant on Friday in two months' time (57%)

This experiment revealed that an initial clear majority who wanted the nice (i.e. French) meal first was almost overturned once the decision was presented as part of a sequence. This reversal of expressed preference seems to be motivated by a desire to have a steadily improving set of outcomes.

Such a way of thinking, modelled on the 'How can we keep them down on the farm now that they've seen Paris?' mindset is easily recognizable. Indeed it is this very psychology that underpins a huge literature in market-based accounting on 'meeting and beating' analysts' consensus forecasts of earnings (see Abarbanell & Lehavy 2003, Graham *et al.* 2005, Kasznik & McNichols 2002). Managers appear to feel under incredible pressure to produce a steady stream of growing earnings-per-share figures and issue 'earnings guidance' to prepare analysts for any deviation from the out-standing consensus forecast. Analysts, like the experimental subjects in the above example, seem to wish to hear slowly improving news about the prospects of the companies they follow. The trends in news releases, as well as their overall implication for the long-run performance of the stock, are clearly important for CEOs and analysts alike.

3.4 Investment Behaviour When Discount Rates are Declining: Investing in a 'Golden Egg'

Laibson (1997) provides a model in which the impact of the adoption of a declining discount rate on the future value of consumption and hence savings and investment can be considered. In this world an investor can discount consumption delayed until next year more than he discounts consumption delayed from a decade to 11 years ahead. To do this consider an investor's portfolios to be made up of two types of assets. The first asset, x_t, is a liquid asset that can be sold at any date t to raise income for consumption at date t. The second is an illiquid asset, z_t, that can be sold at date t to obtain income for consumption in the next period, $t+1$. Laibson (1997) assumes for convenience that both assets offer the same return which I initialize here to be one. The purchase of illiquid asset is then a method by which the investor can pre-commit himself to reducing consumption in this period and the next. Laibson (1997, p.445) interprets the use made of such investments as being similar to 'the goose that laid the golden egg' because it promises long-term benefits in return for short-term cost (you have to remember not to have the goose for dinner). A number of investment vehicles have this sort of property of restrictions on withdrawals, Christmas savings clubs, 'saver' accounts which require notice of a withdrawal and some ISA products sold in the UK.

The investor allocates his consumption across time periods 1 to T, where T is the last period of the investor's life. Every time period is divided into four segments, characterized by some activity/decision as follows:

1. Production occurs and the investor's assets x_t and z_t, chosen at date $t-1$, both yield the same return, $R_t = 1 + r_t$ and the investor supplies one unit of labour regardless of the wage to be paid for it.

2. A wage y_t is paid for the labour performed in segment 1 of the time period and the proceeds of investment in the liquid asset are paid out, $R_t x_{t-1}$.
3. A choice regarding current consumption is made, so $c_t \leq y_t + R_t x_{t-1}$ which keeps current consumption within the bounds of current income, y_t plus currently realizable investment income R_{xt-1} (given only x is liquid and even if you sold z you would have to wait until the next time period to get the proceeds of selling z now). Finally, $R_t = (1 + r_t)$, where r is the discount rate applicable to the consumption stream at date t.
4. A new asset allocation across the liquid and illiquid asset (x_t and z_t) is made to satisfy the budget constraint

$$y_t + R_t(z_{t-1} + x_{t-1}) - c_t = z_t + x_t$$
$$x_t, z_t \geq 0$$

and the investor $x_0, z_0 \geq 0$. So resources left over from the immediately prior period, $t - 1$ (the left-hand side of the above budget constraint), are the only source of investment funds to buy either the liquid asset x or the illiquid asset z at time t. The requirement that balances of the liquid and illiquid assets, x and z, may not go negative rules out short-selling equilibria and so greatly simplifies the modelling process.

Laibson (1997) assumes the investor can borrow against his holding of the illiquid asset, z_t, to fund present consumption for the next period. These asset reallocations are undertaken in segment 4 of each time period. The investor's utility is then a function of present and future expected utility and his utility function takes the form

$$U_t = E_t \left[u(c_t) + \beta \sum_{\tau=1}^{T-t} \delta^\tau u'(c_{t+\tau}) \right] \tag{3.12}$$

where future consumption no longer matters to the investor on the last date T as there is no more future left at that point and τ indicates increments in time forwards until some terminal date $T-t$. Equation (3.12) differs from the usual lifetime consumption-based utility function by the intervention of the function β in the process of discounting future consumption, where β will act to capture investors' impatience to consume in the model. That is, impatience is reflected in the degree to which investors apply short-term discount rates in excess of long-term discount rates for the same span of inter-temporal reallocation of consumption.

Assume $0 < \beta < 1$ in Equation (3.12) captures the essential impact of a declining discount rate on the investor's inter-temporal allocation of consumption and assume

$$\text{discount factor} = \begin{cases} 1 & \text{if } \tau = 0 \\ \beta \delta^\tau & \text{if } \tau > 0 \end{cases} \tag{3.13}$$

where the per-period discount rate between τ and $\tau + 1$ is $1 - \beta\delta/\beta\delta$, or zero, but beyond that horizon is simply $(1 - \delta)/\delta$ and the restriction

$$\frac{1-\delta}{\delta} < \frac{1-\beta\delta}{\beta\delta} \tag{3.14}$$

holds because $\beta < 1$. So for a very simple case where both δ and β take on a value of 0.9, the above inequality reduces to $(1 - 0.9)/0.9 < (1 - 0.92)/0.92$ or $0.11 < 0.23$. So after the current period the discount rate applied by investors to the future stream of consumption exhibits a once and for all drop beyond $\tau = 1$ (Frederick, Lowenstein & O'Donoghue 2002, p.366).

3.5 Hyperbolic Discount Factors

This class of discount factor model, sometimes denoted as the 'hyperbolic' discount rate model, allows the discount rate applied in evaluating future consumption to decline over the investor's forecast horizon. It turns out that a simple hyperbola function of the form

$$(1 + \alpha\tau)^{\frac{\gamma}{\alpha}} \quad \alpha, \gamma > 0$$

represents such a discounting process well. Here $\gamma, \alpha > 0$ and γ is the pure rate of time preference and the instantaneous discount function, τ, of such a function for this model takes the form at time τ as follows

$$\frac{-f'(\tau)}{f(\tau)}$$

where $f'(\tau)$ is the first derivative of the discount function $f(\tau)$. So this function tells us how much discount rates fall proportionately as the time period considered (τ) grows. While $f(\tau)$ for the standard constant discount rate model we all know and love is simply $1/\delta$, in the declining discount rate case of the hyperbolic function $f(\tau)$ becomes

$$\frac{\gamma}{(1 + \alpha\tau)}$$

And so the applicable discount rate declines as the investment horizon lengthens. This form of 'hyperbolic' discount function will be considered later in the chapter. For now it is enough to notice that the discount rate which applies to consumption decisions declines in the delay, τ, by a factor α.

Figure 3.1 displays the impact of varying γ and α relative to each other. A high rate of pure time preference, γ, relative to the impact of a time delay, α makes for a more shallow (hyperbolic style) discount function.

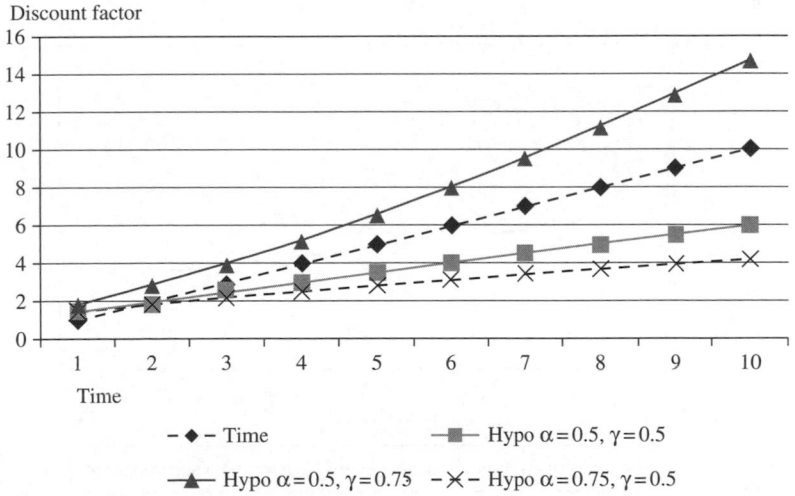

Figure 3.1 Choices of hyperbolic discounting function

A numerical example of quasi-hyperbolic discounting

The impact of transforming the discount rate applied in this way can be illustrated by a simple numerical example employing a discount factor δ of 0.97 (or a discount rate, r, of about 3%, recall $\delta = 1/(1 + r)$) in the constant discount rate case and higher at 0.99 for the 'quasi-hyperbolic' discount rate case (or a higher short-term discount rate, r, of 1%). As can be seen from Figure 3.2, while the hyperbolic discount rate function has a more shallow slope, reflecting the lower discount rate (higher discount factor) being applied, the most dramatic difference is reflected by the drop in the discount factor in period 1, induced by the parameter β. This kink in the discount factor is that implied by Equation (3.13) above. Outcomes in the immediate future are quite heavily discounted relative to those beyond the immediate horizon.

This makes sense of course. Beyond the immediate future it is more difficult to plan ahead. I may prefer a night off with my wife tomorrow night rather than in a week's time. But in a month's time it is hard to say which evening will be more convenient and/or pleasant for me to relax on. In the even more distant future I may lose my job, or even die, and so may feel indifferent about delaying the meal a week.

The form of the hyperbolic discount factor means that the preferences regarding future consumption are not consistent across all dates. My preferences regarding the delay of time off with my wife depend on how far ahead I evaluate the delay from. If the delay is considered from a date close to the meal the delay will upset me more than if I consider a similar delay far into the future.

In my numerical example in Figure 3.2 my attitude to a delay changes at or around 25 time periods (say days). Prior to the passage of 25 days using a constant exponential discount factor produces the same result as a more complicated hyperbolic discount factor, but after that date the discounted value of the delayed reward is greater under the exponential than the hyperbolic discount regime. That is, the exponential discount factor applied is lower than that inferred from using the quasi-hyperbolic discount specification. Recall the discount rate is δ, but $(1 - \delta)$ is the exponential discount factor.

To illustrate this consider winning a small or a big treat. Let say it's England winning through to the final of the World Cup in 2010 (in South Africa) or alternatively winning the World Cup in Wembley

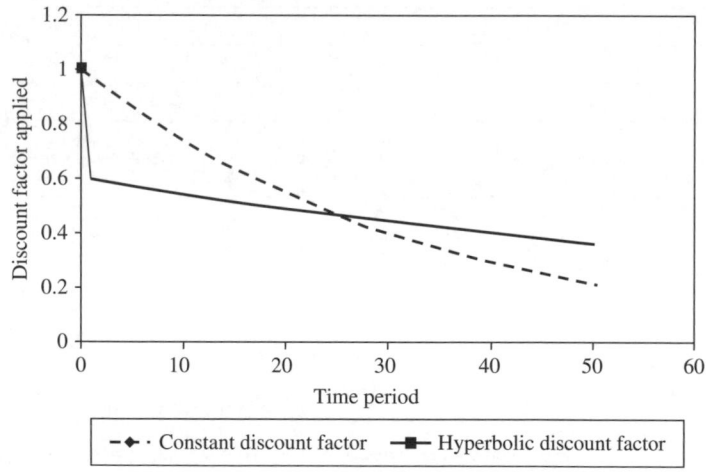

Figure 3.2 Alternative discount factors

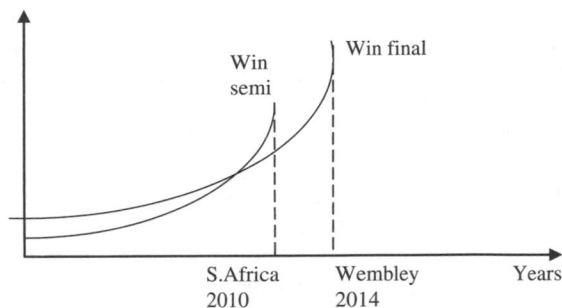

Figure 3.3 Time-inconsistent choice over whether to win 2010 or 2014 World Cup

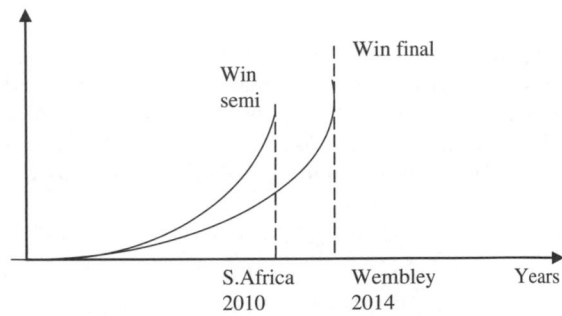

Figure 3.4 Time-consistent choice over whether to win 2010 or 2014 World Cup

(where else) against Germany (who else) in 2014. We might expect our preferences over these two outcomes to look something like Figure 3.4 (based on Lowenstein 1992b, p.97).

This choice makes clear that while dispassionately I might realize it is better to wait until 2014 to fully restore national honour, when the kick-off time arrives in Johannesburg in 2010 I may be willing to sacrifice a lot to see England progress to the final. The passion of my desire for football glory makes my choices, while understandable, inconsistent.

This pattern of choice is not consistent with a representation employing a constant exponential discount rate, e^r. The same choice as in Figure 3.3, using a constant exponential representation, which is in almost universal usage in modern finance, would look something like Figure 3.4.

While the strength of preference for a 2014 outright victory increases over time the basic structure of preferences prevails and hence the resulting choice made never changes.

3.6 Valuation by Using the Matching Law

The convenience and intuitive appeal of the constant exponential discount function makes us loath to discard it in favour of some diffuse alternative capable of rationalizing the preference for more immediate, but less valuable, alternatives. Fortunately a number of fairly easy-to-use alternative discount factors do exist, which are both tractable and consistent with the choices investors actually make, rather than those a standard discount utility framework implies they should make. Following

Ainslie and Haslam (1992) I discuss one common choice suggested by Herrnstein (Herrnstein 1961, Chung & Herrnstein 1967). Herrnstein considered a choice between an award A available at time T, with probability RR (the 'reward rate') and some greater award A' available with some later date T' with probability RR'. He suggested the relative values of award A and A' at dates T and T' respectively were given by a 'matching principle' as follows

$$\frac{V}{V'} = \frac{RR}{RR'} \cdot \frac{A}{A'} \cdot \frac{T'-t}{T-t} \qquad (3.15)$$

From Ainslie and Haslam (1992, pp.65–7) I assume the reward rate is always one (the investor is sure to get his award, A or A') so we can drop RR out of the solution to give the expression

$$\frac{V}{V'} = \frac{A}{A'} \cdot \frac{1 + (T+\Delta) - t}{1 + T - t} = 1 \qquad (3.16)$$

which derives from setting the length of the delay, t, to a value which makes the investor indifferent between the award A and some higher award A', so that he regards them as offering equivalent value, $V = V'$. So simple rearrangement gives a solution for the delay that makes the investor indifferent between receiving A at T and A' at $1 + T + \Delta$. Begin by noting $V'/V = 1$ and then multiplying both sides of Equation (3.16) by A and then pre-multiplying both sides by t we obtain

$$-A' = \frac{A[1 + (1 + T + \Delta) - t]}{1 + T - t}$$
$$\Rightarrow -A'(1 + T - t) = A.[1 + (T + \Delta) - t]$$
$$\Rightarrow -A'(1 + T) - t(A - A') = A.[1 + (T + \Delta)]$$
$$\Rightarrow -t(A - A') = A[1 + (T + \Delta)] - A'(1 + T)$$
$$\Rightarrow t = \frac{A.(1 + T + \Delta) - A'.(1 + T)}{A' - A}$$

where t is the delay which equates the value of award A at T and the higher award A' at $T+\Delta$. Consider a numerical example where we increment A' relative to A for a given value of Δ of 3; t, the delay, then 'matches' the investor's implied valuations of A and A' in accordance with the 'matching law' of Equation (3.15).

In the classic tradition of behaviourism Herrnstein's evidence is collected from pigeons pecking mounted keys for a reward of corn. He noted a close linear correspondence between the relative frequency of responding (pecking the key) and reinforcement offered (corn released to the pigeon). While care is needed, because investors are not pigeons (nor are pigeons investors so far as I know), the insight into behaviour motivated to maximize amongst our feathered friends might be transferable from pigeons to humans.

The essential insight of Herrnstein's 'matching law' is the prediction that an agent (pigeon or investor) will choose the alternative offering the highest ratio of award/reward (A) to delay in receiving it (D). So an investor (pigeon) faced with the alternatives of receiving £1 in a day ($A/D = 1/1 = 1$) or £2 in 10 days' time ($A/D = 2/10 = 0.2$) will choose the first, less valuable, but more immediate, option.

Consider another choice under the matching law, this time receiving £1 in six days' time ($A/D = 0.166$) compared to receiving £2 in 10 days ($A/D = 0.2$). Here the matching law predicts a patient wait by the investor for the more valuable, but delayed, alternative. Now suppose after five days have elapsed we ask the investor (we can just tell the pigeon) to revisit his prior choice. Now it appears the investor perceives the same choice rather differently. The first alternative is transformed into the prospect of £1 in a day's time ($A/D = 1$). The second alternative is transformed into £2 in five days' time ($A/D = 0.4$). Now the matching law predicts the same-choice alternative results in the lower value, but the more immediately received alternative being chosen. The investor's choices are unstable, and/or inconsistent, over time and the choice the investor makes depends on how far ahead the rewards are relative to each other. Life has just got complicated.[4] No wonder the discounted utility model is so popular!

This conflict is called 'time inconsistency' by economists and not surprisingly they try to avoid it in their simpler expository modelling. Constant discount rates exhibit time consistency. How strongly you dislike a delay in consuming something you enjoy just depends on how long the delay is, not what vantage point in time you evaluate the delay from. So it is only worth complicating life to incorporate time-inconsistent preferences if doing so can explain things about financial decisions we are interested in but cannot explain when using the standard constant exponential discount rate model. To see whether this is the case Laibson (1997) examines the sort of decisions investors will make if their evaluation of future consumption is characterized by a 'quasi-hyperbolic' discount factor. For example, the numerical example given in Figure 3.1 suggests that for investments with very long maturities the assumptions we make about the pattern of discount rates that are applicable may not matter that much.

Figure 3.4 makes clear the 'hyperbolic' nature of discount rates that result from an increasing unwillingness by the investor to be fobbed off for a delay in delivery by some incremental increase in the award received. In the numerical example traced in Figure 3.5 based on Equation (3.15), A is set equal to 1, T is 1 and Δ is 3. For these values unit increments in $A'A = 1, 2, 3, \ldots, 20$ are examined to trace their impact on t, the acceptable delay in receiving the reward for the investor.

Figure 3.5 clarifies how greater increments in the final reward granted to the investor can 'buy' his compliance in greater delays, but it does so at a declining rate. Somewhat oddly a delay from two to three days ahead for consumption is much cheaper to buy than a delay of some hours in the receipt of consumption two days ahead.

3.6.1   On Pigeons and Men: Comparing Hyperbolic and Exponential Discounting

Some of the initial evidence in support of the 'matching law' concerned choices made by pigeons required to peck alternative levers to obtain either a small reward now or a bigger

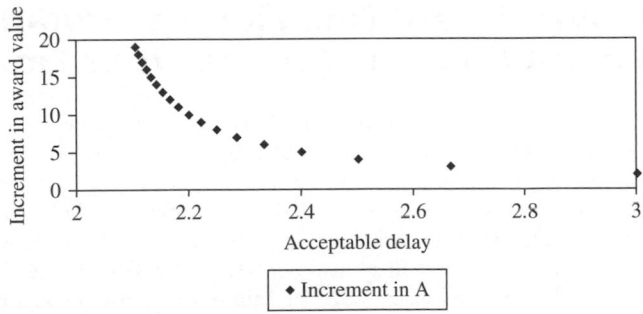

Figure 3.5   How increments in available award make delays more acceptable

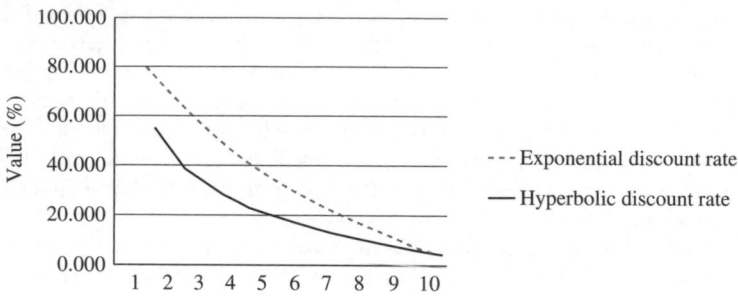

Figure 3.6 Hyperbolic versus exponential discounting and asset value for pigeons

reward in the future (Ainslie 1974). For pigeons the general formula for value in the presence of a hyperbolic discounting

$$\text{Value} = \frac{\text{Award}}{\text{Constant}_1 + (\text{Constant}_2 \times \text{delay})}$$

takes the very simple form *Value = Award*/(1+*delay*), where the *delay* is 1, 2, 3 days/weeks or years in the future because both constants take values of roughly one. Value under our good old friend exponential discounting takes the familiar form

$$\text{Value} = \text{Award} \times (1 - \text{Discount rate}(\%))^{\text{delay}}$$

Figure 3.6 plots the value of an investment over a 10-period horizon for our representative investor (a pigeon in this case). The increasing disparity between value when the reward is discounted exponentially and hyperbolically is clear. While early on the asset has a very similar value to the investor, regardless of how he discounts it, at later dates (like 10 periods' time) the asset has much less value to him (see Ainslie 2001, pp.28–35). So while exponential discounting equally weights discount rates over all time periods in the investor's life, hyperbolic discounters front-end load the discounting process. Much evidence suggests that pigeons are not alone in doing this. Those who borrow on credit cards at rates of interest exceeding 20%, while retaining positive balances in their deposit account, may be guilty of such seeming inconsistency in their choices.

3.7 How Investment Decisions are Made When Discount Factors Decline Over Time

The problem of consistent choice over time and especially the need to develop good habits of self-control have been approached from two alternative paths by both psychiatrists and economists. One approach focuses on weighing rewards to a proposed course of activity and consequent wants which arise. The other emphasizes the hierarchy of wants and how people make judgements between them. I want to go on holiday, but also need to finish this book. How do I adjudicate between these two very reasonable desires contained within myself (Ainslie 2001, p.13)? Thus for (expected) utilitarians, addictive or self-defeating behaviour simply reflects a failure to choose the action yielding the best reward. But maybe we need to be more pressing in our questioning and enquire who the best reward is being given for?

Let the investor have some history of consumption choices, h_t over the period t to $t - 1$ and S_t, where S is a choice set available to the investor in each of the t time periods. So $s|h_t$ is the path of consumption and asset allocation decisions across the whole of the investor's planning horizon from t to T. Finally, let $U_t(s|h_t)$ be the utility of the time t incarnation[5] of the investor from the strategy regarding future consumption conditional upon his recent consumption history h_t. Laibson (1997) is able to identify a unique dynamic equilibrium strategy from date t to T for an investor in this sort of world, from which he will not wish to deviate given his best conjecture about future consumption, discount rates and asset allocations. This strategy constitutes what economic theorists call a 'sub-game perfect equilibrium' for an investor's investment choices. This game is played out over T successive periods with T incarnations of the investor's 'self' in control in each period. A sub-game perfect equilibrium is defined as follows (see Rasmusen 1994, pp.93–6):

A strategy consumption/investment profile is a sub-game perfect Nash equilibrium if:

- it is a Nash equilibrium for all games, $t = 1 \ldots T$; and
- it is also a Nash equilibrium within each separate period on the path from now to T.

John Nash is of course the great, but troubled, Nobel Prize-winning economist portrayed by Russell Crowe in the film *A Beautiful Mind*. Nash solved the problem of how to devise my best/optimal competitive strategy given I am not sure how my opponents are going to reply. The answer Nash said was to solve for the equilibrium in 'best' strategies. So I simply make choices which are best for me, given my assumption my opponents will do what is best for themselves. Knowing this, I will anticipate their actions in constructing my own action plan in a way that best suits me. The concept of sub-game perfection arises from the repeated application over time of this idea.

This way of thinking about decisions is quite testing, so there follows a little example of a sub-game perfect equilibrium for a two-player, two-time period, two-strategies game taken from Rasmusen (1994, p.96). This is in order to try to make the meaning and application of the concept of sub-game perfection in financial models clearer.

3.7.1 A Simple Example of a Sub-Game Perfect Equilibrium

Consider an investor facing the problem of funding future consumption. Let the investor have two separate 'incarnations' of himself that he needs to rationalize: these are himself today that I call 'Mr Now' and himself tomorrow which I call 'Mr Then'. Let these two distinct incarnations or 'selves' have strategy sets as follows:

Mr Now = {Invest/Buy z_t, Consume/Sell z_t}
Mr Then = {Invest/Buy z_t, Consume/Sell z_t}

These strategies can be represented in a payoff table on the assumption that Mr Now has a total of 2.1 units of consumption to invest. This derives from 1 unit earned as labour income (recall the first segment of each time period in Laibson's (1997) model) and 1.1 the payoff to his holding of the illiquid asset z. So if he consumes now he can consume 2.1 immediately and nothing later (Then). If he invests, however, he can only consume 1.1 now, but gets 1.1 in the future (by which time he has metamorphosized into Mr Then), assuming the interest is 10%. If he has enough control to invest both now and in the future he can earn a cumulative return of $1.21 = 1.1^2$. Assume if the investor does invest he must buy one unit of the illiquid asset, z, costing 1. We can represent the game in normal form as shown in Figure 3.7.

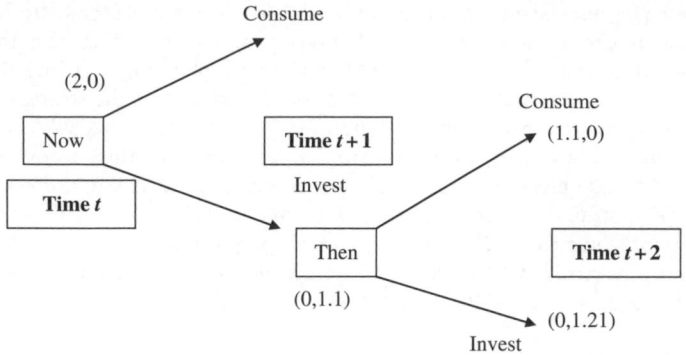

Figure 3.7 A sub-game imperfect equilibrium with a constant discount rate

This payoff matrix results from the fact if Mr Now consumes everything today, including the endowment of 1.1 (from an investment of 1 in *z* yesterday) then there is nothing left for Mr Then to invest. If Mr Then decides to invest, despite the fact Mr Now has left him nothing to invest with, he has to borrow £1 to buy one unit of the illiquid asset *z*. For simplicity I assume borrowing is impossible, otherwise I need to introduce another 'strategy' and this gets more complicated than I wish to be right now. So I assume if he consumed all his wealth in the past he cannot now invest (see the upper right-hand cell). But if Mr Now invests in one unit of the illiquid asset *z* at a cost of £1 then Mr Then inherits Mr Now's £1 investment plus his interest of 10p (£1.1 in all, this is the bottom left-hand cell). If Mr Then decides to follow Mr Now's example and also invests, his future payoff is £1.21, but he has nothing to live on now (the bottom right-hand cell).

The very same game, but twice repeated at *t* and *t* + 1, can be represented in extensive form as the payoff 'tree' in Figure 3.7.

From Figure 3.7 it is clear that Mr Now would choose to consume in the first period as it offers him a better payoff. But Mr Then prefers Mr Now to invest, but he is not making the choice. In the second of the successive games Mr Then is the new Mr Now. Once again Mr Then (the Mr Now of *t* + 1) will choose not to invest. So the sub-game individual period equilibria here are not equilibria for the game as a whole. So this game, with its current payoffs, does not result in a sub-game perfect equilibrium because each individual game has a solution (Consume now), but this is not the optimal solution to the game overall.

Now consider an alternative case of exactly the same game as that above but where the discount rate falls in the second game, compared to the first. Let's go crazy and assume that the interest rate is zero in the second game! Consider this an extreme form of hyperbolic discounting. It is just a game after all. We repeat the lay-out of the payoff of the game in normal and extensive form (over *t* to *t* + 2) in Figure 3.8.

Now we have a sub-game perfect equilibrium to the game. Just keep consuming. Mr Now prefers to consume as before, because the payoff to him from doing so is higher than investing. But when Mr Then, the new Mr Now (of the second game), faces the same decision he will decide to consume too. Investing has no payoff any more, because the rate of return to it has gone to zero by assumption. From the point of view of Mr Then both the Invest and Consume options offer the same return 1 now or after one or two periods, 1.1. Investing is pointless. From Mr Then's perspective he gets a payoff of 1.1 whatever he does. So consuming in the first game and forgetting about the illiquid asset *z* makes good sense at both dates (Figure 3.8).

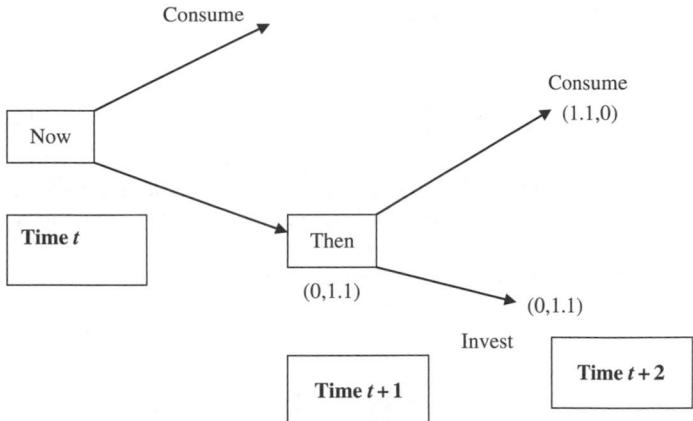

Figure 3.8 A sub-game perfect equilibrium with a declining (to zero) discount rate

3.7.2 The Properties of a Sub-Game Perfect Investment Strategy Equilibrium

Laibson (1997) uses the same intuition as in my simple example above to characterize an equilibrium investment strategy for investors applying hyperbolic discount rates. These conditions (see original paper for notation) begin with an upper bound on the utility the investor can gain from labour income, this is

$$u'(y_t) \geq \beta\delta^\tau \left(\prod_{i=1}^{\tau} R_{t+i} \right) u'(y_{t+\tau}) \quad \forall \; t, \tau \geq 1 \quad (A1) \tag{3.17}$$

This states the utility of current labour income, y_t is bounded above that of future discounted labour income, with the tightness of that restriction being determined by β, the degree to which future discount rates decline relative to the present rate. For an equilibrium to exist the utility of labour income must not only be positive, but also growing. This makes sense as attempts to transfer labour income across time at dates following t produce no gain in utility otherwise (the right-hand side of Equation (3.17) is zero). In a constant discount rate model, where discount rates simply never change so $\beta = 1$, the condition requires equality of marginal rates of discounted consumption at each and every date.

The next condition requires that present consumption income has at least as much value as that at any time in the future so

$$u'(c_t) = \mathop{Max}_{\tau \in \{1, \ldots T-t\}} \beta\delta^\tau \left(\prod_{i=1}^{\tau} R_{t+i} \right) u'(c_{t+\tau}) \quad (P1)$$

This condition is just a standard Euler equation for an economy with liquidity constraints. If the investor gets more joy from deferred than current consumption then he should simply save more to equalize the consumption's value at each date. The second condition relates to when the investor's budget constraint is binding and he is limited in his consumption by his income. This requires

$$u'(c_t) > \max_{\tau \in \{1..., T-\tau\}} \beta \delta^\tau \left(\prod_{i=1}^{\tau} R_{t+i} \right) u'(c_{t+\tau}) \Rightarrow c_t = y_t + R_t x_{t-1} \quad (P2)$$

This simply states that if current consumption has greater utility at the margin than at any date in the future this can only be because he has no more money to spend on consumer goods at the moment. If he could afford to do so he would just keep on spending.

The final two conditions Laibson (1997) imposes on the path of investment chosen reflect strategic choices the investor makes in allocating his assets between the liquid and illiquid assets, x and z. These are:

$$u'(c_{t+1}) < \max_{\tau \in \{1,...T-t-1\}} \delta^\tau \left(\prod_{i=1}^{\tau} R_{t+1} \right) u'(c_{t+1+\tau}) \Rightarrow x_t = 0 \quad (P3)$$

$$u'(c_{t+1}) > \max_{\tau \in \{1,...T-t-1\}} \delta^\tau \left(\prod_{i=1}^{\tau} R_{t+1} \right) u'(c_{t+1+\tau}) \Rightarrow z_t = 0 \quad (P4)$$

The condition $P3$ arises from the desire of the investor's Self t incarnation to limit his Self $t+1$ incarnation to not spend too much by liquidating all liquid assets, i.e. all the assets Self $t+1$ could sell off to fund his immediate consumption ambitions. The investor's Mr Now incarnation realizes that Mr Then will have low marginal utility of consumption in the future, at $t+1$, so he liquidates all liquid assets in advance to avoid them being wasted on consumption at $t+1$ by his future incarnation Mr Then. Conversely, $P4$ is Self t's way of letting his Self $t+1$ incarnation consume as much as he wants next period if the marginal value of consumption is especially high at that date. Mr Now at date t realizes his Mr Then incarnation at date $t+1$ will face the highest marginal utility of consumption available at any date in his future life to T. This requires very high period $t+1$ consumption to allow his $t+1$ incarnation to avail himself of the opportunity to consume all available income and so he desires to maximize the amount of liquid assets at Mr Then's disposal to consume.

3.7.3 How Do Declining Discount Rates Affect Investment Behaviour?

If investors have access to 'golden egg' type investments (as modelled by Laibson 1997) what sort of investment behaviour would we expect to see? If we know this and observed such behaviour in the real world then maybe it's worth moving away from our nice tractable discounted utility model into the more messy world of time-inconsistent inter-temporal preferences.

One piece of evidence that may be seen as giving credence to the importance of hyperbolic discounting is the very close correspondence between current consumption and current income. Rational expectations models of consumption/investment behaviour suggest that we decide on saving and hence current consumption based on our 'permanent' or lifetime income. So if I get promoted at work I should increase my consumption to reflect my new elevated status in life and not just the addition to this month's pay-packet alone. But if I win £10,000 pounds in the National Lottery my current consumption should increase by a far smaller amount since this is just a bit of one-off luck that might have to last me a lifetime. Much empirical work has confirmed the very close relationship between current consumption and current income. This correspondence is much stronger than any estimable relation between current consumption and any reasonable estimate of what I might expect my lifetime future income to be. This may also explain why investors are quite so averse to short-term volatility in equity prices, an issue I explore more in a later chapter.

A further fact that the 'golden egg' model of Laibson (1997) may shed light on is the sharp decline in the savings rate in the United States and elsewhere and its coincidence with the diffusion of widespread consumer credit in the form of credit cards from Visa, MasterCard and others. While these financial innovations certainly increased consumer choice they may also undermine consumer techniques for self-control. Economists typically present more choice as inherently a good thing. But if self-control as a personal trait is valued by consumers, then it follows that techniques that induce it may also be valuable to them. Financial innovations that lead the consumer's current incarnation to undermine his future well-being may be contrary to his welfare. This may be seen as one root cause underpinning the rise in personal debt in the early part of this century and the subsequent 'credit crunch' of 2007 onwards.

3.8 Conclusion and Summary

Once we accept hyperbolic discounting as the norm for decision making and exponential discounting as a normative objective of how we would like to make investment decisions, modelling investors' choices becomes a more messy business than standard finance typically likes to admit. Each intertemporal choice between consuming now and then, that investment by its nature requires, becomes a struggle for self-command and decision-making autonomy. Ainslie (2001, p.39) states the case for its adoption as follows:

> Exchanging hyperbolic discounting for the exponential kind in the reward-maximizing process supplies utility theory with its missing element. Utility theory can now explain the seductiveness of self-defeating choices; and the assumption that a person has to maximize her expected, discounted, reward explains why she doesn't automatically learn to be objective, the way she does with sizes and distances. Reward has its effect directly and intellectual adjustment takes place only tangentially.

This chapter has considered some of the effects of declining discount rates in the investor's evaluation of possible future consumption streams. A wide range of experimental and market-based evidence suggests that this is a more reasonable assumption than the constant exponential discount rate embedded in the standard discounted utility model. Even the limited study given to the topic here suggests that life gets a lot more complicated once we step outside the confines of the standard discounted utility framework. It was therefore not surprising that Paul Samuelson's advancement of this simplifying technology was so widely hailed as a major contribution and its subsequent diffusion was so rapid. A particular problem for any attempt to move away from the discounted utility model is the inability to rely on the equation of marginal utility of consumption in each time period. Indeed, it is in the essence of hyperbolic (declining) discount rates that choices regarding consumption in each period are time inconsistent. This complication is a major price to pay unless these inconsistencies are a primary part of the behaviour we wish to explore. Consequently I will continue to make use of the constant discount rate discounted utility framework in this book; apart from in the chapter on entrepreneurship where the issue of self-control is one of the central issues I want to illuminate.

Appendix: Timely Choice: Euler Equations – Dynamics and Inter-Temporal Choice

Investment has choices at different dates at its heart. Good investors maximize the total value of their consumption over the whole life, by saving in feast years in anticipation of future famine. So much is clear even at the basic level of this teaching text aimed at final year undergraduate and Master's degree students in Europe. The problem for us is that this sort of inter-temporal optimization problem requires a level of mathematical sophistication not common amongst students enrolled in most business school programmes for example. So in this Appendix I briefly give a little hint about techniques used to study dynamic optimization and guide students to where more serious treatments of these issues can be found.

Return for a moment to our problem of maximizing the value of lifetime consumption in Equation (3.12) of the main chapter

$$U_t = E_t \left[u(c_t) + \beta \sum_{\tau=1}^{T-t} \delta^\tau u'(c_{t+\tau}) \right]$$

subject to the budget constraint that the investor cannot spend more money than he has earned or gained through previous investment

$$c_t \leq y_t + R_t x_{t-1}$$

The investor ensures he achieves his best lifetime consumption plan from his current age t to his year of death T by seeking to equate the discounted present value of consumption from each pound spent in the window t to T, that is his remaining lifetime

$$u'(c_t) = \underset{\tau \in \{1, \ldots T-t\}}{Max} \beta \delta^\tau \left(\prod_{i=1}^{\tau} R_{t+i} \right) u'(c_{t+\tau})$$

This is, of course, simply condition $P1$ in the Laibson (1997) model above.

This type of dynamic optimization of value received for resources invested lies at the heart of so many economic problems that a considerable literature has developed around the issue of dynamic optimization in economics.

Our hyperbolic investor's dynamic optimization problem takes the general form

$$Max \ U[c] = \int_t^T F[t, c(t), c'(t)] dt$$
$$\text{subject to } c(0) = A \quad \text{and} \quad c(T) = Z$$

which says the investor should maximize utility of his lifetime consumption as some function F, which is itself a function of the level of consumption each period, $c(t)$, and its marginal utility in that same period $c'(t)$ (Chiang 1999). Here utility is regarded as being maximized in continuous time rather than the discrete time problem considered by Laibson (1997). This simply means we add up changes over infinitely small nanoseconds of time to express the investor's total lifetime accumulated utility and hence use the integral methods of calculus rather than the summations of Equation (3.12) in the main body of this chapter. This integration happens over a time window t to T of the investor's expected life. So the trick of good investment is to choose the level of labour income and its target growth rate $y'(t)$ to maximize his lifetime utility, $U[y]$. In doing this the investor must take his current endowment of wealth, A, as given and set a path which will let him die with some level of consumption Z remaining for others to enjoy. The optimal trajectory of consumption is defined as passing from the endowment A to the terminal point Z according to time path defined by the time derivative $dU(c_t)/dt$, denoted $c'(t)$ in the above maximand. The Euler equation defining this path was first devised in 1744 by one of the legends of mathematics Leonhard Euler.

In order to isolate this unique path where utility is maximized consider slight deviations from it induced by slight perturbations around that optimal path that maximizes lifetime income, $c^*(t)$. So we have

$$c(t) = c^*(t) + \varepsilon(t)$$
$$\Rightarrow c'(t) = c^{*\prime}(t) + \varepsilon'(t)$$

Since consumption is maximized on the dynamic path $c^{*\prime}(t)$ and nowhere else it makes sense that the error around the optimal path of this perturbation is zero. So a defining characteristic of the dynamic path which maximizes lifetime consumption from A to Z is

$$\frac{dU(c)}{dt}\Big|_{\varepsilon=0} = 0$$

And this becomes the defining necessary condition for the optimal path of consumption. This optimal (sometimes termed 'extremal') path of consumption, which will maximize the investor's lifetime consumption, is given by a solution to a so-called 'Euler equation' of the form

$$u'(c(0)) = E_{y(1)|y(0)}\beta R_{(0)}u'\big(R_{(0)}\big(A_{(0)} + y_{(0)} - c_{(0)}\big) + y_{(0)}\big)$$

So in setting today's level of consumption $c(0)$ the investor makes some projection about his future income ($y(1)$) and consumption ($c(1)$) in order to defer or accelerate current consumption depending on his belief about his future needs.

While I try to avoid delving into complexities of the mathematical methods of economic dynamics in this book a number of excellent sources on that subject exist. These include Adda and Cooper (2003), Gandolfo (1997) and Shone (2002).

Questions

1. Refer to Figure 3.6. In that example I modelled the value of the investment as $1/(1 + T)$ but I also mentioned that in general the formula for the value was

$$\text{Value} = \frac{\text{Award}}{\text{Constant}_1 + (\text{Constant}_2 \times \text{delay})}$$

   Now assume that the second constant is 2, not 1. The value of 1 came from the pigeons. Investors are not pigeons so we need to consider such stuff. So our revised value function is now $1/(1 + 2 \times delay)$. What does the revised value function look like? Do you find it a more convincing description of how investors value assets?
2. We know that investors like to get bad things out of the way so they can get on and enjoy life, without thinking of repaying their student loan, or whatever. Refer to Figure 3.7 and the Mr Now/Mr Then consumption game and consider the impact of a negative discount rate of -10.0, which applies to Mr Then's investment. For Mr Now continue to assume his investments earn a rate of return of 10%. What is the sub-game perfect equilibrium investment strategy in this case (if there is one)?
3. I stressed how hyperbolic discount rates can be tricky to incorporate into financial decision making. For what issues do you think the effort may be justified?

Notes

1. The necessary notation is D is the dividend paid, r is the discount rate applicable, g is the expected growth rate of dividends and B is the principal/face value of the bond.
2. It is worthwhile noting that Samuelson himself was acutely aware of what a special case the discounted utility function was and certainly did not advance it for the ubiquity of usage it later enjoyed.
3. Richard Herrnstein was later to gain notoriety, if not ignominy, as a co-author of *The Bell Curve* (Herrnstein & Charles 1996). This text correlated race, poverty and IQ measures and was seen as some as seeking to justify the poor conditions of the urban black population in the United States.
4. This example is modelled on Rachlin and Laibson (1997, p.103).
5. I adopt this term from Benabou and Tirole (2002).

References

Abarbanell, J. & R. Lehavy (2003). Biased forecasts of earnings? The role of reported earnings in explaining apparent bias and over/under-reaction in analysts' earnings forecasts. *Journal of Accounting and Economics*, **36**: 105–46.

Adda, J. & R. Cooper (2003). *Dynamic Economics: Quantitative Methods Applications*. Boston, MA: MIT Press.

Ainslie, G. (1974). Impulse control in pigeons. *Journal of the Experimental Analysis of Behavior*, **21**: 485–9.

Ainslie, G. (2001). *Breakdown of Will*. Cambridge: Cambridge University Press.

Ainslie, G. & N. Haslam (1992). Hyperbolic discounting. In G. Lowenstein & J. Elster (eds), *Choice over Time*. New York: Russell Sage Foundation.

Benabou, R. & J. Tirole (2002). Self-confidence and personal motivation. *Quarterly Journal of Economics*, **117**: 871–913.

Chiang, A. (1999). *Elements of Dynamic Optimization*. Long Grove, IL: Waveland Press.

Chung, S.-H. & R. Herrnstein (1967). Choice and delay of reinforcement. *Journal of the Experimental Analysis of Behavior*, **10**: 67–74.

Frederick, S., G. Lowenstein & T. O' Donoghue (2002). Time discounting and time preference: a critical review. *Journal of Economic Literature*, **60**: 351–401.

Friedman, M. & L. Savage (1948). The utility analysis of choice involving risk. *Journal of Political Economy*, **48**: 279–304.

Gandolfo, G. (1997). *Economic Dynamics: Study Edition*. Berlin: Springer.

Graham, J., H. Campbell *et al.* (2005). The economic implications of corporate financial reporting. *Journal of Accounting and Economics*, **40**: 3–73.

Herrnstein, R. (1961). Relative and absolute strength of response as a function of frequency of reinforcement. *Journal of the Experimental Analysis of Behavior*, **4**: 267–72.

Herrnstein, R. & M. Charles (1996). *The Bell Curve: Intelligence and Class Structure in American Life*. New York: Free Press.

Kasznik, R. & M. McNichols (2002). Does meeting earnings expectation matter? Evidence from analysts' forecasts revisions and share prices. *Journal of Accounting Research*, **40**: 727–59.

Laibson, D. (1997). Golden eggs and hyperbolic discounting. *Quarterly Journal of Economics*, **112**: 443–77.

Lowenstein, G. (1988). Frames of mind in intertemporal choice. *Management Science*, **34**: 200–14.

Lowenstein, G. (1992a). The fall and rise of psychological explanations in the economics of intertemporal choice. In G. Lowenstein & J. Elster (eds), *Choice over Time*. New York: Russell Sage Foundation.

Lowenstein, G. (1992b). Intertemporal choice. In R. Thaler (ed.), *The Winner's Curse: Paradoxes and Anomalies in Economic Life*. Princeton, NJ: Princeton University Press.

Lowenstein, G. & D. Prelec (1992). Anomalies of intertemporal choice: evidence and interpretation. *Quarterly Journal of Economics*, **107**: 573–98.

Lowenstein, G. & D. Prelec (1993). Preferences for sequences of outcomes. *Psychological Review*, **100**: 91–108.

Lowenstein, G., D. Read & R. Baumeister (2003). *Time and Decision: Economic and Psychological Perspectives on Intertemporal Choice*. New York: Russell Sage Foundation.

Rachlin, H. & D. Laibson (eds) (1997). *The Matching Law: Papers in Psychology and Economics*. Cambridge, MA: Harvard University Press.

Rasmusen, E. (1994). *Games and Information: An Introduction to Game Theory*. Oxford: Blackwell.

Samuelson, P. (1937). A note on the measurement of utility. *Review of Economic Studies*, **4**: 155–61.

Shone, R. (2002). *Economic Dynamics: Phase Diagrams and their Economic Applications*. Cambridge: Cambridge University Press.

Thaler, R. (1981). Some empirical evidence on dynamic inconsistency. *Economic Letters*, **8**: 201–7.

Thaler, R. & H. Shefrin (1981). An economic theory of self-control. *Journal of Political Economy*, **89**: 392–406.

Weber, M. (1930). *The Protestant Ethic and the Spirit of Capitalism*. London: Routledge.

Chapter 4

Learning

❝ Nowadays most people die of a sort of creeping common sense, and discover when it is too late that the only things one never regrets are one's mistakes ❞

(Wilde 1891).

There is a danger we regard all mistakes by investors as evidence they are irrational. But in many other areas of life we regard making mistakes in a protected environment as means of learning. Hopefully subsequent editions of this book will remove errors, add new insights, etc. This does not prove its author is irrational (hopefully), but only capable of learning and improving his understanding of his chosen subject. This chapter examines the way in which investors learn and whether it is possible the supposed evidence of investors' irrationality is simply traces of their ability to learn.

4.1 Illustration and Structure

Moneyball (Lewis 2003) tells the story of how baseball manager Billy Beane took the Oakland A's from mid-league obscurity to supremacy by a systematic study of performance statistics little heeded by his peers. By 2002 top table players like the Toronto Blue Jays and the Boston Red Sox were emulating Beane's methods and even trying to recruit him. Lewis summarizes the success of Beane and the Oakland A's thus:

> Oakland had a willingness to rethink baseball: how it is managed, how it is played, who is best suited to play it and why. Understanding that he would never have a Yankee-sized check book, the Oakland A's general manager, Billy Beane, had set about looking for inefficiencies in the game. Looking for, in essence, new baseball knowledge

(Lewis 2003, p.xiv).

As students of finance the creation of new knowledge, or the recognition and exploitation of pre-existing trends, is central to what we seek to achieve. It certainly appears that Billy Beane found plenty of inefficiency in the US professional baseball league to exploit. The central terrain on which this new knowledge could be applied in baseball was in the initial draft of players into professional baseball squads from amateur college and high school teams. It was here that an awareness and understanding of past performance differentiated Billy Beane from all his peers. Beane projected future performance based on past performance as opposed to rankings based on occasional sighting by visiting scouts.

Standard finance assumes the best way to learn is the Bayesian way and Section 4.2 explains what I mean by that. It does so by presenting a number of simple numerical examples of how optimal/Bayesian learning occurs. But clearly some people, like Billy Beane, learn quicker and better than others. Section 4.3 asks why this is and why we might fail to follow Bayesian methods of updating our expectations in light of new evidence. Section 4.4 introduces some psychological evidence regarding a common problem in pattern recognition we are all prey to. This is the representativeness heuristic which states that we construct the anticipated distribution of future financial outcomes according to distribution of the impressions made by previous outcomes. So, extreme past outcomes will be overweighted when we consider the likelihood of future outcomes. This error in the way we process financial data has played such a central part in the development of behavioural finance as a subject, it forms the central core of Shefrin's landmark behavioural approach to asset pricing (Shefrin 2005). Finally, Section 4.5 reconsiders the operation of the capital asset pricing model (CAPM), where some investors learn more quickly than others or may simply not learn at all. Section 4.6 summarizes and concludes the chapter. An appendix to this chapter discusses Billy Beane and his use of statistical analysis of players' performance to bring the Oakland A's baseball team to the play-offs of the US professional baseball World Series. In doing so, Beane learned in ways his peers had failed to and created a new set of performance metrics for judging both his own and rival teams' performance.

From this chapter the reader should:

- Learn what rational, Bayesian learning is and how to construct and apply simple numerical applications.
- Understand why investors may not learn in a rational Bayesian way.
- Know how this process of learning impacts upon standard asset pricing models, like the CAPM.

4.2   Rational Learning

If investors are not irrational, but simply learning how to invest better, how do they learn? Once we know this we are in a better position to conclude that investors are not learning properly and are in fact in some sense irrational. Economists have a very simple answer to this question. Rational learning is undertaken in accordance with Bayes' rule. The Reverend Thomas Bayes of Tunbridge Wells in Kent was a well-known mathematician of his time and active member of the Royal Society. Following his death in 1761 Bayes' friend Richard Price ensured the publication of Bayes' most famous work (1763), which rescued his famous theorem for posterity. (Bellhouse (2004) gives a biography of Bayes, which reviews his numerous contributions to mathematics.)

4.2.1   Bayes' Rule

Bayes' rule is such a standard piece of the economist's toolkit that many textbook discussions exist (Hey 1979, 1983, Hirshleifer & Riley 1992, Howson & Urbach 2006). I draw on these sources heavily in this section, indicating particular sources where appropriate. Bayes' rule is a means for inferring the outcome of some event given the occurrence of another.

I consider one such event drawn from the currently ongoing 'credit crunch' resulting from the implosion of the market for securitized debt. One notable victim of the crisis was Bear Stearns, at the time the fifth-largest investment bank in the world. On 17 March Bear Stearns was acquired for $236 million, or $2 a share, by JP Morgan (*Economist* 2008). On the announcement of the deal, hurriedly put together with the help of the Federal Reserve, JP Morgan's share price jumped to add $14 billion to its value. This was such a good deal that this bid was later raised to $10, to value Bear Stearns at $2.1 billion. Given Bear Stearns had traded at $170 a share a year earlier JP Morgan could have a warm fuzzy feeling about the acquisition.

Let the occurrence of the considered event, here a bailout of Bear Sterns, be denoted by $X = x$, where X takes the form:

$X =$ {Bear Sterns is bailed out, Bear Stearns is not bailed out and so has to be liquidated}

This event occurs given the state of affairs y, where the set of states Y might be:

$Y =$ { JP Morgan meets with Bear Stearns under New York Federal Reserve guidance,
JP Morgan bids for Bear Stearns at \$2 per share,
JP Morgan bids for Bear Stearns at \$10 per share }

In what follows I denote the event $x = X$ as simply x and the state of the world $y = Y$ as y.

We can denote the conjunction of the considered event, given a particular state of affairs, as $\Pr[x|y]$. The conditional probability that $x = X$ given $y = Y$, for example JP Morgan acquires Bear Sterns following a \$10 bid, is given by

$$\Pr[x|y] = \frac{\Pr[x \cap y]}{\Pr[y]} \tag{4.1}$$

where the operator 'I' denotes conditional upon some state of the world and the upside-down cup shape captures the intersection of x and y, or just those occasions when the state y leads to the state x. So the above statements imply the conditional probability of X taking the value x, given Y takes the value y, is given by the probability of both conditions being fulfilled given the state world y has arisen. If Y is unlikely to ever equal the value y, for example if JP Morgan refuses to raise its offer for Bear Stearns above \$2 per share, then the conditional event becomes less likely to happen. But if Y is certain to equal y then the conditional probability of X equalling x is unaffected by uncertainty regarding Y.

At this point it is worthwhile recalling some basic properties of probabilities. These include:

1. For any given event the chance of $x = X$ occurring is bounded between impossibility and certainty, $0 \leq \Pr[x] \leq 1$.
2. If x and y are exclusive events (JP Morgan either acquires Bearn Stearns or it doesn't) then the probability of either of them occurring is simply the sum of each event occurring, $\Pr[x$ or $z] = \Pr[x] + \Pr[z]$ where z in our example would be JP Morgan not acquiring Bear Stearns.
3. Finally, the joint probability of x and y occurring is simply the probability of the state of the world given the event multiplied by the unconditional probability of that event, i.e. $\Pr[x \cap y] = \Pr[y|x]\Pr[x]$. Similarly, the joint probability of x and y is simply the probability of the event x conditional on the state of the world y multiplied by the unconditional probability of the state of the world y. So,

$$\Pr[x \cap y] = \Pr[x|y]\Pr[y] = \Pr[y|x]\Pr[x].$$

To see this imagine a \$10 a share bid makes an acquisition of Bear Stearns by JP Morgan a certainty. If that is the case then $\Pr[x|y]$ converges on 1 and the only determinant of the joint probability is whether JP Morgan will bid \$10 a share ($\Pr[y]$). In a similar way assume that JP Morgan pre-commits itself to bid a \$10 a share bid for Bear Stearns, so $\Pr[y] = 1$. In that event the only thing that matters is how attractive Bear Sterns finds such a bid.

Taking this third property of probabilities on board let us now return to Equation (4.1). It can now be restated using the third property of probabilities listed above:

$$\Pr[x|y] = \frac{\Pr[x \cap y]}{\Pr[y]}$$

$$\Pr[x|y] = \frac{\Pr[y|x]\Pr[x]}{\Pr[y]}$$

$$\frac{\Pr[x|y]}{\Pr[x]} = \frac{\Pr[y|x]}{\Pr[y]}$$

$$\Pr[y|x] = \frac{\Pr[x|y]\Pr[y]}{\Pr[x]} \tag{4.2}$$

This is the famous Bayes' theorem, where the term in the denominator of the last line is the prior concerning x and the right-hand side is the posterior probability.

We can decompose the determinants of the posterior probability of the state y given the observation of the event x into two parts:

- The prior probability of the state of the world y, $\Pr[y]$.
- The relative likelihood of the event given the state, which is given by the ratio of the conditional probability of the event x given the state y to the unconditional probability of the event x occurring, $\Pr[x|y]/\Pr[x]$.

Returning to Bayes' rule, in Equation (4.2), suppose the likelihood of the event is certain, so $\Pr[x|y]/\Pr[x] = 1$. Here learning about the state of the world, y, tells us nothing about whether the event x will happen or not. The effect x and the state y are said to be independent with the state of the world y having no impact on the probability of x happening. In this event the posterior probability of the state of the world y is not affected by whether the event x has occurred or not.

4.2.2   Elements of Bayesian Revision

Bayes' rule makes clear the conditional probability of some outcome, given the signal received regarding its likelihood is a function both of how likely the signal is in the first place and how much more likely the outcome becomes if we observe the signal is about to happen.[1] Recall $\Pr[x]$ is the probability attached to some outcome occurring before any signal about its likelihood is received (or the unconditional probability of the event $\Pr[x]$). Let the number of conceivable outcomes (x_i) be 2 for the purpose of this illustration, $i = 1, 2$. This probability can itself be broken down into outcomes associated with a number of signals concerning the probability of each of the two outcomes x_i. These elements combine to yield the probability of each state, given the signal received $\Pr[x_i|y_j]$. For illustrative purposes assume there are three states, y_j, where $j = 1, 2, 3$. This representation can be represented in tabular form as shown in Table 4.1.

The investor's beliefs under the process of Bayesian revision reflect a weighted average of expected outcomes (x_i) in the light of various signals concerning each state's likelihood of occurrence. Each signal can foretell (or fail to foretell) one of the two possible outcomes in our example (recall x_i, $i = 1, 2$). Overall the chance of receiving one of the three signals (recall y_j, $j = 1, 2, 3$) is certain. So $\Sigma j \Pr[y_j] = 1$. Similarly one of the two states will occur (which makes it important to envisage all conceivable outcomes, so that the i states are exhaustive). Hence $\Sigma i \, x_i = 1$.

Table 4.1 Joint probability of outcome given the signal received

Signal (y_j)	1	2	3	Posterior probability of state given the signal received
Outcomes (x_i)	$\Pr[x_1|y_1]$	$\Pr[x_1|y_2]$	$\Pr[x_1|y_3]$	$\Pr[x_1|y]$
	$\Pr[x_2|y_1]$	$\Pr[x_2|y_2]$	$\Pr[x_3|y_3]$	$\Pr[x_2|y]$
Probability of ith signal (y_j)	$\Pr[y_1]$	$\Pr[y_2]$	$\Pr[y_3]$	1

An analogous converse decomposition can be constructed to infer the likelihood of observing one of the three possible signals given that one of the two possible outcomes in our illustration will occur (Table 4.2). This gives a likelihood of observing the signal y_j if outcome x_i is about to occur.

The posterior probability of the outcome envisaged is then retrieved by dividing the elements of the joint probability of the event given the likelihood of each signal by the unconditional probability of the event occurring ($\Pr[x]$). Recall again the third property of probabilities discussed in the previous section. This states that the joint probability of the outcome, given the signal, is simply the conditional probability of observing the signal y_j given outcome x_i is about to occur multiplied by the unconditional probability of the ith state occurring, i.e. $\Pr[x_i \cap y_j] = \Pr[y_j|x_i]\Pr[x_i]$. Using this result and dividing the joint probability by the likelihood we obtain a table of inferred posterior probabilities as shown in Table 4.3.

Note here I require the conditional probabilities of the outcome to sum to one. While subjectively formed probabilities need not satisfy this requirement it does seem a fairly intuitive criterion to impose.

Table 4.2 Likelihood of receiving signal (y_j) given that outcome (x_i) is in prospect

Signals (y_j)	y_1	y_2	y_3	Cumulative probability of signal
Outcomes (x_i)	$\Pr[y_1|x_1]$	$\Pr[y_1|x_2]$	$\Pr[y_1|x_3]$	1
	$\Pr[y_2|_1]$	$\Pr[y_2|x_2]$	$\Pr[y_2|x_3]$	1

Table 4.3 Posterior probability of an event x occurring, given signal y has been observed

Signal (y_j)	1	2	3
Outcomes (x_i)	$\Pr[x_1 \cap y_1] =$ $(\Pr[y_1|x_1]\Pr[y_1])/\Pr[x_1]$ $\Pr[x_1 \cap y_3] =$ $(\Pr[y_3|x_1]\Pr[y_3])/\Pr[x_1]$	$\Pr[x_1 \cap y] =$ $(\Pr[y|x_1].\Pr[y2])/\Pr[x_1]$ $\Pr[x_1 \cap y_3] =$ $(\Pr[y_3|x_1]\Pr[y_3])/\Pr[x_1]$	$\Pr[x_1 \cap y_3] =$ $(\Pr[y_3|x_1]\Pr[y_3])/\Pr[x_1]$ $\Pr[x_1 \cap y_3] =$ $(\Pr[y_3|x_1]\Pr[y_3])/\Pr[x_1]$
Cumulative conditional probability of outcome given signal received	1	1	1

4.2.3 The Value of Stock Recommendations

A multi-million pound industry exists in giving investment advice. The best 'superstars' are feted as 'gurus' and are sought out eagerly by investors and CEOs. But how do they know their investment advisors are any good? In April 2003, 10 of the largest investment banks, advising investors trading on the NASDAQ, agreed to pay past clients nearly \$1.4 billion in damages in recompense for bad advice to invest in companies on floatation. I examine this issue in greater depth in Chapter 18.

One very simple way to check this out is to ask whether we learn anything about a company's prospects by listening to an analyst's recommendation regarding that stock.[2] Suppose there are two basic types of shares: winners, whose value rises; and losers, whose value does not rise. So I consider the 'event' to be the share purchased being a winner. Can we learn anything from investment banks' recommendations about whether a given share will be a winner or not?

I will assume a recommendation can take one of three values as indicated below

$$Recom = \{1 = Buy,$$

$$2 = Hold,$$

$$3 = Sell\}$$

Applying Bayes' theorem to this more practical case we have

$$Pr[recom_i|winner] = \frac{Pr[winner|recom_i]Pr[recom_i]}{Pr[winner]} \tag{4.3}$$

Where $Pr[winner]$ is the unconditional probability the share will be a winner, regardless of the recommendation an investment bank makes and $i = 1$ to 3, i.e. buy, hold or sell.

As before, if the probability that a share is a winner is roughly equal across recommendation classes then the likelihood of a stock being a winner conditional on the bank's recommendation is simply the unconditional probability of any stock being a winner, regardless of the analysts' recommendation, $Pr[x] = Pr[x|y]$. In this event the posterior probability that a recommendation is a buy, given the stock will be a winner, is simply the unconditional probability of a buy recommendation. To see the logic behind this we can imagine the decomposition of the denominator term $Pr[winner|recom_i]$ in Equation (4.3) as follows:

$$Pr[winner] = Pr[winner|buy] + Pr[winner|hold] + Pr[winner|sell]$$

Or more compactly

$$Pr[Winner] = \sum_{i=1}^{3} Pr[Winner|recom_i]$$

Upon substitution into Equation (4.3) and application of Bayes' theorem we obtain

$$Pr[recom_i|winner] = \frac{Pr[winner_i|recom_i]Pr[recom_i]}{\sum_{i=1}^{3} Pr[winner|recom_i]Pr[recom_i]}$$

This is the form of the equation I use in the numerical illustrations described below.

A numerical application of Bayes' model

To see Bayes' theorem in action I assign some values to these various notional probabilities to see how the rule might be applied practically. Assume that buy recommendations are 60% of all recommendations (so Pr[*buy*] = 0.6), hold recommendations are 30% of all recommendations (so Pr[*hold*] = 0.3) and, finally, sell recommendations make up 10% of all recommendations (so Pr[*sell*] = 0.1). Let the initial unconditional probability (prior) of the investor regarding the probability he is holding a winning share be 50% (so Pr[*winner*] = 0.5).

What is the posterior probability of each recommendation type being associated with holding a winner? To infer this we need to know more about how confident we are that a buy recommendation truly implies the stock is a winner. So assume a buy recommendation foretells a winning stock 70% of the time, Pr[*winner*l*buy*] = 0.7; a hold recommendation foretells a winning stock 25% of the time, Pr[*winner*l*hold*] = 0.25; and, finally, a sell recommendation foretells a winning stock 5% of the time, Pr[*winner*l*sell*] = 0.05.

Applying Bayes' rule to infer the conditional probability of each recommendation class being associated with a future winner we have

$$\Pr[buy|winner] = \frac{0.7 \times 0.6}{(0.7 \times 0.6) + (0.25 \times 0.3) + (0.05 \times 0.1)} = \frac{0.42}{0.42 + 0.075 + 0.005} = \frac{0.42}{0.5} = 0.84$$

$$\Pr[hold|winner] = \frac{0.25 \times 0.3}{(0.7 \times 0.6) + (0.25 \times 0.3) + (0.05 \times 0.1)} = \frac{0.075}{0.5} = 0.15$$

$$\Pr[sell|winner] = \frac{(0.05 \times 0.1)}{(0.7 \times 0.6) + (0.25 \times 0.3) + (0.05 \times 0.1)} = \frac{0.005}{0.5} = 0.01$$

These revised Bayesian posterior priors can now be used as inputs into further iterative revisions of the prior held by the investor. Figure 4.1 graphically depicts this process for six subsequent iterations of applying Bayes' rule to update priors and those iterations are listed in Table 4.4. At each revision the updated revision attaches a higher posterior probability that a share attracting a further buy recommendation is a winner. So after six successive buy recommendations the stock is regarded as almost certain to be a winner. Similarly, after six hold or sell recommendations, investors' posterior that a

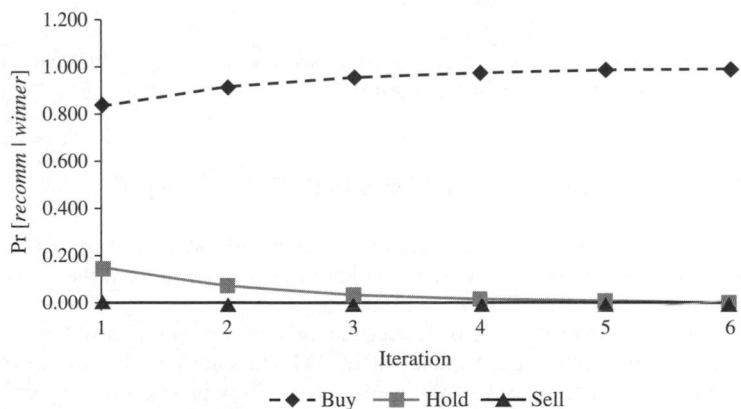

Figure 4.1 Bayesian revision of recommendation *being associated with winning stock*

Table 4.4 Iterative convergence of beliefs conditional on Bayesian beliefs as more buy recommendations are issued for a stock

Iteration	Buy	Hold	Sell
1	0.840	0.150	0.010
2	0.916	0.082	0.002
3	0.957	0.043	0.000
4	0.978	0.022	0.000
5	0.989	0.011	0.000
6	0.994	0.006	0.000

Table 4.5 Joint probability of the share being a winner given the outstanding recommendation

Signal (y_j)	Buy	Hold	Sell	Posterior probability of state given the signal received
Outcomes (x_i)	Pr[*winner|buy*]	Pr[*winner|hold*]	Pr[*winner|sell*]	Pr[*winner|recommendation*]
	Pr[*loser|buy*]	Pr[*loser|hold*]	Pr[*loser|sell*]	Pr[*loser|recommendation*]
Probability of ith signal (y_j)	Pr[*buy*]	Pr[*hold*]	Pr[*sell*]	1

Source: Based on Hirshleifer and Riley (1992) Table 5.1, p. 171.

Table 4.6 Joint probability of the share being a winner given the outstanding recommendation

Signal (y_j)	Buy	Hold	Sell	Posterior probability of state given the signal received
Outcomes (x_i)	0.6	0.3	0.1	Pr[*winner|recommendation*]
	0.4	0.1	0.9	Pr[*loser|recommendation*]
Probability of ith signal (y_j)	0.6	0.3	1	1

Source: Based on Hirshleifer and Riley (1992) Table 5.1, p. 171.

share is a winner is almost zero. Repeatedly similar signals regarding value leads to a complete separation of prospective investments in the market.

4.3 Do We Learn the Bayesian Way?

Bayes' rule sets the standard for how we might expect rational investors to learn from their mistakes. Rational investors need not always be right. But at least they can learn from their mistakes in a way that accords with, or improves upon, Bayesian learning.

As so often in this book we can learn from experimental evidence about how people decide things. David Grether (1980) undertook experiments with 341 students enrolled in various colleges in southern California. The experiment was designed to assess how people learn. Specifically, Grether focused on separating out the two elements of learning in Bayes' theorem about how we can optimally learn from new information. Recall these are:

- the prior probability, $Pr[y]$;
- the relative likelihood of the event given the state, $Pr[x|y]/Pr[x]$.

Since both elements of optimal learning are clearly necessary Grether (1980) designed his experiments to discern their separate presence and isolate their effect on the probability of an outcome. To undertake the experiment he used three bingo ball boxes. One bingo box is seen by the student experimental subjects, two others are hidden from them. These boxes had the following properties:

- The visible bingo box has six balls of the same colour with small numbers on the base detectable to the experimenter who draws then, but not the students in the class.
- A hidden bingo box, Box A, which again has six balls in it, four with the letter N on the base, two with G on the base.
- Finally, a hidden bingo box, Box B, which also contains six balls, three with the letter N on the base, three with G on the base.

In the experiment students were told that if numbers up to two (or three, or sometimes four) were drawn from the visible bingo box all six subsequent draws will be made from the hidden bingo Box A (with a 2/3 chance of drawing a ball marked N). If the number drawn from the visible box is greater than the announced limit (three, four, five or six if the limit is announced to be two) then all six subsequent draws will be from hidden bingo Box B (giving a 1/2 chance of a drawing a ball marked N). Having established this structure the experimenter draws from the visible box and announces the markings on six balls (from the hidden box) chosen in sequence. The hidden box chosen reflects the announced limit and the prior drawing from the visible bingo box. At the end of the six announced draws from the hidden chosen box student participants were asked: 'Which box (A or B) do you think the draw was made from?'

The sequential structure of the draws and the rules used to draw balls ensure that the announcement of the limit for drawing from the visible box (greater than two, three and four, etc.) defines the students' prior probability of drawing an N marked ball in the subsequent hidden draw. If the limit is two then there is a 1/3 probability of drawing from Box A (the box with 2/3 of N balls in it). If the limit is three there is half a chance of draws being made from Box A. Finally, if the limit is four there is a 2/3 chance of draws being made from Box A. Of course, the announced values of the markings on balls drawn from the chosen hidden box itself is quite informative about whether the chosen box contains more than three or four N balls. Indeed, it is quite likely in any drawing of six balls many will produce a three out of six N balls, or a four out of six N balls sequence regardless of whether hidden Box A or B was sampled.

This experiment revealed that very often the students instantly concluded a drawing from the hidden box of three N and three G balls must have come from Box B (which contains three N and three G). Similarly, a drawing of four N and two G from the hidden box almost always led students to conclude the drawing had been made from hidden Box A. In general student participants seemed happy to conclude balls had been drawn from Box A if most of the draws were N and bingo Box B, otherwise, regardless of their initial prior probability (determined by the announcement that draws above two, three or four would mean drawn from Box A in the hidden draw). It appears in deciding what kind of distribution was generating the announced sequence of balls too much weight was attached by the experimental subjects to the relative likelihood of a draw from bingo Box A and not enough weight was attached to the prior provided in the visible draw.

Grether (1980) supports his results with various statistical tests all of which confirm the underweighting of priors in decision making. In control experiments Grether does find experience in making these sorts of choices erodes the bias partially, but strangely financial incentives to make wise choices (prizes for sensible answers) do not. The underweighting of priors, or overweighting of relative likelihoods, seems both substantial and widespread. Indeed this feature of decision making was so well known that even before Grether's experiments it had a name: 'representation bias' or the 'representativeness heuristic'.

4.3.1   Representativeness

Like so much else in behavioural finance the underweighting of prior probabilities in decision making was first chronicled by Daniel Kahneman and Amos Tversky. You may now be thinking 'Will I ever escape these men?' The answer is probably not. Not as long as you want to study behavioural finance anyway. Their joint and separate work is just too important in all sorts of areas.

Kahneman and Tversky (1972) introduced the idea of a bias towards 'constructing the distribution of expected outcomes to conform to distribution of impressions'. They attributed representativeness bias to those who

> evaluate the probability of an uncertain event, or a sample, by the degree to which it is: (i) similar in essential properties to the parent population; and (ii) reflects the salient features of the process by which it is generated

> (Kahneman and Tversky 1972, p.33).

So in making a conjecture about a set of data, the overwhelming consideration we have is 'what does it look like?' not 'what is it most likely to be like?'. Kahneman and Tversky (1972) give a memorable example of such characterization. In London during the Second World War victims thought they perceived an order to the resulting carnage. The government took this conjecture so seriously they mapped in detail bomb damage in small areas of south London. They found that the distribution of bomb damage almost perfectly conformed to a Poisson distribution which would be expected to prevail given a random bombing strategy. The localized clusters in a randomly generated sequence trick us into believing it must have some predictable order. This tendency to find order where none exists combines with the 'law of small numbers' to induce unjustified extrapolation of often spurious trends.

4.3.2   Representation Bias in the Market: Analysts' Overreaction to Earnings

It is easy enough to accept that college students make silly mistakes in characterizing data. If they make such mistakes frequently, then college is a good place for them to be, but direct evidence drawn from records of the activities of finance market professionals confirms they are subject to very similar biases to students used in psychologists' classroom tests.

In a landmark paper on behavioural finance Werner De Bondt and his PhD supervisor Richard Thaler studied the predictions that financial analysts made of earnings-per-share announced by companies (De Bondt & Thaler, 1990).[3] Financial analysts are an important group of finance professionals to understand as De Bondt and Thaler (1990) point out because:

- Analysts' forecasts do seem to influence the stock market, implying their views are respected.
- Analysts do seem to have some skill in predicting earnings and appear to beat most reasonable statistical models most of the time.
- Analysts are well-paid, highly motivated, smart professionals. If they are making simple predictable mistakes it causes despair for simple folk like us.

De Bondt and Thaler (1990) report evidence of analysts' 'overreaction' to recent earnings changes in formulating their prediction of the current and next year's earnings-per-share. Overreaction is defined here to mean excessive revision of the analyst's earnings forecasts relative to that implied by Bayes' rule.

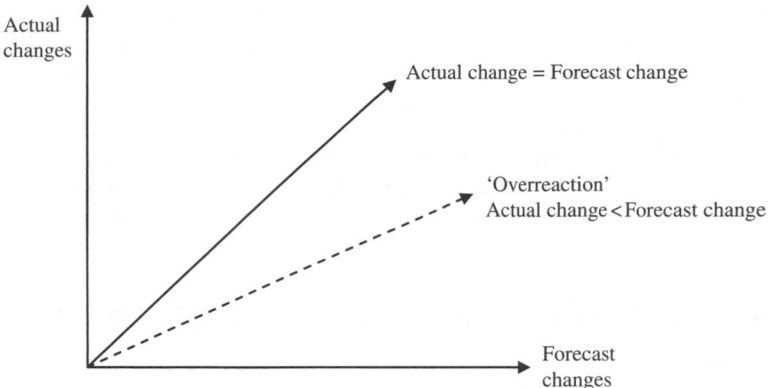

Figure 4.2   Overreaction in analyst forecasts

Figure 4.2 depicts the 45-degree line where forecast and actual changes in earnings-per-share move broadly in sync with each other. In reality analysts forecasted changes in earnings plot along a line to the lower right of the 45-degree line. De Bondt and Thaler (1990, p.685) conclude, 'Forecast changes are simply far too extreme to be considered rational' and as a result:

> When practitioners describe market crashes as panics, produced by investor overreaction, perhaps they are right. After all, are not these very practitioners the very same 'smart money' that is supposed to be keep markets rational?

It is usually assumed that individual, poorly capitalized investors add 'noise' into rationally set asset prices. These are investors who will never accumulate much money because of the naive, predictable, mistakes to which they are prone. The 'smart money' arbitrages against the 'dumb'/amateur-hour players to ensure speculative bubbles are damped down. Results like those in the De Bondt and Thaler (1990) study cast doubt on this soothing perspective.

4.3.3   A Once and For All Lesson?

We can conceive of two types of probability assessments:

- *Objective probabilities*, drawn from a distribution representing the frequency of occurrence of the event in the population. This works well where I encounter very similar situations repeatedly. It will work pretty well if I want to know will my train to work be late. Or, how many students will fail my first year accounting exam?
- *Personal probabilities*, drawn from my personal judgement of a situation. Suppose I am guessing will students and teachers like my textbook. Or will the Labour Party win a fourth term of government? Here I have no prior experience to guide me. I have not encountered such situations before and perhaps could not. In these situations I am thrown back on my subjective judgement of probability.

If we accept both perspectives are valid it is tempting to conclude most large risks are associated with situations where personal probability judgements appear to make most sense. If I invest in a hedge fund the basic level of risk is captured pretty well by data on past risk and return in that volatile sector. But what about the chance of encountering a Nick Leeson (Barings) or Andrew Fastow (Enron), or it is alleged Jérôme Kerviel[4] (Société Générale) type of conman? Such individuals are still so mercifully rare that it is unlikely any such characters have worked for UK hedge funds. The United States has already had its Mr Larry Madoff and Allen Stanford moments. But the demise of long-term venture capital shows how quickly such a fund can implode even without fraud. In such a context an investor must assess the risk of a very low probability, but potentially devastating, event. Here subjective probability assessments come into their own in assessing risk.

4.4   Over Inference and the Law of Small Numbers

As we have already seen in Chapter 2 most of us, including academics who should know better, read too much into small samples. That is, given how small the sample is relative to the population about which we seek to make predictions, we believe we have learned more than we actually have from observing the sample which gives rise to our prediction. This very simple 'law of small numbers' has been used to throw light on two of the most commonly investigated market anomalies by behavioural finance researchers. These are:

- Short-run continuation of returns, as good/bad news enters the market, this is often called under-reaction or *momentum*. I study this phenomenon in Chapter 10.
- Longer term reversals of these prior trends in returns so winners (on the back of good news) become losers later on and losers (in response to bad news) subsequently become winners. This is often called *overreaction* and I study this in Chapter 9.

In both cases the appropriateness of the pattern in observed returns is judged relative to Bayes' rule. In a very simple, but insightful, paper Matthew Rabin (2002) has captured both these phenomena as products of 'over inference' in a financial market where investors are believers in the law of small numbers.

Rabin captures this belief in the law of small numbers in a highly stylized, but very tractable, model. He imagines an investor who draws balls from an urn to determine the quality of an investment fund he is considering investing in. Let his draws be either of winning stocks, 'stars', or losers, 'dogs'. Based on his prior beliefs and what sort of outcomes he observes when drawing from the urn he forms his belief about the proportion of balls in the urn (the population) and so whether the urn represents a good fund (mainly star drawings) or a bad one (full of mainly dog drawings). But Rabin's investor draws balls from the urn in the belief that they are not replaced afterwards, so he believes the urn will be replenished to its original proportions every second draw. In even draws the investor believes that if he drew a star last time a star is less likely next draw, even if his prior was the urn containing equal numbers of stars and dogs. This is a bit like the 'gambler's fallacy' that dictates when you are $100,000 down on the tables in Las Vegas it's best to stay 'because you're due some good luck'.

Rabin gives the following example of how his model might work (Rabin, 2002, p.788). Suppose there is a fund manager who can be any one of three types of manager: good, bad or indifferent. Let good managers pick star stocks three-quarters of the time. Bad managers pick star stocks a quarter of the time, and indifferent managers draw star and dog stocks in equal proportion. So the proportions in the 'urn of the fund manager' the investor draws from has the proportions for good, bad and indifferent fund managers {3/4, 1/4, 1/2}. So for a good fund manager three-quarters of the balls are stars, for a bad a quarter are stars and for an average fund manager half the balls drawn are stars and half dogs.

Now suppose the investor draws out two star stocks from an urn in a row. Is the urn representative of a good, a bad, or an indifferent fund manager, given the sample drawing, which is two draws both stars? A Bayesian will believe that for a good manager a two successive star draw occurs 3/42 = 9/16 of the time, for a bad manager 1/42 = 1/12 of the time, and finally an average fund manager a two stars in a row draw happens 1/22 or 1/4 of the time. A believer in the 'law of small numbers', who thinks the star has not been put back in the urn and so has less chance of recurring, will believe the chance of the urn of a two stars in a row draw is a half for a good fund manager (or 3/4 × (3 − 1)/(4 − 1) = 6/12 = 1/2), zero for a bad fund manager (1/4 × (1 − 1)/3) and, finally a sixth (2/4 × (2 − 1)/(4 − 3)) if an average fund manager controls the urn/draw. So whichever type of manager we consider a believer in the law of small numbers gives little weight to drawing two stars in a row.

The 'over inference' comes about because given these only 'quasi-Bayesian', rather than truly Bayesian priors, any observed sequence, two stars or two dogs in a row, is seen as more surprising than it should be (if he was a clever Bayesian). The investor too quickly concludes that two stars drawn in succession can only mean a good fund or two dogs drawn in succession can only come from a bad fund. That is to say the believer in the law of small numbers overreacts to the signal about fund quality his two draws have given him.

4.5   Disagreement, Tastes and the Capital Asset Pricing Model

A basic assumption of the standard finance capital asset pricing model (Sharpe 1964, Lintner 1965) is that all investors agree on the joint distribution of asset returns and this convergence of beliefs is upon the true distribution (Fama & French 2007). But if agents learn, possibly at different rates, then the CAPM framework may become quite misleading throwing into doubt many of the certainties of standard finance texts.

Recently Fama and French (2007) have provided a simple framework for considering the impact of disagreements over probabilities, tastes and outcomes within the standard CAPM framework. The authors consider a CAPM world in which there are two types of investor:

- Informed investors, A, who hold the tangency portfolio to the mean-variance efficient frontier, call it T.
- Misinformed or simply uninformed investors, D, who overweight some assets relative to the mean-variance efficient market portfolio and underweight others. Call the weighted portfolio bought by the misinformed H and the underweighted portfolio divested by the misinformed G.

For the stock market to clear requires that the value-weighted market portfolio of risky assets is a wealth-weighted aggregate of portfolio D, held by the misinformed or uninformed and T the true tangency portfolio held by informed investors who calculate the true expected value of the distribution. So if x is the proportion of the market held by informed investors the market return, RM, is formed by the linear combination

$$R_M = xR_T + (1 - x)R_D$$

Under the CAPM assumptions for the market to clear the value-weighted market portfolio of risky assets M is simply the wealth-weighted portfolio of that held by the misinformed, D, and the true mean-variance efficient market portfolio T.

The market portfolio can only be the mean-variant efficient portfolio if and only if the uninformed happen to settle on the market portfolio M as their chosen investment portfolio. I denote this

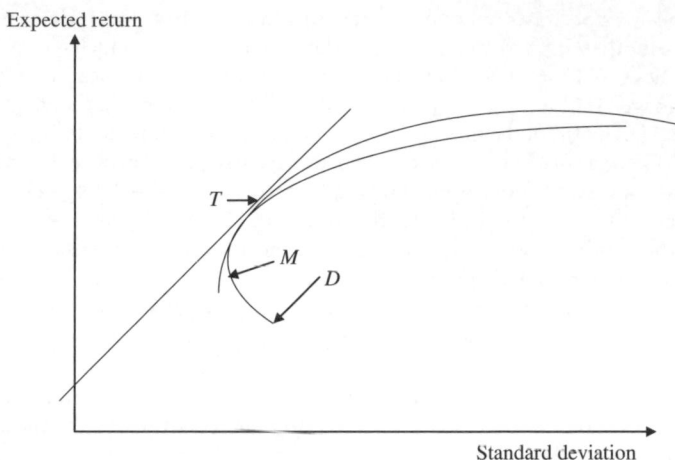

Figure 4.3   The CAPM when investors disagree

wealth-weighted portfolio M and draw the resulting equilibrium in Figure 4.3 (Figure 1 in Fama & French 2007). This can really only happen if their various conflicting errors made by uninformed investors cancel out in aggregate. Any systematic error that aggregates up across the individual uninformed investors causes a problem for the standard CAPM pricing model. Even in such a world the CAPM model still requires the market to clear at the prices set in the economy. So the informed must overweight in their portfolio the very set of assets the uninformed underweight in theirs and they must underweight those very assets and asset classes the uninformed overweight. This makes the standard CAPM outcome a very special case indeed.

Note the market portfolio M deviates from the mean-variant efficient tangency portfolio T by a factor determined by the weighting on investments in the mean-variant inefficient sub-optimal portfolio, D, held by misinformed/uninformed investors. M earns a lower return for bearing the same amount of risk as the mean-variance optimal portfolio T. By trading in the risky asset the misinformed/uninformed investors who buy portfolio D could access portfolio T instead.

If the trades of the misinformed are essentially random and cancel each other out it is unlikely they will have any systematic impact on price. But if for some reason the uninformed herd or follow fads which motivate their overweighting of their chosen portfolio then mispricing can become larger and more sustained. As Fama and French (2007) point out, what is needed is a more explicit theorization of what motivates misinformed, or simply uninformed, 'noise' trades. I follow this up at the start of the asset pricing section of this book when a role for 'noise traders' in asset pricing is formally modelled.

A numerical illustration of the CAPM with disagreement model

Here I briefly consider a version of the Fama–French model by generating a standard efficient frontier and tangency portfolio. I do this by considering two assets A and B which have the following properties of offering returns 7.5% and 15%, respectively, with standard deviations in those returns of 22% and 40%, respectively. So A is a low-risk/low-return stock and B a high-risk/high-return stock in comparison. The investor's mean-variance frontier can be traced out by combining A and B in a series of possible portfolio combinations from holding 95% of your assets in A and 5% in B to holding 5% in A and 95% in B. This locus is plotted in Figure 4.4.

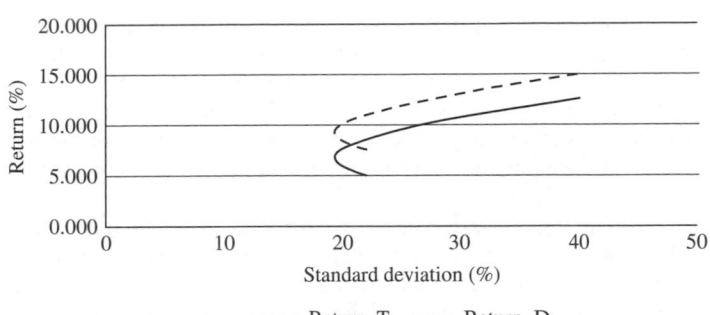

Figure 4.4 Numerical example of calculating joint probability of share being a winner given the outstanding recommendations against it

Table 4.7 Illustrative values for CAPM with disagreement amongst investors

Stock	Company A	Company B	Company C	Company D
Average return (%)	7.5	15	5	13
Standard deviation (%)	22	40	22	40

   Imagine an investor who failed his finance exam at college and really never understood portfolio theory. Out of ignorance he ends up holding stocks C and D. These offer returns of 5% and 13%, respectively. Suppose C has the same standard deviation of returns as A, 22%, and D has the same standard deviation as B, 40%. So doing badly in finance exams is obviously a bad move. This foolish investor is getting less return than his CAPM-following colleague, but for the same exposure to risk. I summarize the characteristics of the assets as shown in Table 4.7.

   Finally assume companies A and C shares have the same correlation with each other, say 15% for illustrative purposes. Following Fama and French (2007) I call the return to CAPM investors, purchasing the tangency portfolio Return_T and that to those who disagree with them (because they don't know much about finance) Return_D. Figure 4.4 traces out the risk–return combinations both investors face, given the assets they invest in.

   The Return_D portfolio is clearly stochastically dominated by the tangency portfolio Return_T. This is because the latter portfolio offers more return for the same risk. So what is the return to the market portfolio averaging across both CAPM investors and those who agree with them? The average return to CAPM investors is 11.25% ((7.5 + 15)/2) or from holding the tangency portfolio, those who disagree with them receive a lower return of 9% ((13 + 5)/2) [Return_T] = 11.25% and E[Return_D] = 9%). If both type of investors invest equal amounts in the market the overall market return will be 10.125%, leaving 1.25% of return unattained compared to the tangency portfolio (E[Return_T] − R_M = 1.125%).

4.6 Conclusion and Summary

This chapter outlines what is understood by optimal learning in standard finance theory and why that theory may not be observed in practice. One problem being the tendency we all have to give too much weight to extreme events relative to well-developed trends. Failures to learn well, or to make systematic mistakes, abound in driving, managing our family and friends, as well as financial markets. The forecasts of analysts of companies' future prospects is one clear example here. One reason such mistakes occur is we cannot always get lots of chances to learn on the same task. For example global warming has happened before, thousands of years ago. But I need to know what to do now since neither my parents nor my grandparents really encountered this problem before. Hence data on probabilities of past occurrence may be either absent or seem irrelevant to my important decision on climate change.

Does this failure, or inability, to learn well matter for students of financial markets? Maybe the slow learners will lose money and leave the market, leaving the 'smart money' to dominate trade. Whether this happens depends to some extent on whether uninformed traders make unrelated errors which cancel out or make more systematic, predictable, mistakes that tend to aggregate up. The appeal of the latter case is developed in Chapter 6.

Appendix: Case Study – Baseball the Bayesian Way

In *Moneyball* (Lewis 2003) Michael Lewis tells the story of how general manager Billy Beane raised the Oakland Athletics or 'Oakland A's' baseball team from small-town obscurity to greatness by the systematic exploitation of performance statistics in college games in picking players for purchase at the beginning of year player draft. Getting good players is vital to success for small-time US baseball teams since once drafted the acquiring team has contractual rights over them for the next six years. If the top table want access to emergent talent on the books of lucky acquirers they have to buy out their contract. So getting young good players cheap in the draft can propel a relatively impoverished mediocre side like the Oakland A's into greatness.

But to work this transformation Beane had to take on the accumulated wisdom of his own coaching staff, who did the hard slog of travelling around high school and college campus fixtures to talent spot potential recruits. To facilitate this process, scouts, who were typically ex-baseball players, had developed a whole lexicon of desirable and unwanted characteristics. Recruits should have a 'great' not a 'soft' body, be able to throw a 'fastball', have 'wheels', or the ability to run between bases very fast, a big 'hose' hand to launch big throws (near 100 miles per hour) and have definitely no 'bad makeup' (prison record, history of psychiatric problems or other personal problems). The characterization went so far as to include the idea that great baseball players had a 'good face' (Lewis 2003, p. 7).

Billy Beane himself knew about such things being in possession of the 'good face' himself. Beane also bore out the essential fallacy of this sort of reasoning, having been recruited in the draft by the New York Mets on the basis of a very brief period of outstanding performance in high school in California only to sorely disappoint later. In his junior year in high school Beane's batting average was half a run for each hit, by his senior year it had already fallen to 0.3 of a run per strike. Appearances can be deceptive it seems and Beane was determined to delve beneath the mask of baseball players entering the 2001 draft.

He did this by supplanting the pick advice of experienced scouts with statistical analysts like his Harvard-educated assistant general manager Paul DePodesta. DePodesta based his picks on a strict adherence to a projection from past performance recorded in college baseball statistics and club websites. He regarded generalizations based on what a club scout had seen in a wet midweek fixture as little more than guesswork (Lewis 2003, p.18). To DePodesta it was all in the spreadsheet. This led him to focus on college players where consistent performance data existed, as against high school players where far more sketchy data existed. This also was heresy to scouts for whom a cult of youth strongly persisted. Bill James, an early statistical analyst of baseball achievements, saw the paucity of interest in drafting college players as part of an underlying anti-intellectualism in American culture (Lewis 2003, p.99) – a culture he felt strongly needed to change, if for no other reason than to produce better baseball teams. James's most ardent disciple distinguished himself most sharply by his willingness to pick players who did not fulfil the usual stereotype – overweight but big-hitting, well-educated, players fitted perfectly into the Oakland A's new gameplan.

> What begins as a failure of the imagination ends as a market inefficiency; when you rule out an entire class of people from doing a job simply by their appearance, you are less likely to find the best person for the job

(Lewis 2003, p.115).

Like many truly radical steps the Oakland A's experiment was a response to failure not success. In 1991 the Oakland A's had the largest payroll in professional baseball courtesy of their wealthy owner, Walter Haas, a local philanthropist businessman. Somewhat awkwardly Haas died in 1995 and his estate sold off the team to two local businessmen, Steve Schott and Ken Hoffman, who made it clear they were going to run the Oakland A's for profit and not glory (Lewis, 2003, p.58). The search was on to discover some alchemy of baseball that would produce a great team for very little cash invested up front.

The first suggestion of how this might be done came in the form of a short pamphlet commissioned by the Oakland A's manager Sandy Alderson, by Eric Walker, a space engineer. Walker pointed out the centrality of not being stuck with any systematic plan in order to dominate professional baseball. Three strikes and you are out – the innings at the plate being over. So good teams frustrate opponents' attempts to strike out their team and strike out their opponents with minimal pitches. The central performance metric for producing a great score was therefore a high on-base percentage, or the lowest possible probability of being thrown off the batting plate (Lewis 2003, p.58). But Walker's intense use of on-base percentages had a precursor in the form of a set of detailed baseball performance metrics by Bill James, published in the late 1970s (Lewis 2003, p.63).

James's work founded a whole new field of statistical analysis of baseball data, entitled sabermetrics, which continues to grow to this day. James did not create this field of study, pioneers such as an English journalist Henry Chadwick had already perfected the 'box score' as a measure of baseball excellence.[5] This score records both the individual and team performance in the game as reported to baseball's governing authorities.

James's genius lay not in his presentation of baseball performance metrics, but in the understanding that they might be used to predict future performance in the league. To aid in this James even advanced a new summary statistic entitled the 'runs created statistic' which took the form:

$$\text{Runs created} = (\text{Hits} + \text{Walks}) \times (\text{Total bases}/(\text{At bats} + \text{Walks}))$$

This formula gave a prediction regarding the number of runs attained given its hits, walks, etc. The formula did a pretty good job of explaining runs attained when used with historic data regarding baseball league fixtures. Previously most team managers focused closely on batting averages as guides to the best players. James's ranking did not even include this figure. At first James thought top teams would be queuing up to receive his advice on managing and improving team performance by focusing on key drivers of runs attained. Nothing could be further from the truth.

Dick Cramer, previously a researcher at SmithKline Beecham (now GlaxoSmithKline), set up a company, STATS Inc, to collate such performance metrics with a view to selling it on, with interpretative analysis, to professional teams. Finally Cramer snagged some attention from Al Rosen, general manager of the Houston Astros, who was interested in the likely impact of a narrowing of the ground in which his team was located on their future performance. STATS Inc advised that the Astros' strength in catching wide field strikes meant such a move was not a good idea. Rosen's response was to continue narrowing the field of play of the Astros, but seek to gag disclosure of the likely impact of such a move on his team's league position. This attitude characterized a dilemma of which Bill James became increasingly aware. Professional baseball teams only survived because of public interest in the game and competing teams' ability to play it, but this did not mean they felt comfortable with the public knowing more than a bare minimum about what the teams did.

The 2002 Draft

The draft of 2 June 2002 was the launch pad for Billy Beane's assault on US professional baseball. That year's draft was a potential turning point for the Oakland A's since they had an almost unheard of seven picks in the season's draft. A good draft held out the opportunity to transform their side on the basis of historical performance statistics. To give some scale of the problem he faced it may be worth noting that Beane had a total budget of $9.4 million for all his draft picks. This budget might have to stretch over 35 players. Given Steve Boras, a major baseball player agent, was asking $20 million for a package involving the purchase of a pitcher named James Guthrie, this was not a task inspiring too much hope. The average salary of a big league player was $2.3 million a year. The opening bid of the Oakland A's was just below $1.5 million, so astute negotiations were a prerequisite of success.

To make the budget stretch Beane had his target players contacted before the draft day to informally agree terms well below prevailing rates. Given that many of the players that Beane was most eagerly searching were just not on the scanner of other teams or baseball agents, or had been passed over in the past, this was not hard to do.

A perfect example of an Oakland A's pick was Jeremy Brown who held the record as a catcher in the University of Alabama college team. Since the clear priority in the draft was in recruiting good pitchers and batters, Brown was an utter no-hoper. Oakland A's contacted him prior to the draft and got his verbal acceptance of a salary of $350,000 a year. This was maybe a million less than the last players picked in the draft could normally expect to secure. Not surprisingly Brown accepted the offer with good grace. He could hardly believe his luck that anyone was interested in drafting him.

But DePodesta's selection methods did not always select players off the radar of other scouts. Beane's best friend J.P. Ricciardi, general manager of the Toronto Blue Jays, was also in pursuit of Nick Swisher, a baseman/centerfielder from West Virginia who was the son of baseball legend Steve Swisher. But most of Beane's picks in the early rounds of the draft would not expect to be selected at any stage in the draft.

The overwhelming response of fellow scouts to Oakland's picks was derision and disbelief. A number of clubs started to click off from the web-cast draft conference call so that the world would not hear them chuckling as Oakland announced its picks (Lewis 2003, p.115). After the first seven rounds the Oakland A's picked up five hitters off their original wish list. The basis of Oakland A's baseball league revival had been laid.

In entering the draft DePodesta had a very clear objective: to enter the play-offs to win the league he calculated the Oakland A's needed to win 95 games or so. To achieve this goal required about 800 to 820 runs as against 670 or so conceded. In fact in the 2002 season the Oakland A's scored 800 runs to 673 conceded. The art of achieving this lay in their pattern of acquisitions but also in their willingness to sell on players who were believed to be overrated because of the distorted performance metrics then used by professional baseball scouts.

In particular Beane placed very little weight on 'saves' in the game by 'closers'. Closers were typically relief or standby pitchers who lacked the reliability of starting pitchers, but could perform some magic at the base to finish the game, 'save' the match, when the team was on the ninth base. A great starting pitcher, who is in the twilight of his career, can develop into a great closer. But closing only becomes crucial if the team enters the ninth and final base fewer than three runs ahead. Oakland A's in 1999–2001 retained one of the greatest closers ever in the game, Jason Isringhausen. Beane sold Isringhausen to the St. Louis Cardinals for two picks in the 2002 draft as he acquired the status of a free agent and started to make inflated wage demands. Beane believed excessive prominence of the 'save' statistic in baseball scouts' minds led to an 'availability bias' that induced overpricing in the market for closers.

For DePodesta and Beane there were really only two performance metrics that were central guides to forming a team capable of winning the league. These were the on-base and slugging percentage. If every hitter was on base, so the on-base percentage was a perfect 1, the team would never be out and so never lose. The batter would always reach the chosen base without being run out. A perfect slugging percentage only told you the team gained a base for each hitter that took the field. How many runs resulted from this depended on how swift the hitter was, how good the opposing field was in catching him out, etc. So the central statistic was clearly the on-base percentage with the slugging percentage playing a secondary role. A perfect slugging percentage could, for example, result either from one hitter hitting a home run, or three hitters being struck out without moving a single base. But even if you knew being on base was the central indicator of purchasing more runs how many more runs do you need to win? You needed to know this to effectively build the best possible team based on the available archive of past performance by players on your team and available for drafting. DePodesta's new insight was to realize that a player's on-base average bought about three times the runs of a good slugging average, while slugging percentages had long been regarded as the central performance metric. After all it was central to the construction of James's 'runs created' metric discussed above. The Oakland A's, guided by DePodesta, focused far more narrowly on maximizing this performance metric than was common in professional baseball at that time.

Trading Bases: AVM and the Market for Baseball Talent

The quantification of baseball talent reached a new intensity once former Wall Street derivatives traders Ken Mauriello and Jack Armbruster left the Chicago Mercantile's trading floor to establish AVM, a company designed to answer the question of exactly how each attribute of a player adds to the expected run average of the side he plays for. In the case of a great pitcher or hitter this may not be too difficult to calculate. But for fielders and other position plays the answer is not so obvious. Even for a pitcher, the consequence of a great pitch in reducing the opponent's run count rather depends on the hitter he faces. If he pitched against Babe Ruth, no matter how good he was, he might expect to have little impact in reducing the opposing team's score. The real question was then what was a good pitcher's 'expected' impact on total runs, or his value in normal conditions averaged out over especially good and bad hitters he might have to face. To make this sort of statement you needed to know a lot about a long history of baseball games. AVM began to compile 10-year profiles of the impact in terms of resulting runs of various types of strikes, runs, fielding strategies, etc. From this they inferred the deviation from average run capability of various types of players and contrasting styles of play.

But even then to talk of pitches and hits seemed somewhat crude in an age when the camera's eye caught almost every move of opposing teams on the baseball field. Soon AVM were classifying hits with trajectory x and velocity y, hit from a point z on the plate. For any given move in a game there had certainly been hundreds, if not thousands, of similar if not identical plays in the last 10 years. The exponential rise in computing power since Bill James commenced his investigations of statistical patterns in baseball scores meant AVM could minutely dissect and compare baseball plays for predictive purposes. An example of such dissection is the scoring of a 'double', where a hit allows the hitter to run onwards to second base.

An Island of Misfit Toys

The quest for cheap talent awakened Beane's interest in the 'rejects' left behind after other professional baseball teams had done their work. Lewis (2003, p.158) finds the Oakland A's locker room to be the 'island of misfit toys', gathered off the floor of baseball fields in a search for cheap talent. Amazingly one Oakland A's player, Jim Mecir, even had a club foot. Mecir's attraction was the screwball he threw due to his disability which was very difficult for left-hand hitters to respond too.

The contrary nature of the Oakland A's selection methods can be illustrated by the case of Jason Giambi, their star hitter, sold in December 2001 to the New York Yankees in a $120 million deal. Giambi had an on-base average 50 points above any other player in the league (0.477 to Seattle's Edgar Martinez's 0.423). Finding someone with an on-base average as good as Guthrie was clearly impossible, he was simply the best on that crucial metric. The astonishing thing was, however, how cheap it was to enhance your team's on-base average collectively even if the improvement did not come in the form of one star player, but was spread over three slightly more modestly gifted players who could collectively enhance the team's on-base average by the same amount. As Beane would state:

> The important thing is not to recreate the individual. The important thing is recreate the aggregate

> (Lewis 2003, p.141).

But to buy increases, in on-base average sufficiently cheaply to maintain Oakland A's tight budget required deviating from stereotypes of what a world-class athlete should look like. The Oakland A's team looked too overweight and old by the prevailing standards in the professional league. A case in point was the 36-year-old, ex-husband of film star Halle Berry, David Justice. Justice earned his place in the Oakland A's because, despite his relative decrepitude, he still retained a very healthy on-base average. His record had declined in recent years from his peak, a fact Justice felt very keenly, but still remained firmly bound above those lesser gifted mortals in the baseball league.

Acquiring good players was critical since it had become clear to Beane that many central characteristics of a great baseball hitter could not be learned and seemed almost innate from birth, or at least infancy. One such trait was the ability to detect balls thrown outside the strike zone and resist the temptation to attempt to play them. What differentiated the top and bottom half of the Oakland A's team, when ranked on on-base average, was this trait more than anything else. Curiously the bottom half was also those players who had come up from Oakland A's youth squad – Beane and his coaching squad had been drumming in the importance of judging a ball before attempting to play it from the teenage years of his players. All this had almost no impact. An ability to judge the position of an incoming ball in the strike zone is clearly fairly innate and impervious to training.

Another fallen angel recruited to the Oakland A's cause was Scott Hatteberg, a famous catcher who had dislocated his arm while catching for the Boston Red Sox. The Red Sox soon palmed him off onto Colorado Rockies, which, in his sixth year in the league, were more than happy to let him be a free agent in the hope of unloading him onto some unwitting opponent (Lewis 2003, p.163). One minute after Hatteberg was contractually bound to Colorado he got the call from Oakland A's. Not only were they offering more money, but they actually wanted him to play, an almost unknown request since his injury and subsequent corrective surgery on his shoulder. However, Beane wanted him to restyle his game as a hitter, not a pitcher, a testing task for any player.

The attraction of Hatteberg to Beane flowed from the latter's obsession with winning by maximizing his team's on-base average. While with the Red Sox, Hatteberg had an on-base average 25 points better than the league average, even though he had played while injured, and even then fairly sporadically. Hatteberg was especially skilled at winning the right to 'walk' to first base after receiving four fair balls from the opposing side's pitcher. In fact his ratio of walks to strike outs was amongst the highest in the whole league and Beane just loved the opposing batter being forced to walk (Lewis 2003, p.144). Beane's central game plan relied on a war of attrition, where the opposing side's pitcher's arms were to be forced into submission. Weirdly the Red Sox had seen Hatteberg's proclivity to walk as a major weakness reflecting an underlying lack of aggression. For Beane and DePodesta walking was Hatteberg's tour de force.

What Beane and DePodesta were seeking was nothing less than a whole new way of seeing baseball play and baseball players. They were aiming to take every action or characteristic of a player and convert each attribute into its notional 'expected run value' which could then be compared to league averages. Once this was done all that remained was a linear programming problem of assembling the least cost set of attributes required to win 95 games in a season with 880 runs or so.

The institutional vagaries of US professional baseball meant it was not just the ability of individual players' attributes to contribute to run totals that were incorrectly valued. The way in which the players' labour market was controlled by their powerful unions also created a number of arbitrage opportunities that Beane seized upon with vigour. Central amongst these institutional rigidities in the baseball player labour market is players' release from their initial contracts after six years to become free agents. Beane and DePodesta noticed that weaker players still in the last year of their contract were held to be almost valueless by most teams' management. While this might be a fair assessment of many of the players' worth, it ignored another important institutional feature of the professional baseball player market. This was that when in the sixth year of his contract a player was declared a free agent, his team received an extra free pick in the upcoming season's draft. This option was wildly undervalued. Hence all that was needed was to find a moderately gifted player in the final year of his contract and the game was on. As a bonus ball if a player ranked in the top 20% in his position in the league, i.e. he was a 'Type A' player in baseball lingo, his passage into free contractual status conferred two free picks in the draft. Ray Durham, a second baseman in the Chicago White Sox, was such a player. Cliff Floyd of the Boston Red Sox was a very similar prospect. The Oakland A's signed both in 2002, which was the backdrop to the remarkable seven free picks they were awarded in the draft that year. Since both Durham and Floyd were Type A players their emergence into free contract status gave the Oakland A's four of their total seven picks. The way Beane saw it, given these facts, they needed to be pretty awful players not to justify at least a low ball bid prior to the season's opening.

Buying Skill Instead of Luck

The key to Oakland A's scouting of talent was an ability to differentiate skilled players from lucky players. Once again Beane's awareness of this difference reflected his own experience of the game. Indeed Beane even viewed himself as the 'Forrest Gump of American professional baseball', always present when great things happened but never making great things happen himself exactly (Lewis 2003, p.51). He was on the bench when the Minnesota Twins won the 1987 World Series and the Oakland A's in 1989. In short Beane was lucky and he knew it. But that made him even less willing to pay for lucky players to clutter up a dressing room he wanted packed with raw skill.

Some tools for differentiating lucky and skilful players were developed by Voros McCracken, a Chicago lawyer bored with his case load of clients. To relieve his boredom he mused about how to best select a pitcher for his fantasy baseball team. It soon became clear to McCracken that differentiating a pitcher from one pitching for a team which had a solid defence was almost impossible. Simply observing outcomes of run totals alone was not enough to allocate the glory of winning between pitcher and defence. McCracken separated out performance statistics that a pitcher could directly affect, like hits and earned runs, from those over which he appeared to have little control, which included strike outs, walks and home runs (Lewis 2003, p.236). If pitcher performance was attributable to skill, not luck, you might expect the same pitchers to consistently perform well. If pitching was pure luck, star pitchers would change each season. McCracken found small, but statistically significant, predictability in pitcher ability, even in outcomes not directly under his control, e.g. walks and home runs. Despite all this it appeared that there was no clear predictability in hits per ball in play. It appeared very few, if any platers, could consistently hit fair balls even if, when they did, they played them in a reasonably consistent fashion.

Up until McCracken most analysts of the game assumed great pitchers pitched in a way that made scoring a run less likely. Analysis of the data suggested this was simply not true. In fact renowned league pitchers like Randy Johnson and Greg Maddox actually created opportunities for hitters to create many more runs than their far less lauded peers.

So McCracken began a search for a performance metric for pitchers which netted out the impact of them playing in teams with good defensive players. Once he began selecting pitchers in this way he soon honed in on Chad Bradford. Bradford was a man who had for a long time been in the eyes of the Oakland A's. Controlling for the ability of the defence to cover pitcher errors, Bradford was simply the best pitcher in US professional baseball. Bradford had long been languishing in the Chicago White Triple A side in Armour Square, Chicago. In 1999 he briefly played for the main team only to struggle and return once more to obscurity. The reason for this was not hard to discern. Bradford was an underarm pitcher at around 84 miles an hour. He simply looked terrible at the plate to both scouts and fans alike. But he was nevertheless highly effective at negating the opposition's ability to score runs. Hitters just found it very hard to deal with his style of pitch, largely because just about no one else pitched like him. His underarm pitch rose then fell with a disturbing topspin that made it perilous to attempt to control. In particular once landed the pitch arrived so close to the ground it was hard to get enough traction even to reach first base, never mind a home run.

Even at the zenith of Oakland A's powers in September 2002 when they faced the Kansas City Royals to win a record-breaking twentieth consecutive match DePodesta was still calculating the probabilities. He attached a roughly 14 in a million chance to pulling this particular plan off (Lewis, 2003, p.257). Subsequent events were to confirm his scepticism as the Oakland A's veered from an 11–0 lead to 11–11 before Scott Hatteberg came down the tunnel as a relief pitcher to hit a home run.

Beane and DePodesta remained clear that their own philosophy of the game implied that the statistical fluke of their success would soon be followed by a reversal of fortune. Indeed reversion to average performance was a central part of Bill James's original creed of baseball play. Exceptional performance by its very nature is unlikely to persist, although it may give great joy while it lasts. Because of this power of statistical aggregates to dominate individual human characters, Beane felt:

> There was no point trying to get inside players' heads, for instance, to reshape their approach to the game. They will be who they will be

(Lewis 2003, p.249).

Strangely given this dispassionate view Beane himself was completely unable to let his players be. In reality he constantly badgered them for minor adjustments in their play. A passive investment strategy appealed in theory, but was hard to follow in practice. Given the amount of luck in the game of baseball, doing nothing in the face of random defeats can seem a bit smug and does not play well with fans and the baseball press. Baseball commentators have little to say about a style of management based on accepting your fate.

Ultimately luck does have a huge role to play, especially when it matters most in the five games of the end of season play-offs. Here the Oakland A's 103 victories of the season counted for nothing more than an entry ticket to this stage. Over a five-game play-off, the law of large numbers, and the statistical reasoning that it gives rise to, seem almost irrelevant. At this point reason goes out the window and blind luck takes over. This very fact creates the space for the old guard with their endless quest for the 'good face', etc.

Indeed Beane himself seemed to falter in his belief that skill and sound judgement could give a consistent competitive edge. Having already traded to produce a relatively cheap on-base maximizing team capable of winning 95+ games in the league, he had little more to aim for. Briefly he considered selling out at the top and negotiated a $12.5 million five-year contract to manage the Boston Red Sox under their new owner John Henry. Henry had already retained the services of Bill James and Voros McCracken, two inspirational figures of the Oak A project, but ultimately emotion dominated reason in Beane's life and he refused to sign the final contract. Reason had been a good servant, but an unattractive master in his life.

Questions

1. Look at Figure 4.1 and the example of learning whether a stock is a winner using analysts' recommendations of when to buy, sell or hold stock. Originally I assumed a buy recommendation foretells a winning stock 70% of the time, $\Pr[winner|buy] = 0.7$, a hold recommendation foretells a winning stock 25% of the time, $\Pr[winner|hold] = 0.25$, and a buy recommendation foretells a winning stock 5% of the time, $\Pr[winner|sell] = 0.05$. What happens if recommendations don't tell you anything about whether a stock is a winner or not initially? So $\Pr[winner|buy] = \Pr[winner|hold] = Prob[winner|sell] = 0.33$. Recalculate Figure 4.1 and comment on the revised learning process the investor undertakes.

2. Go back to Figure 4.4. Suppose the CAPM investor meets the investor who disagrees with him. The other investor thinks all this CAPM stuff is just great. He immediately wants to sell C and D and buy A and B stocks.

    The reason he didn't do much finance at college is because he did a really great business ethics course which really affected his view of how he should live. Before selling C and D he checks on what A and B actually do. He discovers B oppresses workers in South America and may even use child labour there. He decides to just sell C and replace it in his portfolio with A. He retains his D holding, reinvesting the proceeds of selling C in A's stock. Comment on how this transaction affects the market portfolio and the overall efficiency of the stock market in a mean-variance efficiency sense.

3. Read the case study on baseball at the end of this chapter. Obviously big money, television rights etc., have made sport a major industry in itself with a lot of money involved. But are there any lessons in this case study for trading in assets like stocks, bonds and foreign currencies? If so what are they?

Notes

1. This section follows Hirshleifer and Riley (1992, pp.170–8) quite closely.
2. See Hey (1983, pp.88–95) here.
3. De Bondt and Thaler (1985), which first addressed overreaction in stock markets, is one of the most cited, discussed and criticized papers in the history of behavioural finance.
4. Mr Kerviel remains innocent until proven otherwise at the time of my writing.
5. In baseball, the statistical summary of a game is reported in a box score. An abbreviated version of the box score, duplicated from the field scoreboard, is the line score.

References

Bayes, T. (1763). An essay towards solving a problem in the doctrine of chances. *Philosophical Transactions*, **53**: 370–418.

Bellhouse, D. (2004). The Reverend Thomas Bayes, FRS: a biography to celebrate the tercentenary of his birth. *Statistical Science*, **19**: 3–43.

De Bondt, W. & R. Thaler (1985). Does the stock market overreact? *Journal of Finance*, **60**: 793–807.

De Bondt, W. & R. Thaler (1990). Do analysts overreact? *American Economic Review*, **80**: 678–85.

Economist (2008). Wall Street's crisis: what went wrong? pp. 91–6.

Fama, E. & K. French (2004). The capital asset pricing model: theory and evidence. *Journal of Economic Perspectives*, **18**: 25–46.

Fama, E. & K. French (2007). Disagreements, tastes and asset prices. *Journal of Financial Economics*, **83**: 667–89.

Grether, D. (1980). Bayes' rule as a descriptive model: the representativeness heuristic. *Quarterly Journal of Economics*, **95**: 537–57.

Hey, J. (1979). *Uncertainty in Microeconomics*. Oxford: Martin Robertson.

Hey, J. (1983). *Data in Doubt: An Introduction to Bayesian Statistical Inference*. Oxford: Martin Robertson.

Hirshleifer, J. & J. Riley (1992). *The Analytics of Uncertainty and Information*. Cambridge: Cambridge University Press.

Howson, C. & P. Urbach (2006). *Scientific Reasoning: The Bayesian Approach*. London: Open Court.

Kahneman, D. & A. Tversky (1972). Subjective probability: a judgement of representativeness. *Cognitive Psychology*, **3**: 430–54.

Lewis, M. (2003). *Moneyball: The Art of Winning an Unfair Game*. New York: Norton.

Lintner, J. (1965). The valuation of risk assets and the selection of risky investments in stock portfolios and capital budgets. *Review of Economics and Statistics*, **47**: 13–37.

Rabin, M. (2002). Inference by believers in the law of small numbers. *Quarterly Journal of Economics*, August: 775–814.

Sharpe, W. (1964). Capital asset prices: a theory of market equilibrium under conditions of risk. *Journal of Finance*, **19**: 425–42.

Shefrin, H. (2005). *A Behavioral Approach to Asset Pricing*. New York: Elsevier.

Wilde, O. (1891). The Picture of *Dorian Gray*. London: Ward, Lock & Co.

Chapter 5

Bubbles

The volatility of financial markets is both disruptive and costly. Episodes of speculative frenzy followed by market collapse seem the norm of our history. The advent of transformative new technology like the railways, or the Internet, often acts as the trigger to such episodes (see Miller 2003). The crashes of 1929, 1987[1] and most recently the Internet boom collapse of early 2000 are testimony to the ability of financial markets to destroy, as well as create, wealth. Speculative financial bubbles may be more than the illusion of paper wealth, which puff up then crush hopes of huge riches amongst the populace. De Bondt (2005) states:

> Asset market bubbles are worrisome because they misallocate scarce resources and because they lead to economic stagnation. Even if a bubble at first remains confined to one sector, contagion and spill-over effects can cause further damage. Bubbles also redistribute wealth. Sometimes good people get hurt. Financial earthquakes undermine the public's trust in the integrity of the financial system.

This erosion of trust is most probably well placed given the range of dubious dealings associated with sharp rises in the stock market. This creates possible grounds for public policy intervention to prevent the worst excesses of bubbles. Robert Shiller in his commentary of the most recent bubble argues,

> It is a serious mistake for public figures to acquiesce in the ups and downs of market valuations, to remain silent about the implications of valuations and leave all commentary to market analysts who specialize in the nearly impossible task of forecasting the market over the short term and who may share interests with investment banks, broker-dealers, home-builders or realtors. The valuation of our markets is an important national – indeed international – issue

> (Shiller 2005, p.208).

One legitimate ground for government intervention is public fear (Sunstein 2005). We are afraid of many things, diseases, like avian flu or AIDS, and environmental threats, like global warming or nuclear waste. Sometimes we do not understand or fear threats we should, like high blood pressure, the 'silent killer', or obesity. Financial speculation may be a threat of this type. While speculators have much fun at the height of the boom the law may need to be aware, and make the public aware, of the possible consequences. President George W. Bush in justifying the invasion of Iraq in 2002 stated, 'If we wait for threats fully to materialize, we will have waited too long'.[2] While this view was highly controversial, a very similar 'precautionary principle' suggests the state may need to spike financial bubbles in their infancy.

We should not overplay our ability to learn the lessons of financial history. However, Nicholas Taleb points out the limit on our learning from our past:

When you look at the past, the past will always be deterministic, since only one single observation took place. Our minds will interpret most events not with the preceding ones in mind, but the following ones.... While we look at the past we know that history flows forward, it is difficult to realize we envision it backwards. Psychologists call this over-estimation of what we knew at the time of the event due to subsequent events the hindsight bias, the 'I knew it all along' effect

(Taleb 2004, p.56).

5.1   Illustration and Structure

One graphic illustration of how a speculative bubble (on this occasion in the Internet sector) can impact on the real economy is the merger of AOL and Time Warner at the height of the Internet boom and its subsequent unravelling in the wake of the boom's end. Such damaging outcomes from financial bubbles bring inevitable calls for, and acquiescence in, state intervention. Shiller's statement above suggests a policy response to the inflation of financial bubbles is indeed desirable. Certainly the SEC's response to the AOL–Time Warner deal was not long in coming. But is the state's intervention best seen as a corrective to market instability or simply part of the social propagation that generates bubbles? Recently Berenson (2003) has traced how poor regulation of financial markets and financial reporting by companies underpinned much of the froth of the most recent speculative boom in our history. He finds something new and disturbing in the history leading up to the late 1990s' boom. Berenson (2003, p.210) states:

In earlier years the government's data and the S&P500 figures had tracked each other closely. Between 1986 and 1996, for example, both government data and the S&P500 found that profits had roughly tripled. The gap between the late 1990s' data offers strong evidence that much of the growth that public companies reported during that period was a mirage.

Berenson places the blame for gross misevaluation of stocks in the late 1990s squarely at the feet of the accounting profession and its regulators. The state here is an enthusiastic participant in the financial speculation not a dispassionate overseer of it.

I consider this argument before delving further into the history of financial bubbles. I do not provide a full historical overview here (many excellent books already serve such a purpose, e.g. Kindleberger & Aliber 2005 and Chancellor 1999), but rather focus more narrowly on the government's view as the cause of financial bubbles as opposed to a source of amelioration of their impact. Market 'irrationality' is often seen as a justification for state intervention and regulation. Here I focus on the government's part in generating the problem of financial bubbles it purports to cure.

Section 5.2 asks what we can learn from revisiting stories of past financial bubbles and whether the histories we have of them are more informative about their authors' perspective than the events whose history they seek to retell. It does so with reference to the Dutch tulipmania of 1637, an issue I discuss in greater depth in an appendix to this chapter. Section 5.3 comes right up to date by considering some causes and effects of the most recent new-economy bubble of the last year or so of the previous century. Section 5.4 gives some reflections on what motivates our continued interest in the extremities of financial market failure. In Section 5.5, I revisit many earlier themes in a case study of what is in many ways the granddaddy of all stock-market crashes, the 1929 crash. Section 5.6 asks should we just accept that free markets overheat into speculative bubbles sometimes and stop bothering with devising complicated regulatory regimes to save foolish investors from the fruits of their folly? Can government intervention just make matters worse? Or, even more alarmingly, could the state be one of the chief architects of financial collapses we periodically observe? Finally, Section 5.7 summarizes and concludes the chapter.

After reading this chapter the reader should:

- Be aware that discussions of optimism (in Chapter 7), overreaction (Chapter 9) and herding (Chapter 11) are not 'merely academic' and reflect some of the most vital aspects of our financial history.
- Realize that there is 'nothing new under the sun' in the most recent financial crisis/'credit crunch'. The recent crisis is the latest manifestation of a collective madness we have long been subject to bouts of.

5.2 Tulipmania and the Didactic Value of Bubbles

Tulipmania, a surge in the demand for tulip bulbs in the Netherlands in 1637 is the mother of all subsequent bubble narratives. The original story is often recounted based on Charles Mackay's (1841) classic text *Extraordinary Popular Delusions and the Madness of Crowds*. Mackay tells how, following the introduction of the tulip to Europe in the mid-sixteenth century, its popularity grew amongst the prosperous Dutch merchant classes in the mid-seventeenth century. Importation of tulips from Constantinople to Amsterdam was soon a boom market. Mackay states,

> In 1634 the degree of rage amongst the Dutch to possess them was so great that the ordinary industry of the country was neglected, and the population, even to its lowest dregs, embarked in the tulip trade

> (1841, p.115).

Mackay proceeds to outline the lunacy of the ensuing speculative attack that peaked in February 1937, including a sailor imprisoned for mistaking his employer's rare bulb for an onion and eating it for his breakfast.

Tulipmania is the classic bubble story in many ways. But it is largely perhaps just that, an iconic story. Such stories form an important social and rhetorical purpose in our history and are open to strategic, if not manipulative, use by those opposed to the diffusion of the market process. Peter Garber in a series of papers has argued that the tulipmania story constitutes just such a handy myth which propagates even to this day (Garber 2001). Garber (2001, p.11) illustrates his general thesis by reference to lead articles in the *Financial Times* about the 1998 Long-Term Capital Management crisis. He points out that, far from the dizzy prices reported in these historical accounts relating to tulip bulbs in general, the bubble developed only in a narrow strain of 'broken' bulbs infected with a viral condition that produced flaring, or discolouration, of the tulip stem, which could in some cases be extremely beautiful. It was these very rare bulbs, not the general mass of bulbs, which soared in price.

Unbroken single-coloured bulbs displayed little price movements apart from in the final frenzy of the speculation in early 1637. By this time the States of Holland[3] had rendered futures contracts for the delivery of tulip bulbs unenforceable at law. During a time when bubonic plague raged in Amsterdam, and there was a good chance traders may not be around to see the expiry of their futures contracts, trading in basic, unbroken, bulbs took on something of a 'drinking game' (Garber 2001, p.38) to be played while death pressed in from every side. Everyone knew that the futures contracts were unenforceable, so if you were lucky enough to survive the bubonic plague your trading losses in tulip bulbs would certainly not be of concern.

For Garber (2001) the tulipmania story tells us something important about how 'bubble' histories are used in structuring debate about financial markets. He concludes:

> The wonderful tales from the tulipmania are catnip, irresistible to those with a taste for crying bubble, even when the stories are so obviously untrue. So perfect are they for use that financial moralizers will always be ready to find a market for them in a world filled with investors ever fearful of financial Armageddon

> (Garber 2001, p.83).

So if the tulipmania story has less factual basis than rhetorical intent, what is the story telling us about the life and values of the mercantile classes in the Netherlands of the late seventeenth century? A recent book by Anne Goldgar (2007) explores this theme. I discuss this book in an appendix to this chapter. I do so in many ways as an antidote the more formal modelling that dominates much of the remainder of this book and as a reminder of the importance of capturing the full social, economic and cultural context in which alleged deviations from investor rationality occur.

5.3   The Regulatory Origins of the Most Recent Bubble

The defining characteristic of a financial bubble is the uncoupling of price from value. Fortunately by the late 1990s this pattern was well understood and indeed underpinned the legislative response to the previous 'great crash' of 1929, which was the fruit of America's 'roaring twenties'. The 1933 Securities Acts were the US government's response to popular wrath against the speculators and the robber barons who were seen to profit from the misery of the common people. Men like J.P. Morgan and Andrew Mellon became figures of public scorn and the Acts were in part designed to exact public revenge on them. The Glass–Steagall (or Banking) Act of 1933 forced a separation of two types of banking as the basis for privately owned banks (Berenson 2003, p. 21). These were

- Commercial banking, or the offering of loans and taking of savings deposits.
- Investment banking, or the sale, marketing and transfer of securities.

The Act at least prevented a recurrence of generous loans for margin trading amongst individual investors, who were being led to slaughter as the smart money quietly exited the market. With almost surreal mistiming President Clinton finally repealed the already highly compromised Glass–Steagall legislation in November 1999 (perhaps in a 'one more for the road' spirit).

5.3.1   Long-Term Capital Management

Even before this the Federal Reserve, panicked by market disorder induced by the collapse of Long-Term Capital Management (LTCM), a story graphically told in a popular classic of behavioural finance *When Genius Failed* by Roger Lowenstein (2002), moved swiftly to lower short-term interest rates. LTCM hit trading problems in September 1998. The New York branch of the Federal Reserve organized a $4 billion dollar recapitalization/private-sector bailout of LTCM. As September closed, Alan Greenspan cut short-term interest rates by a quarter of a percentage point. As the scale and awareness of LTCM's problems grew Greenspan cut interest rates by a further quarter percent.

LTCM's demise is a graphic illustration of the principle that brains are not protection against financial disaster. Originally established in early 1994 by John Meriwether, the ex-head of the Merrill Lynch Arbitrage Group, the partnership collapsed spectacularly in the summer of 1998.

The partnership gathered a group of all-star partners including two Nobel Prize-winners, Myron Scholes and Robert Merton. *Business Week* swooned that 'never was so much talent given so much money to bet with' (Lowenstein 2002, p.47). And investors flocked in: Michael Ovitz, the Hollywood agent; Phillip Knight, chief executive of Nike; Sumitomo Bank in Japan, Dresdner Bank and Julius Baer in Europe (Lowenstein 2002, p.38).

With this power came a little arrogance. When a trader challenged the projected profits for LTCM during the initial funding road show, Scholes coolly replied they could easily attain this level of profit 'because of fools like you' (and presumably because of very clever people like Scholes). Greg Hawkins, an LTCM trader, asked an ex-colleague at Salomon the rhetorical question, 'Do you know why we make more money than you?'. Hawkins told him the simple truth was, 'It's because we're smarter' (Lowenstein 2002, p.89).

Following Meriwether's success in heading the Arbitrage Group within Salomon Brothers, LTCM specialized in trades based on the relative, not absolute, value assets in their portfolio. These typically involved exploiting very small spreads but doing so with vast amounts of capital. So even if assets were only mispriced a little, LTCM could make this opportunity worthwhile by throwing bucket loads of money at the problem. Scholes likened this process to 'hoovering up the nickels' which we all see, but few bother to capture (Lowenstein 2002, p.34).

An early trade by LTCM illustrates the sort of style they adopted (described in Lowenstein 2002, p.43). This was based on the fact that after initial issue 30-year Treasury bonds depreciate a little in favour of the latest issue. So since 30-year Treasury bonds are issued every six months, when a new issue falls due, the 'off-the-run' issue (issued six months back) falls in price relative to the most recently issued, or 'on-the-run' bonds. The only difference between the two bonds is the fact that 'on-the-run' bonds repay in 30 years while 'off-the-run' bonds repay in 29 years and six months. In the long run we are all dead, so the difference in such a lengthy maturity seems no big deal. But 'on-the-run' and 'off-the-run' bonds have a yield spread of 12 basis points, which opens up on the day the 'on-the-run' new issue is made. Obviously at repayment, or some time prior, the yields on the two bonds must converge. It was this very convergence process that LTCM became wizards at betting on.

Sadly one such gamble on rouble versus dollar-denominated Russian debt went wildly wrong in the summer of 1998. This caused William McDonough, head of the New York Federal Reserve, to summon a meeting of major Wall Street investment banks to organize a private bailout to cover its estimated $1 trillion exposure to financial market risk.

In many ways LTCM's downfall was a result of its success at 'hoovering up the nickels' and this very success brought many imitators, of which Swiss Bank was a leading exponent. This meant as soon as spreads opened up they seemed to be competed away, when rates offered converged. In search of stable, exploitable profits LTCM was pushed into lines of trade outside bonds in which it had little comparative advantage. In equities LTCM exploited 'paired trades in Royal Dutch and Shell Petroleum listings of Royal Dutch Shell and Volkswagen's ordinary and preference share listing (pp.98–9). More rashly it also began to move into 'risk arbitrage', based on second guessing the final outcome of merger/acquisition announcements. This was an area about which LTCM knew nothing and many others already did. Inevitably LTCM lost money in this sort of trade, for example

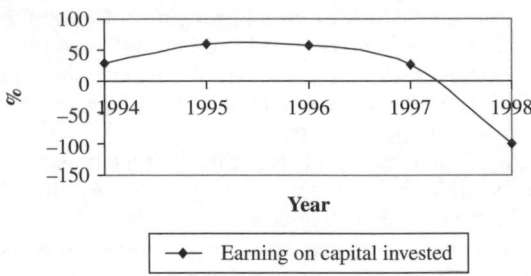

Figure 5.1   Earnings on LTCM investments before fees

when the MCI/British Telecom deal fell apart (Lowenstein 2002, p.112). By the end of 1997 LTCM was forced to concede defeat and returned $2.7 billion of its capital to investors. Returns on investment fell to a very healthy 25%, but far less than the nearly 60% return of the fund's early days. Figure 5.1 leaves little doubt about the stellar performance of the LTCM fund prior to its sudden implosion.

But in many ways the failure of LTCM was not a break in its luck but rather a design flaw in the logic of applying standard finance models. LTCM calculated its risk exposure based on historic volatility measures, such as the 'value at risk' measure of J.P. Morgan and RiskMetrics. Indeed in 1994 in an addendum to shareholders, Meriwether, Merton and Scholes felt confident enough to state that they expected LTCM to lose 5% of its investors' money in 12% of the quarters they participated in over the fund (Lowenstein 2002, pp.61–2). But, at least since empirical work by Fama in the early 1960s, it has been known that volatilities themselves are volatile. Sharp discontinuous 'jumps' in asset price distributions, like October 1987 or 1927, throw such neat calculations out of whack. LTCM's trading strategies coped well with risky trades, where a stable clearly defined asset return exists. But their trading models (and perhaps any model) struggled to manage true uncertainty, which by its nature involves sharp discontinuous transformations of asset returns. Commenting on his student's (Myron Scholes) work, Paul Samuelson, another Nobel Laureate, commented

> This is very important in the Long-Term story. The essence of the Black–Scholes formula is that you know, with certainty, not what the deal of the cards will be but what kind of universe is being sampled, which gives you the assumption of the log-normal process

> (Lowenstein 2002, pp.70–1).

In reality the distribution of asset returns in general is far from log-normally distributed. For a log-normal process a standard deviation of five times the mean in daily data might be expected every 7000 years. In reality such spikes seem to occur every four years or so in financial markets (Lowenstein 2002, p.71).

A major reason for this discontinuity in markets is the failure of the independently, identically, distributed assumption for asset return distributions. If the market falls today I may face margin calls to cover my trading positions. This makes me more likely to sell today to raise revenue. Or, if I see fellow fund managers selling up, it may be less likely I could defend my holding as 'reasonable' in any subsequent litigation by my investors. This raises the spectre of 'herding' in investment practice, a theme I explore more fully in Chapter 11 of this text.

5.3.2   The Federal Reserve and Market Restraint

Apparently William McChesney Martin, a previous holder of Greenspan's post as head of the Federal Reserve, had seen the job as requiring him to 'take away the punchbowl before the party really gets started' (Berenson 2003, p.173). It appears under Greenspan that the Federal Reserve was reluctant to lock the drinks cabinet. This created the so-called 'Greenspan put', which was believed to underpin the market's rise. Soon the bull market resumed with a vengeance with some investors feeling almost any amount of stupidity would be condoned by generous state subsidy in the form of interest rate declines. Some aspects of the financial bailout package of 2008, when $700 billion of financial support was given to US banks, appear to suggest the same 'moral hazard' of reckless behaviour being induced on a gargantuan scale.

Already by the summer of 1998 the S&P500 was trading at 1150 implying a price–earnings ratio of 25. The S&P index rose 27% in 1998 alone. The NASDAQ index, dominated by technology companies, had broken the psychological barrier of 2000 by the end of 1998 – a 25% rise during the year. Even after LTCM the rise in the NASDAQ resumed, finally reaching 2192 at the year close – a 40% annual rise. The Dow Jones index of 30 leading industrial stock climbed 16% in 1998 to 9181, with predictions of '10 by 2' being common amongst investment analysts (i.e. a prediction that the Dow Jones would reach 10,000 by the start of the new millennium on 1 January 2000).

All this was just the prelude to the final crescendo to the Internet boom of 1999. Figure 5.2 plots the market's large swings in the last 13 years.

In 1999 the NASDAQ gained 86% (I am not making this up), the S&P500 gained 20% and a book entitled *Dow 36,000* was published to wide acclaim (Berenson 2003, pp. 174–5). By now the Federal Reserve was well aware that a full-blown speculative bubble was in swing and began to raise short-term interest rates to slow the ascent. But even in the first three months of the new millennium the NASDAQ rose from 4000 to 5000, reaching a peak at 5048 on the last day of February. The S&P500 index peaked in March at 1572, implying an average price–earnings ratio of 29 and a dividend yield of 1% (Berenson 2003, p.179). At that point in the market only seven out of 1000 recommendations issued by analysts were either sell or strong sell. The bulls had run themselves ragged and the market reversal began.

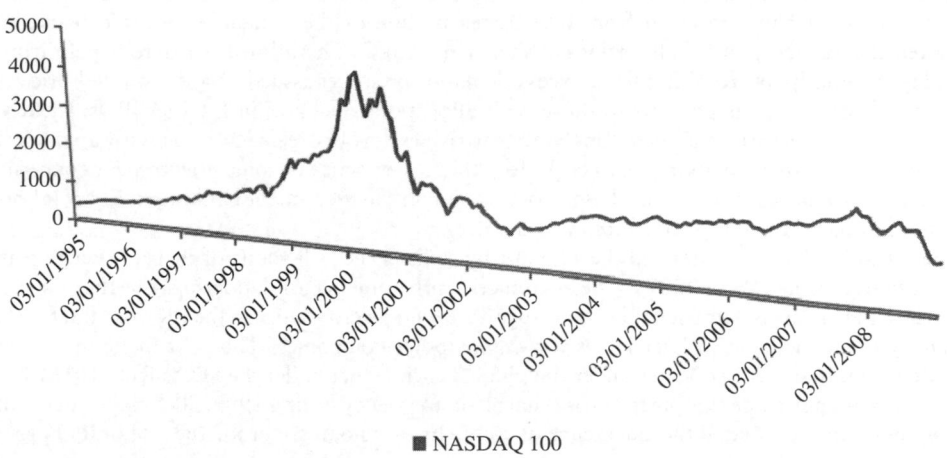

■ NASDAQ 100

Figure 5.2   NASDAQ 1995–2008 index

To chronicle the role of the state in every aspect of the most recent speculative bubble would be a huge task, but I concentrate here on four themes discussed by Berenson (2003) underpinning the inflation of the late 1990s' bubble. These are the structure and operation of the initial public offering of shares to the public. Secondly, I discuss the promulgation and enforcement of accounting standards and the quality of auditing of accounts undertaken by accounting firms. Thirdly, I consider the role of the SEC as a regulator of financial markets. Finally the development of 'conflicts of interest' for investment analysts, who were supposed to be advancing impartial investment advice while in reality often being pressurized by their employers to market the stock of a client as strongly as possible. Part of the reason I choose to discuss these four areas is that three of them will form the basis for later chapters in this book. So while I hope to shed light on the role of government in inducing financial bubbles I also try to introduce topics treated in greater depth later on.

The structure and operation of the initial public offering of shares

The Netscape initial public offering (IPO) was undertaken on 9 August 1995. An IPO is the first opportunity that outside investors get to invest in newly formed companies. Or conversely it is the first opportunity that founders and venture capitalists get to dilute their equity holding in the business (which in the case of the founder is usually the only capital he has). The Internet boom has been called the 'greatest legal creation of wealth in all time' by John Doerr, one of the venture capitalists involved in Netscape, eBay, Google and many other lucrative deals. Part of the reason for this was the fairly fixed rate of fees on offer to investment banks for underwriting the offer. Underwriting an issue requires that the bank be willing to buy up unsold shares at the IPO at a previously agreed price. The 'going rate' for this service seems to be 7% of the IPO proceeds. In the case of Netscape, when even the idea of what the company produced was unclear to many, such insurance was no doubt prudent and paying 7% of the capital raised does not seem that unreasonable. Netscape had originally planned to sell 3.5 million shares at $14 each, raising about $500 million in equity capital, but the strong demand at the IPO meant its merchant bank, Morgan Stanley, decided to offer 5 million shares at an opening price of $28 – this raised the IPO proceeds to more than $1.4 billion. This meant Morgan Stanley received the better part of $100 million for its work on the deal. Floating Netscape required selling a totally new idea into a market that did not yet exist, so we might expect an institution assuming the risk of doing so to be well paid. What is more difficult to understand is the consistency of the 7% of proceeds fee margin as Internet IPOs became almost a one-way bet. Nor were the 7% fees the only benefit merchant banks received from IPO representation of their client, very often bankers and favoured clients were granted allocations of shares in the IPO. This allowed them to benefit from the first-day trading 'pops' resulting from excess demand for shares issued at a discounted price. This could result in very large pay-offs to those with allocations of shares in Internet IPOs. Clearly the presence of such persistent and seemingly almost riskless profits seems at odds with a competitive provision of investment banking services. Indeed there is evidence of some government concern, but little action, about the lack of price-based competition in the investment banking industry (although competition based on non-price factors was intense).

These leading banks maintained their favour by sharing the rich spoils of their IPO engagements with favoured clients (Hao 2007). One such tactic is the practice of 'laddering' the IPO issue. This practice arises from investment banks requiring those who receive shares in the IPO also bid for shares issued by the same bank in later issues for this or other companies. This sort of tie-in strategy is already illegal in the United States under the 1934 Securities Act under the SEC's Rule 101M. If SEC settlements are any guide this practice rose sharply in frequency during 1999. Such tie-ins of clients to investment banks prevented the emergence of competitors who might erode the 7% of IPO proceeds that incumbents were enjoying.

Table 5.1 (excerpted from Morrison & Wilhem 2007, p.17) gives historical data concerning the concentration of the underwriting of share issues in the United States (this data covers both IPOs and

Table 5.1 Underwritten common stock (thousands of US $) US transactions

1960–9		1970		1980		1990		2003	
First Boston	3,989	Merrill Lynch	591	Merrill Lynch	2,233	Alex, Brown	2,975	Merrill Lynch	20,184
Merrill Lynch	3,721	First Boston	345	Morgan Stanley	1,623	Goldman Sachs	2,634	Citigroup	19,256
Lehman Brothers	3,218	Kidder, Peabody	321	Kidder, Peabody	1,118	Salomon Brothers	1,736	Goldman Sachs	14,554
Blyth	2,732	Blyth	262	Goldman Sachs	952	Merrill Lynch	1,596	Morgan Stanley	12,116
White Weld	2,546	Eastman Dillon	256	First Boston	818	Lehman Brothers	1,013	UBS	10,273
Morgan Stanley	2,258	Stone & Webster	239	Dean Witter	758	First Boston	929	CS First Boston	7,355
Goldman Sachs	2,220	Morgan Stanley	211	Blyth, Eastman	639	Paine Weber	911	Lehman Brothers	6,375
Dean Witter	2,000	White Weld	135	Lehman Brothers	629	Morgan Stanley	911	JP Morgan	6,031
Kuhn, Loeb	1,931	Lehman Brothers	134	EF Hutton	465	Smith Barney	807	Bank of America	4,069
Kidder, Peabody	1,891	Smith Barney	132	Salomon Brothers	454	Dean Witter	759	AG Edwards	2,708
Total market	43,022		4224		12,841		20,082		119,503
Top 5 market share	38%		42%		53%		50%		64%
Top 10 market share	62%		62%		75%		71%		86%

Source: Securities Data Corporation. Morrison, A. and W. Wilhem (2007). *Investment Banking: Institutions, Politics and the Law*. Oxford: Oxford University Press.

seasoned equity offerings). Concentration is both high and rising with 87% of the market being dominated by the top 10 investment banks in 2003. Even the top five firms took 64% of the total underwriting market in 2003 with the same names recurring over a long period: Merrill Lynch, First Boston, Goldman Sachs, etc.

The role of accounting practice and the accounting profession

It is a sad commentary on the accounting profession that the 1997–9 winners of the US *CFO Magazine* Excellence awards, Mark Swartz of Tyco International, Scott Sullivan of WorldCom and Andrew Fastow of Enron, all later faced criminal charges (Lowenstein 2004, p.67). It appears the crooks really were in control on Wall Street and were publicly lauded during their reign.

The demise in the authority of the accounting profession and especially of the auditing of published accounts as providing a 'true and fair view' of the company's financial state is one of the most striking features of the most recent speculative boom. Certainly the diminished authority of the accounting profession underpinned much of the legislative response to the bubble's implosion included in the Sarbanes–Oxley legislation. Yet the weakness of regulatory constraint both in the United States and the United Kingdom seems to be the result of a rather studied indifference on the part of elected politicians.

An initial opportunity to curtail the excesses of the accounting profession arose from the misuse of merger accounting in the growth of pyramid scheme-like conglomerates such as Ling Industries (Berenson 2003, p.48). The trick to maintaining this sort of growth is for a high price–earnings ratio to acquire less highly valued target companies.

Imagine a corporation called Ping PLC, which has earnings of £10 million with 10 million shares in issue, so its earnings-per-share is £1. Suppose it has a price–earnings ratio of 40 implying a market capitalization of Ping PLC of £400 million. Now Ping PLC's directors notice Pong PLC also has £10 million earnings and 10 million shares in issue. But Pong PLC has a lower price–earnings ratio of 15. Therefore Pong's market valuation is £150 (£10 million in earnings times its PE ratio of 15). So rejoicing Ping PLC offer £200 million to acquire Pong PLC from its shareholders in a share-only offer of one Ping PLC share for two Pong shares (so half Pong's market capitalization, a £200 million offer). Now suppose the stock market values Ping-Pong PLC, the newly created joint firm, at the similar price–earnings ratio to the original acquirer Ping PLC. It has earnings of £20 million with 15 million Ping-Pong PLC shares in issue (Ping PLC's original 10 million, plus an additional 5 million to fund the acquisition of Pong PLC). This yields an apparent earning-per-share for the newly formed Ping-Pong PLC of 1.33 (£20 million in earnings divided by the 15 million shares in issue). If the stock-market values the newly formed entity at the same price–earnings ratio as the original firm then its price will be £53.33 (40 × 1.33) and a market capitalization of £800 (53.33 times 15 million shares). It appears the merged firm magically creates earnings and stock-market value despite the fact that Ping PLC paid an acquisition premium of a third of its original price (£200 million for assets currently valued at £150 million).

The danger of reporting the effect of acquisitions in this way was condemned in late 1966 by the Accounting Principles Board (APB), a forerunner of the US Financial Accounting Standards Board (FASB). The APB suggested a reform that would prevent the use of merger accounting in acquisitions, where the highly valued firm cashed in on its current stock-market popularity. But the late 1960s' slump in the stock market brought a natural end to such tricks and little was done. Nevertheless, public concern about such accounting scams was met by the usual lame politicians' response to voter wrath in the establishment of a Committee. Here the Committee was set up in 1971 under the chairmanship of Francis Wheat, a former SEC Commissioner. The fruit of the Wheat Committee and its recommendations came in 1973 with the establishment of the FASB to replace the APB in 1973. But the game had changed in little but name and no real reform occurred. Indeed since the FASB was funded by the accounting profession, one expert described its members as 'like goldfish in a bowl of sharks' (Berenson 2003, p. 62). Further meek complaints about the accounting profession continued in a Senate sub-committee report of 1976 which stated:

> the traditional public image of the Big Eight accounting firms as impartial objective experts is not founded in fact.... As political partisans and purveyors of non-accounting services, they become loyal agents of the clients which employ their services'
>
> (Berenson 2003, p.63).

It was not until the 1980s that the whirlwind of poor accounting practice would be reaped. The rise of new technology firms like Microsoft saw a move away from the payment of dividends in favour of intensive internal investment via the retention of earnings. Now companies were no longer held accountable by the need to 'show money' by the payment of dividends. Earnings are a figure at the bottom of the profit and loss account, but 'you can eat dividends' and their payment constitutes a real return of value to shareholders. The weakening of managerial accountability due to the decline in dividend payment intensified the crisis within the profession.

The 1980s also saw the emergence of hostile takeovers often funded by 'junk' (below investment-grade) bonds often issued by Michael Milken and his group at Drexel Burnham Lambert on the West Coast. Managers were now forced to deliver or yield control to junk-bond financed 'raiders'. When Ron Perelman, an almost unknown Milken-funded raider, acquired Revlon in 1985 the starting gun was fired for an assault on the control of S&P500 companies (Lowenstein 2004, p.10). The leverage, junk-financed buyout threatened to give poorly managed corporations, only held accountable to a diversified base of shareholders, often only represented by a crony packed board of directors, over to new owners who had a major stake in making the corporation profitable and capable of paying down its debt schedule.

The corporate response was a clarion call to shareholder value and the rise of the payment of managers in options was seen as a way of motivating them to manage the company in a way that would maximize the share price. A call option (a right to buy at a fixed price) has value only if the share price moves above the value set in the contract (the 'exercise' price). By issuing a call option to buy the share at its current value strong incentives to boost the share price from its level were given to managers. Every penny the stock price moves above the current level brings proportionate benefit to the manager receiving call options. If the manager is granted thousands of call options, as was and is common, this incentive to deliver can be very large indeed. Options are at least 'costless' at the grant date, if issued as a right to buy at the current share price, but upon exercise they have a clear dilutive effect on current equity owners' stake in the firm. Often these dilutions were pretty massive, Charles Lazurus, the CEO of Toys R Us, earned nearly $60 million in 1987 alone and Michael Eisner received $40 million in 1998 (Berenson 2003, p.97). The generosity of these awards meant the average S&P500 CEO in 1997 was taking home 326 times a factory worker's wage in basic salary and options alone (ignoring pensions, golden parachutes etc.).

It was not until 1993 that the FASB was willing to act. In that year the FASB recommended a rule which would require companies to infer the cost of the grant issue (using something like the Black–Scholes option pricing model) and record that cost as an expense against income on the option grant date. But corporate vested interests led to intense lobbying pressure under the direction of Democratic Senator Joe Lieberman. Bizarrely there was even a public march in Silicon Valley to the chant 'Give stock a chance!' (Lowenstein 2004, p.44). This forced the FASB to backtrack on its promise to exercise some control on managerial option grants in 1994.

The Securities and Exchange Commission

With so much bad accounting practice and misleading advice to investors during the bubble's expansion one might not unreasonably ask what was the Securities and Exchange Commission, the body set up to oversee the operation of financial markets in the United States, doing during the Internet bubble. The Commission had been founded in 1934 with Joseph Kennedy, the forefather of the Kennedy dynasty, at its head. Kennedy was a former organizer of stock-market 'pools', coordinators of speculative buy-ups of stocks only to dump them as other less savvy investors rushed in.[4] President Roosevelt joked he had 'set a thief to catch a thief' and certainly the crash had flushed out a few notorious thieves (Lowenstein 2004, p.79). Such an astute adjudicator instilled panic in the post-crash market and most investment banks simply withdrew from underwriting new issues for a couple of years after SEC's establishment. Nevertheless by the end of the Second World War the SEC had gained respect for its intervention and curtailment of bad practice.

The principal protection it sought for investors was disclosure. So links to investment banks, management compensation and membership of all key corporate committees (audit, remuneration, board nomination committee, etc.) had to be disclosed. Buyers needed to be beware and if they were not they must accept the cost of their own foolishness. All this made huge demands on the cognitive abilities of individual investors, an expectation of ability that much of this book suggests may be misplaced.

When Arthur Levitt became head of the SEC in 1993, the boom of the Clinton years was just getting under way after the wipe-out of the junk-bond market in the early 1990s. Levitt started to raise noises about an 'unholy alliance' of bankers, analysts and CEOs in what I will later call the 'market for information' about corporate financial performance (Lowenstein 2002, p.82). Indeed exposing and dismantling this alliance was to become something of a personal crusade for Levitt during his eight years as head of the SEC.

Unfortunately for Levitt by 1994 any support President Clinton could give him was compromised by the radical Republican Congress, headed by Newt Gingrich. By 1995 the deregulation bandwagon was rolling full steam ahead in consumer affairs, antitrust policy as well as securities legislation. Further, despite a record number of earnings misstatements and SEC rule violations being successfully prosecuted, the SEC's budget was cut and its profile in Washington downplayed. Ironically, on recognizing the way he was being undermined, Levitt felt liberated into a more outspoken critique of financial market professionals, especially accountants and analysts.

Economists often claim regulatory agencies are captured by the regulatory constituencies they oversee (for example the UK's gas industry regulator OFGAS has an alleged cosy relationship with British Gas). While voters are a poorly informed disparate constituency towards whom the regulatory agency is in principle accountable, the banks they oversee are tightly organized, well funded and motivated to undermine the public interest agenda of the regulatory body (see Stigler 1971 and Becker 1983). Whatever the general merit of the 'capture' theory of the development of regulatory powers it seems somewhat unsuited to describe the observed behaviour of the SEC. Successive SEC commissioners have had few problems over open confrontation with finance professionals, like bankers and accountants (Joel Seligman (2003) provides a full history of the SEC since its inception). This may not be unrelated to the fact that the commissionership of the SEC is often seen as a springboard for higher political ambitions.

One piece of success Levitt and the SEC did obtain was regulation fair disclosure (FD). Regulation FD ensured that companies publicly disclosed all information disclosed semi-privately amongst a charmed circle of favoured analysts and fund managers. Conference calls between management and analysts are now routinely broadcast live on the web. This at least in theory undermines the role of 'whisper forecast' guidance by management to analysts to make sure the consensus forecast is attainable by the corporation (Lowenstein 2004, p.86).

Analysts' conflicts of interest induced by the investment banking advice of their employer

Analysts are often seen as the 'eager postmen' (according to Warren Buffett in Berkshire Hathaway's *Annual Report* quoted in Penman 2003)[5] of the latest speculative bubble. The $1.4 billion global settlement of 10 US merchant banks involved in NASDAQ IPOs suggests they played an enthusiastic role in propagating the most recent boom. While I discuss the culpability of analysts in more detail in Chapter 18 it is worthwhile to remember that their role was well understood during the height of the boom itself. Regulation FD was one government attempt to curb their distorting role on trading in financial markets although more regulation was to follow in the Sarbanes–Oxley legislative response to the bubble.

5.4 Bubbles: Past, Present and Future

A common element of many speculative bubbles, if not scams, is the belief that the world has entered a new bright dawn of history which will liberate man from his life of want and struggle. In the late 1990s it was common to believe the Internet and the knowledge economy more generally had fundamentally transformed both society and the productive possibilities open to mankind. In its most extreme form this sort of belief imagined a sort of 'digital sublime' which promised almost unlimited wealth (Mosco 2004). Indeed this 'new age' zeitgeist served an important unifying role for those engaged in the investment and development of the new economy almost regardless of its truth. Mosco (2004) states:

> It is important to emphasize the need to resist the peculiarly modern temptation to regard myth as falsehood. Enticing as it is for people influenced by science to assess stories as true (accurate) or false (myth), this is myopic and beside the point.

Instead of listening to stories like this, even when backed up by the rigors of a historical analysis of price–earnings ratios and other statistical indicators, people continued to bid up stock prices. Rather than allow the myth to be undermined by facts proving it false, many people, including some experts, answered with myths of their own.

A classic of the genre of manifestos for the transformative effect of the information revolution is Bill Gates's text *Business @ the Speed of Thought* (Gates & Hemingway 1999). While readers may have suspected a self-serving tone in the book, it is unlikely a man as wealthy as Gates would be entirely debased by selfish motives. Indeed he seems quite busy giving large parts of his fortune away.[6] Illustrative of fairly widespread 'new economy' beliefs is Gates's comment in that book:

> As tough and uncertain as the digital world makes it for business – it evolves rapidly or dies – we will all be beneficiaries. We are going to get improved products and services, more responsiveness to complaints, lower costs, and more choices. We are going to get better government and social services at substantially less expense ... This world is coming

> (Gates & Hemingway 1999, p.414).

The future seemed set fair if not transcendental in many ways. Companies held as icons of the 'new economy' soared to almost surreal valuations. In April 1999 Amazon, the online bookstore, had a market value of $30 billion. This was almost 10 times the combined market value of its two biggest non-Internet based competitors, Barnes & Noble and Borders, each of which had over 1000 bookshops across the world at that time. Similarly, the online toy seller, eToys, in October 1999 had a market capitalization bigger than Toys R Us, the world's biggest non-Internet toy-shop chain with over 1600 branches worldwide (Siegal 2005, p.73).

Yet within months of Gates's manifesto appearing the Internet bubble was in full implosion and we had entered a new hasher reality. High-tech companies from start-ups to blue-chip began to be battered in bear trading.

Some scale of shareholder wealth destroyed by the Internet bubble's implosion is provided by a roll call of individual corporate implosions. Between March 2000 and March 2003 Microsoft lost 53%, Intel fell 73%, Lucent 97% (an accounting scandal and consequent earnings restatements added fuel to its funeral pyre), Cisco fell 81% and many other titans of the new economy moved in tandem. Of course many smaller fish simply imploded overnight.

5.4.1 Financial Bubbles and Infrastructure Technology

The successful introduction of a radical new technology does not necessarily result in systematic rises in securities associated with this productive process. Conversely such a radical economic shift is almost inevitably disruptive, unsteady and destructive. A perfect illustration of this sort of evolution is the recurrent financial speculations in railway and canal companies in the nineteenth century (see Miller 2003). Both the laying down of a rail network and the diffusion of the Internet constituted a huge infrastructure investment in the productive economy. For example in the years 1870 to 1911 the railway grid in the United States grew from 70,000 miles to 250,000 miles of track. This sort of growth could only be attained by considerable state pump-priming investment (see Baskin & Miranti 1999, p. 134). Of the $188 million total investment in the US railroad system in years 1815–60 three-quarters of it came from government sources. This need for the state to at least coordinate infrastructure investment means it often actively participates in bubbles inspired by the diffusion of network technologies like the telegraph system, railways, canals and the Internet. The Internet itself has its origin with the US Department of Defense's ARAP project to facilitate command and control in a post-nuclear apocalypse world.

In Britain funding the canal and railroad system that facilitated the industrial revolution produced a wellspring of pressure to repeal the 'Bubble Act' of 1720, which forbade the use of the corporate form unless explicitly enacted by legislation. The Bubble Act was finally rescinded in 1825 and follow-on legislation in 1855 and 1862 eliminated entirely the need for Parliamentary legislation to incorporate. The corporate form has been such a dramatic engine of economic growth that I cover its merits and nature in Chapter 14.

But the building of the canals and railways contributed to another part of organizational heritage. The stark problems of asymmetric information raised by network technologies requiring a large managerial class induced the first clear separation of ownership and control. Specifically this separation promoted state awareness of a need for the preparation and presentation of consistent sets of financial accounts. This recognition came in the 1879 Companies Act which first required companies to file audited accounts at Companies House. The 1906 Hepburn Act in the United States similarly required the submission of audited accounts prepared according to a standardized template. I discuss the purpose and valuation usefulness of contemporary accounting in Chapter 19.

Each bubble brings its own 'new era' doctrine. In accepting the Presidential nomination from the Republican Party in 1928 Herbert Hoover declared,

> We in America today are nearer to the final triumph over poverty than ever before in the history of our land. We will soon with the help of God be in sight of the day when poverty will be banished from the earth

(quoted in Klein 2001, p.5).

In all these industrial transformations it was never clear that shareholders would be the principal beneficiaries of these transformative technologies. Rather the competitive process is always likely to erode producer surpluses (and their return to shareholders) and return them to consumers. Indeed, the very rationale for Internet usage is often social, as the growth of social networking and content-sharing sites, MySpace, Friends Reunited, YouTube, etc. suggest. Because of this capturing the return to investments in the technology as a private return is rendered complex by the social nature of its use and the non-appropriable nature of the 'content' being sold. Indeed many aspects of the 'new economy' are very well understood through the lens of good old-fashioned microeconomics (see Shapiro & Varian 1999).

5.4.2　Are Bubbles Just Part of the Market Process?

There has been a marked reluctance in public policy discussion to accept a market-based allocation of investment capital. John Galbraith in reviewing the history of financial speculation has pointed to reluctance to accept that securities markets may by their very nature admit occasional gross distortions of capital allocation. He states:

> That the months and years before the 1987 crash were characterized by intense speculation no one will seriously deny. But in the aftermath of that crash, little or no importance was attributed to that speculation.... Markets in our culture are a totem; to them can be ascribed no inherent aberrant tendency

> (Galbraith 1993, p.24).

I imagine Gailbraith, were he alive today, would say the very same thing about the Sarbanes–Oxley response to the most recent speculative bubble. We struggle with the notion that the great benefits of a free, competitive, economy do have some costs. One of these costs is an occasional decline into speculative madness by market participants. Governments are therefore to be blamed for insisting on imposing remedies to failings that are an inherent part of market allocation.

In Galbraith's famous history of the bubble in 1929 (Galbraith 1975) he draws specific implications for regulatory reform of such a perspective. Galbraith states:

> Since 1929 we have enacted numerous laws designed to make securities speculation more honest and, it is hoped, more readily restrained. None of these is a perfect safeguard. The signal feature of the mass escape from reality in 1929 and before – and which characterized every previous bubble from the South Sea bubble to the Florida land boom – was that it carried Authority with it. Governments were either bemused as were the speculators or they deemed it unwise to be sane at a time when sanity exposed one to ridicule, condemnation for spoiling the game, or the threat of severe retribution.

Government cannot restrain or prevent speculative financial market surges and consequent crashes because so often it is complicit in them or they are at least afraid to move clearly against their force. In order to explore this further I discuss the origin and consequence of the Wall Street crash in 1929 in more detail below.

While today we often recoil at the viscous greed of competition in financial markets it is easy to forget that the financial world of city 'gentlemen' (not 'players') in the era before the First World War was hardly any better. The 'club' of J.P. Morgan and Kuhn, Loeb, linked back to England and Germany respectively was an all-white male affair that shunned ambitious Jews or Catholics seeking to enter their midst (Klein, 2001, p.47). Women were simply not considered for club membership. Customer focus was not an issue deemed important to 'club' membership. Klein (2001, p.48) describes the bank J.P. Morgan as follows:

> They had no branch offices and refused to take on new companies unless the move was first cleared with the former banker. The idea was not to compete, at least not too openly, which meant no advertising, no price competition, and no raiding of other's clients.

The bubble of the 1920s was in large part a result of these traditions being broken and a new 'market for information' about security value emerging. This market for detailed knowledge about asset value, corporate prospects, and technological advance remains vital to the operation of financial markets and I discuss it in more detail in Chapter 15.

5.5   The 1929 Stock-Market Crash

In many ways the 1929 crash is 'the big one' everyone fears may one day recur. While the recent Internet boom undoubtedly had its share of victims it did not lead to mass unemployment, trade wars and open public strife. No doubt to some degree this is because we have learned some lessons from the intensity of the suffering caused by the 1929 crash. In order that we might continue to benefit from this lesson of history I revisit part of the 1929 story. As before, I focus largely upon the government's role in inciting, managing and overcoming the crash. I draw heavily upon J.K. Galbraith's (1975) classic account of the crash.

5.5.1   Early Signs

The commencement of the run-up to the 1929 crash flowed on swiftly from the implosion of a prior speculative bubble based on purchase and part-purchase of property in Florida in the early 1920s. Florida became something of an Eldorado location within the United States as the summer 'trip south' to vacation became popular with the urban middle-class of the east coast during the 'roaring 20s'. House prices of beachfront locations soared and when they were all bought up sellers simply exaggerated the proximity of the property sold to the sea. So swampland became an 'ideal holiday location'. Famously a speculator schemed to sell properties 'near Jacksonville' (although in reality 65 miles west of that city using the investment of later depositors to repay earlier ones their expected rental income). The 1925 collapse of the Florida land boom cut land values from over $1.5 million in 1929 to just under $150,000 in 1928 (Galbraith 1975, p.35).

However, even this erosion of real estate values could not deny the generally healthy economic development of the 1920s. Between 1925 and 1929 the value of output rose by a third from $60 billion to $80 billion. Car production rose from 4.3 million to 5.35 million in the years 1924 to 1929. More generally earnings grew and manufacturing industry exhibited sustained grown. Keynes famously quipped in his general theory:

> Speculators may do no harm as bubbles on a steady stream of enterprise. But the position is serious when enterprise becomes the bubble of a whirlpool of speculation

(Keynes 1936).

It seems there was some rationale for confidence in the performance of the real economy to justify at least the relatively modest stock-market gains up to 1927. So judging when justified confidence tips over into unjustifiable speculation is a subtle art.

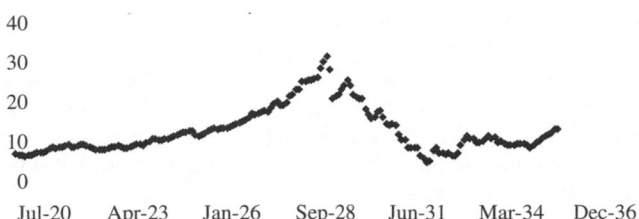

40
30
20
10
0

Jul-20   Apr-23   Jan-26   Sep-28   Jun-31   Mar-34   Dec-36

Figure 5.3   S&P composite value 1920–35

Indeed the surge in equity values funded a merger boom that consolidated many industrial sectors. Figure 5.3 shows the movements in the S&P500 in the years 1920 to 1935, the dramatic plunge between 1929 and 1931 is clear. Well-known companies today, such as International Harvester, United States Steel Corporation and American Tobacco date from this era (Galbraith 1975, p.70). Similarly local utility companies, for example water and electricity, were consolidated into national holding companies as dominant local players used financial leverage to subvert product market competition.

Perhaps the most iconic creation of the era is General Motors (GM), a product of the acquisition spree of Billy Durant, a hyperactive, highly optimistic car-maker, at the start of the twentieth century. Durant built a motor giant from the obscure beginnings of an investment in the Buick Motor Company in Michigan (see Klein 2001, pp.32–3). He took the struggling Buick brand and grew it rapidly from 1905. Sadly he grew Buick too rapidly and the economic stall of 1907 left him with thousands of unsold cars and huge debts. But Durant used this unsteady base to launch an acquisition spree that produced an industrial empire by 1910 of 25 separate companies with 14,000 workers producing 20% of US cars. By 1919, with investment from John Raskob and Pierre du Pont, GM was an industrial giant with earnings in excess of half a billion dollars. In 1920 J.P. Morgan invested to rescue GM during a market downturn. This eased Durant out and on to further speculative adventures (Klein, 2001, pp.38–9).

5.5.2 The Boom is On

In 1927 the stock-market surge really began in earnest with a 69% increase in the *Times* index. In that year Henry Ford shifted from Model T to Model A production in a new car plant. Britain, having moved back on to the gold standard, had been actively lobbying the United States to lower interest rates and follow an 'easy money' policy. By doing so it hoped to stem the flow of capital investment out of Britain in response to the 1925 currency appreciation necessitated by the return to gold. In response to this request the New York Reserve Bank cut its lending rate from 4% to 3.5%. This allowed speculators to obtain cheap funds for equity investment and the final rush to the precipice was on. Lionel Robbins, a professor at the London School of Economics, commented, 'From that date, according to all evidence, the situation got completely out of control' (Galbraith 1975, p.39).

From 1928 onwards an almost delusional optimism spread through the market. The market rose in leaps rather than in a steady stream. Big players, like John Raskob, a director at General Motors and chairman of the Democratic National Committee, talked the market up. The volume of shares traded rose dramatically especially in occasional market fall-offs like on the 12 June 1928 when over five million shares exchanged hands. The total number of shares traded in 1928 rose to just above $9 million from just above $5 million in 1927 (Galbraith 1975, p.45).

On 6 November 1928 Herbert Hoover replaced Calvin Coolidge as President. Hoover as the previous Secretary of Commerce had repeatedly attempted to deflate the boom in progress, but feared inducing overreaction and a consequent market crash. Coolidge had famously declared that the market was 'absolutely sound' and shares were 'cheap at current prices', before departing to let Hoover face the collapse. Despite the election of a more cautious President the stock market surged once more in November with a 'victory boom' (Galbraith 1975, p.45). Hoover's chosen Secretary of the Treasury, Andrew Mellon, did little and so by default restraint passed to the Federal Reserve Board. The Board was above much of the pettiness motivating a great deal of state intervention in the economy. As Galbraith (1975, p.53) states:

> The regulation of economic activity is without doubt the most inelegant and unrewarding of public endeavours. Almost everyone is opposed to it in principle; its justification always relies on the unprepossessing case of the lesser evil. Regulation originates in raucous debates in Congress in which the naked interest of pressure groups may at times involve an exposure bordering on the obscene.

Sadly the Federal Reserve Board did not prove up to the task. The two policy instruments open to it were raising rates and selling gilts to mop up speculative funds. Belatedly it tried both. But by the end of 1928 the Federal Reserve had only $228 million of government securities left to counter the growing tide of speculative investment (Galbraith 1975, p.56). In mid-February 1929 it raised the rediscount rate by one percentage point to 6% with little effect.

Nevertheless Andrew Mellon, originally appointed as Secretary to the Treasury in 1921 by President William Harding, soon established himself as the dominant political figure of the 1920s. Mellon was a keen tax cutter, especially for the wealthy like himself, a fact that made him deeply unpopular as many were pushed into deep poverty in the wake of the 1929 crash (Klein, 2001, p.71).

5.5.3   Innovation and Speculation

Central elements of any financial speculation are financial innovations designed to facilitate an increased volume of trade. New conceptualizations of the allocation of ownership rights facilitate growing volumes of trade. Very often these new strategies come down to exercising the magic of leverage on a portfolio, which in a rising market appears to offer far greater return without any apparent risk (think of options and other derivatives here). Of course the downturn will expose the naivety of this strategy.

The latest fuel to the fire in the late 1920s was trading 'on margin'. This allowed investors to buy stocks by putting up 10% or so of the purchase price in a bank as collateral, as long as they agreed to leave the security certificate with the bank as further collateral. If the investor failed to meet calls for refinancing the bank simply sold the stock. As long as prices kept rising this was a perfect arrangement for a speculator. He could buy a £10 share for £1 from the bank. If its price rose to £11 he took a 100% return on his investment. But if prices fell things became more tricky, the investor was required to 'make margin' or make good the bank's losses. So if the £10 share fell to £9, the investor had to return that £1 to the bank, or take a 100% loss on his initial investment of £10 when the stock is sold by the bank.

5.5.4   Investment Trusts in the Boom's Growth

From 1927 loans by investment brokers to their clients, a good index of margin trading, rose alarmingly. By the end of 1927 about $3.5 billion was outstanding in such loans, this rose to $6 billion by the end of 1928 (Galbraith 1975, p.48). By the summer of 1929 brokers' loans outstanding reached $7 billion (Galbraith 1975, p.92). Since margin loans were secured by stocks they were issued to purchase they were very attractive to lenders also. Initially such loans were made at something close to the riskless rate of 5%. But by 1928 margin loans attracted a return of 12% and many manufacturing companies realized it was pointless to try and find productive projects offering a higher return. Many companies used retained profits and cash reserves to make margin loans for speculation often in their own stock. Dementia was in full swing.

Rapidly formed, but very fast-growing, investment trusts became the most common vehicle for individual investors' participation in the spiralling out-of-control boom. During 1928, 186 such investment trusts were organized although they were not allowed to list on the New York Stock Exchange until 1929. Once again the power of leverage was harvested by investment trusts by levered trusts birthing yet more subsidiary trusts, which then took on more debt. The effect was to geometrically expand both the potential return to and risk exposure of the founding trust. The Shenandoah Trust, established by Goldman Sachs in July 1929 with $102,000 worth of securities issued, was promptly sold to the investing public at $5 million. Shenandoah went on to sponsor the formation of the Blue Ridge Trust with capital of $142,000 sold for over $6 million (Galbraith 1975, p.86). Highly geared investment strategies had a new Trojan horse to assault the market with.

Since a bust was by now almost inevitable some deemed drastic measures acceptable. In late March 1929 Charles Mitchell, a director at the New York Federal Reserve, promised that his bank, the National City Bank, would ensure a reasonable interest rate by making $5 million available to lenders for each percentage point increase in the rediscount rate (the rate at which margin investors could finance their position). It would borrow from the Federal Reserve and pass the funds on at no additional cost to investors. This made a mockery of the Federal Reserve's attempt to put the squeeze on speculators. Senator Glass (of Glass–Steagall fame above) called for Mitchell's dismissal from the Federal Reserve, but nothing was done. Implosion was now just a matter of time and the government's main concern was to avoid being blamed.

The bubble was finally spiked on 3 September 1929 following a gloomy speech by an academic, statistician and all-round market pundit Roger Babson to the Annual National Business Conference of that year. Despite being denounced by no less an authority than the Yale economist Irving Fisher, the market began a slow retreat that grew by late October into a rout.

5.5.5 The Final Implosion

The final implosion was a jagged collapse over the week from Saturday 19 October, when the market opened for a brief trading session. The *Times* index fell 12 points with three million shares changing hands. Sunday's papers only spread panic further to presage a bloodbath of trading on Monday 21 October. Friday morning brought some relief with organized intervention by J.P. Morgan, Charles Mitchell and other leading institutional investors.

Tuesday 29 October is often held to be 'the day' of the crash. The *Times* index fell 43 points, enough to wipe out all the gains of the previous year. Over 16 million shares were sold on that day, over three times the volume on previous heavy trading days (Galbraith 1975, p.133). The stock market had entered a brief period of free-fall. The market was only to stabilize following a close of the stock market for the election of the New York Mayor on 5 November, but the market continued to ratchet down until mid-November.

5.6 Should Government Burst the Bubble?

As illustrated above the state is often either heavily implicated in the emergence of financial bubbles or at least ill-equipped to deflate them. By the time policy-makers know the economy is in the grip of a bubble to act at all runs the risk of precipitating a crash and consequent political censure. So should the government just leave speculators, no matter how unwise, to their inevitable fate? To do so would certainly be consistent with the *laissez-faire* tradition of liberal societies.

The danger here is that in requiring government to short-circuit the market process we degrade the formational role of prices and so distort the allocation of productive capital equity that market competition facilitates. A treasury minister or a financial service authority/securities exchange official may be very wise, but it is impossible for him or her to aggregate information as effectively as competitive asset markets. This is because what prices in a competitive market give us is not the insights of one wise authority, but the disparate and perhaps tentative judgements of a myriad of market participants seeking personal enrichment through informational arbitrage. Friedrich Hayek (1945, pp.77–8) comments on the state regulator's problem as follows:

> The peculiar problem of a rational economic order is determined precisely by the fact that the knowledge of the circumstances of which we must make use never exists in concentrated or integrated form but solely as dispersed bits of incomplete and frequently contradictory knowledge which all the individuals possess. Or, to put it briefly, it is a problem of the utilization of knowledge not given to anyone in its totality.

Hence the problem for the government in calling the bubble and intervening to anticipate speculative mania is that the market as a whole has a far richer and more subtle information set to condition its actions. Some of this knowledge may be 'tacit' and no more than informed speculation or hunches.

Recently in the UK, government ministers were derided for giving misleading replies to queries about the number of migrants entering the UK from recent EU accession counties (Poland, the Ukraine etc.). But in reality the official estimates are based on surveys and official forms submitted. They are just (hopefully) good guesses. Markets allocate resources based on this sort of guess every day, but few ministers would feel confident in their ability to survive democratic accountability by stating, 'I guess there are too many East European migrants here'. So perhaps we should not expect too much from government intervention in financial markets. They do not have the span of knowledge that market participants have as a community. Nor are they empowered to use that knowledge in the same way.

Insofar as elected politicians are representatives of their constituencies, not chosen delegates sent by them, prospect theory suggests that there may be a case for state intervention. Loss aversion implies insurance against a sudden catastrophic loss will be valued at more than its expected value by investors. So suppose you have to choose between losing £1, up front, and a 1% chance of losing £100, most of us will accept the £1 loss rather than take the remote chance of losing a lot more. If the electorate is loss averse maybe their elected politicians should be as well (Sunstein 2005, p.26). Even if the 'new era' does allow capital gains beyond our wildest dreams the precautionary principle means acting against unjustified speculation makes sense. Specifically, acting in anticipation of possible investor losses may be justified when a number of behavioural biases are believed to be at work in the market (Sunstein, 2005, p.35). These include:

- *The availability heuristic*, investors respond to risks they feel they recognize intuitively, so if many new, possibly naive, investors enter a market this may be their first experience of a bubble. Shiller (2005, p.41) has noted the prevalence of 'baby-boom' investors in the Internet boom, due to relatively high birth rates in the years 1946–66. Or they might think 'this time it's different' and sceptics simply don't 'get it'. A wiser legislator might try to bring to mind the amount of entropy in the system, recalling 'what goes up, must come down'.
- *Probability neglect*, which can lead to a focus on 'worst-case' scenarios.
- *Loss aversion*, which may mean investors quickly forget the joy of speculative gains once the bust occurs.
- *A belief in the benevolence of natural processes*, including 'the market', which may lead to a search for scapegoats, like Jack Grubman or Jeff Skilling in recent times. Investors may forget markets perform the very process of 'creative destruction' that drives economic growth.
- *System neglect*, a failure to see how markets interact, for example, how dips in the futures market push down the stock market via implied spot rates.

While it may be argued that the government has no role in engaging in such paternalism it is not clear that brokers and the marketing departments of investment banks will resist exploiting such biases where they are clearly exposed.

At the very least it might be thought prudent for effective government to exercise 'liberal paternalism' in setting some guidelines for individual investors and those investing on their behalf. This might be implemented by setting limits on the 'value at risk' or 'shortfall probability' of taking a loss on some portfolios (Estrada 2005 discusses these techniques). Individuals could be left free to override the standard guideline portfolio, but explicit assent to doing so could be required of authorized sellers of investment products, ISAs, PEPs, etc.

5.7 Conclusion and Summary

Bubbles are a constant but unpredictable star in our financial history. Anecdotes of investor foolishness comfort us that there is nothing new under the sun in financial markets and we are all now too smart to be gulled as easily as our ancestors. Sadly financial innovations to support margin trading, programme trading, or securitization of debt often just reinvent the levered portfolio wheel, which yields superb returns in the boom while disguising downside risk.

Accepting this, what can be done about it? Are we all 'just human all too human' and best left to the school of hard knocks? Certainly the state comes under intense pressure to isolate those who 'caused' investors' losses, Bernie Ebbers, Jeff Skilling and Ken Lay being the most recent crop of sacrifices to public wrath at financial crashes.

Apart from the occasional show trial can the government really do much? As Keynes pointed out the global investment community cannot provide its own liquidity, as every buyer needs a matching seller, and in a market panic everyone wants to sell. Can the government, with taxpayers' money, serve this role?

This seems unlikely as governments often induce, if not actively participate in, speculative bubbles. Certainly interventions to 'pop' bubbles are often seen as unproductive and possibly likely to induce the very crisis it seeks to prevent. More helpful is an approach which seeks to entrench investment norms which protect the most venerable investors from downside risk by setting default portfolio options that limit downside risk. This policy would aim to leave 'smart money' to drive speculative bubbles and face the risk of doing so. If 'smart money' exhibits very similar cognitive errors to everyone else, as I will later argue, this is only a partial solution of course.

Appendix: Tulips as Assets and Art

Almost inevitably in a textbook of this sort the trade in tulips in the early part of the seventeenth century in the Netherlands is portrayed as a commercial activity motivated by a desire for profit. Goldgar (2007) seeks to redress this balance by making clear the way in which tulips formed part of a culture of collecting in this period of rapid economic development and the first flourishing of a market economy around Antwerp, Amsterdam and Haarlem. The cultivation and collection of tulips formed one part of a broader culture of collection which also included shells, paintings, dogs and other exotica. Such a habit of collection grew out of the mercantile classes' desire to define themselves by a knowledge of science and the arts as well as just their wealth. The development, expression and indulgence of taste in art and horticulture formed part of a new assertion of self-consciousness almost unheard of prior to the growth of an active market economy.

For Goldgar then tulipmania reflects a broader social tension in the development of a Dutch mercantile class. She points out,

> Communities find themselves at a loss when value is thrown into doubt. Tulipmania did exactly this
>
> (p.17).

In particular the commoditization and trading of tulip bulbs threw into doubt who were the arbiters of what was beautiful and good. Slowly *liefhebbers*, or horticultural connoisseurs, were being displaced by *bloemisten*, or flower traders, in a move that mirrored the intrusion of the market into previously barter- or gift-based transactions. Tulipmania captured what many contemporaries saw as a moral and spiritual decline of healthy, curiosity based, collection and classification into a debased and corrupting greed for possession and wealth. An essential part of the initial motivation for gardening was a desire to share an experience of beauty with others, especially one's social peers. An essential part of such fraternal relations, often held to characterize the Dutch as a people, is the *discussiecultuur*, which allowed both scientific knowledge and norms of artistic beauty to evolve. Tulipmania ruptured this tradition of social cohesion and so challenged the very identity of the emerging Dutch mercantile class. For Goldgar (2007, p.7),

> People in the 1630s found tulipmania a wonder, something to be marvelled at, like a fireball, a child with two heads, or a plague of mice. But it was also a warning.

Perhaps it was this awareness that what mattered was what tulipmania meant about the end of a distinct community, as the market supplanted its function and legitimacy, allowed the exact details of what occurred to become less important to contemporary commentators. What mattered is the set of social and cultural anxieties made manifest in the speculation, not the exact details of that speculation itself. In this view Garber (2001) is certainly correct to challenge the irrationality and disruptive economic impact of the tulipmania speculation. But what he ignores is the greater underlying fracture in social relations made manifest in the tulipmania incident.

> Tulips and wild flowers in general had for many centuries held a fascination for the Turkish social elite while Europe descended into the darkness of the Middle Ages. By 1630 Constantinople boasted some 80 shops selling flowering bulbs. A visitor to Constantinople in 1591 was staggered by the beauty of its gardens, feeling he was walking in a vision of Paradise to come
>
> (Goldgar 2007, p.30).

The introduction of tulips to Europe in the mid-sixteenth century is sometimes ascribed to the travels of the Flemish envoy of the Holy Roman Empire, Ogier Ghislain de Busbecq, but the opening of the East to commercial trade brought in its wake a scientific and artistic heritage of dizzying variety. Tulips were just part of a broader cultural exchange and mutual fascination then rife at the eastern border of Europe, now, finally, emerging from the darkness of medieval isolation.

This new self-awareness is perhaps most visible in the fashion of the newly wealthy for self-portraits, such as those by Rembrandt and Fran Hals. Still-life painting offered a related opportunity to define oneself by what one owned, or liked (not to say coveted). Hendrick Goltzius painted Jan Govertz van der Aer surrounded with his precious collection of shells in 1603, this being one of eight such portraits of him and his collection or a still-life of his shells alone. Both shells and tulips stood at a crossing point of art and nature, where nature was sufficiently malleable to allow human expression an active role in its design. Hence the fascination which developed in variegated, stripped or freckled, tulips. Their very off-beat nature became an expression of the owner and a way in which he could express his command and mutation of nature. This much valued mutation in tulip leaves formed part of a broader aesthetic of marble itself and a marbling, or veined, appearance. Tulips formed just one part of a complex tapestry of *artificialia* which included worked coral and painted or gilded ostrich eggs. Gold cups and goblets worked into the shape of nautilus shells were another object of veneration amongst the Dutch mercantile elite (Goldgar 2007, p.77)

In such strange markings devout *liefhebbers* saw the glory of God and his majestic creation (Goldgar 2007, p.89). Still-life paintings of such exotic flowers seemed to fix their glory forever and allow an appreciation of that beauty out of the flower's usual season. Seventeenth-century gardeners did not understand that the stripes and flaring on 'broken' bulbs were in fact the product of infestation with the aphid-borne mosaic virus, but methods of producing such effects abounded, including splitting bulbs and grafting them onto another variety in the hope of producing a cross-breed. But their very novelty and rarity gave at least certain types of tulips a talismanic value as defining a new aesthetic in a newly emerging urban elite in northern Europe.

Collective Madness or Overconfident Expertise?

A surface reading of Mackay's (1841) original account of the tulip bubble suggests a descent into collective madness as normal life ground to a halt to allow wholehearted participation in the bubble. Mackay's account is very unlikely to be reliable, however, since his primary source material is drawn from an account by Johann Beckmann originally published in 1797, over 150 years after the speculative bubble. Beckmann's account was based largely on the earlier work of a botanist, Abraham Munting. Munting's father was also a botanist and had been cleaned out by the market implosion of early 1637. Hence his son Abraham was no fan of the tulip speculation which had stolen his inheritance. Even more authoritative sources in Dutch society largely rely on lurid accounts based on pamphlets published by those preaching against the dangers of serving mammon rather than God.

Goldgar's investigation into who was trading bulbs and why reveals a very different perspective to the standard account. Trading in tulips was concentrated amongst the mercantile, trading and artisan classes with certain professions being particularly prominent. Bakers, innkeepers and notaries feature widely as do brewers and shopkeepers. Traders seemed to come from the affluent middle-class and not the more wealthy landed nobility.

Common threads linking traders are both family and religious ties. By means of detailed archival research in three trading centres, Amsterdam, Haarlem and Enkhuizen, Goldgar (2007, p.137) was able to identify 400 serial traders in tulip bulbs in the 1630s. Haarlem as the national centre of tulip trading produced 285 such identifiable traders, Amsterdam, 60 and Enkhuizen (a major municipality in the province North Holland), 60. So if trading in bulbs was a niche interest, who fitted the niche?

Typical of such clusters of traders were the extended Wynant family of Haarlem, headed by Pieter Wynant, a prosperous Haarlem merchant. The Wynant family as Mennonites were bound together by a common religious faith which excluded them from serving in the civic militia and so public office.

With families, religious and vocational ties being so strong between traders you might expect to observe most trades to be between family members, co-religionists or co-workers. But Goldgar reports almost the reverse of this outcome. Related traders tended to take the same side of the trade, buying or selling together. This meant they could avoid profiting at the expense of a family member or other brethren at church. So what was the purpose of these close interpersonal relations between traders?

Goldgar answers that the family, church or profession formed a useful ground for sharing information about tulips and their relative value. Central to profitable trading of tulips was good access to the 'market for information' about tulips and the tulip trade. What were the new breeds? What were possible scams or deceptions (like boring out bulbs to prevent germination and so replication)? What were benchmark prices for each breed and where were they heading? Such questions were easily discussed at home, at church or in the pub.

All Fall Down: Dispute Resolution Amongst the Blomisten

Fortunately legal documents and records of arbitrations give us a pretty good record of what happened at a sale conducted at the height of the tulipmania bubble. While much of the tulipmania legend is of dubious veracity we can be more confident about what happened at the tulip sales conducted on 5 February 1637 in aid of the orphan of Wouter Bartholemeusz. At this auction there were some amazingly high prices for certain rare bulbs, for example a Viceroy bulb sold for 4203 florins and an Admirael van Enchuysen sold for 5200 florins. Total sale value at the auction topped 90,000 florins. This huge value set the background to the subsequent litigation and arbitration as buyers had second thoughts about their purchases in light of plummeting prices.

To understand the nature of the subsequent disputes one needs to know more about how tulip bulbs were traded and the uncertainties regarding their value. Tulips bloom in April through June and flower for a couple of weeks. In September the bulb can once more be replanted to flower again the following year. So anyone buying bulbs in February for example is actually buying the right to obtain the bulb in four or five months' time. Payment would typically be made on delivery. So the 5200-florin Admirael van Enchuysen would not be handed over on 5 February 1637, nor would the payment for it. The buyer only buys the right to receive the bulb when it is dug up in June or July. This obviously leaves a period when:

• the quality of the bulb's bloom is uncertain;
• the right to obtain the bulb can be resold, by the trader waiting to receive it.

Hence the bulb market became a typical futures market in which delivery was not necessarily wanted or expected. Such contracts were fine as long as buyers saw trading as a one-way bet. In the downturn life became a lot more unpleasant.

It was then that honour and family, or religious, ties became particularly useful to wronged parties. Tulip deals were commonly understood to be sealed by the payment of *wijnkoop* (wine money), this was usually about one-fortieth of the total price, up to a maximum of three florins. Contracts could be dissolved upon payment of *rouwkoop* (grief money) to compensate the counterparty for the cancelled contract.

Such trading may seem highly precarious and fraught with risk to those used to highly structured modern futures markets, with their marking to market and regulatory boards, LIFFE or CBOT. But as Goldgar points out (2007, p.221), all trade in this era was almost a form of gambling rather than investment as we think of it today. The susceptibility of normal foreign trade in goods to piracy or petty theft or deception made tulip trading just one exotic aspect of a generally tumultuous developing market economy. Tulip traders were often the same people as grain or textiles traders and all associated risks would have been perceived in this context. So in taking losses in the crash most had the benefits of a diversified portfolio.

Tulipmania and its Legacy

So apart from a few rich folk losing a few florins why should we care about tulipmania? Or why did religious pamphleteers feel so angry against those who participated in the bubble? Mackay (1841) implies that the aftermath of tulipmania in the Netherlands was widespread economic distress. Evidence of the link between stock-market crashes and wider distress in the real economy is mixed. The effect of the 1929 crash was clearly catastrophic. Monetarists like Milton Friedman might argue it was the government's economic policy following the crash that propagated its effect, but without the crash the depression would not have occurred. The 1987 stock-market crash had almost no detectable impact on those outside financial markets, although the impact on individual finance professionals was pretty dire.

Goldgar can find almost no signs of widespread bankruptcies amongst tulip traders and much evidence that traders simply took these losses in their stride as part of the general hazards associated with commercial life (2007, p.247). By March 1638, after much hectic negotiation and blame shifting, the burghers of Haarlem gave notice that such contracts could be set aside by the buyer if he paid 3.5% of the contract value as a grieving money payment to the would-be seller, while the seller could keep his bulb and pray for an appreciation in its value. Where this was done most frustrated sellers just accepted it and moved on.

So what caused the clearly widespread anxiety associated with this bubble and the public moral condemnation of its principal architects, the *blomisten*? Goldgar suggests it was the recognition that individual agreements were made on trust between members of often the same extended family, religion or trade. The crucial damage was the breach of honour not the financial loss. For Goldgar (2007, p.251)

> Tulipmania did have a profound effect upon society, even if it was not a financial one.
> It fractured social relations by reminding burghers how fragile their relations were.

So tulipmania may be as much a story of cultural and social transformation as financial meltdown. Its misrepresentation in the literature should remind us that a model is just a model and may leave much of the central underlying phenomena being studied left on the cutting-room floor. In what remains of this book I try to model what is essential and make clear when the process of simplification distracts from more qualitative, but important, issues.

Questions

1. This is a game for your family, or tutorial group or flatmates. Write down any number between zero and 100 for submission in today's class to your teacher. Keep your chosen number secret. The winner will be the person whose guess is two-thirds of the average of all guesses made. Now go to it. Good luck in winning the prize!
2. On reading the chapter what do you think our government can do to stop losses like those following the Internet bubble, or the sub-prime debt crisis? What are the dangers of intervening to prevent bubbles? Do they outweigh the costs of letting investors make their own bed and then watching them lie on it unaided?
3. Read the Appendix concerning the tulipmania speculation. Are there any lessons, similarities and important differences between the tulip bubble of 1637 and the Internet bubble, starting from Netscape's floatation in 1997? Have the intervening years fundamentally changed the elements of a financial bubble? If so, have they changed the need for state intervention to pre-empt their effect?

Notes

1. In the UK an oil shortage following war in the Middle East and rampant inflation combined to produced our worst ever decline in stock prices.
2. Quoted in Sunstein (2005, p.4).
3. That is South and North Holland, two states in the nation called the Netherlands (although we often use the words Holland and the Netherlands to mean the same thing).
4. Together with John Raskob and Mike Meehan, Kennedy had bought up Pathe Pictures stock, and began a rumour that they were going to make a takeover bid, only to promptly dump their shareholding at a profit (Klein, 2001, p.11).
5. Or go to Berkshire Hathaway website, www.berkshirehathaway.com.
6. According to *Business Week*'s 2006 ranking, Bill and Melinda Gates had given $28 billion to health and development charities. Only Warren Buffett gave more, $40.7 billion.

References

Baskin, J. & P. Miranti (1999). *A History of Corporate Finance*. Cambridge: Cambridge University Press.

Becker, G. (1983). A theory of competition among pressure groups for political influence. *Quarterly Journal of Economics*, 98: 371.

Berenson, A. (2003). *The Number: How America's Balance Sheet Rocked the World's Financial Markets*. London: Pocket Books.

Chancellor, E. (1999). *The Devil Take the Hindmost: A History of Financial Speculation*. London: Macmillan.

De Bondt, W. (2005). Bubble psychology. In W.C. Hunter, G.G. Kaufman & M. Pomerleano (eds), *Asset Price Bubbles: The Implications for Monetary, Regulatory, and International Policies*. Cambridge, MA: MIT Press.

Estrada, J. (2005). *Finance in a Nutshell: A No-Nonsense Guide to the Tools and Techniques of Finance*. Harlow: FT-Prentice Hall.

Galbraith, J. (1975). *The Great Crash 1929*. London: Penguin.

Galbraith, J. (1993). *A Short History of Financial Euphoria*. London: Penguin.

Garber, P. (2001). *Famous First Bubbles: The Fundamentals of Early Manias*. Cambridge, MA: MIT Press.

Gates, B. & C. Hemingway (1999). *Business @ the Speed of Thought: Succeeding in the Digital Economy*. New York: Warner Books.

Goldgar, A. (2007). *Tulipmania: Money, Honor and Knowledge in the Dutch Golden Age*. Chicago: University of Chicago Press.

Hao, G. (2007). Laddering in initial public offerings. *Journal of Financial Economics*, **85**: 102–22.

Hayek, F. (1945). The use of knowledge in society. In F. Hayek (ed.), *Individualism and Economic Order*. Chicago: University of Chicago Press.

Keynes, J.M. (1936). *General Theory of Employment Interest and Money*. London: Macmillan.

Kindleberger, C. & R. Aliber (2005). *Manias, Panics and Crashes: A History of Financial Crises*. Chichester: John Wiley & Sons, Ltd.

Klein, M. (2001). *Rainbow's End: The Crash of 1929*. New York: Oxford University Press.

Lowenstein, R. (2002). *When Genius Failed: The Rise and Fall of Long-Term Capital Management*. London: Fourth Estate.

Lowenstein, R. (2004). *Origins of the Crash: The Great Bubble and its Undoing*. New York: Penguin.

Mackay, C. (1841). *Extraordinary Popular Delusions and the Madness of Crowds*. New York: John Wiley-Marketplace Books.

Miller, R. (2003). *Railway.Com*. London: Institute of Economic Affairs.

Morrison, A. & W. Wilhem (2007). *Investment Banking: Institutions, Politics and the Law*. Oxford: Oxford University Press.

Mosco, V. (2004). *The Digital Sublime: Myth, Power and Cyberspace*. Cambridge, MA: MIT Press.

Penman, S. (2003). The quality of financial statements: perspectives from the recent stock market bubble. *Accounting Horizons*, **17**: 77–96.

Seligman, J. (2003). *The Transformation of Wall Street: A History of the Securities and Exchange Commission and Corporate Finance*. New York: Aspen.

Shapiro, C. & H. Varian (1999). *Information Rules: A Strategic Guide to the Network Economy*. Boston, MA: Harvard Business School Press.

Shiller, R. (2005). *Irrational Exuberance*. Princeton, NJ: Princeton University Press.

Siegal, J. (2005). *The Future for Investors: Why the Tried and True Triumph over the Bold and the New*. New York: Crown Business.

Stigler, G. (1971). The theory of economic regulation. *Bell Journal of Economics*, **2** (spring): 3–21.

Sunstein, C. (2005). *The Law of Fear: Beyond the Precautionary Principle*. Cambridge: Cambridge University Press.

Taleb, N. (2004). *Fooled by Randomness*. New York: Random House.

Part II
Asset Pricing

Chapter 6

Noise Traders

One of the most puzzling facts about modern financial markets is the sheer volume of trade that occurs. Given that most modest consumption needs, for holidays, a new car, etc. can be met by loans, the sheer scale of trading seems phenomenal. Table 6.1 shows that by 2004 over £50 billion worth of trades were made each year on the UK main equity market alone. It is hard to believe that this level of trade is driven only by investors' needs to rebalance their portfolio. Figure 6.1 shows the huge growth in the economic importance of financial markets in Britain. Can it really be true that the British are trading three times the value of their annual gross domestic product (GDP) for reasons motivated by 'fundamental value'? We live in interesting times, but maybe not quite so interesting as this dramatic rise in trading volume suggests. The main reason for trading in traditional finance models is either to fund new consumption or to profit from arbitrage when you receive information about an asset which you suspect very few other people have. This implies there is huge scope for arbitrage within modern financial markets. But, in standard models, homogeneous agents evaluate the value of the traded assets in the same way, so it is hard to see where such large arbitrage profits come from within a normal classroom treatment of asset pricing.

'Noise traders' first appeared in the finance literature as a possible escape clause for the inability of standard models to explain the occurrence of any trade at all (Grossman & Stiglitz 1980, Milgrom & Stokey 1982; see Dow & Gorton 2008 for a review). In standard theory well-informed, highly motivated, well-capitalized traders face each other in the market on an equal footing. Each investor is likely to have very similar beliefs about an asset's true 'fundamental' value (the discounted stream of future cash-flows, the correct multiple of earnings, etc.). If a seller offers to sell at a price reflecting his or her conjecture regarding the asset's true value, few bidders will appear. This is because since price equals value there is little incentive to buy (or even sell) for speculative reasons. Unless you just happen to want an extra vote at General Motors' next annual shareholders meeting, a barrel of oil, or a pork-belly in three months' time, there is little reason to either buy or sell anything we see traded each day in financial markets in such huge volumes.

Given this volume of trading in financial securities, and the sometimes less than transparent relation between investor demand and traditional metrics of asset value, a central part of the behavioural finance literature explores the behaviour of those who trade despite having no new information to impound into the stock price. In the words of Fisher Black, these 'noise' (non-fundamental value) based traders,

> are willing to trade even when from an objective point of view they would be better off not trading. Perhaps they think the noise they are trading on is information. Or perhaps they just like to trade

> (Black, 1986).

As such 'noise traders' sound like very bad fellows indeed, inducing unwanted volatility in share prices for no sensible reason. But, as Black points out, the presence of noise traders creates a feeding frenzy amongst informed investors who do pay attention to fundamental value. This draws the informed into the

Table 6.1   UK equity turnover

	Value (£m)	Number of bargains	Shares traded (m)	Average value per day (£000s)	Average value per bargain (£)	Average number of bargains per day	Number of days
1965	3,478.6	3,417,395	—	13,642	1,018	13,402	255
1970	8,812.7	4,097,903	—	34,560	2,151	16,070	255
1975	17,546.5	4,768,515	—	69,081	3,680	18,774	254
1980	30,801.4	4,230,737	—	121,265	7,280	16,656	254
1985	101,263.0	5,236,292	53,655.0	400,249	19,339	20,697	253
1990	315,625.0	6,910,820	134,040.7	1,247,530	45,671	27,315	253
1995	646,332.0	9,817,204	230,318.6	2,564,810	65,837	38,957	252
2000	1,895,533.8	29,427,308	472,733.5	7,521,960	64,414	116,775	252
2004	2,316,194.5	53,907,459	881,989.4	9,118,876	42,966	212,234	254

Source: London Stock Exchange http://www.londonstockexchange.com/en-gb/about/statistics/factsheets/smfs.htm.

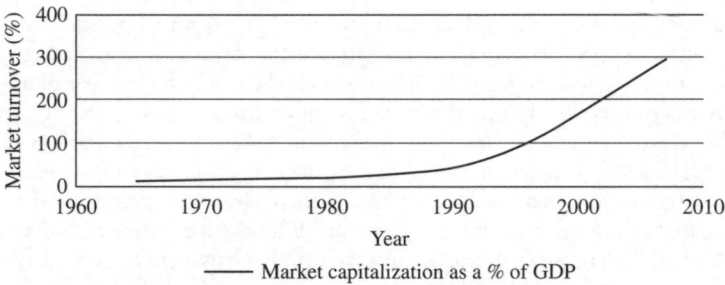

Figure 6.1   Market turnover as a percentage of GDP
Source: 'Something big in the city' by Jonathon Ford, *FT Weekend*, 15/16 November 2008.

market. If the noise traders were not there the informed would stand toe to toe with one other. If all informed investors are roughly equally smart and well connected they face a zero sum, but very viciously fought, game. Fortunately there is 'a noise trader born every minute' and this provides the bait to tempt informed investors with accurate information about the 'true' value of the share into the market.

Noise traders 'create their own space' by inducing a new self-created form of risk. This is the risk that one will meet someone willing to bet that the price is other than its 'true value'. That person is a 'noise trader' and his impact on asset pricing is the topic of this chapter.

6.1   Illustration and Structure

Equity prices are contingent claims on the dividends paid by the companies that issue the shares. So the equity price movements reflect changes in conjectures about the stream of future dividends payable by the firm. Not so, it seems, according to a neat little curiosity explored by Froot and Debora (1999). These authors ask why 'Siamese twin' stocks like Royal Dutch Shell and Shell Transport, Unilever NV and Unilever PLC, or SmithKline Beckman and the Beecham Group seem to offer returns that differ according to which of the separate parts of the 'twin' you invest in. To understand the difficulty, it might be worth giving some detail about how the Royal Dutch Petroleum/ Shell Transport alliance operates.

As a result of an agreement made in 1907 Royal Dutch Petroleum and Shell Transport are incorporated in the United Kingdom and the Netherlands, respectively, and split all cash-flows arising from their trading activity so 60% goes to Royal Dutch shareholders and 40% to Shell Transport. Everyone who invests in the alliance knows this, the details are disclosed in the published accounts and the alliance briefs analysts covering the stock on how it is internally structured and the allocation of shareholder rights including cash-flows to those shareholders.

So one Royal Dutch Petroleum share must be worth one and a half times a Shell Transport PLC? Not so, it seems. Neither are the shares in Unilever NV worth what they should be relative to Unilever PLC. Same thing with SmithKline Beckman and the Beecham Group, following their 1989 merger. In every case the deviations from expected relative values are both high on average and pretty volatile. These are large, highly liquid stocks which typically feature in the major stock-market indices of their home markets. You could struggle to make some market microstructure or tax treatment story fit the facts, but neither of these would help explain why deviations in relative valuations display considerable monthly volatility. It seems these companies' shares, perhaps in common with all shares, reflect a national sentiment that 'it's a new era' or 'this country is falling apart', almost irrespective of any reasonable conjecture about cash-flows deriving from holding these particular stocks in your portfolio.

More details of empirical manifestations of noise trader activity can be found in Montier (2006) in Section 2.7. Montier decomposes noise-trader risk into horizon, margin and short-cover risk and provides evidence regarding each type.

This chapter takes the idea that trades unrelated to cash-flows deriving from holding the stock might influence share price movement seriously. Section 6.2 presents a fairly straightforward model to capture the impact of noise traders' presence on the market on price of equity and the return it offers. I also assess what are the conditions necessary for such noise traders to survive the competitive onslaught of smarter, more rational, peers trying to drive equity values back to their fundamental value based on earnings, dividends, order book flows, etc. In Section 6.3 I ask how reasonable is it to think sentiments, emotions, fads and fashion have a persistent clear role in setting equity prices? A third and final section concludes and summarizes the chapter. The chapter may feel quite 'technology driven' compared to Part I of the book. The reason for this is that the noise trader modelling framework explained here will be repeatedly employed throughout this book and it is worth developing a solid foundation if such modelling strategies are to reap the fruits of their application later on.

After reading this chapter the reader should:

- Understand the role of noise traders in asset pricing, how it can arise, persist and the conditions under which it might grow.
- Put bounds on the growth of noise traders' impact on asset pricing according to the characteristic of the stock and the market it trades in.
- Understand the psychological evidence that mood swings, sentiment and caprice do impact on asset pricing, almost regardless of the underlying fundamentals, of expected discounted cash-flows, deriving from holding the asset.

6.2 The De Long, Shleifer, Summers and Waldmann Model

The impact of noise traders was first modelled by De Long, Shleifer, Summers and Waldmann (DSSW) in 1990.[1] The DSSW model has become something of a workhorse of the behavioural finance literature and we often rediscover it in later, more difficult to understand, research. For this reason it is explored at some length in the chapter and drawn on extensively in later chapters.

6.2.1   The Basic Set Up

Perhaps the most attractive element of the DSSW model is its recognition that both rational, or informed, traders (denoted by the superscript i) and noise traders (denoted by the superscript n) must coexist in the market. There is assumed to be a proportion μ of noise traders inhabiting the market, leaving the remainder of the market to be populated by a proportion $(1 - \mu)$ of informed traders. Total demand for the risky asset, u, is composed of noise trader demand and informed investor demand λ_t^i and as a result the following restriction holds

$$(1 - \mu)\lambda_t^i + \lambda_t^n \mu = 1$$

This equation simply states that the weighted sum of informed and noise traders' demands for the risky asset u must equal total demand for u. The DSSW model investigates whether the proportion of noise traders in the market, μ, falls over time to zero, in other words, will 'noise traders die out?'

Importantly, both informed and noisy traders trade for mutual advantage. Later research papers retain this basic structure, while sometimes using different terminology such as speculators and liquidity traders, informed and uninformed traders, or (for especially hard-nosed authors) smart and dumb traders.

Traders meet in a simple two-period model in which they invest in period 0 when 'young' to maximize period 1 consumption when they are 'old'. Each period, new traders, who must decide their own type, arrive in the market. This type of 'overlapping generation' framework means that although individual lives are described in a very stylized way, the continuity of financial markets can still be captured.

6.2.2   Modelling Mispricing

Both types of traders meet in a market with two types of assets. First, a 'safe' asset (called s), which is in fixed supply, pays a certain dividend r and has a known fixed price forever of one. Think of s as short-term bonds. Secondly, a risky asset (called u), which also pays a return of r forever but has a price and level of supply which varies with the degree to which noise traders misperceive price. Noise traders are assumed to misperceive the value of the unsafe asset u by a time-varying amount ρ_t, which has mean ρ^* and variance $\sigma_{\rho t}^2$. So ρ^* is the average amount of 'bullishness/bearishness' of the noise traders around which individual values of ρ_t vary each time period. Note that all variance in the price of the unsafe asset u is induced by variations in the misperceptions of price held by noise traders, ρ_t. If the noise traders could just be killed off by the arbitrage of informed traders the safe and unsafe assets would be perfect substitutes, both paying r forever. The price of both the safe (s) and unsafe asset (u) would both go to one and everyone could forget trading and get on with their lives. The trading horizon is across two dates only in the stylized world of DSSW. To make life simple, DSSW further assumes that ρ_t has a normal distribution. So we have

$$\rho_t \sim N(\rho^*, \sigma_\rho^2)$$

Given this set up noise traders must maximize their utility when old, given

- the dividend payable, r;
- the expected price of the unsafe asset, p_t;
- their perception of mispricing, ρ_t.

6.2.3   What Investors Want

DSSW assumes that investors possess an exponential absolute risk-aversion form of utility function defined by terminal-period wealth, w

$$U = -e^{-(2\gamma)w}$$

where w denotes investor wealth and γ is a risk-aversion parameter reflecting the fact that investors don't like risk. To make further progress we need to make some assumption about the distribution of wealth and hence the nature of the risk that the investor faces. DSSW assumes, in common with much of finance literature, that the distribution of wealth is normally distributed. The normal distribution can be entirely characterized by its mean and variance. The expected value of the distribution of wealth is simply its average value, $\overline{w}$, and the dispersion, or risk to wealth, is measured by its variance σ_w^2. In such a simple world, the investor's expected utility is given by

$$E(U) = \overline{w} - \gamma\sigma_w^2 \tag{6.1}$$

So his utility rises in his average wealth, but falls the more risk there is to attaining that level of expected wealth. This is no more than a simple restatement of the standard Markovitzian portfolio theory we know and love from our introductory finance class. If the investor's utility falls further, the more risk averse he personally is to variations around his average level of wealth, i.e. the higher γ.

As will become obvious in later chapters, many of the pricing 'anomalies' are the result of a risk-seeking love of gambles in certain situations. Further, many empirical studies have attested to the non-normality of share-price return distributions. However the elegance and ease of manipulation of the DSSW model is achieved at some cost. Let us accept this cost for the moment for the sake of developing a simple tractable model.

Noise traders seek to maximize their utility by maximizing wealth subject to the constraint that they bear as little risk as possible. This simple linear model reflects the normality assumption with regard to the distribution of noise traders' misperception of true value.

Given their utility functions, informed investors maximize their wealth/consumption when old in deciding how to invest across the safe and unsafe asset when young. This involves maximizing a standard Lagrangian form of the type shown in Equation (6.2), which decomposes the objective of investors into the maximization of return, which is attained subject to the condition that the lowest possible amount of risk is assumed to earn a given rate of return. For the simple utility linear function in Equation (6.1) I now solve for the optimal proportion of investment in each type of asset. The relevant Lagrangian optimization equation takes the following form for informed investors

$$\begin{aligned}
E(U) &= \overline{w} - \gamma\sigma_w^2 \\
&= c_0 + \lambda_t^i[r +_t p_{t+1} - p_t(1+r)] - \gamma(\lambda_t^i)^2 \left(_t\sigma_{p,t+1}^2\right)
\end{aligned} \tag{6.2}$$

which can be decomposed into three constituents:

1. An endowment of consumption carried over from when you were young, think of Auntie Ethel's bequest to you in her will, c_0.
2. The return on holding the unsafe asset, u, which itself has two parts: the dividend payable r and the expected capital gain on holding some of the unsafe asset u in your portfolio $(_t p_{t+1} - p_t(1+r))$. Here $_t p_{t+1}$ denotes the conditional expectation of the price of u at date $t+1$, formed at date t.

3. The risk to wealth which investors seek to avoid if at all possible. As the term $(\lambda_t^i)^2 \gamma_t \sigma_{pt+1}^2$ makes clear, the intensity of sacrifice experienced by investors increases with each unit of anticipated price volatility $_t\sigma_{pt+1}^2$ which is defined to be

$$_t\sigma_{pt+1}^2 = E_t\left\{[p_{t+1} - E_t(p_{t+1})]^2\right\}$$

which is simply the conditional expectation of the price variance between date t and $t + 1$ formed at date t.

6.2.4   Choosing Optimal Asset Allocations Across the Safe and Risky Asset

To obtain the optimum allocation of the portfolio to the unsafe asset for informed investors we need to maximize the Lagrangian in Equation (6.2) with respect to the proportion in the total market portfolio of the unsafe asset, u, at date t held by informed investors i.e. λ_t^i.

$$\frac{\partial E(U)}{\partial \lambda_t^i} = 0 \Rightarrow r + _tp_{t+1} - (1+r)p_t - 2\gamma(\lambda_t^i)(_t\sigma_{pt+1}^2)$$

$$\Rightarrow 2\gamma\lambda_t^i{}_t(\sigma_{pt+1}^2) = r + _tp_{t+1} - (1+r)p_t$$

$$\Rightarrow \lambda_t^i = \frac{r + _tp_{t+1} - (1+r)p_t}{2\gamma(_t\sigma_{pt+1}^2)}$$

Note the endowment, c_0, has no role in determining the proportion of total asset demand for u taken by informed investors, λ_t^i. So the mere fact that informed investors inherit a fortune will not entice them to buy more of the risky asset necessarily. This implies risk aversion does not decrease as wealth increases – an odd property.

A similar calculation of the necessary proportion of the risky asset, u, in the noise traders' portfolio to maximize their utility, can be undertaken as follows:

$$\frac{\partial E(U)}{\partial \lambda_t^n} = 0 \Rightarrow \lambda_t^n = \frac{r + _tp_{t+1} - (1+r)p_t}{2\gamma(_t\sigma_{pt+1}^2)} + \frac{\rho_t}{2\gamma\left(_t\sigma_{pt+1}^2\right)}$$

Note this condition is the same as that for the informed, apart from the last term relating to the period's level of mispricing, ρ_t. Recalling the restriction that the weighted sum of total asset demands must equal one, I now obtain the expression

$$(1-\mu)\lambda_t^i + \lambda_t^n\mu = 1$$

$$\Rightarrow 1 = (1-\mu)\left[\frac{r + _tp_{t+1} - (1+r)p_t}{2\gamma(_t\sigma_{pt+1}^2)}\right] + \mu\left[\frac{r + _tp_{t+1} - (1+r)p_t}{2\gamma(_t\sigma_{t+1}^2)} + \frac{\mu}{2\gamma(\sigma_{pt+1}^2)}\right]$$

$$1 = \frac{r + _tp_{t+1} - (1+r)p_t}{2\gamma\left(_t\sigma_{pt+1}^2\right)} + \frac{\mu\rho_t}{2\gamma\left(_t\sigma_{pt+1}^2\right)}$$

$$0 = \frac{r + _tp_{t+1} - (1+r)p_t}{2\gamma\left(_t\sigma_{pt+1}^2\right)} + \frac{\mu\rho_t}{2\gamma\left(_t\sigma_{pt+1}^2\right)} - 1$$

$$0 = r + {}_tp_{t+1} - (1+r)p_t + \mu\rho_t - 2\gamma\left({}_t\sigma^2_{pt+1}\right)$$

$$p_t = \frac{1}{1+r}\left[r + {}_tp_{t+1} - 2\gamma\left({}_t\sigma^2_{pt+1}\right) + \mu\rho_t\right] \tag{6.3}$$

6.2.5 The Pricing Equation

Price is set to be the discounted value of the risk-adjusted expected holding period gain to both types of investors (dividend, r, plus expected future resale price (${}_tp_{t+1}$) adjusted for risk, $2\gamma{}_t\sigma_{t+1}$) and the presence of bullishness amongst the noise traders, $\mu\rho$.

A clear problem with the above solution for price in Equation (6.3) is that it solves only for current price in terms of future price realizations, leaving the ultimate foundations of the price level unclear. To side-step this problem a procedure of iterative substitution of successive future values of expected price for the current one in the next time period can be employed.

$$p_t = \frac{1}{1+r}\left[r + {}_tp_{t+1} - 2\gamma\left({}_t\sigma^2_{pt+1}\right) + \mu\rho_t\right]$$

$$\Rightarrow p_t = \frac{1}{1+r}\left[r + \frac{1}{1+r}\left\{r + {}_{t+1}p_{t+2} - 2\gamma\left({}_{t+1}\sigma^2_{pt+2}\right) + \mu\rho_{t+1}\right\} - 2\gamma\left({}_t\sigma^2_{pt+1}\right) + \mu\rho_t\right]$$

$$\Rightarrow p_t = \frac{1}{1+r}\left[r + \frac{1}{1+r}\left\{r + \frac{1}{1+r}\left(r + {}_{t+2}p_{t+3} - 2\gamma\left({}_{t+2}\sigma^2_{pt+3}\right) + \mu\rho_{t+2}\right)\right.\right.$$

$$\left.\left. -2\gamma\left({}_{t+1}\sigma^2_{pt+2}\right) + \mu\rho_{t+1}\right\} - 2\gamma\left({}_t\sigma^2_{pt+1}\right) + \mu\rho_t\right] \tag{6.4}$$

Therefore price becomes a discounted weighted average of:

- future dividends, r;
- expected future realizations (one-step-ahead predictions), ${}_tp_{t+1}$, ${}_{t+1}p_{t+2}$, ${}_{t+2}p_{t+3}$, etc.;
- current (one-step-ahead) predictions of future price volatility, ${}_t\sigma_{t+1}$, ${}_{t+1}\sigma_{t+2}$, ${}_{t+2}\sigma_{t+3}$, etc.;
- and, finally, noise traders' future misperceptions of price, $\mu\rho_t$, $\mu\rho_{t+1}$, $\mu\rho_{t+2}$, etc.

The endless iteration forward in time of the expansion in Equation (6.4) allows us to finally drive out future expected values of price in the final form of the solution for current price

$$p_t = 1 + \frac{\mu(\rho_t - \rho^*)}{1+r} + \frac{\mu\rho^*}{r} - \frac{2\gamma}{r}\left({}_t\sigma^2_{pt+1}\right) \tag{6.5}$$

which leaves the price of u as being equal to 'true value' of one, plus the discounted value of the deviation of the next period's noise traders' misevaluation from their average misperception of value $(\rho_t - \rho^*)$, plus a perpetuity in noise traders' average misperception of value, $\mu\rho^*/r$, adjusted for risk as a result of the next period's price volatility:

$$2\gamma\frac{\left({}_t\sigma^2_{pt+1}\right)}{r}$$

So at time period t price rises and falls according to whether noise traders are optimistic, when $(\rho_t - \rho^*) > 0$, or pessimistic, that is $(\rho_t - \rho^*) < 0$. But noise traders create risk and since investors don't like risk this pushes down price. This is the role of the last term in Equation (6.5). Noise trader induced risk creates 'price pressure' downwards and does so more dramatically as investors' risk aversion increases.

All the variation in price is induced by movement in noise traders' misperception of price around its long-term mean, $\mu(\rho_t - \rho^*)/(1 + r)$, discounted by one time period. In setting price each period, investors look ahead to whether the bullishness/bearishness of noise traders is expected to be particularly marked over the next time period. If, for example, next period noise traders are just averagely bullish, so that $\mu(\rho_t - \rho^*) = 0$, then price is just one plus the value of a perpetuity in the average amount of mispricing by noise traders, $\mu\rho^*/r$, adjusted for risk. In such a financial market all the volatility in price is driven by volatility in noise traders' misperception of price σ_ρ^2.

Note that the second moment of the price distribution is simply the implied variance of the process outlined in Equation (6.5) above. Given all but the second term in that equation are constants we obtain an expression for the variance of one-period-ahead prices as follows:

$$_t\sigma_{pt+1}^2 = \sigma_{pt+1}^2 = \frac{\mu^2\sigma_\rho^2}{(1 + r)^2}$$

Substituting back into the long-run solution for price in Equation (6.5), the following solution holds for current price of the risky asset u:

$$p_t = 1 + \frac{\mu(\rho_t - \rho^*)}{1 + r} + \frac{\mu\rho^*}{r} - \frac{(2\gamma)\mu^2\sigma_\rho^2}{r(1 + r)^2} \tag{6.6}$$

Numerical illustrations of the price equation

In this section I consider a few simple comparative static exercises of varying assumptions about the proportion of noise traders in a given market, increasing risk aversion amongst noise traders, etc., using some simple illustrative values of the various variables involved. Allowing variations in one factor, holding all the others constant, will give you some idea of how the mechanics of the model work in practice. Of course real-world financial markets don't oblige us by changing in this way. In reality everything is changing all at once and sometimes with complex, or offsetting, impacts on price.

Any numerical exercise is only as credible and sensible as the assumed parameter values going into it. One central restriction in the current case is the need to ensure price does not turn negative. This will occur whenever the final term in Equation (6.6) overwhelms the three terms that precede it.

Negative prices do make intuitive sense as 'shadow prices', i.e. the price you would pay to be rid of the asset. Such shadow prices occasionally feature in finance, in the discussion of limited liability as a put option for example. But such a usage seems forced here, so I avoid it by setting the values in Table 6.2 accordingly to rule out negative price.

In the numerical illustrations of the price equation (6.6) given here assume the values given in Table 6.2 unless otherwise stated. Figures 6.2, 6.3 and 6.4 consider simple variations in one of these price parameters holding all the other assumed values in Table 6.2 constant.

Figure 6.2 considers the impact on price of an increasing proportion of noise traders entering the market, i.e. increasing μ in Equation (6.6), in 10% increments. I consider increases in the percentage of noise traders from 10% upwards to 100%. Price rises since noise traders are assumed to be unusually optimistic ($\rho - \rho^* = 7\% - 3\% = 4\%$).

Table 6.2 Assumed values in numerical illustration of pricing formation using Equation (6.6)

Parameter	Value
Dividend (r)	12.5% of value (0.125, remember the 'true value' is assumed to be one)
Current level of optimism (ρt)	7% of value
Average optimism (ρ^*)	3% of value
% of noise traders in market (μ)	33%
Risk-aversion coefficient (γ)	0.3

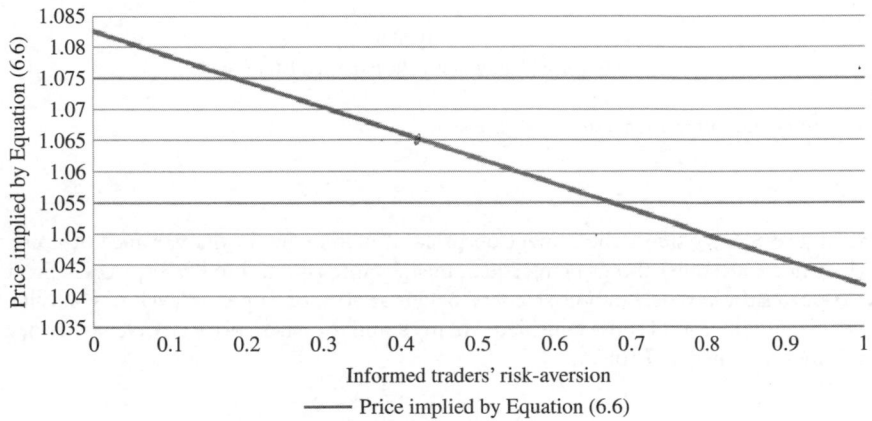

Figure 6.2 Price implied by Equation (6.6) as risk aversion of informed traders increases

Figure 6.3 considers the impact on price of increasing informed investor risk aversion, or increasing γ in Equation (6.6) by increments of 2.5%. The dampening impact on prices is clear, informed traders become sceptical about selling to optimistic noise traders, preventing them from pushing up price.

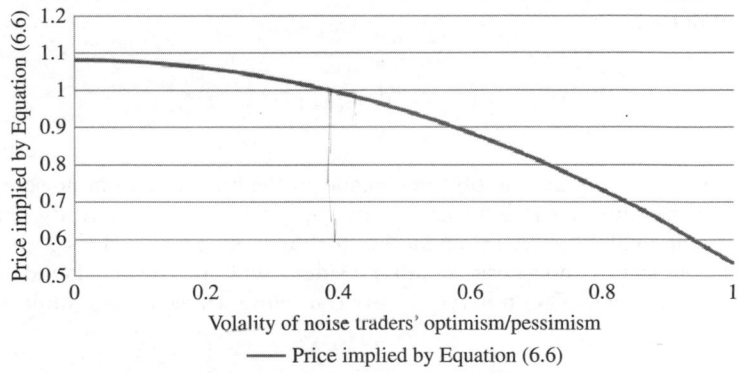

Figure 6.3 Price implied by Equation (6.6) as volality of noise-traders optimism/pessimism increases

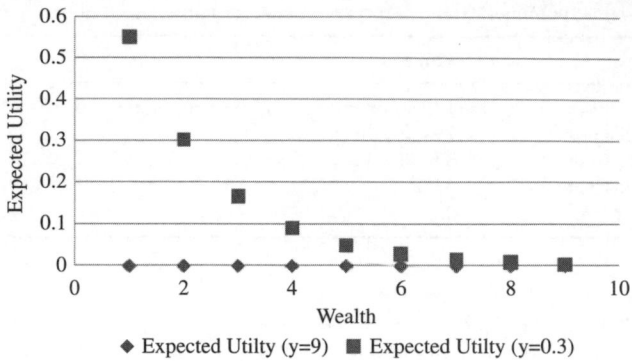

Figure 6.4   Utility and informed investors' risk-aversion

Finally, Figure 6.4 considers the impact on price of increments in the variance of noise traders' beliefs. More noise, all other things being equal, means more risk and so lower prices. The numerical example truncates the variance of noise traders' beliefs at 30% of value. At levels of volatility of noise traders' beliefs, much beyond those considered in my simulation here price is driven to zero, given the base case values assumed in Table 6.2.

6.2.6   Will Noise Traders Die Out?

It is often argued that noise traders (or 'dumb traders'), beautiful as they are, must die young because they are not clever enough to understand true value, like informed (or 'smart') traders, and hence will lose money and so be condemned to an early grave. While their presence in the market might impede the process fundamental, efficiency, it cannot ultimately stop it prevailing according to this view. In this section the conditions for this benign view of noise traders' impact on market efficiency are examined.

Define the difference between the return earned by noise traders and informed traders to be an expected margin of the form

$$\Delta R_{n-i} = \left(\lambda_t^i - \lambda_t^n\right)\left[r_{+t}p_{t+1} - (1+r)p_t\right] \tag{6.7}$$

This expression is derived by netting off the demand of the informed from noise-trader demand to produce a net demand across both groups of traders (λ_t^n and λ_t^i already derived above), which influences the final price set in the market for the risky asset, u. This is shown below. If this margin is consistently non-positive noise traders will not be a significant force in a financial market for long. The difference between noise traders' and informed investors' demands:

$$\left(\lambda_t^t - \lambda_t^i\right) = \frac{\rho_t}{(2\gamma)_t \sigma_{pt+1}^2} \tag{6.8}$$

Recall

$$_t\sigma_{pt+1}^2 = \sigma_{pt+1}^2 = \frac{\mu^2\rho^2}{(1+r)^2}$$

which when substituted into the divergence of demands Equation (6.8) yields

$$\lambda_t^n - \lambda_t^i = \frac{\rho_t}{2\gamma\left\{\frac{\mu^2\sigma_{pt+1}^2}{(1+r)^2}\right\}} = \frac{(1+r)^2\rho_t}{(2\gamma)\mu^2\sigma_\rho^2} \tag{6.9}$$

As the proportion of noise traders left in the market, μ, declines, the noise traders are forced to face the other end of infinite bets by informed traders trying to kill them off. So, if the asset is overpriced, $\rho_t > 0$, informed traders constantly try to short-sell huge amounts of u forcing noise traders to swallow never-ending supplies of u, or accept price declines. Given practical limitations on large amounts of short-selling the lives of noise traders are threatened by these types of large counter-trades by pessimistic (or simply clear-headed) informed investors.

If we consider the normal expected return to holding u to be the dividend payable r, plus the resale price, p_{t+1} we can decompose the pricing equation, Equation (6.3), into a normal and some excess return component. Once this is done the expected excess return on u, the unsafe asset, is given by

$$_t[r + p_{t+1} - p_t(1+r)] = (2\gamma)\mu^2(\sigma_{pt+1}^2) - \mu\rho_t$$

This expression equates the equilibrium return on the risky asset, u, with the risk to holding it, including the noise trader risk in the second term. Given these constituent elements we can solve for the conditional expectation of the premium/discount available to noise traders from introducing valuation risk into a market otherwise devoid of it. This will allow us to judge the longevity of noise traders in the market. Denoting the premium/discount return earned by noise traders as ΔR_{n-i} we have:

$$(\Delta R_{n-i}) = \left[(\lambda_t^n - \lambda_t^i)_t[r + p_{t+1} - p_t(1+r)]\right]$$

recalling

$$\lambda_t^n - \lambda_t^i = \frac{(1+r)^2\rho_t}{(2\gamma)\mu^2\sigma_\rho^2}$$

yields

$$\frac{(1+r)^2\rho_t}{(2\gamma)\mu^2\sigma_\rho^2}\left[\frac{(2\gamma)\mu^2\sigma_\rho^2}{(1+r)^2} - \mu\rho\right] = \rho_t - \frac{(1+r)^2\rho_t}{2\gamma\mu\sigma_\rho^2} \tag{6.10}$$

As trade continues and successive generations of traders live and die we need to consider the expectation of the premium to noise trading in the distant future. To do this we consider the payoff to noise trading in u, given the average level of mispricing, ρ^*, over all future dates, ρ_t, into the infinite future. So the noise traders' mark-up for motivating trade to occur is:

$$E(\Delta R_{n-i}) = \rho^* - \frac{(1+r)^2\rho^{*2} + (1+r)^2\sigma_\rho^2}{2\gamma\mu\sigma_\rho^2} \tag{6.11}$$

If ΔR_{n-i} is small enough noise traders will be a minor part of fundamentals-based trading in the market. But if ΔR_{n-i} starts to grow then fundamentals-based trading can become lost in a sea of noise trades. Since fundamental value is assumed to be one by informed traders, all trade is motivated by noise in the DSSW model. So if ΔR_{n-i} is too small for too long all trading in the unsafe asset u will cease.

6.2.7 Decomposing Noise Traders' Profits

This expectation of future profits to noise traders, given by Equation (6.11), can be decomposed into a number of separable parts:

1. The incentive for noise traders to emerge increases with the average 'bullishness' of their own perception (or reduces in their bearishness if $\rho^* < 0$). This is what DSSW call the 'hold-more' effect.
2. The first part of the second term's numerator captures the fact that, as u becomes more mispriced, its expected return falls as informed investors become reluctant to purchase a clearly grossly overpriced asset. Such apprehension by informed traders creates price pressure for the price of u to fall, reducing noise traders' relative returns in the market. DSSW denote this as the 'price-pressure' effect of noise-trader risk in reducing price.
3. The second part of the numerator in the second term captures the fact that noise traders, by their nature, mistime their trades, buying when the market is low and selling when it is high. They do so since misunderstanding asset value is their defining characteristic.
4. The second term's denominator captures the fact that noise traders 'create their own space', by creating unnecessary volatility in price σ_ρ unjustified by any variance in fundamental value. To see how noise traders set about 'creating their own space' consider a thought experiment of setting σ_ρ^2 to some very small value as noise traders are pushed to the very limits of the market, so that they have almost no effect on price. This makes the mark-up to their presence, as expressed by Equation (6.11), become strongly negative. To maintain their margin in the market noise traders have to do their job and always be noisy as possible!

There is no risk posed to fundamental value in the DSSW framework, because the unsafe asset u, like the safe asset s, always pays a dividend r. But the noise introduced into prices by noise traders means that the unsafe asset offers an additional source of return, albeit at a greater risk. The extent to which this is possible increases in the degree of risk aversion displayed by noise traders γ. Increases in their risk aversion make informed traders less willing to tackle noise-trader risk by counter-trading u's value back to its true fundamental value of one. This is because γ appears in the denominator of the second term of Equation (6.11). So increasing γ, to capture the greater risk aversion of informed traders in taking noise traders on, reduces the second term's negative size and raises the mark-up earned by noise traders. Only if the proportion of noise trader in the market, μ, or their ability to generate volatility in the price, σ_p, declines below some threshold level will the expected return to noise trading, compared to trading on fundamentals, $_t\Delta R_{(n-i)}$, be driven negative. So, as long as noise traders remain optimistic about asset value and are capable of moving price, they will not 'die out' as a breed although some unfortunate individuals will of course.

The relative return to noise traders, compared to their informed peers (that is $_t\Delta R_{(n-i)}$), is not clear from theory alone. The impact of effect (1) and (4) (the hold-more and creating-their-own-space effect) favours the emergence of noise traders. But the weight of effects (2) and (3) (market mistiming and the price pressure of overvaluation) tends to suppress returns to noise trading. Hence complacency regarding the long-term impact of noise traders on the attachment of price to fundamental value is likely to be misplaced.

Looking beyond the confines of the stylized world of the DSSW model, a number of factors suggest that reports of noise traders' impending death may be premature. First, in any real-life financial market it is likely that some doubt about the correct fundamental value of stock will persist. This is especially the case in equities where some degree of uncertainty regarding the correct 'fundamental' value of the company is usually regarded as being present. The survival of a large industry of active fund managers suggests this is the case. The increasing role for knowledge-based intangibles in valuation, employees' skills, patents, etc., suggests such uncertainty regarding 'true' value can only increase over time.

If noise traders are to die out it is not clear who their executioner will be. Informed investors are unlikely to do so since the presence of noise traders simply allows them to benefit from diversification into a more risky asset. Informed traders would simply be left with two safe assets called u and s both worth, and selling at, a price of one in return for paying a certain dividend r. Such a world offers the informed a more boring and less profitable life.

In parallel to the development of the 'noise trader' literature, a large literature concerning how information disseminates from the informed to the uninformed in the process of trade has developed. These sorts of models, sometimes labelled 'market microstructure' models, illustrate a process of dissemination of information through a population of rational investors. I enquire into this process more deeply in Chapter 12 when I consider one model of the impact of informed/insider traders on asset prices.

In one classic paper, Glosten and Milgrom (1985) model how a market-maker aggregates bid-and-ask offers from investors to form a price, using the bid–ask spread as an insurance premium against meeting an investor better informed than himself. These models constitute an alternative route into many of the issues discussed in this chapter and the rest of the book.

Numerical illustration of determination of noise-trader profits

Equation (6.11) tells us what determines the profitability of trading on noise and therefore the incentive to doing so. In this section I enquire into what sort of markets would be profitable for noise traders to operate in. I do this by a numerical illustration of Equation (6.11) above. A simple place to start would be with the same initializing values I used in Table 6.2 to examine price formation. Unfortunately doing this never produces a positive value for the mark-up of noise trader over informed trader profits, therefore I do not isolate market conditions under which noise traders enter and stay in the market for a financial market. To examine this I make some changes to the assumptions regarding initial values.

First, I allow noise traders to be more optimistic by raising the average level of noise-trader optimism, ρ^*, 3% to 10% of value. Since current optimism, ρ_t, does not feature in Equation (6.11) we can keep that value unchanged. The big change comes in the amount of informed trader risk aversion that seems to be needed to make a noise trader's trading strategy more profitable than that adopted by the informed. At lower levels of informed investor risk aversion, γ, noise trading never seems to be profitable, given the assumptions made in Table 6.2 (now amended to increase average optimism to 10% of asset value). Fairly major increases in informed investor risk aversion are needed even at near saturation levels of noise trading in the market, i.e. when informed traders have given up and quit the field in favour of noise traders.

To understand this it might be worthwhile to examine more clearly how increasing risk aversion impacts on the noise trader's utility. Return to the basic form of the informed investor's utility

$$U = -e^{-2\gamma w}$$

Here the parameter γ captures the extent to which informed investors dislike risk. To give some idea of how much more risk averse informed investors have to be in order to be consistent with the initial values of Table 6.2 (allowing for a 3% increase in mean noise trader optimism, ρ^* to 10%), I compare the shape of the utility function used in modelling price setting (using Equation (6.6)) and that used here in simulating variations in the premium that noise traders earn in financial markets (using Equation (6.11)). In moving from simulating Equations (6.6) and (6.11) a thirty-fold increase in informed investors' risk aversion is assumed. This implicitly assumes informed traders have become vastly more afraid of counter-trading against noise traders than in our previous numerical simulation of the condition in Equation (6.6). Note, this may be a very extreme modelling assumption to make. Equation (6.11) tells us how much more profitable it is for noise traders to trade, as against informed peers. Of course becoming informed may not be cheap and noise traders bear none of the costs of acquiring information. So the relative trading profits of noise traders net of information acquisition costs, as compared to informed traders, may be much higher than in my example here.

Table 6.3 summarizes the revised set of numerical values assigned to the various elements in Equation (6.11) made in constructing the numerical illustrations provided here including the sharp thirty-fold increase in γ.

Figure 6.5 examines the impact of allowing the proportion of noise traders present in the market to increase by 10% increments, until they saturate the market. As noise traders enter a market they induce noise-trader risk and deter participation by the informed who dislike such risk (in my example a great deal because γ takes a value of 9, see Table 6.3). Only when noise traders have

Table 6.3 Assumed values in numerical illustration of noise traders' mark up using Equation (6.11)

Parameter	Value
Dividend (r)	12.5% of value
Current level of optimism (ρ_t)	Not in Equation (6.11)
Average optimism (ρ^*)	10% of value
% of noise traders in market (μ)	33%
Risk-aversion coefficient (γ)	9 (Note: 30-fold increase from Table 6.2)

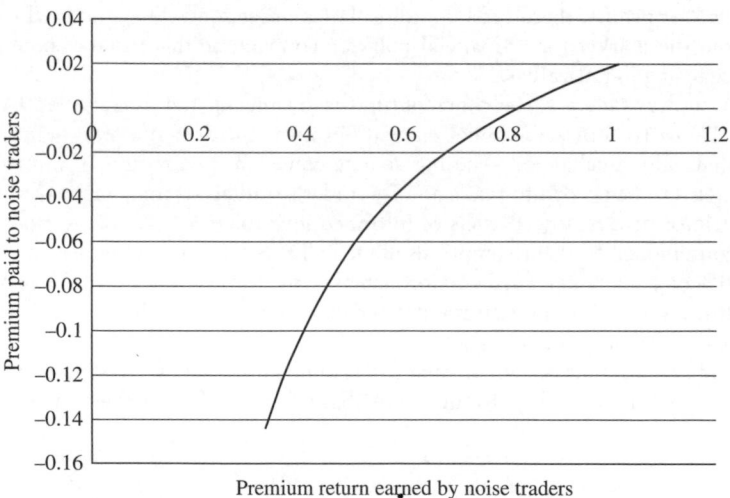

Figure 6.5 Returns to noise trading as more noise traders enter market

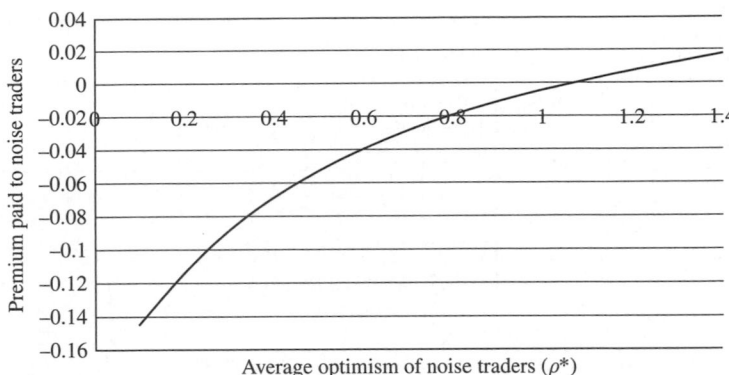

Figure 6.6   Returns to noise trading as noise traders' optimism grows

come to clearly predominate in the market (attracting over 80% of all trades) does a noise-trader strategy earn a mark-up. This suggests noise traders may need to market niche in sectors of the financial markets where fundamentals are fuzzy and informed traders feel particular trepidation taking them on.

Figure 6.6 considers the impact of increments in noise trader average optimism of 15% on the mark-up to noise-trading strategies over and above that earned by their informed peers in the market. Once again, given the working assumptions of Table 6.3, it appears only very optimistic noise traders can consistently earn a mark-up to their trading strategies. Such wildly optimistic conjectures about value may not be consistent with sectors, like utilities, where cash-flows and discount rates are fairly stable. Only high-technology, intangible-rich, sectors of the economy can perhaps sustain such optimism.

6.3   Can Investors Get Emotional?

A clear role exists in the DSSW model for variations in the extent of mispricing induced by noise traders. What causes such swings in the misperception of price, or 'investor sentiment'? At least since the work of the Cambridge economist John Maynard Keynes, such issues have fascinated both those who work in financial markets and those who study them.

That investment is a social process, affected by fads and fashion, like the consumption it funds, should not surprise us. Reflection on our own behaviour, together with a mass of evidence in social psychology, suggests how much we are creatures of habit and fashion. Shiller (1984) points out that the inability of investors to predict stock prices is not compelling evidence for prices being a useful metric of 'fundamental' value. Shiller (1984, p.458) calls this 'one of the most remarkable errors in the history of economic thought'.

The implicit assumption made by efficient-market advocates seems to be that observed prices hover around a sensible estimate of fundamental value (as implied by discounted future dividends for example). An alternative hypothesis is that stock price movements are driven largely by fad and fancies, which are hard to understand or, more ambitiously, predict. This 'market sentiment', or 'noise', is at least as much deserving of our attention as movements in dividends or earnings.

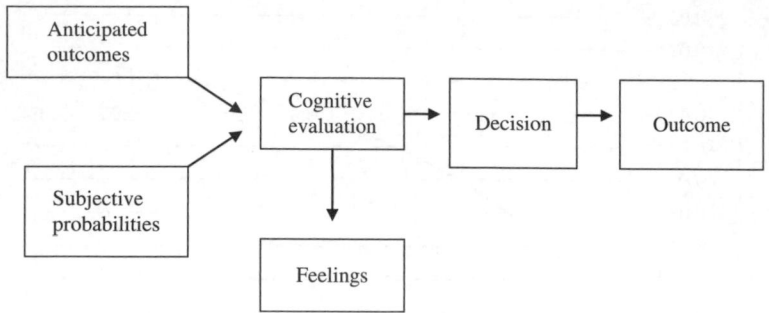

Figure 6.7   The consequentialist perspective on decision making under risk
Source: Figure 1 in Lowenstein *et al*. (2001, p. 268).

6.3.1   Feeling the Risk

In standard finance risks are usually evaluated by looking at the consequences of proposed actions; this is sometimes termed a consequentialist perspective on risk. According to the consequentialist perspective, risk is evaluated by looking at the payoffs to a proposed course of action, weighing each possible payoff by the probability of it being received to determine a prospect's value. So the expected value of a gamble/prospect paying either £1 or nothing with equal probability will be 50 pence in this view.

This consequentialist form of reasoning is represented in Figure 6.7. Beginning in the left-hand side, anticipated outcomes are weighted by subjective probabilities of their outcome to produce some cognitive evaluation of the risk, which yields a decision based on expected values and the cost of the gamble and some associated outcome (win, lose or draw). The consequentialist framework allows that the decision maker may have feelings about the risky prospect (for example 'three is my lucky number'), but simply denies that they can affect decision making and hence outcomes.

While this seems all very sensible Lowenstein *et al*. (2001) have pointed out this may not be the whole story on how investors, or anyone else, make decisions. Despite the chiding of our long-suffering partners and co-workers in telling us not to 'get emotional' in making decisions, it appears the majority of us do. There are very good evolutionary reasons for this. When our ancestors encountered wild animals in the jungle, expected utility theory may not have been particularly useful. Such 'fight-or-flight' instincts remain with us and can be useful in extreme situations, for example, in a car smash, or when approached by a potential mugger. Lowenstein *et al*. (2001) point out that emotions remain important in the general evaluation of risk in (at least) three ways:

- Risk is perceived to be greater if it is of a more vivid type. For example people who are willing to pay more for insurance because they know someone who has been flooded (Browne & Hoyt 2000) or have been flooded themselves at a different address. Similarly airline passengers have seemed willing to pay more for insurance against 'death by terrorist attack' than 'death by all possible causes' (Johnson *et al*. 1993). In each case, the fact we can quickly identify with being flooded or being on a hijacked plane explains the choice rather than any objective assessment of the risk involved.
- Risk is often evaluated with little regard to the probability of the event over a large range. Once an event is seen as possible, or clearly imaginable, its exact probability may have little effect on the perceived level of threat/risk it poses. So we may not be willing to pay that much more for a 1 in

10,000 chance of £100 million than a 1 in 10,000,000 chance. This is because in both cases we see getting the £100 million as 'a bit of a long-shot' (Damasio 1994).

• Risk, and especially the fear of it, is often a social process. This is especially so in the case of extreme market movements of boom or bust. Shiller (1989, p. 374) points to the strength of popular models in financial markets, especially in the form of 'feedback' from price to trading. Typically we would envisage consumers as deciding on how much a loaf of bread is worth to them, observing the price, then deciding whether to buy or not. But survey research on financial markets shows investors often sell simply because they hear about large price drops, almost without thinking if selling makes sense. An example from the October 1987 stock-market crash is considered below.

The reality of decision making is that risk and our emotional response to encountering it are often intertwined. Lowenstein *et al.* (2001) suggest an amendment to the standard expected utility framework to incorporate the reality that perceptions of risk may be a result of a 'feeling', or emotion, and not just an arithmetic calculation of costs relative to expected values. Figure 6.8 presents the Lowenstein *et al.* (2001) 'risk-as-feeling' model of decision making under risk in diagrammatic form. Beginning in the left-hand side, note that anticipated outcomes and their subjective probabilities of these outcomes are joined as inputs in agents' decision making by feelings regarding the vividness, immediacy and social context of the risk faced. The agent's decision is mediated through both a cognitive response to expected payoffs and an underlying emotional response to facing that particular risk. Rational calculation and simultaneous emotional responses and their interaction jointly produce a decision. Importantly, the outcome from the decision arrived at has an emotional impact which causes the agent to reflect upon her attitude to future risks (for example 'Burglary just happens. Deal with it!').

6.3.2 The Affect Heuristic

A wide array of evidence suggests that moods and/or emotions, as rational calculations of expected payoffs, can guide human behaviour. We might ask why it is that a beautiful, talented, woman like

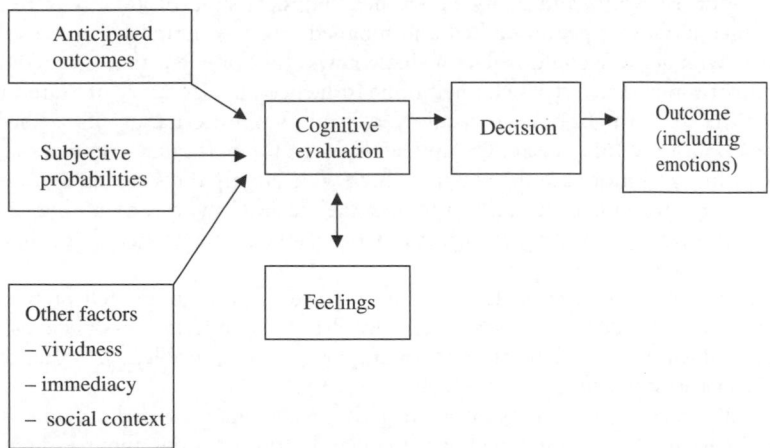

Figure 6.8   The 'risk-as-feeling' perspective on risk
Source: Figure 3 from Lowenstein *et al.* (2001, p.269).

Frances Gumm decided to rename herself Judy Garland before presenting herself to the public? Or why did the musical career of Robert Zimmerman require that he recast himself as Bob Dylan for success? This is clearly because the name brings a certain expectation to the artist's performance for an audience. More generally Slovic *et al.* (2002) argue that there is an 'affect heuristic' human judgement that frames an object of consideration as either good or bad almost without, or at least before, thought. Decision makers inhabit an experiential, as well as consequential, world. Past associations of words like garland, flowers, etc. with pleasure, fragrance, romance, etc. imprint upon a new person in our acquaintance, like Judy Garland, in a way that Frances Gumm does not.[2] In a very similar way we might perceive recently launched companies seeking to hype their own stock as the 'new Cisco Systems' or some other favourable idyll.

6.3.3 Panic and Feedback Trading During the 1987 Stock-Market Crash

Monday, 19 October 1987, saw the biggest fall in stock-market prices in the S&P500 index ever recorded: it fell by 22.6%. To give some idea of the scale of this event – the previous worst day in the US market, 28 October 1929, only produced a market decline of 12.8%. Fortuitously, Professor Robert Shiller and his colleague John Pound just happened to be engaged in a routine of regular surveys of investor attitudes to the stock market around that time. As the stock market dived Professor Shiller rushed to post his questionnaire asking investors if they traded on 19 October, or immediately after, and if they did what motivated them to do so. Shiller (1989) posted two small sample pilot studies of individual investors, which each produced 51 usable replies and two more major questionnaires: one to thousands of individual investors and the other to institutional investors. The individual investor questionnaire produced 605 usable replies and the institutional questionnaire 284 usable responses. Therefore he obtained a good basis for uncovering at least what investors claimed motivated their response to the stock-market crash.

Perhaps the most shocking finding from Shiller's questionnaire-based studies is that very few of his respondents reported trading at all (only 5.2% of the sample), despite the fact that most had strong views about the events and many experienced physical signs of anxiety in response to the crash. Inertia meant a lot of people talked and moaned, but few actually acted on their fears or hopes. Of those who did few could isolate a single news story or event that provoked their trade. A minority of institutional investors claimed to be influenced by Secretary of State James Baker's prediction that the dollar might have to be allowed to fall, but few other events seemed to induce a discernible reaction. Of course earnings, dividends, sales for particular companies, or forecasts thereof, were unlikely to motivate the crash as these were largely the same as the week or month before. So no clear 'news' item seemed to provoke the crash. However, a number of respondents cited contact with friends, brokers, colleagues at work as the immediate cause of their decision to trade (though few did of course).

If few people bothered to trade on 19 October, a quarter of the sample felt pretty shook up by events. Shiller asked respondents if they exhibited any physical manifestations of being stressed by the market decline (difficulty in concentrating, sweating or breathing problems). A quarter of respondents claimed to have manifested physical signs of anxiety.

One important 'image' mentioned by investors in the questionnaires was the vividness of the belief that it was '1929 again'. This claim, which was frequent in conversations about and reporting of the crash as it unfolded, crystallized investors' fears. This claim was a particularly vivid trigger for selling shares during the crash.

Reflecting on his questionnaires as a group and the responses given, Shiller (1989, p.398) concludes:

> There were two channels by which price declines could feed back into further price declines: first, a price-to-price channel – investors on October 19th were reacting to price changes; second, a psychological channel – investors were responding to each other ... both feedback channels were operating fast enough amongst the broad masses of investors to play an important role in the hour-to-hour movements in the market.

6.3.4 The Diminishing Roar of Noise

As important as noise is and as much as I wish to employ the noise-trader modelling later in the book it is important not to overplay the noise-trader issue. A lot of disturbances in financial markets are simply that, random shocks that go nowhere. Such short-term reversible shocks do die out and finance has long had the technology for calculating the impact of such random, reversible, shocks as opposed to the self-generative 'noise' I have focused upon in this chapter.

Taleb (2004) discusses the case of a dentist considering throwing in his drill bit for a life as a day trader. He just doesn't want to make a loss and dig into his accumulated pension. Now suppose the dentist expects the market to deliver a 15% return on average but knows that it has a standard deviation of returns 10% either way. So any given year the market on average can vary by 10% above or below his target of 15%. Now in about 68 out of 100 years, if asset returns follow a normal distribution (they do not), the dentist can expect a return of between 5% and 25%, i.e. within one standard deviation of the mean. He can be very confident, 95% of the time, he will take a loss of no more than −5% and receive a gain of no more than 35%, i.e. the asset will give a return within two standard deviations of the mean. But this is over a year. With a shorter trading period the situation can look much worse. If the dentist is of a nervous disposition he might give up the day-trader job too early, before he can see his luck average out.

The probability the dentist will achieve his desired target return is given by the formula (see Estrada 2005, p.146):

$$z^* = \frac{ln(1 + R^*) - \overline{R}}{\sigma_R / \sqrt{1}} \tag{6.12}$$

where R^* is some target return the dentist sets for himself, here 0 (i.e. he is happy as long as he never takes a loss), ln denotes the natural logarithm of a variable, $\overline{R}$ is the average annual return, here 15%, σ_R is the standard deviation around that mean return, here 10%, and T is the evaluation period, here 1 year initially. The value z^* is a drawing from the unit normal distribution. What's the chance of the dentist avoiding a loss on his trading as his first year of day trading proceeds? Well looking at Equation (6.12) this obviously depends on the period over which the evaluation of performance is made, T. So for the evaluation period of a year we have upon substituting into Equation (6.12) a probability of avoiding a loss of

$$\frac{ln(1 + 0) - 0.15}{0.1 / \sqrt{1}} = -1.5$$

Looking at our standard normal tables we find a value of 1.5 (telling us it is the chance of doing as badly as receiving nothing, given the average return is 15%) is about 93%. But what if the dentist gets nervous after three months and leaves? How likely is he to have reached his target (no losses) by then? Returning to Equation (6.12):

$$\frac{ln(1+0) - 0.15}{0.1/\sqrt{0.25}} = -0.75$$

The probability of avoiding a loss over any three-month period is only 77%. Over any month it is only 67%, over any given day it is 54%. So, patience is a virtue in a market characterized by truly random, reversible, shocks.

Noise-trader models are a very helpful modelling tool for understanding behaviour in financial markets and I will use that framework to integrate much of my discussion in the rest of this book. However, I mean self-generative 'noise' that 'creates its own space' not just the roar of random events that cancels out over any longer period. So for noise-trader models to have some predictive value we require a decent proportion of the noise to feed upon itself and not simply be cancelled out in the next trading round.

6.4   Conclusion and Summary

This chapter has considered the role of noise traders in financial markets and in particular one classic model of the impact of trade occurring almost regardless of fundamentals by DSSW. The model was explicitly solved and its mechanics treated in some detail because it is this sort of informed and uninformed, or smart and dumb, trader model that is the workhorse model of much of behavioural finance (and in all finance in fact). It takes centre-stage in Andrei Shleifer's (2000) classic textbook on behavioural finance, *Inefficient Markets*, for example. So time spent conquering the details of the DSSW model will be repaid by easier comprehension of later chapters where its mechanics reappears in a slightly fancier guise.

The DSSW model argues that noise traders create their own space because of a systemic mispricing of the risky asset being traded. Later in the chapter we presented some research that this might indeed be a credible starting point for analysing trading in financial markets. Emotion, bias and social networks all impinge on decision making under risk as well as cognitive evaluations of risks and rewards. This allows noise traders to survive, and perhaps thrive, in financial markets.

Questions

1. In Table 6.2 let the coefficient of risk aversion fall to 0.1 (from 0.3) and keep all other values the same. Now redraw Figure 6.3 and comment on the changed relationship between noise-trader optimism and implied price. How has the decline in informed traders' risk aversion changed the relationship represented in Figure 6.3?
2. In Table 6.3 let the proportion of noise traders fall by two-thirds, so there are now only 11% in the market. Now redraw Figure 6.6 and comment upon how the relation between the returns to trading on noise and the noise traders' optimism has changed. How has the diminished proportion of noise traders now populating the market changed the relationship represented in Figure 6.6?
3. What strategies have security market regulators taken to reduce 'noise' in stock markets? How successful have these authorities been in achieving their objective of purging the financial market of 'noisy' elements in asset pricing?

Notes

1. Shleifer's (2000) textbook contains a more simplified version of the model together with examples of its use. We draw on both versions in the present chapter.
2. If 1940s' film stars are not your strong point then it might be worth adding that Judy Garland was a child prodigy who played Dorothy in *The Wizard of Oz* (1939) and went on to many unhappy marriages. Her daughter is Liza Minnelli.

References

Black, F. (1986). Noise. *Journal of Finance*, **61**: 529–43.

Browne, M. & R. Hoyt (2000). The demand for flood insurance: empirical evidence. *Journal of Risk and Uncertainty*, **20**: 271–89.

Damasio, A. (1994). *Descartes' Error: Emotion, Reason and the Human Brain*. New York: Putnam Books.

De Long, B., A. Shleifer, L. Summers & R. Waldmann (1990). Noise trader risk in financial markets. *Journal of Political Economy*, **98**: 703–38.

Dow, J. & G. Gorton (2008). Noise traders. In S. Durlauf & L. Blume (eds), *A New Palgrave Dictionary of Economics*. New York: Macmillan.

Estrada, J. (2005). *Finance in a Nutshell: A No-Nonsense Guide to the Tools and Techniques of Finance*. Harlow: FT-Prentice Hall.

Froot, K. & E. Debora (1999). How are stock prices affected by the location of trade? *Journal of Financial Economics*, **52**: 189–216.

Glosten, L. & J. Milgrom (1985). Bid, ask and transaction prices in a specialist market with heterogeneously informed traders. *Journal of Financial Economics*, **14**: 71–100.

Grossman, S. & J. Stiglitz (1980). On the impossibility of informationally efficient markets. *American Economic Review*, **70**: 393–408.

Johnson, E., J. Hershey, J. Meszaros & H. Kunreuther (1993). Framing, probability distortions and insurance decisions. *Journal of Risk and Uncertainty*, **7**: 35–51.

Lowenstein, G., C. Hsee, E. Weber & N. Welch (2001). Risk as feelings. *Psychological Bulletin*, **127**: 267–86.

Milgrom, J. & N. Stokey (1982). Information, trade and common knowledge. *Journal of Economic Theory*, **26** (February): 17–27.

Montier, J. (2006). *Behavioural Finance: Insights into Irrational Minds and Markets*. Chichester: John Wiley & Sons, Ltd.

Shiller, R. (1984). Stock prices and social dynamics. *Brookings Papers in Economic Activity*, **2**: 457–510.

Shiller, R. (1989). Investor behavior in the October 1987 stock market crash. In R. Shiller (ed.), *Market Volatility*. Cambridge, MA: MIT Press.

Shleifer, A. (2000). *Inefficient Markets: An Introduction to Behavioural Finance*. Oxford: Oxford University Press.

Slovic, P., M. Finucane, E. Peters & D. McGregor (2002). The affect heuristic. In T. Gilovich, D. Griffin & Daniel K. (eds), *Heuristics and Biases: The Psychology of Intuitive Judgement*. Cambridge: Cambridge University Press.

Taleb, N. (2004). *Fooled by Randomness*. New York: Random House.

Chapter 7

Overconfidence and Optimism

‘ There is a dangerous cliché in the financial world [that] everything depends on confidence. One could better argue for the importance of unremitting suspicion ’

(Galbraith, 1975).

We often value a cheerful, 'can do' disposition. Who wants to work with, or marry, a misery guts? In psychological tests the only people who rank their own abilities at anything like that of others around them are those suffering from clinical depression. So optimism, even in the face of counter-vailing evidence, seems to be a socially valued personally trait. Hence we should not be surprised that investors are optimistic and we need to take that optimism into account when modelling their decision making.

I may be confusing two biases here. One is optimism, believing I will earn a 15% return on my portfolio, when in reality I will be lucky to earn 10%. The other is optimism about my ability to invest well, choose a portfolio that will produce a 15% return, when I am so dim I should be grateful for 10%. I might call this quite separate trait overconfidence. Since the outcome of these two differentiable biases is often the same behaviour I simply note the difference before proceeding to ignore it.

Optimism denotes a swelling of the mean belief about asset value relative to that which is reasonable, or rational, given later outcomes. Overconfidence means the dispersion of my beliefs about future asset value is not set wide enough to be consistent with actual outcomes. But if I am over-confident in high returns these two biases may begin to look like the same thing. However, this should not mask over the clear difference between overconfidence and optimism. Here I focus on the trading behavior of overconfident optimists.

Nor is overconfidence in my ability always the childlike optimism of the 'somewhere over a rainbow' variety. A large number of studies attest to the overconfidence of various types of 'experts' – doctors, lawyers and investment professionals.[1] This is understandable, they are experts after all. So in the same way as optimism is pervasive in all other aspects of life we might expect to observe its impact in financial markets. The huge volume of trade conducted in financial markets suggests this is the case. After all for every winner to a trade there must be a loser and who is to say which side you will end up on?

In this chapter I consider a model developed by Terrence Odean (1998). As in the previous chapter, where I discussed the DSSW model, the focus is on what noise traders do compared with what a rational trader would do, but in this model there simply is no exogenous noise, outside that produced by overconfident traders' misplaced beliefs. The only deviations from true value that arise are those induced by the inappropriate weighting of information about value by overconfident traders in the market. A rational trader appears as a benchmark, rather than as an active participant in such a model. The focus shifts from maintaining the presence of noise, and hence trade motivated by its presence, to characterizing the nature of misperceptions about value that the process of trade creates in such a noisy world.

7.1   Illustration and Structure

The \$183 billion share offer of AOL for Time Warner was, in early 2000, the largest in history. The deal closed against the background of a deflating Internet bubble, which debased the currency in which AOL had paid for Time Warner. In its wake, the value of the nearly formed entity declined some 70% from its prior combined value. The two chief architects of the deal were pushed out the door, leaving an army of furious investors. Why do such clever men do such stupid things? Could even people as clever as us do something similar?

This chapter models the impact of investor overconfidence on asset prices and returns. In Section 7.2 I focus on one fairly prominent model of how overconfidence in your own abilities (and deprecation of others' insights) can impact on the operation of financial markets. In Section 7.3 I ask is it likely that investors are overconfident? The answer is they almost certainly are. So I look at some of the evidence about how such overconfidence affects their behaviour in financial decision making. In order to ground these ideas in a particular example I discuss the AOL–Time Warner deal in more depth in the appendix.

After reading this chapter the reader should:

- Understand how optimism impacts upon behaviour, and especially the determination of asset price returns in financial markets.
- Know some of the widespread evidence concerning the presence of optimism in financial markets and its effect.
- Understand that mispricing of assets, compared to a 'rational', or reasonable, outcome can occur even if no 'noise' or 'noise traders' are present in the market, if those trading the asset know different things and act as if what they do know is more important than what others appear to know given their asset demands.

7.2   A Model of Trading Amongst Optimistic Investors

Odean (1998) models the trading of two types of assets:[2]

- A *risky* asset, u, which has a payoff $\tilde{v}$ in the last period. We denote demand for the risky asset as x, so x_{it} denotes the ith investor's demand for the risky asset at date t. The expected value of the terminal payoff has fixed mean and variance so

$$\tilde{v} \sim \left(\tilde{v}, \frac{1}{\sigma_v^2} \right)$$

and the $\sim$ placed over the terminal value of the risky asset reminds us it is a random variable.
- A *riskless* asset, s, which pays off one in each period.

Trade occurs between two types of market participant

- *Price-taking*, ordinary Joe, investors, the uninformed, or at least only partially informed only receiving one of the M private signals circulating in the market.
- *Market-makers*, who try to balance the order flow from uninformed price-taking investors.

Hence Odean's model does not only discuss the market impact of optimism upon share prices, it also discusses the important issue of who is optimistic and how we might expect that optimism to impact upon price.

Trade in these two assets occurs over three dates, $t = 1, 2, 3$, with the payoff to holding the risky asset, u, being paid out in the fourth and final period, $t = 4$, after trade has ceased. Initial asset demands are formed at date 1 prior to any information being received by investors. There are N traders who each receive one of the M distinct private signals conveyed in the market. By assumption $M < N$ and N approaches an infinitely large number of traders ($N \rightarrow \infty$), so each investor is a price–taker having little proportionate impact on asset demand and therefore price.

As in the previous chapter investors seek to maximize their payoff at the end of trade in period 4 when the final true value of the risky asset, u, is revealed. For the ith investor we can express his wealth as follows

$$W_{4i} = f_{3i} + \tilde{v}x_{3i}$$

So terminal wealth is composed of holdings of both the riskless asset, s, f_{3i} and the risky asset, u, $\tilde{v}x_{3t}$ held over from the third day, the final trading date.

7.2.1   The Model

For simplicity Odean assumes an equal number of investors receive each signal, so N is some multiple of M (M is one-third of N for the three-signal case, M is one-sixth or one-third N for the six-signal case, etc.). Further, each investor knows another M/N investors also share receipt of his private signal regarding asset value. So he not only knows his own private signal about value, but also how influential that information signal is in the equity market. While no private signal is received at date 1, at dates 2 and 3 each trader i receives one of M private signals in the market, $\varepsilon_{11}, \varepsilon_{12}, \ldots, \varepsilon_{1M}$ for signal 1; $\varepsilon_{21}, \varepsilon_{22}, \ldots, \varepsilon_{2N}$ for signal 2, all the way up to $\varepsilon_{M1}, \varepsilon_{M2}, \ldots, \varepsilon_{MM}$ for the final signal M. Each private signal about value is independent of the rest and can be seen to relate to a different fragment of value, the price–earnings ratio, sales growth, technological or regulatory risk, etc. So each trader has a signal about value y that combines public information about asset value and his own private information signal.

$$\tilde{y} = \tilde{v} + \tilde{\varepsilon}_{tm}$$

where

$$\tilde{\varepsilon} \sim N(0, \frac{1}{\sigma_\varepsilon^2})$$

The investor believes the precision of the signal he receives to be $\kappa \frac{1}{\sigma_v^2}$, where κ is a parameter which reflects the extent to which the investor is overconfident in his own private signal (i.e. the degree to which he overweights his own information as opposed to publicly known sources about value ($\tilde{v}$)), where v is true value.

7.2.2   Price Setting

Price is set conditional on information about fundamental value and the average value of the private information signals investors receive, denoted $\overline{y}$ here. Each of the N traders knows another M traders are receiving the same signal as he does. He estimates the precision of the private signal he receives to be $\kappa \frac{1}{\sigma_\varepsilon^2}$, and $\kappa \geq 0$, where σ_ε^2 is simply the true variance of the signal he has received and κ is some scaling-up factor that captures his overconfidence in the precision of the private signal received. So the parameter κ in Odean's (1998) model captures the investor's overconfidence in the sense of his unjustified belief in the precision of the information on which he trades. In a similar way the investor is also aware that other investors are receiving other signals (even though he does not know what they are). He only observes how these other partially informed traders put their inferences about value, based on the private signal they have received, into price. The market-makers and other, presumed only partially informed, investors are inferred by the price-taking investor to receive $2M - 2$ signals with a precision $\gamma \frac{1}{\sigma_\varepsilon^2}$, where $\gamma \leq 1$, and γ captures the scale of the price-taking (uninformed) investor's underestimate of the true precision of signals given to others. So uninformed investors struggle on two fronts in the Odean model:

- They are overconfident about the private information signals they receive, this is the impact of κ.
- They are too dismissive of the private information signals that others receive, this is the impact of γ.

In short they underestimate others' prescience and overestimate their own insights into market value. The only thing that all the market participants can agree on is the precision of the common public signal about value v, all agree this is $\eta \frac{1}{\sigma_v^2}$, where $\eta \leq 1$. So η captures a common failure to take heed of public information about value that all humans, even the smartest traders, are prone to.

7.2.3   Conditions for Overconfident Pricing of the Risky Asset

A sufficient condition for a price-taking trader to be too confident in his prior about share values is

$$\eta \frac{1}{\sigma_v^2} + 2(\kappa + (M-1)\gamma)\frac{1}{\sigma_\varepsilon^2} \geq \frac{1}{\sigma_v^2} + 2M\frac{1}{\sigma_\varepsilon^2} \tag{7.1}$$

where the right-hand side of Equation (7.1) captures the degree of belief of the 'rational' trader and the left-hand side balances the overconfidence of the price-taking, partially informed, investor in his own signal ε_{mi} (captured by κ) and his dismissal of the precision of others' signals (captured by γ).

Investors have the fairly standard constant absolute risk-averse utility function, already encountered in Chapter 6, which if not particularly realistic, at least has the upside of being easy to manipulate mathematically. So the price-taker's utility function takes the general form $-\alpha\exp(W_{it})$, where W is his wealth and the parameter α captures risk aversion. So a higher value of α implies the investor's risk tolerance has fallen. At each of the three dates $t = 1, 2, 3$, the ith price-taking trader solves an inter-temporal allocation problem of the form

$$Max_{x_{ti}}E[-\exp(-\alpha(W_{t+1i}))|\Phi_{ti}]$$

subject to

$$P_t x_{ti} + f_{ti} \leq P_t x_{t-1i} + f_{t-1i} \tag{7.2}$$

where α is the investor's degree of risk aversion and Φ is the information set on which the price-taking investor bases his decision. This includes both commonly held information about value, $\tilde{v}$, and his own private signal about the terminal value of the risky asset, ε_i, and, finally, the price-taking investor's conjectures about the value of the private signals other market participants are receiving given the observed price of the asset.

A numerical illustration of how overconfidence can affect prices

In this section I examine the conditions that make it likely that investors will indeed be overconfident and the various predictions of Odean's (1998) model might be validated on data taken from actual financial markets. Table 7.1 considers some of the various assumptions I make in undertaking the comparative static exercises discussed below. I consider a market with four separate, distinct, private signals split across the N investors. So one-quarter of all investors get each signal. For illustrative purposes I consider the case where the precision of the private signal regarding value is more precisely defined than the underlying distribution of terminal value itself. So I set $\sigma_\varepsilon^2 < \sigma_v^2$ or $\frac{1}{\sigma_\varepsilon^2} > \frac{1}{\sigma_v^2}$. In the numerical illustration given here I simply ignore under- or overconfidence in the public signal regarding value by setting η equal to one throughout. In the base case simulation I consider a set up where the investor mildly overweights his own private signal regarding value (by 10%), but hugely underweights the predictive value of other investors' signals regarding value (by 90%). I consider deviations from these slightly extreme characterizations of the market in the numerical illustrations below.

The first such comparative exercise in Figure 7.1 considers consecutive 10% reductions in the variance of the private signal received by the ith investor, or alternatively expressed, a 10% increase in the precision attached to other investors' signals. When investors give other investors full weight in their calculation of asset value, then $\gamma = 1$, no overconfidence is present in the market and the condition (7.1) above is not fulfilled. Once they begin to do so, at values of $\gamma = 0.9$ or less, then increasing confidence appears and condition (7.1) is satisfied.

The next comparative static exercise in Figure 7.2 considers the converse weight of an investor overweighting his own signal, even if the investor gives full weight to other investors' signals regarding value (which he certainly does not in this set of calculations, note $\gamma = 0.1$ in Table 7.1). I consider incremental 30% increases in the weight attached to the investor's private signal regarding value, ε_i. Starting from a 10% overweighting of his own private signal (in Table 7.1), I consider successive increases in his confidence about the precision of his own private signal regarding value ($\kappa = 1.1, 1.4, \ldots, 3.8$) until he is assumed to almost quadruple

Table 7.1   Values of variables used in simulation of price movements in the Odean (1998) model

Variable	Value
Number of separate private signals (M)	4
Variance of private signal investor receives (ε)	0.15
Variance of terminal value of asset ($\tilde{v}$)	0.25
Degree of confidence in public signal η (where appropriate)	1
Degree of overconfidence in private signal (κ)	1.1
Degree to which investor underweights other investors' valuation signals (γ)	0.1
Terminal value of risky asset ($\tilde{v}$)	1
Risk aversion to date 3 price volatility (a)	0.3
Mean demand for risky asset ($\bar{x}$)	1
Conditional volatility of period 3 price, given information at date 2 ($\mathrm{Var}_b(P_3|\varphi_2)$)	0.25

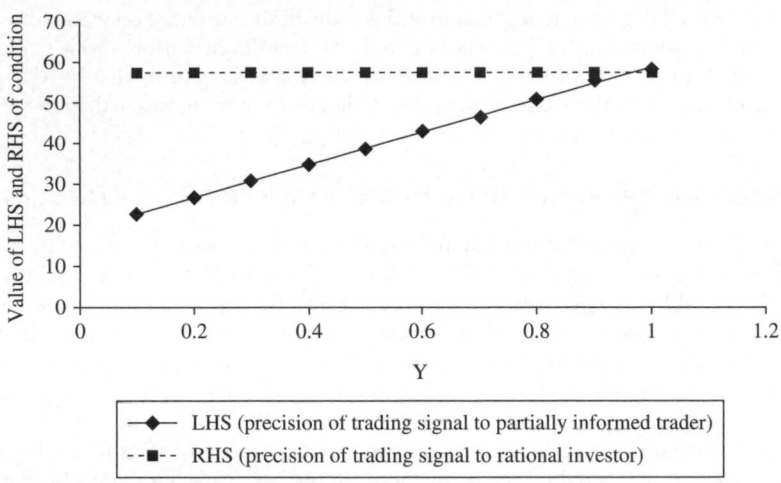

Figure 7.1   Effect of deprecation of informational content on others' signals in Equation (7.1)

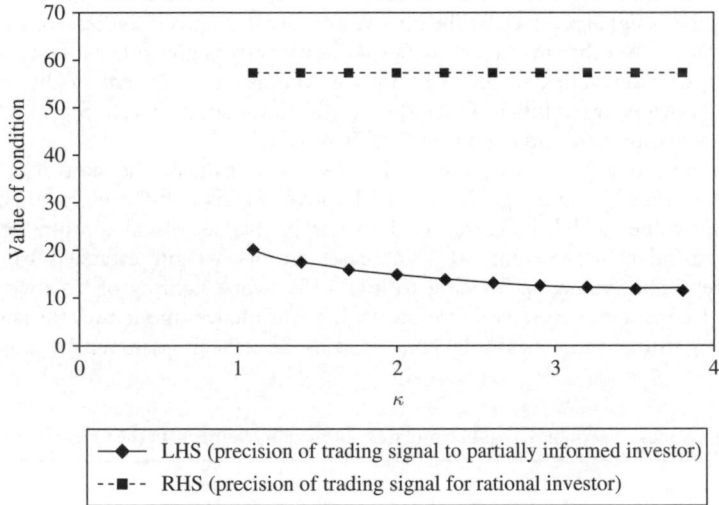

Figure 7.2   Impact of investor overconfidence concerning her own private signal

the actual precision of his private signal in judging the true value of the asset. Even when the investor has only mild overconfidence in his own signal ($\kappa = 1.1$), his marked underweighting of other investors' private signals value in predicting terminal value (recall $\gamma = 0.1$ in the base case of Table 7.1) induces substantial optimism and so the satisfaction of condition (7.1) above. Increases in the precision he attaches to his own private information just exacerbate this situation.

7.2.4 Pricing in Odean's Model

To solve the resulting inter-temporal utility problem given by Equation (7.2), price-taking traders assume prices are set as a function of the average signals received about value by themselves and other market participants. So prices are given by the expression

$$P_3 = \alpha_{31} + \alpha_{32}\overline{Y}_2 + \alpha_{33}\overline{Y}_3$$

$$P_2 = \alpha_{21} + \alpha_{22}\overline{Y}_2 \tag{7.3}$$

Where $\overline{Y}_T$ is the average value of signals received by the ith investor regarding value aggregating over all N investors and all M signals received and α_{ti} are various response coefficients in the model which collectively define the dynamic trajectory of price.

These conjectures are shared by all price-taking investors in the market and result in an equilibrium which has coefficients of the form

$$\alpha_{31} = \frac{\eta\frac{1}{\sigma_\nu^2}\tilde{\nu} - \alpha\overline{x}}{\eta\frac{1}{\sigma_\nu^2} + 2(\kappa + \gamma M - \gamma)\frac{1}{\sigma_\varepsilon^2}}$$

$$\alpha_{22} = \frac{(\kappa + \gamma M - \gamma)\frac{1}{\sigma_\varepsilon^2}}{\eta\frac{1}{\sigma_\nu^2} + (\kappa + \gamma M - \gamma)\frac{1}{\sigma_\varepsilon^2}}$$

$$\alpha_{32} = \alpha_{33} = \frac{(\kappa + \gamma M - \gamma)\frac{1}{\sigma_\varepsilon^2}}{\eta\frac{1}{\sigma_\nu^2} + 2(\kappa + \gamma M - \gamma)\frac{1}{\sigma_\varepsilon^2}}$$

$$\alpha_{21} = \alpha_{31} + (\alpha_{32} + \alpha_{33})\tilde{\nu} - a\overline{x}\mathrm{var}_b(P_3|\Phi_3)$$

$$+ \frac{\tilde{\nu}\left(\alpha_{33}(\gamma + \gamma M - \kappa)\frac{1}{\sigma_\varepsilon^2} + \alpha_{32}\left(\eta\frac{1}{\sigma_\nu^2} + (\kappa + \gamma M - \gamma)\right)\frac{1}{\sigma_\varepsilon^2}\right)}{\eta\frac{1}{\sigma_\nu^2} + (\kappa + \gamma M - \gamma)\frac{1}{\sigma_\varepsilon^2}} \tag{7.4}$$

which gives a solution for date 1 price as follows

$$P_1 = \alpha_{21} + \alpha_{22}\overline{\nu} + \alpha\overline{x}\alpha_{22}^2\left(\frac{1}{\eta\frac{1}{\sigma_\nu^2}} + \frac{\gamma + \kappa M - \kappa}{\kappa\gamma\frac{1}{\sigma_\varepsilon^2}M^2}\right) \tag{7.5}$$

The solution for these coefficients is fairly intricate, but very illuminating about how Odean's (1998) model works. Hence I present this derivation in an appendix to the chapter so as not to interrupt the flow of exposition for those who are happy to take such results on trust.

Focus for a moment on the solution for the price-response coefficients α_{22}, α_{32}, α_{33}. The price response to variation in the per capita supply of the risky asset, $\bar{x}$, relative to that expected in a 'rational' market (devoid of overconfident price-taking investors) is determined by the term $n \frac{1}{\sigma_v^2}$ in the denominator of the solution for the price-response coefficients above. Since $\eta \leq 1$ and $\frac{1}{\sigma_v^2} > 0$, any increase in η serves to diminish price changes in response to changes in the supply of the risky asset, x, making security markets less volatile. In the case of the second and third coefficients private signals received at date 3, i.e. price responses α_{32} and α_{33}, which capture overconfidence, operating via an increase in the precision of the private signal received, $\frac{1}{\sigma_\varepsilon^2}$, has twice the impact of a signal received at date 2, i.e. in the solution for date 2 price response α_{22}. This is because the impact of this overconfidence has been felt repeatedly at date 3, but only once at date 2. Price-taking investors not only respond to the public signal received, but also respond excessively due to their overconfidence in the information the public signal yields about asset value.

Conversely any increase in risk aversion, α, serves to increase the volatility of prices as price-taking investors move to unload risky assets on to others. One possible match to price-taking investors' trades are 'smart' insiders who have less reason to fear price disturbances unrelated to underlying value because they know these positions will be unwound. However, if they are unwilling to stand at the other end of uninformed traders' bids and sales, the partially informed are forced to furiously trade amongst themselves.

A numerical illustration of pricing in Odean's model

In this section I consider some comparative statics of the impact of various parameters in Odean's (1998) model on asset price movements and hence returns. Very often the simulations I take you through in this book have pretty obvious outcomes. But looking at Equations (7.4) and (7.5) above it is fairly clear that disentangling the impact of various offsetting effects, which often interact in a nonlinear way, is very far from being a simple intuitive task. It is obvious that simulations, undertaken here in a set of Excel spreadsheets, really come into their own in yielding predictions about how offsetting effects aggregate up to influence the path of prices in this model. To undertake this sort of simulation exercise I need to make a few more assumptions than I did in modelling the condition for optimism to be present in the market, given by Equation (7.1). See Table 7.1 for these additional assumptions.

I begin as in the previous numerical simulation by considering successive 10% increases in weight attached to other traders' private signals ($\gamma = 0.1, 0.2, \ldots, 1$). The results presented in Figure 7.3 show how increasing confidence about other traders' price signals, holding your own confidence about the informative value of your own private signal constant ($\kappa = 1.1$, see Table 7.1), sharply reduces returns and indeed drives them heavily negative in the movement from date 2 to 3. In the final period, the value of the asset can only be maintained if traders substantially devalue the informative value of other traders' private signals relative to their own. The movement from attaching 10% to 30% of their true informative value to other traders' private signals drops particularly sharply in the final period of trade, $P_3 - P_2$. This indicates the considerable importance of not discounting what others think they know about value in order to maintain an active trading market. If investors do so the informational role of prices in conveying information about asset value can break down. When γ is almost zero (say 0.1), prices change little because they are regarded as conveying almost no information about price. But as γ goes towards one the informational value of other traders' trading is regarded as almost as informative as your own. For the simulation values in Table 7.1 this leads to a sharp decline in implied price.

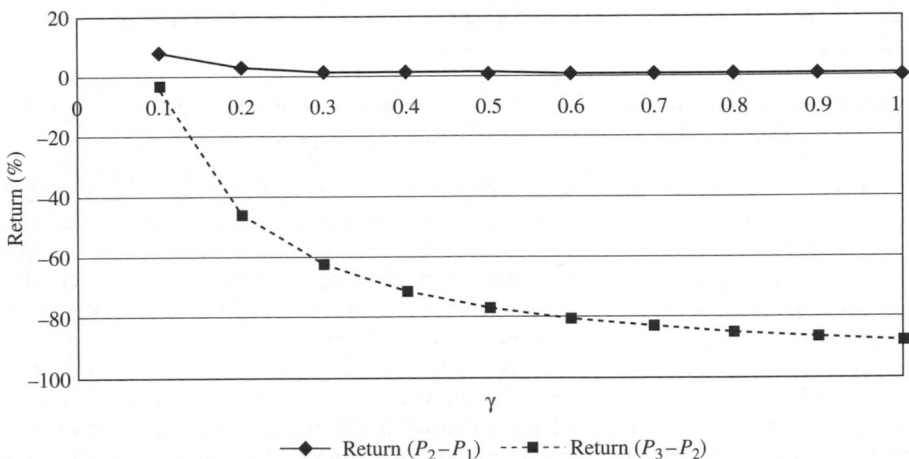

Figure 7.3 Impact of underweighting other traders' private signals on return

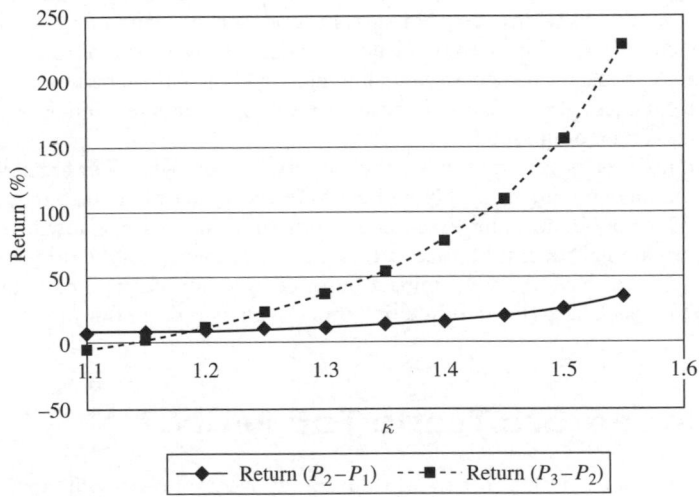

Figure 7.4 Impact of rising optimism about traders' own private signal on returns

Figure 7.4 shows the almost converse effect of increasing confidence by a private, partially informed, trader in his own signal on final period asset returns. I consider 5% increases in investor confidence in his own private signal ($\kappa = 1.1, 1.15, \ldots, 1.55$). Returns rise sharply in response, especially so in the last trading period, $P_3 - P_2$. Investor overconfidence in his own private signal (rising κ) pumps up asset value in much the same way as an increasing belief in the wisdom of others' insights into value (rising γ) undermines it. Returns in this market then reflect the battle between these two offsetting effects.

7.2.5 The Implications of Odean's Model for Financial Markets

The structure and solution to Odean's model have some very clear and important implications for how financial markets will behave. Primary amongst these are the predictions that:

1. Trading volume increases when price-taking investors are overconfident (because there is a diversity of information $M \geq 2$). Each trader overestimates the precision of his own signal and devalues the reflection of other traders' signals he sees impounded into price. This makes him more assertive in his trading, swelling his purchases and sales relative to that of a rational trader.
2. Overconfident traders overcommit in their trades and so induce momentum in price by pushing prices too far in the direction of value change indicated by their private signal. So an initial upward valuation may be subsequently reduced as positions are subsequently unwound as the investor's optimism in his ability to predict value is found to be unjustified. This may induce a form of post-event drift around, earnings announcements, initial public offerings, season equity offerings and other key events in corporate life. This might explain the momentum observed in equity markets, which I discuss in Chapter 10.
3. The overconfidence of traders reduces the utility they derive from trading. So being an insider and hence 'being in the know' (or at least believing you are) can damage your well-being if it makes you trade more aggressively. Being happily ignorant can save you the trauma of wealth-destroying trades. An investor may be the wisest investor if he realizes he does not know anything and so holds back from trading too much. In particular, overconfidence may deceive investors into the attractions of active fund management strategy when buying and holding would serve them better.
4. Overconfidence induces greater liquidity because more investors are willing to trade even if they would be better off not doing so.
5. Overconfident insiders, or 'smart money', who hopefully know what they are doing, can raise the informative content of pricing by disseminating inside knowledge about how much the company is really worth. Overconfident, uninformed or partially informed (who know only ε_i) traders just garble the informational content of prices regarding the true worth of the risky asset. Of course, a misguided insider will have the same impact on price as an uninformed price-taking investor in Odean's (1998) model. So to be an insider is simply to guess right in this model.

7.3 Do Investors Trade Too Much?

A major prediction from Odean's theory regarding how overconfidence will affect trading is that investors will trade too much. This is because investors give too much credence to their own private signal about value, while failing to recognize the predictive value of their fellow traders' private signals. So they are too confident about their own ability to 'beat the market'. Odean (1999) reports the results of tests of this very hypothesis for 10,000 clients of a major US brokerage service in the years 1987–93. This sample frame produces records for 97,483 trades of over 31 million shares. Odean asks, are these trades profitable after controlling for the cost of trading, or do investors just trade too much? Figure 7.5 summarizes the results of his study, recording the increasing losses to lengthening trading windows.

The clear answer to this question is yes, investors do trade too much. The trades are unprofitable even before allowance for trading costs. One of the major reasons for this is that investors ignore mean reversion and so buy 'winners' who later become 'losers'. For all three time periods over which trades are followed, 84, 252 and 504 days, the gains in sold shares always exceeded those in purchased shares.

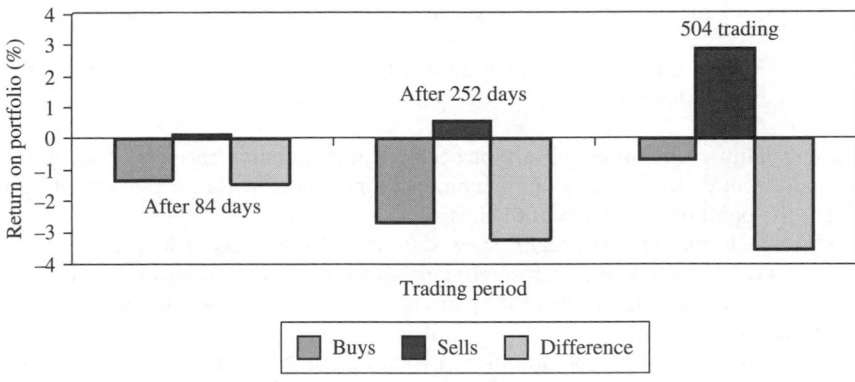

Figure 7.5   Return to Odean's (1999) broker–client trading strategies

7.3.1 Optimism in Corporate Finance

Odean (1998) discusses the impact of overconfidence in liquid markets with very well-informed and highly motivated traders. But it is perhaps in the context of corporate finance that the most devastating impact of optimism, if not self-delusion, is most easily observed. Even the briefest exposure to working life throws up examples of arrogant, delusional and downright foolhardy actions (often, sadly, our own). We do not have to look too far for examples of 'Emperor Eisner' or the 'Court of Lord Conrad Black', even ignoring the darkness of Howard Hughes's final years (Brown & Broeske 1996).

Heaton (2002) develops a simple model of how an optimism bias might affect the decisions of managers. He explains two offsetting trends that are very often observed in a major corporation's investment policy. These are:

- Optimistic managers believe financial markets undervalue their firms and hence pass up positive net present value, because the managers believe 'the market does not understand our value'.
- Optimistic managers overestimate their own ability to manage new projects and so accept negative net present value projects, such managers are 'always wrong but never in doubt'.

Heaton (2002) characterizes a typology of outcomes in which such under- and/or overinvestment equilibria can occur. In particular he links optimism to Jensen's (1986) free cash-flow perspective of the corporate finance. The very reason why managers cannot be trusted with free cash-flow is that they are subject to the offsetting biases given above. While the capital markets outside the company are also subject to the effects of optimism bias, its impact is likely to be more bounded than within the darkened recesses of inefficiently managed giant corporations. This is because the policing pressure of arbitrage is far less in this context.

7.3.2 Facing Failure

Accepting defeat is tough. I feel sure I will go to my grave ashamed of my inability to speak any language other than English. Hope springs eternal, although the teachers of my French and Dutch classes may not share this view. Business failure in particular has many offspring but few fathers willing to confess all (but see Wolff 1998 for an admission of frank defeat in the recent Internet boom).

Business failure has at least three possible causes which each have different interpretations for the role of cognitive bias in that failure:

- Early business failure may simply reflect the fleeting nature of much business opportunity. The 'hit and run' nature of many business opportunities means failure within a year of set up is almost expected at the point of the launch of the business.
- The payoff to the business may be highly skewed to reward a few very lucky players, so the 'winner takes all'. This is what motivates the formation of so many college bands (one of whom may be the next Coldplay) or the fact nearly everyone plans to write, or is writing, a book (and somebody has to be the next J.K. Rowling).
- Finally, entrepreneurs may just be optimistic by nature and be unable to see defeat even when it stares them in the face, they 'refuse to lose' until all is finally lost.

Only the last possibility is indicative of any cognitive bias and many business failures most probably derive from a mixture of all three. In any real-world case study it can be hard to disentangle the exact role of the above three viewpoints as an engine of failure and hence calibrate the relative magnitude of influence. Hence, Camerer and Lovallo (1999) devised an experiment which would allow them to unpick the various motivations for early business failure in a carefully contrived setting.

The entry game

A number of experimental subjects are gathered and asked to decide whether to enter a particular industry without further communication with other players. The capacity of the market, i.e. the number of entrants that can safely enter before profits fall is given by c. The actual number of players choosing to enter is then given by E. They are told they will be paid an amount K ($50 in the experiments reported) if they choose not to enter and an amount $K + rK(c - E)$ (r was set equal to 1 and E was set equal to 10 in the experiments reported) if they choose to enter the industry and produce output. The amount is termed the 'industry profit' or the reward for playing the game, as opposed to bottling out and not entering the industry. Once $c - E$ becomes negative industry losses are shared out over the E entrants to the industry. So if E exceeds c, $c - E$ is negative, the excessive entry drives industry profit down below the reward for not entering. If five too many entrants came into the market the payoff to entry was driven to zero, as against $50 for not entering, i.e. $K = 50$. The 'entry game' was repeatedly played 24 times by the subjects in Camerer and Lovallo's experiments.

Before deciding whether to enter each player was asked for their best guess about how many people would choose to enter the market, i.e. how optimistic were players about the possibility of making money by deciding to enter. If they guessed correctly they were given a $25 reward. After all players had decided whether to enter or not each player was told how many had entered. But no other feedback on their performance in the game was given.

Previous work, using very similar experiments, had already discovered that for the vast majority of plays of the 'entry game' with 10 players, E lies within two entrants of c. So potential entrants, even without the ability to communicate with others, seem pretty savvy and guess industry capacity fairly well. As finance scholars we might expect people to get this sort of calculus right but other social scientists are more wary. Daniel Kahneman (1988), the Nobel Prize winner, expresses amazement at the prescience of would-be entrants, 'To a psychologist this looks like magic''.

7.3.3   Who Dares Loses?

The particular interest of the Camerer and Lovallo (1999) study is the conditioning of the entrance into the game on either some measure of skill or self-selection. Participants in the game were ranked according to their ability to solve simple 'brain teaser' puzzles, or answer Trivial Pursuit type trivia questions. These ranks were not disclosed to the players themselves. The 'entry game' was played either with a random drawing of players or a self-selection of them, where each player was told his payoff from playing would be affected by his 'ability', as measured by the puzzles or trivia questions.

Camerer and Lovallo (1999) then focused on two questions regarding how the manner of play affects its outcome as recorded by the 'industry profits' paid out to those who decided to enter, i.e. $K + rK(c - E)$. So more optimistic conjectures about how few players will enter the game, a higher expected value of E, result in lower industry profits as $c - E$ becomes more negative.

Camerer and Lovallo (1999) report that self-selection, as opposed to random selection, makes players more optimistic about their ability to correctly conjecture how many players will enter and so industry profits are high. Therefore self-selection tends to produce games with lower industry profits because too many people enter, E rises way above c. Agents believe that since they chose to play the game because they had skill (even though this is not skill in playing the 'entry game'), they can be more confident of playing it well than if they were playing as a randomly drawn player. After all they are an elect group, even though they elected themselves.

This sort of behaviour ignores the fact that if you chose to play the game because you 'know you're smart' then other players in all likelihood have made a very similar choice. All the stupid players have bailed out, so now winning the game, by correctly guessing the magnitude of $c - E$, will be really hard! This sort of 'reference group neglect' is quite common in practice and Camerer and Lovallo (1999) quote the answer given by Joe Roth of Disney Studios to the enquiry, 'Why do all the best "blockbuster" films (by Arnie and friends) typically have their release dates clustered on two or three weekends each year?' (Thanksgiving, Memorial Day, etc.). Roth explained this apparent stupidity as follows:

> Hubris, Hubris. If you think about your own business, you think 'I've got a good story department, I've got a good marketing department, we're going to go out and do this'. And you don't think everybody else is thinking the same way.

But hubris is certainly not just a monopoly of larger than life movie moguls as I will now show.

7.3.4   The Hubris Theory of Takeovers

Why do we see so many great companies ruined by empire building? Think about GEC, Hollinger International, Grand Metropolitan or AOL (my case study below). We all know the story of the overreaching acquirer who brings the acquiring corporation crashing to the ground. Since these stories are so commonplace why do CEOs and their boards of directors continue to destroy shareholder wealth in this way? Roll (1986) has a very simple story about why such stories recur throughout our corporate history. This is that many acquirers simply overvalue the target. They are guilty of hubris in believing they can extract more shareholder value from the target than they will subsequently be able to in practice.

Takeovers require the bidder to value the target company and this process, like any other, is fraught with error. Roll (1986) points out that since no target will accept a bid below the existing market value of the company we can only observe overvaluations in a sample of successful acquisitions. The distribution of valuation errors around the true value may be perfectly symmetric for the sample of all potential bidders, but all bids under the current market price fail. This is true even if the stock market overvalues the target company. So, in the sample of observed acquisitions, finding an average overvaluation is not really convincing evidence of market irrationality, or even overconfidence. If we regard the current price of the target to be a fairly accurate assessment of its true value only bids at the true value or overestimates of its value can produce outcomes that lead to a successful acquisition of the firm. Roll (1986) points out that much of the statistical evidence we have about the impact of acquisitions on shareholder wealth is at least consistent with the hubris theory of takeovers.

If there are in truth no synergistic or other gains to acquiring the target company, the central prediction of the hubris theory of takeovers is that the target shareholder's gains are more than compensated for by the bidder shareholder's losses. Sadly, most current published studies do not really address this issue at all. Bidders are generally much bigger than targets. AOL was roughly twice the market capitalization of Time Warner on the acquisition date for example. So a given percentage decline in shareholder wealth destroys far more monetary value for the bidder company than the target in terms of total money wasted. This is roughly what much of the empirical takeover literature reports, small, statistically insignificant, losses to big bidders and large, statistically very significant, gains to target shareholders. But when weighted by market capitalization there is little doubt that on average takeovers destroy shareholder value when netted across large bidding companies and their smaller target prey.

In the case study at the close of this chapter I consider the AOL–Time Warner merger as an example of this hubris theory of takeovers. In reviewing this deal I pay particular attention to details that seem to indicate the presence of hubris or overconfidence in the ensuing implosion of the merged firm (which lost over 70% of its market capitalization before both the authors of the deal were finally shown the door).

The AOL–Time Warner case study is easy to use because of two popular accounts of its progress (Klein 2003 and Swisher & Dickey 2003). Towards the end of Klein's account of the deal (2003, p.254) he quotes a Time Warner executive thus:

> 'There was hubris in every meeting that they had,' said a Time Warner official. 'It was all about "what can you do for me" not "what can we do for each other"'. Many at Time Warner were stunned by what they considered the audacity of AOL officials to demand things they should have known were not appropriate.[5]

This was perhaps the driving force of the cultural disjuncture that rent the two parties apart. I trace the theme of arrogance, overreaching and hubris in my discussion of the AOL–Time Warner deal below.

7.4   Conclusion and Summary

This chapter discusses the impact of a cognitive bias for which there is overwhelming psychological evidence. Not only are we optimistic, it is most probably rational to be so. Life is just more fun if the glass is half full. This chapter reviews some of the likely impacts of this bias on trading in financial markets. Chief amongst these is overtrading.

In Chapter 6 we saw how noise traders 'create their own space' and maybe they do so by means of optimistic forecasts of future trading gains. As such noise traders are not irrational but simply normal jolly folk like us.

Deviations from rationality do not require the presence or maintenance of 'noise' in asset prices. They can simply arise from differences in what information is deemed relevant for valuation and an excess of zeal in applying those beliefs to pricing the asset.

Appendix A: Hubris at Work: The AOL–Time Warner Merger

Michael Bromley, a business development officer at AOL in the late 1990s, is quoted as saying:

> The Internet bubble ended the day we announced the AOL–Time Warner deal. That was the day we realized the Internet could not stand on its own

> (Klein 2003, p.100).

The deal also marked a moment of transition in the history of the digital economy as Swisher and Dickey (2003, p.14) comment:

> The moment the deal was struck has become a kind of Internet Rubicon. It stopped the bubble that needed stopping and ushered the nascent industry into maturity with a rough shove.

The $183 billion share offer of AOL for Time Warner was at the time the largest in history. The deal closed against the background of a deflating Internet bubble, which debased the currency in which AOL had paid for Time Warner. Since the regulatory processes needed to clear the deal took over a year, it was constantly subject to derailment by AOL's shares being devalued.

AOL's CEO, Steve Case, was certainly very aware of the need for a contrarian trading strategy in reinvesting the proceeds of AOL's stellar success. If the dot.com bubble was about to implode it was best to bale out by purchasing real assets with AOL's currently overpriced stock. In an internal memo he stated (Swisher & Dickey 2003, p.125):

> I like the idea of buying fallen stars that have real assets versus chasing high fliers that are fluffy and will inevitably come crashing to ground.

The threat of the debasing of the acquisition currency of the bidder is normally dealt with by the imposition of a 'collar', which specifies how much the bidder's shares can fall before the share offer has to be renegotiated. The AOL offer valued a Time Warner share as being equal to 45% of a share in the newly merged joint entity AOL Time Warner, while AOL shares were valued at 55% of a share in the newly formed company. In many ways this seemed an amazingly high valuation of Time Warner's languishing stock. At the time of negotiation AOL's market capitalization of $160 billion was roughly twice that of Time Warner, but the relative market capitalization of the two companies seemed out of whack with pretty much every other comparative valuation metric. Time Warner contributed 80% of the joint revenues of the merged entity and was really the only partner with any fixed assets to speak of beyond a few computer hard drives (Klein 2003, p.94). Initially Time Warner was canny enough to insist on the imposition of a collar to guard against an implosion in AOL's share value. AOL simply refused to accede to this demand. Finally, Gerald Levin, the long-time Time Warner CEO, personally took responsibility for not requiring a collar, a decision he came to regret.

This personal intervention was characteristic of the whole negotiation of the deal, which was brokered over dinners at Case's home and private dining rooms. Indeed the majority of both companies' boards of directors knew little about the prospect of a merger until summoned to emergency meetings at the start of the year. General Al Haig on AOL's board was one of the few to question the deal's logic, but his questioning never seemed to threaten the return of a unanimous decision to support the merger.

Levin, in particular, had long seemed to encourage a personality cult based on his own cryptic leadership. Klein (2003, p.82) comments:

> Levin evolved into an elusive CEO offering cryptic remarks. 'Jerry became incredibly stealth like', said a former Time Warner official. 'His standard phrase was "Not to worry" ', said one who heard it often. 'He always said that to people. He was almost like a Buddhist monk, like the Dalai Lama.'

Here, as in so much of this text, one is struck by how deeply personal much of high finance is and how ill suited to description by atomistic price-taking models of standard finance interpretations. The fate of huge financial deals often seems more driven by the quirks of personality of those involved than by dispassionate projections of future discounted cash-flows, etc.

Levin and the whole of the Time Warner management team approached the AOL deal with the baggage of two previous attempts at a 'transformational deal'. Ten years earlier, Time publications, the offspring of patrician publisher Henry Luce, had merged with Warner productions run in a far more go-getting 'Hollywood' style. The product, Time Warner, became a series of disparate feudal empires with occasional turf wars between them. Levin sat as the remote adjudicator between the various factions. In 1995 Levin added Ted Turner's CNN empire into the already heady mix. The charismatic Turner, a victim of a bipolar mental disorder, proved a handful to manage, but as the largest shareholder, with an excellent track record of business success, Levin was forced to keep him on the board.

By 1997 Levin was ready to launch Time Warner into the digital age, which he did by establishing the Full Service Network (FSN) in Orlando, Florida. But there was nothing Mickey Mouse about the attempt to link houses to shops, news and information services via their television sets. While the technology eventually worked it was very expensive and impractical. The competing technology of web-based access simply drove the FSN out of the market, despite the bravery of the effort involved. The computer, not the television, was to be the gateway into the digital world. Levin had backed the wrong horse. Nevertheless Levin remained a technology geek at heart despite the setbacks. Swisher and Dickey (2003, p.77) quote Henry Luce III, the son of *Time* magazine's founder, as follows:

> Levin put a lot of energy and commitment into automation of the media and of advances through technology, as well as company money .... It was always a big miss. But he always believed in it.

Even in retirement in 2003 Levin remained hopeful of being eventually proved right in his digital vision. Swisher and Dickey (2003, p.67) quote him reflecting on his years in leadership as follows:

> I know we got punished for the Time and Warner merger, and then the Turner merger ... [the AOL Time Warner merger] is a large transaction and it doesn't matter how smart or well intentioned you are, it is always off the mark .... Until it shakes out into something right, which it will in the end.

It was this constant vision of a 'digital sublime' held by Gerald Levin that drove much of the subsequent history of the deal.

In Chapter 5 I made much of the image of the 'digital sublime' as a 'new era' psychology underpinning the most recent speculative mania to grip financial markets (a new outbreak of financial speculation is almost certain to date this commentary). At the time of the AOL–Time Warner deal much was made of the need of a 'new-economy' technology stock like AOL to seek stability through the acquisition of a veteran media company like Time Warner. Indeed many have seen the deal as a smart move by Steve Case, AOL's CEO, to 'cash in' AOL's overvalued new-economy chips at the height of the Internet bubble. One AOL executive, quoted by Klein (2003, p.106), called it 'Steve's masterstroke', acquiring Time Warner's prime assets on the cheap with the debased currency of AOL stock.

From its inception the stock-market response to the deal was mixed at best. The deal was announced after an intense and brief set of negotiations on 10 January 2000. Two days after this AOL's stock price dropped 17%, matched by a 12% decline in Time Warner's share price. As the merger's closure and clearance by various regulatory agencies, the Federal Trade Commission (FTC), the Federal Communication Commission (FCC) and the European Union's merger body was still awaited, the exposure of the deal to a decline in AOL's market capitalization intensified. Since this process took a whole year and a day, this became a large and growing problem as time went on. To address this problem the deal's parents, Gerald Levin (Time Warner CEO) and Steve Case (AOL CEO), hatched a plan. The plan was 'Project Confidence'.

Project Confidence

'Project Confidence' was an intense earning management project focused especially on maintaining advertising revenue to achieve a rather brutal set of targets pre-announced to analysts at the time of the merger's announcement. These targets related to growth in revenue achieved from selling advertising, pop-ups and other advertisements on the AOL site. By the late 1990s AOL's business model had changed from an hourly rate of usage subscription model to a flat-fee 'all you can eat' service, where variable revenue was driven by attracting subscribers to premium content. One major manifestation of this change of direction was the appointment of Bob Pittman as head of AOL Networks, one of the three primary divisions of AOL.[3] Klein (2003, p.193) records the following confrontation between Bob Pittman and Myer Berlow, head of advertising, in September 2000:

> Pittman just wanted to know whether Berlow expected AOL to hit its advertising revenue target for calendar 2001 – about $2.7 billion. Berlow tried to pick up where he left off, shuffling the slides fast and furiously – until Pittman cut him to the chase: Are we going to hit our number? Chastened, Berlow finally owned up: 'No'.

However, this admission only came after much sharp practice to mask over the implosion in advertising revenue. I return to the subject of earnings targets and earnings manipulation in general in Chapter 19 and especially in a case study of the demise of Enron Corporation, but it is worth recounting here some of the sheer audacity and reckless brutality of those charged with maximizing the advertising revenue stream at AOL.

Dave Coburn and the Drive to Generate Advertising Revenues

The central thrust to AOL Time Warner's attack on the advertising market was led by Myer Berlow, the head of advertising and Dave Coburn, the head of Business Affairs, charged with drawing up the terms of the advertising contracts Berlow's team had brought in. The teams worked at a time when advertising on the Internet, through banner advertisements that invited AOL subscribers to 'click through' to learn more about the product, was an emergent advertising innovation. The precise extent to which this drove additional sales to advertising companies was as yet unknown, but what was known was that any Internet venture seeking to launch an initial public offering needed an AOL deal as an imprimatur of quality. At this time 45% of those accessing the Internet did so via dial-up connections, of which AOL and its recent acquisition CompuServe had by far the greatest proportion (Klein 2003, p.166). The acquisition of Time Warner placed the merged entity in a very good position to dominate the cable access, broadband market as well.

The fact that AOL Time Warner had Internet companies seeking to launch an IPO in a tight spot dawned on Myers Berlow during a final contract review of an $8 million on-line advertising contract with Music Boulevard. The deal was most probably worth the $8 million paid by Music Boulevard in terms of extra sales generated, but in a moment of epiphany Myers realized that the forthcoming IPO of Music Boulevard by its parent company was going to make the management team, sitting before them to finalize the advertising contract, instantly rich. It seemed a shame to miss out on such easy money. Berlow inserted a change in the price from $8 million to $16 million (Klein 2003, p.163). Even Dave Coburn, perhaps not the most morally scrupulous of business executives, balked at this. In a swift caucus meeting outside the negotiating room Myers explained that the fate of Music Boulevard's IPO most probably lay in their hands and it seemed crazy not to get a part of the gravy available from the IPO proceeds for themselves. Coburn found himself easily persuaded of the wisdom of this insight.

This incident set the precedent for a systematic looting of Internet ventures seeking an advertising deal with AOL as a prelude to drawing up an IPO prospectus. In each Internet space, groceries (e.g. Homestore versus Webvan), travel (Expedia versus Priceline), health (WebMD versus Healtheon), for example, AOL chose just one company to give its imprimatur of an advertising deal to. Dave Sickert, a former director of AOL's on-line shopping arm, is quoted by Klein (2003, p.167):

> You had so many people walking through the door with wads of cash. It was life or death to them if they couldn't cut a deal with AOL. It was ludicrous.

The desperation of AOL's suitors soon induced a certain mean streak in the Business Affairs negotiators. Soon they were playing very hard ball indeed. Klein describes the attitude to clients (2003, p.178):

> Informally AOL's goal was to get a minimum of 50% of a dot.com's venture capital funding. '[Kill] 'em'.[4] That was our mantra. We'd say that all the time. We took it to heart. 'Destroy them. [Kill] 'em. You lived by that.

In negotiating deals with companies, another AOL official said the aim finally reached this basic level: annihilation.

The problem was that Business Affairs achieved this objective only too well. By late summer 2000 the bonfire of the dot.com vanities was in full swing. For the 30 September fiscal quarter close alone the company saw $23.2 million of advertising revenue jeopardized by cancellation or renegotiation. An internal memo suggested as much as $108 million of advertising revenue could disappear in the fiscal year 2001 (Klein 2003). Collapses, or major restructuring, at Living.com, Bigedge.com and Owners.com, all added to falling projected advertising revenue. Project confidence dictated that termination of contract payments was booked as current advertising revenue and a raft of other conceits were used to cover over these losses until the merger could be completed.

None of these shenanigans worked, therefore in the first quarter of 2002 AOL Time Warner was forced to write off $40 billion in acquired goodwill. Later a non-cash charge of $54 billion pushed the merged company's share price down to a three-year low at $26.40. The price of past hubris had to be paid.

Business Affairs 'Specials'

As the AOL Time Warner ship began to sink, strong-arm tactics, no matter how bizarre, were no longer enough and Business Affairs 'specials' to manipulate, if not create, revenue began in earnest. Many of these would form the basis of SEC investigations and subsequent accounting restatements.

One particularly dramatic example of such a 'special' deal designed to massage advertising revenue was with a British company. Wembley PLC owed AOL about $22.8 million as a result of a legal settlement in 1995 with one of its subsidiary companies Moviefone Inc. Business Affairs negotiated that rather than simply pay up as the court required, Wembley purchase $23.8 million of on-line advertising on AOL's homepage. This had the major advantage to AOL of plugging a gaping hole in its third quarter of 2000 earnings target. But Wembley executives were struggling to understand why a UK gambling conglomerate would bother advertising on a US Internet site. Conveniently someone noticed Wembley were about to launch an Internet site for gambling on the outcome of dog racing meets. Suddenly the AOL homepage was awash with pop-up dogs jumping up to advertise 24dogs.com. Klein describes the scene (2003, p.184):

> To maximize the amount of revenue it could generate, AOL ran three or four Wembley ads on a single webpage. [This included pop-ups on AOL's Internet radio webpage Spinner.com.] The number of greyhound ads got a little too much, even for some at AOL. It got so bad a Spinner.com official on the West Coast felt compelled to call an AOL official. 'Dude', the Spinner man complained, 'my home page looks like a dog site'.

This deal was signed off as generating $23.8 million of advertising revenue by both Dave Coburn, as head of Business Affairs, and by AOL's internal accountants. Unfortunately for AOL this deal was accurately described in Wembley's annual report to investors thus creating an audit trail for the SEC to follow in its subsequent investigation of this and other Business Affairs 'special' deals.

But not everyone in AOL was happy to join in the conspiracy to deceive investors. On New Year's day 2001, Robert O'Connor, an AOL VP for finance within Myer Berlow's advertising division, noticed banner advertisements for Telefonica SA, the Spanish Telecom giant, on his AOL webpage. This seemed odd since he knew that the contract to advertise Telefonica terminated at the end of December. He assumed the problem was simply an oversight by those required to update the site. Nevertheless on his return to work O'Connor challenged the continuation of the banner adverts with a colleague inside Business Affairs. He was told the continuation was no oversight but the specific result of an oral agreement with Telefonica. O'Connor went straight to AOL's head of the internal accounting function: 'I think we have a problem' (Klein 2003, p.209). It turned out the problem was the product of a Business Affairs 'special'.

Once again AOL was short of its advertising target, this time for the fourth quarter of 2000. The solution this time was a $15 million deal to run banner ads for Telefonica SA. To book the full $15 million that quarter all the banner ads had to appear by 31 December. The problem was Telefonica was unwilling to pay $15 million for such a spike in web presence. Telefonica counter-proposed that, while the written agreement remain as $15 million for banner ads in December, it should be informally understood that the banners would continue to appear after that date.

The truly remarkable thing about this story is that even after O'Connor exposed the wrongdoing, Berlow still felt able to berate O'Connor (rather than thank him) for exposing this deception. Klein quotes Berlow as telling O'Connor

> What the hell are you doing talking to accounting? You work for me I don't want you talking to accounting anymore

(Klein 2003, p.212).

Business Affairs as 'Boys' Town'

A very marked characteristic of the Business Affairs culture (and perhaps other degenerate business units like Enron's trading floor) was the very macho culture. It appeared that negotiators often vied to be the most brutal of all the thugs. Klein (2003, p.176) quotes a rare female negotiator as calling Business Affairs 'Boys' Town'. She stated 'AOL was nothing but the Boys Club of America'. Swisher and Dickey (2003, p.116) comment upon the underlying aggression at AOL as follows:

> As AOL's power grew, its potential partners increasingly began to feel they were being subjected to an AOL shakedown, although AOL sold itself as partner friendly. As the old saying goes, if you're a hammer everything looks like a nail. And AOL was a proficient carpenter – Coburn often joked to his colleagues about his rotten reputation, 'I'd better make a lot of money at AOL, since I'll never be able to get another job again'.

In empirical work on the habits of Internet day traders, Barber and Odean (2001) confirm the greater overconfidence and hence aggression in trading of men. Barber and Odean studied data for 35,000 clients of a large US brokerage firm over the years 1991 to 1997. They found that men trade far more than women and do so far less profitably than their female counterparts.

Case and Levin's Role in Obtaining Regulatory Clearance for the Merger

If an arrogant, aggressive attitude characterized the early days of the AOL–Time Warner deal it is fairly clear where it came from. The organizational arrogance flowed down from the top team. Steve Case (CEO of AOL) and Gerald Levin (CEO of Time Warner) bore the brunt of the pressure of doing the necessary political work to obtain regulatory clearance by the FTC, FCC and EU.

A particular problem with the deal from the regulatory authorities' perspective was its possible usage of Time Warner's large cable network and AOL's subscriber network to lock other competitors out of emerging digital technologies like broadband access to the web and Instant Messaging. AOL Time Warner addressed this in February 2000 by announcing a 'memorandum of understanding' regarding the terms on which other companies could access its cable network. One company that had legitimate fears about being shut out of Time Warner's cable network was Disney's cable television ABC.

In what seems like an act of crass stupidity Time Warner chose 1 May 2000 as a good day to shut ABC out of its cable network over a dispute over the cost of programme content. In the middle of the wildly popular *Who wants to be a Millionaire?* the screen went blank and an odd message appeared saying Time Warner would not let Disney make its cable channel viewers 'walk the plank one more time' (Klein 2003, p.124). Sure enough Rudy Giuliani, the Republican politician, soon weighed in:

> This is what happens when you allow monopolies to get too big and they become too predatory and the consumer is hurt

(Klein 2003, p.125).

One of the consumers damaged was Mozelle

W. Thompson one of the five FTC Commissioners deciding the deal's fate was also a *Millionaire* fan. Nobody at Time Warner seemed to understand the political sensitivity of completing the biggest merger deal in history. In relation to the problem of competitors accessing AOL Time Warner's market to disseminate interactive television content, Levin bridled at the FTC Commissioners' concerns. In his evidence to them he stated (Klein 2003, p.138):

> You don't know what interactive TV is. It's a new market. How can you seek relief where there isn't a product area?

Klein (2003, p.140) comments on the impact of this type of arrogance on the regulatory procedure as follows:

> Levin and Case miscalculated the government's resolve and the two executives had shown little respect in the process. 'The proper stance in coming to talk to the Commission is really on bended knee, strategy wise; they didn't do that', said a former FTC official.

Since regulatory clearance was the primary driver of the stasis that the combined company was in, this arrogance was costly indeed. Waiting for the deal to complete drove the accounting shenanigans designed to support AOL's share price previously commented on. At very senior level the hubris of senior management stymied the process of successful integration of the merged entity.

Lessons from the Case Study

The AOL–Time Warner deal was obviously a bridge too far for its authors. Having achieved so much in their respective industries they yielded to the dream of a 'transformative deal'. But with the dot.com bubble bursting they needed a miracle not a transformation. AOL was set for a fall anyway along with other web-based corporations. The effective takeover of Time Warner was undertaken using debased coinage of AOL bubbling over stock. But the subsequent resentment soon ejected Case, leaving a flailing ship to be rescued by others.

Appendix B: Derivation of Results in Odean's Model

To begin the derivation return to Equation (7.3). We set it up as a Lagrangian optimization problem of the type already discussed in Chapter 6. In this case we seek to maximize the investor's utility by choosing the optimal demand for the asset each period, x_{it}. This yields

$$U = -\exp(-\alpha(W_{4i})\Phi_{ti}) - \lambda[P_3 x_{ti} + f_{3i} - P_2 x_{t-1i} + f_{2i}]$$

Substituting in *from* Equation (7.3) and recalling how W_{t+1} is defined

$$W_{ti} = f_{ti} + P_t \tilde{v}$$

we obtain

$$U = -exp(-\alpha(f_{3i} + \tilde{v} x_{3i})|\Phi_{ti}) - \lambda\big[(\alpha_{31} + \alpha_{32}\overline{Y}_2 + \alpha_{33}\overline{Y}_3)x_{3i} + f_{3i} - (\alpha_{21} + \alpha_{22}\overline{Y}_2)x_{2i} + f_{2i}\big]$$
(7.6)

Maximizing utility with respect to the choice of x, the demand for the risky asset, across the two time periods yields the following solution to the inter-temporal maximization problem. We begin by setting demand for the risky asset x to its equilibrium per capital value $\bar{x}$, which is its expected value in the absence of any evidence of the ith trader's skill or luck in trading

$$\frac{\delta U}{\delta \bar{x}} \Rightarrow -\alpha + (\alpha_{31} + \alpha_{32}\overline{Y}_2 + \alpha_{33}\overline{Y}_3) - (\alpha_{21} + \alpha_{22}\overline{Y}_2) = 0$$

Now recall that the market signals concerning asset value at each date, $\overline{Y}_2$, $\overline{Y}_3$ are simply averaged values of the M signals regarding value received by N individual price-taking investors, which take the form

$$\tilde{y}_{ti} = \tilde{\nu} + \varepsilon_{tm}$$

$$\overline{Y}_t = \sum_{t=1}^{N} \frac{y_{ti}}{N} = \sum_{m=1}^{M} \frac{y_{tm}}{M}$$

where each signal has to be weighted by the posterior probability of the signal received being truly informative about value. After the receipt of both signals (when terminal wealth W_4 is to be maximized), this precision of signals received is given by

$$\eta\frac{1}{\sigma_\nu^2} + 2(\kappa + (M-1)\gamma)\frac{1}{\sigma_\varepsilon^2}$$

where the first part of this expression for precision relates to the publicly available signal regarding value ν and the remainder relates to the precision of the private signals received by price-taking investor i and another M such traders. Remember all traders overestimate the informational value of their own signal by some value κ and underweight the informational value of other traders' signals by some factor γ. Further, the condition $\eta \leq 1$ implies price-taking investors underestimate the precision of public signals about value, ν. Further, $\kappa \geq 1$, so the price-taking investor regards his own signals as conveying more precise information about asset value than it actually does. Finally, Odean assumes $\gamma \leq 1$, because price-taking investors are assumed to dismiss the $2M - 2$ signals (he doesn't receive) received by other price-taking investors as being less precise in their instruction about asset value than they actually are. So the impact of information received in equilibrium trades off the overconfidence of price-taking investors about their own signals embedded in κ and the dismissal of the truths contained in signals received by other price-taking investors embedded in γ. Now assume in equilibrium no new information about asset value is revealed at date 3, i.e. we are in an expectational equilibrium and hence $\overline{Y}_2 = \overline{Y}_3 = \overline{Y}$. The Lagrangian solution, which maximizes utility with respect to asset demands, can be restated to read

$$-\alpha\bar{x} - \alpha_{31} - \alpha_{32}[\kappa + M\gamma - \gamma]\bar{x} + \alpha_{33}\left[\eta\frac{1}{\sigma_\nu^2} + 2(k - (M-1)\gamma)\bar{x}\right]$$

$$-\alpha_{21} - \alpha_{22}\left[\eta\frac{1}{\sigma_\nu^2} + 2(k - (M-1)\gamma)\bar{x}\right] = 0$$

$$\Rightarrow \alpha_{32} = \alpha_{33} = \frac{(\kappa + \gamma M - \gamma)\frac{1}{\sigma_\varepsilon^2}}{\eta\frac{1}{\sigma_\nu^2} + 2(\kappa + M\gamma - \gamma)\frac{1}{\sigma_\varepsilon^2}}$$

which makes clear the response of price to private signals received is largely a function of price-taking investors' excessive beliefs in the precision of this public signal about value, ν. If it were not for the term, $\eta \frac{1}{\sigma_v^2}$, in the denominator of the above solution all the price responses to private signals, α_{22}, α_{32} and α_{33} would be fixed at unity. Then price would be a simple weighted average of signals received by investors about the risky asset's terminal value at date 4. For given precision of the public signal about value, $\frac{1}{\sigma_p^2}$, the response of price to a growth in overconfidence about the informational value of the public signal received, η, is proportional. The fact that $\eta \le 1$ and $\frac{1}{\sigma_\varepsilon^2} > 0$ means that overconfidence in the ability to interpret the public signal boosts the price responses of price-taking investors to changes in the per-capita supply of the risky asset.

Questions

1. Return to the numerical simulations of the condition that optimism is present in the market based on Equation (7.1) in the chapter, using the initializing values in Table 7.1. What is the impact of decreasing precision in the private signal received by the partially informed investor (a fall in $\left(\frac{1}{\sigma_\varepsilon^2} \right)$)? Is it more or less likely that investors display overconfidence in their trades and why do you think this is so?
2. Return to the numerical simulation of price setting using Equations (7.4) and (7.5) and the initializing values in Table 7.1 We know from Figure 7.3 that growing confidence in other traders' private signals (γ rising) drives down returns and increasing confidence in the informational value of your own signal (κ rising) pushes returns up. How does this trade-off occur exactly? Try to determine which of these two opposing effects is stronger. How would increased variance in the private signal received by investors (falling $\left(\frac{1}{\sigma_\varepsilon^2} \right)$) impact upon that trade-off calculus?
3. Read the AOL case study at the end of the chapter. How are such internal conflicts, produced by the need to 'deliver to the City/Wall Street' best managed? Is there a role for corporate 'whistle-blowers' to uncover such bad practice? What are the costs of defending the rights of employees to 'blow the whistle' on their employers if they break their fiduciary duty to their shareholders?

Notes

1. Quoted in *The Economist*, Christmas Issue, 22 December, 2007.
2. Many very similar papers adopt different notation in the literature. To make life a little bit easier where I can I retain a common notation as I move from chapter to chapter in this book. I cannot claim perfection in this matter, sadly, so you may still find very similar things denoted by different letters and symbols even within this one book.
3. The three divisions within AOL, created in 1996 after the shift to a flat-fee service, were (i) ANS Communications, headed by Bruce Bond; (ii) AOL Studios, headed by Ted Leonsis; (iii) AOL Networks, headed by Bob Pittman (Swisher, 1998).
4. Language within business affairs was more crude than I let on here.
5. Stealing time: Steve Case, Jerry Levin, and the Collapse of AOL Time Warner by Alec Klein. Copyright © 2003 by Alec Klein. Reprinted with the permission of Simon & Schuster and International Creative Management, Inc.

References

Barber, B. & T. Odean (2001). Boys will be boys: gender, overconfidence and common stock investment. *Quarterly Journal of Economics*, 116: 1149–87.
Brown, P. & P. Broeske (1996). *Howard Hughes: The Untold Story*. London: Time Warner.

Camerer, C. & D. Lovallo (1999). Overconfidence and strategic entry: an experimental approach. *American Economic Review*, 89: 306–18.

Galbraith, J. (1975). *The Great Crash 1929*. London: Penguin.

Heaton, J. (2002). Managerial optimism and corporate finance. *Financial Management*, 31: 33–45.

Jensen, M. (1986). Agency costs of free cash-flow, corporate finance and takeovers. *American Economic Review*, 76: 323–9.

Kahneman, D. (1988). Experimental economics: a psychological perspective. In R. Tietz, W. Albers & R. Selton (eds), *Bounded Rational Behaviour in Experimental Games and Markets*. Berlin: Springer-Verlag.

Klein, A. (2003). *Stealing Time: Steve Case, Jerry Levin and the Collapse of AOL Time Warner*. New York: Simon & Schuster.

Odean, T. (1998). Volatility, price and profit when all traders are above average. *Journal of Finance*, 53: 1887–934.

Odean, T. (1999). Do investors trade too much? *American Economic Association*, 89: 1279–98.

Roll, R. (1986). The hubris hypothesis of corporate takeovers. *Journal of Business*, 59: 195–216.

Swisher, K. (1998). *AOL.Com, How Steve Case Beat Bill Gates, Nailed the Netheads and Made Millions in the War for the Web*. New York: Random House.

Swisher, K. & L. Dickey (2003). *There must be a Pony in Here Somewhere: The AOL–Time Warner Debacle and the Quest for the Digital Future*. New York: Crown Business.

Wolff, M. (1998). *Burn Rate: How I Survived the Gold Rush Years in the Internet*. New York: Touchstone.

Chapter 8

Asset Pricing under Prospect Theory

The original version of prospect theory was advanced as a positive description of how people make decisions under uncertainty as a counterpoint to the von Neumann–Morgenstern axioms about how they should make decisions. I considered some of the most basic features of that theory in Part I of this book, in Chapter 2. It may be worth just reminding yourself of the material there before seeing how I apply it to financial markets in this chapter. Prospect theory splits decision making under uncertainty into two discrete sequential phases.

- The first phase is *editing* of the decision to make it more easily processed in the next stage.
- The second phase is the *evaluation* stage in which the recently characterized decision is processed.

I focus in this chapter on the second stage, although it is noteworthy that the first stage has not yet received the attention it deserves within finance scholarship.

8.1   Illustration and Structure

If you are in a hole, stop digging, it is often advised. But it can be difficult to follow such advice. We wish to 'gamble for resurrection' in the belief that our chosen strategy to support Manchester City, or retake the driving test one more time, will finally pay off. Hersh Shefrin and Meir Statman (another great coupling of researchers in behavioural finance, like Daniel Kahneman and Amos Tversky or Werner De Bondt and Richard Thaler) present evidence that a very similar mode of thought may apply to investing.

Shefrin and Statman (1985) studied the disposition of investors to sell winners too early in order to lock into current gains and to hold on to losing stocks in order to avoid the pain of realizing a loss. This 'disposition' effect arises from the very asymmetric response to gains and losses which prospect theory seeks to capture. Shefrin and Statman (1985) quote research that does indeed confirm that investors sell winning stocks quickly to bank their gains, but ride their losses in an eternal, and often frustrated, hope of gains (see Schlarbaum *et al.* 1984 or Shefrin 2002, Chapter 9). Montier (2006) is also very strong on evidence regarding prospect theory induced phenomena in financial markets. Section 1.3 of Montier's text introduces this topic and it frequently recurs throughout the book.

Section 8.2 explains the basics of prospect theory. Following Milton Friedman we might ask whether prospect theory earns its keep by yielding credible predictions about the behavior that we observe in finance markets. In Section 8.3 I ask whether prospect theory can explain the Internet bubble observed at the end of the last century and underpricing of IPOs. I find some reasons to believe prospect theory may yet yield important insights into those two questions, which are usually seen as problems for standard models. Section 8.4 extends our understanding of prospect theory to its cumulative form to help us understand new problems in finance. In this section I discuss the evolution of prospect theory into cumulative prospect theory by a later contribution of Kahneman and Tversky. Section 8.5 examines applications of the cumulative version of prospect theory to help understand initial public offerings and other areas standard finance theory struggles with. Section 8.6 summarizes and concludes the chapter. The appendix provides more detail about a piece of technology used a lot in this book: the constant absolute risk aversion (CARA) utility function. If you are happy to take results provided on trust then you do not need to read this section, but since such simplifying assumptions often let you down when you need your valuation model most, I suggest you read it.

After reading this chapter the reader should:

- Understand how prospect theory can contribute to a greater understanding of how asset pricing may be modelled.
- See how a prospect theory of asset pricing may help us understand financial behaviour that standard theories seem to struggle to explain.

8.2   The Basics of Prospect Theory

The value of an edited prospect, V, is expressed in terms of two scales: a decision weight, π and the outcome it operates on, ν. Each probability p has a weighting π which is associated with it and which transforms that probability into an operator denied many of the characteristics associated with standard objective probability measures.

Prospect theory's evaluation of outcomes is encapsulated in the equation

$$V(x, p; y, q) = \pi(p)\nu(x) + \pi(q)\nu(y)$$

where $\nu(0) = 0$, $\pi(0) = 0$, and $\pi(1) = 1$. Hence V is defined over weighted outcomes or 'prospects'. Prospects are decomposed into two parts:

- a riskless, or certain, part;
- a risky prospect, the additional gain, or loss, that the prospect involves, relative to the investor's reference point y.

If $p + q = 1$ and $x > y > 0$ or $x < y < 0$ then

$$V(x, p; y, q) = \nu(y) + \pi(p)[\nu(x) - \nu(y)]$$

Under prospect theory the value of any outcome equals the value of the riskless component plus the weighted difference between the prospective outcomes. Note that the decision weight π operates only upon the value difference implied by the decision being faced, not the riskless part $\nu(y)$. Hence the metric for choice is changes in wealth, not the resulting level of wealth as incorporated in standard utility theory of the von Neumann–Morgenstern axioms. This accords with the idea that a reduction in wealth from some level, to which we have become accustomed, is often particularly painful. This brings into focus the need to isolate clear reference points of wealth, deviations from which are then weighted by π in the prospect theory evaluation framework.

A central aspect of prospect theory is the recognition that the response to losses and gains in wealth is often asymmetric, with the former being felt far more keenly than the latter. The simplest reference point is often zero, or the current level of wealth. In the case of analysts' forecasts of earnings, De George *et al.* (1999) have suggested a hierarchy of implicit benchmarks used by management which takes the form

(a) zero earnings, or the avoidance of losses;
(b) last year's/quarter's earnings, or the avoidance of declines in earnings;
(c) the outstanding consensus forecast.

Whichever benchmark is chosen the role of benchmark utility in setting prices in financial markets seems well established. Barberis, Huang and Santos (BHS; 2001) provide a modelling framework for understanding how these effects impact upon trade in financial markets. I discuss that model and its implications in the remainder of this section.

8.2.1   Prospect Theory's Application to Finance

A landmark paper in the application of psychological insights into how financial markets work is the development and application of the BHS model and I discuss that paper in some depth here. In doing so I attempt to isolate its implications for episodes like the recent Internet bubble and to determine if they are consistent with some sensible notion of rational behaviour on the part of the investment community caught up in it.

Barberis et $al.$ (2001) return to the classic inter-temporal consumption-based CAPM under constant relative risk aversion, under which investors/consumers allocate consumption to maximize a utility function of the form

$$U(c_t) = \left[\sum_{t=0}^{\infty} \rho^t \frac{C_t^{1-\gamma}}{1-\gamma} \right] \tag{8.1}$$

where c is consumption, ρ is a discount factor ($\rho = (1/(1+r)$, r is some discount rate), so $r = 10\%$ implies $'\rho = 1.1$) and γ is a coefficient of risk aversion, with $\gamma > 0$ ensuring the concavity of the utility function in expected utility–wealth space. This sort of consumption-based asset-pricing model has become the principal workhorse of most standard finance theorists. It locates the origin of changes in speculative asset prices in movements in the future consumption profile they are held to fund. This framework portrays investors as having constant absolute risk aversion (CARA) in the preferences towards risky prospects. This form of specification, while very tractable for theoretical modelling, has fairly strong implications about how investors assess risk. Therefore I comment briefly on the properties of CARA utility functions in the appendix. This will hopefully alert you to what my modelling omits.

Barberis et $al.$ (2001) expand this framework to account for the fact that recent gains in financial wealth (X) may make investors less risk averse, or more risk loving. Similarly, recent losses may make investors more risk averse. This is incorporated in an expanded version of the consumption-based inter-temporal CAPM of the form:

$$U(c_t) = E \left[\sum_{t=0}^{\infty} \left(\rho^t \frac{C_t^{1-\gamma}}{1-\gamma} + b_t \rho^{t+1} v(X_{t+1}, H_t, z_t) \right) \right] \tag{8.2}$$

where the second term captures a dynamic adjustment of consumption-based utility to the recently past trajectory of financial wealth. The impact of these changes in wealth, X, reflects not only their relative size, but also H_t, the size of the investor's current holdings of risky assets in his or her portfolio and a state variable, Z_t, is some benchmark/reference change in wealth to which current changes are implicitly compared by the investor. The ratio, z_t, captures the impact of past gains and losses on the change in utility deriving from a present loss/gain, X_t. It is the dynamics of z_t's effect upon current utility that I focus upon in much of the remainder of this chapter.

It is worth noting here that the incorporation of past losses and gains into an investor's utility does not necessarily require any irrationality on his part. Indeed it may simply reflect a prudent revision in an investor's belief in his or her ability to invest wisely. An investor who has recently made huge losses may not unreasonably feel more risk averse as he/she stands to lose all. Alternatively a man as rich as Warren Buffett or Bill Gates may feel at this point that losing a couple of billion dollars is no big deal.

8.2.2   Benchmarks, Gains and Losses and the Dynamics of Utility under Prospect Theory

Discussion of gains and losses implies the existence of some implicit benchmarks for what 'normal' or 'expected' utility might be. One simple benchmark is that expected wealth or consumption is simply current wealth or consumption. This implies a zero change in wealth is the reference level from which departures are measured. In contrast to this Barberis *et al.* suggest the reference level of growth in financial wealth is given by a risk-free asset. This benchmark level of utility is henceforth denoted Z_t. So the benchmark change in financial wealth on an investor's current asset portfolio H_t becomes

$$X_t = H_t R_{t+1} - H_t R_{f,t}$$

where $R_{f,t}$ is the risk-free rate and R_t is the market rate of return on the asset. Here $H_t R_{t+1}$ captures how the market has recently swelled, or shrunk, the value of an investor's portfolio and $H_t R_{f,t+1}$ gives an indication of how that investor would have done if he simply left his money in a building society account. This implies if an investor finds out he earned less on his stock-market holdings than he did on his building society, or post-office account, he might feel slightly cheated.

The impact of *recent changes* in financial wealth is set equal to $z_t = Z_t/H_t$. So $z_t < 1$ implies good times are here, that is, the value of asset portfolio H_t exceeds the benchmark the investor sets for it, Z_t. By contrast $z_t > 1$ implies austerity because the value of the investor's current portfolio H_t lies below its benchmark value when z_t, the value of your portfolio, exceeds what you would have earned by investing the same amount in the risk-free asset. But if $z_t > 1$ then you would have done better not investing in the risky asset and would have profited more from holding your money on deposit at the risk-free rate of interest. This set up allows for three conceivable ways in which recent changes in wealth may impact on current utility:

- No impact, because financial wealth has not changed much recently, or $z_t = 1$. In the absence of prior losses investors are far more sensitive to losses than to gains, so $z_t < 1$ $\lambda > 0$, that is, investors are loss averse. In this case the response to prior changes in financial wealth is given by

$$v(X_{t+1}, H_t, 1) = \begin{cases} X_{t+1} & X_{t+1} \geq 0 \\ \text{or} \\ \lambda X_{t+1} & X_{t+1} < 0 \end{cases}$$

- Recently the investor has had increases in financial wealth over and above her benchmark level, i.e. $X > 0$ in past periods and so $z_t < 1$. This is expressed by the upper arm of the above expression. In this case losses are cushioned by prior gains in their impact on the investor's wealth. The investor may feel he was playing with 'house money' which was never really used to fund a higher lifestyle anyway. Perhaps because he or she felt 'they had it coming' after the recent good times.
- Recently the investor has had losses in financial wealth over and above his or her benchmark level, i.e. $X < 0$ in past periods. The lower branch of the expression where $z_t > 1$ captures when the holding portfolio H_t underperforms the benchmark set H_t. This is expressed in the lower branch of the above expression where the intensity of past losses is reflected in the amplification of past losses by the factor λ, set equal to 2.25 by Bernartzi and Thaler (2001).

8.2.3 Integration or Segregation of Losses and Gains in the Presence of Loss Aversion

The idea that recent losses might make an investor more risk averse may seem at odds with the whole notion of 'risk seeking in the loss domain' associated with the development of prospect theory in Chapter 2. Whether this tendency of investors to accept desperate measures to get out of a hole applies to successive losses, or gains, depends on whether each successive loss or gain is 'integrated' with its predecessor to make one big loss or not. If such integration occurs then a trading period will be seen by the investor as producing one big loss and we might expect to observe 'risk seeking in the loss domain' as he struggles to dig himself out. Alternatively the investor might 'segregate' each prospective gamble regarding each trading day as a clean slate, the results of which have not been written up. The conditions under which investors integrate, or segregate, losses or gains are discussed further in the context of dividends in Chapter 16. I will consider such choices in the case of 'money left on the table' in IPOs later in the chapter, but for now it suffices to say the BHS model relies for its power to some degree on the segregation, as opposed to integration, of successive losses/gains experienced by investors.

To illustrate this, suppose that the current holding of the risky asset is $H_t = \$100$. Let the benchmark level of financial wealth be \$90, $Z_t = \$90$, so $z_t = 0.9$, where the cushion of \$10 (i.e. $H_t - Z_t$) helps soften the blow of any recent loss. If the stock market now falls to $H_t R_{t+1} = \$80$, assuming $z_t = 1$ we have

$$(80 - 100)\lambda = -40 \text{ for } \lambda = 2$$

This may overstate the loss felt by the investor if he has a cushion of $H_t - Z_t = \$100 - \$90 = \$10$ to ease the loss of the first \$10. Only after the initial \$10 loss has been exceeded do losses start to 'bite' at the full rate. So the revised calculation of perceived loss becomes

$$(90 - 100)1 + (80 - 90)\lambda = -10 + (-10)2 = -30 \text{ for } \lambda = 2$$

Or more generally

$$(Z_t - H_t).1 + (H_t R_{t+1} - Z_t)\lambda = H_t(z_t - 1).1 + H_t(R_{t+1} - z_t)\lambda$$

If the loss is less than \$10 then the whole loss can be weighted at the lower rate 1, since no uncushioned losses arise. Hence the summary response to current losses in the wake of prior gains, when $z_t < 1$ can be described as follows

$$v(X_{t+1}, ..., H_t, z_t) = \begin{cases} H_t R_{t+1} - H_t R_{f,t} & R_{t+1} \geq z_t R_f \\ & \text{for} \\ H_t(z_t R_{f,t} - R_{f,t}) + \lambda H_t(R_{t+1} - z_t R_{f,t}) & R_{t+1} < z_t R_f \end{cases}$$

where the analogous expression for utility given past losses, or when $z_t > 1$, is as follows

$$v(X_{t+1}, H_t, z_t) = \begin{cases} X_{t+1} & X_{t+1} \geq 0, \\ & \text{for} \\ \lambda(z_t) X_{t+1} & X_{t+1} < 0. \end{cases}$$

$$\lambda(z_t) = \lambda + k(z_t - 1)$$

and $k > 0$, so the weight put on current losses becomes a weighted average of past losses and the extent to which they aggravate any current loss, X_t.

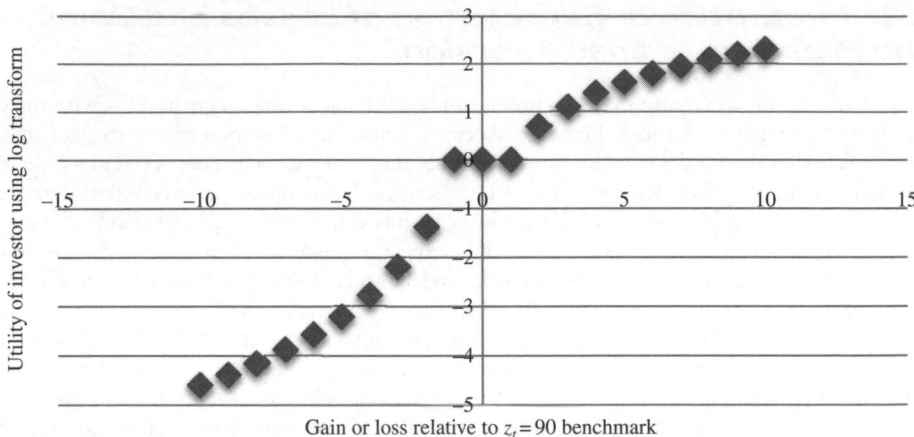

Figure 8.1   Utility relative to benchmark of $90

Figure 8.1 traces out a logarithmic transform of gains and losses as the value of the investor's portfolio moves relative to some benchmark wealth level, here set equal to $90.

8.2.4   The Evolution of Investor Benchmarks

The response of investors to past losses/gains evolves with the history of trading. But how? Is our response to a prospective loss fully determined by our prior history of trading? Is each session on the trading floor a bright new day? Or are prior losses/gains fully integrated into current prospective trades? Barberis *et al.* (2001) opt for an agnostic view on this matter by adopting the following specification for the evolution of $z_t + 1$, the state variable in the model which captures investors' attitudes to gains and losses in wealth relative to some benchmark expected value. So $\lambda(z_t)$ is the weighting given to losses in reducing investor utility

$$\lambda(z_t) = \lambda + k(z_t - 1)$$

$$z_{t+1} = \eta\left(z_t \frac{\overline{R}}{R_{t+1}}\right) + (1 - \eta)1$$

where η is the degree of integration of past losses into the current evaluation of investment prospects. So for the case of full integration where $\eta = 1$ we have

$$z_{t+1} = z_t \frac{\overline{R}}{R_{t+1}}$$

Therefore the investor becomes less sensitive to risk the higher recent returns have been relative to their historic average ($\overline{R}$) and conversely the more sensitive to risk the more they have recently fallen below some historic average value.

8.2.5 Price Formation in a Market Populated By Investors With Prospect Theory Utility Functions

Barberis *et al*. (2001) derive prices in a competitive asset market in which agents are characterized by the type of prospect theory utility functions over future consumption outcomes just described. This implies

$$U(c){=}E\left[\sum_{t=0}^{\infty}\rho^t\frac{C_t^{1-\gamma}}{1-\gamma}+b_0\overline{C}_t^{-\gamma}\rho^{t+1}v(X_{t+1},H_t,z_t)\right]$$

subject to

$$X_{t+1} = HR_{t+1} - R_{f,t} \tag{8.3}$$

Barberis *et al*. (2001) consider the impact of investors having prospect theory utility functions in the context of two different types of economy. The first is that usually considered in standard finance theory when asset prices are modelled using the consumption-based asset-pricing model as stated in Equation (8.1). In this model all shocks to asset price value must emanate from consumption. Barberis *et al*. (2001) call this sort of asset pricing their Economy 1 benchmark. In fact the most simple interpretation of the consumption variable in this model is that of a stream of dividends. The major problem with this sort of model is that it contradicts everything we know about consumption, dividends and asset price volatility in the real world. While share prices are highly volatile both consumption and the dividends that fund our pattern of consumption are very smooth. Shiller (1981) reported that US share prices were 'excessively volatile' relative to the dividends that gave rise to them, with share prices being 5 to 13 times more volatile than the dividend stream, which gave rise to that price in the first place. It's a neat theory, but it doesn't seem to work that well.

Given the lack of realism of the Economy 1 model of asset pricing (routinely used in standard finance theory), Barberis *et al*. (2001) advance an alternative to that model. Economy 2 models asset pricing in a world where the growth rate of dividends and consumption can grow at different rates. Such a divergence may emerge from other sources of income, like a salary or benefit payments. This could cause a less than full integration, or partial segregation, of successive investment losses or gains.

8.2.6 Pricing in the Standard Inter-Temporal Consumption-Based Asset-Pricing Model or Economy I

In the standard inter-temporal consumption-based asset-pricing model of the type described by Equation (8.1) the growth paths of consumption (g_c) and dividends are interlocked since dividends are the only source of funding for consumption, hence:

$$\log\left(\frac{\overline{C}_{t+1}}{\overline{C}_t}\right) = \log\left(\frac{\overline{D}_{t+1}}{D_t}\right) = g_c + \sigma_C\varepsilon_{t+1}$$
$$\text{where} \quad \varepsilon_t \sim N(0,1)$$

where the normality assumption in respect of the distribution of shocks to consumption, ϵ_t (or 'news' about consumption), is crucial to fully characterize the asset price distribution by reference to the mean and standard deviation alone and ϵ_t are assumed independently identically distributed. Further, the use of the standard normal distribution (of mean zero and unit variance, the 'unit normal' distribution as it is described) means the value of any given shock can be read from the statistical tables found in any decent statistical textbook. Finally, the statistical independence of the shocks (or the iid requirement, that is identically independently distributed assumption, regarding the error) in the expression above for ϵ_t assures that no momentum or mean-reversion/overreaction is allowed to enter the standard asset-pricing model by the back door. In this Economy 1 type model, economy returns follow a simple dynamic process reflecting the gains to holding the asset and the investor's responsiveness to those gains given his recent trading losses or gains.

$$R_{t+1} = \frac{1 + f(z_{t+1})}{f(z_t)} e^{g_c + \sigma_C \epsilon_{t+1}} \tag{8.4}$$

So returns are a positive linear function of the growth rate of consumption and its riskiness. The function f then captures the sensitivity of asset demand to the pattern of past trading gains and losses. Good times, when $z_t < 1$, have heightened responses of returns to growth in consumption, unless times are expected to be even better in the future ($z_{t+1} < z_t$, while both z_{t+1} and z_t lie below 1). So the response of asset returns is intensified if investors feel they are entering relatively good times. This may be because recent times have actually been bad, or the future is just seen to be 'better than ever'.

8.3   Does Prospect Theory Work?

8.3.1   Can Prospect Theory Explain the Internet Bubble?

In Chapter 5 I discussed a not uncommon belief which characterized investors at the end of the last century as on the cusp of history and entering some 'digital sublime' in which want was abolished and technology would liberate humans from their life of toil. A very simple way to stylize such a belief is to set z_t to some low level, say 0.25, but z_{t+1} to a far lower level, say 0.05, so life has got five times as good in the transition from date t to $t + 1$. Let the function used be simply the square root function. So $z_{t+1} = 0.25$ implies $f(z_t) = 0.5$. Substituting into Equation (8.4) we solve for a multiplier on returns $(1 + f(z_{t+1}))/f(z_t)$ of $0.55/0.22 = 2.24$ – a less dramatic movement in z_t implies a lower multiplier. Suppose $z_t = 0.25$ again and $z_{t+1} = 0.1$. In this case the multiplier falls to $0.5/0.316 = 1.582$. Recall lower values of z_t imply better times are coming in this model. So $z_t = z_{t+1} = 0.25$. In this case the multiplier rises once again to 5.

Of course we are not discussing z_t and $z_t + 1$ themselves but rather a function f of them both, that is $f(z_t)$ and $f(z_{t+1})$, so I recalculate the previous example using the square-root function as a way of mapping changes in z into changes in returns. In the case of our initial values condition, where $z_t = 0.25$ and $z_{t+1} = 0.05$, then $f(z_t) = 0.5$ and $f(z_{t+1}) = 0.223$. So the multiplier implied by a square-root function is $1.5/0.223$ or 6.71. Figure 8.2 traces out the value of the multiplier, holding z_t constant at 0.25, i.e. currently holdings are four times their benchmark value, z, and varying z_{t+1} in 5% increments, 0.05 to 0.45, implying the value of future shareholdings will vary from 20 times their benchmark value to just over twice the value of current holdings.

A similar exercise for the exponential function with the same illustrative values as in the square-root case implies initial values of $f(z_t)$ is -1.38 and $f(z_{t+1})$ is -2.99 and so a multiplier of $-1.99/-1.38 = 1.44$. Figure 8.2 traces out the remainder of the function as z_t stays at 0.25 and $f(z_t)$ is 0.5 and $f(z_{t+1})$ rises over the interval 0.223 to 0.45.

A higher growth rate of consumption is identical to a higher growth rate of dividends in the Economy 1 type world, so it is not hard to see why returns rise in g_c, the growth rate of consumption. Similarly, standard arguments from finance tell us that investors will need to be compensated for assuming additional risk, in this case via increased dispersion of future consumption, or equivalently dividend payments, $\sigma_c \epsilon_{t+1}$. As the consumption path offered by the risky asset becomes more volatile risk-averse investors will increasingly shift their portfolio into the riskless asset offering a fixed return R_f.

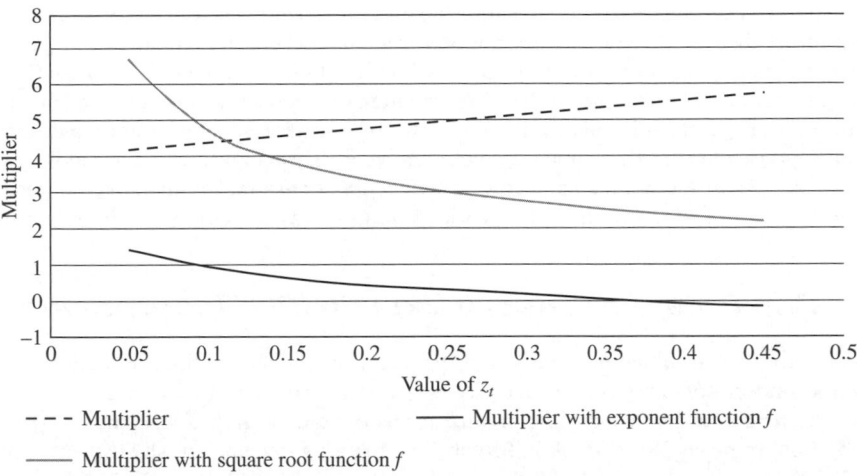

Figure 8.2   The impact of alternative transformative function on the multiplier of returns $(1 + z(t + 1))/z(t)$

Whether the square root or the exponential function is chosen as the transformative function to construct the multiplier in Equation (8.4), the underlying message is the same. The effect of a belief that 'things can only get better', even though they may be pretty good now, amplifies the impact of changes in expectations regarding consumption growth on returns. How strong this effect is rather depends on the function chosen. The multiplier is far larger and grows more as future prospects rise in the case of the square-root transform. Such a multiplier may be consistent with the Internet bubble of the latter months of the last century, as share prices uncoupled from fundamental values to enter the 'digital sublime'.

For an Economy 1 model, in Barberis *et al.* (2001)'s terms, they prove the following: denoted *Proposition 1* of their paper. In an Economy 1 security market there exists an equilibrium in which the following pricing relationships hold:

$$R_f = \rho^{-1} e^{\gamma g_C - \gamma^2 \sigma_C^2 / 2}$$

So once again the investor's exponential utility rises in average growth rate of consumption, g_c, and falls in the level of risk emanating from 'news' about consumption $\frac{\gamma^2 \sigma_C^2}{2}$.

For such an economy the state variable constructed from the history of past trading losses or gains evolves so as to ensure the following restriction on expected exponential utility holds.

$$1 = \rho E_t \left[\frac{1 + f(z_{t+1})}{f(z_t)} e^{(1-\gamma)(g_C + \sigma_C \varepsilon_{t+1})} \right] + b_0 \rho E_t \left[\hat{v} \left(\frac{1 + f(z_{t+1})}{f(z_t)} e^{g_C + \sigma_C \varepsilon_{t+1}}, \ z_t \right) \right]$$

where for $Z_i \leq 1$,

$$\tilde{v}(R_{t+1}, z_t) = \begin{cases} R_{t+1} - R_{f,t} & \text{for } R_{t+1} \geq z_t R_{ft} \\ (z_t R_{ft} - R_{f,t}) + \lambda(R_{t+1} - z_t R_{ft}) & \text{for } R_{t+1} < z_t R_{ft} \end{cases}$$

and for $z_t > 1$,

$$\tilde{v}(R_{t+1}, z_t) = \begin{cases} R_{t+1} - R_{f,t} & \text{for } R_{t+1} \geq R_{f,t} \\ \lambda(z_t)(R_{t+1} - R_{f,t}) & \text{for } R_{t+1} < R_{f,t} \end{cases}$$

This states that the trajectory of future consumption moves in such a way as to ensure that the marginal utility of a future discounted unit of consumption is the same whether it is enjoyed in a period of glut when current consumption is above average ($C_t > \overline{C}$) in Equation (8.3), or below average $C_t < \overline{C}$. This, of course, is our good old friend the fundamental theorem of risk bearing, discussed in Chapter 2. Like Joseph during the biblical famine in Egypt, the investor reallocates resources to smooth out famine and feast years. Suppose returns to investment are counter-cyclical, being low in boom periods, when lots of investors are keen to invest, but high in recessions when greater risk makes investors less keen to invest unless offered a very good return. In such a world, holding equity serves to smooth out consumption.

8.3.2   Can Prospect Theory Explain IPO Underpricing?

One problem that has troubled those raised in the tradition of classical finance theory is the ease of making large amounts of money on the one-day 'pop', or increase in price, on shares being sold to the public for the first time. In fact the UK privatizations of state monopolies created a generation of 'Sids'[1] who bought newly issued stock in British Gas, British Telecom, British Steel, etc. only to 'flip the stock', selling out the day after they received their allocation. Indeed many saw the availability of such easy money as a way of making such sales of publicly held assets to private concerns more popular with voters. Nor was the UK Thatcher government unique in its generosity in this respect, Loughran and Ritter (2002) estimate that in the period 1990–8 US IPO issuers left $27 billion on the table in the form of a discount of the issue price compared to that prevailing at the end of the first day of trading in the stock. This compares to $13 billion paid to investment fees to underwrite the issues. It appears that company owners are unusually keen to let others share in their good fortune on IPO days. Why would anybody in their right mind act like this?

Loughran and Ritter (2002) present a prospect theory rationalization of this seemingly very odd behaviour. Recall that an investor characterized by a prospect theory utility function focuses on changes in wealth, not the absolute level of wealth as used in standard theory. These authors point out that those holding pre-issue equity, typically, the founding entrepreneur and key employees, normally attain a vast increase in their wealth anyway and may not be too concerned about a few million dollars of crumbs 'left on the table'. Rather they may integrate the losses from the first day 'pop' and the gains from sales of their share of the equity to end up overall with a warm fuzzy feeling of being seriously rich.

Loughran and Ritter consider the case of Jim Clarke and the Netscape IPO in 1997 (a story recounted by Lewis 2000). As a founder member of the corporation Clarke held 9.34 million shares at the IPO date. About a month before the IPO in August 1997 Netscape's investment bank Morgan Stanley (home of influential analyst Mary Meeker, the 'Queen of the Internet') filed an IPO prospectus with a target range of $12–14. At this price Clarke stood to take home $121 million from the IPO. In reality, Netscape shares were issued at $28 a share on 9 August 1997. At the close of trade on that first day Netscape's shares stood at $71. Clarke's stake was worth $544 million if he could sell out that night (in reality 'lock-in' provisions precluded him from doing so). One way to look at this is to say Jim Clarke was an idiot and could have made himself a billionaire on the day of the IPO by offering the stock at $70 a share, but some may feel, like Clarke, that a tripling of expected return in a month was an event worth celebrating.

Loughran and Ritter (2002) place this integration of the loss of wealth 'left on the table' and the gains from stock held at the pre-issue date into the standard prospect theory framework. They devise a typology of possible outcomes from the IPO offering depending on how much money is 'left on the table' by the selling-out founders and their increase in anticipated wealth from the date the prospectus was filed to when the IPO date is traded off. In the right-hand upper quadrant of Figure 8.3, very little money is lost by being 'left on table' (so there is little or no loss through this source), but there is a big boost to the pre-issue equity owner's wealth through the revision upwards of their personal wealth

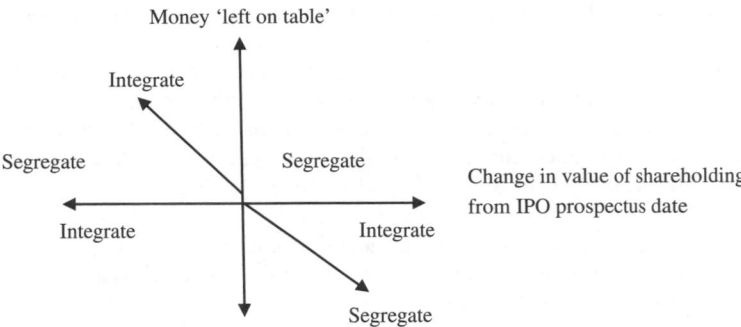

Figure 8.3 A prospect theory perspective on IPOs

post IPO from the date the prospectus was filed to the moment the issue price is set. Here the large gain from the increase in expected personal wealth, post IPO, is segregated out from that small loss. This is so that the large gain can be 'savoured' unsullied by the chump change passed on to the first day of trading share purchasers.

Conversely, in the upper-left hand quadrant of Figure 8.3 pre-issue equity stakeholders make no gain in their wealth as they approach the IPO, and a loss if the issue price is discounted from that set in the IPO prospectus, and also manage to leave a lot of money 'on the table' at the issue date. So their loss is the first day of trading share purchasers' gain. Prospect theory teaches us that losses are especially painful to investors and so here we find the two different types of losses are segregated:

1. the decline in expected post-IPO wealth from the prospectus submission date; and
2. money handed over to those who buy the issue in the form of a first day of trading 'pop' in the price.

Segregation of these two types of loss reduces the pain investors feel at incurring the total loss. It is then not seen as just one big painful loss.

But it is when losses from one source and gains from another need to be traded off that a prospect theory intuition regarding the evaluation of their return to the IPO enters its own. The lower right-hand quadrant of Figure 8.3 shows the usual case where the founder trades off money 'left on the table' against the huge upward revision in his personal wealth as he nears the IPO date (here measured as the revision of offer price from that placed in the prospectus filed with the SEC and the issue price itself set on the day of IPO). Here the small loss of money from being 'left on the table' at the IPO is offset by the huge gain in the founder's personal wealth attributable to upward revision in the issue price as the IPO approaches.

Ljungqvist and Wilhelm (2005) have confirmed some of the intuition of the Loughran and Ritter (2002) prospect theory rationalization of IPO issue underpricing. These authors examine choices regarding a company's decisions whether to re-employ the investment bank that underwrote their original IPO. They find that, controlling for other factors, the greater the integrated gain from the IPO to the company's founding management the greater the probability the original merchant bank retained to underwrite the IPO will be re-employed. Examining a sample of US IPOs in the years 1993–2000 they find sample companies are far more likely to switch investment bank representation as the integrated gain at the IPO date declines. Such switching of investment bank representation is most probably a pretty good proxy for whether the company founders are happy with the deal they got from floating the company.

8.3.3   Prospect Theory Here, There and Everywhere

Regardless of how convincing you find the two applications previously discussed there is little doubt that prospect theory is working its way through a myriad of phenomena that standard economic theory seems to struggle with. Colin Camerer in a review of applications of prospect theory (Camerer 2000) lists 10 areas where prospect theory has made an impact on our understanding of how people behave. These include, as well as the disposition effect, the following:

- Cabbies, at least in New York, often have a 'target fair' for each day. So they stay a long time at the stand on quiet days and get off home early on days when the meter is whizzing along. This of course is the reverse of what an upward-sloping labour supply curve leads us to expect, when a higher hourly wage encourages us to work longer, not shorter, hours. Cabbies rush to bank gains, but gamble to rectify perceived losses on dead days at the stand.
- The stickiness of consumption downwards, the permanent income hypothesis suggests that I form some reasonable guess about how much a university teacher will be paid and form a lifetime consumption plan accordingly. So I might borrow now in the belief that I will get paid more when I am promoted later, but in reality there is a fairly close relationship between consumption now and my income now, so most people when they retire sharply reduce their consumption. It appears losses from income undershooting our reasonable expectation are particularly painful and to be avoided if at all possible. So we are risk averse to losses and cut our current consumption when our current income falls even if we always anticipated this fall as part of our lifetime consumption profile.
- Consumers are far more sensitive to price rises than gains in setting their demand. A 10% discount in a sale may not drag in much more trade, but raising prices 10% soon silences the tills. Shoppers are loss averse and retailers are acutely aware of this.

8.4   The Cumulative Probability Version of Prospect Theory

The cumulative version of prospect theory uses information about the cumulative gains, or losses, an individual faces as he or she moves away from some benchmark/reference level of wealth. Consider S, a set of states of nature, subsets of which are called events. Let O be a set of outcomes, associated with the S states of nature, and A_i be some partition of that space. O is assumed to include some neutral outcome with a value of zero and all gains/losses are then defined relative to that outcome.

An uncertain prospect f is defined to be a mapping of S into X outcomes associated with those states of nature, showing how for any event, s, an element in S, results in an outcome x, $f(s) = x$. So a 'prospect' f is represented as the pair (x_i, A_i), which is the outcome x_i that arises because of the set of events A_i in the space of all events O. Because of the previously discussed asymmetric response to gains and losses around some suitable reference point, positive and negative prospects are separated out and denoted f^+ and f^- respectively. So the revised valuation equation becomes

$$V(f) = V(f^+) + V(f^-)$$

$$V(f^+) = \sum_{i=0}^{n} \pi_i^+ v(x_i), \quad V = \sum_{-m}^{0} \pi_i^- v(x_i)$$

where the decision weights $\pi^+(f^+) = (\pi_0^+, \ldots, \pi_n^+)$ and $\pi^-(f^-) = (\pi_0^-, \ldots, \pi_n^-)$ are defined as being for $\pi^+(f^+)$ 'the outcome is at least as good as x_i' or 'the outcome is strictly better than x_i' and for $\pi^-(f^-)$ 'the outcome is at least as bad as x_i' or 'the outcome is strictly worse than x_i'. In this way a decision weight can be interpreted as the marginal contribution to the individual's wealth of that prospective event, or set of events, A_i.

Each prospect $f(x_i, A_i)$ is generated from a distribution of underlying events $p(A_i)$, where p is a standard objective probability with all its usual properties. As such $f(x_i, A_i)$ is a risky (rather than uncertain) prospect (x_i, p_i). So decision weights are defined in the following terms

$$\pi_n^+ = \omega^+(p_n), \; \pi_{-m}^- = \omega^-(p_{-m})$$
$$\pi_i^+ = \omega^+(p_i + \ldots + p_n) - \omega^+(p_{i+1} + \ldots + p_n), \; 0 \le i \le n-1$$
$$\pi_i^- = \omega^-(p_{-m} + \ldots + p_i) - \omega^-(p_{-m} + \ldots + p_{i-1}), \; 1-m \le i \le 0$$

Tversky and Kahneman (2000) provide an illustration of how this cumulative value of a prospect might be calculated. The illustrative 'event' is the roll of a die, producing outcomes $1, \ldots, 6$. If x is even you receive x, but if it is odd you must pay x. So the probability distribution is $x = (-1, 2, -3, 4, -5, 6)$ where each outcome could occur with equal probability of $1/6$. So $f^+ = (0, 1/2, 2, 1/6, 4, 1/6, 6, 1/6)$ and $f^- = (-5, 1/6, -3, 1/6, -1, 1/6, 0, 1/2)$. Starting with f^+ we note half the distribution lies to the left of zero, one-sixth to the left of 2 (i.e. the outcome -1), a further sixth to the left of 4 (i.e. the outcome -3) etc. A direct application of the cumulative version of the valuation equation then implies

$$V = V(f^+) + V(f^-)$$
$$= v(2)[w^+(1/2) - w^+(1/3)] + v(4)[w^+(1/3) - w^+(1/6)]$$
$$+ v(6)[w^+(1/6) - w^+(0)] + v(-5)[w^-(1/6) - w^-(0)]$$
$$+ v(-3)[w^-(1/3) - w^-(1/6)] + v(-1)[w^-(1/2) - w^-(1/3)]$$

Note that in this valuation framework the attitude to risk is jointly determined by the value function and cumulative probability. The trick here is to note the extra flexibility that this framework offers for capturing movements in cumulative probabilities even when it is hard to say much about exact individual probabilities. This holds out the possibility of applying cumulative prospect theory to uncertain, as opposed to simply risky, prospects, because it is possible to discuss movements in probability even when individual probabilities themselves are hard to calculate with any precision.

8.5 Does Cumulative Prospect Theory Work?

Tversky and Kahneman (2000) report experimental evidence that confirms the realism of the cumulative prospect theory insights into how games played under uncertain conditions are assessed. Examining the choices of 26 graduate students enrolled in Berkeley and Stanford they find them to be risk seeking for small probabilities of gains and risk averse in their evaluation of the prospect of a small loss. This is, of course, very different to what standard prospect theory leads us to expect. Prospect theory, as originally discussed by Kahneman and Tversky (1989), predicts risk aversion over gains combined with risk seeking in the loss domain. Rather Tversky and Kahneman's (2000) experimental evidence suggests a fourfold separation of attitudes to risk. This takes the form shown in Table 8.1. So for gambles involving significant probabilities (say above 10%) the original statement of prospect theory seems to work fine. It is just at the tails of the distribution at near certainties, or near impossibilities, that an inversion of attitudes to risk appears to occur.

Table 8.1 Fourfold separation of attitudes to risk

	High probability	Low probability
Gain	Risk averse	Risk seeking
Loss	Risk seeking	Risk averse

Tversky and Kahneman (2000) asked 26 student subjects to give cash amounts that they would be willing to accept in return for gambles involving the outcomes of four simple events. So, for example, one trial paid the student $150 or $50 depending on the extent of the gap in scores at a forthcoming Stanford–Berkeley football game. In another prospect study 156 money managers were asked to evaluate prospective changes in the Dow Jones index in the near future. In this second example money managers were told they would be paid $25,000 if the Dow Jones moved up 30 points by the close and nothing if it did not. How much would money managers pay to be allowed to accept this gamble for real? This is what is sometimes called the 'certainty equivalent' of the gamble. How much do you need to be paid up front to let the prospect go?

Tversky and Kahneman (2000) repeated this exercise for each of the four types of prospects shown in Table 8.1, losses and gains of high and low probability. They examined the correlation between stated certainty equivalents, offered by experimental subjects to forgo the gamble offered. Two strong negative associations stand out when examining correlations between certainty equivalents. The amount needed to compensate for the surrender of a gamble offering a low probability of an expected gain (L^+) is negatively correlated with the amount the same subject is willing to accept to pay to avoid a low probability of a loss (L^-) given in Figure 8.4 as –0.23. This point of inflection within the domain of losses is not part of standard prospect theory as it was originally outlined (see Kahneman &

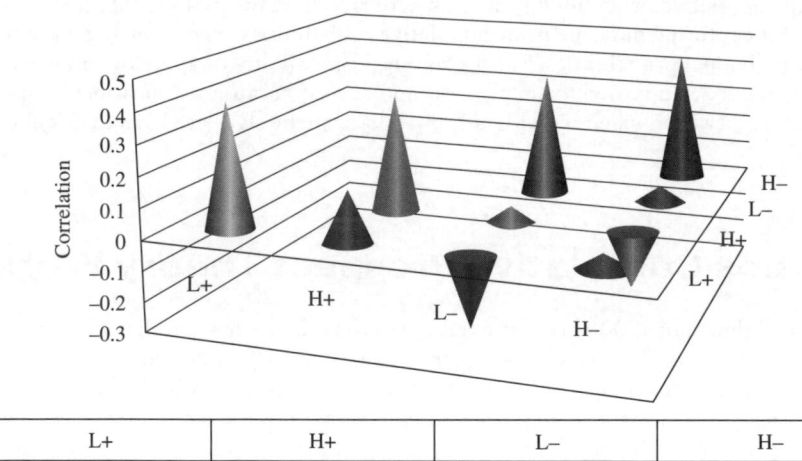

	L+	H+	L−	H−
■ L+	0.41	0.17	−0.23	0.05
■ H+		0.39	0.05	−0.18
■ L−			0.4	0.06
■ H−				0.44

Figure 8.4 Average correlations between certainty equivalents over four prospect types

Tversky 1989). A very similar point of inflection is implied by the negative correlation between certainty equivalents offered to retain gains attained with near certainty (H^+) and those which are almost impossible to achieve (H^-), which is given in Figure 8.4 as –0.18. The degree of reversal of risk preference is lower here (a correlation of –18% against –23% for the equivalent movement from almost sure losses to highly doubtful ones). This pattern is outlined in Figure 8.4, but overall these correlations suggest a simple inflection of investors' utility around some reference point is not the best description of how they evaluate uncertain outcomes. The inflection point contains a fairly flat portion over which investors are risk seeking with regard to gains attained with low probability and then risk averse over losses taken with a low probability. Only at the tails of the cumulative probability distribution does the asymmetry of risk aversion to large gains achieved with high probability and risk seeking with respect to large losses taken with high probability kick in.

8.5.1 Cumulative Prospect Theory and Asset Pricing

One important property of the weighting function is its tendency to overweight the tails of the distribution, expressing an investor's preference for skewness in the return distribution. Barberis and Huang (2005) used these properties of cumulative prospect theory as a way of understanding a number of disparate anomalies in financial markets (for example IPO underpricing and the implied volatility 'smile' of out-of-the-money options). One possibility is that the 'lottery-like' nature of stocks engaged in 'winner-takes-all' competition within an Internet sector made them more enticing to investors. Barberis and Huang (2008) show that a security with a skewed return can become overpriced, offering a negative average excess return. Even in an economy populated by investors with homogeneous preferences (such as that envisaged in the CAPM world), some investors may choose to take a large undiversified position in the skewed security, in doing so they convert some of their contingent claims into lottery-like claims on future wealth. Because their utility function is constructed under the axioms of cumulative prospect theory this outcome seems attractive. This property of a skewed return distribution is so valuable to some investors that they are willing to pay a high price to obtain the security, even at the expense of receiving a return that is on average negative.

The preference by investors for a skewed investor return has been examined by a number of authors. The unusual point here is the preference that investors express for idiosyncratic skew for a single stock rather than skewness in a diversified portfolio's return. Barberis and Huang (2008) show the relevance of a cumulative prospect theory specification of utility to understanding a number of anomalies that have troubled standard finance. These include:

- The poor performance of initial public offerings. Such IPOs are likely to be dominated by offerings with a large proportion of the value in growth opportunities, to implement frontier technologies or create new markets (think eBay here). Such a market might become dominated by investors willing to accept low, or even negative, asset returns in return for a few 'big hits' which arise in the extreme right-hand tail of the distribution.
- The preference for investors for relatively undiversified investment portfolios (remember De Bondt's (1998) 'Fox Valley' investors). Such a practice may reflect a desire to hold a good chunk of the company's equity in case it turns into 'the next Cisco/Google'.

A numerical illustration of prospect theory

Reconsider the simple die-rolling gamble I used to illustrate cumulative prospect theory in Section 8.4. If the die landed on an even number you received that number of dollars, otherwise you paid the uneven number shown on the face of the die. So if the die landed on 1 you had to pay a dollar, if it landed on 2 you were paid two dollars. Now we know that investors are typically risk seeking over gains with small expected values and risk averse to losses with small expected values. I capture this in Table 8.2 by reducing the cumulative prospect theory weight attached to a gain of two dollars by 7.5% compared to its objective probability of a sixth ($p = 1/6 = 16.7\%$, so the cumulative prospect theory weight $w = 16.7\% - 7.5\% = 9.2\%$). Similarly we know investors are risk averse to losses that are small in expected value, so suppose I increase the cumulative probability weight attached by the investor to a loss of $1 by 7.5% to give it a cumulative prospect weighting of 24% (or $16.67\% + 7.5\%$). Small losses are now felt intensely by investors, once bigger losses emerge they will become risk seeking once more as standard prospect theory emerges. Having 'kinked' or 'tweaked' the cumulative prospect theory weighting function relative to the standard objective probability function around the transition from a dollar loss to a two-dollar gain I reweight the remainder of the function appropriately. The objective probability function attaches a weighting of $1/6 = 16.7\%$ to each outcome, but the cumulative prospect theory attaches a 9.2% weight to a two-dollar gain and 24% weight to a small loss. This still leaves two-thirds of the mass of the distribution to be spread over the other four outcomes. So outside the segment of payoffs, negative one dollar to two dollars, the objective probability function (p) and the cumulative probability weighting function (w) largely overlap. Figure 8.5 maps the two functions for the values given in Table 8.2.

Table 8.2 Cumulative prospect theory weights versus objective probabilities for dice-rolling example

Payoffs	Objective probability (p)	Prospect theory weight (w)	Payoffs	Cumulative objective probability	Cumulative prospect theory weighting
−5	0.17	0.17	−5	0.17	0.17
−3	0.17	0.17	−3	0.33	0.33
−1	0.17	0.09	−1	0.50	0.43
2	0.17	0.24	2	0.67	0.67
4	0.17	0.17	4	0.83	0.83
6	0.17	0.17	6	1.00	1.00

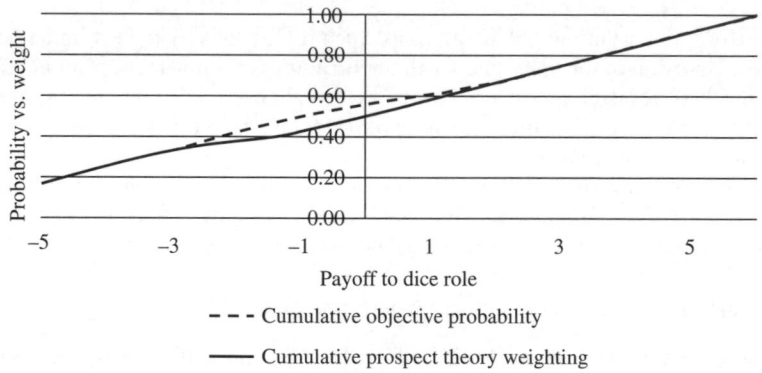

Figure 8.5 Cumulative prospect theory weights (w) versus objective probabilities (p) in dice-throwing example

8.6 Conclusion and Summary

Prospect theory is perhaps the brand leader of the products of behavioural economics and its application to finance. Barberis *et al.* (2001) show that when a prospect theory utility function is incorporated into a simple asset-pricing model it explains many things that standard theory has struggled with, while retaining the standard consumption-based capital asset-pricing model within itself as a special case. Furthermore, experimental evidence suggests many of the principal predictions of the cumulative prospect theory which Barberis *et al.* (2001) employ to model asset pricing accord with how we actually evaluate uncertain outcomes. Currently the potential for widespread application of prospect theory to understanding investment is clear. We can only await the harvest of that application with interest at this early stage of our understanding.

Appendix: CARA Utility

Consider an investor's uncertain level of future consumption c subject to a disturbance e. A market measure of risk would be how much would a person be willing to avoid the risk resulting from the disturbance to his payoff c implied by e? We might call the amount our consumer is willing to pay the risk premium, p, so we have

$$U(c - p) = E(u(c + e))$$

The curvature of the utility of the consumer's utility function, or how $(c - p)$ changes with increments in the expected value of c, can be determined by taking a Taylor's series expansion of successively higher derivatives of the consumer's utility function. Such a series has the general form

$$u(c - p) = u(c) + \frac{\partial u}{\partial c}e + \frac{\partial u^2}{2\partial c^2}e^2 + \frac{\partial u^3}{3\partial c^3}e^3 + \ldots$$

where the expansion evaluates the impact on investors' utility of an increasing series of powers of the disturbance e. Given the normality assumption usually made in the sort of simple theoretical models I consider in this text we can safely ignore powers beyond the second moment (remember the scale and scope of the normal distribution is entirely characterized by its mean and standard deviation). So the Taylor's series expansion contracts to

$$u(c - p) = u(c) - p\frac{\partial u}{\partial c}e + \frac{\delta u^2}{2\partial c^2}e^2$$

$$\Rightarrow u(c - p) = u(c) - p\frac{\partial u}{\partial c}e + \frac{\partial u^2}{\partial c^2}e^2 + higher\ order\ terms$$

Taking expectations and recalling the expected value of the disturbance to consumption, e, is zero (otherwise there is nothing very disturbing about it!) we obtain

$$u(c) - p = u(c) + \frac{\partial u}{\partial c}0 + \frac{\partial u^2}{\partial c^2}\mathrm{var}(e)$$

$$p = -\frac{\frac{\partial u^2}{\delta c^2}}{2\frac{\partial u}{\partial c}}\mathrm{var}(e)$$

where this measure is the Arrow–Pratt measure of risk aversion (Pratt 1964, Arrow 1970), which I denote r_{AP} (following Shefrin 2005). We can apply this risk measure to the utility function used to measure the utility of the future path of consumption in Equation (8.1), where we have

$$\frac{\delta u}{\delta c} = c^{-\gamma}$$

$$\frac{\partial^2 u}{\partial c^2} = -\gamma c^{-\gamma - 1}$$

$$cr_{AP}(c) = \frac{-c\left(-\gamma c^{-\gamma - 1}\right)}{c^{-\gamma}}$$

Recall the investor is willing to pay some premium p to avoid an uncertain path of future income, i.e. to be able to guarantee future consumption. Here this premium is just a per-unit of risk assumed ($\delta u/\delta c = c - y$) constant that does not vary as that uncertainty increases. This seems to contradict the intuition that as we assume more risk we demand a higher price to bear it.

Questions

1. Consider a stock in Bim PLC you bought for $50 a month ago. You notice it is now trading at $40. What do you do, sell your Bim PLC share or not? Assume there are no taxes or other costs of trading. Explain your choice of action.

   Now suppose there was a tax offset that you could claim on capital losses, which there generally are. You notice that Bom PLC has a very similar price to Bim PLC and offers a very similar average return to Bim PLC for a very similar risk profile (market beta and factor loadings on various other priced characteristics like size and the market-to-book ratio). Maybe you could go for a 'tax swap', selling your Bim PLC share, buying one in Bom PLC and getting that nice bit of tax relief from your losses on holding Bim? What do you think? Explain your choice to go for the 'tax swap' or not.

2. Return to Table 8.2 and Figure 8.5 in the numerical illustration of cumulative prospect theory. Suppose the rules of the game change. If you roll the die and it comes up an even number you pay (not receive) that amount, if it lands on an odd amount you receive, not pay, that amount. What do the objective probability function (p) and cumulative probability weight function (w) look like now?

3. In my discussion of the experimental evidence I told you investors are risk seeking over low probability gains, but risk averse to small probability losses. Does my numerical example exactly capture this distinction? How would it deal with a 'worst-case scenario' (Sunstein 2007) of landing a five in the original example, or a six in the revised version given in Question 2?

4. Prospect theory seems to get everywhere, the Internet bubble, IPOs, the race-track, etc. Camerer (2000) gives 10 such illustrative applications. Can you think of financial decisions, problems, about where prospect theory decision making might apply or explain phenomena that standard theory struggles with?

Note

1. 'Sid' appeared in adverts for the British Gas privatization. Sid bought stock because 'he just wanted to be part of it', easy money being too base a motive for public utterance it appears.

References

Arrow, K. (1970). *Essays in the Theory of Risk Bearing*. Amsterdam: North-Holland.

Barberis, N. & M. Huang (2008). Stocks as lotteries: implications of probability weighting for security prices. *American Economic Review*, December: 2066–100.

Barberis, N., M. Huang & T. Santos (2001). Prospect theory and asset prices. *Quarterly Journal of Economics*, **116**(1): 1–53.

Bernartzi, S. & R. Thaler (2001). Myopic risk-aversion and the equity premium puzzle. *Quarterly Journal of Economics*, **116**(1): 1–53.

Camerer, C. (2000). Prospect theory in the wild: evidence from the field. In D. Kahneman & A. Tversky (eds), *Choice Values and Frames*. New York: Cambridge University Press.

De Bondt, W. (1998). A portrait of the individual investor. *European Economic Review*, **42**: 831–44.

De George, F., J. Patel *et al.* (1999). Earnings management to exceed thresholds. *Journal of Business*, **72**(1): 1–33.

Kahneman, D. & A. Tversky (1989). Prospect theory: an analysis of decision under risk. *Econometrica*, **47**(2): 263–91.

Lewis, M. (2000). *The Next New Thing: A Silicon Valley Story*. New York: W.W. Norton.

Ljungqvist, A. & W. Wilhelm (2005). Does prospect theory explain IPO market behaviour? *Journal of Finance*, **60**(4): 1759–90.

Loughran, T. & J. Ritter (2002). Why don't issuers get upset about leaving money on the table in IPOs? *Review of Financial Studies*, **15**(2): 413–43.

Montier, J. (2006). *Behavioural Finance: Insights into Irrational Minds and Markets*. Chichester: John Wiley & Sons, Ltd.

Pratt, J. (1964). Risk aversion in the small and the large. *Econometrica*, **32**: 122–36.

Schlarbaum, R. *et al.* (1984). Realized returns on common stock investments. *Journal of Business*: 299–325.

Shefrin, H. (2002). *Beyond Greed and Fear: Understanding Behavioral Finance and the Psychology of Investing*. Oxford: Oxford University Press.

Shefrin, H. (2005). *A Behavioral Approach to Asset Pricing*. New York: Elsevier.

Shefrin, H. & M. Statman (1985). The disposition to sell winners too early and ride losers too long. *Journal of Finance*, **XL**(3): 777–90.

Shiller, R. (1981). Do stock prices move too much to be justified by subsequent changes in dividends? *American Economic Review*, **71**(3): 421–36.

Sunstein, C. (2007). *Worst-Case Scenarios*. Cambridge, MA: Harvard University Press.

Tversky, A. & D. Kahneman (2000). Advances in prospect theory: cumulative representation of uncertainty. In D. Kahneman & A. Tversky (eds), *Choice Values and Frames*. Cambridge: Cambridge University Press.

Chapter 9

Overreaction and/or Underreaction

The tendency to follow trends is one of the basic traits of human nature and in much of financial decision making too. The BRICs (Brazil, Russia, India and China) are today's hot-ticket investment, so I will follow the crowd and pile in. This proclivity was discussed in Chapter 3 where I introduced the representativeness heuristic resulting from excessive weighting being put on recent trends by investors, relative to the secular, base case, prior probability. For Shefrin (2005), in his construction of a complete behavioural theory of asset pricing, this is the single defining characteristic of the behavioural approach.

It was the recognition that simple contrarian trading strategies could be profitable that was in many ways the starting gun for a resurgence of interest in fundamentals-based valuation analysis and much of the behavioural finance research that parallels these trends (in Chapter 19 I examine the use of accounting valuation metrics in valuing equities). This chapter focuses on the emergence of such trends, their dissipation and reversal. It does so using the noise-trader modelling framework of Chapter 6. This chapter should help you understand that model more, as well as the insights that the noise-trader structure can give to the emergence of stock price trends and their reversal.

9.1   Illustration and Structure

Investors follow trends. One of the central lessons of the behavioural approach is that they follow them too closely, failing to realize what goes up must come down and may do so with an unpleasant bump. Lakonishok *et al.* (1994) examine a number of fairly simple-minded strategies based on selling stocks that appear overvalued on the basis of simple ratios like price-to-book value, earnings-to-book value and price-to cash-flow (sometimes called 'glamour' stocks because they seem so shiny and glamorous), using the proceeds to purchase those that appear undervalued on the basis of the same ratios (the so-called 'value' stock because they seem cheap at the price given their fundamentals). The theory underlying such simple contrarian strategies derives from our good old favourite the Gordon growth model, $D_t + 1/(r - g)$, which states price as a function of future discounted (at some discount rate r) dividends (D) and their expected future growth rate (g, $g < r$). Higher cash-flows, or earnings, now come at the cost of future investment and so high price-to-earnings or price-to-cash-flow stocks should be heading for a fall; their shiny glamour denoting troubles ahead. Lakonishok *et al.* (1994) find that this is indeed the case with numerous single ratio based trading strategies of this type yielding almost absurdly high returns to buying and holding for five years. The obvious explanation, which might bring some comfort to efficient market theory fans, is risk, but such simple-minded contrarian strategies seem to work particularly well in market downturns, when investors really need the cash, and are certainly no worse overall.

How can such a simple trading strategy make money? Lakonishok *et al.* (1994) argue that investors may simply extrapolate current performance, but they do so too far and ignore the fact that extraordinarily good performance is just that, out of the ordinary, and ultimately a reversal of fortune is very likely to occur. Lakonishok *et al.* (1994, p.543) state the extrapolation hypothesis as follows:

> Contrarian strategies work because they exploit expectational errors implicit in stock prices. Specifically, the differences in expected growth rates between glamour and value stocks implicit in their relative valuation significantly overestimate actual future growth differences.

More empirical evidence can be found in Montier (2006, especially Section 3.8). Montier divides value strategy drivers into profitability, leverage and liquidity and operating efficiency and discusses the evidence for each type.

Section 9.2 presents a unified model of stock-market overreaction and a resulting corrective phase together with some casual evidence to suggest investors do indeed 'extrapolate' trends too much in their trades and are then forced to unwind the resulting positions in their portfolio. Where do these trends come from? Section 9.3 gives one answer, earnings expectations as captured by consensus analysts' forecasts of future earnings.

After reading this chapter the reader should:

- Understand how stock-market overreaction and underreaction fit together in a common analytical framework.
- Know what might drives them both, i.e. changes in earnings expectations.
- Understand what the pattern of overreaction and corrective underreaction looks like in actual markets.

9.2 The DHS Model

Daniel, Hirshleifer and Subrahmanyam (1998) constructed a model (hereafter the DHS model) of two types of investors trading across four time periods. The two sorts of investors are informed investors, I, who each receive a 'private' information signal in the second time period; and uninformed investors, who are reliant on public information alone to value the asset. The 'time line' of the model's investment process is given in Figure 9.1. Investors start in time period 0 with an endowment. At this point all investors are equally well informed. Later in period 1 the informed investors receive

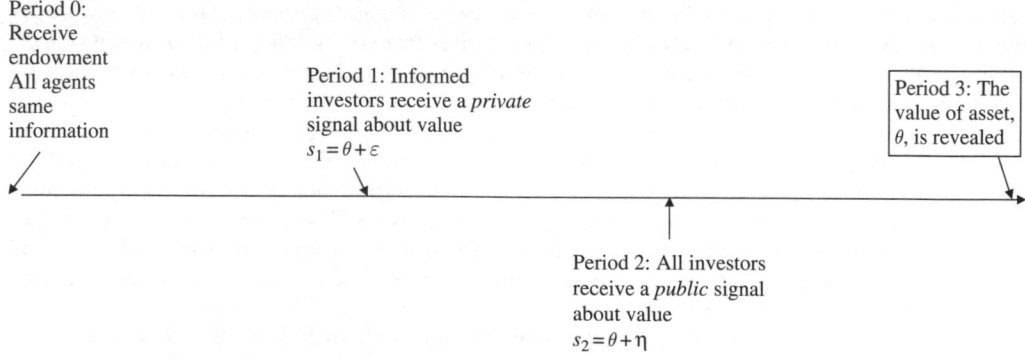

Figure 9.1 The time line of trade in the DHS model

signals about the value of the asset, s_1 at period 1 and an analogous signal regarding true asset value s_2 at period 2 of the form

$$s_1 = \theta + \varepsilon$$
$$s_2 = \theta + \eta$$

where θ is the true value of the asset and ε is some private signal only received by the informed at period 1 and η is a public signal received by all investors at period 2. Further the DHS model assumes

$$\theta \sim N(\overline{\theta}, \sigma_\theta^2)$$
$$\varepsilon \sim N(0, \sigma_\varepsilon^2)$$

Finally, it is assumed that θ, the dividend finally paid out to investors, equals zero for ease of calculation.[1]

At this point the difference between informed and uninformed investors can be introduced. The Bayesian precision of the time period 1 signal about value is $1/\sigma_\varepsilon^2$, however, in the DHS framework informed investors are overconfident and so perceive the precision of ε to be above its true level, that is $\sigma_C^2 < \sigma_\varepsilon^2$.

The pricing of the asset in this market reflects the expectations agents have about the asset's true value, θ, at each point in time:

$$P_1 = E_C[\theta | \theta + \varepsilon],$$
$$P_2 = E_C[\theta | \theta + \varepsilon, \theta + \eta],$$
$$P_3 = \theta$$

Relying on the properties of normally distributed variables:

$$P_1 = \frac{\sigma_\theta^2}{(\sigma_\theta^2 + \sigma_C^2)}(\theta + \varepsilon),$$

$$P_2 = \frac{\sigma_\theta^2(\sigma_C^2 + \sigma_p^2)}{D}\theta + \frac{\sigma_\theta^2 \sigma_p^2}{D}\varepsilon + \frac{\sigma_\theta^2 \sigma_C^2}{D}\eta$$

$$\text{and} \quad D \equiv \sigma_\theta^2(\sigma_C^2 + \sigma_p^2) + \sigma_C^2 \sigma_p^2 \tag{9.1}$$

To see the impact of informed investor overconfidence, suppose for a moment that informed investors become so confident that σ_C^2 converges to zero in value, then the revised pricing formulae become:

$$P_1 = \frac{\sigma_\theta^2}{\sigma_\theta^2}(\theta + \varepsilon) = \theta + \varepsilon$$

$$P_2 = \frac{\sigma_\theta^2 \sigma_C^2}{D}\theta + \frac{\sigma_\theta^2 \sigma_p^2}{D}\varepsilon$$

Note also under complete certainty of the informed investor's signal, ε, the denominator, D, of the second time period pricing expression is also changed to yield:

$$D_C = \sigma_\theta^2 \sigma_p^2$$

$$\Rightarrow P_2 = \frac{\sigma_\theta^2 \sigma_p^2}{\sigma_\theta^2 \sigma_p^2}\theta + \frac{\sigma_\theta^2 \sigma_p^2}{\sigma_\theta^2 \sigma_p^2}\varepsilon = \theta + \varepsilon \tag{9.2}$$

So if informed investors become supremely confident of the value of their private signal about the asset in time period 2, ε, the stock market no longer reflects the information in the second period's public signal and price changes between periods 1 and 2 would be driven to zero. Returns between periods 1 and 2 are a diminishing function of informed investors' confidence. Informed investors are unshakable in their belief in the predictive power of the private signal, ε, and so cannot be moved to trade based upon new information in the public signal, η, received at period 2. Such a world requires that informed investors retain a little bit of doubt about how useful the period 2 private signal they receive about asset value, ε, actually is in predicting the liquidating dividend θ.

9.2.1 Reversals of Fortune

Figure 9.2 shows the pattern of price movements predicted by the DHS modelling framework. After an initial overreaction between periods 0 (the initial period when no-one knows anything about value) and 1 due to informed investors' overconfidence in the signal they receive, ε, at period 1, a correction sets in between periods 1 and 2. This correction is motivated by the arrival of the public signal, η, received by all investors regardless of whether they received a private signal or not. This gives the market a nudge towards the true value, θ, before it is, finally, shoved into place when the liquidating dividend is paid at period 3. Consequently the model predicts price increases between periods 1 and 2, motivated by the overconfidence of informed investors in their private signals, s_1 and s_2, will be reversed between periods 2 and 3 when the true value is ultimately revealed as θ. So period 1 to 2 returns are negatively correlated with period 2 to 3 returns, or their covariance is negative, $\text{Cov}(P_2 - P_1, P_1 - P_0) < 0$.

This market correction, or reversal of fortune, occurs in two stages in the DHS framework. First the public signal, η (recall nobody is overconfident about the value of that), so if it has any informative value about θ it will push price towards true value. The final stage of the market correction is at period 3 and the liquidating dividend is paid. Given all this we expect the covariance of security returns between periods 1 and 2 and periods 2 and 3 to be positive as the full body of the correction phase unwinds, so $\text{Cov}(P_3 - P_2, P_2 - P_1) > 0$. So post-event 'drift' following events like earnings announcements, which give public signals regarding company value, are a direct implication of the DHS model. I try to illustrate how this might occur in practice using some numerical illustrations below.

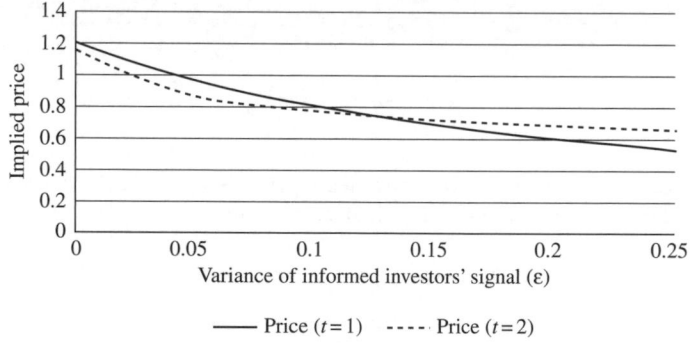

Figure 9.2 Price changes with informed investor confidence in the DHS model

Heads I win. Tails it's chance

Informed investors' optimism about their private signal is not the full story; that is, it is not solely optimism that drives the post value-relevant event. This arises from the combination of informed investor optimism with another important psychological trait: self-attribution bias, or our belief that good things happen because we are smart, but bad things happen because the world is stupid. Some of my research papers are published because they are brilliant contributions to world knowledge. Sadly, others are suppressed by ignorant editors and referees who just cannot understand how great my work is. Daniel *et al.* (1998) term this sort of bias 'Heads I win. Tails it's chance'. Students might recognize this as our tendency as teachers to assume good pass rates are achieved because we are great teachers, but attribute high failure rates to the laziness of our students (or to your own hard work if you are a student who passes your exam, but to a poor teacher if you failed).

In order to capture this in their model Daniel *et al.* (1998) consider a very simple version of the period 2 public signal η. This is termed the simplified signal s_2 and it has one of two possible values: either 1 ('good news') or -1 ('bad news'). The model allows for, but does not impose, informed investor overconfidence in the private signal they receive about the value, i.e. $\sigma_C^2 \leq \sigma_\varepsilon^2$. However, the model is adjusted so informed investors get a bit ahead of themselves in believing in the wisdom of their private signal if the public signal, s_2, confirms their private signal ε. Informed investor confidence thus follows the rule.

If $\text{sign}(\theta + \varepsilon) = \text{sign}(s_2)$ then informed investor confidence contracts to

$$\sigma_C^2 - k, \quad k > 0 \tag{9.3}$$

If the signs of the public and private signals disagree then no diminution in confidence occurs. So it truly is 'Heads I win. Tails it's chance'. If the public signal, s_2, confirms the prior private signal received by informed investors, ε, then they increase their confidence in the private signal's worth in predicting true value. But when the public signal flatly contradicts the prior private signal informed investors received, then best not to worry, and they carry on as if nothing has changed from period 1, or as if s_2 doesn't exist.

9.2.2 Pricing When Confidence Levels Depend on the Relation Between the Public and Private Signals

By now you might be thinking stop making life so complicated! The original DHS model, with confident informed investors, worked really well. Why bother about whether that overconfidence fluctuates with its relation to the public signal, s_2, announced at period 2? At period 1 you would be absolutely right, of course, introducing outcome-dependent overconfidence has no effect on the solution for period 1 price, which remains as it was in our original version of the DHS model as presented in Equation (9.1). As before we have

$$P_1 = \frac{\sigma_\theta^2}{(\sigma_\theta^2 + \sigma_C^2)} (\theta + \varepsilon)$$

where for a perfectly trusted signal price at period 1 price once again degenerates to $\theta + \varepsilon$.

It is at period 2 that the outcome-dependent confidence model comes into its own, because the solution for price at period 2 changes from that in the original model and presented in Equation (9.1). Recall the presence of overconfidence in the value of the private signal the informed investors receive in period 2, s_2, if that private signal confirms the prior private signal about asset value the informed investors received at period 1, i.e. ε. This contracts the noise attributed to that signal s_2 by the 'early' informed so $\sigma_C^2 \leq \sigma_\varepsilon^2$. So the revised solution for the period 2 price in the presence of outcome-dependent confidence becomes:

$$P_{2C} = \frac{\sigma_\theta^2}{\sigma_\theta^2 + \sigma_C^2 - k}(\theta + \varepsilon) \tag{9.4}$$

where the subscript C on period 2 price captures its dependence on the informed investors' confidence. The parameter k captures the step increase in confidence in the precision of the informed investors' private signal about value, ε. Here greater confidence raises price responsiveness to investors' understanding of true value, given here by conjectures about the distribution of the liquidating dividend payable, and the informed investors' private signal, i.e. $\theta + \varepsilon$.

Daniel *et al.* (1998) focus in particular on when company management can 'select' the public event. Often this is the case, think for example of management chances, rights issues or the decision to go public. Even in an earnings announcement some 'earnings management' can nudge announced earnings per share in line with analysts' expectations. Daniel *et al.* (1998) focus on such 'selection' of the public signal, η, sent by managers in response to their perception of how well the current stock price reflects fundamental value.

A simulated numerical example

We have already determined that if informed investors feel perfectly confident in their private signal, prices will not change as we pass from period 1 to 2. But let's say they are just a teeny bit worried, what then? Figure 9.3 undertakes a comparative statistic exercise using the solutions for price given in Equation (9.1). I do this invoking the base case valuation assumptions given in Table 9.1.

Figure 9.3 also makes clear the impact of diminishing confidence in the informed investors' signal, ε, is felt fairly early on (at values of σ_C^2 between 0.05 and 0.1, recall we are modelling the overconfident beliefs about value here and so $\sigma_C^2 \leq \sigma_\varepsilon^2$), but dies out fairly quickly. Once the variability of the informed investors' signal rises above 0.2, at 0.25, the informed investor is better

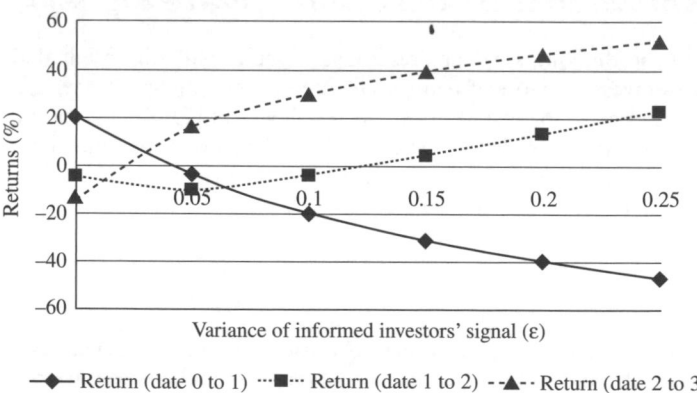

Figure 9.3   Return trajectories over four trading periods in the DHS model

Table 9.1   Base case values for numerical illustrations of the
DHS model

Parameter	Value
Θ	1
$(\theta + \varepsilon)$	1.2
$(\theta + \eta)$	1.15
$\sigma_\theta^2 = \sigma_C^2$	0.2

off ignoring it in favour of the period 0 indication of value, θ. This makes sense of course. Why bother about trying to impound into prices the impact of such an unreliable signal? If it's that bad maybe you're better off ignoring it.

Given the implied solutions for prices at each period in the DHS model I now proceed to explore the implicit patterns of returns and hence covariances derived from these solutions for price. Figure 9.3 plots returns for between periods 0 and 1, 1 and 2 and, finally, between periods 2 and 3. Recall the initial values of our numerical illustration, given in Table 9.1, allow for an optimistic shock to expectations of value amongst informed investors, ε indicates asset value is 1.2, not its real value θ of 1. This initiates an overreaction of price between periods 0 and 1, as informed investors place too much weight on their private signal about value ε. The public signal at least partially corrects that misleading idea about value taking, indicating a value of 1.15. This public signals starts the 'correction' phase, which is finished the next period between periods 2 and 3 prior to the payment of terminal dividend of θ. Figure 9.3 confirms this basic pattern, at least when informed investors are fairly confident in the private signal about true value they receive. Recall for $\sigma_C^2 > 0.2$ or $\frac{1}{\sigma_C^2} > 5$ the numerical illustration here. As informed investors become less confident in the private signal about value they receive periods 1 to 2 and 2 to 3 returns slowly converge. Recall no one is overconfident about the public signal, η, but the informed investors are overconfident about their private signal, ε, so $\sigma_C^2 \leq \sigma_\varepsilon^2$, i.e. as informed investors see their private signal, ε, as more precise than it truly is. In this numerical simulation I fix the variance of the public signal, σ_p^2 or to be 0.2. So the area to the left near the horizontal axis is indeed the place where one expects to find the DHS model's predictions regarding market corrections to prior overreactions to be verified. My numerical illustration here may give us a little bit of confidence that the DHS model could be a credible story of market over-/underreactions to events signalling the future value of assets.

Numerical example with outcome-dependent confidence

What happens when we allow informed investors' confidence to depend on whether the public signal received at 2η confirms or refutes their private signal from period 1? If it does then informed investors become a lot more confident. I undertake this numerical illustration retaining all the initial values in Table 9.1, but keep informed investor confidence in the private signal, σ_C^2, at 0.2, while increasing k in Equation (9.4) by 5% increments from 0 to 25%. Figures 9.4 and 9.5 show the results of this numerical exercise on prices at periods 1 and 2 and returns across periods 0 to 3, respectively.

The impact of a boost to informed investor confidence, rising k, is to boost period 2 price (see Figure 9.4) and so raise period 1 to 2 returns on the traded risky asset (see Figure 9.5). As in the simple case without outcome-dependent confidence (presented in Figures 9.2 and 9.3), the greater the period 1 overreaction the greater the period 2 to 3 resulting correction.

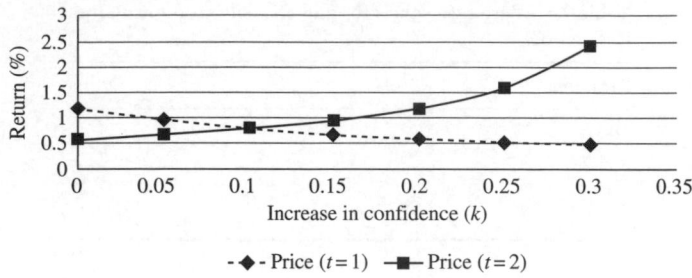

Figure 9.4   Pricing in the DHS model when public signal confirms private signal

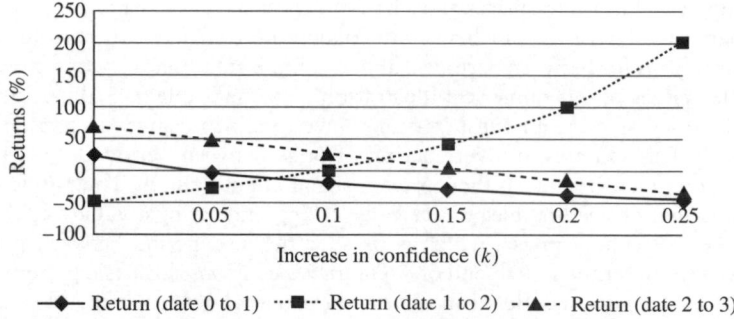

Figure 9.5   Return on periods 0 to 3 when public signal confirms private signal

9.2.3   *Investor Extrapolation and Reversals of Fortune*

The DHS model of an initial overreaction followed by a subsequent correction phase does seem broadly consistent with the 'extrapolation hypothesis' advanced by Lakonishok *et al.* (1994) mentioned briefly in Section 9.1. Those authors tested a number of trading strategies based on buying and holding portfolios of stocks on the New York Stock Exchange in the years 1968–90. These strategies buy 'value' stocks, i.e. stocks that seem good value in the sense of having high book-to-market values, or earnings-to-price ratios, and funding the purchase by selling 'glamour' stocks, which have the reverse characteristics. The authors begin by ranking stocks on the NYSE from most 'glamorous', those in the lowest book-to-market decile (portfolio 1), to the most 'valuable' in the tenth decile, of highest book-to-market and earnings-to-price stocks (portfolio 10). They then sell glamour stocks in portfolio 1 and buy value stocks in portfolio 10 and hold the resulting net position for five years. The profits from this strategy are shown in Figure 9.6 for the book-to-market ratio trading strategy and Figure 9.7 gives the profits to a similar trading strategy based on the earnings-to-price ratio.

9.2.4   *Many Theories in Search of a Decisive Verification*

The confluence of initial overreaction, followed by subsequent market correction, has become the central problem for behavioural approaches to asset pricing. One very straightforward, if sceptical,

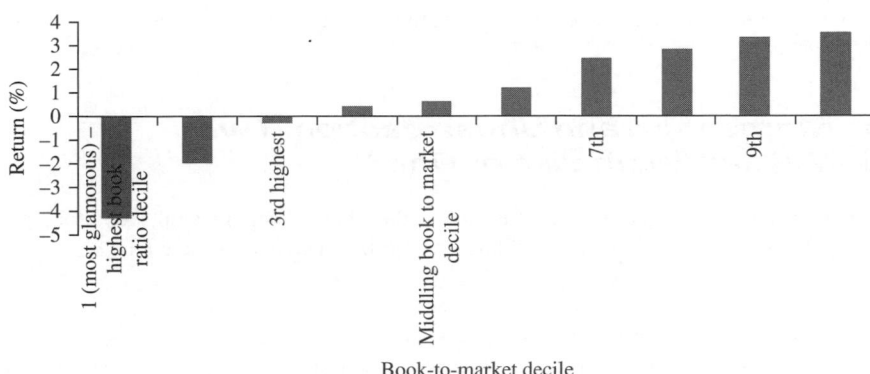

Figure 9.6   Return to 'value/glamour' five-year buy and hold strategy based on book-to-market decile

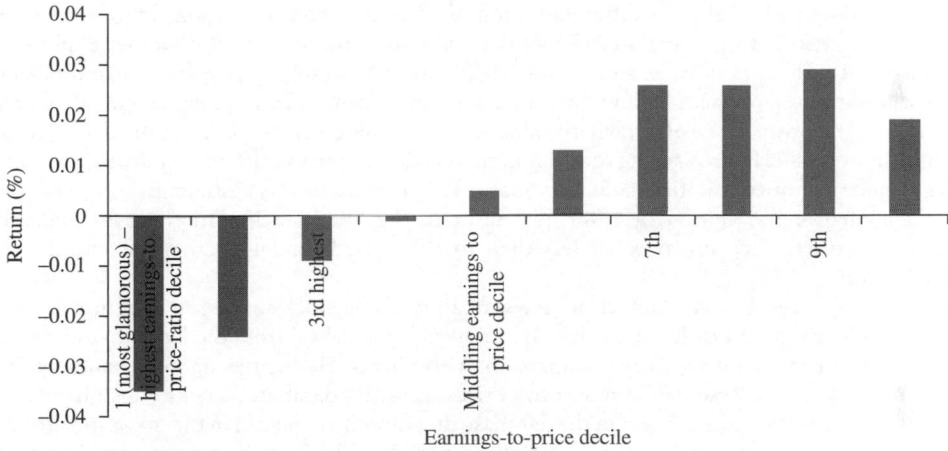

Figure 9.7   Return to five-year 'value vs. glamour' strategy based on the earnings-to-price ratio

approach to the issue is that of Eugene Fama (1998). Fama observes that if some researchers find overreaction in security markets and others find underreaction it is possible that some average across all the evidence simply implies that in most cases the market prices assets at near what they are worth. After all when using a 95% statistical confidence interval 1 in 20 studies will find a significant result even if in truth there is no pattern at all of consequence in the data. Researchers and academic journals like to publish positive results, 'we find this', not 'we tortured the data, but it just would not confess'. So it is possible that reported results are just a statistical mirage.

Yet the finance research literature almost groans under the weight of competing reconciliations of overreaction and underreaction phenomena. Is it overconfidence in private signals, as modelled by the DHS model? Or some market outcome produced by the meeting of trend chasing and partially informed fundamental traders in the market, as suggested by Harrison Hong and Jeremy Stein (1999)? Or, alternatively, something to do with investors' inability to learn the time-series properties of earnings from observed outcomes (Barberis *et al.* 1998)? We appear theory rich, but results poor, and we seem to await a decisive set of results to motivate both underreaction and overreaction in security markets.

9.2.5 Momentum and Underreaction: Two Stock-Market Anomalies or One?

Many 'event studies' record the impact of events in the life of companies on their stock price. The appendix to Daniel *et al.* (1998) gives an exhaustive list but such events include:

- mergers;
- dividend initiations and omissions;
- chief executive turnover, due to death or poor performance;
- initial public offerings of equity to the public;
- (seasoned) equity offerings by companies already listed on an exchange;
- earnings announcements.

These studies invoke a slightly different notion of efficiency than the standard threefold categorization of Harry Roberts ((Roberts 1967): weak, semi-strong and strong). Rather they explore some more vague idea that prices are in some sense 'right', given the resulting payoffs to investors and the rate of discount used on them by investors. Prices are inefficient in this 'fundamental value' sense if they drift too far from 'true value', where value is the discounted value of future dividends, or some multiple of forecasted future earnings etc. It is hard to say when prices drift 'too far' from fundamental values, rendering prices inefficient in this sense. Fisher Black in his Presidential Address to the American Finance Association in 1986 (just prior to the 1987 stock-market crash) suggested a boundary of price being no more or less than twice implied fundamental made intuitive sense (Black 1986).

Chan (2003) focuses on the impact of 'news' of all types on stock-market momentum and reversion. Chan identifies a portfolio of stocks who received some 'news' from the Dow Jones Interactive Publications, a large database of newspapers and periodicals. He focuses upon a randomly drawn quarter of the Chicago Research into Security Prices securities database. Stocks which have at least one 'news' story written about them in the database that month are placed in the 'news' portfolio, the remainder of stocks enter the 'no news' portfolio. Chan then observes the sequences of returns over subsequent months. He finds that momentum is clustered in the 'news' portfolio, with price shocks to the 'no news' portfolio being negated the following month. The impact of 'bad news' is markedly strong with negative shocks, motivated by bad news, and persists for a year or more. This implies that investors are particularly slow to impound bad news about a company into its price.

9.3 No News Is ...?

While Chan draws out the importance of news for market mispricing, a large prior literature speaks of the significance of 'non-events', or 'noise' for security pricing. Cutler *et al.* (1989) report a study of large price movements in the United States in the years 1926–85. These authors divide value-relevant news about equities into two types:

- Standard quantitative metrics, dividends, interest rates, money supply, etc.
- Major events, the Cuban missile crisis in 1962, President Eisenhower's heart attack in 1955, the assassination of President Kennedy in 1963.

Focusing on large stock price movements over the study period, Cutler *et al.* find little correspondence between stock price movements and either news from changes in quantitative metrics or major events. Combining all observable sources of news, Cutler *et al.* can explain less than half the variance in stock prices over the period by reference to observable news events. Indeed many major stock-market movements, such as the October 1987 crash, appear to be associated with only the most ephemeral news items. The authors conclude their work by suggesting that often large movements in stock prices result from a reinterpretation of existing facts, no new facts as such.

Trading is a social process that 'propagates' relatively small changes in cash-flow or discount-rate projections into far larger anticipated movements in price as the information diffuses through the market and so induces 'excess volatility'. Hence noise traders can create their own, often widening, space without any change in the fundamental indicators of value for traded stocks.

Andrew Jackson and Tim Johnson (2006) have suggested that this attempt to reconcile over-reaction and underreaction may be pointless since both are in reality manifestations of the same phenomenon, the arrival of news, especially about earnings, into the stock market.

9.3.1   The Jackson and Johnson (JJ) Model's Message

Jackson and Johnson constructed a model of overreaction/momentum and underreaction/reversion as a part of a unified cycle of response to news about firm value conveyed by earnings. 'News' in the present context is given a very specific definition, that is news about value or innovations in value (via earnings or dividends) are deviations from investors' conditional expectations of that value attribute. Is it possible what we call 'momentum' in stock prices is just the aggregate aftershocks of all the good and bad news about individual companies? Of course Chan's (2003) study already tries to address this issue by simply looking at all news reported about companies. This is a truly mammoth task, given the vast range of possible stories and fora for discussion now available to investors via for example newspapers, blogs and Internet chat rooms. Jackson and Johnson (2006) seek out an easier solution by constructing a measure of what constitutes 'news' about shareholder value in real-world security markets. News is clearly some deviation from what investors currently expect, given the information they have – what statisticians call our benchmark expectation. It is devising such an appropriate benchmark that is the core of Jackson and Johnson's contribution.

Jackson and Johnson find that the key variable underpinning investors' conditional expectation of future stock returns is expectations of future earnings as captured by monthly consensus forecasts of earnings. They believe their results open the possibility of uncovering a common cause of both momentum and underreaction in their emergence from news about earnings. Jackson and Johnson state (2006, p.77):

> Our findings are that both momentum and drift observed after several previously studied types of event are coincident with changes in either expected earnings or expected earnings growth and that changes in the latter two quantities account for all subsequently observed abnormal performance. Holding these expectations fixed there is no momentum effect.

So the JJ model finds momentum in stock returns. But this momentum exists because stock price movements presage and predict future changes in earnings. The part of past price changes that is not indicative of future earnings and future earnings growth is of no use in predicting future stock returns.

Most of the drift associated with various corporate events results from their ability to embed market expectations of future earnings levels and growth on that level of earnings. So once we control for such shocks to earnings expectations such events have no further predictive power.

Jackson and Johnson test the hypothesis that the predictability of major corporate events derives from what those events divulge about changes in earnings expectations by examining four types of corporate event:

- seasoned equity offerings;
- share repurchases;
- stock-financed mergers;
- dividend initiations and omissions.

In each case after controlling for changes in investors' expectations regarding the future level and growth in earnings these various events have no ability to predict earnings.

What does this all mean? Jackson and Johnson suggest two possible interpretations of their results:

- Analysts' forecasts of earnings could just be very good proxies for all the short-sighted, ignorant, errors that stock prices impound, this tends to favour behavioural perspectives on asset pricing.
- Alternatively, investors could just be very smart and pick up straight away the implications for future earnings of various types of earnings and adjust asset prices appropriately. This second interpretation sees behavioural theories as rushing to solve a puzzle or problem where none exists. If this second story is to hold true we need pretty clear theories of how an event like a seasoned equity offering tells investors so much about the path of future earnings.

9.3.2   How the JJ Model Works

The conditional expectation of a variable is that expectation which minimizes the prediction error made using information available to the decision maker. More formally the conditional expectation of some price (P), given that dividends (D) take a particular value d for future dividend payments, $g(P,D)$ dividend $D = d$ is expressed (Moody et $al.$ 1974, p.157) as:

$$\varepsilon[g(P,D)|D=d] = \int_{-\infty}^{\infty} g(p,d) f_{p|d}(p|d)$$

if (P,D) are jointly continuous, and

$$\varepsilon[g(P,D)|D=d] = \sum_{j} (p,d_j) f_{p|d}(d_j|p)$$

if they are jointly discrete, where the summation is performed over all possible values of the dividend payable. In both cases the conditional expectation is simply possible outcomes multiplied by the possibility of their occurrence once we have observed current price.

To begin let i_t^* be a vector of parameters that impact upon firm value and $\{i_t\}$ is a noisy series that will eventually converge on i^*_t. Then

$$E_t(i^*) = i_t + E_t \sum_{k=0}^{\infty} E_t(\Delta i_{t+k}). \tag{9.5}$$

So the true measure of the amount of news about, or 'shock' to, firm value captured by ξ is a measure of innovations in available information about firm value, where

$$\xi_t \equiv E_t(i^*) - E_{t-1}(i^*) = \sum_{k=0}^{\infty} [E_t(\Delta i_{t+k}) - E_{t-1}(\Delta i_{t+k})] \tag{9.6}$$

Our estimate of ξ remains valid even if the estimate we make for it never converges to 'true' i_t. All that is required is that any element of bias in estimating ξ is stationary and hence declines in importance over time. For ease of exposition we follow Jackson and Johnson in assuming that $\{i\}$ is a series of monthly consensus forecasts of earnings.

Jackson and Johnson begin by letting the stock-market return in month t be a function of last month's innovation ξ_{t1}, so we have:

$$r_t = \alpha_0 + \alpha_1' \xi_{t-1} + \varepsilon_t^{(0)} \tag{9.7}$$

Hence stock returns are a function of 'news' about fundamentals alone. Here I consider only Jackson and Johnson's basic model with one-period ahead effects (so $E(r_t + 2)$ is a constant).

While movements in stock returns are purely a function of last period's 'news' (about earnings), recent stock returns are part of 'news' conveyed by Δ_i. So Δ_i becomes a dynamic function of its own past and stock returns' past history

$$\Delta i_t = \mu + A(L)\Delta i_{t-1} + a(L)\tilde{r}_{t-1} + \varepsilon_t^{(1)}$$

where A is a sequence of p lagged values of Δ_i and r_t, where a third-order 'polynomial' implies an expression of the form

$$\Delta i = \mu + A_1 \Delta i_{t-1} + A_2 \Delta i_{t-2} + A_3 \Delta i_{t-3} + a_1 \tilde{r}_{t-1} + a_2 r_{t-2} + a_3 r_{t-3} + \varepsilon_t^{(1)}$$

for example, where $\varepsilon_t^{(1)}$ is simply unpredictable 'noise' in observed innovations about value.

While Δ_{it} determines r_t, r_t is itself a function of Δ_{it}. In the resulting simultaneous equation system conditional expectations are generated as follows:

$$\mathbf{F} = [I - \mathbf{A}(1) - \boldsymbol{\alpha}(1)\boldsymbol{\alpha}_1']^{-1}$$

$$\mathbf{E} = \mathbf{F}\mathbf{a}(1)\boldsymbol{\alpha}_1'$$

$$\lambda_t = \left[\varepsilon_t^{(1)} + \mathbf{a}(1)\tilde{r}_t\right] \tag{9.8}$$

where $\mathbf{A}, \mathbf{E}, \mathbf{F}, \boldsymbol{\alpha}$ and $\mathbf{a}$ are matrices/vectors of parameters capturing the relation between current stock prices and past 'news' including the path of stock returns last month.

Substituting into the return generating equation, Equation (9.7), we obtain

$$r_t = \alpha_0 + \alpha_1'(I + \mathbf{E}L)^{-1}\mathbf{F}\lambda_{t-1} + \varepsilon_t^{(0)} \tag{9.9}$$

which is a simple regression of stock returns on the 'filtered' series $\{\lambda\}$. The relatively straightforward regression of r_t on 'corrected' innovations in (earnings) news is rendered more complex by the dependence of the parameter matrices $\mathbf{E}$ and $\mathbf{F}$ on α_1'. Therefore even though the JJ model posits only simple linear dynamics in 'news' and past stock returns, this nevertheless results in a nonlinear model for predicting returns.

Jackson and Johnson estimate the innovations in Equation (9.6) by ordinary least squares inserting its product of monthly estimated innovations λ_t into the returns equation (9.9), which they then estimate by nonlinear least squares.

Given the above set up the innovations in 'news' (about earnings) in Equation (9.6) can be expressed as follows:

$$\xi_t - A\xi_t = \varepsilon_t^{(1)} + \alpha(1)\tilde{r}_t + a(1)\alpha_1'\xi_t - a(1)\alpha_1'\xi_{t-1}$$

or

$$\xi_t = (I - A)^{-1}\{\varepsilon_t^1 + a(1)[\tilde{r}_t - \alpha_1'(\xi_{t-1} - \xi_t)]\}$$

where the latter expression comes from expanding out the individual terms of Equation (9.6). Since it is clear that the level of earnings i has no effect on 'news' (about earnings), as opposed to the level of value itself Jackson and Johnson set μ to zero without loss of generality. We observe

$$E_t(\Delta i_t) = \Delta i_t$$

$$E_t(\Delta i_{t+1}) = A\Delta i_t + a(L)E_t(\tilde{r}_{t+1})$$

$$E(\Delta i_{t+2}) = AE_t(\Delta i_{t+1}) + \mathbf{a}(L)E_t(\tilde{r}_{t+1})$$

$$= AE_t(\Delta i_{t+1}) + a_0(\alpha_1'\xi_t) + a_1\tilde{r}_t + \dots$$

$$E_t(\Delta i_{t+3}) = AE_t(\Delta i_{t+2}) + a_1(\alpha_1'\xi_t) + a_2\tilde{r}_t \qquad (9.10)$$

continuing on until, finally,

$$E_t(\Delta i_{t+k}) = AE_t(\Delta i_{t+k-1})$$

for k with a polynomial lag greater than 3.

An expression like Equation (9.9) does look rather foreboding. But the intuition underlying it underlies many problems we encounter in finance and economics. Jackson and Johnson consider the analogy of calculating the impact of 'news' about earnings on stock prices with estimating the permanent-income hypothesis consumption function. Recall the permanent-income hypothesis states that current income raises consumption to the extent of my expectation of future income. So getting promoted should increase my consumption a lot, but getting a one-off bonus payment should have almost no effect on my spending. The first thing I need to work out is how closely current and future income are related. I can do this by a regression of income on its own past values. This is an expression like Equation (9.5) for 'shocks' to permanent income, giving some idea how quickly these shocks decay. We then might ask how much a certain 'shock' to permanent consumption might affect observed spending. This might be done by means of an equation like Equation (9.7). The final test of the validity of the permanent-income hypothesis is not if current income affects consumption, but rather whether current income affects current consumption to the extent it raises the consumers' estimate of their own permanent future income: so it is important we only let current income enter the determination of current consumption in a constrained way. This is what a set of simultaneous equations like Equation (9.10) does.

Equation (9.10) tells us how shocks to expectations about the level of future earnings and the growth of that level impact upon returns, but it only allows that part of the change in earnings expectations which no one could reasonably predict, given past experience to enter the process generating returns.

9.3.3 Stock-Market Responses to News and No News

The JJ model of how news (about earnings) builds on a whole history of empirical work suggesting stock-market volatility reflects the diffusion of value-relevant information about assets, but the evidence suggesting the presence of seemingly inexplicable stock-market volatility or 'noise' should also be noted.

9.4 Conclusion and Summary

This chapter has looked at two separate stock-market anomalies that have featured heavily in behavioural finance research. I have argued that these two phenomena are best not seen as separable violations of market efficiency but as two manifestations of a common underlying cause. Daniel, Hirshleifer and Subrahmanyam emphasize the role of events 'selected' by managers to signal company value to investors, especially earning announcements. Jackson and Johnson emphasize the origin of stock-market momentum and underreaction to changes in investors' earnings expectations and how they will grow. Earnings and how they enter company valuation will be the subject of the last substantive chapter of this book (Chapter 19). But perhaps this is an area where the quip that finance is an area with much theory and no clearly supporting facts and many stylized facts for which we have no credible theory is painfully true. To this extent this chapter is a spur to challenge current ignorance rather than a statement of knowledge.

Questions

1. Return to Figures 9.2 and 9.3. Those examples modelled the impact of increasing informed investors' confidence in the period 1 signal they received, so declining σ_C^2, but what happens if informed investors just felt more confident about asset value in general, regardless of the private signal they received? Leave ε and σ_C^2 at their base values from Table 9.1 and explore reduction in the variability of θ, that is σ_θ^2 on the solution for period 1 and 2 prices and period 0 through three returns. How could investor confidence about fundamental value be increased? Is it worth the effort?
2. For the outcome-dependent confidence model I modelled a rise in investor confidence as a result of a confirmatory public signal, η, at period 2. The results are given in Figures 9.4 and 9.5. But what if the period 2 signal, η, refutes prior private signal, ε? How would the path of prices at periods 1 and 2 and returns across periods 0 to 3 change then?
3. Daniel, Hirshleifer and Subrahmanyam devote a great deal of effort to discussing earnings announcements and how they affect stock-price movements. Suppose you are Jackson and Johnson and after presenting your research results someone stands up and asks, 'You model four types of corporate events, but not earnings announcements. What you got to say about them?' How would you reply?

Note

1. Informed investors as risk-neutral investors will accept fair bets. If ε becomes very small or zero then investors face the prospect of investing for zero return. So since they are indifferent between accepting and rejecting gambles offering a zero payoff Daniel *et al.* consider the case where all informed investors accept no return to investment activity. What considerations could motivate trade despite there being no expected return to trading?

References

Barberis, N., A. Shleifer *et al.* (1998). A model of investor sentiment. *Journal of Financial Economics*, 49(3): 307–43.

Black, F. (1986). Noise. *Journal of Finance*, 61: 529–43.

Chan, W. (2003). Stock market reaction to news and no news: drift and reversal after headlines. *Journal of Financial Economics*, 70: 223–60.

Cutler, D., J. Poterba & L. Summers (1989). What moves stock prices? Moves in stock prices reflect something other than news about fundamental values. *Journal of Portfolio Management*, 15: 4–12.

Daniel, K., D. Hirshleifer & A. Subrahmanyam (1998). Investor psychology and security market under- and overreaction. *Journal of Finance*, 52: 1–33.

Fama, E. (1998). Market efficiency, long-term returns, and behavioural finance. *Journal of Financial Economics*, 49(3): 283–306.

Hong, H. & J. Stein (1999). A unified theory of underreaction, momentum, trading and overreaction in assets markets. *Journal of Finance*, 54: 2143–84.

Jackson A. & T. Johnson (2006). Unifying underreaction anomalies. *Journal of Business*, 79: 75–114.

Lakonishok, J., A. Shleifer *et al.* (1994). Contrarian investment, extrapolation and risk. *Journal of Finance*, 49(5): 1541–78.

Montier, J. (2006). *Behavioural Finance: Insights into Irrational Minds and Markets*. Chichester: John Wiley & Sons, Ltd.

Moody, A., F. Graybill & D. Boes (1974). *Introduction to the Theory of Statistics*. Singapore: McGraw-Hill.

Roberts, H. (1967). Statistical versus clinic prediction of the stock market, unpublished paper from Seminar on the Analysis of Security Prices, Chicago.

Shefrin, H. (2005). *A Behavioral Approach to Asset Pricing*. New York: Elsevier.

Chapter 10

Momentum

Trending patterns in share prices, especially following the announcement of company earnings, seems a very basic violation of stock-market efficiency indeed. The attempt to find patterns in the entrails of past prices was perhaps the original 'get rich quick' spark for serious intellectual interest in financial markets. Certainly many great minds, like the brilliant Sir Isaac Newton, lost huge amounts of money in financial speculation. The identification of 'drift' or slow dissipation of earnings 'news' through the market, occurred many years ago by Ball and Brown (1968), and as I will show, has been confirmed by more recent work. Even Eugene Fama, the father of the efficient-market hypothesis, has confessed to finding the post-earnings-announcement drift (PEAD) research evidence as 'an anomaly above suspicion' (Fama 1998). In a very similar spirit Michael Brennan (1991)* of UCLA has commented,

> Perhaps the most severe challenge to financial theorists posed on recent work to earnings announcements is the finding by Bernard and Thomas (1989, 1990) that market reaction to the current quarters' earnings can be predicted on the basis of information contained in the previous quarter's announcement, and that this phenomenon can be explained by a model in which the market uses a naive model of the stochastic process of earnings.

Is it possible that patterns in share price returns are largely driven by news about earnings? This chapter explores this possibility that stock price momentum is a consequence of a sluggish response to news about earnings.

Momentum profits from following short-run price trends are recorded by Jegadeesh and Titman (1993) for the United States and Rouwenhorst (1998) for many other countries. Jegadeesh and Titman (2005) see such trends in price and PEAD in company stock price returns as the two central anomalies in financial markets creating a demand for behavioural explanations of financial phenomena. Indeed these two phenomena may emerge from a common source of the stock market's difficulty in understanding the consequences of recent earnings information for future stock-market value (see also Chordia & Shivakumar 2006).

10.1   Illustration and Structure

Jegadeesh and Titman (1993) report the profitability of forming a portfolio over J months ($J = 3$ to 12) and holding it for K months ($K = 3$ to 12) to see how profitable short-run trend-chasing strategies can be. The answer is such momentum strategies work very well. The sort of profits recorded by Jegadeesh and Titman (1993) are given in Figures 10.1 and 10.2. The Jegadeesh and Titman (1993) original study, for which there have been many follow-up investigations on different markets and sectors, looked at the stock-market performance of the New York Stock Exchange and American Stock Exchange (NYSE-AMEX) over the years 1965–89. For both long (one year) and short (three months) portfolio formation periods this momentum trading strategy seems to yield a reliable profit.

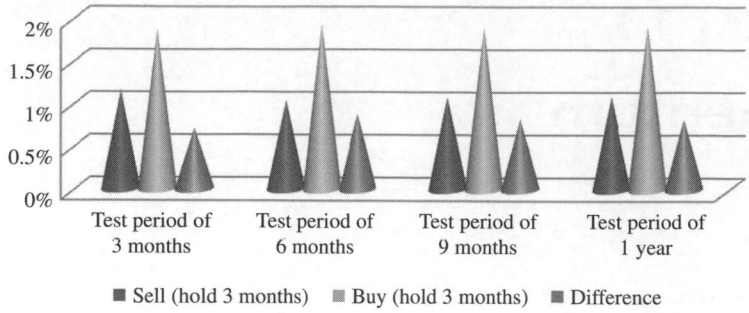

Figure 10.1   Returns to momentum trading strategy based on three-month holding period

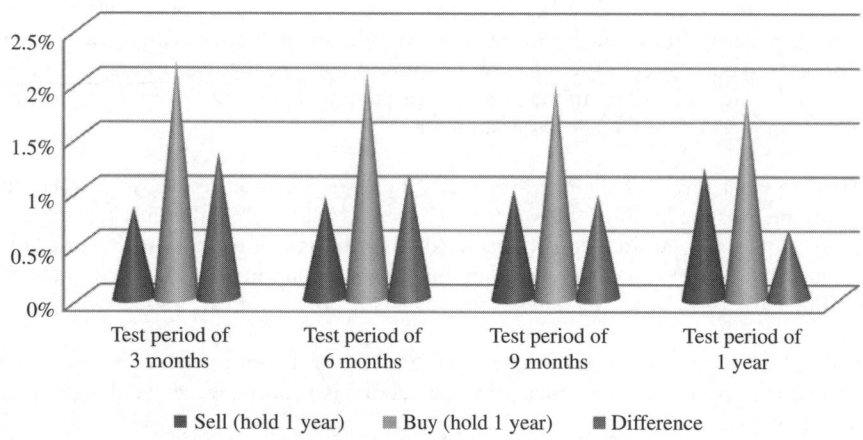

Figure 10.2   Returns to momentum trading strategy based on one-year holding period

Montier (2006, especially Section 2.9) provides evidence on the motivation and scale of momentum trading. One reason for this, which he discusses in greater length than is possible here, is the existence of limits to arbitrage to remove mispricing.

Section 10.2 discusses a simple model of stock-market momentum in response to announcements about earnings, clearly a very important indicator. This model builds on the prospect theory discussed in Chapter 2 and already used in Chapter 8 to model asset prices. Once again the role of benchmark values and particularly a failure to attain them is central to the way this model works. This chapter also attempts to bring together two modelling strategies kept apart until now.

Noise traders characterized by prospect theory style utility functions are also discussed. Noise traders and prospect theory investors have been two of the major modelling devices used to propel a uniquely behavioural understanding of financial markets. The marriage of the two 'big beasts' of the behavioural approach is obviously a major milestone in the development of the subject. I examine some tentative progress in that direction in this chapter.

In Section 10.3 I ask how credible is it that stock-market momentum is a product of the slow response of investors to news about earnings? In Section 10.4 I look at alternative explanations for

PEAD other than investors' underreaction to news about earnings. Section 10.5 summarizes and concludes the chapter.

After reading this chapter the reader should

- Be able to integrate stock price momentum in response to earnings news into a prospect theory model of asset pricing.
- Understand the evidence that it is indeed earnings news that drives observed continuation in short-run stock price trends, or stock price momentum.

10.2   Grinblatt and Han's (2005) Model

Grinblatt and Han (2005) develop and empirically implement a model which combines the presence of traders subject to two well-documented cognitive biases:

- A utility function which exhibits prospect theory style properties, where agents are risk averse in the domain of gains, but risk seeking with respect to losses (Barberis, Huang & Santos 2001).
- The maintenance of 'mental accounts' in which responses to risk are evaluated separately, rather than as part of an integrated portfolio, allowing for contrasting attitudes to risk over rather similar types of gambles (see Thaler & Johnson 1990).

Investors characterized by these two characteristics are called PTMA (prospect theory with mental accounting) investors. The utility function of PTMA investors is represented diagrammatically as kinked around some reference point R in Figure 10.3. The reference point can be defined with respect to any subjective/objective notion of what the stock is 'worth', but Grinblatt and Han define R simply with respect to what PTMA investors paid to acquire the risky asset. So points above R represent unrealized gains, those below unrealized capital losses. A reduction in unrealized losses from wealth level A to B yields the investor a greater increase in utility than a similarly sized increase in unrealized gains, from C to D. This reflects the prospect theory characteristic of PTMA investors who, while risk averse over gambles concerning gains, nevertheless become risk seeking in the loss domain. More formally, the structure of this loss-making PTMA utility function can be expressed as follows:

$$U(W) = \frac{(W - R)^{1-\gamma}}{1 - \gamma} \quad \text{if} \ \ W \geq R$$

$$U(W) = -\lambda \frac{(R - W)^{1-\gamma}}{1 - \gamma} \quad \text{if} \ \ W < R \tag{10.1}$$

Grinblatt and Han follow experimental evidence in Kahneman and Tversky (1979) and Tversky and Kahneman (2000) in choosing values of γ equal to a half and λ equal to 2.25 for illustrative purposes. I retain this assumption in the numerical illustrations discussed below.

The GH model is inhabited by a mixture of two types of investors:

- A proportion μ of rational investors whose trades reflect fundamental value.
- A proportion $(1 - \mu)$ of PTMA investors, whose utility is characterized by Equation (10.1) above.

Hence the Grinblatt and Han (GH) model has the noise-trader structure of Chapter 6, but with the additional feature that the utility function of investors has the prospect theory properties discussed in Chapters 2 and 8.

The GH model further assumes:

- The risky asset to be priced by the model is in fixed supply, normalized to be 1.
- Public information about the stock, F_t, arrives at the start of the trading period t. If all PTMA investors were driven from the market the price would converge on fundamental value.
- Fundamental values evolve as a random walk through random shocks to value, and so:

$$F_{t+1} = F_t + \varepsilon_{t+1} \tag{10.2}$$

10.2.1   Modelling Asset Demand in the GH Model

Total demand for the risky asset is a weighted average of rational and PTMA investors' demand

$$D_t^{RATIONAL} = 1 + b_t(F_t - P_t)$$

$$D_t^{PTMA} = 1 + b_t[(F_t - P_t) + \lambda(R_t - P_t)] \tag{10.3}$$

where R_t is the 'reference' price, or value, around which the slope of the PTMA utility function changes; b_t is the slope of the rational investors' demand; and λ is the time-invariant responsiveness of PTMA investors to, as yet unrealized, capital gains/losses relative to the reference point R_t. Combined market demand sets price, given the asset is in fixed supply. Since demand equals supply in equilibrium and supply of the risky asset is arbitrarily set at 1, then total asset demand must also equal 1 to clear the market.

Recall that total asset demand for the risky asset equals 1 by assumption. Total asset demand can be decomposed into a proportion μ of PTMA investors and the remainder $(1 - \mu)$ of rational investors. Since equilibrium supply equals demand we have

$$D = 1 = (1 - \mu)[1 + b_t(F_t - P_t)] + \mu[1 + b_t\{(F_t - P_t) + \lambda(R_t - P_t)\}]$$

$$1 = 1 + b_t(F_t - P_t) - \mu[1 + b_t(F_t - P_t)] + \mu[1 + b_t(F_t - P_t) + \lambda b_t(R_t - P_t)]$$

$$1 = 1 + b_t(F_t - P_t) + \mu\lambda b_t(R_t - P_t)$$

$$0 = b_t(F_t - P_t) + \mu\lambda b_t(R_t - P_t)$$

$$0 = F_t - P_t + \mu\lambda R_t - \mu\lambda P_t$$

$$P_t = \frac{F_t + \mu\lambda R_t}{1 + \mu\lambda}$$

$$P_t = wF_t + (1 - w)R_t \tag{10.4}$$

In equilibrium the price of the risky asset is set as a linear combination of fundamental value, F, and the reference price perceived by PTMA investors, where the weight placed upon fundamental price, w_t, declines as more PTMA investors enter the market.

The evolution of the reference point, R, in each time period t, is defined in the process of trade, as it is assumed PTMA investors value their stock holdings on a cost basis. This cost basis for valuation implies that the more trade occurs (i.e. the higher volume at date t denoted here as V_t) the closer R_t

moves towards current price, P_t. So this period's reference point for PTMA investors becomes a weighted average of last period's reference point and current price:

$$R_{t+1} = V_t P_t + (1 - V_t) R_t \tag{10.5}$$

where the relative weight on P_t and R_t depends on the turnover of claims to the risky asset V_t. For an asset where 100% of the claims change hand each time period, $V_t = 1$, the reference point simply becomes this period's price. So if R_t follows a random walk and $E(R_t) = R_t + 1$, or is simply assumed to be constant, we have $E(R_t) = P_t$. So the expression for equilibrium price becomes:

$$P_t = wF_t + (1 - w)P_t$$
$$\Rightarrow 0 = wF_t + (1 - w)P_t - P_t$$
$$0 = wF_t - wP_t$$
$$P_t = F_t \tag{10.6}$$

In the case of full turnover, $V_t = 1$ of the risky asset and R_t evolving as a random walk price converges on fundamental value, even while PTMA investors remain active in the market.

Grinblatt and Han examine the dynamics of market price setting under the assumption that the proportion of PTMA investors remains fixed period to period, $w_t = w_t + 1 = w$. So we have

$$P_{t+1} - P_t = w(F_{t+1} - F_t) + (1 - w)(R_{t+1} - R_t) \tag{10.7}$$

where expected changes in F are zero by definition of the 'fundamental' value of a stock, so $F_{t+1} - F_t = 0$, that is price changes proportionately reflect revisions in the reference price of PTMA investors. Note that since w declines as PTMA investors dominate the market, i.e. μ increases, the above expression implies expected returns are increasing in the proportion of PTMA investors in the market and the revision in their reference point. More formally

$$E[(P_{t+1} - P_t)] = (1 - w)[R_{t+1} - R_t]$$

given

$$E[R_{t+1}] = VP_t + (1 - V)R_t$$
$$\Rightarrow E(P_{t+1} - P_t) = (1 - w)[\{VP_t + (1 - V)R_t\} - R_t]$$
$$E(P_{t+1} - P_t) = (1 - w)[V_t(P_t - R_t)]$$
$$E\left[\frac{P_{t+1} - P_t}{P_t}\right] = (1 - w)V_t \frac{(P_t - R_t)}{P_t} \tag{10.8}$$

Hence in the GH model returns are a function of the deviation of the current price from PTMA investors' reference point, $(P_t - R_t) P_t$, the degree of turnover in the risky asset, and the weight put on the reference point by PTMA investors in the formation of price, $(1 - w)$.

A numerical illustration of the GH model

This section presents some simple spreadsheet-based numerical illustrations of using the model and considers the impact of relaxing some of the assumptions embedded in its structure. We begin by

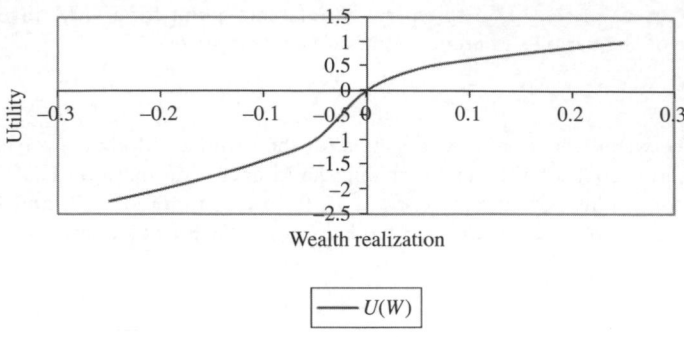

Figure 10.3 PTMA investors' utility function ($\gamma = 0.5$, $\lambda = 2.25$)

constructing the PTMA investor's utility functions using the base assumptions, $\gamma = 0.5$ and $\lambda = 2.25$. An initial plotting of such a function is given in Figure 10.3.

The concavity of the utility function and its convexity below the reference point, chosen here to be zero, is clear. Increasing risk aversion, as captured by λ, set initially to 2.25, increases the slope of the PTMA utility function symmetrically around the origin. This kink in the investor's utility function is sharpened as risk aversion above and risk loving below the chosen reference value of zero. This is illustrated by a revised graph shown in Figure 10.4.

A similar comparative static exercise reveals the impact of variations in λ, the time-invariant responsiveness of PTMA investors to as yet unrealized capital gains or losses (relative to the reference point R_t) on their attitude to risk. This is shown in Figure 10.5, where λ is now increased to 3.25 (from 2.25). Increasing λ, PTMA investors' sensitivity to unrealized gains and losses leads to increases in the asymmetry of the PTMA utility function around zero. Higher λ means PTMA investors shun risk over gains and become more acquiescent in facing possible losses.

Turning to the pricing equation we observe that equilibrium price is a linear combination of fundamental value, F_t, at time t and the reference point for value in period t, where R_t is set here arbitrarily to zero. The individual weightings on F_t and R_t fluctuate with the weight, w, where $w = 1/(1 + (\mu/\lambda))$. So $P = wF_t + (1 - w)R_t$. If fundamental investors could drive PTMA investors out of the market, so $\mu \rightarrow 0$, then $w = 0$ and price of the risky asset converges on its fundamental value, set here arbitrarily to one. So simply plotting price against (μ/λ) reveals how this convergence occurs.

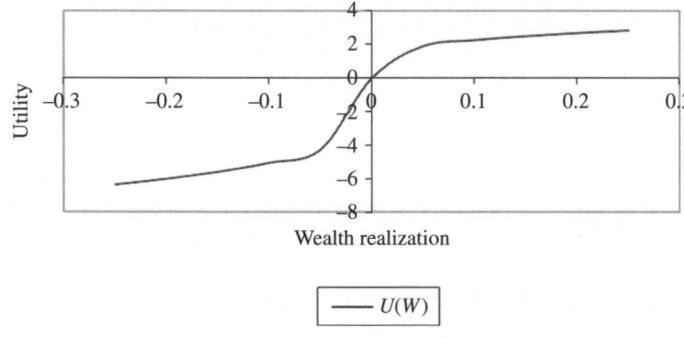

Figure 10.4 PTMA investors' utility function ($\gamma = 0.75$, $\lambda = 2.25$)

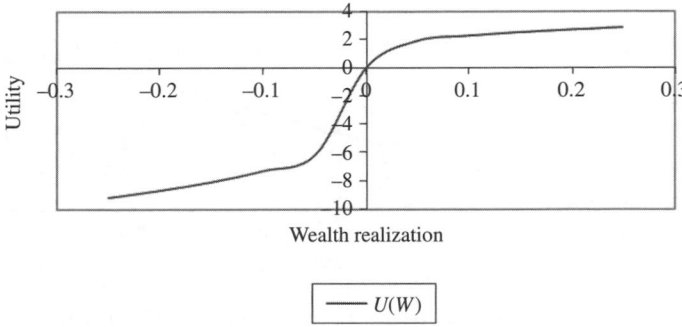

Figure 10.5 PTMA investors' utility function ($\gamma = 0.75$, $\lambda = 3.25$)

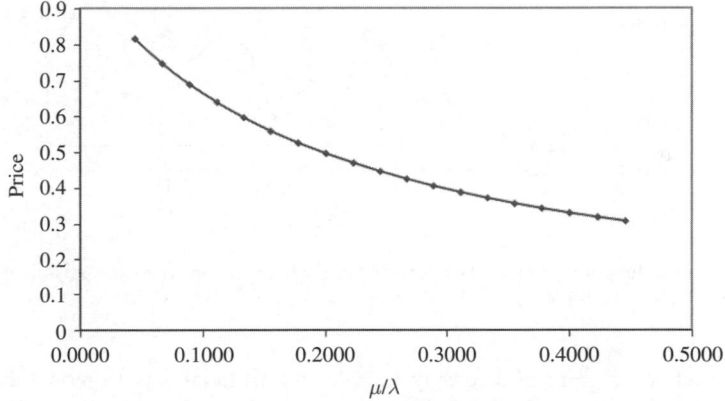

Figure 10.6 Price as a function of ratio of PTMA investors to their risk aversion (μ/λ)

Figure 10.6 shows a value of λ set to the typical assumption of 2.25. Increasing PTMA investors' responsiveness to unrealized gains and losses simply increases the concavity of the curve. The crucial determinant of deviation of price around the fixed fundamental value (of 1) is the evolution of the reference point R over time and the ratio of PTMA participating investors in the market.

Figure 10.7 shows the simple linear relation between return and price for a reference point of zero, since all capital gains feed directly into increases in investors' utility.

Returns are a linear function of the deviation of price from fundamental value ($P_t - F_t$), as mediated at each date through the volume of trade V_t and the proportion of PTMA investors present in the market.

10.2.2 Investor Returns and the Evolution of the Reference Point

Returns rise as price deviates from the fundamental value of one. The only impact of increasing turnover of the risky asset is to increase returns, because of the more rapid updating of the reference point R. Similarly a greater proportion of PTMA investors raises returns across all prices.

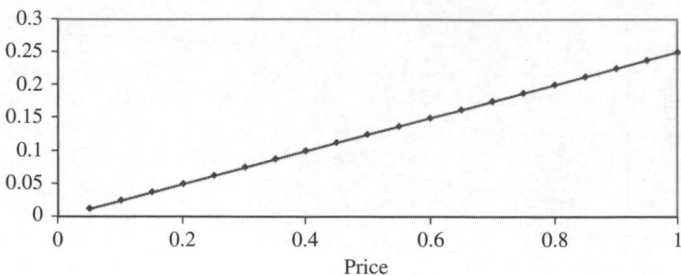

Figure 10.7   Return as a function of price for reference point of zero ($V = 5\%$, $w = 50\%$)

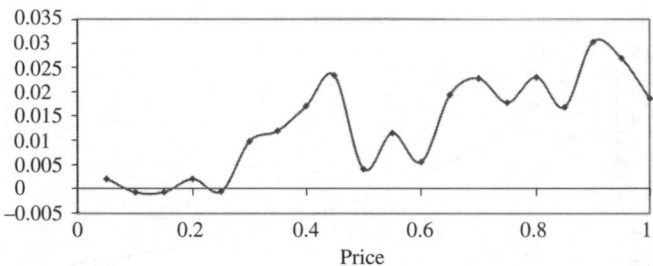

Figure 10.8   Return as a function of price for reference point of zero mean with normally distributed shocks to R ($sd = 0.25$; $V = 5\%$, $w = 50\%$)

While a fixed reference point of zero may seem a very artificial way to model the price-setting process, little is changed fundamentally by allowing the reference point to randomly fluctuate around zero (in this example with a standard deviation of 0.25; Figure 10.8) as price rises towards one, which is arbitrarily set to be the fundamental value of the risky asset of our numerical example (i.e. moves away from the average value of the reference point).

The stochastic nature of the reference point makes returns far more volatile, but the basic comparative static properties of the model remain unchanged. As price diverges from the reference point (which retains a mean of zero), observed returns to the risky asset rise. As before, in Equation (10.5), returns to the risky asset are scalable in turnover.

10.3   What Drives Stock-Market Momentum?

Following Ball and Brown's initial reporting that stocks receiving 'good news' about their earnings saw their share price rise (and vice versa for 'bad-news' stock) there subsequently developed a minor cottage industry of similar follow-up studies (see Jones & Litzenberger 1970 and Foster, Olsen & Shevlin 1984 for fairly prominent examples of the genre). However, even though the presence of drift upwards in share returns following an earnings announcement of good news about earnings and of drift downwards following bad news is widely accepted its cause is still very much in contention. Behavioural finance researchers, following De Bondt and Thaler (1990), suggest that financial analysts, and so the investors they advise, 'overreact' to recent earnings information and enter a 'correction' phase once earnings are announced with prices slowly adjusting to the reality of recently announced earnings (Daniel, Hirshleifer & Subrahmanyam 1998). This, of course, implies poor processing of one of the most basic pieces of financial data. This is a conclusion that adherents to the efficient-markets hypothesis, like Eugene Fama, are reluctant to accept. If investors cannot interpret such a basic piece of value-relevant information it does not give us much hope that the overall market is informationally efficient with respect to the vast array of more discreetly transmitted and subtle information available.

10.3.1 Evidence of PEAD

In a fascinating trilogy of papers Bernard and Thomas explored the scale of and potential explanation for PEAD (Bernard 1993; Bernard & Thomas 1989, 1990). These papers and the claims made for the manner in which financial markets process news about earnings have induced a steady stream of commentaries and supposed refutations some of which I study below. I begin by simply explaining what Bernard and Thomas claimed to show. Bernard and Thomas (1989) examined roughly quarterly 85,000 earnings announcement on the NYSE-AMEX in the United States in the years 1974–85 – the data came from 37 separate industries.

In order to capture the theoretical construct of 'news' that investors receive about earnings Bernard and Thomas needed some benchmark 'expected' level of earnings, which investors are deemed to anticipate. Deviations from that benchmark are then defined to be 'news' about earnings. They adopted a benchmark from an earlier classic paper recording PEAD in the US market by Foster *et al.* (1984) – that is, this quarter's earnings (Q_t) are likely to be very similar to the same quarter last year. So if last year the first quarter produced earnings of 25 cents, a good guess of this quarter's earnings might be 25 cents again. This quarter's market expectation of quarterly earnings, $E^M[Q_t]$, is given by the expression

$$E^M[Q_t] = \delta + Q_{t-4} \tag{10.9}$$

where the constant term δ captures some expected 'drift' in earnings due to inflation, or changes in the technological and/or regulatory environment of the firm. Hence news 'about' company earnings is simply the difference between the actual and benchmark values. So the observed 'abnormal return' (AR) in the share's price, relative to some relevant benchmark return, like the CAPM, or the return on the FTSE 100 index, is given by:

$$AR_t = \lambda(Q_t - E^M[Q_t]) = \lambda(Q_t - Q_{t-4} - \delta)$$

That is, the expected abnormal return is given by deviations from a detrended seasonal difference in earnings. This method of constructing an earnings 'news' metric implies the first of the hypotheses regarding PEAD tested by Bernard and Thomas (1990).

Hypothesis 1

If earnings expectations are formed by Equation (10.9) above we expect quarterly earnings announcements to be greeted by positively related abnormal share price returns in the first three quarters, $t-1$, $t-2$, $t-3$, but to a declining degree, and to experience negative abnormal returns in the fourth quarter, $t-4$.

Bernard and Thomas record large differences in the returns to good and bad news firms in the period following earnings announcements. They calculate cumulative abnormal returns relative to

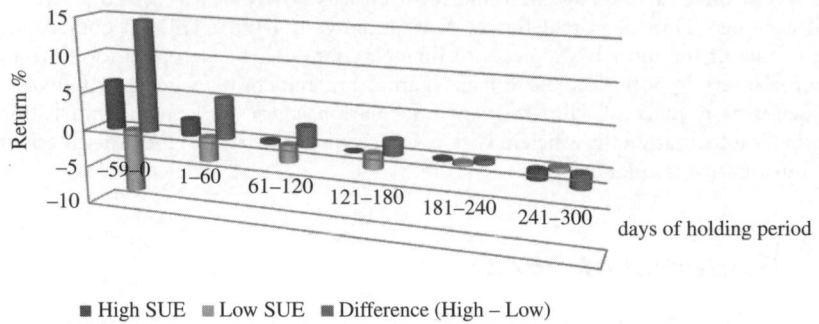

Figure 10.9   Cumulative abnormal returns following earnings announcements for small good/bad news firms

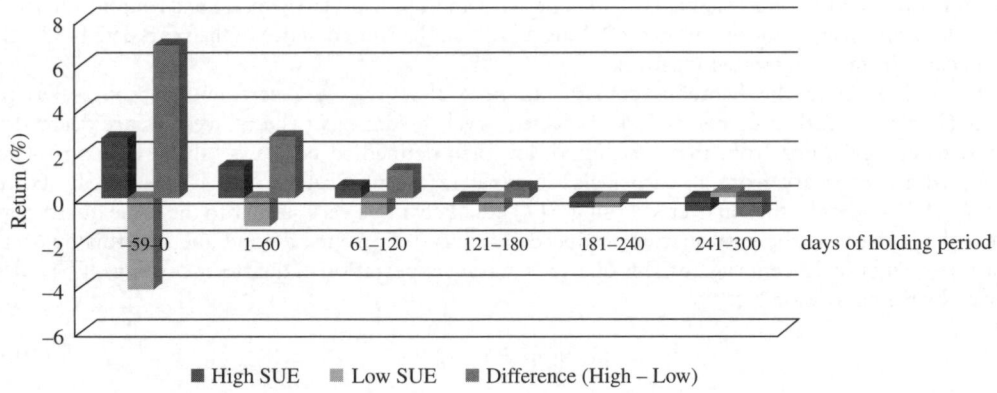

Figure 10.10   Cumulative abnormal returns following earnings announcements for large good/bad news firms

firms of equivalent size over various holding periods both before and after the earnings announcement. They measure earnings 'shocks' by a standardized unexpected earnings (or SUE) metric. Figure 10.9 gives the results for the smallest group of firms in their sample. Figure 10.10 gives an analogous set of results for the largest firms in their sample. They find evidence of PEAD clustered in small- and medium-sized portfolios, but clearly present in all portfolios. In the first three months (or 60 trading days) following quarterly earnings announcements the difference between the 10% of firms with the best news and the 10% of firms with the worst news about earnings is almost 15% in the smallest firm deciles. Even after 180 days (or nine trading months) a difference of 2% in post-earnings-announcement returns remains. The calculation is made by adding up the daily abnormal share price returns over successive days following quarterly earnings announcements. The post-earnings-announcement returns reported by Bernard and Thomas are shown in Table 10.1. For the largest group of companies a similar pattern of results was obtained, but of roughly half the size.

The basic intuition is that over the year increases in earnings might be expected to persist, so a good first quarter implies a good second quarter, etc., but year-to-year earnings changes are partially negated as earnings mean-revert in accordance with the normal pressures of market competition. It is hard to be the greatest of all times, even if you can manage to be so momentarily.

Table 10.1 Numerical example of the Bernard and Thomas equation

Quarter	Year 0	Year 1	Year 2
1st quarter	10	11	10.76
2nd quarter	10	10.34	
3rd quarter	10	10.19	
4th quarter	20	20.6	

Source: Bernard, V. and J. Thomas (1990). Reproduced with permission.

Shocks to expectations in quarterly earnings cumulate during the year and then dissipate over the years. Bernard and Thomas (1990) seek to capture this pattern of correlation by estimating the coefficients of a partial adjustment model for earnings of the form:

$$Q_t = \delta + Q_{t-4} + \phi(Q_{t-1} - Q_{t-5}) + \theta\varepsilon_{t-4} + \varepsilon_t \tag{10.10}$$

where the second term captures the catch-up effect of this quarter's earnings to the growth in earnings over the year, so $\phi > 0$ but also $\phi < 1$. Similarly, we expect 'shocks' to be reversed next year (otherwise they would not be very shocking), so $\theta < 0$, implying shocks to earnings are self-reversing over the years.

Hypothesis 2

If prices reflect expectations formed using Equation (10.9) above there should be positive but declining association between the abnormal share price return in the first three quarters of the financial year, with a reversal of trend in the fourth quarter.

Bernard and Thomas (1990) considered the consequences of actual earnings following a pattern determined by an equation of the form of Equation (10.9) above, while expectations of them formed by investors following Equation (10.10). This implies stock-market responses to earnings take the form of an adjustment to the growth path of earnings in the past year and a reversion from the shock-to-earnings expectations in the same quarter last year (when earnings expectations were formed by the same expectations formation mechanism as they are now). This follows from the fact that 'earnings surprises' made manifest in stock returns immediately following earnings quarterly announcements take the form given in Equation (10.11):

$$Q_t - E^M[Q_t] = \delta + Q_{t-4} - [\delta + Q_{t-4} + \phi(Q_{t-1} - Q_{t-5}) + \theta\varepsilon_{t-4}]$$

$$\Rightarrow Q_t - E^M[Q_t] = \phi(Q_{t-1} - Q_{t-5}) + \theta\varepsilon_{t-4} \tag{10.11}$$

Since $Q_{t-1} - Q_{t-5}$ is just the 'earnings surprise', or quarterly earnings change from the previous quarter, the equation for earnings surprises reduces to a geometrically declining series in quarterly earning shocks deriving from annual earning changes, as measured in the first through fourth quarters.

$$Q_t - E^M[Q_t] = \lambda\varepsilon_t + \lambda\phi\varepsilon_{t-1} + \lambda\phi^2\varepsilon_{t-2} + \lambda\phi^3\varepsilon_{t-3} + (\theta + \phi^4)\varepsilon_{t-4} + \lambda\nu_t \tag{10.12}$$

The predicted pattern of share price return movements at each successive earnings announcement is that suggested by Equation (10.12).

If earnings surprises are formed by a mechanism like Equation (10.9), but actually are generated by a statistical process such as Equation (10.10), then the autocorrelation in share price returns around

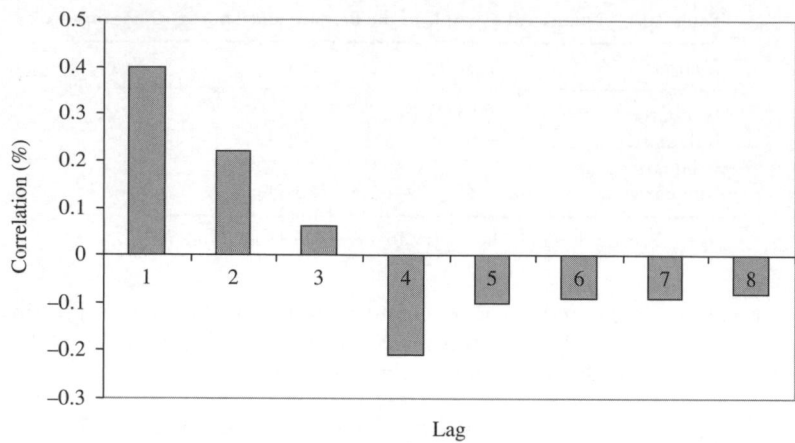

Figure 10.11   Correlation in quarterly 'earnings surprises' (SUEs) across eight prior quarters

Source: Bernard, V. and J. Thomas (1990). Evidence that stock prices do not fully reflect the implications of current earnings for future earnings. *Journal of Accounting and Economics*, 13(4): 305–40. Reproduced with permission.

earnings announcement should display a positive correlation at the first, second and third quarterly lag and a negative correlation at the fourth.

The evidence from Bernard and Thomas's (1990) own data confirms this intuition as shown in Figure 10.11.

The quarterly distribution of PEAD does indeed seem rather consistent with a simple failure to properly anticipate the future trajectory of earnings. Investors appear to make very predictable mistakes in interpreting one of the most fundamental pieces of financial information. Not surprisingly this assertion of a basic failure of the market to adequately impound clearly value-relevant information caused some consternation and it was not long before the search was on to explain Bernard and Thomas's results.

10.4   What Causes PEAD?

10.4.1   Is PEAD Due to Changes in Risk?

One very simple explanation of PEAD is that earnings news brings with it changes in the perceived risk of shares and for that reason return patterns change in response. Such an explanation of PEAD is perfectly consistent with efficient markets and standard asset-pricing models like the CAPM, or arbitrage pricing theory. Of course the risk explanation must be a little convoluted here because 'good news' stocks become more risky, while 'bad news' stocks become less risky and this is just hard to believe. But for completeness's sake Bernard and Thomas give this angle on the PEAD anomaly a decent shot.

At least a partial risk-based explanation of PEAD has been advanced by Ball, Kothari and Watts (1993). They note that the earnings reported by companies, which enter calculations of the 'earnings surprises' in PEAD studies themselves, reflect the equity cost of capital. As we know from our first-year finance class every project evaluation requires us to discount projected cash-flows to determine if it is worthwhile to undertake the project or not. Ball *et al.* (1993, p.623) write:

We argue that changes in expected earnings and stock returns are jointly determined by changes in the firm's investment risks and in its leverage. Thus part of the observed association between changes in earnings and stock returns is predicted to be attributable to changes in equities' risks and, hence expected returns.

So companies facing more risk, and hence attracting a higher cost of capital on their chosen bundle of projects, reject low net present value projects and therefore earn higher rents/earnings on the reduced set of projects they choose to undertake. Such firms undertake a small number of more lucrative, but risky, projects. So an upward shift in the equity risk of a stock raises its cost of capital pushing it further along the net present value schedule, raising the earnings number it reports. Ball *et al.* also note that this positive relation between equity risk and earnings 'surprises' will be masked by the negative relation between debt on the balance sheet and earnings, moderated via interest charges made against reported earnings in the profit and loss account.

The results for US companies in the years 1950–88 suggest that the underlying reverse causality running from changes in equity risk to earnings 'surprises' does indeed exist in the data. Ball *et al.* report that even controlling for shifts in risk, by re-estimating CAPM betas for each year of their sample, observed PEAD remains statistically significant, while of diminished economic importance. Nevertheless, even with changes in risk controlled for, the rank correlation between abnormal share price returns and earnings 'shocks' at the annual earnings announcement date is 0.56 and this remains statistically significant at the 91% confidence interval. Hence Ball *et al.* conclude rational variation in equity risk profiles are at best a partial explanation of observed PEAD.

10.4.2   Are Prices Following Themselves or Following Earnings?

Most evidence of price momentum records how price run-ups perpetuate themselves and downward spirals gather speed over time (Jegadeesh & Titman 1993). The impression given is that prices are following themselves as investors 'pile in' to the stock market following on others' prior trades. Such investors are often characterized as 'trend chasers' jumping on the latest boom/bust (Hong & Stein 1999).

Chan (2003) studied a unique database recording news headlines about companies in the United States in the years 1980 to 2000. The Dow Jones Interactive Publications Library (DJIPL) records abstracts and articles from a variety of business and financial newspapers and newswires in the United States and certainly captures all the usual suspects, the *Wall Street Journal*, *Fortune*, *Business Week*, *Barrons*, etc. Because hand collation of these news items can be very tedious work Chan focused on a random subsample of firms included in the Center for Research into Security Prices (CRSP) US share returns database. Nevertheless Chan's study still includes some 766 stocks which were already in existence at the start of the sample period of 1980.

Having identified the subsample of stocks for his study Chan allocated them to 'news' and 'no news' portfolios each month according to whether the DJIPL database records a news story for that month. If it does attract a story in the news service the firm is allocated to the 'news' portfolio for that month in which the portfolio is formed. If no news item is found for the company in the portfolio formation month it is allocated to the 'no news' portfolio in Chan's tests. Within both 'news' and 'no news' portfolios a subset of 'winning' and 'losing' stocks are identified in each portfolio formation month. Shares included in the 'winning' portfolio are in the upper third of recorded share return performance in the month the portfolio was formed. Conversely shares included in the 'losing' portfolio are in the lower third of recorded share return performance in the month the portfolio was formed. Chan observes the behaviour of the share's returns over the three years following the portfolio formation period. The results are reported in Figures 10.12 and 10.13.

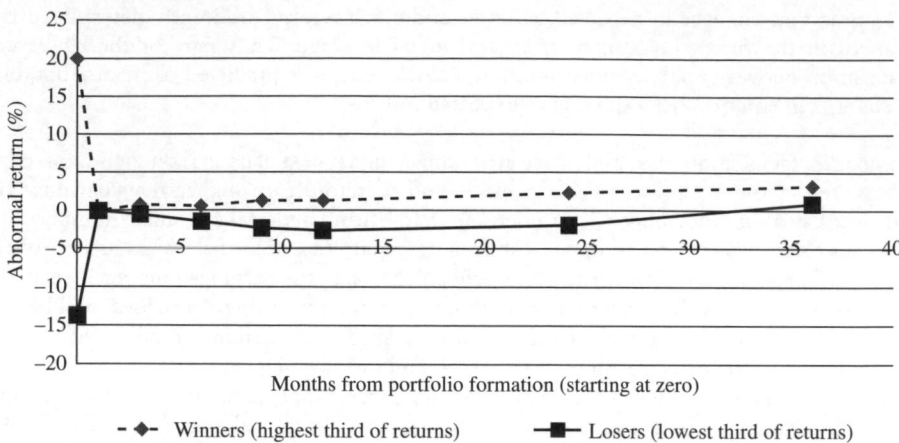

Figure 10.12   Winners and losers in the 'news' portfolio of stocks 1980–2000

Source: Chan, W. (2003). Stock price reaction to news and no news: drift and reversal after headlines. *Journal of Financial Economics*, 70(2): 223–60. Reproduced with permission.

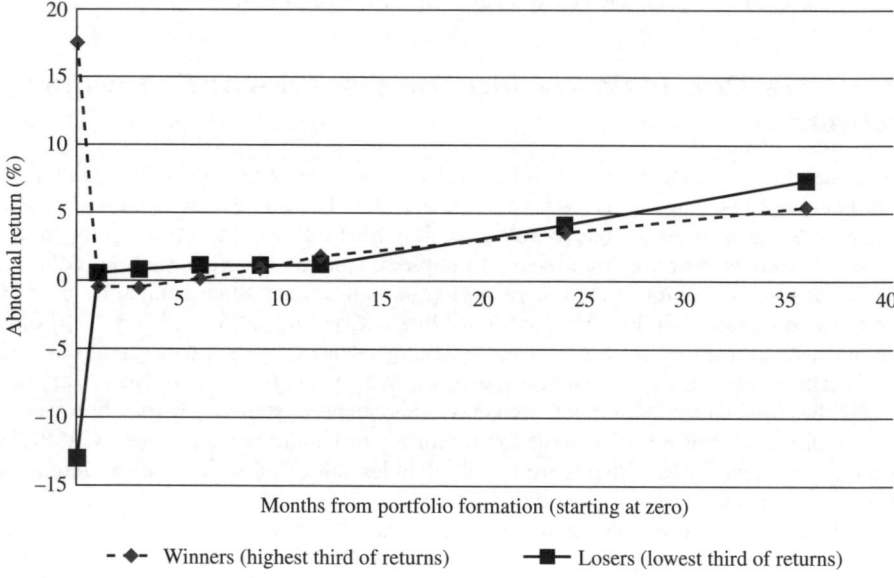

Figure 10.13   Winners and losers in the 'no news' portfolio of stocks 1980–2000

Source: Chan, W. (2003). Stock price reaction to news and no news: drift and reversal after headlines. *Journal of Financial Economics*, 70(2): 223–60. Reproduced with permission.

Figure 10.12 gives the abnormal returns for the three years following portfolio formation for the portfolio with 'news' items recorded in the DJIPL database. Figure 10.13 gives the abnormal returns for the three years following portfolio formation for the portfolio without 'news' items recorded in the DJIPL database. Comparing the two plots there is a clear difference between 'winners' and 'losers', i.e. the best and worst third of shares in the appropriate portfolio is only really discernible for those shares that have had some 'news' reported that month. The difference between portfolio formation returns is fairly large (over 30%) in both cases, but only the newsworthy portfolios show the characteristic overreaction and consequent mean reversion that we associate with phenomena like post-earnings-announcement drift in share prices.

Of course the 'news' items Chan (2003) considers do not exclusively, or even mainly, concern earnings. So we cannot take these results as evidence earnings momentum causes, or is indirectly the same phenomenon as, stock price momentum. Indeed Chan repeats the same tests excluding all company months which span the earnings announcement date. He finds a reduced difference between the news and no news portfolios, but still a very statistically significant difference. Hence it appears that it is not just news about earnings that induces price momentum. Chan concludes (2003, p.253) as follows:

> Post-earnings-announcement drift is important but does not drive all of the underreaction I have found. Excluding stocks that had earnings announcements eliminates any trace of post-news-winner drift. Investors do not appear to underreact to good news, aside from positive earnings announcements.

10.4.3 Is PEAD in the Market or in the Eye of the Researcher?

Typically the research of Bernard and Thomas on PEAD is seen as supporting the idea that investors' expectations about earnings are naive in the sense that while they believe that quarterly earnings evolve according to a seasonal random walk of the form of Equation (10.9), quarterly earnings actually follow a process of the form of Equation (10.10). This results in 'earnings surprises' of the form of Equation (10.11). This happens because investors underestimate the extent to which earnings mean-revert with past earnings 'shocks' being subsequently reversed.

Jacob *et al.* (2000) have advanced a very different interpretation of Bernard and Thomas's results based on a possible error in their proposed measure of earnings 'surprises'. Jacob *et al.* note that differencing quarterly earnings may itself induce the mean-reversion that Bernard and Thomas report. Recall the basic model of investors' earnings expectations

$$E_t^M[Q_t] = \delta + Q_{t-4}$$

which when quarterly earnings follows a random walk implies

$$Q_{t-4} - E^M[Q_t] = \delta$$

Therefore shocks to earnings expectations are given by δ, the 'trend' in earnings attributable to inflation and/or industrial restructuring, plus other random shocks.

If quarterly earnings display some mild tendency to mean-revert over time, instead of Equation (10.9), which assumes a seasonal random walk, we actually have

$$Q_t = \delta + 0.98Q_{t-4} \tag{10.13}$$

Now we have a revised solution for the changes in quarterly earnings of the form

$$\Delta Q_t - 0.02Q_{t-4} = \delta$$
$$\Delta Q_t = \delta + 0.02Q_{t-4}$$

So if earnings do not follow a seasonal random walk, but rather slowly revert to some historic value established at the same time last year, then earnings changes will be anchored in past quarterly earnings values. So returning to Equation (10.11), Bernard and Thomas's expression for investors' earnings surprise becomes:

$$Q_t - E^M[Q_t] = \phi(Q_{t-1} - Q_{t-5}) + \theta\varepsilon_{t-4}$$

which for a mean-reverting quarterly earnings series of the form described by Equation (10.12) can be rewritten as:

$$Q_t - E^M[Q_t] = \phi(Q_{t-1} - Q_{t-5}) - \phi Q_{t-5} + \theta\varepsilon_{t-4}$$

Recall that $\varphi > 0$, so for mean-reverting earnings series we also expect to observe mean reversions in earnings according to past quarterly earnings levels, rather than a correction of past trends.

Jacob *et al.* (2000) examined the time-series properties of individual companies with Bernard and Thomas's original dataset. They tried to separate out companies whose quarterly earnings seemed to follow seasonal random walks, as described by Equation (10.9), and those companies whose earnings appeared to mean-revert, in accordance with Equation (10.13). They found that PEAD is heavily clustered in portfolios of companies for which quarterly earnings seemed to mean-revert, in accordance with Equation (10.13). This suggests reported PEAD may have more to say about how we test market efficiency with respect to earnings information than about stock-market efficiency with respect to earnings information as such.

10.4.4   Show Me the Money

If Bernard and Thomas are right and naive investors make predictable errors in forecasting which move stock prices in an easily predictable way following the quarterly earnings announcement perhaps I have better things to do with my time than write this book. I should just get on-line and start trading against the PEAD induced by less clever investors than myself. Whether this is a feasible strategy depends on the trading costs of selling short a 'good news' shareholding at the earnings announcement and using the proceeds to buy a portfolio of stocks receiving bad news at the earnings announcement date.

But to successfully arbitrage against PEAD requires that the investor undertaking the counter-trade against naive investors can move price to exploit the perceived mispricing based on naive investors' predictable mispricing. This may not be that easy to do. Recent evidence in a PEAD study by Battalio and Mendenhall (2005) shows that trades in large blocks of shares (the very ones that tend to move price most) do not exhibit the same naive earnings expectations (portrayed in Equation (10.9)) evoked by Bernard and Thomas to explain PEAD.

Coincidentally Battalio and Mendenhall confirm the presence of substantial, statistically significant and economically valuable returns to following a counter-PEAD trading strategy even when no time-series benchmark of earnings expectations is used. Even when the expectations of earnings in the market are inferred from outstanding analysts' forecasts of quarterly earnings substantial, and sometimes more sharp, evidence of PEAD is found. Hence Jacob *et al.*'s (2000) claim that PEAD may simply be an artefact of Bernard and Thomas's research method is not wholly convincing.

Certainly, any potential arbitrageur of the PEAD phenomenon will face substantial costs in exploiting the share mispricing he observes to be present. Ravi Bhushan (1994) argues for an 'informational perspective' on reported PEAD. This perspective simply points out that the mere fact that mispricing is present does not mean it is a profitable strategy for even the smartest and most prescient of investors to try and exploit. He reports results suggesting the distribution of PEAD across the market does indeed correlate with various proxies for transaction costs faced by traders seeking to arbitrage on the basis of risk; these include the volume of trade in the stock and the number of analysts covering its fortunes. Of course, if high transactions costs do explain the failure of PEAD to be arbitraged away this still leaves us searching for the motivation of PEAD's presence in the first place.

10.5   Conclusion and Summary

This chapter has examined one of the most famous illustrations of share price momentum. This is that news about earnings seems to diffuse slowly through markets after the announcement of earnings, rather than being swiftly impounded into price as we might expect in an efficient market. It is fairly clear that price momentum is associated with 'news' about companies, but far less clear if it is news about earnings that is the central piece of information inducing price momentum.

Because of its iconic role in the development of the behavioural finance literature I have concentrated on PEAD as a central aspect of stock-price momentum. Attempts to dismiss it as partly, or largely, an artefact of a narrowly specified research design seem premature. The Grinblatt and Han (2005) model explains PEAD as a product of a prospect theory style utility function combined with a use of separable mental accounts by investors.

Questions

1. Return to Figure 10.3 and the PTMA utility function. The more perceptive of you might be thinking, 'Hold on, in Chapter 8 you made a big deal of cumulative prospect theory and how it is a wonderful new step in understanding how prospect theory works. Why has cumulative prospect theory gone out the window now?'

   It is true I have not built a cumulative prospect theory perspective into my treatment of the GH model, but how could Figure10.3, in particular, be changed to reflect the adjustment of a standard prospect theory approach (which I follow in my numerical example in the chapter) to that required by the adoption of a cumulative prospect theory perspective on the same problem that Grinblatt and Han study?

2. Return to Table 10.1 and the equation for the stock-market's expectation of earnings (Equation (10.9) above) assumed to take the form:

$$E^M[Q_t] = 0.05 + Q_{t-4}$$

   And let the process assumed to actually generate earnings (Equation 10.10 above) take the form:

$$Q_t = \delta + Q_{t-4} + 0.25(Q_{t-1} - Q_{t-5}) + 0.\varepsilon_{t-4} + \varepsilon_t$$

   What are the predicted markets' expectations, predicted actual outcomes and resulting market forecast error in forecasting year 2 quarters 2 and 3 earnings? If you carried on generating expected market expectations and predicted actual outcomes and so predicted forecast errors, by iteratively applying the version of Equations (10.9), (10.10) and (10.11) until the end of year 3, i.e. seven quarters ahead, what happens to the quality and quantity/level of the forecasts produced? [Note:

you can set ε_t, the moving average error part of the predictive model, Equation (10.10), to zero to make life a bit easier in solving the question.]

3. In this chapter I have made great play of stock-market momentum as a response to movements in earnings, however, Earnings = Levered Cash-flow + Accrual (see Penman 2004, p.134), and we know properties of accruals and cash-flows are very different. How might the distinction between the cash-flow and accruals elements of earnings be important in modelling the relations discussed in this chapter?

Note

* Brennan, M. (1991). "A perspective on accounting and stock prices." *The Accounting Review*, **66**: 67–9. American Accounting Association. Reproduced by permission.

References

Ball, R. & P. Brown (1968). An empirical evaluation of the accounting income numbers. *Journal of Accounting Research*, 159–78.

Ball, R., S.P. Kothari & R. Watts (1993). The economic determinants of the relation between earnings changes and stock returns. *Accounting Review*, **68**: 622–38.

Barberis, N., M. Huang & T. Santos (2001). Prospect theory and asset prices. *Quarterly Journal of Economics*, **116**: 1–53.

Battalio, R. & R. Mendenhall (2005). Earnings expectations, investor trade size and anomalous returns around earnings announcements. *Journal of Financial Economics*, **77**: 289–319.

Bernard, V. (1993). Stock price reactions to earnings announcements: a summary of recent anomalous evidence and possible explanations. In R. Thaler (ed.), *Advances in Behavioral Finance*. New York: Russell Sage Foundation.

Bernard, V. & J. Thomas (1989). Post-earnings-announcement drift: delayed price response or risk-premium? *Journal of Accounting Research*, **27**: 1–36.

Bernard, V. & J. Thomas (1990). Evidence that stock prices do not fully reflect the implications of current earnings for future earnings. *Journal of Accounting and Economics*, **13**: 305–40.

Bhushan, R. (1994). An informational efficiency perspective on the post-earning announcement drift. *Journal of Accounting and Economics*, **18**: 45–65.

Brennan, M. (1991). A perspective on accounting and stock prices. *The Accounting Review*, **66**: 67–9.

Chan, W. (2003). Stock market reaction to news and no news: drift and reversal after headlines. *Journal of Financial Economics*, **70**(2): 223–60.

Chordia, T. & L. Shivakumar (2006). Earnings and price momentum. *Journal of Financial Economics*, **80**(3): 627–56.

Daniel, K., D. Hirshleifer & A. Subrahmanyam (1998). Investor psychology and security market under- and overreaction. *Journal of Finance*, **52**: 1–33.

De Bondt, W. & R. Thaler (1990). Do analysts overreact? *American Economic Review*, **80**: 678–85.

Fama, E. (1998). Market efficiency, long-term returns and behavioural finance. *Journal of Financial Economics*, **49**: 283–306.

Foster, G., C. Olsen & T. Shevlin (1984). Earnings releases, anomalies and the behaviour of security returns. *Accounting Review*, **59**: 574–603.

Grinblatt, M. & B. Han (2005). Prospect theory, mental accounting and momentum. *Journal of Financial Economics*, **78**: 311–39.

Hong, H. and J. Stein (1999). A unified theory of underreaction, momentum, trading and overreaction in assets markets. *Journal of Finance*, 54: 2143–84.

Jacob, J., T. Lys *et al.* (2000). Autocorrelation structure of forecast errors from time-series models: alternative assessments of the causes of post-earnings announcement drift. *Journal of Accounting and Economics*, 28: 329–58.

Jegadeesh, N. & S. Titman (1993). Returns to buying winners and selling losers: implications for market efficiency. *Journal of Finance*, 48: 65–91.

Jegadeesh, N. & S. Titman (2005). Momentum. In R. Thaler (ed.), *Advances in Behavioural Finance*, Volume 2. Princeton, NJ: Princeton University Press.

Jones, O & R. Litzenberger (1970). Quarterly earnings reports and intermediate stock price trends. *Journal of Finance*, 25: 143–8.

Kahneman, D. & A. Tversky (1979). Prospect theory: an analysis of decision under risk. *Econometrica*, 47: 263–91.

Montier, J. (2006). *Behavioural Finance: Insights into Irrational Minds and Markets*. Chichester: John Wiley & Sons, Ltd.

Penman, S. (2004). *Financial Statement Analysis and Security Valuation*. New York: McGraw-Hill.

Rouwenhorst, G. (1998). International momentum strategies. *Journal of Finance*, 53: 265–95.

Thaler, R. & E. Johnson (1990). Gambling with the house money and trying to break even: effects of prior outcomes on risky choice. *Management Science*, 36: 643–60.

Tversky, A. & D. Kahneman (eds) (2000). *Advances in Prospect Theory: Cumulative Representation of Uncertainty*. New York: Cambridge University Press.

Chapter 11

Herding

❝ Public opinion only exists where there are no ideas ❞

(Wilde 1894).

A basic requirement of market efficiency is that price reflects a diverse set of information about asset value. But how is the selection of information which is impounded into price made? This chapter investigates some of these issues. As the above quote from Oscar Wilde implies, understanding of complex corporations is often quite fragile and subject to opposing credible theorizations. In such circumstances the rule of the swinish mob can easily come to prevail. The ability of markets to aggregate information about investment opportunities has long been seen as part of their social function. What if, instead of aggregating information, they serve to stifle it in an echo chamber of repeated platitudes? This chapter investigates some of the challenges of herding to the proper economic functioning of financial markets.

11.1 Illustration and Structure

The fact that we observe herding in financial markets should not really surprise us given the extent of conformity in both product markets and investment or the productive technology to make goods in high demand. Many goods are really only of value if other people that I know use them. I read newspapers written for and read by people like myself (see Rohlfs 2001). I join social clubs and movements agreeable to my personality and social background. Often the very technology of production requires that consumers of the product agree on some industry standard about how the product is made. It is pointless for me to write my book in Microsoft's Word if my publisher only accepts manuscripts submitted in WordPerfect, LaTeX, or some other word-processing package.

One behemoth of contemporary standardization is Microsoft. Rohlfs (2001, p.8) states:

> Bill Gates [is] the supreme virtuoso of the management of bandwagon effects. Gates has become the real-life personification of the revenge of the nerds.

Part of this revenge was extracted by the promulgation of a standard for accessing the Internet. Specifically, Bill Gates managed to ensure Internet Explorer's adoption as the primary tool for gaining access to the World-Wide Web in the face of a clear viable competitor. This may be because Microsoft's Internet Explorer was simply the better product, of course, but the US Supreme Court and the European Court of Justice did not seem to think so. I explore how a false conformity on an inferior, or more costly, alternative can occur in an appendix to this chapter.

Following the 'noise-trader' modelling strategy for capturing limitations in the cognitive ability of investors deployed in Chapters 6, 9 and 10, I examine the model of herding developed by Froot, Scharstein and Stein (1992) – henceforth the FSS model-in Section 11.2. Remember, a model is just a model, therefore Section 11.3 examines the evidence that investors herd in their trading behaviour and those advising them promote that tendency. Section 11.4 summarizes and concludes the chapter. An appendix considers the US government's case against Microsoft for monopolization of software for use on personal computers as an illustration of how herding in financial markets reflects a deeper tendency towards conformity in markets as a whole.

After reading this chapter the reader should:

- Gain insight into how and why herding occurs and what makes herding more intense.
- Understand the evidence that herding does occur in financial markets.
- Know the roots of herding in human psychology and how that has been captured under experimental conditions.

11.2 The FSS Model

11.2.1 The Basic Set Up

The FSS model considers trading between informed speculators and uninformed, or liquidity/noise, traders, as mediated by a competing set of market-makers. The market-makers collect buy and sell orders, made by informed and uninformed traders, and try to set a market clearing price. Informed/speculative traders look to asset value, v, in setting their demand for the asset. Value is assumed to have two distinct attributes: a and b. So $v = a + b$. To model the dissemination of value-relevant information Froot *et al.* (1992) assume speculators learn about either a or b before submitting orders to the market-makers but importantly not both. This modelling device allows uninformed, or liquidity/noise, traders to submit orders in periods 1 and 2 regardless of true asset value, v. These are denoted ε_1 in period 1 and ε_2 in period 2. Since noise traders trade with no regard to true value, v, knowing neither a nor b, the market-makers would simply ignore their orders in setting price if they could distinguish the informed and uninformed. However, because the market-makers cannot make this distinction, price becomes an inadequate guide to true value.

The time line of trade is as portrayed in Figure 11.1. At the start of trade, in period 0, informed traders decide on their orders, given knowledge of either one of the valuation attributes, a or b. In period 1 the market-maker randomly clears half the trades of both a and b types of informed traders. In period 1 the market-maker sets the price p_1 for the asset, based on the first half of trades. In period 2 a price p_2 is set which reflects all the orders the market-maker has received. In period 3 the value of the asset is revealed with probability α. If it is not revealed in period 3, the value is then revealed in period 4 – this occurs with probability $(1 - \alpha)$.

The FSS model allows for the staggering of the true value's, v, revelation until period 4 to allow for the impact of variations in the trading horizon of the informed traders. If v is not revealed until period 4 then it does not matter to the informed when their trade is cleared, i.e. early at period 1, or later. In the case where $\alpha = 1$ and hence value is sure to be revealed at period 3, informed investors become 'short-sighted'. It is this very short-termism that will serve to induce a form of herding in the FSS model.

Each type of informed trader infers asset value on the basis of either one of the valuation attributes, a or b. Whatever the informed trader's type he acts as if the other valuation attribute, which is unknown to him, does not exist. The FSS model assumes there are n_a informed traders who collect and use information on the valuation attribute a, the remainder, n_b informed traders,

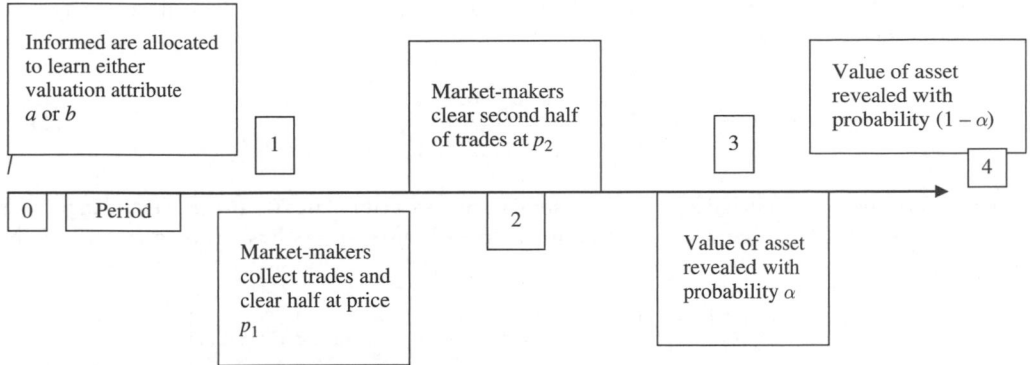

Figure 11.1 The time line of trade in the FSS model

collect and use information on the valuation attribute b. So $n = n_a + n_b$. It is simple to extend the FSS model to the case of three or more sources of information, so the model (like all others) is a simple illustration of principle. At each of periods 1 and 2, informed trader demand, D, is as follows:

$$D_t^a = \frac{n_a}{2} q_a + \frac{n_b}{2} q_b + \varepsilon_t \qquad (11.1)$$

where q_a and q_b are the informed trader's demands, given their respective knowledge of the two alternative valuation attributes a or b, and ε_t, noise trader demand. Recall noise trader demand, ε_1, being unrelated to value has no systematic impact on price.

At the end of the trading periods 1 and 2 noise traders simply unwind their position (since the informed have withdrawn from the market) to await the revelation of v (which occurs with probability α at period 3 and $(1 - \alpha)$ in period 4). Hence $(\varepsilon_1 + \varepsilon_2) = \varepsilon_3$.

Therefore α is a simple device to capture the length of informed investors' forecast horizon. If informed speculators believe value will be revealed at period 3, then $p_2 = p_1$, and it becomes vital to get their trades executed quickly. So $\alpha = 1$ implies that informed speculators become 'short-termist' in their horizon. This type of investor short-termism will suffice to generate herding in the FSS model.

11.2.2 The Price-Setting Mechanism Used by Market-Makers

Market-makers adjust price to clear the trades they receive. In doing so they use the order flow they receive to infer value. The price inference process results from projecting implied asset value, v, into the order flow the market-maker receives. The resulting responsiveness of the price set by the market-maker can be seen as the result of standard ordinary least squares regression where the slope coefficient, b, is set by the ratio of the covariance of the variable to be explained (y) and that doing the explaining (x) divided by the variance of the explanatory variable, x. That is $b = \text{Cov}(x,y)/ \text{Var}(x)$.[1] Denoting the responsiveness of inferred value by market-makers, given the flow of orders to them, λ_t, and applying the ordinary least squares formula we obtain

$$\lambda_1 = \frac{Cov[v, D_1]}{var[D_1]} = \frac{Cov\left[a + b, \frac{n_a}{2} q_a + \frac{n_b}{2} q_b + \varepsilon_1\right]}{Var\left[\frac{n_a}{2} q_a + \frac{n_b}{2} q_b + \varepsilon_1\right]} \tag{11.2}$$

The responsiveness of period 2 price is very similar, but now cumulates the orders cleared in periods 1 and 2 to better infer value once the total order flow of informed traders has been cleared by the market-maker:

$$\lambda_2 = \frac{cov\left[v, \frac{D_1 + D_2}{2}\right]}{var\left[\frac{D_1 + D_2}{2}\right]} = \frac{cov\left[a + b, \frac{n_a}{2} q_a + \frac{n_b}{2} q_b + \frac{1}{2}(\varepsilon_1 + \varepsilon_2)\right]}{var\left[\frac{n_a}{2} q_a + \frac{n_b}{2} q_b + \frac{1}{2}(\varepsilon_1 + \varepsilon_2)\right]} \tag{11.3}$$

As all the information about informed investors' orders is only known in the second period, then $\lambda_2 > \lambda_1$. Here the 'noise' of ε_1 and ε_2 on our estimates λ_1 and λ_2 nets off since it appears in both the numerator and the denominator of the expressions for λ_t above. So 'noise', being by nature unrelated to fundamental value, has no impact on our mapping of prices into fundamental value attributes.

11.2.3 Informed Speculators' Demands

Assume one of the informed speculators, i, observes the valuation attribute a (rather than b) in period 0. The speculator knows he randomly has half a chance that his trade will be executed in period 1, the remainder being processed by market-makers in period 2. So the expected profit from trading for the speculator in period 1 is given by

$$E\left[v - \frac{1}{2}(p_1 + p_2)|a\right] \tag{11.4}$$

In placing an order at period 1 the speculator does not know if his order will be cleared at period 1 or 2, so in calculating the expected profit on his trade the speculator uses an average price across both periods. By period 2 the price is set, but if the speculator's profit is constrained to be zero because no new information arrives at period 3, $p_3 = p_2$, and no profit is to be gained by buying or selling in period 2 to unwind the position in period 3. Hence the only chance of making a profit is if his trade is cleared, by the market-maker, at period 1, when the profit to be made is

$$E[p_2 - p_1|a]$$

Since value is revealed at period 3, with probability α, the speculator's utility from trading, via the market-maker, can be expressed as

$$\begin{aligned}
U_a^i &= q_a^i E\left[\alpha\left(v - \frac{p_1 + p_2}{2}\right) + (1 - \alpha)\frac{p_2 - p_1}{2}|a\right] \\
&= q_a^i\left[\alpha v - \frac{\alpha p_1}{2} - \frac{\alpha p_2}{2} + \frac{p_2}{2} - \frac{p_1}{2} - \frac{\alpha p_2}{2} + \frac{\alpha p_1}{2}\right] \\
&= q_a^i\left[\alpha v - \frac{p_1}{2} + \frac{p_2}{2}(1 - 2\alpha)\right]
\end{aligned} \tag{11.5}$$

where the first line of the above set of expressions decomposes the speculator's utility into that expected to prevail if his trade is cleared 'early', at period 1. The second part of the expression in square brackets, records the utility gained by holding the asset if his trade clears 'late' at period 2. If the speculator's trade clears early then he gains, or loses, the difference between the average price he pays and what the asset is truly worth; but if his trade clears late he receives the capital gain on holding the asset based on the difference between what he paid for it at period 1 and what it's now worth at period 2.

So if the ith speculator trading upon valuation attribute a can get his trade executed at period 1, he expects the price to be

$$E[p_2|a] = \lambda_1 E[D_1|a] = \lambda_1 \left(q_a^i + \left(\frac{n_a}{2} - 1 \right) \bar{q}_a \right) \tag{11.6}$$

where D_1 is the period 1 order flow for the asset at period 1, $\frac{n_a}{2}$ is the half of informed speculators who have their trades executed 'early' at period 1. Price is determined by the ith informed speculator's demand, q_a^i plus that of the $(n_a - 1)$ other informed speculators trading on the basis of valuation attribute a, where these are assumed to have an average demand of $\bar{q}_a$. A very similar expression for period 2 price results from the aggregation of the order flows cleared at both periods 1 and 2, $(D_1 + D_2)$

$$E[p_2|a] = \lambda_2 E\left[\frac{D_1 + D_2}{2} |a \right] = \lambda_2 \left(\frac{q_a^i + (n_a - 1)\bar{q}_a}{2} \right) \tag{11.7}$$

Given these expectations, when an informed speculator trades he seeks to maximize a utility function of the form

$$U_a^i = q_a^i \left\{ \alpha a - \frac{\lambda_1}{2} \left(q_a^i + \left(\frac{n_a}{2} - 1 \right) \bar{q}_a \right) + \frac{\lambda_2}{4} (1 - 2\alpha)(q_a^i + (n_a - 1)\bar{q}_a) \right\} \tag{11.8}$$

We can see the effect of varying informed speculators' degree of short-sightedness by considering this utility function when speculators have varying trading horizons. We begin by seeing what happens if value, v, is certain to be revealed at period 3, so $\alpha = 1$. Under these circumstances there is no benefit to informed speculators who trade late, $p_2 = p_3$, because no new information arrives after period 2, all trades now have to be cleared through the market-maker. Here the utility of speculators informed about a becomes

$$U_a^i = q_a^i \left\{ a - \frac{\lambda_1}{2} \left(q_a^i + \left(\frac{n_a}{2} - 1 \right) \bar{q}_a \right) + \frac{\lambda_2}{4} (1 - \alpha)(q_a^i + (n_a - 1)\bar{q}_a) \right\}$$

$$\Rightarrow q_a^i \left\{ a - \frac{\lambda_1}{2} \left(q_a^i + \left(\frac{n_a}{2} - 1 \right) \bar{q}_a \right) - \frac{\lambda_2}{4} (q_a^i + (n_a - 1)\bar{q}_a) \right\} \text{ if } \alpha = 1 \tag{11.9}$$

In this expression the search for information about the first valuation attribute, a, only reduces the utility of those who searched for it first. If informed speculators can get information about value attribute a into price in period 1, they can profit when the terminating value is revealed in period 4. If such an informed trader trades early the value of his information is dissipated in the next period (between periods 2 and 3), as others follow his lead. If they do not (because they collect information about the other element of terminating value b, for example), they do not push price closer to value, which can only erode the informed speculator's profit from trading on the value attribute a ($E[v - 1/2(p_1 + p_2)|a]$). So informed speculators have no incentive to herd and every incentive to divert interest amongst other traders from the fragment of value they concentrate their research upon. This encourages the collection and use of a wide variety of information in trading. Thus price is rendered a sufficient statistic of value.

Assume conversely $\alpha = 0$, because dividends are sure to be announced in period 4, and so there will be no change in price between periods 2 and 3. If there is no price change possible (because no new information is revealed about v) speculation is short term in the sense that all hope of profiting from the trade is focused in the near term, between periods 1 and 2. Since value is not revealed at period 3 the speculators' only hope is to correctly guess what information will be impounded into price by those who have their order cleared 'late', i.e. between periods 2 and 3. In these circumstances short-term informed speculators have a utility function of the form

$$U_a^i = q_a^i \left\{ \alpha a - \frac{\lambda_1}{2} \left(q_a^i + \left(\frac{n_a}{2} - 1 \right) \overline{q}_a \right) + \frac{\lambda_2}{4} (1 - 2\alpha)(q_a^i + (n_a - 1)\overline{q}_a) \right\} \text{ if } \alpha = 1 \qquad (11.10)$$

In this expression a greater number of investors following the information source regarding true asset value, a, concerning value, v, the higher the ith informed speculator's utility if he trades on the basis of information about value contained in value attribute a. If only such a speculator can get his trade cleared 'early', he profits from later imitators, who follow his introduction of information about asset value, a, into price, so collecting information.

Now price becomes fixated on one aspect of value alone and the true importance of that fragment may not matter that much. What matters is to focus on an information source others will later be easily able to pick up on. Hence collecting truly fundamental, value-relevant, information may be rendered as less important than collecting eye-catching, but ultimately uninformative, gossip about a stock.

A numerical illustration of the FSS model

To illustrate how contraction of the investor's prospective horizon affects the utility of investors trading on the basis of value attribute a, I consider some simple comparative static exercises using Equation (11.5). As in other such exercises I provide some initial values used in the numerical illustrations (see Table 11.1).

I begin by considering the effect of slowly making the investor, trading on the basis of some value attribute a, more convinced that he needs to get his trade cleared 'early', i.e. at period 1, by allowing the probability the liquidating dividend will be paid at period 3, α, to slowly converge on certainty. Figure 11.2 shows the impact of the contracting investment horizon on the utility of an investor trading on information regarding value attribute a alone. As the probability of trading ending at period 3, α, rises towards 1 (i.e. right-hand side of Figure 11.2), the investor's utility is solely determined by the difference between what the asset is finally worth ($v = 10$ in this example) and the average price he pays to obtain it across periods 1 and 2 $((10 + 11)/2 = 10.5)$. So when an early end to trading is certain, $\alpha = 1$, then utility equals -0.5 (i.e., $1 \times (10 - 11)/2$).

Table 11.1   Initial values for numerical illustration of investors' utility for those trading on the basis of value attribute a (Equation (11.5))

Parameter	Value
q_a (quantity demanded by investors trading on value attribute a)	1
v ('true value' of asset at end of trade)	10
α (probability of liquidating dividend, v, paid early at period 3)	0.5
p_1 (price at period 1)	10
p_2 (price at period 2)	11

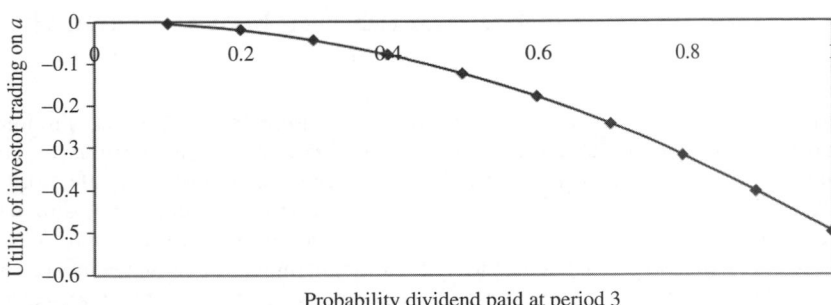

Figure 11.2 Investor's utility if he trades on a as a function of probability dividend paid at period 3 (α)

In the next comparative static exercise I hold the probability of trading ending early at period 3, α, equal to 50%. Now I consider a slowly increasing period 2 price or, alternatively, put a slowly growing percentage return between periods 1 and 2. Examining Equation (11.5) for the utility of an investor trading on the basis of some value attribute a, it is clear a rising price at period 2 relative to period 1 has two offsetting effects:

- It reduces the first part of expression (11.5) because it raises the average price paid to obtain the asset. Since the first part of the expression is given by value minus average price paid to obtain the asset rising period 2 price makes this term more negative,
- It raises the value of the second part of the expression, which is actually the horizontal axis in Figure 11.3. Rising period 2 price, p_2, holding period 1 price, p_1, constant increases the second term proportionately, given the probability of an early end to trade, α, is now fixed at a half in this example.

As is clear from Figure 11.3, given the numerical initial values supplied in Table 11.1, the diminutive impact of the first term dominates in this example and rising period 2 price tends to reduce investors' utility if they trade on the basis of value attribute a. The holding gains if their trade clears early are greater, but this effect is overwhelmed by the increased cost of acquiring the asset if their trade is cleared late, at period 2 (so they actually pay the higher price p_2 to acquire the asset).

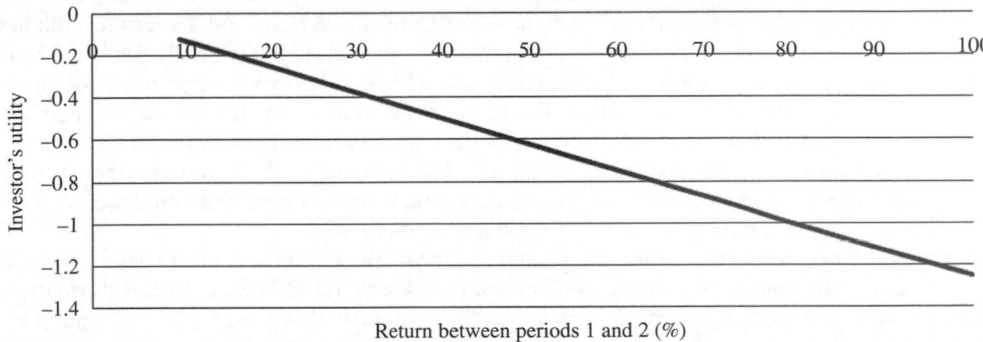

Figure 11.3 Investor's utility if he trades on a as a function of return (%) between periods 1 and 2

11.3 Conformity as a Force for Social Good and Evil

Few can doubt that some degree of social conformity is a useful thing. If drivers randomly chose whether to drive on the right- or left-hand side of the road, life could get tricky. Similarly some degree of conformity in styles of dress, degree of familiarity and punctuality just make life more pleasant. Shiller (1995) points out the centrality of polite conversation, small talk and even gossip in making a social polity cohere. But, following the rise of communist/authoritarian states and the scourge of Nazism in Europe, psychologists started to study the more pathological consequences of conformity (Shiller 2005). These studies tried to understand how mature, mentally stable, married men could submit children and grandmothers, very like their own, into a gas chamber. If such decent ordinary folk could do that, could I be brought to such animalistic behaviour too?

One such famous experiment by Solomon Asch (1952) asked participants to answer very straight-forward questions about the relative length of two pieces of string. Left to their own devices, participants correctly stated which string was longer almost without error. However, Asch now introduced some 'stooges' who deliberately gave the wrong answer. Asch then asked participants to give their answer to questions about the lengths of the pieces of string in sequence and he ensured the lying stooges went first. Upon hearing the lying stooges' (clearly incorrect) answers almost one-third of non-stooge/true participants started to give answers they must have known to be false. In Asch's original version of the study, the true participant could see the stooges and so may have made some connection with them. The decision to give obviously incorrect answers to simple questions may have been induced by fear of the social consequences of not doing so. Later Deutsch and Gerard (1955) repeated the experiment with anonymous unseen stooges. Again about one-third of non-stooge/true participants gave the wrong answers to these obvious questions. The only explanation here seems to be that we truly value others' judgements and often conform, even if doing so defies our own internal logic. It may simply be that others with more up-to-date information know more than we do.

The hideous lengths to which conformity can go were shockingly revealed in an experiment by Stanley Milgram in the 1960s. Milgram (1974) asked experimental subjects to punish participants in a quiz for incorrect answers. Initially the shocks given by the experimental subjects were merely irritating and designed to alert those taking the quiz that they were performing poorly. But over time Milgram increased the voltage of the shock until the quiz participant cried out in agony. Fortunately for all involved Milgram arranged for the quiz candidates to be actors who simply feigned a response to the electric shock. Disturbingly, even when the quiz participant/actor was clearly screaming in agony, many participants were happy to carry on pushing the button.

In the recent movie version of *The Smartest Guys in the Room* (McLean & Elkind 2003), footage of the Milgram experiments is shown to explain how institutionalized fraud and deception could have propagated through Enron. In the footage chosen the experimental subject is clearly distressed by the quiz participant's/actor's response and repeatedly asks Milgram, 'Do you accept responsibility for this?' before continuing to hit the button. The clear implication is that the scientific expertise of Milgram makes it all right to ignore the evidence of the experimental subject's eyes that he is causing another person great pain and possible lasting injury. The relevance to the Enron story here is that if Jeff Skilling and Ken Lay as 'the smartest guys in the room' believed Enron had found a great way to make money, who were their less 'smart' subordinates to doubt it?

This 'informational effect' of observing what other (possibly smarter) people do before you act is modelled as an 'informational cascade' (Bikhchandani, Hirshleifer & Welch 1992). Informational cascade models are just one form of 'rational herding' models that try to explain herding as a consequence of behaviour, which while individually rational, nevertheless has socially damaging effects (see Devenow & Welch 1996). Such models are part of the wide range of models in behavioural finance which consider a 'representative agent'. All investors have the same attitude to risk and face the same payoffs to alternative courses of action, they only differ in their place in the queue of decision-makers. Such models give an important alternative perspective on behavioural bias in financial decision making to that emphasized in the current text, which focuses largely on 'noise-trader' type models. Here I focus on trade between different types of traders, ignoring the conflicts within individual traders' choices. Representative agent type models are better at capturing the impact of biases in individual traders' utility behaviour, but often do so at the expense of ignoring how these biases work themselves out in the process of trading an asset. So the type of model you focus upon contains a trade-off because neither representative agent models nor noise-trader models do a complete job in capturing the full range of behavioural phenomena observed in financial markets.

11.3.1   Evidence on Herding and its Effect

Often many forms of stock-market anomalies are seen as a consequence of the participation of ignorant, poorly capitalized, individual investors. Strangely, Nofsinger and Sias (1999) present evidence that the herding in equity markets may be primarily driven by the trading of institutional investors. These researchers examined monthly returns in the years 1977–96 for stocks that they could match in each October of each year to Standard & Poor's data on institutional ownership. This led to a sample of between 1200 and 1500 stocks in each year of their 20-year sample. Consequently their study was performed on a sample of over 24,000 firm-years. In October each stock is assigned to an institutional ownership decile (say decile 1 is the 10% most dominated by institutional stock holding, while decile 10 is that most dominated by individual investors), and a similar allocation within each ownership decile is made on the basis of the degree of the change in institutional ownership. Nofsinger and Sias (1999) found that institutions consistently pile into a fairly narrow set of stocks driving their price and returns to holding them up; leaving securities in the deciles they have left to perform poorly. To some extent this reflects the fact that institutions follow the market and seek out shares that are already rising. This means that the impact of attracting institutional investors on price is to some degree an artefact of the momentum effect already documented (Jegadeesh & Titman 1993). But Nofsinger and Sias (1999) confirmed that, even allowing for the confounding effect of momentum, institutional shareholders isolate, enter and reap profits in narrow segments of equity markets.

This evidence confirms more general evidence concerning the dubious value of 'expert' opinion. Hilton (2003), in a review of the evidence, notes professionals like doctors and lawyers:

- use too few cues, or indicators, of the correct path forward, to make decisions;
- use cues which differ greatly depending on the 'expert' consulted;
- seem to have little insight into either the range or nature of the cues they use to characterize a particular decision to be made.

It appears that both doctors and fund managers differ in unsystematic ways and those that consult them suffer as a result.

This conclusion accords with the traditional understanding that few financial institutions exhibit any stock-picking ability (Jensen 1968). But Nofsinger and Sias (1999) point out that most tests of the skill of financial institutions have been confined to mutual funds and it is possible other players, such as unit trusts and hedge funds, have more success. Indeed the very rise of hedge funds as significant forces in financial markets suggests that active institutional investment may play a role that efficient markets hypothesis advocates would seek to deny it.

11.3.2   Herding in Investment Advice

One reason why investors may tend to agree is because of the nature of the advice they receive from stock brokers and market commentators. Welch (2000) studied the clustering of analysts' recommendations to buy, sell or hold a stock in a client's portfolio. Importantly, Welch warns us that herding is more than simply agreement. Two advisors may agree simply because the salient facts all point in one direction. If all doctors now advise their patients against smoking, whereas only a third did so in the 1950s, we would not say doctors are 'herding' on the advice that smoking harms our health. We just know so much more about how smoking causes cancer, and many other nasty conditions, now. Doctors' advice has changed to reflect the balance of medical evidence. So herding is agreement which cannot be explained by reference to the facts other than the behaviour of their peers.

The problem faced by tests for the presence of herding, as Welch points out, is that we can never really know what the dispersion of analysts' recommendations would look like if they did not herd. In order to make some progress in judging the extent of herding in investment advice, Welch (2000) advances one simple, if extreme, assumption about what the distributions of analysts' recommendations would look like if no herding was present. Welch simply assumes that the overall distribution of analysts' recommendations we observe exhibits no herding on average. So for Welch (2000), the distribution of analysts' recommendations under the null of no herding is simply the observed distribution of recommendations at any point in time. Welch (2000) then compares how the distribution of recommendations changes with the prevailing consensus amongst analysts. Only when analysts' revisions of their recommendations (not the recommendation level itself) gravitate towards the overall consensus can we conclude analysts herd in their recommendations. So a high proportion of revisions of analysts' recommendations from strong buy (coded 1) to sell (coded 4) does not in itself imply herding, but a higher proportion of revisions from strong buy to sell implies more herding is more probable when the consensus is sell than when it is hold (coded 2) does imply herding in Welch's (2000) tests. Any base tendency to herd towards the consensus, regardless of its level, is thus excluded from the measurement of herding in this form of test.

Welch (2000) studied over 50,000 recommendations issued by 226 different brokerage houses in the US Zacks database in the years 1989–94. This sample results from the exclusion of stocks attracting fewer than 16 recommendations, to focus on large well-covered corporations where herding is most likely to impact on the market. Despite the inherent conservatism of Welch's (2000) herding metric, he finds considerable evidence that recommendation revisions herd towards the prevailing consensus regardless of the underlying distribution of advice given. Importantly he finds the strength of herding toward the consensus is not affected by whether the consensus recommendation is a good predictor of future stock price performance or not. This finding suggests that security analysts may indeed focus on almost randomly chosen fragments of information, as opposed to benefiting from information contained in the prior recommendations making up the consensus value. Welch (2000) also reports the tendency to herd is stronger during market booms than busts. This implies market rises are more fragile and ill considered than subsequent declines.

11.3.3   Words which Cannot be Spoken

One of the most recognized failures of competitive financial markets is their inability to impound bad news about company performance. Hong, Lim and Stei (2000) tell us 'bad news travels slowly'. Conrad, Cornell and Landsman (2002) find the impact of bad news regarding company performance is particularly devastating in rising markets. Later work by Conrad et al. (2006) confirms that price-following behaviour by analysts is particularly marked for sell recommendations. Analysts, it seems, will only downgrade a stock once the fact the company has fallen apart is public knowledge. Sticking the knife into company management does not come naturally to analysts it seems.

Two examples of brave journalism exposing blemishes on shiny exteriors illustrate the costs of bucking the trends of being held in thrall to a seemingly successful management team. The first, by Bethany McLean of *Fortune* in February 2001, was entitled 'Is Enron overpriced?', built on the concerns of Jim Chanos of the Kynikos Associates hedge fund that had begun to short sell Enron stock (McLean & Elkind 2003). Upon checking some financial facts with Jeff Skilling, the CEO of Enron, on 14 February, McLean was visited the next day by a three-man team to 'guide her' through the intricate details of Enron's accounts – this included Andrew Fastow, later portrayed by Jeff Skilling and Ken Lay as the chief architect of Enron's chicanery. Skilling and McLean were joined in this meeting by two of McLean's superiors on the editorial team at *Fortune* to focus her attention. After an initial market downturn in March the bubble continued to inflate. Goldman Sachs' analyst David Fleischer dismissed her concerns stating, 'Investors have focused on issues we view as almost insignificant for valuation'.

A second example of brave journalism relates to an article in the *Washington Post* in July 2002. Alex Klein points to how AOL had used 'unconventional deals' to prop up advertising revenue in the period after the dot.com collapse (Klein 2003, pp.287–8; see also Swisher & Dickey 2003, pp.231–8). Klein pointed out that AOL had booked the whole of eBay's on-line advertising budget as part of its own advertising revenue as well as the recognition of other 'bartered' revenue from reciprocal advertising deals (where no cash actually passed at all!) with Sun Microsystems and others. After initial opposition from Time Warner's outside attorney, Thomas Yanucci, and some reassuring noises from the new CEO, Richard Parsons, Time Warner began to implode. The two Klein articles broke the 'informational cascade' that depicted AOL as the gold standard of the remaining new economy. The whole house of cards tumbled down with little more than two investigative reporting articles that summarized what was already known concerning strange accounting practice within Time Warner. The consensus of support for Time Warner though tight proved very fragile.

It is in the nature of speculative bubbles that they breed a political consensus to maintain its grip. As Galbraith (1993, p.5) points out:

> Those involved with the speculation are experiencing an increase in wealth – getting rich or being further enriched. No one wishes to believe this is fortuitous or undeserved; all wish to think it is the result of their superior insight or intuition.

Once a speculative bubble takes grip, defusing it may be a thankless task.

11.3.4 Private Truths and Public Lies

The rapid evaporation of a positive consensus regarding a company's 'value creation' story might be seen as analogous to the rapid demise of political tyrannies, such as when the Berlin Wall unexpectedly 'fell down' in 1990. Timur Kuran in his book *Private Truths and Public Lies* (1997) presents a theory of the falsification of expressed preferences and its consequences. Such falsification is everywhere and often benign in character. For example, I may pretend to be comfortable with a Muslim colleague's wearing of the veil in order to avoid an embarrassing scene. Similarly, a Muslim colleague might choose not to wear her veil to work so as to avoid being thought 'extreme'. But sometimes, as Kuran writes, the preference falsification can induce rapid swings in the prevailing public consensus. Kuran points out the presence of three forms of utility from public decisions:

- *Intrinsic utility*, the instrumental utility of getting what I really want, for example unveiled colleagues, or the freedom to cover my face in public as I believe my faith requires.
- *Expressive utility* from our freedom to express who we truly are and feel, if my religious faith is very important to me I may value highly a public statement of it.
- *Reputational utility*, which derives from others' response to our decision, for example claims of racism, or dangerous religious extremism.

The utility we experience is the sum of all three elements. When sitting in a Glasgow pub concern about reputational utility may make me cheer 'our boys' on in a more muted way than at home in England. Figure 11.4 shows how total utility aggregates all subcomponents to lead to 'preference reversals' in the sense that publicly expressed preferences refute private preferences at least for a large percentage of the population.

Following an illustration of Kuran's model, suggested by Robert Frank in his book review (Frank, 1996), consider an imaginary despot called Elvis who insists on public adoration by his people, anything less being ruthlessly crushed. Opponents to Elvis's rule are willing to voice their discontent at differing levels of public support. Dissident A will always speak out against Elvis as a lone voice. But dissidents B and C, being weaker willed, will only speak out against Elvis if 20% of his subjects also do so. Dissident D will join A, B and C in opposing the Elvis regime if 30% of Elvis's subjects rebel, etc. We can consider the opposition to Elvis lined up according to their degree of outspokenness as shown in Table 11.2.

In this sort of society A is marginalized easily, perhaps even imprisoned, or simply regarded as odd for not appreciating how wonderful Elvis, the glorious leader, truly is. Now suppose either B or C just happen to have a nasty experience with one of Elvis's hired thugs. Let B or C decide to speak out, because he is annoyed, even though currently only $1/7 = 14.28\%$ of Elvis's subjects dare to oppose

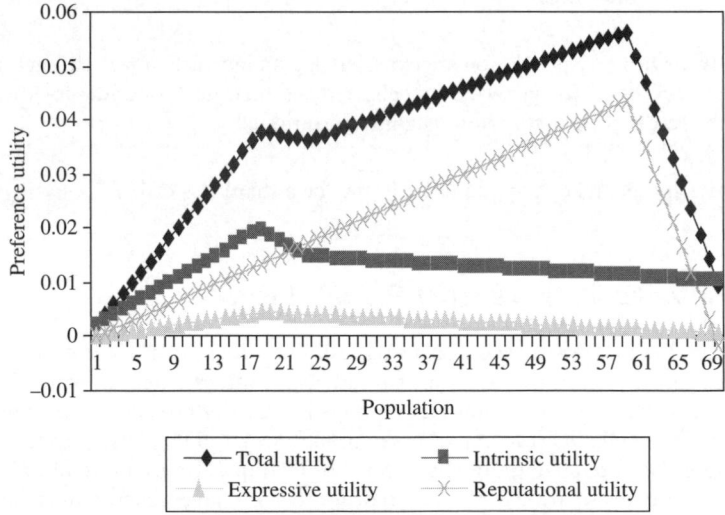

Figure 11.4   Kuran's 'preference reversal'

Table 11.2 Numerical illustration of Kuran's preference falsification

Dissident	A	B	C	D	E	F	G
Support required to rebel	0	20%	20%	30%	40%	50%	60%

him. Once either B or C joins with A to oppose Elvis the other joins him. Opposition has grown to 28% and B will join the opposition if C already has and C will join if B already has. The opposition swells to A, B and C. So with 3/7 or 42% of the population opposing, E joins the opposition. Now with 5/7 or 71% of the population opposing Elvis even timid F and G will join the coup. The game is up for Elvis just because of a casual act of brutality by one of his bag carriers.

Sunstein gives two examples of recent recognition of the gathering around and subsequent rapid dissolution of a 'group think' consensus within US government agencies (Sunstein 2006). The first was the 2004 Select Committee's report on the CIA's decision to support invasion of Iraq, despite clear doubts about Iraq's immediate threat to international peace. The second was NASA's 2003 report into the decision to launch the *Challenger* space shuttle on a freezing January morning in 1986, despite evidence that the sealant 'O rings' on the booster rockets could fail at low temperatures. In both cases the move from optimistic action to a defensive search for scapegoats was rapid.

The importance of these tales for finance is the rapidity with which a firm consensus surrounding a company can dissolve. In this environment small cue variables, such as those incorporated in simple decision heuristics, count.

11.3.5 The Herd in History

Since Gustave Le Bon we have been all too aware that we live in the 'era of crowds' (Le Bon 1895). It appears every generation must experience the scourge of financial contagion at least once. Historians of financial crises are so well supplied with materials that they can provide a top 10 list of such events (Kindleberger & Aliber 2005, p.8). These include:

- the Dutch 'tulip bulb' bubble of 1636 (recall the case study in the appendix to Chapter 5);
- the South Sea bubble of 1720;
- the 1929 stock-market crash; and
- the dot.com bubble at the end of the 1990s.

Each of these financial bubbles/manias gave rise to social transformations in their formation and sharp regulatory responses to their demise. None seems to have exhausted investor credulity and we must accept that we are simply in the interregnum between the last bubble and the next, even though the current crisis of 2008 seems the 'mother of all meltdowns' right now. In a separate chapter, I chronicle some of the history of financial bubbles and consider how well existing evidence fits the 'noise-trader' interpretation of how bubbles take grip and implode.

11.4 Conclusion and Summary

This chapter presents a theoretical illustration of how an inappropriate level of agreement can arise amongst financial agents. In such circumstances herding can occur in financial markets. As Hayek has pointed out the beauty of financial markets and their fast-moving prices is their ability to aggregate more information about investor demands than any one trader could reasonably hope to know. This information aggregation property is part of the 'magic of the market'. The FSS model shows how the market, far from aggregating a vast disparate array of information, can fixate on a narrow strand of value-irrelevant company attributes. I also present evidence that herding occurs in financial markets, even amongst professionals. Later in the chapter I try to give some idea of why herding occurs and why the swiftly emerging, tight-bound, consensus about a company's or market's prospects once created can prove so fragile.

Appendix: *The United States vs. Microsoft*

On 18 May 1998 the US government, 19 states and the District of Columbia sued Microsoft Corporation, claiming it had monopolized the personal computer operating software industry and was using unfair competitive tactics against rivals like Sun Microsystems, producers of Java-based technologies, and Netscape, producers of the famous rival browser. This suit constituted a return to the big 'trust-busting' litigation of the late eighteenth century against John Rockefeller's Standard Oil, IBM in the 1960s and ATT in the 1970s. My discussion of this case is largely based on an account by William Page and John Lopatka, two lawyers heavily involved in preparing the government's case against Microsoft (Page & Lopatka 2007). However, this case was so massive and influential it has spawned a whole literature in and of itself within industrial organization and law and economics.

Central to this literature is the impact and appropriate public policy response to 'network externalities' especially in the development and use of new information technologies. Such 'network externalities' are everywhere in modern life. My television will stop working in the UK soon unless I 'go digital'. Even then I must do this in a particular prespecified way. Such network effects are all around us and are of two types:

- *Network externalities*, this occurs when we need to agree a common technical standard to coordinate our use of technology. Linking railway stations is a classic example of this. Suppose the gauges of railway tracks running between Bristol and London are different. Commuters will have to choose, when travelling between these two cities, from trains distinguished on the basis of the width of their wheels, as well as time of departure and cost. Separate rail companies will have separate terminals with varying width of track and never the two trains will meet. In the modern age, standards for bandwidth, data transfer speeds, etc., pose similar challenges.
- *Complementary bandwagon effects*, these arise if my usage of a specific technology makes it cheaper or better for those I deal with to use it as well. So I choose to have the same mobile phone company as my wife, because our calls and texts are cheaper that way. Or I might fly with the same airline company as my colleagues, so we can pool free 'air miles' savings. Here there is no technical barrier to personally stylized usage. It is just a shared frame of use or it is cheaper or more fun for me to travel that way.

You may be wondering why a book on behavioural finance has wondered off into industrial organization, even in an appendix, but it is important to understand that financial markets service the investment needs of the companies traded in them. Conformity in investment and product development induces conformity in the purchase of equity of rival software producers. A 'neglected stock' may become so, not because of analysts or investment bankers, but because of clever lawyers or cantankerous judges. Nor is the consumer the only player in the determination of who makes what software and under what competitive conditions. The state in the form of a myriad of regulatory authorities also determines the shape of supply for new technologies and acceptable practice in their development and marketing. The US Department of Justice (DoJ), from the late 1980s, raised at least four separate actions against Microsoft for various types of anti-competitive practice against software rivals. These were:

1. Following a discontinued initial action by the Federal Trade Commission in 1989 the DoJ intervened to prevent Microsoft's suppression of IBM's rival operating system the OS/2. This resulted in Microsoft having to amend its 'per processor' licence agreement that imposed payment of a licensing fee irrespective of whether Microsoft's MS-DOS or the icon-driven 'middleware' system 'Windows' was used.
2. The DoJ challenged Microsoft's planned acquisition of Intuit, the manufacturers of the personal accounts software product Quicken, following its IPO in 1993. Quicken was a strong competitor to the Microsoft Money program in 1995. Microsoft backed off and abandoned the acquisition.
3. The DoJ challenged the bundling of Internet access software, the Microsoft Service Network, into its Windows 95 upgrade of the Windows system.
4. From August 1996 the DoJ began to concentrate all its antitrust fire against Microsoft for the way in which it responded to the arrival of perhaps its first credible competitor in the software market – Mark Andreessen and Jim Clark's Netscape (the history of which is told fairly entertainingly in *Netscape Time*: Clark & Edwards 2000).

I will focus here on the fourth point, following Page and Lopatka (2007), and it is indeed the 'browser wars' that have been the most contentious part of litigation against Microsoft for abuse of its dominant position. The case against Microsoft alleging monopolization spanned over 150 separate legal rulings (including appeals and dissenting legal judgements), so what I give here can only be regarded as the high points of that litigation. All such common law cases, requiring interpretation of primary antimonopoly legislation, such as the 1890 Sherman Act, involve balancing two opposing approaches to regulation of monopolized markets:

• *An evolutionary approach*, which holds that monopolists sow the seeds of their own downfall, creating huge profits to attract competitors and soon becoming lazy, insufficiently cost conscious and crucially lacking in innovative verve. This view tends to favour the courts holding back and awaiting the monopolist's downfall at the hands of his own greed.
• *An interventionist approach*, which worries about monopoly capitalism compromising the proper operation of markets, via brute force, bribes and intimidation of rivals. This perspective favours court action to remedy wrongs done to plaintiffs before the court.

Microsoft's history certainly gave scope for both interpretations to make sense. Microsoft did largely miss out on the early stages of Internet development and allowed rivals, like AOL, to displace them. But as disclosures in the various trials would point out there was no shortage of evidence of Bill Gates's iron fist inside the velvet glove he presented to the courts.

A central document in feeding the case for an interventionist approach to Microsoft's emergence as a monopolist in the software market was a white paper submitted to the DoJ by Gary Reback and Susan Creighton on behalf of Netscape. This 191-page document set out what Page and Lopakta (2007, p.29) call the 'guiding narrative' of the claim of monopolization against Microsoft. Once established all plaintiffs made their claims on derivative versions of this central document. The Reback and Creighton 1996 white paper stated:

> At very bottom this is a simple case. It is about a monopolist (Microsoft) that has maintained its monopoly for more than 10 years. That monopoly is threatened by the introduction of new technology (Web software) that is a partial substitute – and could in time become a

complete substitute for the monopoly product. Before that can happen the monopolist decides to eliminate its rival Netscape

The threat that software resident on a website, but executable on an individual personal computer, posed to the Windows' monopoly had already been publicly recognized by Gates, making the white paper's claim quite credible. Computer applications written in Sun Microsystems's Java language could now be accessed via Netscape and executed locally, although the requisite source code was resident on a remote computer. This sowed the seeds for bypassing the need for an operating system and accompanying computing applications on each individual's personal computer. Such a trajectory for new software development effectively unravelled Microsoft's headlock on the software market. Microsoft was not slow to protect its turf. The question remained what the DoJ could do about it, if anything.

Very little, it turned out – the initial ruling of Judge Thomas Penfield Jackson that Microsoft was in violation of Sections 1 and 2 of the Sherman Act led him to recommend the break-up of Microsoft in 2000 into an applications software house and an entirely separate operating systems provider with strong restrictions on the way products of the two companies could be cross-marketed and designed so as to facilitate simultaneous use.

In June 2001 the Court of Appeal overturned Jackson's proposed remedy and remanded a re-hearing of the case by Judge Kollar-Kotelly, but not before making some observations that were to later derail the DoJ's case. In particular, the Court of Appeal did not accept the government had proved the browser market was a separate market capable of being monopolized. Nor did it accept the view Judge Jackson had taken of Microsoft's attitude to competitors, that is, Netscape, Sun Microsystems, IBM, etc., as constituting monopolizing behaviour 'on the whole'. The Court of Appeal preferred to consider individual markets and products and apply legislative standards of conduct. In November 2002 Judge Kollar-Kotelly approved a settlement between Microsoft, the DoJ and nine plaintiff states. Microsoft was initially ordered to comply with the consent decree for five years. In June 2004 a Federal Appeals Court approved the settlement between Microsoft and the DoJ, rejecting objections, raised by the State of Massachusetts, that the sanctions were inadequate to meet the damage caused. The consent decree was extended in January 2008, after Judge Kollar-Kotelly again reprimanded Microsoft for failing to release requisite documentation to facilitate compatibility with its products to rival software producers. The consent decree thus stays in force until November 2009 at the earliest.

Questions

1. Return to Equation (11.5), the expression for an investor's utility if he trades upon the basis of value attribute a. Figure 11.2 showed how, given the initial values provided in Table 11.1, an investor's utility for trading on the basis of value attribute a fell as period 2 price, p_2, rose. Suppose you hear a rumour that it is very unlikely a liquidating dividend will be paid early. Now you feel confident setting $\alpha = 5\%$ in evaluating the investor's utility from trading on a (i.e. calculating Equation (11.5) above). How does a rising period 2 price, p_2, from 11 to 20 impact on an investor's utility from trading on value attribute a? Redraw Figure 11.2 for $\alpha = 0.5$ and interpret your results to answer this question. Interpret the relation between the redrawn Figure 11.2 and the original provided.

2. Remember the kingdom of Elvis in Table 11.2 and how B or C got beaten up by Elvis's thugs? A news flash has arrived. It was B who was beaten up. But he will be OK so don't worry. C has always hated B, it's a long story, and always hoped someone would sort him out. On hearing B has got his just desserts C rejoices, glad to have the great Elvis's protective hand on his life. So now he

too (like D) will only rise up if 30% of all subjects rise up against Elvis. What is the impact of the A and B backed insurgency against Elvis?

3. Read the appendix on the Microsoft litigation. Do you think the extent of 'herding' on to Microsoft products (for word-processing, producing presentations and data analysis) can be justified in terms of consumer well-being? What dangers, if any, do you see in such 'herding' occurring?

Note

1. The OLS technology is explained is most econometrics textbooks but Madala (1992) and Greene (2003) are very readable classics.

References

Asch, S. (1952). *Social Psychology*. Englewood Cliffs, NJ: Prentice-Hall.

Bikhchandani, S., D. Hirshleifer & I. Welch (1992). A theory of fashion fads, custom and cultural changes as informational cascades. *Journal of Political Economy*, **1000**: 992–1026.

Clark, J. & O. Edwards (2000). *Netscape Time: The Making of the Billion-Dollar Start-up that Took on Microsoft*. New York: St Martin's Griffin.

Conrad, J., B. Cornell & W. Landsman (2002). When is bad news really bad news? *Journal of Finance*, **57**: 2507–23.

Conrad, J., B. Cornell, W. Landsman & B. Rowntree (2006). How do analysts' recommendations respond to major news? *Journal of Financial and Quantitative Analysis*, **41**: 25–49.

Deutsch, M. & H. Gerard (1955). A study of normative and informational influences upon individual decision making. *Journal of Abnormal and Social Psychology*, **51**: 629–36.

Devenow, A. & I. Welch (1996). Rational herding in financial markets. *European Economic Review*, **40**: 603–15.

Frank, R. (1996). The political economy of preference falsification in Timur Kuran's *Private Truth, Public Lies*. *Journal of Economic Literature* **34**(March): 115–123.

Froot, K., D. Scharstein & J. Stein (1992). Herd on the street. Informational efficiency in a market short-term speculation. *Journal of Finance*, **47**: 1451–84.

Galbraith, J. (1993). *A Short History of Financial Euphoria*. New York: Penguin.

Greene, W. (2003). *Econometric Analysis*. Englewood Cliffs, NJ: Prentice-Hall.

Hilton, D. (2003). Psychology and financial markets: applications to understanding and remedying irrational decision-making. In I. Brocas & J. Carrillo (eds), *The Psychology of Economic Decisions: Volume 1: Rationality and Well-Being*. Oxford: Oxford University Press.

Hong, H., T. Lim & J. Stei (2000). Bad news travels slowly: size, analyst coverage and the profitability of momentum strategies. *Journal of Finance*, **55**: 265–95.

Jegadeesh, N. & S. Titman (1993). Returns to buying winners and selling losers: implications for market efficiency. *Journal of Finance*, **48**: 65–91.

Jensen, M. (1968). The performance of mutual funds in the period 1945–1964. *Journal of Finance*, **23**: 389–416.

Kindleberger, C. & R. Aliber (2005). *Manias, Panics and Crashes: A History of Financial Crises*, fifth edition. Basingstoke, England: Palgrave.

Klein, A. (2003). *Stealing Time: Jerry Levin and the Collapse of AOL Time Warner*. New York: Simon & Schuster.

Kuran, T. (1997). *Private Truths and Public Lies: The Social Consequences of Preference Falsification*. Cambridge, MA: Harvard University Press.

LeBon, G. (1895). *The Crowd*. New Brunswick: Rutgers State University Press.

Madala, G.S. (1992). *Introduction to Econometrics*. Englewood Cliffs, NJ: Prentice-Hall.

McLean, B. & P. Elkind (2003). *The Smartest Guys in the Room: The Amazing Rise and Scandalous Fall of Enron*. New York: Portfolio.

Milgram, S. (1974). *Obedience to Authority*. New York: Harper & Row.

Nofsinger, J. & R. Sias (1999). Herding and feedback trading by institutional and individual investors. *Journal of Finance*, 54: 2263–95.

Page, W. & J. Lopatka (2007). *The Microsoft Case: Antitrust, High Technology and Consumer Welfare*. Chicago: Chicago University Press.

Rohlfs, J. (2001). *Bandwagon Effects in High Technology Industries*. Cambridge, MA: MIT Press.

Shiller, R. (1995). Conversation, information and herd behavior. *American Economic Review*, 54: 181–5.

Shiller, R. (2005). *Irrational Exuberance*. Princeton: Princeton University Press.

Sunstein, C. (2006). *Infotopia: How Many Minds Produce Knowledge*. Oxford: Oxford University Press.

Swisher, K. & L. Dickey (2003). *There must be a Pony in Here Somewhere: The AOL Time Warner Debacle and the Quest for the Digital Future*. New York: Crown Business.

Welch, I. (2000). Herding amongst security analysts. *Journal of Financial Economics*, 58: 369–96.

Wilde, O. (1894). A few maxims for the instruction of the overeducated. *Saturday Review*.

Chapter 12

Insider Trading

A large literature in both finance and the economic analysis of law discusses the rationale and effectiveness of insider trading legislation (see Bainbridge 2001 for a review). In this chapter the argument is advanced that recent contributions to the behavioural finance literature uncover a little-discussed benefit of insider trading – it provides company management an incentive to disclose private information to financial markets. Stories of corporate helmsmen, such as Steve Case, ex AOL Time Warner Captain, selling his own stake as he encouraged others to accept the proposed merger of AOL and Time Warner (then the biggest in history) have rightly attracted legal sanction, but in this chapter I argue the proposed remedy of further restrictions on management self-dealing ('insider trading' if the moral obloquy could be removed from that term) contains a hidden cost. This comes in the form of the constraints it places on incentives for managers to put value-relevant information into price.[1] This is indeed the impact of the tightening of the window between self-dealing and disclosure required by Section 403 of the Sarbanes–Oxley Act, which came into effect on 27 August 2002. While under the old reporting regime 'Section 16' (of the 1934 Securities Act) officers had to report their trades by at least the tenth day in the month following their trade, this is now reduced to a delay of two business days from the date of the trade.

Recently theorists working in the field of behavioural finance have suggested earnings might be constructed or 'selected' by company management in response to their private perception of the extent to which the company they manage is over- or undervalued. That selection, or tactical manipulation, of earnings seems rife is clear from both survey evidence (Graham *et al.* 2005) and market-based accounting research (Abarbanell & Lehavy 2003). Montier (2006) discusses empirical evidence regarding the impact of insider trading in Section 7.7.3 of his book. That managers' self-dealing may be a good indication of the construction of future earnings numbers has already been suggested by a variety of authors. For example Beneish and Vargus (2002) state:

> We expect managers to have private information about the likelihood that income-increasing accruals will result in higher future earnings and the likelihood that income-decreasing accruals will result in lower future earnings.

This process of earnings selection and discreet trading based on foreknowledge of critical events in the corporation's development will be seen to underpin three seeming anomalies in stock-market pricing of assets discussed in previous chapters. These are:

- momentum (in Chapter 10);
- overreaction (in Chapter 9);
- herding (in Chapter 11).

This is done in the context of the development of a noise-trading framework with which you will hopefully feel comfortable by now. So the present chapter has an integrative role as well as a focus on the important policy issue of how we encourage prices to be as reflective of value of possible, without encouraging morally debased leadership of publicly traded corporations.

Public policy must trade-off the greater informational efficiency that insider trading tends to induce against the often adverse distributional consequences of its presence. We might be willing to tolerate some self-serving greed amongst egotistical managers to move price towards a better reflection of fundamental value, but outright looting of shareholder value by those charged to protect it is likely to prove a bit more difficult to swallow. The models discussed in this chapter should give you a better understanding of the conditions under which these trade-offs are made by regulators and the courts.

12.1   Illustration and Structure

Ivan Boesky, a risk arbitrageur in the mid to late 1980s, in many ways embodies the dark heart of the insider trader that the SEC and others warn us against. On 14 November 1986 Boesky pleaded guilty to charges of insider trading, paid a fine of $100 million, and agreed to 'cooperate' with SEC investigators. Soon his confessions led investigators to Dennis Levine, a lawyer at Drexel Burnham Lambert. From Levine's confessions the investigation proceeded to charge bankers at many other major investment banks, Goldman Sachs, Shearson Lehman and others. But the big fish only Boesky could help nail was Drexel's star 'junk bond' trader Michael Milken (see Bruck 1989). Milken's 'junk bond' (beneath investment grade) financed takeovers, undertaken by a series of corporate raiders, were slowly restructuring corporate America.

As so often with insider trades, rather than the case turning on Milken getting a tip-off and buying stock based upon it, the SEC case against Milken involved a complex web of co-conspirators and ambiguous transactions. The SEC focused especially on a payment of $5.3 million by Boesky to Drexel, Milken's employer for 'consulting'. The SEC claimed this was actually a reward to Boesky for 'parking' stock for Milken, this is simply buying and holding stock until the person you have 'parked' for needs to call on it. Specifically it appeared Boesky had purchased equity in Fischbach Corporation. Fischbach was a target of Victor Posner, one of Milken's many 'corporate raider' friends, who bought up corporations on Drexel's 'junk bond' debt and tried to turn them around. Posner was bound from 1980 onwards by a 'standstill agreement' with Fischbach's board that prohibited him from acquiring more than 24.9% of Fischbach's equity. But this, of course, would not prevent Posner getting a little help from his friends Milken and Boesky. By the summer of 1984 Boesky had amassed 13.4% of Fischbach stock, more than enough to give Posner control if he needed to take it. In reality Boesky sold out his position in Fischbach to a Posner-related company, Pennsylvania Engineering, in February 1985. Posner finally acquired Fischbach in October 1985. These transactions were certainly worthwhile from Milken's standpoint as the man who financed all of Posner's deals.

By September 1988 the SEC was able to compile and file a 184-page document containing charges against Drexel and Milken's trading desk. Despite the weight of evidence Milken eventually went to jail for violation of the Racketeer-Influenced Corrupt Organizations (or RICO) laws. These laws were introduced to combat the Mafia, but the strong evidential requirement of insider trading legislation often makes their invocation a preferable route for the SEC.

Section 12.2 introduces the problem of insider trading. I consider the moral rights and wrongs of this practice as well as its practical impact on markets. I also consider the costs of getting tough on insider trading – how much insider trading is too much? Can we tolerate any insider trading at all? Section 12.3 presents a model that captures the impact of insider trading on asset pricing in a world characterized by a number of the biases we have already considered, namely, momentum, overreaction and herding. This model allows us to revisit some old chestnuts in a more flexible 'noise-trader' framework as well as breaking new ground. The potential costs and benefits of insider trading and how that welfare calculus operates are discussed and some determinants of its outcome considered. Section 12.4 examines how insider trading and how the desire of managers to profit from engaging in insider trading influence the reporting of company earnings and so public perceptions of corporate performance. Section 12.5 considers how insider trading positions may influence managers to undertake strategic manipulation of earnings and other signals of company value to investors. This allows us to understand some of the real costs of insider trading beyond a reallocation of wealth to those 'in the know' from those who are not. Section 12.6 concludes and summarizes the chapter.

After the reading this chapter the reader should:

- Understand why insider trading is outlawed and some of its damaging consequences for the integrity and healthy functioning of financial markets.
- Understand some of the possible benefits derivable from allowing insider trading to occur and gain insight into theoretical frameworks that allow the costs and benefits of insider trading to be traded-off.
- Gain insight into a model of how insider trading affects asset pricing within a theoretical model that incorporates a number of the psychological biases already encountered, notably, momentum, overreaction and herding. As such this chapter serves an integrative function for material previously considered as well as breaking new ground.

12.2 Insider Trading Here for Better or Worse

Most upstanding members of the financial community take a pretty dim view of insider trading. Arthur Levitt, then chairman of the SEC, stated:

> Trading based on privileged access to information can demoralize investors and destabilize investment. It has utterly no place in any fair minded, law abiding economy. It's a chronic danger. It's all too evident in today's marketplace. And it's a crime. The American people see it, bluntly, as a form of cheating. They – along with the SEC – have zero tolerance for the crime of insider trading. Let's state clearly, and in the unambiguous terms it deserves. Insider dealing is legally forbidden. It's morally wrong. And it's economically dangerous.[2]

The current head of enforcement at the UK's Financial Services Authority, as if not to be outdone, stated this in a speech to the American Bar Association in October 2007:[3]

> We do see market abuse – of which insider dealing is the highest profile aspect – as posing a risk to our statutory objectives. It is a financial crime – it may not attract the immediate moral outrage of a violent crime against a person, but it is, in our view, and in the view of the UK government, a serious white-collar crime with potential sentences of up to seven years imprisonment.

It seems churlish to demur from such an unambiguous condemnation from such noble voices. Yet what insiders do when they trade is simply put information into price about the company and its prospects. Isn't this a good thing? The answer to this question requires a fairly finely balanced calculus that the initial moral outrage at 'cheating' tends to obscure (see Leland 1992).

The proposed benefits to allowing open insider trading include:

- It facilitates more informed trading ensuring the share price better reflects the value of the asset.
- Since price more accurately reflects value investment is encouraged and asset values raised as demand is increased.

Against this must be set the alleged costs of insider trading:

- If the integrity of financial markets is placed in doubt and the stock market becomes viewed as a 'rigged game' then shareholders will vote with their feet and withdraw, reducing liquidity, the cost of capital and the general well-being of society.
- Insiders, especially if operating in groups (like the infamous 'stock pools' organized by Jay Gould and others in the 1930s or Michael Milken and Ivan Boesky in the late 1980s) may induce greater volatility and thus risk in financial markets and so inhibit investment.

Prohibition, in this case of certain trading practices, is a violation of our basic economic freedom to trade for our own personal benefit. Of course with any right comes a corresponding responsibility not to harm others, in this case those to whom managers, or regulators, owe a fiduciary duty of care. However, prohibitions by their very nature entail some costly sacrifices against which any benefits must be offset to justify their imposition. These include (see Meadowcroft 2008):

- Criminalizing trading by insiders tends to push those who undertake it into the hands of those with the necessary know-how and capitalization to pull it off, such people are often already established criminals.
- By prohibiting insiders from trading on price-sensitive information obtained though their insider status, more regulated, controllable, forms of trading regimes are prevented from emerging.
- Given the heavy legal sanctions to insider trading the costs of detection, prosecution and punishment are not small, so any benefits from a reduction in the incidence of insider trading must be offset against these costs of enforcement.
- Finally, and perhaps most damning of all, is the almost certain failure of prohibition when some insider traders still see it as strongly in their interests to trade despite the legal sanction attached to doing so. After prohibiting alcohol from 1920 to 1933 the US government just gave up and no doubt had a pint to drown their sorrows at their failure. Those who study and work in UK universities can have little doubt about how ineffective current drug laws against ecstasy and cannabis are. Prohibiting activities many find unexceptional, or even beneficial, is almost surely a bad road for regulatory policy to take.

12.2.1   The Distributional Impact of Insider Trading

Insider trading pushes prices towards being a reflection of value. The only question is who should get the benefit of any price 'correction', as previously unknown, but value-relevant, information emerges. Allowing insider trading lets the senior management team, corporate bankers and others walk off with the profits from a resulting price correction. Insider trading laws simply pass profits from a price correction to the shareholders of the company subject to the revaluation of its worth, but this reallocation only occurs if insider trading laws work, by making insider trading prohibitively expensive once fines, confiscation of profits and possible (if unlikely) jail sentences are considered.

Arturo Bris (2005) of Yale University has reported evidence that far from reallocating price correction profits to outsiders, as intended, insider trading laws simply serve to reduce the incidence of insider trading, while greatly enhancing the profits to those few insiders bold, or foolish, enough to bear the increased risk of continuing to trade on price-sensitive information. An analogy Bris gives is the impact of prohibition on American drinking habits in the 1920s: while the amount of alcohol consumed fell by 60–70%, its price almost tripled. The inelasticity of demand for alcohol fed a generation of gangsters, like Al Capone, to ride the surging revenues from underground speakeasies (Bris 2005, p.270). In the same way Bris argues insider trading laws increase profits to suppliers of price-sensitive information by allowing monopolization of supply of price-sensitive information.

Bris supports this conclusion with a study of 4451 takeover announcements in 52 separate countries with various degrees of insider trading prohibition, or tolerance thereof. Bris compares trading profits across these alternative national regulatory regimes. Sadly, insider traders are not the sort of decent chaps who post summary profit and loss accounts on their personal webpage, so their profits need to be inferred or observed by some proxy of their hidden presence.

12.2.2 When does Trading become Insider Trading?

Bris (2005) provides such a measure of insider trading based on share price movements and volume of trades in the run-up to the takeover announcement. Bris (2005, p.285) advances a measure of insider profits, Π:

$$\Pi_i = \frac{\sum_{t=-T}^{-5} \dfrac{B_i - P_{it}}{B_{it} - P_{i0}} Vol_{it}^*}{N_i} \times 100$$

where

$$Vol_{it}^* = \begin{cases} Vol_{it} - \left[\overline{Vol_i} + 2\sigma_{VOL} \right] & \text{if } Vol_{it} > \overline{Vol_i} + 2\sigma_{VOL} \\ 0 & \text{otherwise} \end{cases}$$

where B_i is the bid price for the ith target company, P_{it} is the share price of the ith target in the five days preceding the bid and P_{i0} is the price five days before the bid is publicly announced. Vol is volume and $\overline{Vol}$ its average value before the initiation of the bid, σ_{VOL} is the standard deviation of volatility and N_i is the number of shares. Insider profits are captured by the metric Π_i set equal to the cumulative mark-up of the bid price over the prevailing five days prior to the bid, that is $B_i - P_{it}$, normalized by the pre-bid price run-up in the T days preceding the fifth day prior to the bid relative to the final bid price, $B_i - P_{i0}$. If the numerator of the first expression in Π_i, $B_i - P_{it}$ captures the cost of acquiring control of the target, i.e. the mark-up over the prevailing price five days prior to the bid. Then the expression for Π's denominator $B_i - P_{i0}$ can be seen as capturing how much such a bid was anticipated by the market in the T days preceding the five days prior to the bid. Bids characterized by sudden jumps in the price in the last five days prior to the bid's announcement, where $B_i - P_{it}$ is high relative to $B_i - P_{i0}$, are regarded as prima facie evidence of insider trading. Such bids are seen as offering high insider profits.

How do we know insiders caused the price spike in the last five days prior to the bid? Maybe the target is just generally recognized to be a really great acquisition target and there is widespread market recognition that it is 'in play'? This is where the 'dummy' variable Vol^* comes in. Bris (2005) only calculates the insider profits from the bid if trading volume five days before the bid is more than twice its 'normal' value in the five days prior to the acquisition. Recall for a normal distribution 95% of the mass of the distribution is contained within the bounds of two standard deviations from the mean, $\overline{Vol}$, so Bris (2005) calculates insider profits only if there are suspiciously high levels of trade occurring just before the bid, that is five days prior to the deal's final announcement to the market. Otherwise insider profits, captured by the proxy Π_i, are set to zero.

In summary the Bris (2005) metric of insider profits seeks to identify sudden spikes in target prices, just before the bid, associated with large surges in volume relative to that normally observed in the target's shares. Once insider trading is deemed to have occurred the measured amount is proportional to the price rise in the last five days prior to the bid relative to that in the T days prior to the five-day bid window examined.

Bris (2005) reaches the slightly depressing conclusion that tough insider trading regulatory regimes are associated with bigger profits, Π_i, to insiders. The reason for this is simply the presence of anti-insider regulation increases the cost and risk of entering the insider trading industry and so those who do so attract handsome monopoly profits. Who dares wins even when punitive legislation makes fewer willing to trade. Insider trading laws, and Sarbanes–Oxley in particular, may simply serve to make the distribution of profits to insider trading more skewed towards a high return for a few aggressive amoral traders willing to enter the market for the provision of 'inside' information, despite the criminal sanction.

12.2.3 Insiders on Trial: Proof of Guilt or Innocence?

While regulators and politicians huff and puff about the evils of insider trading it is still most probably a better basis for a criminal career than stealing cigarettes from your local newsagent. Profits are high and convictions are so low as to be almost non-existent. Being a wealthy, well-connected, insider trader may look attractive and might understandably be seen as a good way to turn a responsible, but modestly paid, job into huge riches very quickly.

Engelen (2006), in a case study of the 1994 *Bekaert* case in Belgium, shows how confusing such cases can appear to the courts. The *Bekaert* case involved a Belgium manufacturer of steel wire, largely for radial car tyres, and its collaboration with a Japanese tyre manufacturer, Bridgestone. In 1992 Bekaert and Bridgestone decided to list its joint venture on the second market of the Japanese Stock Exchange. This transaction was expected to raise €26 million and as a result of this Bekaert planned to announce a special dividend of €2.48 per share on 20 December. This was discussed and agreed at a board of directors' meeting in November on which the first defendant sat. In the three weeks prior to the announcement of the special dividend the first defendant's husband, the second defendant, bought 400 Bekaert shares worth roughly €130,000. The Belgium authorities spotted the trades and traced them despite the use of a shell company called Batibo NV. The criminal court in Ghent convicted the couple of insider dealing, accusing them of 'pillow talk', leading the husband to trade privileged information, obtained by the wife, on the Bekaert board in the previous month to the trade. The Court of Appeal overturned the conviction arguing some link (presumably beyond sharing a bedroom) had to be shown between the trader and the person with the privileged information. Different judges hold different standards it seems.

An additional problem that Engelen (2006) points out for obtaining a conviction is that it is not clear that the special dividend, as opposed to the sale of the joint venture, which was already known to the market, was the value-relevant disclosure. Indeed much standard theory argues dividends are actually irrelevant to company value (although try not to prejudge before you have read Chapter 16 of this text).

Engelen (2006) suggests that the high burden of proof imposed by the Court of Appeal reveals a particular choice between two different types of enforcement errors. If the null hypothesis is the defendant is innocent (as it is by tradition in a criminal trial) the question is then what is the economically and socially appropriate value of the probability of guilt needed to overthrow the null? Should I only convict if I am convinced beyond all, even unreasonable, doubt, let's say I am at least 99.9999% convinced the defendant did it, or could 98% do a better job? So the decision can be portrayed in the form as shown in Table 12.1.

Given the distribution of evidence present for the innocent and guilty in insider trading, it is likely that the tails of the two distributions of evidence will often, if not usually, overlap. The region of intersection can be divided into two halves by a chosen critical value, c. The region of innocent traders falsely accused and convicted is called the β region and where guilty insiders walk free is called the α

Table 12.1 Two types of errors in prosecuting insider trading

Verdict of court	Underlying truth	
	Person did not trade as an insider, i.e. they are really innocent of offence	Person did trade as an insider, i.e. they are really guilty of offence
Innocent (Null H0)	$1 - \alpha$ probability acquit when innocent	Probability of type II error β (guilty go free)
Guilty (the alternative H1)	Probability of type I error α (innocent convicted)	$1 - \beta$ probability convict when guilty

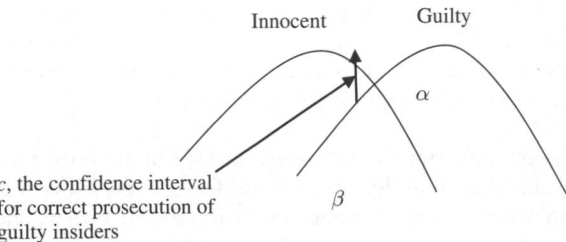

Figure 12.1 Choosing critical point, c, for conviction in insider trading trials

region (Engelen 2006). A prosecutor who is too confident in his ability to bring only the guilty to trial will set c too far to the right, β will swell and the prisons will be flooded with those falsely accused of insider trading. Alternatively a prosecutor who is too timid will set c too far to the left, α will expand and so hardened insiders will escape the net, ready for more misbehaviour. In the diagrammatic illustration given in Figure 12.1 c is slightly to the left of a point equally dissecting the two areas α and β and the regulator is seen to be favouring damning the innocent, rather than let some of the guilty go free. Where exactly the cut-off point, c, should be drawn is a tricky question for regulatory authorities. Such an approach focuses on social losses to insider trading. We need an analytical framework capable of capturing the losses and gains to insider trading. I now proceed to examine such a framework in some detail using the 'noise-trader' style modelling of Chapter 6.

12.3 The Hirshleifer, Subrahmanyam and Titman Model

Hirshleifer, Subrahmanyam and Titman (1994) develop a model of how those with an informational advantage, gained by obtaining information early, set about exploiting that information for profit. In its original conception those who receive information early are seen as private investors or either 'lucky', or just gifted with high ability, but another interpretation is that company managers use their inside position to capture information about earnings early. In the words of Arthur Levitt, ex chairman of the SEC, this includes some 'cheats'/insider traders. In this section we explore the model interpreting the characterization of pricing in an equilibrium with just such an 'insider' group who learn information about true asset value before other investors.

The HST model bears a close resemblance in its structure to the Froot *et al.* (1992) model studied in Chapter 11. The focus there was on herding and indeed in the HST model there is a return to the early informed to trading on the same sort of inside information as others (be that information about earnings, regulatory compliance, or product innovation, etc.). As we shall see later if the early informed trade in a prescient fashion about information that others will trade on later, they can unwind their positions with profit to liquidity traders who do not trade on the basis of any value-relevant information at all ('they trade because they wish to trade'). The strength of the HST model is to integrate two further additional phenomena also discussed in separate chapters of this book. These are:

- *Momentum*, or price-trend chasing, already discussed in Chapter 10, which also manifests itself here in the capacity of the 'later' informed investors to buy up the same stocks purchased by the 'early' informed at some earlier date, when only the early informed had been in the know about the valuation implications of new information about the company.
- *Overreaction*, or the tendency of extreme price movements to be reversed in the medium term. This is built into the current model by the fact that the early informed need to offload the stocks in which they have an informational advantage before the later informed investors start to trade and undermine the informational advantage they currently enjoy.

Therefore the underlying motivation for discussing the HST model is to explain how insider trading impacts on a market inhabited by liquidity or 'noise' traders. Nevertheless the model does allow us to see three biases operating in unison (herding, momentum and overreaction) and observe their interaction and role in propagating each other. As such this chapter is a little more technical and demanding than those encountered up to this point. My hope is the gains in terms of realism in capturing financial decision making justify the investment of time and effort spent in gaining command of the HST model.

12.3.1 Asset Demands and the Determination of Investor's Terminal Wealth in the HST Model

The HST model captures the interaction between three types of agents: informed, risk-averse, investors of two sub-types and a market-maker who aggregates and clears their trades. First, informed investors both those informed early (or insiders) about fundamental value and those investors informed later. Each informed investor is conceived of as a point on a real line, which constitutes a continuum of investors of mass N. Investors informed early make up some subset (M) of that total mass of informed investors N. The time periods 1 and 2 demands of the early informed investors are $x_1(\theta, P_1)$ and $x_2(\theta, P_2)$, while those of the later informed are $y_1(\theta, P_1)$ and $y_2(\theta, P_2)$. Liquidity traders have demand schedules labelled z_1 and z_2 in time periods 1 and 2, respectively. The shocks to demand that liquidity traders generate are distributed normally around zero with variance σ^2_z, so $z \sim N(0, \sigma_z)$. The informed investors trade in the presence of liquidity traders (who 'trade because they wish to trade'; De Long *et al.* 1990) who serve simply to introduce a source of noise into asset demand. Inter-reaction between informed investors and liquidity traders is facilitated by means of risk-neutral market-makers. These market-makers bundle the net demands of informed investors and liquidity traders and settle them at competitive prices.

In summary the HST model is populated by three types of traders:

- informed, risk-averse, traders who receive a signal θ at period 1 or 2;
- liquidity/noise traders who just like to trade (they don't know or care about θ);
- market-makers, risk-neutral traders, who clear the trades of the other two types of traders and try to infer value, F, from the order flow they receive.

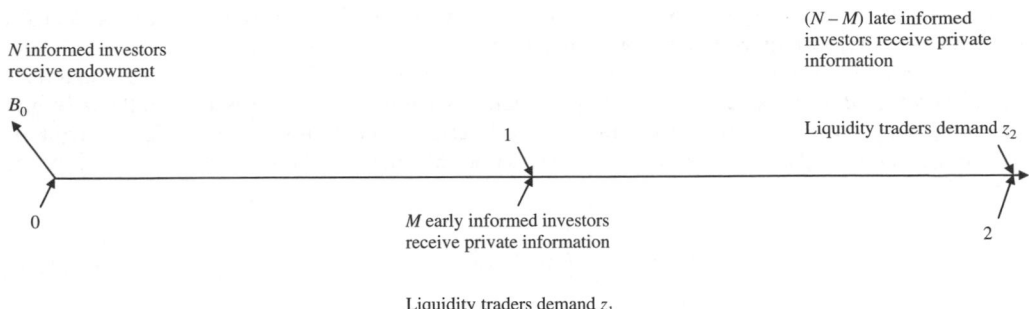

Figure 12.2   The time line of trade in the HST model

The final liquidation value of the asset is given by public information about the asset value, $\overline{F}$, private information regarding asset value is only received by informed traders, θ, and a random shock to value, ε, which is not disclosed to anyone at either of the trading dates. Hence the expression for terminal value is

$$F = \overline{F} + \theta + \varepsilon \tag{12.1}$$

where the bar over F denotes it is F's mean value and both θ and ε are independently normally distributed around a mean of zero.

Investors trade along a time line as drawn in Figure 12.2. At time period 0 all informed agents are granted an endowment of risk-free bonds to fund their subsequent trading, B_0. In time period 1 only the early informed amongst informed traders receive some private signal, θ, about value. Finally, in time period 2, the later informed investors catch up with the early informed by receiving the signal about value received earlier by the early informed in time period 1 and trade ends.

HST begin by conjecturing the existence of an equilibrium in which prices in time periods 1 and 2 are linear functions of public knowledge, $\overline{F}$, the private information only informed investors receive, θ (received by the early informed at period 1 and the later informed at period 2), and shocks to demand from liquidity traders, z_1 and z_2. Substituting in from the expression for public knowledge, $\overline{F}$, entering Equation (12.1) above, price is conjectured to be a linear function of both public and private information and liquidity trader demand, z_1 and z_2 as follows

$$P_2 = \overline{F} + a\theta + bz_1 + cz_2$$
$$P_1 = \overline{F} + e\theta + fz_1 \tag{12.2}$$

Informed investors seek to maximize their terminal, time period 2, wealth which for early and later informed investors takes the form

$$W^E = x_2(\overline{F} + \theta + \varepsilon) + x_1 P_1 + (x_2 - x_1)P_2 + B_0 \tag{12.3}$$

The first part of the expressions for wealth captures the fundamental/intrinsic value of period 2 holdings of the asset. So the first term pre-multiplies the asset's fundamental value by the amount of it held by the early informed at period 2. Note that in time period 2, at the conclusion of all trading, since all informed investors know the full body of public and private information, $F + \theta$, period 2 price converges on the true intrinsic value.[4] The second part of the terminal wealth expression reflects the change in value of the asset bought for P_1 at period 1 prices and held for sale until period 2 at P_2, which may or may not approximate true liquidation value.

Since period 2 terminal wealth is assumed to be normally distributed we can apply standard mean-variance Markovitsian analysis to this wealth portfolio. This reveals that both early and later informed investors choose the same optimal terminal portfolio in period 2, as might be expected given that they by now both have the same information. This portfolio is given by the expression

$$x_2(\theta, P_2) = y_2(\theta, P_2) = \frac{\overline{F} + \theta - P_2}{R\sigma_\varepsilon^2} \tag{12.4}$$

This can be seen as something like a Sharpe ratio in which the mark-up return on the asset, over and above its period 2 price, is scaled by the risk associated with buying it and then discounted back to period 1 using the discount factor $R = 1/(1 + r)$, where r is the risk-free rate.

The period 1 demand of early informed investors is given by

$$x_1(\theta, P_1) = \frac{\overline{P}_2 - P_1}{R} \left(\frac{1}{\sigma_{P_2}^2} + \frac{1}{\sigma_\varepsilon^2} \right) + \frac{\overline{F} + \theta - \overline{P}_2}{R\sigma_\varepsilon^2} \tag{12.5}$$

where $\overline{P}_2$, and $\sigma_{P_2}^2$ are the mean and variance of period 2 prices, respectively. The derivation of this expression is sufficiently intricate for me to leave it to an appendix to the chapter.

So the early informed investor trades at period 1 in order to maximize the discounted sum of two elements of the return on offer to insider trading. Firstly, price-appreciation gains derived from buying early on the receipt of value-relevant information about value, $\theta + \overline{F}$. Recall the mean value of F is assumed to be zero, so terminal value converges on θ in expectation. Secondly, the return to being an astute fundamental investor: the difference between what the early informed believed the asset to be worth and what it actually pays out as a dividend, θ. Note that the size of the initial endowment to the early informed plays no role in the size of early informed investors' asset demands in period 1.

The period 1 asset demand equation suggests early informed investors seek to purchase the asset in period 1, x_1, for two reasons:

1. To make a capital gain on the difference between period 1 and period 2 price, $(P_2 - P_1)$, that is an arbitrage profit, this is captured by the third part of Equation (12.5).
2. To lock into assets with value in excess of the period 2 price and hence extract a premium return to investing on the basis of prescience regarding value, this is captured by the second part of Equation (12.5).

Increases in second period price, P_2, are offset by proportionate declines in the second term, but in period 2 the informational advantage of the early informed evaporates as the later informed also learn, θ.

The first of these elements of the return to insider trading induces redistribution of wealth away from the later informed toward those informed early. Depending on how the early 'in-crowd' got their information, this may not be a desirable reallocation of wealth and something public policy wishes to discourage. The second part of the return to early investors is simply the return to pushing price towards fundamental value. This is a return to making the market in the asset more efficient in a 'fundamental value' sense. It is hard to see, almost irrespective of how this comes about, how this can be regarded as anything other than a good thing from a public policy standpoint.

At period 2 the early informed will seek to unwind their asset position in x, selling it on to uninformed, liquidity motivated, investors. In doing so they will be particularly keen to sell:

1. If their capital gain, between period 1 and 2, $(P_2 - P_1)$, is high, i.e. insiders have a lot of gains to cash-in.
2. Or, if the price in period 2 is fairly close to fundamental value, $(F + \theta - P_2) \approx 0$, i.e. informed investors (both early and later) have no advantage over uninformed liquidity.

So the liquidation of the portfolio of those informed early intensifies with the reduction in the informational advantage regarding future value, θ, which they enjoy. The message for policy-makers is clear: a stock market that allows security prices to drift far from fundamental value is fertile ground for insider traders. To combat insider trading requires many of the same measures that are usually associated with market 'transparency' and the appearance of large gaps between what companies appear to be worth and what they actually turn out to be worth to their shareholders.

The later informed investors do not trade at all in period 1 since they are unable to extract a risk premium to meeting early informed traders. This is because the early informed can simply choose to trade with uninformed, liquidity traders, who demand no such compensation. So, since all the later informed choose to trade only in period 2 we drop the subscript and denote their demand as y.

Recall that the end-period wealth of early informed investors is given by

$$W^E = x_2(\overline{F} + \theta + \varepsilon) - x_1 P_1 - (x_2 - x_1)P_2 + B_0 \tag{12.6}$$

while as derived in Equation (12.4):

$$x_2(\theta, P_2) = \frac{(\overline{F} + \theta - P_2)}{R\sigma_\varepsilon^2} \tag{12.7}$$

Substituting into the terminal wealth Equation (12.6) for the solution for period 2 demand by the informed investor, $x_2(\theta, P_2)$ given by Equation (12.7), we obtain a solution for the informed investor's period 2 demand as follows:

Recall $\quad W^E = x_2(\overline{F} + \theta + \varepsilon) - x_1 P_1 + (x_2 - x_1)P_2 + B_0$

substitute in for x_2

$$= \frac{(\overline{F} + \theta - P_2)}{R\sigma_\varepsilon^2}(\overline{F} + \theta + \varepsilon) - x_1 P_1 - (\frac{(\overline{F} + \theta - P_2)}{R\sigma_\varepsilon^2} - x_1)P_2 + B_0$$

$$= \frac{(\overline{F} + \theta - P_2)}{R\sigma_\varepsilon^2}(\overline{F} + \theta + \varepsilon) - x_1 P_2 - x_1(P_2 - P_1) - \frac{(\overline{F} + \theta - P_2)}{R\sigma_\varepsilon^2}P_2 + B_0$$

$$x_1(P_2 - P_1) = \frac{(\overline{F} + \theta - P_2)}{R\sigma_\varepsilon^2}(\overline{F} + \theta + \varepsilon - P_2) - x_1 P_2 + B_0$$

$$x_1 = \frac{(\overline{F} + \theta - P_2)}{R\sigma_\varepsilon^2}(\overline{F} + \theta + \varepsilon - P_2)(P_2 - P_1) - x_2 P_2 + B_0$$

Let $\quad (\overline{P}_2 - P_1)^2 = \sigma_{P2}^2$

$$x_1(\theta, P_1) = \frac{\overline{P}_2 - P_1}{R}\left(\frac{1}{\sigma_{P2}^2} + \frac{1}{\sigma_\varepsilon^2}\right) + \frac{\overline{F} + \theta - \overline{P}_2}{R\sigma_\varepsilon^2} \tag{12.8}$$

where price at period 2, P_2, has been evaluated at its mean value.

This expression makes clear that the end-period wealth of early informed investors has three distinct components:

1. A price appreciation, capital gain, component earned from holding that amount of the risky asset x_1 from period 1 to 2, $(P_1 - P_2) x_2$, this is the opening part of the first element of Equation (12.8).
2. Gains to investing based on being better informed about fundamental value. This is captured by the difference between what the asset is revealed (to the informed at least) to be truly worth and the price it currently trades at, $(F + \theta - P_2)$, where this is discounted back into the current period by the discount factor R and further risk-adjusted for the precision of the signal about unknown period 2 shocks to asset value, σ^2_ε, this is the first element of Equation (12.8).
3. The initial endowment, which the investor uses to fund trades, the final element of Equation (12.8).

I now proceed to a more detailed study of the price-setting process in the HST model.

At this point in constructing their model Hirshleifer *et al.* draw heavily on the particular properties of the normal/Gaussian distribution from which the various random variables determining value are drawn.

This can get quite cumbersome, so I follow Hirshleifer *et al.* in providing the details of the proof of why informed traders do not trade in period 1 in Appendix A below.

12.3.2 *Pricing in Equilibrium*

Early informed investors faced with the period 1 pricing in Equation (12.2):

$$P_1 = \overline{F} + e\theta + fz_1$$

can infer z_1 given their knowledge of F and θ, while market-makers, liquidity traders and the later informed cannot. So

$$\phi_1 \equiv [\theta, P_1] \equiv [\theta, z_1]$$

Recalling from Equation (12.2) the pricing for period 2:

$$P_2 = \overline{F} + a\theta + bz_1 + cz_2$$

This implies

$$E(P_2|\theta + z_1) = \overline{F}_1 + a\theta + bz_1$$
and
$$\sigma^2_{P_2} = var(P_2|\theta, z_1) = c^2 \sigma^2_z$$

So volatility in period 2 price is solely induced by noise/liquidity traders' demand, since by now all informed traders know the signal regarding fundamental value, θ. The period 1 demand schedule is then

$$x_1(\theta, P_1) = \frac{\overline{P}_2 - P_1}{R} \left(\frac{1}{\sigma^2_{P_2}} + \frac{1}{\sigma^2_\varepsilon} \right) + \frac{\overline{F} + \theta - \overline{P}_2}{R\sigma^2_\varepsilon}$$

Substituting out for expected values of $\overline{P}$ and $\sigma_{P_2}^2$ already obtained above:

$$x_1 = \frac{(\overline{F} + a\theta + bz_1 - P_1)}{R}\left[\frac{1}{c^2\sigma_z^2} + \frac{1}{\sigma_\varepsilon^2}\right] + \left[\frac{(\overline{F} - \theta - (\overline{F} + a\theta + bz_1))}{R\sigma_\varepsilon^2}\right]$$

$$= \frac{(\overline{F} + a\theta + bz_1 - P_1)}{Rc^2\sigma_z^2} + \left[\frac{(\overline{F} + a\theta + bz_1)}{R\sigma_\varepsilon^2}\right] + \left[\frac{(1+a)\theta + bz_1 + P_1}{R\sigma_\varepsilon^2}\right]$$

$$= \theta\left(\frac{a\sigma_\varepsilon^2 + c^2\sigma_z^2}{Rc^2\sigma_\varepsilon^2\sigma_z^2}\right) + z_1\left(\frac{b}{Rc^2\sigma_z^2}\right) + \frac{(\overline{F} - P_1)(\sigma_\varepsilon^2 + c^2\sigma_z^2)}{Rc^2\sigma_\varepsilon^2\sigma_z^2} \qquad (12.9)$$

This derivation results from variation in period 2 prices resulting only from liquidity traders' demands at period 2 (remember they don't trade at all at period 1, since true liquidation value, θ, is fixed regardless of trading behaviour in the market).

Now total period 1 demand for the asset is simply a weighted average of M early and N later informed investors and the noise/liquidity traders' demands as follows:

$$D_1(t) = Mx_1 + Ny_1 + z_1$$

Of course we know that the early informed do not demand the asset at period 1, so we finally obtain

$$D_1(P_1) = M\left[\theta\frac{a\sigma_\varepsilon^2 + c^2\sigma_z^2}{Rc^2\sigma_\varepsilon^2\sigma_z^2} + z_1\frac{b}{Rc^2\sigma_z^2} + \frac{(\overline{F} - P_1)(\sigma_\varepsilon^2 + c^2\sigma_z^2)}{Rc^2\sigma_\varepsilon^2\sigma_z^2}\right] + N(y_1) + z_1$$

Upon substituting into the period 1 demand schedule we obtain a linear solution for price at periods 1 and 2 given by Equation (12.2). I give the details of this derivation and especially solution for the coefficients on the various elements of value, a through f in Appendix B. The requisite algebraic manipulation is fairly prolonged, but knowledge of it will be useful in understanding the comparative static exercises presented in the numerical illustration section that follows.

12.3.3 Trading Behaviour in Equilibrium

The nature of equilibrium implies certain relations between period 1 and 2 prices and the trades of informed agents based on the information they receive θ (be that early or later). Proposition 1 of HST implies that price movements between periods 1 and 2 reflect public and private information such that

$$\text{cov}(P_1 - \overline{F}, \theta) > 0$$

and

$$\text{cov}(P_2 - P_1, \theta) > 0$$

so the deviation between the price of the asset in period 1 and its value on the basis of public information is a product of the early informed traders' demands in response to their private information signal θ. Similarly, price appreciation between periods 1 and 2 reflects the nature of private information that the early informed have received. If θ is good news prices rise, if bad news prices will fall.

Proposition 2 of HST specifies the relation between period 1 and 2 demands of the early informed traders, x_1 and x_2 and price appreciation between periods 1 and 2 ($P_2 - P_1$) and the later informed traders' demand, y. The second proposition of the HST paper comes in two parts. The first states:

$$\text{Cov}(x_1, \theta) > 0$$

and

$$\text{Cov}(x_1, P_2 - P_1) > 0$$

And proposition 2 of the HST paper simply states that good news motivates the early informed to load up their portfolios with the assets, while bad news leads them to sell it. Expected increases in the price of the assets, conditional on private information received about its value, θ, raise the demand of the early informed. Secondly,

$$\text{Cov}(x_2 - x_1, P_2 - P_1) < 0$$

and

$$\text{Cov}(x_2 - x_1, \theta) > 0$$

The greater the run-up in the price between periods 1 and 2 the more the early informed seek to unwind their period 1 position. So if prices rise, the early informed seek to sell off the asset; if prices fall they seek to restore their position in the risky asset. This is because the early informed have their informational advantage, θ, eroded by other later informed traders. Once this occurs, they counter-trade to reap the profit of their period 1, privileged position based on early knowledge of a signal about asset value, θ.

A numerical illustration of the predictions of the HST model

In order to clarify some of predictions of the HST model a simple numerical illustration is undertaken within an Excel spreadsheet which allows the reader to further understand the mechanics of the model, conduct scenario tests etc. In particular the illustration seeks to clarify how the predictions of the HST model follow from its assumptions.[5]

I begin with some simple numerical simulation based on Equation (12.8), which tells us how much of the asset the early informed (who know θ at period 1) will buy. To make progress I provide some initial values for the simulation exercises in Table 12.2.

I initially consider a gradual increase in expected period 2 price, $\bar{P}_2$, and its impact on the demand of the early informed as captured in Equation (12.8). Such an increase in period 2 price has two offsetting effects.

1. To raise the early informed capital gains to holding the asset.
2. To reduce the returns to the investor's fundamental investment skills (*the offsetting effect*).

Table 12.2 Initial values for simulation of HST model of insider trading

Parameter	Value
Price expected at period 2, $\bar{P}_2$	11
Variance of prices, σ_p^2	0.2
Variance of epsilon, σ_ε^2	0.1
Discount factor, R	1.1
Public signal about value, $\bar{F}$	10
Liquidating dividend paid, θ	10

But note that while the impact on the numerator term is proportionate in both the first and second terms, the denominators differ. The denominator of the first price appreciation term is always bigger than the second, return to fundamental investment term. This is because the first term in Equation (12.8) contains an additional term to reflect price turbulence between periods 1 and 2 $\left(\frac{1}{R\sigma_P^2}\right)$. More price turbulence, i.e. smaller $\frac{1}{R\sigma_P^2}$, magnifies the return to price appreciation in the first term of Equation (12.8). This is because the early informed unwind their position less in such an environment. Irrespective of how variation in price impacts upon the early informed demand at period 1, $x_1 (\theta, P_1)$, the presence of price volatility in the denominator of the first and not the second term shrinks that denominator's value and so swells the impact of the first term in Equation (12.8), the price appreciation term, relative to the second, denoting the return to fundamental investing (so long as the product of R and price volatility σ_P^2 is less than 1 at least). So an increase in expected period 2 price, $\overline{P}_2$, increases the incentive of the early informed to buy more of the asset at period 1, i.e. raise x_1. Figure 12.3 shows this pattern for the initial values provided in Table 12.2.

I now consider a similar comparative for changes in the early informed demand for the asset at period 1, x_1, as uncertainty about value, or the volatility of the shocks to value, ε changes. In Figure 12.4 I consider the impact on the early informed asset demand at period 1, x_1, in Equation (12.8), of

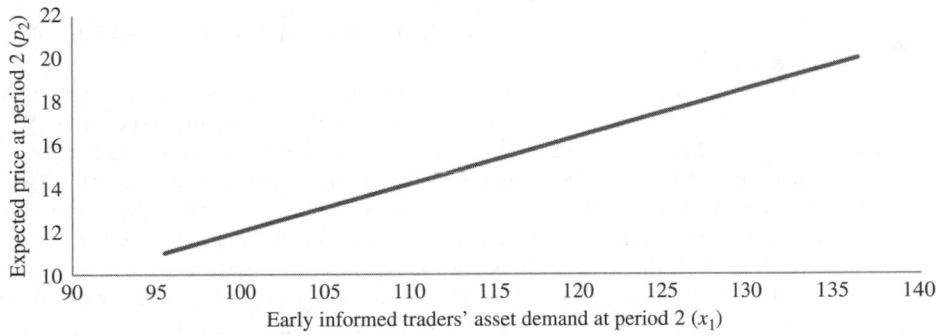

Figure 12.3   Demand schedule for asset by early informed at period 1 as a function of period 2 expected price

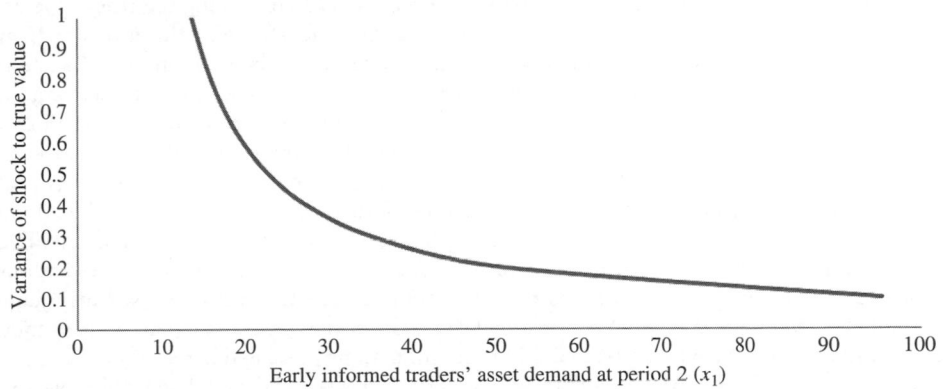

Figure 12.4   Demand schedule for asset by early informed at period 1 as a function of variance of shock to value (ε)

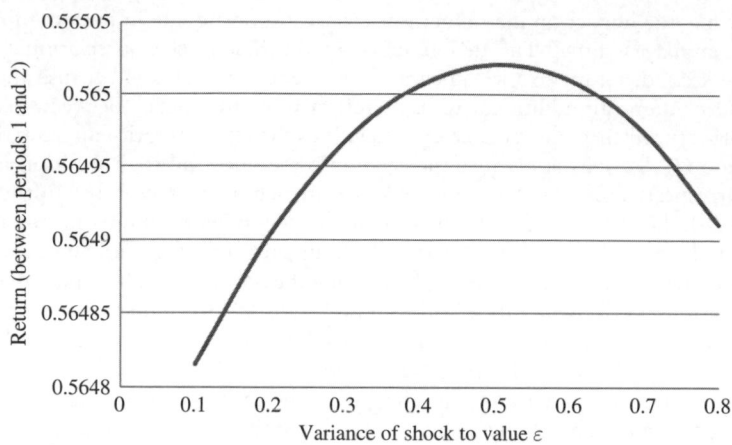

Figure 12.5   Return to holding asset as a function of variance in shocks to value ε $(t = 1$ to $2)$

incremental 10% increases in the volatility of shocks to value, that is σ_ε^2 retaining all the other variables as initialized in Table 12.2.

The HST model provides a linear solution for prices provided in Equation (12.2), but this linear solution in prices is highly nonlinear in the underlying coefficients forming the response coefficients on the right-hand side of Equation (12.2). The way in which these nonlinear coefficients on the various elements of value are formed is detailed at some length in Appendix B. Equations (12.14) and (12.15) outline the nature of the restriction on the roots of the quadratic we solve to obtain these coefficients. So I solve for the nonlinear coefficients, a, b, c, d, e and f in Equations (12.14) and (12.15) subject to the restriction on k, the root to the quadratic equation in Equation (12.15) subject to the restriction given by Equation (12.15). Hence I use the solver routine in Excel to retrieve coefficients a to f and so P_1 and P_2 in Equation (12.2), subject to the restriction on k implied by Equation (12.14). I set $k = 0.25$ for the purpose of the comparative static exercise requirement.

Having set up the solution for the various nonlinear coefficients for prices at periods 1 and 2, P_1 and P_2 in Equation (12.2), using the guidance of Equation (12.13) through (12.15) in the Appendix below, I conduct two separate comparative static exercises using the initial values in Tables 12.2.

In this first exercise I incrementally raise the variance of shocks concerning the true value of the asset, σ_ε^2, by 10% increments from 10% to 100% of price. The effect of doing this is to slowly mask the true value of the asset. Given the increase in risk now faced by the early informed since their informational advantage is being diluted by true uncertainty, which is faced by all traders regarding the asset's true value, return rises. What is more surprising is how small the increment in return is to increase the required rate of return. At relatively higher levels of ignorance regarding the true value of the asset, θ, the early informed may feel they actually now have no comparative advantage by trading the asset early, or at all perhaps, and so their demand falls. Since the later informed never buy the asset at period 1 this means its price will fall after initially rising in volatility in shocks to asset value, ε. Figure 12.5 captures this nonlinearity in return implicit in the set linear pricing equations in Equation (12.3). This nonlinearity derives from the nonlinear coefficients expressed in Equations (12.14) and (12.5). Equation (12.17) requires that the roots of the quadratic equation lie within the unit circle and to this end I set k equal to 0.25 in the simulations presented here.

Using the same set of linear pricing equations in Equation (12.2) and the nonlinear solutions for the coefficients in Equation (12.15) in combination with the initial values given in Table 12.2 I conduct a

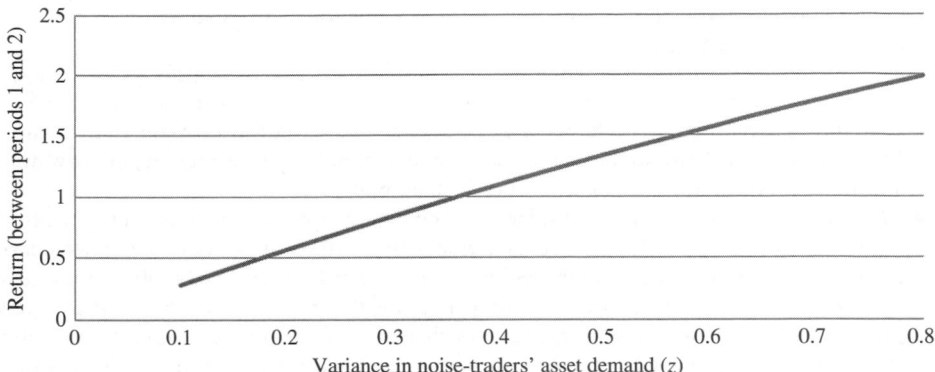

Figure 12.6   Return to holding asset as a function of noise-traders' demand (z) ($t = 1$ to 2)

second comparative static exercise shown in Figure 12.6. Here I raise the volatility of noise-traders' demands at periods 1 and 2 by equal 10% point increments.

As in Chapter 6 noise-trader demand allows them to 'create their own space' making the early informed even more keen to hold the asset, given their informational advantage at period 1. Of course the demands of noise traders are completely unrelated to true asset value, θ, but an increase in the volatility of noise-trader demand does not erode the informational advantage of the early informed relative to those informed later and so even at relatively high levels does not erode their return to holding the asset.

12.4   Insider Trading, Stock Options and the Construction of Earnings

Thus far I have portrayed insider dealing as a way of getting information about fundamental value into price, but managers (who are a large proportion of the insider population) often construct the performance metric out of which fundamental value is inferred – earnings, dividends, sales and investment in research and development. Is it possible that the side of the trade managers have previously taken, either buying or selling their employer's shares, motivates them to boost or depress earnings (if the auditor is sufficiently compliant)? If the CEO of a FTSE 100 company has just been issued with hundreds of thousands of options to buy the stock at the price it was last year is it possible that he has an incentive to seek out new ways to ramp up the forthcoming earning-per-share figure a little?

This suspicion has led to a number of studies regarding the anticipation and reflection of earnings announcements by insiders' trades. Hillier and Marshall (2002) study directors' trades in the United Kingdom, as recorded on the *Directorswatch* database in the years 1992 to 1996. They find that 23% of all director-recorded trades take place within 10 days of the most recent earnings announcement. The UK London Stock Exchange code forbids trading during a 'closed period' of two months prior to the earnings announcement. Since most major corporations make both an interim and a final earnings announcement many managers are locked out of trading their employing corporation's shares for four months of each year. Hillier and Marshall (2002) also find insider trading activity to be clustered near to the 'closed' period surrounding earnings announcements. Interim earnings announcements attract even bigger bursts of insider trades around the dates of closure than the announcement of final earnings. This may be because interim announcements are unaudited and so offer the opportunity for strategic earnings management.

Of course senior managers trading within days of the closed period are highly likely to have their trades closely scrutinized by the financial authorities regulating the market (the Financial Services Authority in the United Kingdom or the Securities and Exchange Commission in the United States), so it is likely that managers of any sophistication will trade to avoid any unwanted regulatory attention to their influence on their employing corporation's share price.

Ke *et al.* (2003) present evidence that insiders can and do anticipate earnings announcements for up to two years ahead. Ke *et al.* (2003) studied the relation between the turning points in quarterly earnings announcements and over 80,000 insider trades by executives employed by over 4000 separate US firms in the years 1989 to 1997. A 'break in a string' of quarterly earnings occurs for Ke *et al.* if this quarter's earnings-per-share figure falls below, or rises above, that of the same quarter last year. These authors focus particularly on whether insiders' trades anticipate a breakage in a successive 'string' of positive, or negative, earnings announcements. They find anticipation of earnings breaks by insider trades for leads of three to nine months prior to the break. Such subtle use of insider information is unlikely to be effectively outlawed unless the senior management team of major corporations are entirely denied the opportunity to trade in their own stock. Since many of them are already partially paid in options to purchase their own company's stock this seems a rather unhelpful situation.

But restriction on insider trading is not imposed solely, or even perhaps the most bitingly, by government. Company boards that are interested in maintaining a high reputation for loyalty to their fiduciary duty to shareholders also impose privately policed restrictions on insider trading. Bettis *et al.* (2000) found 92% of their sample of 403 companies in the United States studied in the mid-1990s imposed restrictions on insider trading and 78% imposed voluntary 'black-out' periods around key events in corporate life, earnings announcements and changes in the executive team. The single most common policy adopted was to disallow any trading by members of the senior management team[6] except in a 10-day window following each successive quarterly earnings announcement.

12.4.1   *Psychological Factors Determining the Exercise of Stock Options*

Senior management of most corporations cannot help trading their employing corporation's equity because much of their pay comes in the form of call options exercisable against their employer's stock. Such options are paid as a way of 'bonding' managers to serve shareholders' interests by 'making managers owners', or at least co-owners, in the shareholders' venture. Heath *et al.* (1999) show clearly that the way in which this form of remuneration is recouped by managers reflects many of the psychological biases so far in this book.

Such behavioural biases in the exercise of managers' stock options contrast with the very successful standard theories of option pricing found in standard finance, such as the Black–Scholes and binomial option pricing models. It is a general prediction of such 'rational' models of option pricing that early exercise of the options granted to managers is most probably unwise. The value of the call is derived to be the maximum of zero and the gap between the value at which the option was written on the grant date (usually prevailing price in the market on the issue date) and the current price of outstanding shares currently trading in the market. Since the return on most shares is positive most months of most years, holding until exercise usually makes sense. Selling for liquidity makes sense, however, if exercising the options held yields cash more cheaply than raising an equivalent loan for the same amount of cash. Therefore Heath *et al.* (1999) control for the relative costs of raising cash by option exercise and an equivalent loan in judging the behavioural motivations of options exercise.

The first behavioural bias that may underpin early exercise of stock options is the tendency of managers to follow trends and seek to anticipate reversals. In particular many follow short-run trends while believing long-run trends will dissipate. Indeed Barberis *et al.* (1998) examine just such a model of investor sentiment in which company stock prices in reality follow a random walk, but investors act in the belief they are characterized by either a trend-chasing or mean-reverting dynamic.[7]

A second behavioural concept, previously discussed in this book, which weighs heavily on the early exercise of senior managers' stock options is the prevalence of 'reference points' in the evaluation of investment returns. Prospect theory, discussed in Chapter 2 and applied to the problem of asset pricing in Chapters 8 and 10, stresses three points of importance for the early exercise of managerial stock options. These are:

1. Utility is defined over changes in wealth, not its level.
2. As we move away from some salient reference point, zero, or last year's bonus received via the option exercise of stock options, the investor's response becomes less sensitive to changes (either through a surfeit of riches or the abandonment of all hope).
3. Losses are felt more keenly than gains, which strongly favours the payment of stock options since their minimum worth is zero while their maximum value is unbounded at the date of their issue.

In their results Heath *et al.* (1999) find an important role for psychological factors in inducing early exercise of stock options granted in part payment of salary. In particular they report a strong inducement to exercise managers' options emanating from the stock reaching the maximum value at which it has traded in the most recent year. When this maximum value is attained managers tend to bail out. Heath *et al.* conclude (1999, p.623):

> Employees are much more likely to exercise their options when stock prices exceed some maximum price that was achieved within the previous year, and that they are even more likely to exercise when subsequent price movements move them past their reference point.

Hence in evaluating the trades of informed insiders it is wise to remember they remain subject to the same trend-chasing and reference point breaking behaviours their peers outside the company exhibit.

12.5 Insider Trading and its Consequence for Outsiders

Leland constructs a model of the impact of insider trading with the following types of traders:

- Insiders have a privileged position within the company that gives them access to superior information regarding future 'shocks' to company value, via takeovers, restructuring or changes in the senior management team.
- Outsiders realize they may unwittingly be trading with insiders who have superior information to them and act accordingly.
- Liquidity traders who trade to transfer consumption between the current and future, or past, periods.

These traders meet in a market into which a company will make a share issue open to each type of trader equally. Once again Leland's (1992) model has clear implications regarding the distributional consequences of insider trading, as opposed to its impact in undermining the efficiency of trading in financial markets.

Leland points to the offsetting impact of insider trading on outsiders trading in the same shares as insiders:

- It reduces their profits on average because they occasionally get stung by insiders who know more than they do.
- It reduces their risk in trading because the prices they trade upon are more informative about true value now that they contain inside information.

Leland notes an additional benefit of insider trading not commonly commented upon in public discussion of the matter. Insider trading may increase the accessibility to capital for entrepreneurs/innovators bringing new products to market. For example suppose a scientist in my university's Science Park is sure he has found an elusive cure for cancer. Allowing him to trade on that knowledge is one easy way to enable him to raise cash to finance his life-saving invention. As the proposed cure clears various medical trials and Federal Drug Agency clearance etc. the money to self-fund his life-changing scientific discovery will roll in.

12.6 Conclusion and Summary

One way to see insider trading is as a stupidity tax on those who don't do their homework fully regarding fundamental value. Recall that all insiders do is get price to fundamental value quicker. It's hard to be an insider dealer on baseless rumours. So insiders might be seen as secret policemen against naive speculators checking bubbles and baseless market cascades. As such the impact of insider trading may not be entirely bad after all.

This chapter has examined the role of insider trading in the evolution of security prices in the contexts of a market characterized by noise trading of the type considered initially in Chapter 6. Such a model, which accommodates investors informed at different stages of trade (some early, some late), is characterized by many of the biases previously discussed in other chapters. These include momentum trading, or price trend chasing considered in Chapter 10, subsequent overreaction and resulting market corrections to such overreaction considered in Chapter 9, and herding of informed investors like analysts and fund managers into a narrow market sector or valuation basis, for example break-up values, or economic value added, of the type considered in Chapter 11.

Regulatory authorities and politicians are given to occasional bouts of moral condemnation concerning the evils of insider trading, but in reality, like sin itself, we are all at it to some degree and this is unlikely ever to change. So the more pressing question is, how much insider trading can be tolerated before market integrity is compromised and outside investors withdraw from the market? In evaluating this we need to consider the costs as well the benefits of insider traders' presence in the market. One clear benefit is the incentive it gives to investors to be active participants in the 'market for information' (which I consider in Chapter 15) and so acquire information about fundamental value early and thus profit from trading on that knowledge. This incentive transfers wealth from liquidity/noise traders to those making the effort to obtain information early and put it into price. As such, insider trading may act as a bulwark to promote healthy financial markets rather than erode their integrity.

Appendix A: Why Don't Later Informed Traders Trade in Period 1 in the HST Model?

Hirshleifer *et al.* make use of one of the properties of the characteristic function of the normal distribution (see Anderson 2003 for a review) to show why the later informed investors delay all their trades until period 2, not trading at all in period 1. The characteristic function of a random vector of i investor's asset demands, $\mathbf{x}$, has the form

$$\phi(t) = E e^{it'x} \quad \forall\, t$$

which characterizes the evolution of $\mathbf{x}$ over time and can be used to check the dynamic stability of asset demands in the model. For some normally distributed, finite variance variable, u, ($u \sim N(\mu,\sigma^2)$), the characteristic function takes the form

$$\phi(t) = E e^{it'x} = e^{it'\mu - \frac{1}{2}t'\sigma t}$$

Hirshleifer *et al.* consider a particular case of such characteristic function containing two elements, $u = W^E$, the end-period wealth of early informed investors and R the discount factor. Combined they capture the discounted terminal period wealth of early informed investors. Recall the density function that generates the normal distribution takes the form

$$f_x = f_x(x; \mu, \sigma) = \frac{1}{\sqrt{2\pi\sigma}} e^{-(x-\mu)/2\sigma}$$

where μ and σ satisfy the condition $-\infty < \mu < \infty$ and $\alpha > 0$: see Mood *et al.* (1974, p.107).

Hence using the properties of the characteristic function of a normal distribution (discussed above)

$$E(\exp(vu)) = E(\exp(\mu v + \frac{1}{2}\sigma^2 v^2))$$

Recall that the early informed investors already know both F and θ at period 1, so in maximizing discounted end-period wealth in period 2 in time period 1 all they need to worry about is the unpredictable random shocks to asset value captured by the shock to value ε. The expression for their wealth maximization becomes Equation (12.8) in the main part of this chapter

$$E(-\exp(R W^E)|\phi_2) = E\left[\left[-\exp\left\{-R\left[B_0 - x_1 P_1 + x_2 P_2 + \frac{(F + \theta - P_2)}{2R\sigma_\varepsilon^2}\right]^2\right\}\right]|\phi_1\right]$$

Here discounted end-period wealth is a function of the three primary elements previously discussed: capital gains on period 1 holdings; gains to sound fundamental investing in period 2; and the early informed initial endowment. But we also know that evolution of terminal wealth is driven by random variables that are drawn from a normal distribution. Hence to determine terminal wealth we need to evaluate (add up or integrate) the whole distribution of possible terminal-wealth outcomes the investor can expect to face. In calculating the area under the distribution of possible, period 2, investor terminal-wealth outcomes we use the fact that we know the distribution of wealth outcomes is normally distributed, since its outcomes are a mixture of known variables, like x_1 and R and other normally distributed random variables, like θ and ε. Incorporating this knowledge into the terminal wealth maximand we obtain

$$-\left[2\pi\sigma_{P_2}^2\right]^{1/2} \int_{-\infty}^{\infty} \exp\left\{-R\left[B_0 + x_1 P_1 + x_1 P_2 + \frac{(\overline{F} + \theta - P_2)^2}{(2R\sigma_\varepsilon^2)}\right] - \frac{1}{2}\frac{(P_2 - \overline{P}_2)}{2R\sigma_\varepsilon^2}\right\} d(P_2 - \overline{P}_2)$$

The exponent part of the expression above can be strategically arranged to allow some simplifications as follows:

$$-\left[\frac{1}{2}(P_2 - \overline{P})^2\left\{\frac{1}{\sigma_{P_2}^2} + \frac{1}{\sigma_\varepsilon^2}\right\} + \left\{Rx_1 + \frac{(\overline{F}+\theta-\overline{P})}{2\sigma_\varepsilon^2}\right\}(P_2 - \overline{P}_2) + Rx_1(\overline{P}_2 - P_1)^2 \right.$$
$$\left. + \frac{(\overline{F}+\theta-\overline{P}_2)^2}{2\sigma_\varepsilon^2} + RB_0\right]$$

which can be written in short-hand form as

$$-\left[\frac{1}{2}w^2 s + hw + l\right]$$

which can be compressed down to read

$$w = (P_2 - \overline{P}_2)$$

$$h = Rx_1 + \frac{(\overline{F}+\theta-\overline{P}_2)}{\sigma_\varepsilon^2}$$

$$s = \frac{1}{\sigma_{P_2}^2} + \frac{1}{\sigma_\varepsilon^2}$$

$$l = Rx_1(\overline{P}_2 - P_1) + \frac{(\overline{F}+\theta-\overline{P}_2)^2}{2\sigma_\varepsilon^2} + RB_0$$

Hence the investor maximizes risk-adjusted returns to both the holding gain on the portfolio held to maturity (hw) subject to the risk associated to holding that portfolio ($w^2 s$). Those holding gains themselves combined both a discounted holding gain earned at period 2 by the early informed to buying the asset with a positive signal at period 1 and selling out to the later informed at period 2 (the first element in l) a return on fundamentally sound investment (the second element in l).

At this point we need to scrub up some high school algebra for solving simple quadratic equations. Recall one of the simplest such quadratic equations (Bostock & Chandler 1994):

$$x^2 - 2x$$

Consider for a moment what happens if we just added one to that expression to give

$$x^2 - 2x + 1$$

We now have the 'perfect square' of the original equation (without the 1 added in)

$$(x-1)(x-1) = x_2 - 2x + 1$$

Now this result isn't actually magic, although it may seem like it. In reality it is a general algebraic rule that

$$x^2 + 2ax + a^2 \equiv (x+a)^2$$

There the magic number to be added to give us our 'perfect square' is always half the coefficient on the x square term in the expression . The coefficient on x in our example $x^2 - 2x$ is 2, so we added 1 in that example. But the general solution to solving quadratics of the form $x^2 + bx$ is to add $(b/2)^2$ to obtain the completed square

$$x^2 + bx + \left(\frac{b}{2}\right)^2 \equiv \left(x + \frac{b}{2}\right)^2$$

Using this technique for solving the roots of a quadratic equation I define

$$u \equiv \sqrt{sw} + \frac{h}{\sqrt{s}}$$

The compressed expression for the discounted value of terminal wealth within the exponent, $-[1/2\ w^2 s + hw + l]$, becomes

$$\frac{1}{2}u^2 + \frac{1}{2}\frac{h^2}{\sqrt{s}} + l$$

So the revised expression for terminal wealth becomes

$$-\left[2\pi\sigma_{P_2}^2 s\right]^{-\frac{1}{2}} \int_{-\infty}^{\infty} \exp\left(\frac{1}{2}u^2 + \frac{1}{2}\frac{h^2}{s} - l\right) du$$

$$= -\frac{1}{(\sigma_{P_2}^2 s)^{\frac{1}{2}}} \exp\left(\frac{1}{2}\frac{h^2}{s} - l\right)$$

This reduction in the above integral relies on the property of the normal distribution integral, which ensures

$$\frac{1}{\sqrt{2\pi}} \int_{-\infty}^{\infty} u^2 e^{\frac{1}{2}u^2} du = 1$$

which simply states that over the whole distribution, between ∞ and $-\infty$, the cumulative distribution contains all the distribution of possible outcomes (see Anderson 2003, p.19). Much of the prior tortuous manipulation is predicated on a desire to invoke this simplifying property of the normal distribution.

The period 1 demand of early informed investors is given by

$$x_1(\theta, P_1) = \frac{\overline{P}_2 - P_1}{R}\left(\frac{1}{\sigma_{P_2}^2} + \frac{1}{\sigma_\varepsilon^2}\right) + \frac{\overline{F} + \theta - \overline{P}_2}{R\sigma_\varepsilon^2}$$

which is just Equation (12.5) in the main body of the chapter.

Appendix B: Deriving Investor Demands as Linear Functions of the Random Variables Underpinning the Model

In this appendix I show how the HST model implies a linear demand function for the risky asset where price is a linear function of the random shocks to value, both fundamental value θ and shocks to that value ε of the form given by Equation (12.2) in the main body of this chapter. So recalling that equation

$$P_2 = \overline{F} + a\theta + bz_1 + cz_2$$
$$P_1 = \overline{F} + e\theta + fz_1 \tag{12.2}$$

where

$$\alpha = \frac{\sigma_\theta^2 \left[(\kappa N - R\sigma_\varepsilon^2)^2 + R^2\sigma_\varepsilon^4 \right]}{D} \tag{12.10}$$

$$b = \frac{\kappa R^2 \sigma_\varepsilon^4 \sigma_\theta^2}{D}$$

$$c = \frac{\kappa R \sigma_\varepsilon^2 \sigma_\theta^2 (\kappa N - R\sigma_\varepsilon^2)}{D}$$

and

$$e = \frac{\sigma_\theta^2}{(\sigma_\theta^2 + \sigma_\varepsilon^2)} \qquad f = \kappa e$$

$$D \equiv \sigma_\theta^2 (\kappa N - R^2\sigma_\varepsilon^2)^2 + R^2\sigma_\varepsilon^4 (\sigma_\varepsilon^2 + \kappa^2\sigma_z^2) \tag{12.11}$$

I now ask what determines the weights on various fragments of value, i.e. a, b, c, e and f. This statement of the linearity of the pricing function is Lemma 1 in the Hirshleifer *et al.* (1994) paper. I begin by defining some characteristics of conditional distribution of period 2 price, when the early and later informed trade for the first time. Recall from Appendix A that the later informed simply don't trade in period 1 because they realize the early informed can fleece them since they know θ while the later informed don't. Liquidity/noise traders trade on oblivious to such subtleties in both periods 1 and 2. The conditional distribution of price in period 2 can be restated as follows

$$\overline{P}_2 = E[P_2|\theta, z_1] = \overline{F} + \theta + bz_1$$

$$\sigma_P^2 = \text{var}[P_2|\theta, z_1] = c\sigma_{P_2}^2$$

which on substituting into Equation (12.5) (which I repeat for convenience below)

$$x_1(\theta, P_1) = \frac{\overline{P}_2 - P_1}{R} \left(\frac{1}{\sigma_{P_2}^2} + \frac{1}{\sigma_\varepsilon^2} \right) + \frac{\overline{F} + \theta - \overline{P}_2}{R\sigma_\varepsilon^2}$$

Recall the solution for the variance of period 2 prices and the period 2 price itself are given as

$$\sigma_{P_2}^2 = c^2\sigma_z^2$$
$$\overline{P}_2 = \overline{F} + a\theta + bz_1$$

And then substituting into the solution for x_1 given by Equation (12.5), we obtain

$$x_1(\theta, P_1) = \theta \frac{a\sigma_{P_2}^2 + c^2\sigma_z^2}{Rc^2\sigma_z^2\sigma_\varepsilon^2} + \frac{b}{Rc^2\sigma_z^2} z_1 + \frac{(\bar{F} - P_1)(\sigma_\varepsilon^2 + c^2\sigma_z^2)}{Rc^2\sigma_\varepsilon^2\sigma_z^2}$$

Total asset demand is given by the sum of demands from the early informed x, the later informed y, and liquidity/noise traders

$$M\left[\theta \frac{a\sigma_\varepsilon^2 + c^2\sigma_z^2}{Rc^2\sigma_\varepsilon^2\sigma_z^2} + z_1 \frac{b}{Rc^2\sigma_z^2} + \frac{(\bar{F} - P_1)(\sigma_\varepsilon^2 + c^2\sigma_z^2)}{Rc^2\sigma_\varepsilon^2\sigma_z^2}\right] + Ny_1(P_1) + z_1$$

Defining τ_1 as follows:

$$\tau_1 \equiv \frac{M(a\sigma_\varepsilon^2 + c^2\sigma_z^2)}{Rc^2\sigma_\varepsilon^2\sigma_z^2}\theta + \frac{Mb + Rc^2\sigma_z^2}{Rc^2} z_1$$

allows us to restate the rearranged expression for x_1 as follows:

$$x_1 = \frac{M(\bar{F} - P_1)(\sigma_\varepsilon^2 + c^2\sigma_z^2)}{Rc^2\sigma_\varepsilon^2\sigma_z^2} + Ny_1(P_1) + \tau_1 \tag{12.12}$$

Since the demand of the later informed in period 1, y_1, is zero as already discussed and the early informed already know θ, the informative part the of demand schedule for setting period 1 price is τ. So period 1 price is set as follows:

$$P_1 = E[\bar{F} + \theta + \varepsilon|\tau_1] = \bar{F} + E[\theta|\tau_1] \tag{12.13}$$

This implies price takes the form of a prediction from the linear projection of θ on τ_1. Let κ denote the coefficient of a regression of θ on τ_1. Hence

$$k \equiv \frac{Mb\sigma_\varepsilon^2 + Rc^2\sigma_\varepsilon^2\sigma_z^2}{M(a\sigma_\varepsilon^2 + c^2\sigma_z^2)} \tag{12.14}$$

so we have

$$P_1 = \bar{F} + \frac{\sigma_\theta^2}{\sigma_\theta^2 + k^2\sigma_z^2}(\theta + \kappa z_1)$$

Returning back to our simple postulate that period 1 price is a linear function of uncertain elements of value

$$P_1 = \bar{F} + e\theta + fz_1$$

and equating both expressions for period 1 price

$$P_1 = \bar{F} + \frac{\sigma_\theta^2}{\sigma_\theta^2 + k^2\sigma_z^2}(\theta + kz_1) = \bar{F} + e\theta + fz_1$$

$$\Rightarrow e = \frac{\sigma_\theta^2}{\sigma_\theta^2 + k^2\sigma_z^2}$$

$$f = ke \tag{12.15}$$

In period 2 the demand schedule sums the demands of the early and later informed together with those of liquidity traders to yield

$$D_2(P_2) = \frac{N}{R\sigma_\varepsilon^2}\,(\overline{F} + \theta - P_2) + z_1 + z_2 \tag{12.16}$$

Note liquidity traders' demands in period 2 are neither a function of price nor the asset's deviation in price from true value. Liquidity traders trade because they wish to trade. As in the case of τ_1 we define τ_2 to simplify the demand equation for period 2 as follows:

$$\tau_2 \equiv \frac{N}{R\sigma_\varepsilon^2}\theta + z_1 + z_2$$

So

$$D_2(P_2) = \frac{N}{R\sigma_\varepsilon^2}\,(\overline{F} - P_2) + \tau_2$$

And the price in period 2 must satisfy the condition

$$P_2 = E[\overline{F} + \theta + \varepsilon | \tau_1, \tau_2]$$

Drawing on properties of conditional normal distributions (Anderson 2003, p.35) to characterize the whole distribution by reference to its mean and variance:

$$(v_1, v_2) \sim N\left[(\mu_1, \mu_2), \left(\begin{matrix} \sum_{11} & \sum_{12} \\ \sum_{21} & \sum_{22} \end{matrix}\right)\right]$$

The conditional distribution of v_1 given the value of v_2 is

$$E(v_1 | v_2 = \mathbf{X}_2) = \mu_1 + \sum_{12} \sum_{22}^{-1}(X_2 - \mu_2)$$

Let

$$v_1 = \theta,$$
$$v_2 = k\tau_1, \frac{R\sigma_\varepsilon^2}{N}\tau_2$$

and the expression for v_2 above is the same in any real world application as $[\tau_1, \tau_2]$.

The various constituent elements of the covariance matrix of v_1 and v_2 are

$$\sum_{11} = \sigma_\theta^2 \sum_{12}$$
$$\sum_{12} = [\sigma_\theta^2, \sigma_\theta^2]$$
$$\sum_{22} = \begin{bmatrix} \sigma_\theta^2 + k\sigma_z^2 & \sigma_\theta^2 + \dfrac{kR\sigma_\varepsilon^2\sigma_z^2}{N} \\[2ex] \sigma_\theta^2 + \dfrac{kR\sigma_\varepsilon^2\sigma_z^2}{N} & \sigma_\theta^2 + \dfrac{2R^2\sigma_\varepsilon^4\sigma_z^2}{N^2} \end{bmatrix}$$

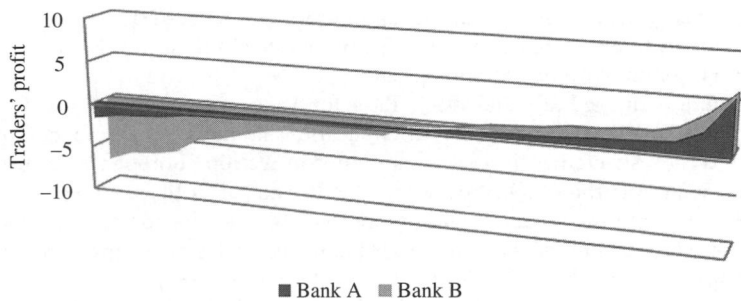

Figure 12.7 Distribution of trading profits: who is an insider and who is a little angel: A or B?

Solving the resulting quadratic equation yields two solutions: one positive, $T+$; one negative, $T-$. It turns out the price movement implied between periods 1 and 2 is greatest by taking positive root $T+$. Two positive real roots to the quadratic are guaranteed if the condition

$$\frac{4MR^2\sigma_\varepsilon^2\sigma_z^2\left[2M\left(\sigma_\varepsilon^2 + \sigma_\theta^2\right) - N\sigma_\theta^2\right] + 4M^2N^2\sigma_\theta^2}{R\sigma_\varepsilon^2\sigma_z^2\sigma_\theta^2} < 1 \tag{12.17}$$

is satisfied.

Questions

1. Return to Figure 12.1. Suppose insider trading is a risky business and you can make money as well as lose it. As head of the Financial Services Authority for a day, your staff present you with two sets of trading profits by Banks A and B (Figure 12.7). Who is the insider and who is the little angel they wonder? Your job is on the line here, so try to get this right. Remember you are a public servant, accountable to politicians, so having some sensible reasons for your decision would help.
2. Return to the numerical simulations considered in Figures 12.5 and Figure 12.6, respectively. Figure 12.5 considers the impact on early informed investors' returns of growing volatility in shocks to fundamental asset value, ε. Figure 12.6 does an analogous comparative static exercise for increases in the volatility of noise-traders' demands for the assets z_1 and z_2. What about increases in volatility of prices at period 2 generally? What would an analogous comparative static exercise based on increases in $\sigma_{P_2}^2$ look like? Explain how returns to the early informed (and so the incentive to become informed) varies as volatility in period 2 prices increases in increments of 10%.
3. You've finally got your dream job as a hedge fund manager with Greed and Fear Associates. Your preferred 'value add' is insider trading in your clients' stock. What stocks would you buy and what pointers would guide you as to when to sell them? Maybe keep your notes in answering this one in a place no one would dream of looking.

Notes

1. Against the cost, highlighted here, we must weight the matching benefit of preventing the 'herding' on to a minority of salient stocks also predicted by the HST model.
2. This quotation is taken from Bris (2005, p.268) and is from a speech given by Levitt in Washington on 27 February 1998 when the bull run in the US economy was in full swing.

3. See http://www.fsa.gov.uk/pages/Library/Communication/Speeches/2007/1004_mc.shtml.
4. Recall that liquidity trader demands are simply random shocks that average out in expectation at least in the final period, with no effect on price.
5. Some useful guides to using Excel and Visual Basic for Applications, or VBA, are Robinson (2004) and Calberg (2002). An excellent source for applications in finance is Benninga (2000).
6. The group of those restricted as 'insiders' is specified in Section 16(a) of the Securities Exchange Act 1934, these include the CEO, President, Chief Financial Officer, Chief Operating Officer and Chief Accountant plus others owning more than 10% of the company's equity.
7. The Barberis *et al.* (1998) model is not discussed in my book despite its great importance in behavioural finance as a whole. This is because it does not fit very easily into the noise-trader structure I choose as a formal modelling device throughout the book. In the Barberis *et al.* (1998) model there is one type of representative trader trading in two perceived regimes, not two (or more) types of trader under a common pricing regime as in noise-trader models.

References

Abarbanell, J. & R. Lehavy (2003). Biased forecasts of earnings? The role of reported earnings in explaining apparent bias and over/underreaction in analysts' earnings forecasts. *Journal of Accounting and Economics*, 36: 105–46.

Anderson, T. (2003). *An Introduction to Multivariate Statistical Analysis*. New York: Wiley & Sons, Inc.

Bainbridge, S. (2001). The Law and Economics of Insider trading: a comprehensive primer, SSRN-id2612, Working Paper on Social Science Research Network (SSRN).

Barberis, N., A. Shleifer *et al.* (1998). A model of investor sentiment. *Journal of Financial Economics*, 49(3): 307–43.

Beneish, M. & M. Vargus (2002). Insider trading earnings quality, and accrual mispricing. *Accounting Review*, 77: 755–91.

Benninga, S. (2000). *Financial Modeling*. Cambridge, MA: MIT Press.

Bettis, C., J. Coles *et al.* (2000). Corporate policies restricting trading by insiders. *Journal of Financial Economics*, 57: 191–220.

Bostock, L. & S. Chandler (1994). *Core Mathematics for Advanced Level*. Cheltenham: Nelson Thomas.

Bris, A. (2005). Do insider trading laws work? *European Financial Management*, 11(3): 267–312.

Bruck, C. (1989). *The Predator's Ball: The Inside Story of Drexel Burnham*. London: Penguin.

Calberg, C. (2002). *Business Analysis with Microsoft Excel*. United States of America: QUE Publishing.

De Long, B., A. Shleifer *et al.* (1990). Noise trader risk in financial markets. *Journal of Political Economy*, 98(4): 703–38.

Engelen, P.-J. (2006). Difficulties in the criminal prosecution of insider trading – a clinical study of the *Bekaert* case. *European Journal of Law and Economics*, 22(2): 121–41.

Froot, K., D. Scharstein *et al.* (1992). Herd on the street. Informational efficiency in a market short-term speculation. *Journal of Finance*, 47 (September): 1451–84.

Graham, J., H. Campbell *et al.* (2005). The economic implications of corporate financial reporting. *Journal of Accounting and Economics*, 40: 3–73.

Heath, H., S. Huddart *et al.* (1999). Psychological factors and stock option exercise. *Quarterly Journal of Economics*, 114: 601–27.

Hillier, D. & A. Marshall (2002). Are trading bans effective? Exchange regulation and corporate insider transactions around earnings announcements. *Journal of Corporate Finance*, 8: 393–410.

Hirshleifer, D., A. Subrahmanyam & S. Titman (1994). Security analysis and trading patterns when some investors receive information before others. *Journal of Finance*, **49**(5): 1665–98.

Ke, B., S. Huddart *et al.* (2003). What insiders know about future earnings and how they use it: evidence from insider trades. *Journal of Accounting and Economics*, **35**: 315–46.

Leland, K. (1992). Insider trading: should it be prohibited? *Journal of Political Economy*, August: 859–87.

Meadowcroft, J. (2008). *Prohibitions*. London: Institute for Economic Affairs.

Montier, J. (2006). *Behavioural Finance: Insights into Irrational Minds and Markets*. Chichester: John Wiley & Sons, Ltd.

Mood, A., F. Graybill *et al.* (1974). *Introduction to the Theory of Statistics*. Singapore: McGraw-Hill.

Robinson, E. (2004). *Excel VBA in Easy Steps*. Southampton: Computer Step.

Chapter 13

Equity Premium Puzzle

Finance teaches us that assets are held by investors in proportion to their risk and return. But much evidence suggests that investors like holding equity to a degree that cannot be explained by its relative risk-adjusted return. Figure 13.1 gives some basic data on the UK equity premium in the years 1900–2000. This data is a small part of the 100-year plus history of international equity entitled *The Triumph of the Optimists* (Dimson, Marsh & Staunton 2002). Over the whole period the arithmetic average of the mark-up of equity over treasury bills in the United Kingdom is 6.1% and even higher elsewhere. Numerous studies in the United States suggest a premium over the year in the range 5.5–8.5%. Given the average equity return over this period was about 12% this suggests that equity earns a return nearly twice that on treasury bills because of additional risk. However, the standard deviation of real equity returns is just over three times that of the mean return and the standard deviation of treasury bill prices is more than six times its mean return, so it appears that in the very long term bonds may be more risky than equity! How can equity earn a premium over treasury bills – a pretty riskless security for a developed country? Not because of risk it seems, or at least not by the risk metrics we normally consider in finance classes.

13.1   Illustration and Structure

Figure 13.1 gives some idea of the scale of the equity premium puzzle in six major financial markets based on the Dimson *et al.* (2002) study. The evidence is enough to tell us that this is a pretty widespread anomaly. The relative return to equity seems too large to be justified by its risk compared to other assets. The mark-up of equity returns over that offered by bonds is widespread (see Montier 2006, Section 1.3.2.4, for a discussion of empirical evidence regarding the premium).

In Section 13.2 I explain the equity premium 'puzzle'. I then investigate one solution to the puzzle, rooted in investors' aversion to losses. Section 13.3 gives more detail about how psychological research is enhancing our ability to understand choices made in relation to distinct 'reference points' of importance to investors, for example historically average performance or current practice. Section 13.4 summarizes and concludes the chapter.

After reading this chapter the reader should:

- Understand the nature of the puzzle surrounding the equity premium.
- Understand how investors' aversion to losses may explain the equity premium puzzle.
- See how the equity premium puzzle fits into a broader range of financial phenomena that reflect the impact of key 'reference points' investors often used in evaluating their portfolio position.

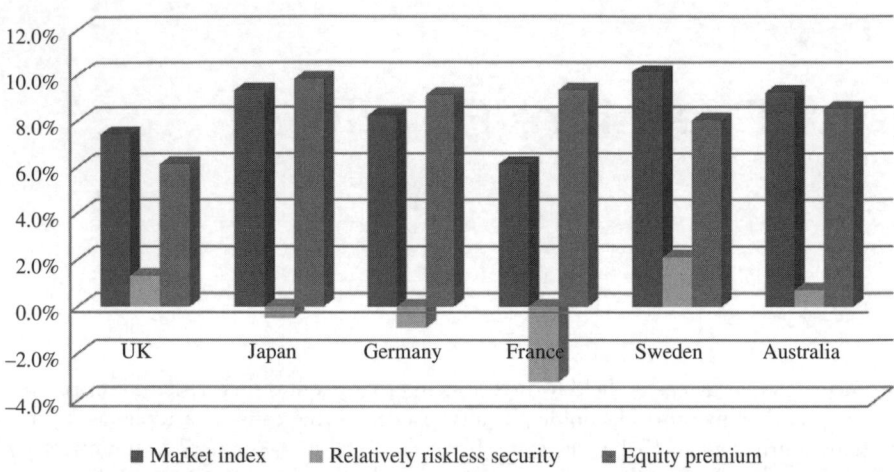

Figure 13.1   Dimson *et al.* (2002) estimates of equity premium in six countries
Source: Table 3 in Merhra and Prescott (2008).

13.2   The Puzzle

A starting point of consumption-based models is that the majority of people dislike sudden changes in their consumption, e.g., downsizing the house, selling the car, etc. Since most of us expect to get richer over the course of our (at least working) lives, one major purpose of capital markets is to allow us to leverage future wealth by getting loans (for an education or to buy a house) on the basis of future expected income. This suggests the presence of a positive rate of interest.

How risky equity actually is depends on the investment horizon you have of course. A well-known property of a 'random-walk' process, which prices follow in an efficient market, is that the standard deviation declines with the square-root of the horizon, so moving from sampling at four-monthly intervals to nine-monthly intervals moves the standard deviation from being a half to a third of its initial month-to-month value as a general rule (Siegel & Thaler 1997). Statistical tests demonstrate that while equity's movements over time exceed these implied bounds, bond yields are constrained within them. Equity thus sometimes 'mean-reverts' with extreme upward and downward movements being fairly swiftly offset over time. Bond yields by contrast 'mean avert' with upward or downward trends being ramified through the entire history of bond prices. Therefore the investment horizon of the investor needs to form an integral part of any solution to the puzzle.

The very existence of the puzzle is founded in three assumptions (Kocherlakota 1998):

- Investors' choices can be characterized by standard von Neumann–Morgenstern utility functions of the type discussed previously in Chapters 2 and 8.
- Secondary markets are complete allowing investors to trade rights to future consumption to the point where the marginal rate of transformation of current and future consumption is equalized.
- Finally, trading is costless thereby facilitating the costless equalization of marginal rates of transformation of today's and tomorrow's consumption.

Given the huge size and variability of the premium it would be great to be able to predict its value. This is all the more so given its central role in the standard capital asset pricing model where expected return = risk-free rate + β (risk premium). To satisfy this curiosity many studies have tried to predict future realizations of the premium. A recent review of these various studies by Welch and Goyal (2008) suggest little reliable ability to predict the premium has been demonstrated by these studies. They are fairly open about adopting a 'kitchen sink' approach to the prediction of the equity premium, giving any reasonable candidate a chance to predict the premia in linear regressions over the years 1926–2005 in the United States. They examine the predictive performance of, among others, the:

- dividend pay-out ratio;
- dividend yield; and
- earnings to price ratio.

They conclude:

> Our article suggests only that the profession is yet to find some variable that has meaningful and robust empirical equity premium forecasting power, both in sample and out of sample

(Welch & Goyal 2008).

In related research Campbell and Thompson (2008) point out that imposing some sensible restrictions on the type of forecasting equation used greatly improves their performance, so that their out-of-sample forecasts beat the historical average. But even once this is done, the explanatory power of the model remains low, typically a little above 1% for the United States in the years since the 1929 crash.

13.2.1 The Mehra and Prescott Statement of the Equity Premium Puzzle

The first formal statement of the equity premium puzzle was by Mehra and Prescott (1985). These authors built upon the consumption-based capital asset pricing model that sees investors' utility as a function of a stream of present and future consumption, the exact pattern of which is determined by their investment decisions. So the utility function of the investor takes the form

$$U(c) = E \frac{\sum_{s=0}^{t} \beta^s (c_s)^{1-\alpha} - 1}{(1-\alpha)} \qquad \alpha \geq 0, \quad 0 < \beta < 1$$

Where $0 < \alpha < c_s$ is the stream of consumption now and in the future, β is a discount factor $1/(1+r)$ discounting future consumption to its present value and α is a risk-aversion coefficient reflecting a dislike of volatility in consumption. So β^s has the form $1/(1+r)$, $1/(1+r)^2$, $1/(1+r)^3$ etc. The ability of the model to explain observed data is then largely driven by the chosen level of risk aversion, α. Increasing values of α imply increasing aversion to growth in consumption, with a preference for a stable consumption profile.

In order to maximize consumption the investor's investment problem must be solved to satisfy the two first-order conditions

$$E\left\{ \left(c_t / c_{t+1} \right)^{-\alpha} \left(R_{t+1}^s - R_{t+1}^b \right) \right\} = 0$$

$$\beta E_t \left\{ \left(c_{t+1} / c_t \right)^{-\alpha} R_{t+1}^b \right\} = 1$$

where R^b is the return on a risk-free asset, like a treasury bill, and R^s is the return on stocks.

These conditions impose nonlinear restrictions on the relation between consumption growth and asset returns. In particular the first condition requires that increases in consumption growth are matched by declines in the equity premium, allowance being made for investors' aversion to risk. This makes sense since growing consumption is reflected in declines in the savings rate, which drives the demand for equity. Of course the first condition could be trivially solved by setting either consumption growth or the equity premium to zero, but more credibly the restriction does require expected consumption growth to be reflected in the future scale of the equity premium. It is only by an indirect impact on constraining bond yields entering the first restriction that the first condition can influence the expected equity premium puzzle.

The second condition states that the discounted risk-adjusted expected value of consumption growth moves in offsetting proportion to the future expected return on bonds. As before this condition reflects the need of the bond market to reflect ebbs and flows in the savings rate. Note it is only the first condition that imposes any condition on the size of the equity premium as such. The second condition only specifies the movement of bond yields, without stating anything about their relation to equity returns.

Imposing these restrictions on historical averages for US consumption growth and asset returns Mehra and Prescott (1985) find the first condition cannot be satisfied for a value of α much below 8.5 in the investor's utility function, $U(c)$, above. The value of β is required to be between zero and one for the discount factor to have any sensible economic meaning.

The basic intuitive insight of the puzzle as stated by Mehra and Prescott is that the investment process is driven by a desire to reallocate consumption across time, since equity and bonds pay off at rather different states and we would expect differences in their return to result. The objective of the investor in reallocating consumption through investment is taken to be to smooth consumption over the investor's life. Bond yields rise in periods of recession when the demand for borrowing, by distressed firms and individuals, is high. Such reallocations of consumption from good times (when the investor is rich) to bad times (when he is poor) are very attractive to investors. Conversely equity pays off in good times (when firms are profitable and keen to invest) and not in bad times (when firms go bankrupt and profits plunge). Such a pro-cyclical pattern of payoffs to investors is likely to be of less value to investors in smoothing consumption over their lives. This makes the much higher payoff to holding equity truly a puzzle from the perspective of the consumption-based CAPM. If you really want to smooth consumption across your life, bonds seem the best way to invest and you might expect the return on bonds to exceed that on equity when averaged over any reasonable period.

13.2.2   Explaining the Risk Premium by Myopic Loss Aversion

One particular rationalization of the equity premium is provided by Benartzi and Thaler (1995) using two well-known behavioural finance concepts. These are:

- loss aversion, investors hate losing more than they love winning;
- mental accounting, investors' tendency to put gains and losses in separate 'pots' (e.g., holiday money, school fees, retirement money), which are reviewed at regular set intervals.

They try to show that the equity premium as large as the one we observe might make sense if investors are very averse to losses and evaluate the performance of their investments each year, asking of their fund managers 'What did you do for me this year?'. In many ways returns to investors are a natural application of the concept of loss aversion. Recall from Chapter 2 or 8 a central tenet of prospect theory that it is changes in wealth (or returns on investment) not the level of wealth itself that triggers a changed response to uncertain outcomes.

Their model begins by assuming investors respond more strongly to losing money than they do to gaining it in the first place. This strikes a chord with many of us who worry about not being able to pay the mortgage, retire at 60, etc. They suggest investors have a value function of the following form:

$$v(x) \begin{cases} x^\alpha & \text{if } x \geq 0 \\ -\lambda(-x)^\beta & \text{if } x < 0 \end{cases} \tag{13.1}$$

where x is the payoff investors receive, λ is a coefficient capturing investors' degree of loss aversion and finally α and β capture risk aversion (as opposed to loss aversion) in the domain of gains and losses, respectively. Figure 13.2 gives a diagrammatic representation of such a value function.

The value attached to any investment is given by a weighted average of expected outcomes from undertaking it:

$$V = \sum_i \pi_i v(x_i) \tag{13.2}$$

where π_i is some nonlinear set of weights transforming standard objective probabilities into the subjective weights used by investors in evaluating risky investment outcomes.

Benartzi and Thaler, following Tversky and Kahneman (1992), suggest the following weighting function mapping objective probabilities into subjective decision-making weights:

$$w(p) = \frac{p^\gamma}{(p^\gamma + (1-p)^\gamma)^{1/\gamma}} \tag{13.3}$$

where γ is some weight placed by investors on traditional probabilities in evaluating investment prospects.

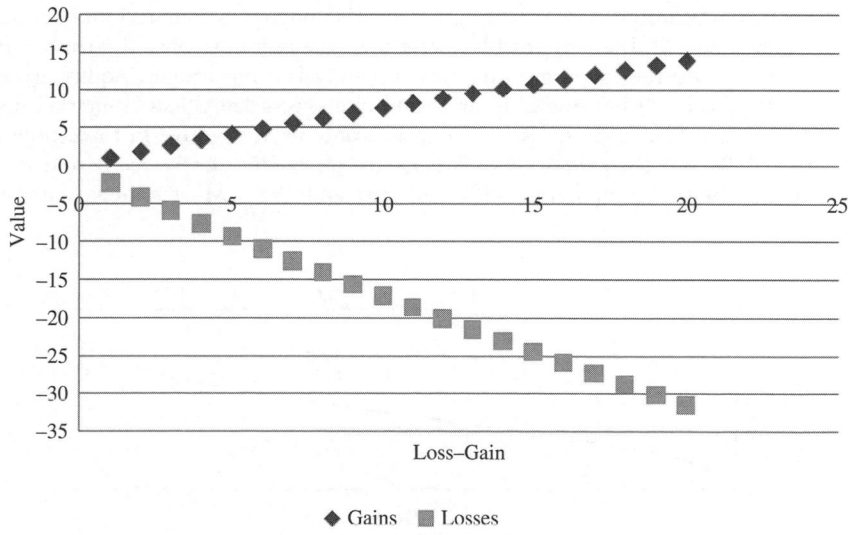

Figure 13.2 Loss-aversion utility function

Benartzi and Thaler (1995) implement this weighting system using a value of γ of 0.61 for probabilities attached to prospective gains and 0.69 for prospective losses. The net effect of this is to raise the perceived probability of very unlikely events and nearly certain events. So an objective probability of a prospective gain of 1% raised to the power 0.61 becomes a subjective probability of 6%, while an objective probability of 99.9% becomes a subjective probability of 99.94%. In the domain of losses a similar calculation using a higher value of γ of 0.69 and a similar transformation of a 1% objective probability of a prospective loss becomes a 4% subjective probability and a 99.9% objective probability is transformed to yield a 99.93% subjective probability. So the skewing of subjective probabilities, relative to their comparable objective probability, is less extreme for prospective losses than for prospective gains.

Plugging probabilities of 1% and 99.9% into the weighting function given by Equation (13.3) we obtain a transformation of 1% into 5.55% and 99% into 91.15%.

Numerical example of the Benartzi and Thaler model

Feeding these transformed values into the $w(p)$ weighting equation, given by Equation (13.3), into the value function of Equation (13.1), we obtain the mapping shown in Figure 13.2. The net effect of the weighting structure is to allow the subjective probabilities of the $w(p)$ function to underweight highly unlikely events but to overweight ones that are objectively almost certain. This can be seen by the points of inflection of the $w(p)$ function at its origin at 0 and termination at 1. The way in which this distorts the standard investor utility function is shown in Figure 13.3.

The Benartzi and Thaler (1995) model applies the weighting function of Figure 13.3, $w(p)$, to the losses and gains investors experience in an attempt to explain the equity premium puzzle. I present such an analysis applying the weighting function in Figure 13.3 using a loss-aversion coefficient of -2.25 ($\lambda = -2.25$ in Equation (13.1) above).

13.2.3   Can Loss Aversion Explain the Puzzle?

Having established a technique for evaluating prospective outcomes Benartzi and Thaler (1995) apply it to stocks and bonds over steadily increasing forecast horizons. Remember from the data in Figure 13.1, over the long-haul investing in equity is a no brainer. Equity always beats bonds or treasury bills in all but one 20-year period in all recorded US stock-market history. In the United States since 1900 the equity premium has only been negative in three brief periods: 1920, the late 1930s and the mid-1970s. The 1930s are by far the worst period for the US market with the premium falling below -40% in 1931 and 1937. Most frequently the mark-up

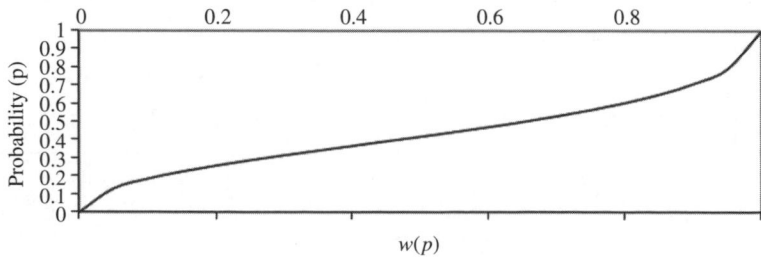

Figure 13.3   The weighting function $w(p)$ as a function of normal probability measure

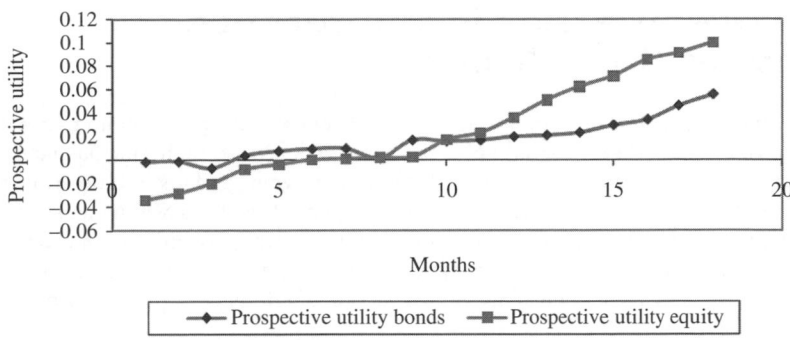

Figure 13.4 Prospective utility and the evaluation period in the Benartzi and Thaler model

of the return on equity over and above that offered by bonds for the period 1900–2000 is of the order of 20% or more (Dimson *et al.* 2002, pp.166–7).

For both equity and bonds Benartzi and Thaler (1995) calculate the prospective utility of investment in the US market over the period 1926–1990 in Equation (13.1) using the probability weighting structure in Equation (13.2). Gains and losses are calculated separately according to the evaluatory mechanism given in Equation (13.3). For random samples of sequential monthly returns and treasury bill index changes, drawn repeatedly from the years 1926–1990, Benartzi and Thaler (1995) calculate prospective utility as described by Equations (13.1) to (13.3) above. For increasing investment horizons of one, two, three months, etc., they ask which offers the higher prospective: utility bonds or equities? The authors repeat this exercise four times for real and nominal bond issues. Figure 13.4 gives the plot of prospective utility produced for nominal returns at increasing evaluation horizons. Note, equity seems to yield higher prospective utility as we pass beyond a 10/11-month evaluation period.

This suggests that the evaluation horizon of one year might be a focal point at which investors decide upon their investment allocation. Hence, at forecast horizons beyond one year, investors' aversion to losses becomes sufficiently attenuated for them to prefer holding equity to bonds. At shorter evaluation horizons, equity's greater risk does not compensate for its better average return. However, at a forecast horizon of around a year, the volatility of equity is sufficiently attractive for even loss-averse investors to want to hold it. For this to occur equity must offer a substantial premium over bond returns, only by doing so can equity overcome investors' natural reluctance to being exposed to a threat of a reduction in wealth.

Benartzi and Thaler (1995) point out that in their simulation it is the introduction of loss aversion that drives most of their results. Indeed if they ditch the $w(p)$ nonlinear transformation of probabilities, of Equation (13.2) above, and revert to using standard objective probabilities to evaluate investment prospects, the basic results obtained do not change that much. So whether we model asset prices using the cumulative form of prospect theory or the original version may not matter that much in practice.

A possible objection to the imposition of a one-year evaluation period in the model is that institutional investors are long-run investors with conceivably infinite corporate lives. While this may be true it is unlikely to be the case for hard-pressed individual fund managers struggling to meet quarterly, or annual, benchmarks for performance with their failure or success being rendered very transparent by business data-providing companies like Morningstar and others.

13.3   Loss Aversion in a Reference-Dependent Utility Model

The Benartzi and Thaler (1995) rationalization of the sheer scale of equity premiums builds on further developments of prospect theory for its explanatory power. Tversky and Kahneman later refined their original model (1979) to make the response of investors to gains and losses a function of where the investor's wealth stands relative to a chosen reference point (Tversky & Kahneman 1991). A central tenet of standard prospect theory is that utility is a function not of wealth but of changes in wealth. The new insight here is that how investors experience changes in wealth depends on where it takes them relative to their reference point. This revised version of reference-dependent prospect theory has three core elements:

- Investor gains and losses are relative to the relevant reference point.
- Investors are loss averse, grieving a loss of a given amount far more than a gain of a similar amount.
- Investors exhibit diminishing gains as losses as they move further away from the reference point.

A very simple experiment to illustrate how these decision heuristics interact is reported by Kahneman *et al.* (1991). Kahneman and his colleagues randomly placed decorated mugs at a third of the seats in their class as students came into the class arranged with seating bearing their student id/library card number (they could not just choose to sit in a seat with a mug). The students were then asked by how much they would be willing to sell their mug for, if they had one. Mugless students were asked how much they would be willing to pay to get a mug from their mug-bearing classmates. Given the allocation of mug-endowed seats was random, we would expect the valuation of the mug to be roughly equal across the minority who did and the majority who did not get a mug, but this was far from the case. The average selling price of the mug-bearing minority was almost twice the average potential buying price set by mugless students in the class. This implies the mere fact of owning a decorated mug can increase your valuation of it (see Kahneman *et al.* 1991 for a helpful review of this area). The select few who received a mug felt special because they were 'chosen'.

A similar sort of reasoning can be applied to the valuation of stocks. Figure 13.5 depicts an investor's choice between stocks characterized by two attributes or dimensions of value, let us say smallness and 'value', a high book value of assets relative to market value (see Fama & French 1992, 1996). Company x has a lot of 'value' but is too big a stock to earn much of a small company premium in the market. Company y is a small stock which exhibits little 'value' and so has little chance of earning much of a value premium.

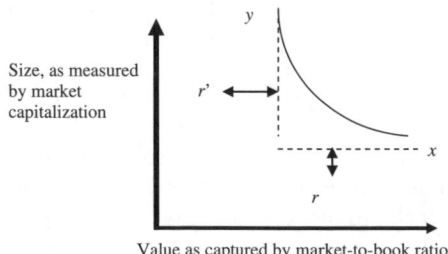

Figure 13.5   Value versus size as a reference-dependent choice

In Figure 13.5 the way an investor evaluates the options between holding small cap and value stocks depends upon his current reference point. An investor with a portfolio tilted towards value stocks will have a reference point r. An investor with a portfolio tilted towards small caps has a reference point r'. The value investor is likely to value a choice x far more than y, while a small-caps investor will do the reverse. No doubt this is partly the result of the fact that value investors tend to construct a reference point r, while those preferring small caps stocks tend to construct a reference point r'. As seen in the example of the mug similar endowment/status quo effects result from random allocation of the reference points. Value investors, with a reference point, r, perceive a move to a portfolio like y as gaining a small size premium on their portfolio, but more importantly, losing the value premium to their low market-to-book holdings in their current portfolio x. Small-caps investors, with reference point r', see a move to x as offering a value premium, but more importantly the surrender of their small firm premium on their current portfolio, y. The dominating feature in each choice is loss of a valued attribute in their current portfolio, as opposed to the gain from the alternative portfolio irrespective of which portfolio they initially hold.

13.3.1 A Reference-Dependent Model of Investor Choice

The advancement in our understanding of prospect theory provided by Kahneman *et al.* (1991) is that the choices made under prospect theory are contingent upon the chooser's reference point. To capture this reality Kahneman *et al.* (1991) introduce the concept of a 'reference structure' for choices faced by investors. Consider a choice set $X = \{x, y, z\}$. Each option involved in the choice offers a bundle of goods x_1, x_2, etc. A reference structure is then an indexed set of preference relations where the index captures the reference point of the individual making the choice. So the orderings $\{x: x \geq r\, y\}$ and $\{x: y \geq r\, x\}$ capture the individual's preference for x over y, or y over x, given his reference point r. The prior absence of such specificity in the formal logic of choice means that choices were regarded as reference independent, but in the presence of status quo/endowment effects this is very unlikely to be the case.

If we accept where you choose from affects what choices you make, we need to be clear about how investors differ in their present reference point and how that impacts on the sort of choice they make. This motivates a description of choice which is not simply a ranking of alternatives, i.e. I like apples more than bananas. Instead we can now describe choice as an indexed set of orderings, one ordering for each current reference point, so I prefer apples to bananas, apart from when bananas first come into season and I have not eaten one for a few months (i.e. my apple endowment has been a bit too high recently).

The introduction of reference dependence into the logic of choice raises further questions about how such reference points are determined. The answer depends on the particular application of the theory. The focus in Kahneman *et al.* (1991) is how the presence of such reference points influences choice. Reference-dependent choices are characterized for illustration by two primary characteristics (say size and value in my example below) which we comment upon below.

13.3.2 Loss Aversion in a Reference-Dependent Model of Choice

A reference structure can be said to exhibit loss aversion if the following condition holds for all x, y, r, s in the choice set $X = \{x, y, z\}$. If $x_1 \geq r_1 > s_1 = y_1, y_2 > x_2$ and $r_2 = s_2$ then $x =_s y$ implies $x >_r y$ and the

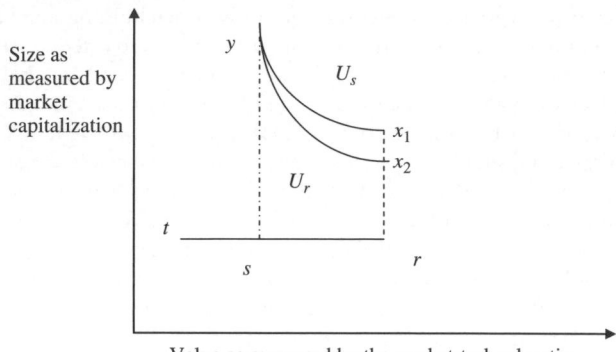

Value as measured by the market-to-book ratio

Figure 13.6   Loss aversion in the rank-dependent utility model of choice

same holds if the subscripts 1 and 2 are interchanged throughout the reference structure. Stated in terms of Figure 13.6, this requires the slope of the investor's utility function, U_r, is steeper when evaluated from a reference point like r, than from a reference point s. Looking at the choice between portfolios y and x from a reference point like s induces a more shallow slope to the investor's utility function (as shown by U_s in Figure 13.6). Since x_1 is preferred to x_2 in an ordering dependent on the reference point r_1 it will also be preferred to all other alternatives in y which are less desirable under a common reference point r. So, if two similar choices are faced with the same reference point, the one offering a loss, compared to the current status-quo position, will be evaluated as being worse than if such a perceived loss was not present. Figure 13.6 graphically illustrates loss aversion in the rank-dependent utility model. While an investor may be indifferent between a small-cap portfolio, like y, and a value-share portfolio from the vantage point of t, from his current reference point, conditioned by his current portfolio allocation, he will prefer to retain a small-cap portfolio from the vantage point of a portfolio like y or a value-based portfolio from the vantage point of a current portfolio like x. So movements towards a value portfolio, like x, yield a lower path of utility, U_r, when judged from vantage point y, than from reference point x U_s^2. So more formally $x =_t y$ but $x >_x y$ and $y <_y x$.

13.3.3   *Diminishing Sensitivity to Losses and Gains*

A second characteristic of the revised version of prospect theory is that the impact of changes in wealth diminishes as they move far beyond the current reference point. This makes some sense. Becoming as rich as Bill Gates seems like an impossible dream to me. Whether I become as rich as Bill before he gave away a few billion to charity is not a big deal from my point of view. A reference structure exhibits diminishing sensitivity if, letting $x_1 > y_1$, $y_2 > x_2$, $s_2 = t_2$, then for all possible portfolios x or y, and all reference points s or t in X, $y =_s x$ implies $y \geq_t x$.

Here the subscript on the operator, s, denotes that the operator locally operates around the reference point s and may not hold or even be reversed elsewhere. Figure 13.6 graphically represents this. If the individual is indifferent between outcomes x and y, from the reference point s, this implies he will prefer x from the perspective of t. This result arises from the property that t and s are equidistant from y, but s is twice as close to x, or alternatively t is twice as far away from x as s. So diminishing sensitivity to gains or losses requires that investor responses to changes in wealth are muted as they move further away from their current point of reference in evaluating wealth changes.

13.3.4 Constant Risk Aversion and the Benartzi and Thaler (1995) Model

Loss aversion underpins the Benartzi and Thaler (1995) proposed rationalization of the equity premium puzzle. Diminishing sensitivity of utility to gains and losses as the individual moves away from his reference point is also important to the way in which prospect theory is invoked by Benartzi and Thaler (1995) to explain the size of the equity puzzle. Diminishing sensitivity implies investors require a higher compensation in terms of a per unit of risk premium paid to get them to accept a move to a moderately risky portfolio from a fairly safe one they have held for a long time as compared to a move from a moderately risky to a very risky one. This assumes that the primary motivator of the investor's choice is a dislike of risk, as opposed to the demand for a constant per unit fee for each portion of risk assumed as standard theory implies. So as the investor moves outside the realm of his own past experience in terms of gains and losses the per unit of risk borne charged on each of the risk assets purchased declines.

Any reference structure can be thought of as being defined on a four-quadrant diagram relative to some reference point. Imagine an investor who ranks stocks on size and 'value' (low market-to-book value of assets). Small undervalued stocks are his dream, large overvalued stocks are his nightmare and he needs a hefty return to even accept them in his portfolio.

Figure 13.7 shows the position of an investor who has most of his portfolio invested in stocks trading at market capitalizations of $100 million and book values of about half that or $50 million dollars. The investor switches his preferences and the risk premia demanded to assume the two risk characteristics around these benchmark values.

An investor's reference structure satisfies the condition of sign dependence if, for all investments x (say an overvalued huge stock) and y (say a small undervalued stock) in his portfolio and all reference points r (market-to-book value of 2) and s (market capitalization of $100 million) describing his portfolio, the following condition holds in Figure 13.5: for all investment opportunities x and y, $x \geq_r y$ if and only if $x \geq_s y$.

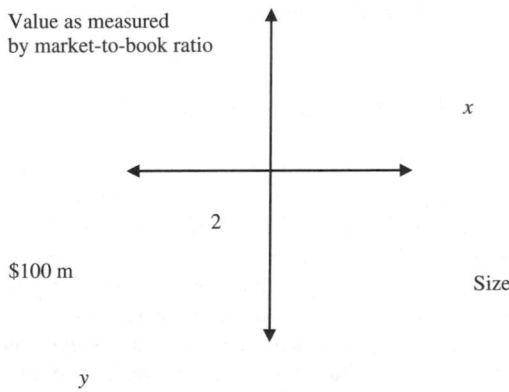

Figure 13.7 Reference-based choice over shares varying by size and value

For the choice described here this requires that if a stock is preferable on the basis of the value for money it offers (given its size), it will also be preferable on the basis of its size (given the value for money of the investment). So this allows the per unit of asset risk premia required for bearing different types of risk to vary, but only once and for all at the reference point. Curvature of the investor's utility function as he moves away from the reference point is ignored. So a mid-cap stock of $500 million and a multinational of many billions of dollars are assumed to attract the same risk premia for each additional reduction of $1 million in its value.

To obtain a utility function of the form used by Benartzi and Thaler (1995) we require an even more constrained form of evaluation of risky outcomes suggested by prospect theory. This is that the utility gained from any investment strategy must be the product of gains and losses relative to the investor's selected reference points alone. So

$$U_r(x_1, x_2) = U(R_1(x_1), R_2(x_2))$$

This means that how a portfolio is evaluated only depends on how its elements vary relative to the benchmarks set (value and size or whatever). This assumption is not an innocuous one since it rules out the possibility that some combinations of characteristics may prove particularly attractive to investors, so a large highly overvalued firm (like Enron) may be seen as particularly risky because its failure can be seen as inducing systemic, portfolio-wide, risk. Standard asset-pricing models, like the arbitrage pricing model, can handle such interactions pretty easily, but they are more difficult to accommodate in the sort of additive separable utility function invoked by the myopic loss function explanation of the equity premium puzzle advanced by Benartzi and Thaler.

13.3.5   Is Loss Aversion Irrational?

While the evidence in favour of loss aversion appears fairly clear cut, its interpretation as a sign of irrationality on the part of investors seems far more dubious. Indeed much of natural selection requires us to habituate to our environment. My daily life most probably requires more cognitive skill and less physical strength than my forefathers 100 years ago. Adapting to that change of relishing mental challenges, but tiring of physical exertion easily, is not irrational, but simply expedient on my part. Further the asymmetric response most of us display to pleasure and pain is just cautious self-preservation. Forgone pleasures, while frustrating, do not pose any threat to my health or survival. Hence loss aversion may be a mental trait hard-wired into us by evolution and it is as well to accept it and build its impact into financial models rather than argue about its desirability.

13.4   Conclusion and Summary

This chapter focuses on one of the longest running motivations for interest in behavioural finance. The equity premium, or just how great equity seems to be as an investment, seemingly offers amazing return per unit of risk assumed. At the start of the chapter we saw that attempts to confirm if the historically huge equity premium will continue have not had much success. When questions of fact are most hotly disputed (for example, 'can equity be such a great investment forever or is the game up at last?') we often need to ask which facts actually matter and what constitutes factual evidence itself. In short we need better theory. Behavioural researchers have answered that call with some modest success as this chapter has tried to show, but the chapter also makes clear how far we are from having a credible, robust, story of the sheer scale of the equity premium. It is hardly surprising we struggle to predict its scale given our inability to properly understand its origin.

Questions

1. Return to the numerical illustration of the Benartzi and Thaler (1995) model in Figures 13.2 through 13.4. In Figure 13.3 I estimated the weighting function assuming a value of γ equal to 0.61 in the domain of gains and 0.69 in the domain of losses. Now the impact of γ comes at the extreme of the distribution we know, making both very low and high probability events seem more likely at the expense of events of intermediate probability. Given this, now suppose γ is again assumed to equal 0.61 over the investor's gains, but now 0.9 (not 0.69) for his losses. How would Figure 13.3 and its application to bonds and stocks in Figure 13.4 change? What would this new sort of weighting function imply about the way in which the investor has changed the way he evaluates games?

2. Return to Figure 13.5. Recall x is an overvalued huge stock and y is a small undervalued stock, and the reference points r (market to book of 2) and s (market capitalization of \$100 million) describe the investor's portfolio. There is a new stock on the block. Stock z is a mid-cap stock with a market-to-book ratio of 2.1. How do you think our investor will feel about z? Can you justify its purchase for his portfolio? Why, or why not?

3. The size of the premium paid to equity (over and above that paid to bondholders) is a problem for standard finance theory, but unless you want to devote your life to the theory of finance this may not bother you too much. Why should ordinary people in investment banks and individual investors care about the size and stability of the equity premium?

References

Benartzi, S. & R. Thaler (1995). Myopic risk-aversion and the equity premium puzzle. *Quarterly Journal of Economics*, **110**(1): 1–53.

Benartzi, S. & R. Thaler (2001). Myopic risk-aversion and the equity premium puzzle. *Quarterly Journal of Economics*, **116**: 1–53.

Campbell, J. & S. Thompson (2008). Predicting excess stock returns out of sample: can anything beat the historical average? *Review of Financial Studies*, **21**: 1509–31.

Dimson, E., P. Marsh & M. Staunton (2002). *The Triumph of the Optimists: 101 Years of Global Investment Returns*. Princeton, NJ: Princeton University Press.

Fama, E. & K. French (1992). The cross-section of expected stock returns. *Journal of Finance*, **47**: 427–65.

Fama, E. & K. French (1996). Multifactor explanations of asset pricing anomalies. *Journal of Finance*, **51**: 55–84.

Kahneman, D., J. Knetch *et al.* (1991). The endowment effect, loss-aversion and the status quo bias. *Journal of Economic Perspectives*, **5**(1): 193–206.

Kahneman, D. & A. Tversky (1979). Prospect theory: an analysis of decision under risk. *Econometrica*, **47**(2): 263–91.

Kocherlakota, N. (1998). The equity premium: it's still a puzzle. *Journal of Economic Literature*, **34**: 42–71.

Mehra, R. & E. Prescott (1985). The equity premium: a puzzle. *Journal of Monetary Economics*, **15**: 145–61.

Mehra, R. & E. Prescott (2008). The equity premium: ABCs. In R. Mehra (ed.), *Handbook of the Equity Premium*. Amsterdam: Elsevier.

Montier, J. (2006). *Behavioural Finance: Insights into Irrational Minds and Markets*. Chichester: John Wiley & Sons, Ltd.

Siegel, J. & R. Thaler (1997). Anomalies: the equity premium puzzle. *Journal of Economic Perspectives* **11**: 191–200.

Tversky, A. & D. Kahneman (1991). Loss aversion in riskless choice: a reference-dependent model. *Quarterly Journal of Economics*, **106**(4): 1039–61.

Tversky, A. & D. Kahneman (1992). Advances in prospect theory: cumulative representation of uncertainty. *Journal of Risk and Uncertainty*, **5**: 297–323.

Welch, I. & A. Goyal (2008). A comprehensive look at the empirical performance of the equity premium prediction. *Review of Financial Studies*, **21**: 1455–508.

Part III
Corporate Finance

Chapter 14

Incorporation

‘ The firm is not an individual. It is a legal fiction which serves as a focus for a complex process in which the conflicting objectives of individuals are brought into equilibrium within the framework of contractual relations ’

(Jensen & Meckling 1976, p.311).

Companies are legal 'persons' controlled by senior officers – the chief executive, chairman and chief financial officer, etc. – sitting on a board of directors. In public discussion companies almost always coalesce into their controllers, so GE was Jack Welch and Stuart Rose is the embodiment of Marks & Spencer's resurgence. Long after Walt Disney's death it is said that Disney employees would ask, 'What would Walt do?', before deciding on a course of action (Camerer & Malmendier 2007). Often these great men lead the corporations they head astray (e.g., Robert Maxwell, Conrad Black or Kenneth Lay) and shareholders rightly look for redress from the law against those responsible for their losses. They often feel that these rogues hid their crimes behind the cloak of incorporation. This chapter tries to delve beneath the legal fiction of the corporation to see how individuals' biases influence corporate decision making.

Behind the 'veil' of incorporation colourful human characters drive the actions of public corporations. These individuals exhibit the same biases and framing effects we are all commonly prone to. Indeed company law has developed a case-law tradition of 'piercing the veil of incorporation' to punish the most venal and/or damaging examples of human weaknesses from harming shareholders' (or other stake-holders') well-being. In this chapter I ask how this separation of the legal fiction of the corporate person and its controllers is made and how the biases and mental frames of its controlling officers can show through. I illustrate this process by a case study of Michael Eisner's period as chief executive at Disney.

Traditional finance has long been aware of the problem of errant managers failing to serve the company shareholders' best interests and has given considerable effort to understanding how such 'agency' conflicts between the managerial agent and his shareholding principal. But once we lift the lid of the incorporated legal entity called the company, a murkier, richer, reality emerges and we try to shed some light upon this here.

14.1 Illustration and Structure

The Walt Disney Company embodies the American dream and its CEO carries the torch on from its founder, Walt Disney, of whom it has been written,

> Arguably no single figure so bestrode American popular culture as Walt Disney. By one estimate, in 1966 alone, the year of his death, 240 million people saw a Disney movie, a weekly audience of 100 million watched a Disney television show

(Gabler 2006, p.xii).

Michael Eisner from 1984 to 2005 carried that iconic presence in American life forward as CEO of the Walt Disney Company. Together with Frank Wells, his trusted president until his sudden death in 1994, Eisner determined to 'ride that Mouse into the ground' (Masters 2001, p.2). This they did, creating and destroying huge wealth in the process.

Eisner is an interesting character not least because he was initially seen as a paragon of a new 'value-based management', which placed shareholder value as its central goal. In Eisner's first six years in the job he was paid $250 million. The head of executive compensation at Stern Stewart & Co., Stephen O'Byrne, calculated that a 200% increase in the shareholder value of the Walt Disney Company, relative to that predicted by the CAPM, would increase Eisner's wealth by 279% (O'Byrne 1992). Nice work if you can get it. Eisner's riches were not at the expense of share-holders, but in reward for their own enrichment. Such close ties between pay and returning value to shareholders might be expected to have kept petty squabbling and empire building in check. So what went wrong?

In this chapter I explore the role of individual bias and its social propagation within the 'black box' of the modern corporation. The economic theorization of organizational form and behaviour has been an area of rapid academic advance in the last three decades (see Milgrom & Roberts 1992 and Roberts 2004). Most of this literature turns standard economics inwards to understand how compa-nies set prices, strategies and priorities. This chapter explores what behavioural perspectives have to offer in this new area of the inner life of corporations.

Section 14.2 examines the origins and development of the corporate form to understand the role of individuals' bias and charisma in their life and actions. Section 14.3 examines and critiques one of the classic attempts by standard finance to understand the internal life of the corporation. An alternative to the standard agency theory framework is advanced which sees senior managers as judges in a series-ascending hierarchy within the corporation, with teamwork and gaining commitment to corporate objectives being a central part of their skill. In Section 14.4 I present some explicitly behavioural approaches to these problems. In general this text is very much an introduction to complex and heavily contested topics, but in the case of this chapter I just give a taste of a whole emergent field of study. An appendix examines the reign of Michael Eisner at Disney to ground some of the ideas discussed in corporate practice. While Eisner had an unusually long run at Disney, he simply typifies a cohort of managers who personally embody their corporation in the way that Steve Jobs is Apple, or Bill Gates is Microsoft.

After reading this chapter the reader should:

- Understand the problems raised for standard finance theory by entering the realities of how firms make decisions, as opposed to what happens when they have decided.
- Understand how the response of standard finance to this problem has been challenged by a 'team-based' (as opposed to agency-based) model of how companies decide what to do.
- Know the way in which bias, if not outright eccentricity and self-aggrandizement, can flourish in major corporations in which shareholders have little day-to-day control. In this context managers are little different from student tutorial groups or staff rooms in being fertile ground for exhibiting all the distortions of group psychology.

14.2 Companies: Where did They Come from and Where will They Go?

Few can doubt the galvanizing impact of public corporations on our economic growth. Yet we are often only dimly aware of the history of their presence and their centrality to our political and cultural life. When considering the evils of Enron, WorldCom and in their wake the Sarbanes–Oxley Act, it is just as well to remember the wheel of fate that returns us to the South Sea Bubble or the robber barons Arthur Mellon, Andrew Carnegie, J.P. Morgan and their role in inducing the 1929 crash and the resulting Securities Acts of the 1930s.

The very word 'company' reflects its Roman origin as a compound of the words *cum* and *panis* with the connotation 'breaking bread together' (Micklethwait & Woolridge 2003, p.18). These companies were an improvement on the prior *societas* which were limited in their capital-raising ability by the extent of their partners' funds. The *compagnia* format allowed for the raising of additional rounds of funds from the founding members, plus time-limited deposits from non-members for specific projects by the Medici and other Florentine merchant families in the twelfth century (Baskin & Miranti 1999, p.38). The initial purposes of these companies were public works like the conquest of foreign lands, trading in slaves and educational progression, thus companies were created as state-granted monopolies to trade in India and beyond (the East India Company formed in 1699) or trading in African slaves (the Royal African Company formed in 1672). As such economic liberals like Adam Smith viewed corporations with suspicion if not derision. But it was with the arrival of the railways and telegraph industries of the 1820s that the UK parliament considered repealing the Bubble Acts making it easier to incorporate for purely private economic objectives. Robert Lowe, the British Governor of the Board of Trade, finally created something like the current freedom to incorporate in his Joint Stock Companies Acts of 1856 and 1862. British common law finally abandoned its historic opposition to the avoidance of creditors' claims by means of limited liability in the landmark case of *Salomon vs. Salomon and Company Ltd*.

While the corporation is often portrayed as part of the missionary drive to propagate market forces it is most probably more accurately seen as a historical artefact of attempts to fund a profligate state, often freshly impoverished by war (Baskin & Miranti 1999, pp.90–113). Following the Treaty of Utrecht in 1713, which ended the War of Spanish Succession, both the French and English states sought to recapitalize their depleted treasuries. The French, in the form of Prince Regent Phillip of Orleans, turned to John Law whose Mississippi Company launched a company aiming to colonize south-west America. In emulation the English Parliament founded the South Sea Company, which targeted Latin American trade as an objective. In 1720 speculative bubbles in the newly operating public markets in these stocks collapsed to huge public outcry and political hand wringing.

The corporation had to cross the Atlantic to see its final flowering in the rise of the huge multi-national corporations of our modern lives. Improved train transport and telegraph communication facilitated the growth of coast-to to-coast companies staffed by a professional life-long elite of managers. Whole swathes of commerce previously served by local independent firms began to disappear within large corporations. As the best-known historians of the era have put it, the 'visible hand' of the managed corporation replaced Adam Smith's 'invisible hand' of market provision (Chandler 1977). The rise of the multidivisional firm, pioneered by Alfred P. Sloan at General Motors, saw large tracts of diverse industrial activity subsumed with huge professionally managed corporations.

As the Internet and information technology more generally reduce the cost of financial and commercial intermediation, the boundaries of the corporation become more porous. Collaboration between smaller owner-managed firms is more feasible, reducing the prominence of physical capital within the corporation. This trend is confirmed by the recent rise in debt-financed acquisitions by private-equity hedge funds. This implies the public corporation may now be reaching a point of inflection in its history. I develop this possibility later in the chapter.

14.2.1 Limited Liability: its Value and its Role in the Emergence of the Corporate Form

Any standard finance textbook informs us that limited liability is valued by investors as a put option to sell off their interest in the firm at the price at which they bought it. As long as their investment has some positive value their limited liability put option is 'out of the money' and so has no value. They are better off selling their shares in the open market rather than exercising their right to limit their liability. Once the company's value is exhausted by creditors' claims the put option is 'in the money'. Rather than having to settle with the firm's creditors the shareholder's loss is capped at the amount of his initial investment.

One curious historical fact is the relatively rapid diffusion of limited liability in the United States during the nineteenth century compared to the British experience (Forbes 1986). One particular blockage to the diffusion of the limited liability form was the presence on the British statute book of the 1720 'Bubble Act' passed to suppress a speculative bubble that included the South Sea Company, companies formed to produce perpetual motion machines and other dubious ventures. Furthermore, the settled industrialists of Britain had less needs than their American counterparts, who were coping with the ravages of the civil war. Established manufacturers, who can fund growth through internally generated profits, have little incentive to offer limited liability, so the comparative advantage of offering limited liability lies with new entrants and fast-growing firms who wish to enter new markets or adopt capital-intensive technologies which require large amounts of funding raised quickly in the open market. These conditions more closely approximated the emergence of the US corporation than its earlier British counterpart.

14.2.2 The Economic Rationale for Granting Limited Liability

While limited liability often seems on the surface just a great wheeze to protect corporate suits from legal responsibility for their actions, in reality there is a fairly compelling case for granting this privilege (Easterbrook & Fischel 1985). Indeed, it might even be argued that if limited liability had not been legally granted, corporations would have found ways to fashion it themselves by getting creditors to insure them against the effects of potentially limitless liability upon their wealth. Arguments that can be advanced to support the granting of limited liability include:

- Limited liability reduces the need of shareholders to monitor managers, second guess their judgement and generally be bothersome to company management – diversification and passive investment then becomes the norm.
- Limited liability reduces the need to monitor other shareholders in your investment. Remember you are personally liable for the debts of an unlimited liability company. So if your fellow investors are all paupers you will be left holding the baby in the event of the threat of liquidation. Under limited liability the financial position of your fellow investors doesn't affect you and you can simply deal with them at arm's length.
- Limited liability by promoting liquidity swells the total amount of funds available for investment, lowers interest rates and so increases the number of positive net present projects that can be undertaken. Society as a whole is better off.
- Limited liability maintains a 'law of one-price' for share dealings. In an unlimited liability company shares are worth less to rich investors as they accept a greater liability when they invest. To understand price formation you need to make speculations about the distribution of wealth amongst each company's shareholder register. This is not an easy thing to do. So prices do less work and are less transparent in a market for unlimited liability companies.

- Limited liability, because of its greater price transparency, allows low share prices to signal poor management and the benefits of a well-timed acquisition. This improves the disciplinary role of the market for corporate control.

What limited liability does is to allow shareholders in the company to unburden some of the risk they carry on to bondholders, suppliers, workers and other stakeholders in the firm. One of the key lessons of standard finance theory is the benefits of diversification and risk sharing. Thus if limited liability did not exist shareholders would have an incentive to invent it by making bondholders and others co-insure them against liability in the event of liquidation.

14.3 Agency, Monitoring and Incorporation

Standard finance has not been slow to open the 'black box' of the company and peer inside to see how shareholder principals and the managerial agents they employ to run their firm interact. Jensen and Meckling (1976) provided the initial theorization of the manager–shareholder agency relationship.

Jensen and Meckling (1976) compare the value of the corporation initially under conditions of owner/manager control and then after the sale by the owner of some portion of his ownership rights in the firm. An owner/manager, prior to any sale of ownership rights, is regarded as simply maximizing the value of his investment in the firm. The owner/manager can consume the return on investment as profits or in the form of non-pecuniary 'perks', for example, charitable donations to the Opera House or just slacking on the job. After the owner/manager sells some of his ownership rights in the firm consumption of non-pecuniary benefits of his remaining control will seem more attractive. This is because as manager he still gets all the benefits of that donor's box at the Opera House, but without having to pay for it all. After diluting his ownership stake the diminution in profits due to his non-pecuniary elements of return are shared with the new owner/non-manager. So the owner/manager's consumption of the perks that come with control of the company increase.

Expectations by new owners of this sort of expropriation by current owners cause them to discount the value of ownership rights on sale from their current owners. This tension between the current owner/manager and the new owner's claims on the company gives rises to three types of agency costs:

- Monitoring costs incurred by new owners/non-managers, to make sure the incumbent owners/managers don't waste money, or sleep on the job, etc.
- Bonding costs incurred by owners/managers to assure new owners/non-managers that they will not loot the firm and hence make it worthwhile to invest.
- A deadweight loss arising from investments forgone because of new owners/non-managers being unwilling to purchase ownership rights from incumbent owners/managers for fear of being fleeced by the seller.

Jensen and Meckling (1976) conduct their analysis of a one-period model under the assumptions of no taxes, all purchased equity is non-voting and that new owners/non-managers can only gain return on their investment through dividends paid out of reported profits. Let x_N denote the list of non-pecuniary 'perks' the owner/manager might enjoy, $C(x_N)$ is the cost of providing these perks, $P(x_N)$ is the benefit to the firm of indulging the owners/managers perks in terms of forgone pecuniary payments to owners/managers. Finally, $B(x_N)$ is the net benefit to the company of allowing the owner/manager to consume his perks in peace, where $B(x_N) = P(x_N) - C(x_N)$. It is further assumed that in equilibrium owners/managers are left to consume their perks until their benefit to the company they control is exhausted, so $\frac{\delta B}{\delta x_N^*} = 0$. Jensen and Meckling (1976) also assume that the expected value of future non-pecuniary perks granted to owners/managers is capitalized by the stock market and impounded into the company's market value. Figure 14.1 displays how the stock market trades off the market value of the company and the consumption of non-pecuniary perks by owners/managers (with resulting lower profits and dividends payable to non-managers/new owners). Non-pecuniary perks are fully priced by the market, resulting in the budget constraint shown with a slope of -1. Every pound paid in gifts to the Opera House, in order to get that donor's box, is a pound off the stock-market value of the company. However, owners/managers do not experience a one-for-one decline in the market value of their remaining equity stake in the firm, rather their loss of value is diluted to reflect their remaining ownership stake of α, so the slope of their own trade-off given by indifference curves U_1 and U_2 is $-1 \times \alpha$ or $-\alpha$. This traces out a locus of company market values and non-pecuniary benefits along a locus A, B etc. At A the owner/manager consumes perks to the value F_0, whereas if he was pushed back to the budget line he would have to reduce consumption of perks to a value of F_1. Each of these outcomes results in some deadweight loss of market value compared to a situation where the manager/owner recognizes the full value of non-pecuniary perks as at point D and so consumes an amount x^* (for which $\delta B(x_N)/\delta x_N = 0$) of such perks, which are valued at F^*.

Given this implicit market discount attached to market equity where owners/managers expropriate value from new owners, via an increased consumption of non-pecuniary benefits of control, owners/managers themselves have an incentive to put in place auditing and accountability measures to anticipate and curtail such temptations to extract rents from new owners in the form of non-pecuniary rents of control. That is, an incumbent shareholder has an incentive to exercise some degree of self-control in their consumption of the perks from controlling the company.

The agency model essentially sees a principal standing on high directing a board of directors to get his strategy implemented by the chief executive officer. In doing so he is aware of the need to incur

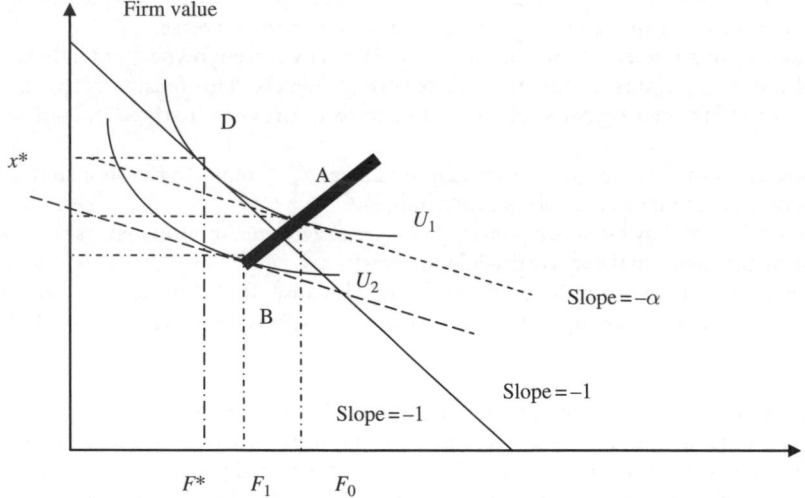

Figure 14.1 The agency theory model of Jensen and Meckling

Source: Jensen, M. and W. Meckling (1976). Theory of the firm: managerial behaviour, agency costs and ownership structure. *Journal of Financial Economics*, 3: 305–60. Reproduced with permission.

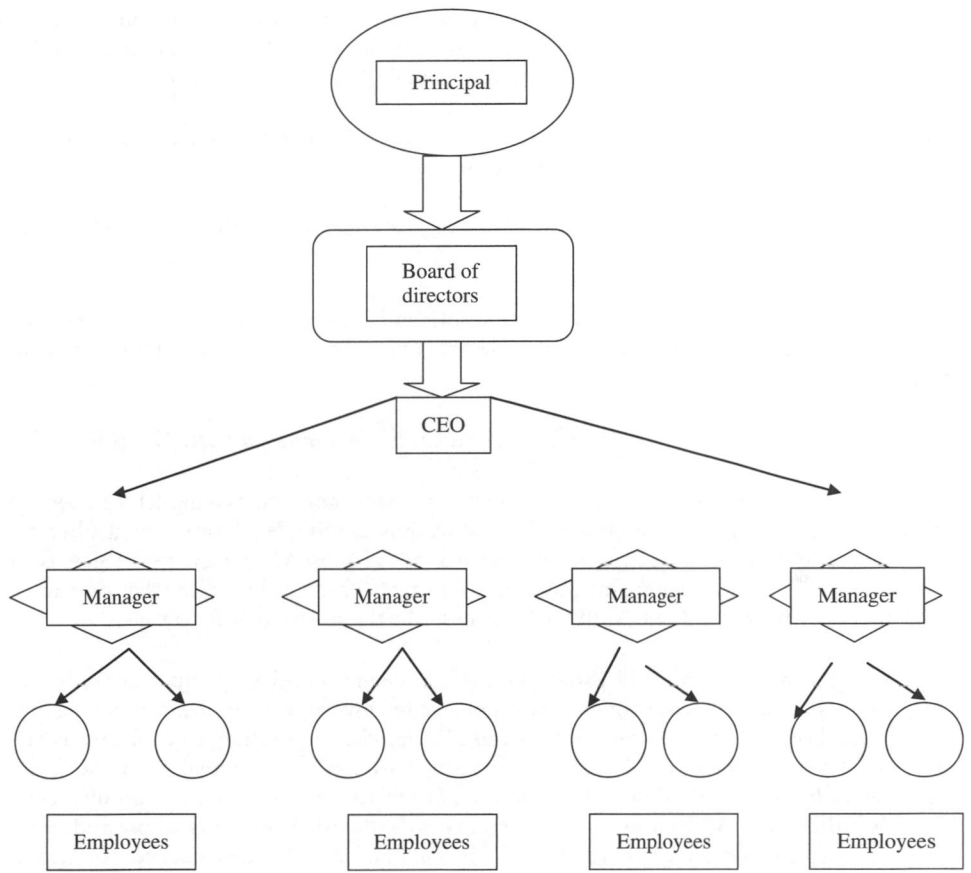

Figure 14.2 The agency theory model

monitoring costs to ensure his will is implemented. Figure 14.2 graphically portrays this model of how companies operate. A principal/CEO's voice shouts down the line to workers scavenging around to execute his will as under the board of directors' supervision. This is not an organizational form that many of us either feel comfortable with or recognize from our working lives. Hence it seems worthwhile to seek out a more credible theory of how corporations make decisions within the 'black box' of their life as portrayed in price theory.

14.3.1 Are Managers Agents or Team Members?

Agency theory assumes that an informed principal/owner can successfully direct a managerial agent to conduct his affairs for best profit. However, the realities of contractual incompleteness where the manager may be asked to oversee a project the owner could not complete or even clearly conceive of (for example manipulating the human genome, or perfecting new Internet search tools), suggest such a conception of how companies are governed may be unrealistic. In reality life-long senior managers with very high levels of company-specific investments may feel some power of control and hence ownership of the firm. Indeed a major characteristic of the new economy is the central role of human capital as a source of competitive advantage. The whole economy has seemingly 'dematerialized', with human capital coming to the fore at the expense of physical capital (Zingales 2000). As Zingales states:

> Employees are not merely automata in charge of valuable operating assets, but valuable assets themselves, operating with commodity-like physical assets.

Similarly Blair and Wallan (2001, p.7) quote a *Washington Post* op ed on the proposed 'break up' of Microsoft as follows:

> Given that no company can establish a monopoly on brains, how do you keep the people that make it work? There are no tangible assets to divest. There is intellectual property and that's about it... and a building

> (Andrew Lloyd Cutler, *Washington Post*, 27 April 2000).

In this more messy, less easily contracted world it may make more sense to model the operation of the corporation as a 'team' sharing joint resources, as opposed to a legal fiction controlled by one party, the shareholders, whose actions are implemented by subservient managers (Blair & Stout 1999). Central to the operation of team and its allocation of control rights across the company is the board of directors. Blair and Stout (1999, p.251)[1] describe the situation as follows:

> In essence the mediating hierarchy solution requires members to give up important rights to a legal entity created by the act of incorporation. In other words corporate assets belong not to the shareholders but *to the corporation itself*. Within the corporation, control over assets is exercised by an internal hierarchy whose job is to coordinate activities of the team members, allocate the resulting production, and mediate disputes among team members over that allocation. At the peak of this hierarchy is the Board of Directors whose authority over the use of corporate assets is virtually absolute and whose independence from team members... is protected by law (original italics)

So it is the shareholders' interests as reflected by decisions of the board of directors that constitutes the legally recognized focus of corporate decision making. It is often thought that great leeway given to boards of directors to ignore second guessing and protests from shareholders reflects the courts' recognition of the strength of market-based disciplines, takeovers, institutional shareholder activism, etc. But this quietism of the courts may rather reflect a different conception of what the purpose of a board of directors actually is. The board is not charged to protect only shareholders, but all those, including other stakeholders, who make company-specific investments. This may be senior managers, like Jerry Katzenberg at Walt Disney, or the 'talent' that draws in the cinema-goers at the box office. The recent post-Enron emphasis on the importance of safeguarding shareholder rights against managerial looting has not been matched by judicial activism to overturn decisions by the board of directors. Rather the courts seem content to accept that the board of directors acted in 'the business interest' of their company as they saw it unless this seems manifestly not to be the case.

As originally conceived by Alchain and Demsetz (1972), the monitoring function of a team was fulfilled by a randomly chosen overseer, appointed by the team of co-workers, to ensure shirking and rent-seeking by team members is minimized and so profits flowing to the team are maximized. However, as Blair and Stout (1999) note, this seems to ignore an essential part of group dynamics within a productive team, that is the need to reconcile and most effectively deploy very different talents which sometimes come with very large egos attached. The intensity of the resulting creative tension will be illustrated by the Disney case study later in the chapter.

Blair and Stout (1999) point out that the key to team membership and participation is not ownership as such, but rather participation in firm-specific investments whose value is lost upon expulsion or resignation from the firm. The central role of the board of directors within the incorporated firm is to act as an independent 'court of appeal' amongst aggrieved team members. Outside interference by the legal courts can only be justified if the internal court of the corporation clearly breaches rules of natural justice or makes decisions which are obviously perverse in some way. The corporation is then best seen as a sequence of ascending hierarchies where the personnel at each level pass unresolved disputes 'up the tree' until they reach the final seat of judgement: the board of directors.

The structure of the team-production model of the corporation as a mediating hierarchy is portrayed in Figure 14.3. At the top of the hierarchy sits not the owner but the board of directors.

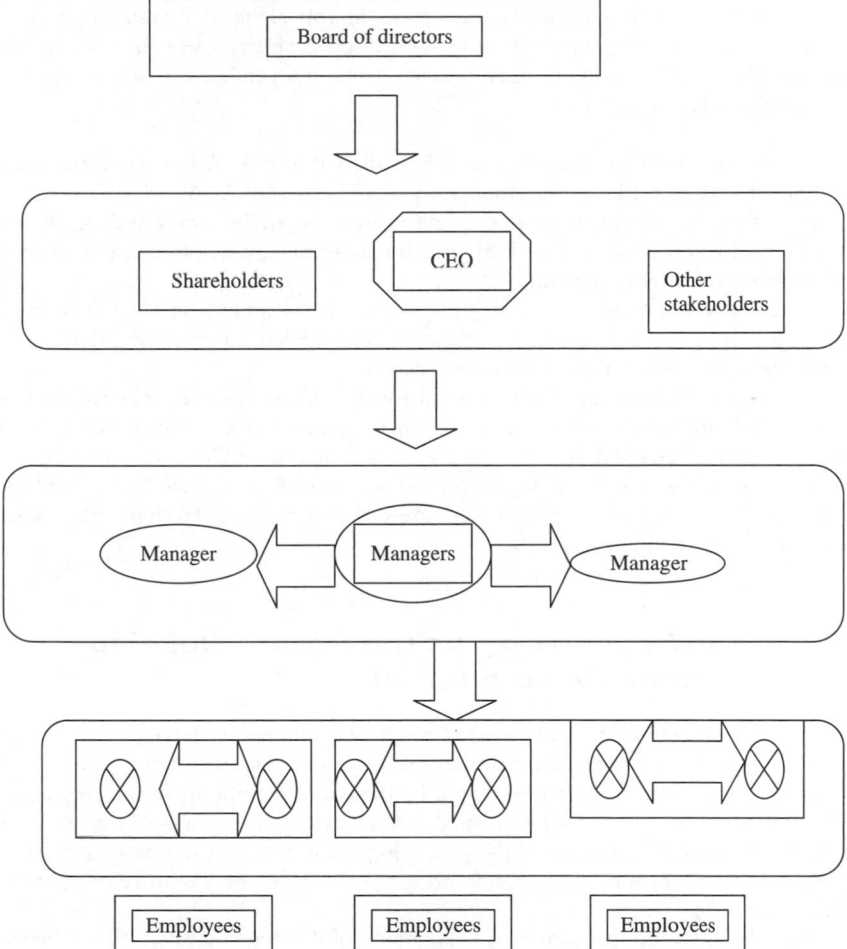

Figure 14.3   The team theory of the corporation

The board acts as a final court of appeal, where the CEO operates as a senior judge for problems that cannot be resolved by employees and managers amongst themselves or for major decisions pertaining to the integrity of the company, takeovers, CEO succession, major new strategic initiatives, etc. Employees are not subordinates in this perspective on the firm but rather simply another team member. The Disney case below is used to illustrate how Michael Eisner, the CEO, found himself hemmed in and dependent on his subordinate managers, especially those on the board.

14.3.2 Psychological Barriers to Arm's Length Contracting

The Jensen and Meckling model assumes the CEO is bound to shareholder interests by contractual conditions imposed by a board of directors, partially composed of 'independent' non-executive directors, who deal with the senior management team 'at arm's length'. Examining the explosion of executive compensation, often even in response to mediocre performance, Bebchuk and Fried (2004) have concluded this 'arm's length contracting' model of corporate governance is largely fictional. They give a number of reasons for this:

- The presence of 'interlocking' directorships where the CEO of AAA PLC is on the board of BBB PLC and the CEO of BBB PLC is simultaneously on the board of AAA.
- Loyalty: often the CEO nominates or at least has a veto over potential new 'independent' directors. So if the CEO got you your spot in the first place it may seem a bit rich to conspire in your patron's downfall even if he is a bit of a chump.
- Most CEOs become CEOs by being rather forceful people. Running an S&P500 company is not really a job for the timid or meek. Given these CEOs are fairly commanding figures confronting them can be bruising and retaliation is to be expected.
- Most of us like to think we do a pretty good job and shun evidence that suggests otherwise. Psychologists call this tendency to discount negative feedback about our performance 'cognitive dissonance'. Many non-executive directors are retired successful CEOs of the company itself or companies in the same sector. Big pay-packets and generous severance terms delivered for them, so they may regard these goodies as in the best interest of shareholders. To think otherwise is to raise the spectre of living off ill-gotten gains.

14.3.3 Group Psychology on the Board, Building Consensus and its Dissimulation

By this point a reader might feel we have strayed a long way into industrial organization for a text on behavioural finance, but in reality these developments in our understanding of how corporations decide things and have their decisions evaluated by the courts remind us of the centrality of group decision making, peer pressure and interpersonal conflict especially as they operate within the board of directors. While the whole subject of the psychology of group decision making is vast I confine myself to studies of boardroom dynamics to prevent the burden of literature overwhelming both author and reader alike.

Boardrooms, like any other gatherings, display many of the dynamics and biases documented by social psychology. Regulation of corporate boards in the UK by the law has largely evolved by means of the promulgation of a series of best practice corporate governance codes. These include the

Turnbull Report (ICAEW 1999), the Higgs Report (Higgs 2003) and the overarching Combined Code (FRC-LSE 2003), which specify the proportion, tenure and duties of board members, but beneath these externally verifiable characteristics great variation in board effectiveness can still persist.

Forbes and Milliken (1999) present a model of how the 'demography' (or external characteristics) of a board of directors can impact upon their effectiveness across two dimensions:

- *Control* of the organization, displayed by getting the correct strategy chosen and implemented.
- *Service* to the CEO, displayed by mentoring, advising and if need be correcting/removing the CEO of the firm.

The relationship between various measures of company financial performance (especially share-holder returns) and various board demography metrics (proportion of outsiders, board tenure, dismissals) have been extensively investigated in the accounting and finance research literature (see Bushman & Smith, 2001 for a review). Frustratingly few robust results have emerged from this burgeoning literature. Forbes and Milliken (1999) point out that the linkage between the board's external demographic characteristics and its impact on performance are likely to be subject to mitigation through a number of well-documented biases associated with decision making by small groups.

Forbes and Milliken (1999) suggest a number of hypotheses concerning how board demography and board effectiveness, in terms of control and service to the CEO, might be related. These are summarized in Figure 14.4.

The diagram in Figure 14.4 synthesizes a number of pressures that exist within the board that impact upon its performance.

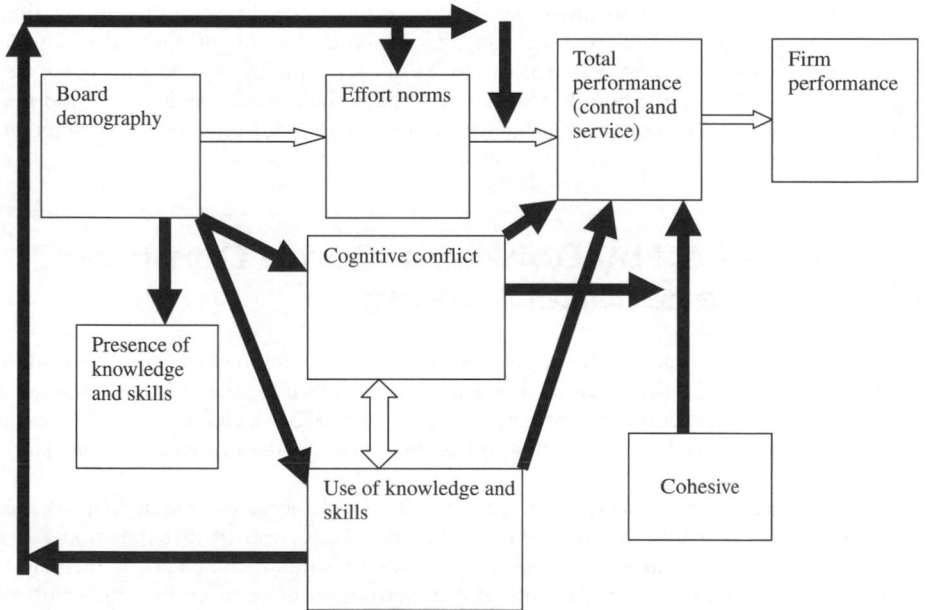

Figure 14.4   The impact of board representation and composition on corporate performance

- The first is the *effort norm*, or benchmark expected level of work/diligence by those on the board. Large boards can be cluttered by big-name time-servers who do little but make the company's headed notepaper look impressive.
- The second is *cognitive conflict*, or the tendency for boards to disagree, squabble or fail to reach a consensus effectively.
- Thirdly, board *cohesiveness* measures the ability of the board to communicate if necessary between meetings to exchange ideas, build commitment and resolve those genuine differences which any creative enterprise will inevitably throw up.
- Finally, board *diversity* measures the width of skills, culture and experience on which the board can draw, from traditional functions in accounting and operations to more niche skills in regulatory compliance and political lobbying, etc.

Forbes and Milliken (1999) suggest four possible testable hypotheses concerning how these biases affect board effectiveness.

- Higher effort norms and the presence of cognitive conflict should help improve board effectiveness (on the criteria given above).
- Cognitive conflict will damage board cohesion.
- Board effectiveness will initially rise in board cohesion. But board effectiveness will decline if the board becomes a rubber stamp packed with Yes men. To prevent such degeneration into a rather smug club, some productive level of cognitive conflict needs to be retained if only to keep board members on their toes and encourage critical thinking.
- Diversity in board membership will raise performance but may also reduce board cohesion, which may work to undermine any improvement in performance that diversity brings.

While Forbes and Milliken (1999) do not provide evidence to correctly sign these various effects they do enough to make us unwilling to put too much weight on univariate relationships between board, size, proportion of outsiders and effectiveness. An effective decision-making process at the board level is a process that cannot be simply induced by conformity to externally imposed rules alone. Hence the board of directors remains the central monitor of 'good practice' since no outside agency is likely to either desire to assume this objective or have competence in discharging it.

14.4   Lions Led by Donkeys. Some Common Failings in Managerial Making

Even the most general knowledge of financial press can make us painfully aware of the weaknesses of our captains of industry. English industry has always had a place for the incompetent amateur, as opposed to properly trained corporate 'players' (see Coleman 1973). Such failings are long enough to fill a book and indeed Max Bazerman's (2006) text *Judgment in Managerial Decision-Making* is a classic in this area.

One well-documented bias, which the presence of outside directors might help to abate, is 'isolation bias'. This arises when managers overplay the uniqueness of their position and hence fail to make prudent inferences from past experience of similar challenges (Coleman 1973). They do not take advantage of the benefits of aggregation on offer from forming a portfolio of similar prospects currently held by the company. This is one of the primary costs of isolation bias.

To understand how this operates consider holding three separate gambles of the form:

- In one gamble you have half a chance of winning $500.
- In two further gambles you have a half a chance of winning $250.

This forms a compound gamble with the following prospects:

- A one in eight chance of winning $1000 (from winning the first, second and third gambles).
- A one in four chance of winning $750, if you win the first and second or third gamble. Or $500 from just winning the first gamble.
- Or, finally, $250 from just winning the second or third gamble.

Recall if you lose all the gambles you get nothing. This implies the compounded value of the gambles can be calculated as follows.

$$0.125 \times 500 + 0.25 \times 750 + 0.25 \times 500 + 0.25 \times 250 = 437.5$$

Individually the gambles have a total value of 500, however

$$(0.5 \times 500) + 2 \times (0.5 \times 250) = 500$$

So whether we aggregate the gambles makes a clear difference to our assessment of their value as a prospect. Here the compound gamble reveals the addition of further gambles especially if they are similar (like the second and third gambles here) and reduce the investor's utility. The company is putting all its eggs in one basket rather than diversifying risk.

14.4.1 Clearing Out the 'Inside View'

Managers by failing to aggregate gambles effectively can become victim to the 'inside view' which sees their actions as creating history rather than being subject to it. This inside view focuses on the job at hand to the exclusion of the larger business and macroeconomic context in which it arises. A particularly common context of this, as we shall see, is when a recession or technological obsolescence implies the necessity of liquidating the company either partially or in full. Such a fixation may be ameliorated by an opposing 'outside view' that sees the case in hand (the product launch or joint venture) as part of a broader trend in industrial restructuring or a macroeconomic change in fortunes. This suggests a clear role for non-executive directors drawn from industry peers.

An intermediate view is that the mingling of insiders and outsiders on the board can act as a symmetrical de-biasing mechanism. While outsiders may help mitigate excessive optimism induced by isolation bias they do not inspire loyalty amongst those competing in tournaments further down the corporation hierarchy for positions on the board. This may lead to a damaging reduction in the effort put into acquiring reputation and status within the organization.

Independent non-executive directors are one clear source of external monitoring. But as Cox and Munsinger (1985) point out their effect is neutralized by an array of biases which make them reluctant to undermine the executive directors, especially the CEO and chairman, who may have appointed them. Often they too quickly adopt the 'inside view', especially when faced with the external threat of shareholder litigation. In the United States non-executives are often used to consider the merits of legal suits that shareholders are seeking against incumbent management (termed 'derivative' suits in the US courts since they derive from shareholders opposing the board of directors' decisions). Cox and Munsinger explain the process of non-executive capture as follows (1985, p.85)[2]:

> A cornerstone of boardroom culture is a near fanatical concern for 'the liability of today's directors', which is documented by studies of director attitudes that repeatedly identify fear of personal liability as a paramount concern about service on the board. Directors' fear of liability is fed by a steady flow of exhortations in executive trade publications and other media warnings of the expanding legal obligations of a director of a publicly held corporation.

With such preconceptions it is unlikely that non-executives will significantly inhibit the actions of incumbent managers. This will be the case especially when outsiders feel there is a conflict between not wishing to be obstructive to the incumbent management which appointed them and exercising detached caution. As another legal commentator has put it:

> The important point is, of course, is that the final awareness of the risk or harm occurs sometime after the point at which, both practically and legally, the responsible actors are likely to be held responsible. This is the optimism-commitment whipsaw effect. As one of the more polite sayings goes the managers find themselves 'knee deep in the big muddy'

> (Langevoort 2000).

14.4.2   Come On Down: the Satisfaction of Recognition

One motivation for the conformity observed on the board of directors is the pleasure taken in being 'recognized' by one's peers. Anyone chosen as treasurer of the local parish council, or social secretary to the scuba club, will recognize this phenomenon. It is nice to be noticed. Work practice studies at Western Electric, a telecommunications company, in the years 1924–32 confirm this effect. These so-called Hawthorne studies conducted in the Hawthorne plant of the Western Electric company in Cicero, Illinois, led by Elton Mayo, a Harvard psychology professor, and colleagues, confirmed the productivity enhancing effect of just watching workers do their job (even if their working conditions were made slightly worse by dimming the lighting). By doing so workers felt 'chosen' or special in some way and this appeared to have a motivating effect. Certainly the inclusion in an elite group such as the board of directors of a FTSE100 (or S&P500) corporation is something most of us would value and be reluctant to surrender once received.

14.4.3   Facing Glory and Defeat: Managers' Resistance to Recognizing Failure

As described in detail later in Chapter 17 a strong characteristic of those who are successful in business and in life is optimism. Success sometimes even requires optimism in the face of strong evidence to refute it. On hearing of his conviction for fraud on charges which could lead to up to 35 years in jail, Lord Conrad Black commented, 'It is a bit of setback', before vowing to fight on. Such a plucky spirit seems almost the essence of a successful manager. Such optimism often characterizes managers' optimism in entering a new market or evaluating a new competitive strategy, for example AOL's adoption of the fixed-price 'all the Internet access you want'/flat-rate strategy in place of charges based on metered usage (see Swisher 1998, pp.161–96). Zajac and

Bazerman (1991) point out that few managers fully account for the consequent (but easily foreseeable) responses of competitors serving the same market. They adopt new strategies largely on the assumption that the competition will sit back and take a beating graciously. In reality price cuts are likely to be matched, technological edge will be eroded, etc. In the case of AOL and its adoption of a flat-rate pricing policy, this led to a huge surge in demand from its membership that no-one within AOL had anticipated, which resulted in sluggish response times and straight computer outages when the creaking system gave way under the pressure of demand. Zajac and Bazerman (1991) suggest three testable hypotheses concerning the way in which cognitive bias and 'blind spots' of managers will inhibit the effective implantation of strategic decision making and especially market entrance. These are:

1. All else being equal, strategic decision makers considering capacity expansion will pay insufficient attention to competitors' contingent decisions, resulting in industry overcapacity.
2. All else being equal, strategic decision makers considering entry into a new business (through internal development) will pay insufficient attention to competitors' contingent decisions, resulting in new-business entry failures.
3. All else being equal, strategic decision makers considering an acquisition will pay insufficient attention to competitors' contingent decisions, resulting in an acquisition premium being charged to acquire control.

14.4.4   Governance in the Long and Short Run

These business failings will be punished by the market and gross errors will no doubt lead to company failures, leaving a less-biased, more rational cohort of companies in the sector. But in the short run individual company market plays are likely to reflect as yet unpunished, or at least uncorrected, bias. This suggests the domain in which a behavioural perspective on corporate behaviour might be most useful. Zajac and Bazerman (1991, p.51)[3] state the case as follows:

> Therefore if the research objective is to analyze the long-run equilibrium of the markets, a rational, economic, game theoretic approach may be highly useful. However, if the research objective is to explain and understand the actual behaviours of individual firms as they interact with competitors, a behaviorally based, competitive decision-making approach may have distinct advantages in shaping future research questions in competitor analysis.

I pick up on this advice below in undertaking a case study of Michael Eisner's rise and fall from grace within the Walt Disney Company over a period of two decades in the final section of this chapter.

However, Jensen (1993) has suggested that failure to face the need to downsize/exit can be extraordinarily costly to the company's shareholders and constitutes another consistent bias of managers. As an example he cites the case of General Motors where:

> The company spent a total of $62.8 billion in excess of depreciation in the period and produced a firm with total ending value of equity of $2.8 billion. Ironically its expenditures were more than enough to pay for the entire equity value of Toyota and Honda which in 1985 totalled $21.5 billion. If it had done this GM would have owned two low-cost, high-quality, automobile manufacturers

(Jensen 1993, p.850)[4].

Clearly the board was far too averse to a 'buying in' of the requisite production capacity and proceeded with a costly and ultimately ineffective 'build' option at their shareholders' expense. Jensen suggests a number of board reforms aimed at reducing such abuse, including:

- A change in board culture to reward competence rather than consensus and conformity.
- Smaller boards to increase accountability and promote frank discussion and if need be disagreement.
- Incentives in the form of equity stakes and equity and option grants to make board members owners. Jensen proposes a minimum stake of $100,000 on joining the board to be enlarged by later equity and option grants as part of board membership compensation.
- Separation of the board chairman and CEO roles (as required by UK governance codes) to prevent the nonsense of the chairman overseeing the possible need to remove himself from the CEO's position. In the long run Eisner's indifference to shareholder interests brought him down, but his downfall was neither automatic nor speedy and reflected many of the biases and frailties discussed here.

14.5   Conclusion and Summary

This chapter has examined the concept of incorporation and the models of internal governance of the firm. Standard finance theory stresses the role of agency and the hierarchy of command. This chapter presented an enticing alternative of the corporation as a 'team' made up of ascending hierarchies with the board as the final court of appeal largely isolated from outside control by judges in common law courts reluctant to second guess what is in the 'business' interest of the firm. So power resides largely unperturbed at board level.

The subsequent case study on Michael Eisner's period as the head of Disney suggests even a board's censure and control can be circumvented by a skilful and well-entrenched CEO. This suggests the 'cult of the leader' and his psychology may be more important for business decisions than much standard finance theory seems keen to allow.

Appendix: Emperor Eisner – A Case Study in the Power of Personal Control in a Corporation

Michael Eisner's 20-year reign at the top of Disney (from 1984–2003) provided him with the longevity necessary to ensure his personality was firmly stamped on the corporation he headed. In this section I describe how Eisner worked the corporate board and senior management to maintain and build his personal power base and how he ultimately lost power as the board and senior managers, some family members, lost confidence in him. I choose Eisner not because he is a crook, or a swindler, but rather because as an icon of US business he better exemplifies the norm of business life (as opposed to Jeff Skilling, or Robert Maxwell, who are recognized by their peer CEOs to be bad apples). In many ways Eisner is a paragon of American business life having been recognized as Pioneer of the Year by the Will Rogers Institute in 2003, an honour previously awarded to Cecil B. De Mille and Jack Warner. Disney Corporation is a straight-out American institution with its ambition of releasing 'the child within us all', as its founder Walt preached. In doing so I plunder a number of excellent accounts of his reign at Disney including one by Eisner himself (Stewart 2005, Masters 2001 and Eisner & Schwartz 1999).

Eisner arrived at Disney during a lull in its distinguished history at the behest of Roy E. Disney, the son of Walt's brother (Roy O. Disney). In the years since Walt's death in 1966 the Disney Corporation had atrophied under his chosen successor, his son-in-law Ron Miller. Miller had stood down in favour of Card Walker two years before. But by 1984, when Roy Disney approached Eisner, Miller's inhibiting presence was still felt. Disney was widely touted as a takeover target and Eisner felt little pressure to accept the initial offer of becoming president of Disney. He told Roy Disney:

> Roy. I'm bigger than you right now at Paramount. I make three times as many pictures and do really well. So if I come here, I want to be President and Chief Operating Officer

> (Stewart 2005, p.47).

Roy Disney had been advised by Stanley Gold, to whom he had handed over his business affairs, that the value of his stake in Disney had fallen from $80 million to $50 million in just the last year (Masters 2001, p.141). Roy had left the board in 1977 and from that point on Gold represented him. Roy increased his shareholding to 4.9% in preparation for ousting Walker.

The Early Years

Eisner had made a name for himself as president at Paramount Studios under Barry Diller's chairmanship. Together Eisner and Diller developed a series of 'high-concept' productions where plot and characterization were considered more important than big movie stars or dramatic locations and special effects. *Saturday Night Fever*, *Grease*, *Terms of Endearment* and *Flashdance* are memorable examples of how this philosophy worked. Eisner articulated the basic idea of how to make a studio work as follows:

> We have no obligation to make Art. We have no obligation to make history. We have no obligation to make a statement. But to make money, it is often important to make history, art, a statement, or all three

> (Stewart 2005, p.32).

Eisner, knowing his own value, held out for a stunning pay package. This was a base salary of $750,000 per year, an equivalent signing-on fee, 2% of all profits over $100 million per year, plus options to buy 510,000 options at the current stock price of $57 per share. By 1988 Eisner would get a bonus of $6.8 million and a further $32.6 million by exercising his options. With a total income of over $40 million that year (plus $50 million worth of unexercised options) Eisner was the highest paid executive in the United States in 1988.

Eisner's position was substantially weakened following his emergency open-heart surgery in July 1994. He felt the need to delegate some tasks. This led him on a quest to find a worthy lieutenant: a mission he was to find difficult and ultimately fruitless (Stewart 2005, p.175). The hierarchy broke down because its principal hierarch could not execute his dominating function effectively. I examine this dissemblance below.

Jeffrey Katzenberg

In reaching this position Eisner had not been slow to wield the knife on Disney's payroll. Over 1000 managerial posts were cut in Eisner's first four years, with many replacements coming in from Paramount. Chief amongst these were Jeffrey Katzenberg. Katzenberg had been Diller's personal assistant at Paramount and his workaholic drive soon led others to notice him. Katzenberg was not unaware of his own worth and on being approached by Eisner constructed an alarming wish list including,

> Two seccys, a beach house, a corporate jet, travel-family, etc., screening room, house maintenance? Butler?

> (Stewart 2005, p.58).

In a concession, which later proved controversial, Katzenberg was offered a 2% annual bonus of all the profits from productions he headed up. Further, Eisner brought in a new chief financial officer from Marriott Hotels, Gary Wilson. As the revenues from Katzenberg's hits rolled in, Frank Wells, the company president and Eisner's chief lieutenant, became concerned about the 2% perpetuity in project proceeds they had granted Katzenberg. This problem became especially prominent after successes like *The Little Mermaid* and *Pretty Woman* made it clear that Katzenberg was capable of producing true box-office magic.

Katzenberg offered to relinquish this entitlement if he was guaranteed at least 75% of Eisner's remuneration. Wells rebuffed this suggestion. This foreshadowed the later rivalry between Eisner and Katzenberg (Stewart 2005, p.100).

By early 1991 the liability to pay the 2% of proceeds to Katzenberg has become so worrying that Wells launched 'project snowball' to calculate its total cost if Katzenberg departed from Disney, which was beginning to look increasingly likely (Stewart 2005, p.117).

Wilson made clear public statements that he intended to transform Disney into a growth company generating a consistent 20% earnings growth and 20% stock-price growth to match. This was what Wilson termed his '20/20' principle (Stewart 2005, p.66). With ambitions like these, pressure to generate income was intense. By 1990 Eisner could sensibly speak of the last 10 years as the 'Disney decade' and upped his projection of future earnings growth to 20% in his dealings with investment analysts. But many Disney insiders were becoming nervous that an unjustifiable arrogance was setting in and Gary Wilson himself unloaded $60 million in stock that year (Stewart 2005, p.113).

Nowhere was this pressure felt more intensely than in the animation division which had been the origin of Disney's greatness as a corporation but which now stood almost idle. Hand production, frame-by-frame, of animated sequences made for labour-intensive slow work. Initially Eisner and Wells intended to shut animation down. The primary opposition to doing so came from Roy Disney to whom Eisner felt beholden because he had got him the CEO's position in the first place. The remarkable resurgence of animation was due to an ambitious young vice-president, Stan Kinsey, who championed the cause of George Lucas's (of *Star Wars* fame) Pixar Advanced Computer Graphics. Pixar's computer-generated graphical images held out the prospect of making films without expensive movie stars and touchy directors with exorbitant budgetary demands. While Katzenberg had no interest in this new technology and preferred to focus on his traditional strength of real-life action dramas, Eisner gave the project funding to proceed, largely to placate Roy Disney, his sponsor. Eisner told Katzenberg,

> Roy wants to do this and he believes in it. I think we have to take a deep breath and say yes

> (Stewart 2005, p.86).

Elsewhere he and Katzenberg implemented the 'high-concept' drama principle that had worked for them at Paramount. These were films with good storylines that appealed to a wide audience, but had no big-name stars or expensive directors attached – *Down and Out in Beverly Hills* and *Three Men and a Baby* were notably successful comedies in this genre.

Eisner's Ambition Grows

Elsewhere a worrying growth in Eisner's self-awareness was becoming visible. Early on in his leadership Eisner decided to relaunch the television show *The Wonderful World of Disney* and to present it himself. This was despite a widespread belief he was a poor presenter and the prospect that Tom Hanks might be willing to take the role. By presenting the television show Eisner placed himself in direct succession to Walt Disney, a mantle for which there was competition from Roy Disney and other family members.

However, it was in the theme parks division that Eisner's more majestic vision came to the fore. The theme parks, Walt Disney World in Florida and Disney World in Anaheim, Los Angeles, had been a pet project of Walt Disney, undertaken in opposition to his brother Roy O. and other family members. By the time of Eisner's arrival the parks were a steady earner, headed by Richard Nunis, one of the few cash-generative businesses Disney had left. The parks allowed Eisner to indulge his more creative/artistic side, especially his love of architecture. While being a total amateur Eisner took a detailed interest in the hotel developments in the parks, holding presentations by competing architectural teams at his home, as well as making detailed comments himself. The more imperial vision of Eisner began to be displayed. Stewart (2005, p.66) quotes him as saying of these projects in a memo to Frank Wells:

> If we are going to stamp our imprint on the world, if we are going to do something more than help people have a good time with Mickey Mouse, if we are going to make aesthetic choices, then we have got to upgrade the level of our architecture and try to leave something behind for others.

By 1991 the Euro Disney costs were out of control having exceeded $2 billion. A construction advisor brought in to reconnoitre the situation reported to Eisner, 'You are headed for one of the biggest failures in construction I've ever seen'. The total cost of the Euro Disney park was ultimately to exceed $4 billion. This left Euro Disney at its opening saddled with $3 billion of debt. Part of the reason for this was Eisner's insistence that the park open 9am sharp on 22 April 1992. This opened Disney up to all sorts of hold-out demands from French construction companies and their somewhat prickly labour unions. Nor was the opening of Euro Disney the end of Eisner's woes. Visitor numbers were far more sensitive to the weather than in the Japanese park, where visitors' patience was legendary, and Euro Disney proved unable to generate sufficient operating income to independently service its debt. Disney by 1994 was forced to pressurize debt bond-holders to accept a restructuring of the debt schedule, which was hardly designed to encourage investment in future Disney projects.

Following on from the Euro Disney debacle Eisner accepted an invitation to become involved in the renovation of the New Amsterdam Theatre and the Times Square area in general. By February 1994 New York Mayor Rudy Giuliani was praising the 'match made in Heaven' that was Times Square and the Disney Corporation. Indeed Euro Disney did not exhaust Eisner's ambitions to build new parks. Eisner also started developing plans for a theme park themed on American history called 'Disney's America' outside Washington, DC (Stewart 2005, p.147). This became one of Eisner's few public failures when it was shut down in the face of 'nimby' protests by Washington residents in 1994.

This high ambition underlay the increasing divergence between Eisner and his close partner Jeffrey Katzenberg. The tension can be illustrated by the development of two projects in the early 1990s. *Dick Tracy* was a standard star-studded blockbuster, featuring Warren Beatty and Madonna, and was favoured by Eisner; *Pretty Woman* was favoured by Katzenberg, a fairytale-type story concerning the love of a high-class call-girl played by a relative newcomer to Hollywood, Julia Roberts. *Dick Tracy* dominated by the co-stars' affair and their expensive demands cost a whopping $47 million and grossed $100 million, a respectable, but not thrilling return. *Pretty Woman* cost $14 million and grossed $463 million, serious money by anyone's standards. But the real power shift from Eisner to Katzenberg occurred because of the huge success of animated productions and the comparatively poor showing of real-life dramas.

By its termination in 1994 the Eisner/Katzenberg partnership had created a company earning $2 billion profits on revenues of $10 billion. Even the live-action studio at last produced a winner in the form of *Pulp Fiction*, a tongue-in-cheek gangster movie from the new enfant terrible of cinema Quentin Tarantino.

The Rift between Katzenberg and Eisner

This contrast led Katzenberg to issue a memo to Disney executives calling for a return to their 'high-concept' story-based, cheap-to-produce, roots which Eisner had pioneered at Paramount but now seemed to be abandoning. This vision of Katzenberg's was articulated in 'The Memo' released in a briefing to analysts in Orlando in early 1991 (but originally intended to be private). He stated (Stewart 2005, p.114):

> Our initial success at Disney was based on our ability to tell good stories well. Big stars, special effects and named directors were of little importance. Of course we started this way out of necessity. We had small budgets and not much respect. So we substituted dollars with creativity and big stars with talent we believed in. Success ensued. With success came bigger budgets and bigger names.

This back to basics call started a rift between Eisner and Katzenberg that would ultimately lead to Katzenberg's departure and the demise of a creative partnership that had dominated the movie business for a decade. Other hits ensued, *Beauty and the Beast* and *The Lion King*, but the old magic was gone.

By 1992 Katzenberg was the golden boy and he knew it. While live-action films and the parks languished, his animation studio generated $500 million in 1992. As if sensing 'project snow-ball's' presence Katzenberg asked Frank Wells to report on the expected pay-out on his 2% of all proceeds on projects he headed. Wells already knew this would amount to $169.4 million. This gave Katzenberg considerable leverage in his negotiations to extend his current contract beyond its current 1994 expiry date.

In this spirit Katzenberg asked Eisner if he could be guaranteed the succession to COO and president if Frank Wells were to leave (as was expected as he was known to harbour political ambitions in the US Senate). Eisner found the approach distasteful, but indicated that Katzenberg could expect to succeed Wells (Stewart 2005, p.139). This began a misunderstanding that would ultimately lead to the courts. Both Wells and Eisner were well aware that it was the teamwork of the trio that had produced the magic of the last decade and were wary of losing Katzenberg and possibly creating a major competitor.

The bubbling conflict inevitably boiled over when Frank Wells died in a helicopter crash on the ski slopes of Nevada on Easter Sunday, 1994. Katzenberg sat until the following Monday awaiting Eisner's call, but in the event he just received a public press release telling him Eisner was assuming Wells's prior roles as COO and president. At a subsequent crisis meeting Katzenberg let Eisner know his true feelings about not being named Eisner's second in command:

> If you can't tell me after 19 years, if you can't tell me [whether I will succeed Wells], then you've told me everything I need to know about my future. I've hit the ceiling I have to move

on. After 19 years together I have earned the right to be your partner. You should know me by now

(Stewart 2005, p.161).

Meanwhile the movie hits in animation just kept coming. *Toy Story*, over which Eisner had doubts, proved another big hit for Katzenberg's studio. *The Lion King*, which opened in June 1994, was dubbed by one analyst 'The most profitable picture in Movie history' (Stewart 2005, p.169).

Despite this, following Eisner's decision to rely on others to recover the situation after his 1994 heart attack, Katzenberg decided to leave Disney and form DreamWorks (SKG) with his friends, the film director Steven Spielberg and David Geffen the famous music impresario. Following his departure his de facto replacement Michael Ovitz sought to negotiate a settlement to Katzenberg's expected bonus payments. Katzenberg seemed willing to accept a $100 million payoff, which was a good deal for Disney, but Eisner felt so bitter about the dispute he refused to settle (Stewart 2005, p.237). While the settlement would certainly enhance shareholder wealth, by maybe $300 million or more, personal dislike got the better of this outcome.

Finally, on 9 April 1996 Katzenberg filed a suit in the Los Angeles superior court claiming a breach of contract and remuneration worth possibly as much as $12.5 billion, as the cumulative value of 2% of all the projects he headed up at Disney during his time there (Stewart 2005, p.449). At this point $100 million seemed like a pretty good offer. Finally, on the 4 July weekend 1999, Stanley Gold was able to negotiate a $280 million settlement of Katzenberg's claim in a deal negotiated by David Geffen on Katzenberg's behalf. But this was only after a public hearing of an arbitration in front of former Judge Paul Breckenridge in which notes taken for an autobiography of Eisner, ghost written by Tony Schwartz, were subpoenaed. This brought into full public view the contempt in which Eisner held Katzenberg, Ovitz and other senior colleagues. The press had a field day.

Michael Ovitz

Eisner, after Wells's death and Katzenberg's departure, became chairman, CEO, COO, president and the creative force behind an animation studio currently enjoying fantastic success. Unsurprisingly, his doctor and wife begged him to delegate some of his duties before the stress of command proved fatal. Eisner was now Disney, but perhaps not in a healthy, balanced, sustainable way. It was at this point that Eisner decided to acquire the ABC television network in a move that would hugely expand both Disney itself and the managerial demands on his time. Eisner had come up through the ranks of ABC 20 years ago. It was now pretty clear Eisner needed help to retain control of such a complex company. He looked to his long-time friend and confidant Michael Ovitz, who was the leading partner in Creative Artists Agency, a partnership that negotiated on behalf of some of Hollywood's leading talent.

Recently Ovitz had emerged as a central matchmaker/dealmaker in Hollywood advising Japanese market entrants into Hollywood like Matsushita Electric Corporation's acquisition of Universal Studios and the Sony Corporation on its acquisition of Columbia and TriStar studios (Stewart 2005, p.171). In fact Ovitz had also been courted by Universal Studios itself with a deal rumoured to offer him $250 million. Eisner enticed Ovitz with the notion that he would be his 'partner' but was reluctant to specify what this meant in terms of a formal position.

Indeed days after Ovitz's arrival he was summoned to Eisner's house (they were family friends prior to his arrival at Disney) to be informed that neither Sandy Litvack, general counsel and vice-chairman of Disney, nor Steve Bollenbach, the CFO, were happy to report to him even though this had been the line of command when Frank Wells was president (Stewart 2005, p.217). Eisner refused to intervene.

One of the reasons Eisner increasingly distrusted Ovitz was his tendency to thrive on a flurry of deals, or near deals. Eisner, at some level, still adhered to his 'high concept', cheap and profitable formula. As he expressed it to Ovitz in a memo on 10 October 1994:

> The 'deal' is not the essence of Disney...Operations are the thing...I feel about acquisitions exactly as I feel about everything else. We don't need them. We don't need the overly expensive movie or television show. We don't need the actor who has priced himself out of the market. We do not need the acquisition that, even if it fits strategically, is economically ridiculous
>
> (Stewart 2005, p.225).

Coming from a man who that year had completed the second-largest acquisition in history, albeit at a low premium, this comment seemed strange. But Eisner's reservations did not just concern the substance of his business approach, he was also concerned about Ovitz's style, especially the lavish Hollywood parties and present giving, which Ovitz had almost adopted as a habit in his days massaging the 'talent's' collective ego.

By June 1996 Ovitz could no longer stand Eisner's interference and undermining. He confronted Eisner in a letter mocking his decision to house the senior executives in a building called 'Team Disney' as follows:

> You're a team destroyer not a team builder. I've had enough trouble inheriting your fights and enemies. Everyday somebody complains to me about something. It is ok because it is human and healthy....I've always had one goal, to protect you, the company and our relationship. Maybe you cannot have a partner. You failed with everyone over the years
>
> (Stewart 2005, p.256).

Despite the external appearance of 'Team Disney', Eisner was unable to share the glory of the undoubted achievement under his reign. He had worked with a number of 'partners', Wells, Katzenberg, Ovitz, each of which in his view had failed him. Eisner recognized the benefits of teamwork yet feared the reality of the dilution of personal control it implied.

Still the hits just kept on coming from the Disney Studios with *The Hunchback of Notre Dame* grossing over $100 million and the 'event' movie of that year, *101 Dalmatians*, taking $136 million in domestic receipts alone despite incurring a high production cost of $45 million.

Ovitz finally departed Disney on 11 December 1996. Strangely in his case Eisner was happy to give the full pay-out due to him for termination under his contract issued 16 months earlier. This included $50 million in cash plus options on five million Disney shares then valued at $40 million. Eisner consulted general counsel Sandy Litvack on whether Ovitz could be simply dismissed for 'just cause'. Certainly, Ovitz had a style of management that grated with Eisner and was more 'showbiz' than was normal at Disney, but ultimately Disney issued a press release announcing Ovitz's departure 'by mutual consent' (Stewart 2005, p.274).

The Studios under Joe Roth and Peter Schneider

With Katzenberg gone the control of the studios passed to Joe Roth. Roth was certainly not a man to be restricted by 'The Memo'. With his new favoured director, Jeffrey Bruckheimer, by his side, Roth jumped straight into production of such classic movie blockbusters as *Armageddon*, the most expensive movie that Disney studios ever made at $140 million. This type of movie (another example is *Con Air*) with huge cost overruns without audiences to match meant the studios reported a loss of $180 million in 1996.

Under pressure to cut costs from Eisner, Roth was told to merge Touchstone, Hollywood Pictures and Walt Disney Pictures Studios into Buena Vista Motion Pictures Group. Hollywood Pictures was a Disney vehicle for making films principally aimed at an adult audience headed by David Vogel and was created at his request. Eisner chose David Vogel to head Walt Disney Picture Studios and he reported to Joe Roth as head of Walt Disney Studios division, which had produced *101 Dalmatians* and had first read and championed the production of M. Night Shyamalan's *The Sixth Sense*. But Vogel too was ultimately deemed disposable by Eisner in order to accommodate the ambitions of Peter Schneider, the head of the animation studio. Schneider was basking in the glory of *Toy Story 2*, a sequel that exceeded the original in both critical acclaim and box-office revenues.

Schneider's principal attraction from Eisner's viewpoint was his willingness to report back directly on his boss Joe Roth which Vogel had not been willing to do (Stewart 2005, p.315). Eisner had created a hierarchy of command but then seemed unwilling to use it since it exposed him to reliance on the local hierarchs beneath him. Instead he preferred to create personal loyalties to be used opportunistically to retain command. Eisner felt this need acutely as the latest Bruckheimer blockbuster, *Pearl Harbor*, spiralled in cost to over $200 million.

Eisner succeeded in facing down the demand of movie stars and producers to a percentage of future net profits (or worse revenues) on the film. On top of these they were also paid a minimum fee for appearing in/producing the film. Since most films are unprofitable these contracts became like a salary (minimum fee) plus options (percentage of profit if any emerges) employment contract. Eisner, himself largely paid in options, challenged the appropriateness of this remuneration structure. Bruckheimer counter-proposed that he and the actors get paid a percentage above the cost of making the film they served on. Later Schneider went on to insist the 13 principal cast members in *Pearl Harbor* were also offered options to employ them in future films. While this made for some unhappy campers on the *Pearl Harbor* set, Schneider and Eisner held the line and began at last to regain cost control in the movie business. Sadly their efforts were not enough and despite high praise for the film in that year's shareholder reports it was a critical and box-office failure. This failure was more difficult to bear when *Pearl Harbor* was eclipsed that summer by *Shrek*, the first animated offering from DreamWorks.

Joe Roth's blockbuster 'event' film strategy was exposed as a failure and Disney returned to the 'high-concept' cheap-to-produce, story-based model. When Peter Schneider departed from Disney Studios in 1999 he was replaced by a more modest double act, with Eisner himself pledging more creative input. Despite all these problems Disney studios began the new millennium in good shape: financially cheap, popular films like *Scary Movie*, which grossed $157 million that year in the US alone, and *Scream 3* both earned good returns even if it was hard to attribute too much artistic merit to them.

Almost as a last hurrah for Eisner's inherent creative talent the studio released one last major success inspired by Eisner's command that Disney divisions seek to find synergy in collaborative projects. The theme parks and Disney studios had already tried this with *The Country Bears*, a film based on Disneyland's singing bears – this was the sort of box-office turkey they seemed to specialize in in recent years. But Jerry Bruckheimer thought of a new approach based on a pirate theme. The twist would be that the pirates were dead and cursed and like Wagner's *Flying Dutchman* roamed the seas in search of atonement. With the addition of Johnny Depp as the exotic Jack Sparrow, the money-machine, *The Pirates of the Caribbean*, was born. *Pirates* opened on 9 July 2003 and grossed $305 million in the US and $348 internationally. Reviews were mixed, but a genuine popular classic had at last been made.

The Acquisition of the Cap Cities/ABC Network

The Disney acquisition of Cap Cities/ABC was finally completed in January 1996. At $20 billion the acquisition was the second biggest in history at the time of its completion. Disney paid $115 per share for shares trading at currently $106 per share. This is a low premium compared to other large deals at the time. This included an 80% holding in ESPN, the very successful sports channel.

Eisner moved swiftly to put his own people in control. Jamie Tarses, second in command at rival network NBC, was selected to replace Ted Harbert, who had been at the helm of NBC for 20 years. Tarses was given the title head of programming. Once again, as with Wilson and Litvack, Eisner allowed her to report to Ovitz and himself rather than Robert Iger, then chief operating officer of ABC.

Problems emerged early when Tarses was delayed in her arrival by a court ruling that she could not breach her existing contract with NBC and simply jump ship to a direct rival. Tarses struggled to exhibit enthusiasm for the sort of cheap family fare that ABC specialized in, like *Roseanne*, now nearing the end of its shelf life. ABC brought in a young English programmer, Michael Davies, to search out cheap and cheerful family entertainment. While at first he seemed obsessed with the gross and prurient, as exhibited by *The Man Show*, which relied heavily on scantily clad girls and performing animals, he eventually struck scheduling gold by bringing the *Who Wants to Be a Millionaire?* game-show format to ABC. While Tarses was trying to bury the project, Eisner's personal approval brought the wildly successful format to ABC viewers.

A clear threat to Jamie Tarses's control of ABC soon appeared in the form of Lloyd Braun, who had previously been president of Brillstein-Grey Entertainment, a television production company frequently used by ABC (Stewart 2005, p.304). Braun rose to fame on the back of commissioning *The Sopranos* from producer David Chase. *The Sopranos*' central conceit is that gangsters have problems too, need to find college fees for their children, placate their wives and deal with the emotional stresses that being ruthless killers brings.

Eisner in the summer of 1999 decided to merge Touchstone Studios and ABC, demoting Tarses to reporting to Braun and Stu Bloomberg the current head of Touchstone. Tarses strongly resented this and went into open revolt against Braun. One manifestation of this was her refusal to commission *CSI: Crime-Scene Investigation*, the first fruit of the Touchstone collaboration. *CSI* is a Las Vegas based dramatization of the work of forensic science investigators and cashed in on public interest in blood-stained gloves and other lurid details following the O.J. Simpson trial and acquittal. *CSI* was produced by Jerry Bruckheimer in his usual expensive style and soon faced large cost overruns. Having been rejected by ABC for inclusion in its schedule Touchstone had a possible disaster on its hands. When a rival television channel CBS picked the show up at the last moment it meant Touchstone was now busting its budget to subsidize a direct competitor. Eisner shut it down, but production of the series continued, funded by CBS.

Once Eisner and Robert Iger decided to run *Millionaire* three times a week on ABC in November 1999 the game was up for Tarses. *Millionaire* attracted 30 million viewers on the last episode of that run, averaging over 24 million a show. Disney was able to double the cost of advertising slots between stages of the quiz. The show had pretty much single-handedly revived ABC's fortunes. Tarses resigned on 27 August 1999 to be replaced by Lloyd Braun.

Problems at ABC

The jaded programming and overexposure of *Millionaire* meant that by the start of 2000 ABC was in deep trouble falling rapidly in viewing polls and hence advertising revenues. Despite his oft-expressed hostility to 'deals' Eisner advanced the prospect of acquiring Rupert Murdoch's Fox Family channel currently aired on the Fox cable network. Eisner also saw it as a way for Disney to regain ground in the 'new media' after the fiasco of Go.com. The big problem from Robert Iger's and other executives' viewpoint was the price of $5.5 billion. A major reason why this seemed exorbitant was that Fox had just signed a $700 million contract for live transmission of major league basketball. The problem was that on the west coast, where ABC predominated, these games went live in the middle of the afternoon when few fans had time to view them. Steve Bornstein, now head of ABC and ex-head of Disney sport-channel ESPN, thought the price ridiculously high and told Eisner so clearly. In mid-July 2000, Stanley Gold, who had put out feelers for the deal, got a call confirming Eisner had agreed to acquire Fox Family for Disney at a price of $5.3 billion.

Once again it appeared Eisner struggled to adhere to his own dictum that it was foolish to overpay for assets, even if the assets themselves were valuable. The central assumption underlying the acquisition was that ABC could use it to 'repurpose' old hits like *Seinfeld* and *Roseanne*, a common use of niche cable channels. Unfortunately no-one had checked whether they held the broadcasting rights to do this. Unfortunately, they did not, so the Fox Family acquisition simply served to further expose the fact that ABC had acres of programming time with little new, or even old, content to fill it with (Stewart 2005, p.366).

The 2001–2 seasons, after the addition of ABC Family (as Fox Family was renamed), were disastrous, ratings and the advertising revenue contingent upon them fell alarmingly. On 7 January 2002 it was Stu Bloomberg's turn to face Eisner's wrath and be dismissed. Since Eisner and Robert Iger had personally dictated most of the terminal decisions in ABC's fate (the saturation deployment of *Millionaire*, the acquisition of Fox Family), Eisner was not on strong ground terminating Bloomberg's employment for 'just cause' and so Eisner agreed to a television programme production contract with equivalent value to the time remaining on Bloomberg's three-year executive employment contract. Bloomberg was replaced by Susan Lyne.

To stem the implosion at ABC Family, Iger brought in Angela Shapiro, a veteran of ABC Daytime. Having no driving ambition of her own Shapiro was able to drive a pretty good deal since she had no deep desire to take the job anyway. Once she had time to familiarize herself with what was happening at ABC Family she became even less keen. In particular Shapiro won the right to report directly to Iger (the Disney president) and Bornstein (head of ABC) rather than Anne Sweeney, the head of ABC's cable division. This meant Shapiro was head of a cable channel, ABC, but had no need to report to the head of the cable television division (Stewart 2005, p.389–91).

Once Shapiro got into her post it became clear that an obvious rebranding strategy was to focus programming and advertising on younger 18–34 aspirant women as a core advertising demographic. Advertisers like this group because they are often key decision makers regarding household disposable income. Anne Sweeney, as head of the cable division, blocked this move pointing out affiliate television stations that syndicated ABC Family's programming had the right to revoke, or renegotiate, their contracts for provision if the family orientation of the provision changed. Shapiro's aim to gain autonomy from Sweeney was stymied (Stewart 2005, pp.396–8).

Even if Shapiro's turn-around strategy was in utter turmoil, the pressure to produce results to pacify now-jumpy investors was intense. Stewart (2005, p.394) reports the following exchange in May 2002 during a presentation of financial results by division heads to Eisner and Iger in preparation for reporting June 2002 second quarter earnings:

> Shapiro: Michael, the finance people will take you through the numbers, but you should know they are incredibly aggressive.
>
> Eisner: Angela, I need you to look at me. Either you are totally exaggerating, and these numbers are not aggressive, or you're saying that we really overpaid for this channel.

Shapiro: I had nothing to do with the purchase of the channel. I can't speak to the reasoning or the purchase price. All I can tell you is that these numbers are more than incredibly aggressive.

Since Eisner had personally agreed the price, to the horror of Iger and Bornstein, the implication was obvious. Eisner walked out of the meeting in frustration.

Ultimately the huge cost of this negotiating error was revealed when ABC's CFO Tom Staggs launched an internal investigation to calculate the net present value of ABC Family in case overpayment brought entitlement to a tax write-off under US IRS rules. An external valuation consultant calculated the true value of ABC Family to be $1.378 billion, rather than the over $3.2 billion paid. While the acquisition had brought other assets and programming rights, this implied Eisner had overpaid for Fox Family by about $1.4 billion, a pretty major error.

Go.com and Threat from the Internet and Cable

As a new millennium dawned the whole future of traditional media was placed in doubt by the rise of Internet service portals like Yahoo! and AOL. In mid-December 1999 Gerry Levin, CEO of Time Warner, invited Eisner to a meal where he suggested a defensive merger of Disney and Time Warner as protection against being consumed by one of the big Internet portals. This made sense since AOL announced a $165 millennium 'merger' (read takeover) of Time Warner in the first days of 2000. From this point Eisner became obsessed with the threat from the 'new' media of the Internet. As a protective strategy Eisner grouped Disney's Internet assets under a company entitled Go.com. He brought in Steve Bornstein from ESPN to run it and when he arrived he found something of a shambles, which he suggested to Eisner might need to be closed down. Nevertheless he reluctantly took the job on regarding it as somewhat of a suicide mission (Stewart 2005, p.338).

A suicide mission is what Go.com eventually proved to be. By February 2000 Bornstein convened a meeting of Disney executives and bluntly told them, 'We cannot compete and win in the Internet portal sector' (Stewart 2005, p. 357). Go.com was closed at a cost of over $1 billion with $790 million being written off in Disney's accounts for the year. Unusually for Disney, Bornstein did not go down with the ship, being transferred to try to turn round the traumatized ABC (he had come from the sports channel ESPN of course).

The threat of the AOL Time Warner juggernaut did contain a silver lining if it could be used to make tactical use of antitrust legislation given the dominant role AOL Time Warner now had in distributing Disney's content. To precipitate this outcome Robert Iger had ABC redraft its terms and conditions sheet for airing Disney programmes to include a requirement that these programmes be treated in the same way as Time Warner's own output. Time Warner estimated the costs of accepting this revised deal as $300 million and not surprisingly they baulked at it. The dispute went public and got quite nasty with Disney taking out full-page advertisements in newspapers to alert cable subscribers to the threat to their viewing of ABC programmes. So on Monday 24 May 2000 Time Warner put out the lights on ABC for a day. Political pressure from Washington on Time Warner eventually gave Disney the victory it sought (Stewart 2005, p.351) (to learn more about this read the AOL Time Warner case study in Chapter 7 of this book).

Eisner Tightens his Grip on Command

Following Ovitz's departure in 1996 Eisner had his status confirmed by the board by a new 10-year contract confirming his $750,000 a year salary but now granting a staggering eight million share options on Disney stock. The compensation consultant valuing the contract suggested a value of $771 million for this package, although this was later revised downwards by Disney to be $195 million in its published accounts. This was the best deal ever given to a chief executive of a public corporation then known (Stewart 2005, p.278).

The generosity of this settlement is perhaps less surprising when one is aware that Eisner's personal attorney, Irwin Russell, was both on the board and chaired the Compensation Committee. Russell simply relinquished the chair to Ray Watson when Eisner's pay was considered. Other board members included the principal (Reveta Bowers) of a private school in West Hollywood, which Eisner's child attended, and the architect (Robert Stern) that Eisner had chosen to build his own home and completed a number of the projects in theme parks (Stewart 2005, p.279). Not that Eisner really needed to massage the board anyway, as the second biggest shareholder after Sid Bass and the Bass family, Eisner had enough voting stock to remove those whom he perceived as awkward.

Early Signs of Eisner's Downfall

Around the time of the Fox Family acquisition in the summer of 2000 two board members, Roy Disney and Stanley Gold, were becoming increasingly concerned about the financial performance of Disney Corporation. While at a company level Disney remained profitable, since 1995 on most standard, ratio-based, metrics of performance (return on equity or assets) it had been heading relentlessly downwards.

Bizarrely at this point when ABC's fortunes looked most precarious, Eisner wrote a new $9 million three-year contract for Stu Bloomberg, chairman at ABC. Both Stanley Gold and Roy Disney protested, but it was awarded anyway. This sowed the seeds of doubts regarding Eisner's judgement that preceded his fall.

Something needed to be done if the illusion of Disney as a growth (as opposed to an income) stock was to be maintained. At around this time Eisner organized a retreat for executives in 'Team Disney'. An outside consultant who was brought in to conduct in-depth interviews with the attending executives concluded, 'my research concludes you guys are not a good team. You're not a team at all. You're not even a group'. On being quizzed about this feedback one participant responded,

> What Michael likes is to put six pit bulls together and see which five die

> (Stewart 2001, p.367).

By 2001 this strategy of divide and rule had left Disney fractious and weak and the harsh reality of post-9/11 America was to cruelly expose this weakness.

Disney, as an American cultural icon, saw itself now directly under threat from Al-Qaeda inspired terrorism. The discovery by Spanish detectives of videos of the Golden Gate Bridge, Universal Studios and Disneyland in an Al-Qaeda cell's apartment caused panic to set in. The fact that the Arabic commentary suggested these were normal light-hearted tourist fare was not sufficient to recover the situation. The immediate threat was perceived to be to the parks where cancellations spiked and bookings fell precipitously. The reflex action drop on the stock market in the days following the attacks hit Disney hard too. Disney shares fell from a value of $23 per share on the morning of the attacks to $17 on Thursday of the following week.

A major consequence of this from Eisner's perspective was that sudden margin calls on the Bass family's holdings forced Sid Bass and his siblings to substantially liquidate their position. Since they held much of their position via only partially paid for stocks (held 'on margin' in stock-market jargon), the sudden price drop forced them to show cash to cover their investment. Although the Bass family had never taken a seat on the board they had given unwavering support to Eisner throughout his years at Disney. The combination of the Bass family's stake and his own substantial shareholding largely liberated Eisner from too many tedious constraints from the board, but the Bass family had noticed the deterioration in financial performance highlighted by Roy Disney and Stanley Gold. So the 9/11 margin calls may not have been an entirely unwelcome opportunity to unload the Disney holding without too much embarrassment (Stewart 2005, pp.372–6). To add to Eisner's woes the proceeds of $1 billion of marketable debt, originally issued to fund the Fox Family acquisition, ended up being diverted into panic buying of Disney's stock in a declining market.

Eisner's Fall

As Disney's financial performance floundered the particular coalition of corporate players that had maintained Eisner's control began to unravel. One irksome problem for Eisner was the impending expiry of the production contract with Steve Jobs's Pixar for computer-generated animation projects. Called before a Senate Committee to give evidence concerning video/DVD piracy and circumvention of intellectual property rights in films and music he lashed out in an unusual display of public emotion:

> There are computer companies – computer companies, that their ads...full page ads, billboards up and down San Francisco and L.A., that say – what do they say? 'Rip, Mix, Burn' . . . In other words they can create a theft and distribute it to all their friends if they buy this particular computer

(Stewart 2005, p.383)[5].

This was a clear reference to Steve Jobs's Apple and their recent statewide adverts for the iMac computer. Eventually the existing concerns of Stanley Gold and Roy Disney found common cause with Steve Jobs, whose initial irritation at Eisner's opposition to doing *Toy Story* had been intensified into rage by his statement to the Senate. A coalition to unseat Eisner had started to emerge.

Once again Euro Disney (now renamed Disneyland Paris) would play a key role in Eisner's fate within Disney. On 16 March 2002, the $533 million 'second gate' of the park was at last opened. The idea behind this new attraction was to attract visitors to extend their stay at the park hotels which had always been a problem at Euro Disney. Eisner attended the opening as did the whole board of directors. One recently appointed director, Andrea van de Kamp, told Robert Iger of her doubts about the wisdom and efficacy of the improvements given their objective. On hearing her objection Eisner insulted her and questioned her loyalty. News on this storm in a teacup spread and soon board members were gossiping about Eisner's ability to take the pressure and successfully turn the company around. When June's second quarter results slowed further slippage on financial targets, Stanley Gold's concern and expression of it grew.

All Fall Down

Concurrent to the steady stream of accounting and corporate scandals, Tyco International, Enron, WorldCom produced the reactionary Sarbanes–Oxley (often shorted to 'Sarbox') Act in their wake. While Disney emerged with its integrity intact from this period it still had to show itself Sarbox-compliant just like everyone else. When internal lawyers began this process they concluded Stanley Gold could no longer formally be regarded as an 'independent' executive since his daughter held a $50,000 per-year job as an advertising representative within Disney. Eisner had the ammunition he needed to crush emergent opposition and promptly asked Gold to resign from the board entirely or at least step down from heading the Nominations Committee of the board. This opportunistic side-step badly backfired when Gold went into open opposition to Eisner by circulating e-mails and memos criticizing him around the board as a whole. An example of their content is given below:

> I have had fund managers tell me they won't buy a share of stock in a company where Michael Eisner is CEO. I have had employees (senior executives) tell me the company would be much better off with a new management team. Morale at the company is at an all-time low

> (Stewart 2005, p.407).

The Final Meltdown

On 23 September 2002 Stanley Gold presented the full scale of the problem. He told the board that since 1995 Disney had deployed an additional $24 billion in invested capital yet operating income had declined. The compounded annual return on Disney stock since 1995 had been 1.9%, lower than the return on treasury bills. Eisner had failed to meet his financial projection every year for the past five years, falling short by 23% in year one, 33% in year two, 47% in year three and 55% in the fourth year. Further, what profitability there was, was solely contingent on the continuing deal with Pixar and more recent hits like *A Bug's Life* and *Finding Nemo*, but Eisner's continuing presence completely undermined any chance of that collaboration continuing. Eisner was shocked and asked the board for a vote of confidence in him. None was given and he was left to limp onwards.

Eisner was finally removed from his position as chairman of Disney as a result of 43% of shareholders withholding their endorsement of his position on the board in an Annual General shareholders meeting on 3 March 2004. He stayed on as CEO for one more year. This unprecedented vote of no confidence resulted from all three of the major 'proxy' shareholder institutions (that hold mandates to vote on behalf of passive shareholders: these are Institutional Shareholders Services (ISS), Glass, Lewis, and the California state pension fund CalPERS). However, Eisner's ouster was supported by the Fidelity investment fund and an array of smaller state pension funds including those in Florida and New York (Stewart 2005, pp.508–14). This last push was partially the result of an Internet-based petition campaign against Eisner called 'Save Disney' organized by Roy Disney and Stanley Gold. Eisner was to be the victim of the impact of the 'new media', but perhaps not in the fashion he expected.

Questions

1. Reflecting on the Disney case study what sort of agency problems do you observe to be present and how well were they dealt with?
2. How well were teams formed at Disney? Did the various teams formed interact for the benefit of shareholders, or to their detriment?
3. I chose Disney to illustrate the issues discussed in this chapter. If you had to make a choice, which company would you choose and why?

Notes

1. Blair, M. and L. Stout (1999). The quote is from page 251. Reproduced by permission.
2. Cox, J. and H. Munsinger (1985). The quote is from page 85. Reproduced by permission of the authors.

3. Zajac, E. and M. Bazerman (1991). The quote is from page 51. Reproduced by permission of the Copyright Clearance Center.
4. Jensen, M. (1993). Quote is from page 850. Reproduced by permission of Michael Jensen and Blackwell Publishing.
5. Stewart, James B (2005). All quotes reproduced by permission of Simon & Schuster UK.

References

Alchain, A. & H. Demsetz (1972). Production, information costs and economic organization. *American Economic Review*, **62**: 777–95.

Baskin, J. & P. Miranti (1999). *A History of Corporate Finance.* Cambridge: Cambridge University Press.

Bazerman, M. (2006). *Judgment in Managerial Decision-Making.* New York: John Wiley & Sons, Inc.

Bebchuk, L. & J. Fried (2004). *Pay Without Performance: The Unfulfilled Promise of Executive Compensation.* Cambridge, MA: Harvard University Press.

Blair, M. & L. Stout (1999). A team production theory of corporate law. *Virginia Law Review*, **85**: 247–328.

Blair, M. & S. Wallan (2001). *Unseen Wealth: Report of the Brooking Task Force on Intangibles.* Washington, DC: Brookings Institution Press.

Bushman, R. & A. Smith (2001). Financial accounting information and corporate governance. *Journal of Accounting and Economics*, **32**: 237–333.

Camerer, C. & U. Malmendier (eds) (2007). *Behavioral Economics of Organizations.* Princeton, NJ: Princeton University Press.

Chandler, A. (1977). *The Visible Hand: The Managerial Revolution in American Business.* Cambridge, MA: The Belknap Press.

Coleman, D. (1973). Gentleman and players. *Economic History Review*, **26**: 92–116.

Cox, J. & H. Munsinger (1985). Bias in the boardroom: psychological foundation and legal implications of corporate cohesion. *Law and Contemporary Problems*, **48**: 83–135.

Easterbrook, F. & D. Fischel (1985). Limited liability and the corporation. *University of Chicago Law Review*, **52**: 87–117.

Eisner, M. & T. Schwartz (1999). *Work in Progress: Risking Failure, Surviving Success.* New York: Hyperion.

Forbes, D. & F. Milliken (1999). Cognition and corporate governance: understanding boards of directors as strategic decision-making groups. *Academy Review of Management*, **24**: 489–505.

Forbes, K. (1986). Limited liability and the development of the business corporation. *Journal of Law, Economics and Organization*, **2**: 163–77.

FRC-LSE (2003). *The Combined Code on Corporate Governance.* London: Financial Reporting Council and London Stock Exchange.

Gabler, N. (2006). *Walt Disney: The Triumph of American Imagination.* New York: Vintage.

Higgs, D. (2003). *Report on the Role and Effectiveness of Non-Executive Directors and Audit Committees.* London: HMSO.

ICAEW (1999). *Internal Control – Guidance for Directors on the Combined Code (Turnbull Report).* London: Institute of Chartered Accountants of England and Wales.

Jensen, M. (1993). The modern industrial revolution, Exit, and the failure of internal control systems. *Journal of Finance*, July: 831–80.

Jensen, M. & W. Meckling (1976). Theory of the firm: managerial behaviour, agency costs and ownership structure. *Journal of Financial Economics*, **3**: 305–60.

Langevoort, D. (ed.) (2000). *Organized Illusions: A Behavioural Theory of Why Corporations Mislead Stock Market Investors (And Other Social Harms)*. Cambridge: Cambridge University Press.

Masters, K. (2001). *The Keys to the Magic Kingdom: The Rise of Michael Eisner and the Fall of Everybody Else*. New York: HarperBusiness.

Micklethwait, J. & A. Woolridge (2003). *The Company: A Short History of a Revolutionary Idea*. London: Random House.

Milgrom, P. & J. Roberts (1992). *Economics, Organization and Management*. Englewood Cliffs, NJ: Prentice-Hall.

O'Byrne, S. (1992). What pay for performance looks like: the case of Michael Eisner. *Journal of Applied Corporate Finance*, **5**: 135–6.

Roberts, J. (2004). *The Modern Firm: Organizational Design for Performance and Growth*. Oxford: Oxford University Press.

Stewart, J. (2005). *DisneyWar: The Battle for the Magic Kingdom*. London: Simon and Schuster.

Swisher, K. (1998). *aol.com. How Steve Case Beat Bill Gates, Nailed the Netheads and Made Millions in the War for the Web*. New York: Random House.

Zajac, E. & M. Bazerman (1991). Blind spots and competitor analysis: implications of interfirm (mis)perceptions for strategic decisions. *Academy of Management Review*, **16**: 37–56.

Zingales, L. (2000). In search of new foundations. *Journal of Finance*, **55**: 1623–53.

Chapter 15

The Market for Information, Noise and Deception

To understand the psychology of markets one needs to understand some of the central players in their drama. As stated in the introduction to this text, a striking feature of neoclassical finance is the degree to which it has been depopulated of agents capable of forming relationships and building understanding of the corporation. This chapter introduces the role of stock-market analysts, fund managers and the chief financial officers who provide investors with information. The chapter portrays their interaction within a 'market for information' which ties their objectives, payoffs and plans together. It describes some of what we know about how this trinity of market agents interact and gives an indication regarding how we might model that interaction. An attraction of this literature for the current author is the dominance of UK researchers in the field, who have thus far shown far more interest in and ambition for the use of case-history, field-based studies than the dominant community of North American finance scholars. Such studies directly ask financial market participants how they make investment and financing decisions rather than simply inferring their motivations from observed market reactions.

While numerous 'event studies' testify to the stock market's ability to impound information about earnings, dividends, mergers, management turnover, etc., into share prices, some uncomfortable gaps in our understanding remain. We know information gets into share price values but are not clear how this happens. Richard Barker (1998) points out that the efficient market hypothesis sheds little light on:

1. What information is brought to the market, i.e. what is deemed the 'value-relevant' information set.
2. How that information actually gets into price.

Sat atop the stock market there lies a market for information relevant to pricing assets. This market is far more intimate, personalized and at times antagonistic than the structured theoretical models that characterize most of finance, including much of behavioural finance theory discussed in this book.

The emergence of a private market for voluntary disclosure by corporations can be seen as analogous to that motivating the emergence of the firm itself. The firm is often seen as the transaction cost minimizing solution to the need to engage numerous factors of production in the cooperative enterprise of production for mutual profit (Coase 1937). In the same way, the relative costs and benefits of private versus public disclosure channels drive much disclosure into a set of implicit relational contracts formed between analysts, fund managers and company managers which constitute the 'market for information' concerning future company performance. These relationships are further mediated by the state and appropriate legislation. This reflects the state interest in building and maintaining the integrity of financial markets. Company management for their part have little desire to explicitly discuss the details of research and development, senior management succession, etc. in public. To publicly reveal such information may hand a competitive edge to a rival firm. Similarly, few analysts or fund managers care to explore their most carefully researched and incisive lines of questioning in public. Further, in step with the market for financial information, there operates a market for managerial talent capable of running a FTSE100 (or S&P500) corporation. This gives senior company management a personal incentive to devise a credible corporate strategy of disclosure.

15.1   Illustration and Structure

On 29 July 1993 a large Swedish investment bank decided to sell out its rather large stake in Ericsson. It began doing so on 3 August and carried on selling until 28 October that year. We know this because Niclas Hellman recorded the trade and the reasons giving for making it in a study of 'Alfa', a large Swedish investment bank (Hellman 1996). The reasons given for the trade were more rumour than hard fact. There was nothing you could put in a spreadsheet exactly. Hellman records the reason advanced by one analyst involved in the decision:

> I became suspicious of the profit margins on some of the foreign deals Ericsson make. By coincidence I heard about it on an occasion, but it was not so precise you could call it information. Let's just say I drew a conclusion from a situation I got into

(Hellman 1996, p.674).

It seems there is more to trading than spreadsheets and algorithms. In this chapter I set out to explore some of the broader context in which trading takes place. Section 15.2 introduces the idea of a market for corporate information, what can be discussed by managers, when and in what forum. Section 15.3 focuses on one key player in such discussions – financial analysts, what they strive to do and their methods for achieving those aims. Section 15.4 discusses the valuation process, given the somewhat complex and intimate social nexus that creates it and can cause it to unravel. Section 15.5 concludes the chapter.

After reading this chapter the reader should:

- Understand the intimate and febrile market for information in which corporate disclosures, outside those in public filings (10ks, press releases, etc.), occur and its role in valuing the corporation.
- Know what analysts try to do and the variant valuation models they use.
- Understand how valuations models evolve and change and the resulting volatility in investor perceptions of corporate value.

15.2   The Boundaries of the Market for Corporate Information

Boundaries for the release of public information are set by compliance with stock-market listing requirements and the prevailing financial accounting standards. In the United Kingdom, listing rules on price-sensitive information[1] and in the United States, SEC Regulation Fair Disclosure require complete public disclosure of information likely to induce immediate material price movements. At the other extreme there is certainly information the board of directors may not wish anyone to know, for example specific acquisition plans, or terminations of senior executives' employment. Between these boundaries the private voluntary disclosure occurs. This is because:

> The transaction costs of exchange in the private relationship were lower than the market and this network mechanism replaced the market mechanism for producing and exchanging this type of information. This is a classic case of market failure and its replacement by a hierarchy or network
>
> (Holland 1998, p.40)*.

Within these close-knit hierarchies the role of price-based arbitrage, as a way to limit deviations from market efficiency, is more remote. In this setting the possibility of a significant and lasting impact for 'noise' or fashion is far more likely.

A central insight of research on the 'market for information' is how compact, personal and relationship-based the contacts between company management and financial markets are. Company management sees the core fund-manager contacts as a 'broadcast system' to mediate between the company and the wider market (Holland 1998, p.43). As such, relations with the core fund-manager group are seen as central to the formation of market sentiment towards the firm. Given the growing concentration of total market capitalization in the hands of no more than 100 financial institutions (on both sides of the Atlantic), this implies that market sentiment and personal sentiment of 'key players' can be hard to separate. Holland (2006, p.104) reports that analysts target a group of 20–30 core fund managers and 10–15 influential analysts, whose views they regard as a 'rough proxy for wider market expectations and consensus'. It is amongst this fairly compact group that information in the market for financial analysis is traded.

Standard game-theoretic interpretations of disclosure policy suggest any natural tendency of with-holding information from the market is unwound by market forces. Consider the case of a qualitative disclosure such as gaining 'investor in people' status as a badge of good employment practice. Certainly any company awarded 'investor in people' status will put the plaque in its entrance hall, on its website, stationery etc. This leaves only those who have not achieved that status. So that the market does not think badly of them, better companies will tell the market how close they are to achieving 'investor in people' status, giving a target date for attaining that status, etc. Ultimately silent companies are seen as just lousy employers who can't make the grade. So market pressures tend to drive disclosure by all but companies with the worst news to tell.

This market pressure to disclose can be frustrated in three types of situation (Lundholm & Van Winkle 2006), when managers

- don't know;
- cannot tell, for competitive reasons; or
- simply don't care about the information that could be potentially disclosed.

In each of this cases the private market for corporate information is required to fulfil market needs.

15.2.1   The Conduct of the Market for Corporate Information

The market for corporate information allows the supply and demand for information about company prospects to interact to set each company's costs of capital. But a company's cost of capital and its decisions regarding voluntary disclosure should most probably be regarded as being simultaneously determined (see Walker 2006).

Much voluntary private disclosure, especially with established core fund managers, is in one-on-one meetings between fund managers and the chief executive and/or chairman of major corporations. These meetings are often fairly intense interactions. Holland (1998, pp.48–9)** quotes one source as follows:

> Essentially the institutions are using company meetings to hard ball the Chairman and see the whites of the eyes of the Chief Executive.... What they are really judging is their confidence in a small selection of top management, their ability to get strategy across to influence strategy and to get the returns.

In later work Holland (2001, p.511) quotes a fund manager as setting the private meeting agenda from the following perspective:

> This is really about us checking against our prior expectations of these matters and seeing there has been no radical change. So much of the information coming through is subjective about strategy, the coherence of strategy, about innovation, about the value of brands, all these intangibles. If they are credible managers then this improves our confidence in our own estimates of the future in terms of risk and return.

It is worth noting from these comments:

- The primacy of personal relationships with the senior management team, especially the CEO, in these meetings.
- The aversion fund managers have to unexpected changes in the direction in the path followed by managers. Fund managers dislike surprises or jolts to their understanding of the value-creation model.
- The qualitative/intangible focus of private discussion around publicly available more quantitative information regarding performance.

Barker (1998, p.17) concludes that:

> Fund managers' 'private' meetings with managers effectively circumvent the public-good information problem and they are of *central* importance to share price determination. These meetings ensure that fund managers are not just passive recipients of information, but there is a feedback and control loop whereby investee companies are held accountable (original italics)

Such findings make abundantly clear that a crucial element of information dissemination in financial markets is conducted via the establishment and maintenance of close personal contact. Barker (1998) found major funds would receive presentations from about a few hundred firms a year, with an additional number of one-off meetings with firms seeking to attract investment or in receipt of a takeover bid, etc. Within these confines core fund managers probe issues including senior management quality and succession plans, management's view of strategy, competition and innovation. Much theoretical and empirical modelling in standard finance sees transactions occurring through faceless 'classical' contracts. In such classical contracts anonymous parties meet on a level playing field to exchange offer and acceptance in return for some consideration never to meet again (Cootner & Ulen 2004). The standard textbook illustration of the classical contract is the purchase of a newspaper from a street vendor in a town you have visited but have no reason to return to.

As the prize for rising to the top of the market for information hierarchy the core fund management group may get access to abnormal trading profits via two possible routes:

1. by predicting future events as illuminated by better 'signposting' of public information in private one-on-one meetings;
2. by exploiting the perceived ignorance and prejudice of 'noise' traders whose sentiments have detached price from value (Holland 1998, p.59).

Contracting in financial markets is thus profoundly 'relational', requiring investment, calibration and readjustment to background change. To uncover this process requires skills of interview-based, case-study research, which few finance academics have comparative advantage in. But it is hard to understand what happens behind the closed door of these one-to-one meetings without asking those involved directly. So this chapter reviews research undertaken by a different research method on the same subject as much of the other parts of this text. The interaction of investors' representatives (analysts and fund managers) and company managers to determine price and allocate capital is studied here as personal and relationship-based rather than as the impersonal price–quantity driven exchange of standard economic theory. This offers a new perspective on issues that were previously discussed.

15.3   What Do Analysts Do?

Analysts communicate with investors through a variety of channels (Francis & Philbrick 1993), which include:

- a forecast of earnings-per-share;
- a resulting recommendation to buy, sell or hold the stock (if previously bought);
- some 'value-creation' story (Holland 2004) covering an individual firm, industry or regulatory regime. This may set the backdrop for the forecast revisions or investment recommendations. Indeed the commitment by fund managers to valuation on the basis of fundamentals may become subject to challenge.

Holland's (2004) longitudinal study of disclosure practices amongst 25 major UK companies revealed:

> The extent to which such company-side 'fundamental' information is used in company valuations was perceived by companies as contingent upon changing user decision needs.

Barker (1998, p.10) finds that analysts attach little importance to accurately predicting earnings in building their credibility with their audience, the fund managers. Rather they see their role as being to provide detailed analysis of a company's financial performance and strategy, via original research which leads to profitable trading recommendations. Within the group of 32 analysts he interviewed, Barker discerned two distinct camps which could be differentiated by their objectives:

- 'Advisors', which constitute the largest group, who see themselves as giving diffuse investment advice based on a detailed understanding of a particular company and the regulatory/competitive environment in which it exists.
- 'Recommenders', who focus on giving profitable trading tips for immediate use and accurate earnings forecasts.

In trying to interpret analysts' forecasts and recommendations fund managers face a number of problems (Holland 2001, p.507), including:

- Unless they get the information on a 'first call' basis, i.e. before their peers in the fund management industry, the price of the share would already impound the recommendation or forecast. This gave fund managers an incentive to keep on good terms with the brightest and best, or at least most influential, analysts.
- Sell-side analysts' marketing function gave them a distinct bias towards sensationalizing stories to drive trade and hence commissions for their house.
- Only lead analysts could determine price, with 'the pack' just chasing, or introducing noise to the market.
- Major, e.g. FTSE100, companies attracted much public interest and sector-wide research. Further, most had very active investor relations functions in house. Hence a lot of information was already in the public domain, via the financial press, interventions by regulatory agencies, etc. This meant analysts needed to make the 'value-added' of their research much more clear for these much-discussed firms.

Fund managers were seen to clearly favour advisors over recommenders. The illiquidity of the relatively large blocks of shares that major funds hold meant the short-term recommendation advice of analysts could simply lead to churning of the portfolio (Barker 1998, p.10). Fund managers had more use for company-specific investigation of various market plays and conditions, possible regulatory decisions, etc.

15.3.1 The Ivkovic and Jegadeesh (IJ) Model

Ivkovic and Jegadeesh (2004) model the stock-market impact of stock-market analysts' forecasts and recommendations in order to determine the nature of their informational advantage, be that as 'advisors' or 'recommenders'. They envisage the potential value of analysts' search for value as coming from two potential sources:

- They may be better at predicting public information. This would be the case if they made clever use of time-series models of earnings prediction or the implication of disclosures about goodwill write-offs and research and development for future value.
- They may be better at extracting private information of the company. This would be the case if analysts by judging the quality of the management, or technology development, could predict company performance and hence value.

Ivkovic and Jegadeesh (2004) incorporate these two potential sources of analysts' advantage into a simple theoretical framework and develop a metric which allows some measurement of the dominance of these competing sources of value. They explore this by examining the precise point in the earnings announcement cycle at which analysts' forecasts and recommendations have most influence upon market prices.

They envisage price as being decomposed into an element on which investors/analysts have perfect foresight, P^*, and a less predictable component, η. So

$$P_t = P_t^* + \eta_t$$

where P^* is the 'perfect forecast' price which would prevail if the complete trajectory of future earnings were known and η_t reflects a pricing error arising from uncertainty regarding future cash-flow.

The pricing error, η_t, is decomposed into two elements:

- An element reflecting true uncertainty about earnings (the sole value-metric in the IJ model), ε_t.
- An element reflecting non-earnings information, ν_t. This is interpreted as cash-flow by Ivkovic and Jegadeesh, but may perhaps be 'noise' introduced by those who trade on information other than earnings, e.g. 'intangible' aspects of value.

Hence

$$\eta_t = \varepsilon_t + \nu_t$$
$$\varepsilon_t \sim N(0, \sigma_\varepsilon^2(t))$$

where the part of pricing error with respect to fundamental value, here future earnings, declines over time as we approach the earnings announcement date. So the stock price is predicted to converge on the true price consistent with full knowledge of earnings, P^*, apart from a divergence produced by uncertainty about non-earnings related aspects of value (cash-flow or other 'noisy' elements of value).

Analysts enter the IJ model by issuing revisions of their forecasts of future earnings. These revisions contain a signal concerning price, θ. This signal about price also contains two elements:

- information about changes in earnings, ε_t;
- a 'noisy' element which may reflect bias, compromise or simply ineptitude on the analyst's part, φ. Whatever their motive the size of φ is not affected by the size of ε at any point in time.

So

$$\theta_t = \varepsilon_t + \varphi_t$$

Ivkovic and Jegadeesh further assume

$$\varphi_t \sim N(0, \sigma_\varphi^2(t))$$

This appears to rule out the possibility of noise traders 'creating their own space', at least by means of conjectures about earnings. The distribution of ν_t in the pricing equation is left unspecified, allowing a role for non-earnings-based valuation errors to generate noisy elements of value. By introducing noise traders the mean value of φ could now be non-zero (and in all likelihood positive). By gradually raising the mean level of φ, 'noise' is allowed to have a systematic and pervasive influence on asset returns.

Given the signal concerning value received by investors at time t, θ_t, investors infer value and so price. This results in a price movement which is contingent upon the information signal, which itself reflects expectations of future value.

$$\Delta P_t = (P_t^{new}|\theta_t) - P_t = \theta_t \left[1 \left/ \left(\frac{\left(1 + \sigma_\varphi^2(t)\right)}{\sigma_\varepsilon^2(t)} \right) \right. \right] \qquad (15.1)$$

where the ratio of signal variances $\frac{(1+\sigma_\varphi^2(t))}{\sigma_\varphi^2(t)}$ is called the analyst information ratio (AIR). Note that the expression for price change in Equation (15.1) above contains effectively the inverse of the AIR function $\frac{\sigma_\varphi^2}{\sigma_\varepsilon^2}$ in the expression in round brackets. As such the AIR is the Bayesian precision of the revision, with respect to earnings information, $\frac{1}{\sigma_\varepsilon^2}$, multiplied by the amount of 'noise' in valuation from non-earnings sources, $\sigma_\varphi^2 P$. Interpret $\frac{1}{\sigma_\varepsilon^2}$ as the Bayesian 'precision' of the signal about value implied from analysts' forecast revision. Now the role of σ_φ^2 is simply to mask the valuation signal conveyed by analysts' forecasts. Reductions in the AIR diminish the power of analysts' forecast revisions to induce movements in price.

To see this consider the case of a perfectly informative 'pure' signal about earnings where $\sigma_\varphi^2 = 0$. For this case

$$\Delta P_t = (P_t^{new}|\theta_t) - P_t = \theta_t \left[1 \Big/ \left(\frac{1}{\sigma_\varepsilon^2(t)} \right) \right]$$

Here increases in the variance of the signal of earnings simply serve to amplify the response of prices to analysts' revisions. This is because the information content of analysts' forecasts/recommendations regarding value is seen to be high, with no disruptive 'noise' being present. The price change conditional on the valuation signal, θ_t, becomes simply the inverse of Bayesian precision of that signal multiplied by the signal's value itself, θ_t. A rising $\frac{\sigma_\varepsilon^2(t)}{\sigma_\varphi^2(t)}$ AIR mutes price responses to the signal contained in the forecast or recommendation. So in this simple 'no noise' case very precise signals mute the signal's impact. With very diffuse signals, for which $\frac{1}{\sigma_\varepsilon^2}$ is small, the impact of the signal is greatly amplified, or 'noisy', in terms of price response. For example, when $\sigma_\varepsilon^2 = \sigma_\varphi^2$ then the noisy price signal is halved compared to when there is no noise present at all. Re-introducing σ_φ^2 now simply serves to dull the impact of analysts' forecast revisions since they can no longer be seen as unambiguous signals regarding stock value.

Examining the temporal distribution of analysts' ability to predict and so to move security prices Ivkovic and Jegadeesh find it to be greatest just before quarterly earnings announcements (in the United States) and least just after them. This implies analysts' contacts with management to gain insight into and even hints concerning future earnings are vital to their ability to satisfy their clientele with valuable advice.

In the IJ model the average value of 'noise' in each trading period must be zero. So 'noise' traders' trades must cancel out in their net effect on price. If noise traders were to 'create their own space' as suggested in Chapter 6 of this text then the result of the IJ model may be very different.

A simple numerical example of the IJ model in action

To illustrate the practical workings of the IJ model I consider the case of a share subject to two different types of shocks to value in each period. These are shocks in value from earnings, ε, and some other 'noisy' information about the share-price value not based on earnings, φ. Following Ivkovic and Jegadeesh we assume both types of news follow the normal distribution. In our example the variance of ε, σ_ε^2, is held constant at 0.125. I consider the effect of increasing the dispersion of the non-earnings news component, σ_φ^2 by 0.01, starting from a value 0.102. In the example we assume mean values of both ε and φ to be 0.05. This implies $\theta = 0.1 = 0.05 + 0.05$. So substituting into the equation

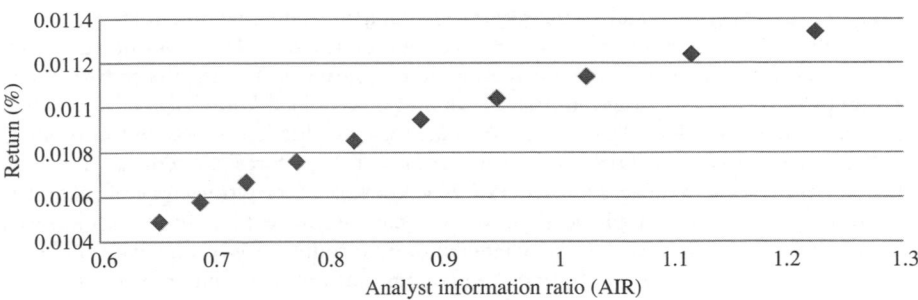

Figure 15.1   Share price return (%) as a function of the AIR

$$\Delta P_t = (P_t^{new}|\theta_t) - P_t = \theta_t \left[1 \Big/ \left(\frac{\left(1 + \sigma_\varphi^2(t)\right)}{\sigma_\varepsilon^2(t)} \right) \right] = 0.1 \left[1 \Big/ \left(\frac{(1 + 0.102)}{0.125} \right) \right]$$

$$= 0.1 \left[1 \Big/ 8.816 \right] = 0.1 \times 0.113 = 0.0113$$

Now for the same illustrative values the AIR is $\frac{\sigma_\varepsilon^2}{\sigma_\varphi^2} = 0.125/0.102 = 1.125$. Plotting each value successively, incrementing σ_φ^2 by 0.01 each time yields Figure 15.1. Increasing the analyst information ratio (i.e. the informativeness of revisions about prices) raises the price response to analysts' forecast revisions (and recommendations). Or alternatively the impact of earnings-relevant 'noise' in forecasts or recommendations is to dull the market's response to analysts' advice since the AIR is simply the inverse of the bracketed term in the calculation of share price changes given by Equation (15.1). So for the first increment we have a decrement in the AIR of 1.122 to 1.106 (as the variance of φ rises from 0.102 to 0.112) and a fall in return implied by Equation (15.1). The same increment in the variance of φ pushes down the share price return from 0.1127 to 0.111 (or 0.1 × (1/8.96) following the same calculative method as above. Of course the IJ model specifies that both ε and φ are drawings from a normal distribution with mean zero, so these simple proportional relationships are likely to be obscured by random components in both processes. Beneath these stochastic elements the underlying tendency of 'noisy' forecasts/signals having a diminished market impact is likely to remain.

15.4   Valuing Investment Advice

The device of imbuing investors with perfect foresight of some accounting value-relevant outcomes, such as future earnings or dividends, to judge their efficacy in inferring true value has already appeared widely in empirical studies. Shiller (1981) looked at the variance of stock prices relative to that of future discounted dividend streams. Examining the profitability of forming hedge portfolios based on an assumed knowledge of future accounting-based value-metrics has already featured strongly in discussions of the usefulness of accounting information to investors.

Francis and Schipper (1999) studied the returns available to trading by investors assumed to have perfect foresight regarding future patterns of accounting information. They considered a number of alternative accounting outcome information sets including earnings changes, the sign or direction of future earnings changes, the change in cash-flows and a combined knowledge of the outcome of future earnings and book values. Their results indicate that such foreknowledge of future accounting value-metric outcomes earns between 17% and 66% of perfect-foresight returns. These perfect-foresight returns are those available to investors who know the future trajectory of price itself and trade accordingly, rather than simply accounting data that partially explain future price movements. This leaves over one-third of price variance that cannot be accounted for by any discernible accounting metric. Francis and Schipper (1999) find the earnings part of accounting information's explanatory power has declined relative to that of book value reported on the balance sheet.

The sharp decline in the 'value-relevance' of accounting value-metrics in the last 20 years has been located by Lev and Zarowin (1999) in the sheer scale of business change and the sharp rise in 'intangible' assets (and liabilities) as a proportion of total value. The 'matching' principle which underpins conventional accrual accounting is decidedly ill-suited to reflect value generation in periods of great economic turmoil. While the costs of lay-offs, plant and equipment write-offs and terminated contracts tend to be expensive, the resulting benefits, manifest in higher productivity, product innovations, etc., from corporate restructuring only appear much later.

15.4.1 The Market for Corporate Information

Lying on top of the equity market is an active market for information regarding the 'fundamental' value of securities trading in it. This market seeks to ensure prices remain a sufficient statistic regarding the value of future cash-flows deriving from holding assets. Figure 15.2 (Figure 1, Barker 1998, p.5) gives a diagrammatic exposition of how this market functions and the purpose it serves.

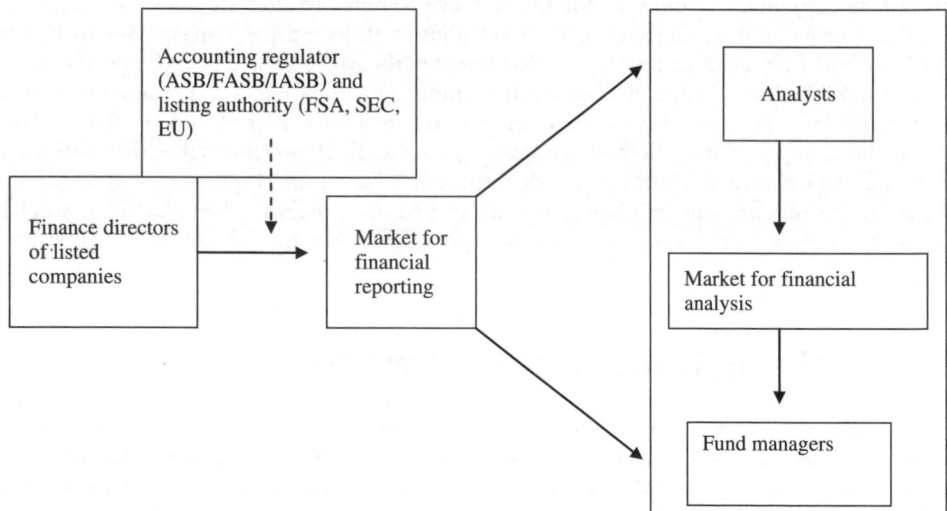

Figure 15.2   The market for information

Source: Figure 1 in Barker, R. (1998). The market for information: evidence from finance directors, analysts and fund managers. *Accounting and Business Research*, **29**(Winter): 3–21. © Wolters Kluwer (UK) Ltd. Reproduced by permission.

Beginning in the left-hand tableaux financial directors, as the drivers of voluntary disclosure by firms, prepare financial reports which form the basis of intense private discussion by analysts and fund managers in an enclosed market for financial analysis of published reports. Overseeing and structuring the preparation of published accounts is the accounting regulatory body (the Accounting Standard Board in the United Kingdom, Financial Accounting Standard Board in the United States, or International Accounting Standard Board more generally) who together with the relevant listing authority (Financial Services Authority in the United Kingdom or Security and Exchange Commission in the United States) dictate the structure and nature of public disclosure. The market for financial analysis/corporate information has no such overseer, however. It is this level of private voluntary disclosure within the market for financial analysis that we discuss below.

Holland (2004) in a study of 25 major UK listed companies undertaken at the height of the dot.com bubble observes a typology of value-creation processes within his sample. Strikingly he observes the extent to which the knowledge economy has moved to the centre stage in fund managers' evaluation of corporate management teams. Holland (2004, p.39) comments that:

> Fund managers view knowledge as *the* critical component in competitive advantage (original italics).

Interrogation of the value-creation processes within corporations is grouped into three complimentary categories:

- *Hierarchical processes*: including board structure, executive pay and its link to share price performance, the quality and coherence of corporate strategy. The senior management team, to which fund managers have regular access, is held personally accountable for these issues.
- *Horizontal processes*: including the transformation of inputs into outputs; these include new product development, 'blue-sky' research with longer-term goals, supply chain management and regulatory compliance. These are largely seen as the concern of middle managers and employees over whom the senior management team have oversight.
- *Network processes*: including the formation of alliances, joint ventures and effective industry lobbying and industry-wide union negotiations. Implementation of these issues, while often diffusing outside the firm, still requires management by the senior management team.

This typology is shown diagrammatically in Figure 15.3, which is a condensed version of a diagram presented in Holland (2004). Holland (2006), in a follow-up study to his earlier work, outlines two types of information suggested by these three types of process:

1. Those suggested by a hierarchical view of process: these include information regarding value creation from current operations, the ability of the board to generate cash-flows, how the board can maintain and build confidence in the company's value-creation processes by more effective use of corporate disclosure.
2. Information pertaining to horizontal and network value-creation processes: these include information regarding both current trading and how strategic options (investment or acquisitions) are being managed to produce growth both in the short, medium and long term, also the record of cash generation recently generated by the exercise of strategic options.

These disparate aspects of value can be interpreted as a reconfigured version of the adjusted present value valuation framework where growth in cash-flows beyond the forecast horizon is used as a sort of 'fudge factor' on standard cash-flow projections (Holland 2006, p.72). The

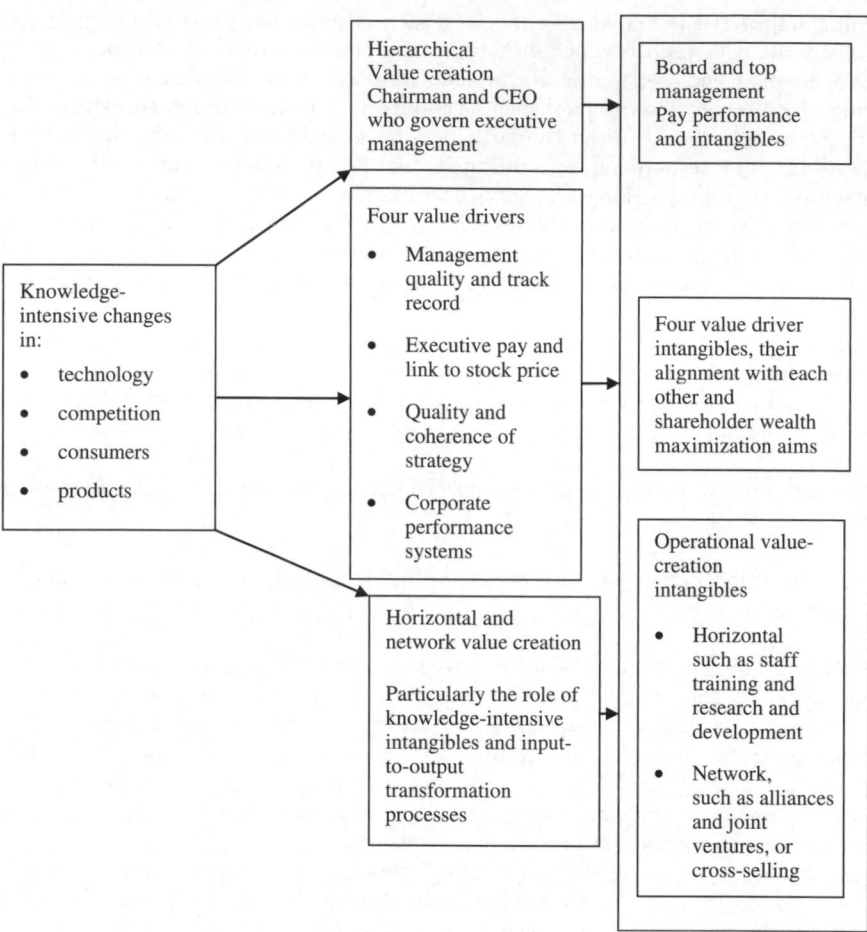

Figure 15.3 The company value creation as a continuous option creation, exercise, use and abandonment process

Source: Diagram 4 in Holland, J. (2006). *A Model of Corporate Financial Communications*. Edinburgh: Institute of Chartered Accountants of Scotland, p.54. Reproduced with permission.

reconfigured adjusted present-value valuation model that emerges from this perspective is portrayed in Figure 15.4. The tableau constructs firm value as the cumulative value from exercising current and future options, including those to abandon past activities. This value-creation process can be used to fund the creation of new options/capabilities which constitute the growth opportunities of the firm.

15.4.2 *What Type of Valuation Models do Analysts Use?*

Before advancing investment advice analysts and fund managers typically interpret the company information/performance metrics through the lens of a valuation model. While a number of variants exist, three basic formulae seem to prevail (Penman 2004 gives a good coverage of these topics):

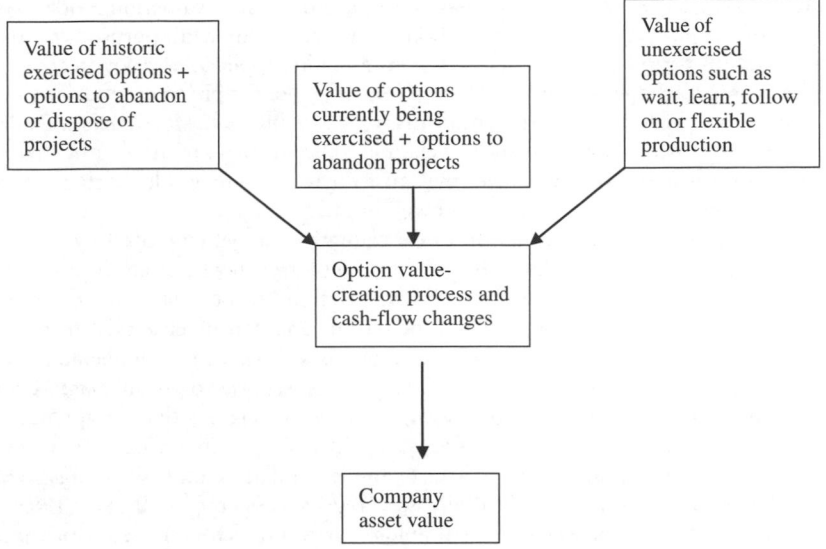

Figure 15.4 Supply side determinants of disclosure agenda

Source: Amended Figure 3.2, p. 42 Holland in (2004). Corporate Intangibles, Value Relevance and Disclosure Content. I.o.C.A.o.Scotland. Edinburgh, Scotland, Institute of Chartered Accountants of Scotland.

- the price–earnings ratio;
- the discounted cash flow (DCF) model of standard finance which calculates value as

$$V = C_0 + \frac{(C_1 - I_1)}{(1+r)} + \ldots + \frac{(C_{T-1} - I_{T-1})}{(1+r)^{T-1}} + \frac{\frac{(C_T - I_T)}{r}}{(1+r)^T}$$

where V is implied value, C is cash, I is investment and r is the market rate of interest. Here the last term, or terminal value, captures cash-flows into a distant future, which is not explicitly the subject of the forecasting process;

- the residual income valuation (RIV) model, which calculates value as

$$V = B_0 + \frac{(E_1 - rB_0)}{(1+r)} + \ldots + \frac{(E_{T-1} - rB_{T-2})}{(1+r)^{T-1}} + \frac{(P_T - B_T)}{(1+r)^T}$$

where E is earnings, B is book value and P_T is an estimate of terminal price.

Demerikos *et al.* (2004) study the absolute and relative frequency of use of the three valuation models in 104 analysts' reports, issued by leading UK brokerage firms on 26 large UK listed firms. The authors chose their industries to observe the choice of valuation model in an intangible rich industry, pharmaceuticals, a 'basic' low technology industry, beverages and an intermediate case, electronics.

They report that use of price relatives, like the price–earnings ratio, is highest in the low-technology beverage industry, but prevalent overall in the economy (it was the dominant model in 55.5% of the reports). Analysts base their investment advice to clients on either the price–earnings ratio or some form of multi-period discounted cash-flow model. But even where a multi-period discounted cash-flow model is used it is not usually the primary basis for dispensing investment advice.

The Demerikos *et al.* study makes clear that analysts choose their valuation model based on the characteristics of the industry rather than having any agreed upon all-purpose 'correct' model. Earnings-based multi-period (RIV) models are seen as more applicable to low-technology, basic, industries like beverages than intangible rich companies like those in pharmaceuticals, however, even when such models are used they are rarely the primary motivating factor for a recommendation. This may be because of the perceived preference of the market audience for simple price comparatives, especially the price–earnings ratio. Whatever the cause the use of simple rules of thumb in valuation, such as the price–earnings ratio, seem alive and well in the market.

Barker (1999) studied industrial variation in the valuation model employed by analysts using a mixture of survey and statistical methods. Barker began by surveying 42 analysts in seven of the top nine brokerage houses. He divided his sample of responses into those from industries dominated by valuation by the price–earnings ratio (services, industrials and consumer goods) from those dominated by valuation using the dividend yield (financial and utilities). In a complementary statistical study Barker asks if the statistical dependence of the companies' price on the analysts' chosen value-metric vindicates their choice of valuation model. His results suggest that companies, where the dividend yield method is employed, display far greater price responsiveness to dividend (as opposed to earnings) changes. So in the utilities industry, for example, regulation makes earnings so predictable the equity can be priced as a bond with the dividend being a sort of coupon. Barker (1999) concludes that analysts' choice of valuation model is justifiable by firm and sector characteristics and reflects a strategic choice to maximize the profitability of the advice that analysts give to their clients.

15.4.3 *The Fragility of Valuation Models*

These separate strands of an overarching value-creation story are interpreted by Holland as an attempt to stylize a hugely complex decision-making problem by means of a simple, but hopefully reasonably reliable, set of heuristics.

> As the intellectual capital element in value-creation, and as value-creation became more invisible, then the story and track record became a more critical method for overcoming the information asymmetry between company insiders and the external market.... The increasing significance of the story and of benchmarks to bridge the information gap can be interpreted as responses to corporate value-creation complexity and to fund-manager cognitive limitations
>
> (Holland 2004, p.51).

The mental frames that are constructed to understand and predict the unfolding story of corporate value-creation can distort and disintegrate in times of sudden technological or regulatory change. Holland gives the example of the management of the UK's Railtrack, which seemed unable to focus on the corporate mission to provide a safe, reliable, railway service at reasonable cost during the privatization of the firm in the late 1990s. The implosion of Enron in the United States and GEC/Marconi in the United Kingdom, as they made the transition from a corporation based on tangible assets (natural gas for Enron, electrical goods for GEC/Marconi) to more ethereal intangibles (contract trading in gas, electricity, broadband width for Enron, broadband spectrum for GEC/Marconi), are more extreme examples of such failures. So the corporate disclosure level that prevails is itself a reflection of the business cycle as captured in the company's cost of capital. As illustrated above in discussing the IJ model, that cost of capital is itself a function on 'noise' which has little value relevance to the fundamental value of a stock.

One source of the instability of financial communication is the strong motivation of analysts to initiate trade amongst fund managers (Barker 1998, p.9). This causes them to focus on change, lack of clarity in the company's 'valuation story' and potential news entering the stock market. So no news is certainly bad news for analysts, or at least for their performance bonuses at the end of the year. In this world it is likely that some cause for trade can be uncovered with sufficient ingenuity.

The contraction of the mental frames used to interpret company information is reciprocated by analysts. Here Holland (2004, p.65) concludes

> There is a strong emphasis on the use of heuristics or 'rules of thumb' in valuation and the use of market-relevant methods of valuation.

We conclude that case-study evidence suggests the use of stylization, framing and straight bias is common in market valuations and especially so when accepted value-creation stories are in transition or under threat. This induces a fragility in the market for information that can induce an implosion in the company's stock price if its corporation value-creation story is seen to unravel or contain inconsistencies. This is particularly likely to happen if discussion with fund managers and analysts is allowed to fixate on a narrow subset of company information (Holland 2006, p.112).

The fragility of the corporate value-creation story is partly a result that is to some degree created in its retelling by company management to their eager audience of fund managers and analysts. Holland quotes an executive from a transport company in his sample thus,

> The basic weakness of the financial report is that it is a one-way view. . ... It is clearly best if the fund managers can spend one hour on their questions. They can ask much better questions. That is better for us and for them and we both learn from this dynamic interchange

> (Holland 2006, p.131).

So the value-creation story is malleable in the process of being contested, reformulated and retold. This simultaneity between the message and the aspirations of those who receive it also underpins much of the explosion of empirical interest in companies 'meeting or beating' the outstanding analysts' forecasts (Abarbanell & Lehavy 2003). Financial directors and chief financial officers were found to be very sensitive to movements in the share price in Barker's study of FTSE100 firms (Barker 1998, p.6). He confirms the fact that fund managers prefer there to be 'no surprises', especially in the announcement of headline earnings (Barker 1998, p.8).

The market for financial information dialogue has some of the distortions and possibilities for implosive dissimulation as Keynes's 'beautiful baby contest' where newspaper readers are asked to rank babies by their attractiveness. Of course in such a competition the winner is not the reader who gives a 'correct', or intrinsically truthful, ranking of the children's beauty. Rather the correct answer is given by the reader who correctly infers the ranking given by the average reader faced with exactly the same inference problem. So Holland states:

> The case companies knew they were guessing about what fund managers, analysts and traders were guessing was in the price

> (Holland 2005, p.260).

Such calculations are likely to produce very unstable outcomes indeed. This is all the more so given the relatively short time horizon used by analysts in evaluating returns on investment by companies

(Barker 1998, p.8). This telescoping of analysts' vision of value-creation is often blamed by managers on the inability of the management team to convey its strategic vision.

15.4.4   A Dynamic Model of the Market for Financial Information

Holland (2005) has advanced a dynamic model of the cumulative learning process which characterizes the market for financial information. This is represented in Figure 15.5 (a version of Figure 2 in Holland 2005). This captures the reflexive dialogue of the market for information from the prior understanding of company managers, often based on past interactions with analysts and fund managers, through to the resolution of that uncertainty in observed market outcomes.

Beginning at the left-hand side of Figure 15.4 we see that company management enter the post-earnings announcement period with priors about its outcome based on what they have learned and especially how they expect fund managers to pursue their increasingly dominant agenda of shareholder wealth maximization. To answer this company management rehearse their opening corporate value-creation story with its hierarchical, horizontal and network components, but they remain ready to reconfigure the story as it is contested and refined through interaction with its audience.

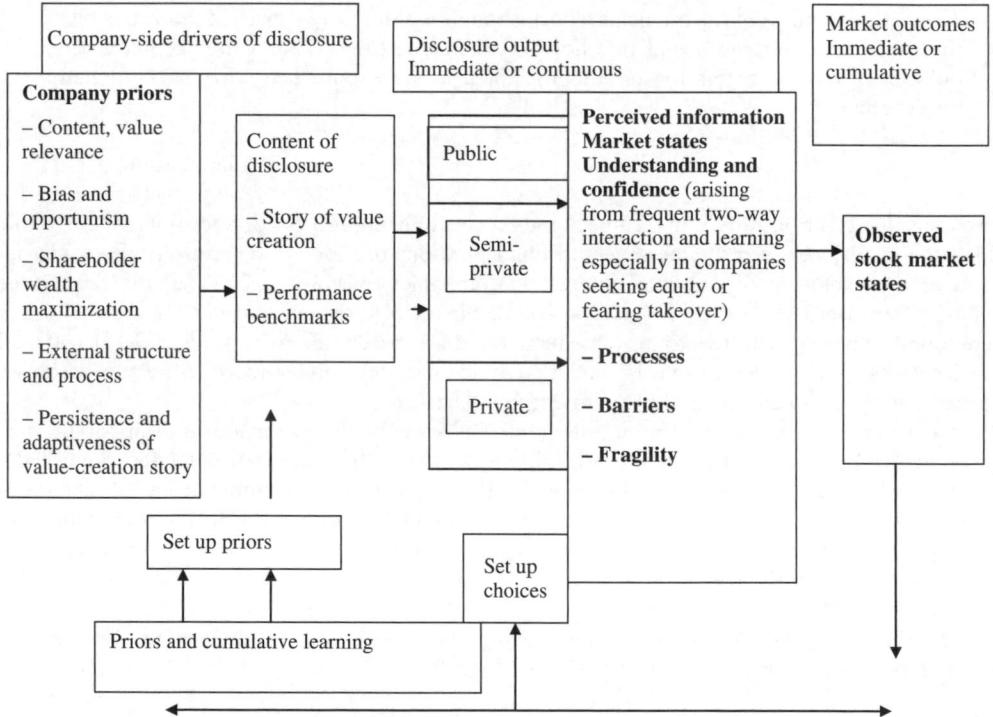

Figure 15.5   Dynamic processes and interactions in the market for corporate disclosure

Source: Figure 2 in Holland, J. (2005). A grounded theory of corporate disclosure. *Accounting and Business Research*, 35(3): 249–67. © Wolters Kluwer (UK) Ltd. Reproduced by permission.

The nature of the revised value-creation story suggests the appropriate avenue for disclosure of corporate information held by senior management in the company. This might be public if likely to cause immediate price movements; or remain secret if likely to undermine competitiveness or aid rivals. In revealing information company management seeks to maintain and increase the markets' understanding and confidence, especially amongst core fund managers and leading analysts.

Finally, the company observes price movements, investment allocations, and responds accordingly at the commencement of the next reporting cycle. In doing this company management needs to be sensitive to external factors changing the environment for value creation and so inducing fragility.

15.4.5   From Inside and Out: Isolation Bias and Risk Taking

A clear danger for both analysts and fund managers is that they swallow the hype presented to them by managers. Indeed some analysts at the height of the dot.com boom made a virtue of their close personal friendship with company management. In 1996 Jack Grubman of Salomon, a future star analyst in the US telecom industry, largely set up and negotiated a deal for Bernie Ebbers's WorldCom to acquire MFS Communications. Grubman later used this deal as a justification for touting WorldCom's stock to his clients. Even though this discrepancy was pointed out to the compliance office at Salomon nothing was done (Gasparino 2005, p.84). At Enron, key analysts were invited to the ski slopes to discuss strategy with chairman Ken Lay and chief operating officer Rich Kinder (McLean & Elkind 2003, p.92).

Even without complicity or duplicity on their part, analysts and fund managers may fail to take an 'outside view' (Kahneman & Lovallo 1993), which maintains a critical view of the problem. In particular they may fail to construct scenarios for failure to match the plan for success, outlined by the management team that they are supposed to be undertaking scrutiny of. Such bias is to some degree a natural byproduct of how we think about possible outcomes. The benefit of an outside view, which analysts are supposed to offer, is the aggregation of seemingly unique scenarios to allow the application of a more dispassionate risk assessment. This may explain one of analysts' more documented traits: the optimism of their forecasts. Management may see objective probabilities of failure as something to be triumphed over rather than accepted. In this view good managers transform history/ fate rather than meekly accepting it. If outside analysts uncritically accept this standpoint then their oversight role can be compromised.

15.5   Conclusion and Summary

Holland (2006, p.195) has noted the importance of case-study/field-based research for an understanding of the psychology of investing and its implications for financial markets. This chapter has tried to draw out some of these aspects of the field research of John Holland and others in order to understand how investment/asset-allocation decisions are made. One thing that this literature makes clear is the intensely personal and at times heated nature of relationships that produce these decisions. Fund managers, far from looking dispassionately at screens of data and plotting ratio distributions to construct portfolios, are drawn into a close, intense and reflexive ongoing dialogue with company management. Out of this emerges a value-creation story, which stylizes the company's business model. The constructions of these value-creation narratives, like other mental frames, may be subject to bias, if not intentional opportunism. The quantitative valuation models used by analysts in devising price targets and recommending purchase or sale allow for wide discretion in finessing the model. This draws judgement, especially regarding the quality of senior management, their strategy and its execution, to the core of investment management.

Questions

1. Return to Equation (15.1) – the IJ model expression for changes in prices. Plot the relationship between movements in the AIR and stock returns for values of $\theta = 1$, $\sigma_\varepsilon^2 = 0.25$ and $\sigma_\varphi^2 = 0.1, 0.11$ etc. to 0.75 in 0.01 increments. How do you interpret the graph you have drawn?
2. Return to Equation (15.1). Let's say analysts' forecasts/recommendations are optimistic, as well as noisy. You can denote this as a shift in θ from a value of 1 to 2. Redraw the figure in question 1 above for this case. Interpret the graph you have drawn.
3. This chapter stresses the intimacy of contact between senior managers, fund managers and analysts. Reflecting on your own knowledge of recent happenings in financial markets can you think of events when one key investor (Warren Buffett or Henry Kravis, for example) was a deal maker or breaker? Give some examples of such a role played by prominent individuals.

Notes

1. UK listing rules concerning price-sensitive information have been in place since 1994 but are currently in the process of revision in light of the need to provide a comparable level of protection to that offered by Regulation Fair Disclosure [FD] in the United States.
* Holland, J. (1998). Quote from p.40. Reproduced by permission of Blackwell Publishing.
** Holland, J. (1998). Quote from p.48–49. Reproduced by permission of Blackwell Publishing.

References

Abarbanell, J. & R. Lehavy (2003). Biased forecasts of earnings? The role of reported earnings in explaining apparent bias and over-/underreaction in analysts' earnings forecasts. *Journal of Accounting and Economics*, **36**: 105–46.

Barker, R. (1998). The market for information: evidence from finance directors, analysts and fund managers. *Accounting and Business Research*, **29**: 3–21.

Barker, R. (1999). Survey and market-based evidence of industry-dependence in analysts' preferences between the dividend yield and price earnings ratio valuation models. *Journal of Business, Finance and Accounting*, **26**: 393–418.

Coase, R. (1937). The nature of the firm. *Economica*, **4**(3): 386–405.

Cootner, R. & T. Ulen (2004). *Law and Economics*. Boston, MA: Addison-Wesley.

Demerikos, E., N. Strong *et al.* (2004). What valuation models do analysts use? *Accounting Horizons*, **18**: 221–40.

Francis, J. & D. Philbrick (1993). Analysts' decisions as products of a multi-task environment. *Journal of Accounting Research*, **31**: 216–30.

Francis, J. & K. Schipper (1999). Have financial statements lost their relevance? *Journal of Accounting Research*, **37**: 319–52.

Gasparino, C. (2005). *Blood on the Street*: *The Sensational Inside Story of How Wall Street Analysts Duped a Generation of Investors*. New York: Free Press.

Hellman, N. (1996). What causes investor action? *European Accounting Review*, **5**(4): 671–91.

Holland, J. (1998). Private voluntary disclosure, financial intermediation and market efficiency. *Journal of Business Finance and Accounting*, **25**: 29–68.

Holland, J. (2001). Financial institutions, intangibles and corporate governance. *Accounting, Auditing and Accountability*, **14**(4): 497–529.

Holland, J. (2004). *Corporate Intangibles, Value Relevance and Disclosure Content*. Edinburgh: Institute of Chartered Accountants of Scotland.

Holland, J. (2005). A grounded theory of corporate disclosure. *Accounting and Business Research*, 35(3): 249–67.

Holland, J. (2006). *A Model of Corporate Financial Communications*. Edinburgh: Institute of Chartered Accountants of Scotland.

Ivkovic, Z. & N. Jegadeesh (2004). The timing and value of forecast and recommendation revisions. *Journal of Financial Economics*, 73(3): 433–63.

Kahneman, D. & D. Lovallo (1993). Timid choices and bold forecasts: a cognitive perspective on risk-taking. *Management Science*, 39: 17–30.

Lev, B. & P. Zarowin (1999). The boundaries of financial reporting and how to extend them. *Journal of Accounting Research*, 37: 353–96.

Lundholm, R. & M. Van Winkle (2006). Motives for disclosure: a framework and review of the evidence. *Accounting and Business Research*, 36: 41–61.

McLean, B. & P. Elkind (2003). *The Smartest Guys in the Room: The Amazing Rise and Scandalous Fall of Enron*. New York: Penguin.

Penman, S. (2004). *Financial Statement Analysis and Security Valuation*. New York: McGraw-Hill.

Shiller, R. (1981). Do stock prices move too much to be justified by subsequent changes in dividends? *American Economic Review*, 71(3): 421–36.

Walker, M. (2006). How can business reporting be improved? *Accounting and Business Research*, 36: 95–105.

Chapter 16

Dividends

Why do companies worry about dividends or ever pay them? In the United Kingdom, under the system of advanced corporation, for many years tax investors were penalized by the 'double taxation of dividends' – yet many companies continued to pay dividends. Shefrin (2007, p.111) reports that 75% of the firms listed in the S&P500 pay dividends. As one of the perennial 'puzzles' of finance it might be hoped that a behavioural approach would help us understand why companies pay dividends when we have so many good reasons to think they need not bother (Miller 1986).

Foundational theoretical research in corporate finance proves that in a stylized form, no taxes, no transaction costs and perfect information, then dividends are deemed 'irrelevant' for firm value. Standard finance theory has reintroduced justifications for paying dividends based on the presence of taxes, asymmetric information, etc. Jensen (1986) argues that paying dividends forces managers to disgorge cash-flow, preventing them from empire building and leading to poor stewardship of the shareholder's money in general. In this chapter I consider one justification for dividend payments based on the 'prospect theory' of investment evaluation previously discussed in Chapters 2 and 8. Before doing so, I revisit the question of why dividend payments given to shareholders are a puzzle at all.

16.1   Illustration and Structure

As the giants of the new economy like Cisco and Microsoft have reached maturity they have become more like other companies. One part of this is the payment of dividends. Shefrin (2007, p.118) discusses the decision by Cisco not to bother initiating a dividend in late 2002. At the time Cisco was sitting on top of $21 billion in cash and generating about $4 billion a year from its operating activities. How to best blow the money? Cisco decided to repurchase $8 billion of its own stock. Why do this and not 'show them the money' by offering a dividend? In fact dividend yields fell in the United States for most of the 1990s, only recovering slightly recently. Why is this?

Section 16.2 revisits the standard model of dividend policy and its effect on value, i.e. none. Section 16.3 presents the most prominent behavioural explanation of how and why dividend payments might affect company value. Section 16.4 discusses some of the empirical evidence on patterns of dividend payment and their effect on company value and asks how much support this evidence gives to the behavioural approach. Section 16.5 summarizes and concludes the chapter.

After reading this chapter the reader should:

- Understand why dividend policy is usually thought to be irrelevant to valuing companies in standard finance and why this conclusion may have been wrongheaded.

- Understand how prospect theory can explain the importance that company management clearly does place on getting its dividend policy right even in frictionless, 'perfect' markets with no taxes, symmetric information, etc.
- Understand how dividend policy has changed in the last decade and how that change has affected corporate valuations.

16.2   The Irrelevance of Dividends to Value

To understand the argument for the irrelevance of the payment of dividends to company value I follow Modigliani and Miller (1961) by considering the determination of the equilibrium price of any share. As in all finance this is given by the discounted value of payoffs to holding a share. So price is given by the expression

$$p_t = \frac{1}{(1+r)}[d_t + p_{t+1} - p_t] \tag{16.1}$$

where d is the dividend paid and p is price. Just play along with the constant discount rate in this chapter. Denote by n_t the number in shares in issue before the dividend is paid and m_t the new number of shares after the dividend so letting $n_t + 1 = n_{t-1} + m_t + 1$ we obtain

$$n_t p_t = \frac{1}{(1+r)}[n_t d_t + n_{t+1} p_{t+1}]$$
$$V_t = \frac{1}{(1+r)}[n_t d_t + n_t p_{t+1}] \tag{16.2}$$

where V is the corporation's market value. Since $n_t = n_{t-1} + 1 - m_t + 1$

$$V_t = \frac{1}{(1+r)}[D_t + V_{t+1} - m_{t+1} p_{t+1}] \tag{16.3}$$

where D_t is the total company-wide dividend ($n_t d_t$). So the company's value at t is simply the discounted value of the dividend payable, plus the market value of the next period net of the value of any shares issued to pay that dividend. Therefore the impact of dividend payment on price nets two effects:

- Increased demand, pushing price upwards, in response to the attraction of dividends to investors.
- Increased supply of shares issued to fund the dividend payment, tending to push prices down.

Recognizing that the value of next period's growth in market value is given by the investment stream of the corporation minus any retained profit X, after dividends D have been paid:

$$m_{t+1} p_{t+1} = I_t - [X_t - D_t]$$

Which is simply to say price movements reflect the net return on investments by the company in each period. Plugging that into the valuation Equation (16.3) gives:

$$V_t = \frac{1}{(1+r)}[D_t + V_{t+1} - (I_t - \{X_t - D_t\})]$$
$$= \frac{1}{(1+r)}[V_{t+1} - I_t + X_t] \tag{16.4}$$

So it appears that in a perfect capital market world dividends have no role to play in corporate valuation. Later in the chapter I will try to cast some doubt on all this, but this conclusion is embedded in so much of the existing research literature it is best not to ditch it too quickly. However, the world is not perfect and dividends can be reintroduced into valuation by many and varied routes. Theories of dividend payments include:

• Dividends are simply a residual paid after setting investment policy.
• Dividends are a signal of value.
• Dividend payments discipline naughty managers/agents on the shareholders'/principals' behalf, stopping them from empire building, losing money on whacky projects, etc.
• Dividends reflect the attributes of the investors they serve whether these are particular tax clients or value/growth investment strategists.

One complicating reality that has drawn enormous attention has been the comparatively favourable tax treatment of capital gains compared to dividend income.

16.2.1   The Puzzle of Dividend Policy

The reason why the payment of dividends is puzzling is the comparatively high tax rate imposed on dividend income compared to capital gains by most tax regimes at most times. Dividends are typically taxed at almost twice the rate of capital gains on shares which retain earned income within the firm (Miller 1986). One reason why retention of capital within the firm may not seem attractive to company management is the lack of attractive, positive net present value projects. But this does not really make sense once one recognizes that any company can invest in other companies, which for a reasonably sensible portfolio should earn the market cost of capital. Alternatively the company can simply use retained earnings to buy back its own shares, directly converting a potential dividend stream into capital gains reaped by investors. The favourable tax treatment of capital gains means any company motivated to maximize after-tax shareholder wealth will cease to pay dividends.

Miller (1986) points out that before rushing in search of behavioural explanations of this puzzle it is most probably prudent to be a little more sceptical about the foundations of the dividend mystery. If earnings are retained within the firm, let's say to be invested in government bonds, this does not offer a watertight tax avoidance plan. Tax must be paid on bond coupons resulting from such internal investments. Now some pension funds and charities, for example the big private university investment funds in the United States, do not pay tax on dividend income at all. These large institutional investors, which often figure prominently on corporate boards, will not be happy if tax-exempt dividend repayments are retained for investment in securities which attract tax on the income they generate. Further, what company wants to generate a cash mountain that just screams 'take me over' to prowling hedge funds and corporate raiders?

The principal route by which value is usually returned to shareholders is by share buybacks and this at least solves the problem of amassing a cash (or near cash) mountain within the firm. But this solution to the dividend puzzle is also clearly problematic; the impact of share-repurchase is uneven across the shareholder base. As Miller (1986, p.274) states,

> The policy of share repurchase, like the quality of mercy, is twice blessed. It blesses not only those who sell but those who do not. In fact, the non-sellers are thrice blessed because their benefit takes the form, not of realized, but of unrealized capital gains.

Capital gains can be held on to by investors until a future date when gains can be offset against future losses to minimize the tax incidence. Further, it is only sensible for managers to suppress dividends in favour of share buybacks if high dividend yield stocks clearly sell at a discount to high capital gain stocks. That is, we can only expect managers to respond to signals conveyed to them via capital market prices. If high dividend yield stocks are cheaper than high capital gain stocks then, and perhaps only then, can we expect managers to act. But the evidence that this discount is observed is unclear at best.

An empirical study by Blume (1980) of the return premium/price discount earned by high dividend yield stocks found clustering of the price discount to high dividend yield stocks amongst those paying least (i.e. nothing) and those paying most (even to the point of full payout of earnings). So investors seem to shun extreme dividend policies, but not high dividend yield stocks as such. It is averaging over the two extremes of dividend policies that produces the conclusion that high dividend yield stocks attract a discount.

16.3   A Prospect Theory Explanation of Dividend Payments

Shefrin and Statman (1984) present a justification of the payment of dividends which invokes Kahneman and Tversky's 'prospect theory' style of utility theory. Recall from Chapters 2 and 8 that under prospect theory an investor evaluates the investment opportunity set based on what it yields relative to some 'benchmark', or expected, outcome which he regards as normal or necessary.

Shefrin and Statman (1984) focus on one aspect of prospect theory that has not been discussed so far: this is the concept of investor 'coding' of risky prospects. This concept arises when we ask how much would an investor be willing to pay to have a probability $p(x)$ of receiving an amount x as payment in a gamble and a separate amount y with $1 - p(x)$. In this context the investor's payoff from accepting the gamble at some opportunity cost s of accepting the gamble is given by the utility function

$$\pi(p(x))v(x - s) + \pi(p(y))v(y - s) \geq v(0) \tag{16.5}$$

where $\pi(p(x))$ is the prospect theory transformation of the standard expected utility payoffs from the von Neumann–Morgenstern axioms and s is some benchmark payoff. One property of this is the probability weighting function $\pi(p(x))$, which Shefrin and Statman (1984) describe as 'subcertainty' – this is the idea that a risk-averse investor will value the complete elimination of all risk much more than simple reductions in risk exposure would suggest. Small dividend payments can make a stock seem riskless if their payment masks any small capital loss that the investor envisages to be the cost of equity investment.

Shefrin and Statman (1984) suggest that rather than evaluating the probability weighted net benefits of alternative outcomes (i.e. $\pi(p(x)v(x - s))$ versus $p(y)v(y - s)$), investors decompose costs and possible benefits to yield a utility function

$$\pi(p(x))v(x) + \pi(p(y))v(y) + v(-s) \geq 0 \tag{16.6}$$

So the price of the gamble is 'segregated' from its benefits for the purpose of evaluating the prospective investment. Shefrin and Statman (1984) build on Thaler's (1980) model of how investors aggregate the 'sure', or at least sticky, return offered by dividends and the far more volatile capital gain on holding the stock.

16.3.1   Coding of Prospects: Combination, Segregation

In evaluating risky prospects, prospect theory envisages two stages of consideration (see Kahneman & Tversky 1979, pp.28–32):

- An editing phase in which the prospect is organized, reformulated and framed.
- An evaluation phase where the decision calculus regarding prospective payoffs and the probabilities are drawn together to decide a course of action occurs.

In the editing phase, before any decision calculus begins, a series of stylizations of the prospect faced occurs. These include:

- *Coding*. Initially any outcome is evaluated as a gain or loss relative to some relevant benchmark (be that zero, or expected return, etc.), which is denoted *s* above.
- *Combination*. Prospects are often simplified by combining outcomes with identical or very similar outcomes.
- *Segregation*. Some prospects contain a riskless component alongside a risky one and these might be separated out in the editing phase of the prospect's consideration. So a prospect of the form (300, 0.8; 200, 0.2) might be separated out into a prospect of the 200 you feel sure to get and the risky prospect of 100 you get with an 80% probability.

In the editing phase of consideration of a prospect one or more of these principles may be applied. When evaluating two or more prospects an investor might apply a further principle:

- *Cancellation*. Prospects which offer shared prospects are eliminated as separate outcomes in decision making. So the choice between two prospects $(200, 0.2; 100, 0.5; -50, 0.30)^1$ and $(200, 0.2; 150, 0.5; -100, 0.3)$ is reduced by editing the prospects to a choice between $(100, 0.5; -50, 0.3)$ and $(150, 0.5; -100, 0.3)$. Here the common outcome of 200 with a 20% probability is removed from consideration by cancellation. Further, extremely unlikely outcomes are likely to be eliminated, as are outcomes deriving from choices which are strictly dominated by other choices.

16.3.2   Shop Until You Should Stop

Thaler (1980) considers the following practical choices

(a) You set off to buy a clock radio at what you believe to be the cheapest store in your area. When you arrive, you find the radio costs $25, a price consistent with your priors (the suggested retail price is $35). As you are about to buy it a reliable friend comes by and tells you the same radio is selling for $20 in another store 10 minutes away. Do you go to the other store? What is the minimum price differential that would induce you to go to the other store?

(b) Now suppose that instead of a radio you are buying a colour television for $500 and your friend tells you it is available at another store for $495. [Answer the] same questions as in (a) above.

Reflecting on this pair of choices suggests a decision heuristic which is to shop around if doing so saves more than a given percentage of price. In choice (a) the saving in going elsewhere is 25%, so it makes sense to take your friend's advice. In choice (b) shopping around saves about 1% of the sales price, so it hardly seems worth the effort.

The point of this example is that the costs and benefits to the choice are integrated in these two choices. The amount I am willing to pay to search for a better buy is evaluated in a proportion of the purchase price. So I ask is it worth shopping around given the percentage saving I can make? For a big purchase like a television (in choice (b)) this makes sense, for a small purchase like a radio (in choice (a)) it does not. Costs of search are not evaluated in isolation by consumers, but rather integrated into total costs of making some purchase.

While standard theory suggests dividend policy is irrelevant, since investors can easily create dividends through 'homemade leverage' (i.e. selling the shares they own to obtain the desired amount of dividend), this proposition may not hold in a world where investors struggle with issues of self-control (discussed in more detail in Chapter 17). The payment of dividends allows the investor to implement the simple consumption rule to maintain capital and always live off the interest on it. If I allow myself the opportunity to dip into capital it is possible my weak will would cause me to 'live as if there is no tomorrow' and regret doing so the next day.

16.3.3   Calculating the Dividend Yield Premium/ Discount

Decompose the return on equity into an amount α which is paid as a dividend and an amount β which is the resale value of the share held. Let ω_α be the reference/benchmark expectation the investor has for dividends and ω_β be the reference benchmark expectation for the resale price. Without loss of generality, assume ω_α, the expected level of dividends, is zero, so the prospect of dividends becomes simply α. Shefrin and Statman (1984) consider the likely attitude of an investor to these two elements of return – dividends and capital gain – as we vary the capital gain payable on the stock. For an investor who integrates the two elements of return his utility is given by

$$v(x) = w\big((\alpha - \omega_\alpha) + (\beta - \omega_\beta)\big) \tag{16.7}$$

while segregation of the two alternative elements of return implies a somewhat different utility function of the form

$$v(x) = w(\alpha - \omega_\alpha) + w\big(\beta - \omega_\beta\big) \tag{16.8}$$

where each element of return is weighted separately in the evaluation of the investment. Suppose the investor can choose whether to integrate or segregate these two elements of return to holding an asset in order to maximize his utility. So the investor now faces a utility function of the form

$$v(x) = \max\big[w\big((\alpha - \omega_\alpha) + (\beta - \omega_\beta)\big), \ w(\alpha - \omega_\alpha) + w\big(\beta - \omega_\beta\big)\big] \tag{16.9}$$

where the branch of the utility function chosen reflects a choice the investor makes to maximize his utility. What will he choose and under what circumstances will he make which choice? Will he segregate the dividend element of the return to holding the stock from the capital gain it offers or not? To get the answer to that we need to make an assumption about the investor's utility function.

As stated above Shefrin and Statman (1984) assume a prospect theory utility function of the form given in Figure 16.1. Gains exhibit the usual law of diminishing returns. Winning a thousand pounds seems great to me, but I might not be bothered if I became a multi-millionaire. This is captured by the concavity (bowing away from the horizontal axis in the upper-right panel) of the utility function in the

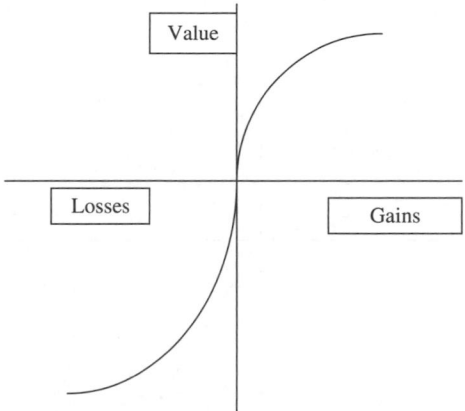

Figure 16.1   A prospect theory utility function

domain for gains. Conversely, in the domain of losses, it is assumed larger losses hurt investors proportionately more compared to more moderate losses. So for me to lose £5000 is a problem, but to lose £10,000 is becoming a serious disaster. It is this intensity, with which I feel large losses, that is expressed by the convexity of the utility function in the domain of losses. This property is captured by the convexity (bowing towards the horizontal axis in the lower-left panel) of the utility function in the loss domain.

What does this form of utility function imply about how dividend payments and capital gains will be integrated/segregated by investors? Clearly we might expect investors' behaviour to change around the pivot points of their expected/benchmark level or return from each source, that is ω_o, assumed to be zero here. Specifically, as investors incur capital losses and so are pushed into the lower-left panel of Figure 16.1 we might expect them to focus on potentially offsetting gains from steady dividend payments. This might imply segregation of equity returns might cluster amongst stocks with capital losses.

Figure 16.2 illustrates how we might expect investors to integrate/segregate the two elements of return as capital gain values. For large gains in value from dividends and capital gains (the upper right-hand panel of Figure 16.2) investors tend to segregate the two elements of return to 'savour' them both separately. This is because of the concavity of the investor's utility function in the domain of gains. Bigger gains produce proportionately less pleasure for the investor and so separate smaller gains are savoured by him. Part of this savouring process may be due to the subcertainty principle, by which investors particularly value a guarantee of avoiding losses. Subcertainty implies an investor will pay more to achieve certainty than a straightforward evaluation of expected values might suggest he would be willing to pay.

When investors make large losses and are required to make capital contributions (the lower left-hand panel of Figure 16.2) they will tend to segregate both elements of the loss. By doing so they seek to diminish the impact of the two separate losses on their total utility by not aggregating these two elements into one big loss. Prospect theory tells us investors suffer the pain of losses far more intensely than they experience the pleasure of gains. This intensity of loss results from the convexity of the investor's utility function in the domain of losses. Integration of the combined losses captures the intensity of the loss investor's experience. Smaller losses are less difficult for the investor to face and he avoids cumulating them into larger more painful losses if he possibly can.

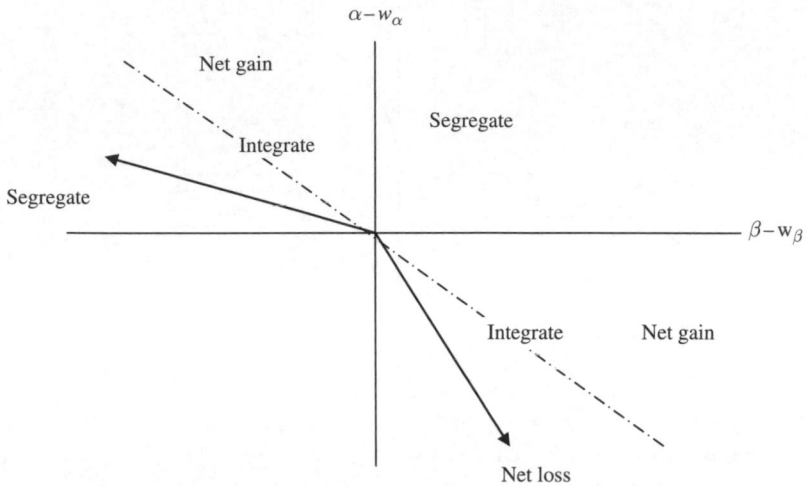

Figure 16.2 Integration and segregation of investment losses for an equity investor

Finally, when dividends are paid to investors who have just taken a small capital loss they are integrated so that the dividend is seen as compensation for the capital loss. Shefrin and Statman (1984) interpret this as the origin of the 'bird in the hand' effect. If I have lost a little in a decline in the price of my shareholdings, a dividend payment may constitute a compensatory gain to ease that loss.

Consider a share which earns a capital loss, but pays a precisely compensating dividend. So $-\alpha = (\beta - \omega_\beta) < 0$ for this share. Integration allows the investor to avoid experiencing any loss at all. Segregation would mean that the investor must separately evaluate the gain and the loss. Since losses are felt more acutely than gains of the same size this separation makes the investor feel worse off. Variations on dividend over this range may be particularly valued due to the subcertainty principle that prospects that guarantee no losses are especially valued by investors.

A numerical example of capital gain and dividend integration/segmentation

In order to give some idea of how the choice between integrating and segmenting capital gains and dividends operates I consider a very simple numerical example. To construct a fairly tractable example I use the functional form of the natural logarithm of each type of benefit to holding shares, dividend payments and capital gains. This has the benefit of yielding a concave function over gains. Hence for losses I use the inverse/mirror function of minus the natural logarithm of the absolute value under consideration. So for the sequence of gains 2 and 4 in the domain of gains we have 0.693 and 1.386 and in the domain of losses we have -0.693 and -1.38.

Using this simple functional form I consider the response of investors' utility over a range of capital gains from a price of 30 all the way down to 1. Initially in Figure 16.3 I consider the effect of varying capital gain against a fixed reference/benchmark price of 10 (so the first capital gain considered is $20 = 30 - 10$, all the way down to a capital gain of -10 at price 0) and at a fixed dividend of 2. I call this my growth stock example. In Figure 16.4 I once again consider the relative utility of integrating and segregating capital gains and dividends from a price of 30 but now with a reference target price of

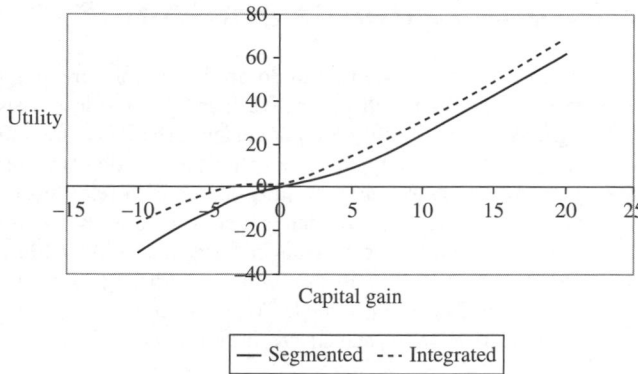

Figure 16.3   Integration vs. segmentation of capital gains and dividends (reference price 10, dividend 2)

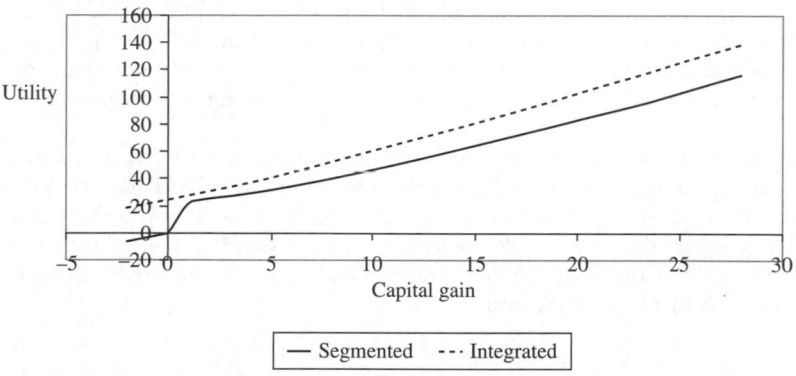

Figure 16.4   Integration vs. segmentation of capital gains and dividends (reference price 2, dividend 0)

2 (so the first capital gain considered is $28 = 30 - 2$ all the way down to a capital gain of -2 if the stock is valueless in the market) and a dividend of 10. I call this my income stock example (the dividend is five times that of the growth stock example and the range of price variation considered is exactly the same).

In both examples the strategy of integrating losses produces higher utility in both the domain of losses and gains. The only effect of moving from the growth stock to the income stock example is that the integration strategy seems more dominant in the income stock example (i.e. in Figure 16.4 as compared to Figure 16.3). This greater favour for integration for income shares makes sense. For income stocks the 'riskless' (or at least less volatile) element of dividends is the predominant determinant of investor return. Only when capital gains are very low does segregation appear at all attractive. Here dividends might be seen as compensating for capital losses. Once a capital loss is incurred, which is too large to be compensated for by the dividend payment (of 2 for the growth stock in Figure 16.3 and 10 for the income stock in Figure 16.4), the intensity with which capital losses are felt leads to integration being the preferred strategy to mask the capital loss by the dividend payment. This strategy serves to reduce the size of the perceived loss.

16.4   Who Pays Dividends and Why?

The answer seems to be those who can afford to and do not have more pressing uses for their cash. These tend to be more mature firms in a cash-generative, relatively modest investment stage of the lifecycle. DeAngelo, DeAngelo and Stulz (2006) present evidence that US companies with a high ratio of retained earnings to total shareholders' equity, book value, pay dividends while those with low, or negative, retained earnings relative to shareholders' equity do not. This relationship holds both for the number of companies that choose to pay dividends and the amount of dividends they pay. DeAngelo *et al.* (2006) studied US non-financial firms in the years 1973 to 2002. Fama and French (2001) have already recorded a steep decline in the number of firms paying dividends during this period. Figure 16.5 summarizes this key result of the DeAngelo *et al.* (2006) paper and illustrates how the proportion of dividend issues rises with each successive segment of the retained earnings to total equity ratio distribution examined.

What DeAngelo *et al.* (2006) add to this is the knowledge that the reduction in dividend payments is heavily concentrated amongst the subgroup of firms most capable of paying them because they have positive retained income to profit ratios. They find a 50% reduction in the propensity to pay dividends derives from amongst this group. They also record a dramatic rise in loss-making companies, up from 11.8% of the sample in 1978 to over half the sample in 2002. Nevertheless the preponderance of dividend terminations is amongst profitable firms who can presumably afford to pay them. So whatever is causing the reduction in the desire to pay dividends it does not appear to be an inability to pay. In fact dividends in aggregate are not even falling as DeAngelo *et al.* (2004) show elsewhere.

The clustering of dividend payments amongst those companies with the most retained earnings suggests that dividends may indeed be playing the disciplinary role that Jensen (1986) envisages for them. If this is the case we might anticipate any reduction in dividend payment is interpreted by the market as a siphoning off of shareholder value to pet projects, probably negative net present value, and a comfortable life more generally for company managers. It is towards evidence on dividend omissions and initiations that I now turn.

16.4.1   Are Dividends Signals of Future Earnings Prospects?

One of the most common explanations given for the payment of future dividends is that they 'signal' future earnings prospects. So an increase in dividends says the company can take the pain of this additional expense. It is a credible and costly signal of future good performance. Similarly, cutting dividends tells the market the company is in trouble and there is no quick way out of it, so the company needs its money back quickly. But is that true?

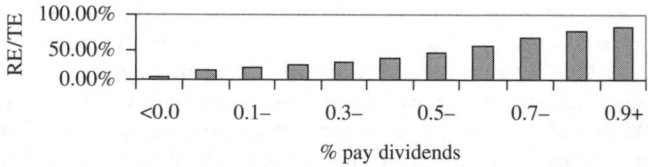

Figure 16.5   Proportion of dividend payers by ratio of retained earnings to total shareholder equity (RE/TE)

A study by Benartzi, Michaely and Thaler (1997) suggests it may not be. Bernartzi *et al.* (1997) examined the earnings performance of New York and US Stock Exchange companies that changed their dividend in the years 1979–91. This generated a sample of 1025 firms and over 7000 firm-year observations. While the authors reported strong correlation between lagged and contemporaneous dividend and earnings changes they found dividend changes cannot really predict future earnings changes, although they may be able to predict a sustained, once and for all, increase in the level of reported earnings. In the two years following dividend increases earnings movements showed no relation to that increase. But their evidence does suggest that dividend increases do signal a permanent increase in the level of earnings. This finding supports conclusions in the early literature by John Lintner (1956) that dividend increases do signal a once and for all increase in the sustainable level of earnings. In this sense dividends tell us a story about what has already happened, that is, earnings power has increased, not what will happen in the future. For this reason share price responses to dividend changes are difficult to reconcile with the standard efficient markets hypothesis.

16.4.2   Dividend Omissions, Initiations and Drift

The omission or initiation of dividends is a major event in any company's life. Omitting a dividend suggests cash-flow problems lie ahead. Initiating a dividend implies either greater cash-flow in the future or possibly a reduction in attractive investment opportunities for the company to exploit. So if initiating a dividend is a sign of corporate maturity, omitting a dividend can be seen as a sign of corporate decline. The share price response to initiations and omissions of dividends can be seen to contain a number of elements (see Michaely, Thaler & Womack 1995, p.573) including:

- *Underreaction*, as the market struggles to interpret the signal being conveyed. This signal may be re-evaluated in light of press commentary and informal briefings and disclosures in the ambient 'market for information' about company prospects. Hence we might expect some drift downwards for companies omitting dividends and upwards for those initiating payments as the impact of these announcements diffuses through the equity market.
- *Overreaction*. Conversely it is well documented that extreme share price returns are almost by their nature reversed in the longer run. Losers become winners and winners become losers as secular trends unwind short-run market turbulence (De Bondt & Thaler 1985).
- *Clientele effects*. If some investment managers prefer to invest in income stocks they might drop companies omitting dividends from their portfolio and replenish their holdings with those who initiate dividend payments. If funds do not pay tax on dividend income, this sort of behaviour will be encouraged.

Examining a sample of 561 cash dividends initiation events and 887 omissions of dividends from the years 1964 to 1988 Michaely *et al.* (1995) observe far larger price responses to omissions than initiations. Price declines in response to omissions are roughly twice the comparative price rises associated with dividend initiations. This is consistent with a prospect theory utility function. The pattern of long-term price response is far more consistent with dividend omission 'drift', as opposed to overreaction to dividend omissions. Indeed the drift observed is larger and more durable than that reported in classic studies of post-earnings-announcement drift (see Bernard 1993). This suggests post-dividend-announcement drift is not a statistical artefact of post-earnings-announcement drift – if anything the reverse must be true.

16.4.3   What Reasons do Managers Give for Paying Dividends?

Since there seems no sensible reason why dividends should be paid, given the tax disincentive to paying them, and the existence of so many theories of why they are nevertheless paid, it appears standard finance has got itself in a bit of a mess about dividends. Realizing this some authors have been audacious enough to consider asking company managers why they pay dividends and, if they do, how they decide how much to pay. This is a radical step for most finance researchers, despite the fact almost every other social science area (marketing, human resources, etc.) regards practitioner surveys as normal practice in research.

In the United States, Brav, Graham and Harvey (2005) surveyed chief financial officers in 384 major companies and held 23 follow-up interviews to discuss company pay-out policy. In many ways we can see their study as revisiting the original study by Lintner (1956), who concluded that:

- Managers are very loath to cut dividends.
- Managers target a specific pay-out ratio and adjust dividends paid to attain that ratio as earnings rise and fall.

Brav *et al.* (2005) found that the adherence to a target pay-out policy has greatly weakened in the half-century since Lintner undertook his research. This makes sense because the world has changed so much in that 50-year period. One major change has been the growth of share buybacks. Such buybacks were unheard of at the time of Modigliani and Miller's research and were essentially unknown in the UK until the new millennium. While the managers in Brav *et al.*'s (2005) survey are fairly rigid in their setting of dividends, they exhibit a far more liberated attitude in the usage of share repurchase. Indeed many managers express regret that they initiated a dividend at all and claim they might stick with share repurchase as a way of returning capital to shareholders if they did not feel condemned by their history to maintain dividend payments. They do not see share repurchases as setting a precedent to which they can be held to account by the market for information and by its chief inhabitants, analysts and fund managers in particular. Nor do managers offer much support for any of our major theories of why dividends are paid. Neither taxes nor promoting internal discipline are mentioned as motivation for dividend payouts. Managers do think changes in dividends convey/ signal some information to the market, but this signal is part of a broader package of communication conveyed in the market for information by company managers. Dividend policy, not very important in itself, becomes important as part of a larger 'value creation story'. In a follow-up interview one chief financial officer called his company's pay-out policy a 'punctuation mark' and not the 'meat in the sentence' of its communication with investors (Brav *et al.* 2005, p.512).

From a survey of 164 UK companies, that is 25% of the companies originally posted questionnaires, Dhanani (2005) finds it is hard to support any particular theory of what determines dividends, but also concludes:

- No relation exists between investment policy, capital structure and dividends.
- Dividends are seen as a signal of value by managers who raise dividends to signal a sustained improvement in company performance.
- Dividends are rarely raised to discipline managers and stop them empire building except in regulated utilities and finance companies.
- Dividends are not seen as important for shareholder value by high-growth firms, but are seen as an important source of return to shareholders by low-growth firms. Tax status seems to have little impact on dividend policy.

Both US and UK evidence tells us that there is still scope for a convincing theory of dividend policy. Filling this gap might be one of the first big hits of a behavioural approach to financial decision making. Certainly the competition from standard theory does not seem very well ordered.

16.4.4   Does Pay-out Policy Matter?

As we have seen much of standard corporate finance theory concerns a search for a rationale for dividend payment given that such payments did not matter for the firm's value in a perfect, zero transaction, no tax, etc., market. But is it possible this conclusion was reached too hastily? While this would mean that many of the attempts to justify the payments of dividends are a wild goose chase, it appears this may be the case.

DeAngelo and DeAngelo (2006) expose a hidden assumption in Modigiani and Miller's reasoning. Returning to Equation (16.4) above they note that it requires full pay-out of free cash-flow in each period. This is because:

$$D_t = X_t - I_t + V_t = FCF + V_t \tag{16.10}$$

where FCF denotes free cash-flow. Since the market value of the company cannot be negative, $V > 0$, the company is implicitly required to pay out all its free cash-flow in each period. That is $FCF_t = X_t - I_t$ at every date. To say dividend policy is not relevant to company valuation in such a world is not saying very much. DeAngelo and DeAngelo (2006) relax this assumption, allowing companies to retain cash within the firm. They then clearly show that the chosen dividend policy does have an impact on company value. To illustrate the impact of relaxing the full cash pay-out restriction DeAngelo and DeAngelo (2006) consider pay-out policy in a simple three-date world. At date $t = 0$ the company invests and this investment generates free cash-flow at date $t = 1$, FCF_1 and free cash-flow received later, FCF_2.

Figure 16.6 portrays how free cash-flow at the two dates following the investment at date 0 are traded off. This trade-off occurs at the market rate of interest r, which determines the slope of the line W_2W_1 in Figure 16.6. The assumption of Modigliani and Miller that the firm pays out all of its free cash-flow in each time period restrains the company to a distribution of cash-flows given at the point A in that figure. Under this assumption all distributions of cash-flow must lie on the line AW_1. Free cash-flow combinations on the line AW_2 cannot be implemented by the firm since that would then require some retention of cash-flow at date 1. Of course, the individual investor can still reach allocations on the line AW_2 but he must do so by borrowing against current shareholdings or other assets. Movements along the line AW_1 represent trades between investors at date 1, with points to the right of A being reached by the company engaging in share repurchase and so generating additional free cash-flow. As DeAngelo and DeAngelo (2006, p.299) sum it up:

> Bottom line, in MM (1961) the only policies the firm can choose entail 100% FCF payout, and that is why payout policies examined by MM are all equally valuable to stockholders and why investment policy is the sole determinant of value....MM does not apply to payout retention decisions since their assumption prohibits retention.

If this is accepted the behavioural approach may be a theory of pay-out policy even in the stylized world of modern finance. In doing so behavioural theories could offer something different from the 'market imperfections' theories based on tax and asymmetric information, etc. Behavioural theories owe their explanatory power not to imperfections in the market, but rather to the way in which investment prospects are evaluated by investors, even in a 'perfect'

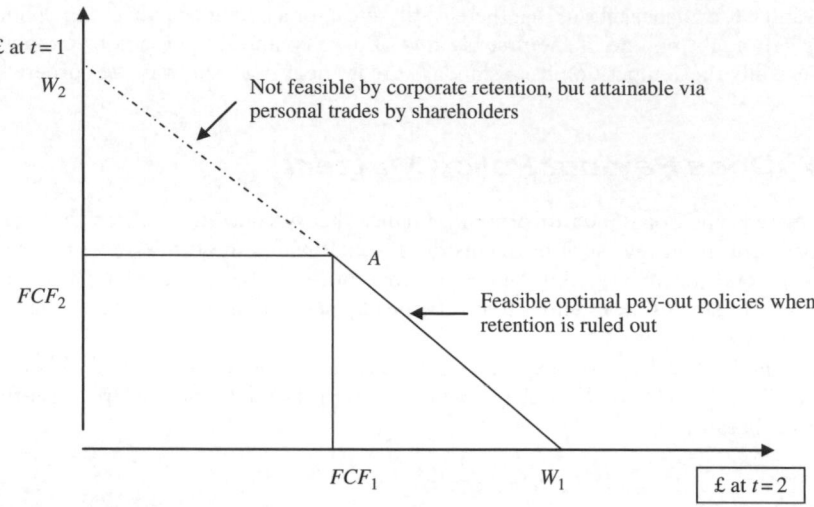

Figure 16.6 Feasible and optimal pay-out policies in three period MM economy

market. If dividend policy is now accepted as being relevant to firm value behavioural theories can help us understand how they are relevant.

16.5 Conclusion and Summary

This chapter applies the prospect theory of investment decisions to the dividend policy of firms. The evidence in favour of this approach is not yet in, but given the penury of credible theory to explain why dividends are paid at all and, if paid, at what level, behavioural researchers are booting in a rotten door here. Indeed even within standard finance theory the orthodoxy is changing. While it was initially thought in some 'perfect' market of finance textbooks that dividends were 'irrelevant' to firm value, this view may now be changing. While most of standard theory explains dividend pay-outs as resulting from various 'market imperfections', the behavioural approach emerges from an understanding of how investment prospects are evaluated by investors. No imperfection in the market is required to facilitate its explanatory power and its relevance pertains as much to the 'perfect' world of classical theory as to our own more messy existence. For this reason behavioural approaches may have a comparative advantage in a time when the relevance of dividends to value is in transition.

Questions

1. Return to the original Modigliani and Miller (1961) model of equations (16.1) to (16.4). Suppose that M&M PLC has a total dividend payable this year of £1 million, next year the company is expected to be worth £10 million and trade at a price of £1 a share. M&M PLC currently has one million shares in issue and has no plans to issue new shares. What is M&M PLC's current value according to the Modigliani and Miller (1961) model of equations (16.1) to (16.4)?

Suppose M&M PLC now plans to issue 10,000 shares next year. How would this affect value?

2. Redraw Figure 16.3 using a dividend of 10 and a target price of 10. Call this the 'balanced growth' stock. Once again consider price movements from 30 down to 0. How do these price movements influence the choices an investor makes between stocks? How do they impact upon the integration/segregation of gains/losses to holding the 'balanced growth' stock?

3. Segregation/integration of investor losses/gains seems like an interesting idea. How could it be applied elsewhere in finance to solve problems that the standard model struggles with?

Note

1. Here the notation is: (payoff if outcome 1 occurs, probability of outcome 1 occurring; payoff if outcome 2 occurs, probability of outcome 2 occurring).

References

Benartzi, S., R. Michaely & R. Thaler (1997). Do changes in dividends signal the future or the past? *Journal of Finance*, **52**: 1007–33.

Bernard, V. (1993). Stock price reactions to earnings announcements: a summary of recent anomalous evidence and possible explanations. In R. Thaler (ed.), *Advances in Behavioral Finance*. New York: Russell Sage Foundation.

Blume, M. (1980). Stock returns and dividend yields: some more evidence. *Review of Economics and Statistics*, **62**: 567–77.

Brav, A., J. Graham & C. Harvey (2005). Payout policy in the 21st century. *Journal of Financial Economics*, **77**: 483–527.

De Bondt, W. & R. Thaler (1985). Does the stock market overreact? *Journal of Finance*, **60**: 793–807.

DeAngelo, H. & L. DeAngelo (2006). The irrelevance of the MM dividend irrelevance theorem. *Journal of Financial Economics*, **79**: 292–315.

DeAngelo, H., L. DeAngelo & R. Stulz (2006). Dividend policy and the earned/contributed capital mix: a test of the life-cycle theory. *Journal Financial Economics*, **81**: 227–54.

DeAngelo, H., L. DeAngelo *et al.* (2004). Are dividends disappearing? Dividend concentration and the consolidation of earnings. *Journal of Financial Economics*, **72**: 425–56.

Dhanani, A. (2005). Corporate dividend policy: the views of British financial managers. *Journal of Business, Finance and Accounting*, **32**: 1625–72.

Fama, E. & K. French (2001). Disappearing dividends: changing firm characteristics or lower propensity to pay? *Journal of Financial Economics*, **60**: 3–43.

Jensen, M. (1986). Agency costs of free cash-flow, corporate finance and takeovers. *American Economic Review*, **76**: 323–9.

Kahneman, D. & A. Tversky (1979). Prospect theory: an analysis of decision under risk. *Econometrica*, **47**: 263–91.

Lintner, J. (1956). Distribution of incomes of corporations, retained earnings and taxes. *American Economic Review*, **46**: 97–113.

Michaely, R., R. Thaler & K. Womack (1995). Price reactions to dividend initiations and omissions: overreaction or drift? *Journal of Finance*, **50**: 573–608.

Miller, M. (1986). Behavioural rationality in finance: the case of dividends. In R. Hogarth & M. Reader (eds), *Rational Choice: The Contrast between Economics and Psychology*. Chicago: University of Chicago Press.

Modigliani, F. & M. Miller (1961). Dividend policy, growth and the valuation of shares. *Journal of Business*, **34**: 411–33.

Shefrin, H. (2007). *Behavioral Corporate Finance: Decisions that Create Value*. Boston, MA: McGraw-Hill Irwin.

Shefrin, H. & M. Statman (1984). Explaining investor preferences for cash dividends. *Journal of Financial Economics*, **13**: 253–82.

Thaler, R. (1980). Towards a positive theory of consumer choice. *Journal of Economic Behavior and Organization*, **1**: 39–60.

Chapter 17

Entrepreneurship

‘ The next step is to break open the black box called the individual and similarly realize because of self-control problems that lead to nonfunctional behaviour the individual cannot be said to maximize in the simple sense we economists have assumed for the last two hundred years ’

(Jensen 1998, p.48).

This chapter examines how two well-documented psychological biases interact to produce predictable behaviour in an area where existing economic theory is seen to be struggling. The entrepreneur is the unspoken hero of contemporary economic theory. Standard economic theory with its focus on comparative statics downplays the role of those who change the scheme of production or distribution. The focus in standard theory is on equilibrium – not on where the evolving settled state came from or may be going. For Joseph Schumpeter (1947, p.151), the entrepreneur was needed to do ‘new things or things that are already being done in a new way’. The entrepreneur therefore is often a marginalized, misunderstood figure in standard economic theory (see Parker (2004) for a review or Huarta de Soto (2008) for an Austrian school perspective).

In this chapter we combine two well-known cognitive biases to try to explain some of the apparent strangeness of the entrepreneur. In particular we consider a model by Roland Benabou and Jean Tirole that incorporates two well-known psychological biases into a model of entrepreneurs' behaviour (Benabou & Tirole 2002). These biases are:

- Optimism.
- A need to exert ‘self-control’ because of inconsistent attitudes to discounting future consumption depending on how close to the present a reward is likely to be received. This is the presence of a hyperbolic discount function applicable to future benefits as described in Chapter 4. In particular, Benabou and Tirole consider the possibility that entrepreneurs are unusual in their ‘resolve’ and delay gratification, or at least find methods of self-control that allow them to make great efforts in the pursuit of a very uncertain profit.

The impact of these biases is illustrated within a model in which the ‘present self’ must make the correct decisions given insight into the weak will or resolve of the ‘future self’ who will soon control his destiny. In this way Benabou and Tirole (2002, p.885) unbundle the ‘self that knows’ and the ‘self that does not know’. While such a schizophrenic perspective may seem somewhat unhinged, it does allow Benabou and Tirole to develop a very flexible framework for understanding a range of what have hitherto been very perplexing phenomena. Benabou and Tirole often mention entrepreneurship and the courage and self-control required to set up a business from scratch as an example of their idea, but they do not make entrepreneurship the focus of their paper. Other papers in the same tradition have done so (Brocas & Carillo 2004, Bernardo & Welch 2001), and I discuss these papers in light of the Benabou and Tirole framework. So the discussion of the Benabou and Tirole (BT) model should be interpreted as illustrative, not definitive, of their ideas.

17.1   Illustration and Structure

The Netscape IPO became the 'starting gun for the greatest legal creation of wealth in history', according to John Doerr, a leading venture capitalist of the time. Jim Clark, who jointly founded Netscape, was a reckless disenchanted academic who had previously founded and left Silicon Graphics. Clark personified the brash attitude of the time. His account of that period quotes him as saying,

> A lot of very smart entrepreneurs are quite rational about how they take chances; they think it through, then work out contingency plans should things go wrong and they need a fall-back position. I'm not good at that. My point of view has always been, Damn the torpedoes. I don't want to think about not being successful. It's a driven state, a mild form of insanity – or at the very least, a kind of selective dumbness

(Clark & Edwards 2000, p.71).

This chapter examines how optimism may be of value in contexts where the decision-maker faces a very challenging task, like launching a new company or producing a new product into a market that does not yet exist. Here a little optimism might give the entrepreneur enough steel to continue, when wiser heads might be crippled by self-doubt.

Section 17.2 presents a model by Roland Benabou and Jean Tirole (the BT model) of how optimism can be valuable in undertaking tasks requiring strong self-command. Section 17.3 examines some of the broader consequences of such behaviour for firms and for the economy as a whole. Section 17.4 summarizes and concludes the chapter. An appendix considers some case studies of entrepreneurs to illustrate the themes of the chapter.

After reading this chapter the reader should:

- Understand how some psychological traits tend to be associated with an entrepreneurial spirit and how the costs and benefits of such traits must be traded off.
- Understand how these psychological traits are often observed in famous entrepreneurs, especially those involved in 'new economy' type enterprises where uncertainty is high and the chances of establishing a viable business low.

17.1.1   The Problem of Self-Control

The problem of self-control characterizes many aspects of our financial and personal lives. As the opening quotation makes clear even senior figures in finance are turning their attention to struggles arising within the financial decision maker's mind. Saving for retirement or your children's education, dieting or sobriety, all require management of our behaviour, even at the expense of satisfying our immediate desires. Thaler and Shefrin (1981) point out the similarity between these situations and the typical 'agency' problem in corporate finance. In the agency problem a principal/employer tries to restrain a self-interested employee from shirking at work in a business he does not own. The same self-control is often necessary for the current self to ensure that his future self will successfully complete certain goals. For Thaler and Shefrin (1981) the same division of labour exists within us all, being manifest in two distinct aspects of our mental capacity, which are:

- The 'planner', our 'good angel', who says save hard for retirement, drink or eat moderately.
- The 'doer', or a voice of temptation, who says enjoy yourself, spend a little, have a glass of wine to wash down the dessert.

Any balanced life requires such an intrapersonal conflict to be resolved. Failure to achieve a good balance between our 'planner' and 'doer' selves threatens to throw us into poverty in old age, miserliness, obesity or anorexia.

An example of the perceived need for self-control comes from the recent collapse of Farepak, a UK 'Christmas club'. Farepak was largely patronized by poorer people with large families prepared to save at below market rates in order to have the security that their children would have a good Christmas. Farepak collected money from clients on a monthly basis throughout the year and then would issue vouchers that could be redeemed at some of the UK's largest retailers, such as Argos and Woolworths. This allowed poorer people to spread their end-of-year payments, and relied on retailers trusting clubs such as Farepak to settle up the bill for their vouchers after Christmas had passed. Unfortunately the decision by major stores not to accept vouchers without prior payment from Farepak caused liquidity problems, which eventually pushed the company under. However, the basic demand for Christmas clubs remains, especially amongst those on low incomes whose desire to spend peaks at times like Christmas.

17.2   The BT Model

Benabou and Tirole model the creation and maintenance of personal self-image, or esteem. As the authors point out the maintenance of an optimistic view of life is the departure point of a whole 'self-help' industry. Since the classic book, *Self Help* by Samuel Smiles, was published in 1882, a whole swathe of literature helps us to 'Think yourself thin!' or 'Get published!'. Indeed the very success of these titles implies a need for keeping ourselves positive, perhaps even against a bleak reality. A cheerful, go-getting attitude is usually seen as an attractive attribute in a potential recruit or friend. Benabou and Tirole note at least three possible advantages to an optimistic view of life:

- Investors may consume optimism as a good, simply because it's more fun than being miserable, this might be called a *personal* benefit.
- Investors may find that if they appear optimistic (because they are), other people perceive them as more able, this is a *reputational* benefit.
- Investors may find optimism helps them succeed in difficult circumstances, believing we shall overcome, this is the *motivational* benefit of optimism.

While optimism and a plucky attitude can be a blessing it obviously becomes a problem if it crosses the line to self-delusion. The band's decision to keep playing as the *Titanic* sank has become an iconic image of futile gallantry. Benabou and Tirole construct a model of why we wish to be self-confident (the demand for self-confidence) and how we might induce the self-confident attitudes we desire (the supply of self-confidence). This process of confident maintenance of optimism in the face of adversity is part of a whole literature on self-control within behavioural finance alluded to at the start of the chapter. I begin by discussing the demand for, or motivation of, self-confidence amongst entrepreneurs in the setting of the BT model.

17.2.1   The Demand for Self-Confidence in the BT Model

Benabou and Tirole consider an agent/entrepreneur who intervenes/creates across three dates. At date 0 the entrepreneur discovers something concerning his nature which may help him undertake a

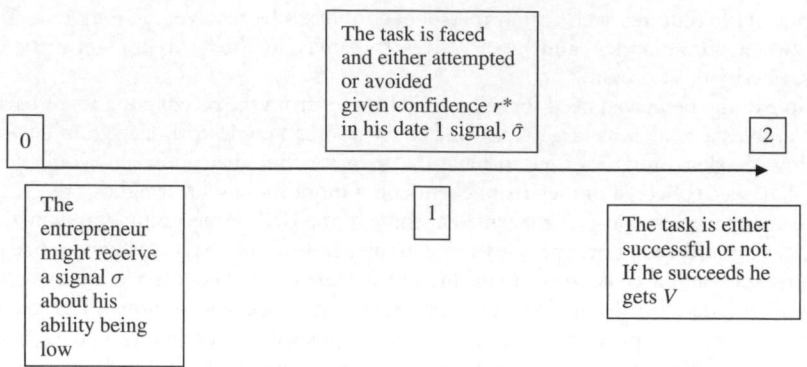

Figure 17.1 Time line for the BT model

task or challenge at date 1. At date 1 the entrepreneur undertakes the task at cost c, or chooses not to do so. The entrepreneur faces this choice with a set of beliefs about his own ability to do the task successfully, θ, which is distributed as $F(\theta)$ at date 0 and $F_1(\theta)$ at date 1. In between dates 0 and 1 information about the entrepreneur's ability to do the task can be strategically 'forgotten', if it is damaging to his ego and so confidence. A reward V for successfully completing the task is received on the final date 2. If he does not attempt the project, or does so and fails, he gets nothing. Figure 17.1 gives the time line of the model. At date 0 the entrepreneur chooses an action and/or receives a signal regarding a choice he will face to undertake a project at date 1.

Benabou and Tirole also assume that a threat for wannabe entrepreneurs is living for the present, lacking self-control, discounting future benefits by more than a simple consideration of prevailing market interest rates would imply. So they discount more heavily benefits receivable in the distant future than those in the near future. That is, they possess a hyperbolic discount function of the type discussed in Chapter 3. Given this, the entrepreneur's perceived utility at date 1, u_1 is given by the expression

$$u_1 + \beta\delta E_1[u_2] = -c + \beta\delta\bar{\theta}_1 V \tag{17.1}$$

if he successfully completes the project and zero if he does not; where $\beta < 1$ and captures the extent to which the entrepreneur discounts future consumption in excess of the usual market interest rate, denoted δ here. The entrepreneur maximizes his present (u_1) and future ($\beta\delta E_1[u_2]$) utility by balancing the cost (c) and benefits ($\beta\delta\bar{\theta}V$) of each of his actions regarding whether to undertake the project or not. If he succeeds he gets V, if he fails he still faces costs of undertaking the project. Note both future utility and the gain it derives from are diminished by an amount β that reflects the 'impatience' (Fisher 1930) of the entrepreneur to consume now. This impatience makes bearing the cost of undertaking the task more difficult to bear and thus a lower chance that it will be performed.

Given his date 1 utility we can infer the entrepreneur's date 0 utility, if he attempts the date 1 project, by backward induction to be

$$u_0 + \beta E_0[\delta u_1 + \delta^2 u_2 | \bar{\theta}_1] = u_0 + \beta\delta[-c + \delta\bar{\theta}_1 V] \tag{17.2}$$

if he successfully completes the project and zero if he does not. Where date 0 utility is set by the discounted value of expected date 1 and 2 utility ($\delta u_1 + \beta\delta_2 u_2$), conditional on his understanding of his ability to successfully complete the date 1 challenge. The right-hand side of the above expression sums initial utility at date 0 and the discounted value of the net payoff to undertaking the task. In the second expression on the right-hand side of Equation (17.2), β captures the impatience, or lack of resolve, of the date 1 entrepreneur's persona in undertaking the task. In performing this calculation the entrepreneur is unsure of his own ability to complete the task successfully, $\bar{\theta}$, and hence his ability to win V at date 2.

Benabou and Tirole (2002) consider the process of the entrepreneur's 'Self at date 0' (which I denote Self 0) deciding on whether to face a trial, which reveals his true ability to successfully complete the task, θ, date 1. In a later article, Benabou and Tirole (2004) refer to these selves separated by the time of their existence as 'incarnations' and I follow that terminology here. At date 0 the entrepreneur does not know his own ability to complete the task, θ. So being risk neutral the entrepreneur simply sets it equal to the sample mean of the ability distribution $F(\theta)$, $\bar{\theta}_F$. Self 1, the entrepreneur at date 1, undertakes the challenge if the probability of him successfully completing it lies above the cost–benefit ratio of completing the task, i.e.

$$\bar{\theta}_F > \frac{c}{\beta \delta V} \tag{17.3}$$

Hence the value Self 0 places on Self 1 learning his ability to complete the task, θ, is given as follows

$$\delta \beta I_F \equiv \beta \delta \left(\int_{\frac{c}{\beta \delta V}}^{1} (\delta \theta V - c) dF(\theta) - (\delta \bar{\theta}_F V - c) = G_F - L_F \right)$$

where

$$G_F = \int_0^{\frac{c}{\delta V}} (c - \delta \theta V) dF(\theta)$$

$$L_F = \int_{\frac{c}{\delta V}}^{\frac{c}{\beta \delta V}} (\delta \bar{\theta}_F V - c) dF(\theta) \tag{17.4}$$

where G_F is the benefit to the entrepreneur of receiving information regarding his ability to success-fully complete the date 1 task and L_F is the cost of receiving that information. L_F reflects the net benefit to Self 1 if he never tried to learn anything about his ability before attempting the task. The gain from acquiring information about his own ability to complete the task successfully comes from a boost it gives to his self-confidence, if the information is encouraging.

The loss comes from the potential deflation of his confidence if he receives bad news about his ability to successfully complete the task.

We evaluate the gain function G_F over a range from certainly rejecting the task ($F(\theta) = 0$) up to the probability of doing so given the impatience, or 'lack of resolve', of the entrepreneur's Self 1 incarnation, that is $F(\theta) = c/\beta \delta V$. Losses, captured by L_F, on the other hand are only evaluated over the range of costs of the project which might be undertaken. The lower bound of this range is given by the cost to Self 0 who knows Self 1 will have to consider undertaking the project next period, that is $F(\theta) = c/\delta V$. The upper bound on losses is given by the greater costs perceived by the entrepreneur's later Self 1 incarnation as he struggles with his own lack of resolve, as captured by β ($F(\theta) = c/\beta \delta V$). Recall $\beta < 1$ so the presence of β in the denominator makes the condition less likely to hold.

If the entrepreneur at date 1 finds his probability of successfully completing the task, θ, lies in the interval $\frac{c}{\delta V} < \theta < \frac{c}{\beta \delta V}$ then he will not attempt the task despite the fact that his Self 0 incarnation would wish him to do so. This 'time-inconsistency' in the entrepreneur's decision whether to undertake the task arises because while Self 0 would discount the period 2 reward to successful completion of the task, i.e. V by the market interest rate alone to give a value $c/\delta V$, the date 1 entrepreneur, Self 1, discounts date 2 benefits more heavily to reflect his high value of current happiness. In the presence of such an accelerated depreciation of the date 2 reward V, the entrepreneur will only undertake the task if $\theta > c/\beta \delta V$, rather than the more lax condition of $\theta > c/\delta V$ preferred by his Self 0 incarnation. Recall $\beta < 1$ so the presence of β in the denominator makes the condition more likely to hold the further it falls below 1 in value.

Here β can be interpreted as Self 1's weakness of resolve to work hard to succeed at the project. So information could become a threat to the self-confidence of the entrepreneur in performing the task if it throws him into the region where Self 0 would undertake the task, but his Self 1 incarnation does not. In this event the value of information about the entrepreneur's ability to complete the task successfully may be rendered negative $I_F < 0$. The possibility of an entrepreneur exhibiting this aversion to information about his ability rises in β. Examining the condition Equation (17.4) above it is clear that increasing β contracts the range over which net gains arise as calculated in Equation (17.4), i.e. $\delta \beta I_F$. So the net gain to acquiring information falls in β as implied by the condition in Equation (17.4).

Figure 17.2 attempts to portray the decomposition of the net value of information to the Self 0 entrepreneur graphically. Here we assume the distribution of implied losses to Self 0 lies entirely within the bounds of the distribution of gains from undertaking all projects offering net benefits from zero to $c/\delta V$. The net benefit of information to the Self 0 entrepreneur, I_F, is given by subtracting the area under the distribution of losses from that under the distribution of gains. In the graphical presentation, given the two distributions are symmetric (with L_F being simply a diminished version of the G_F distribution), information has value to the Self 1 entrepreneur. However, the exact outcome of this calculus will depend on the value of β, which captures the degree of impatience of the Self 1 entrepreneur and the distribution of θ.

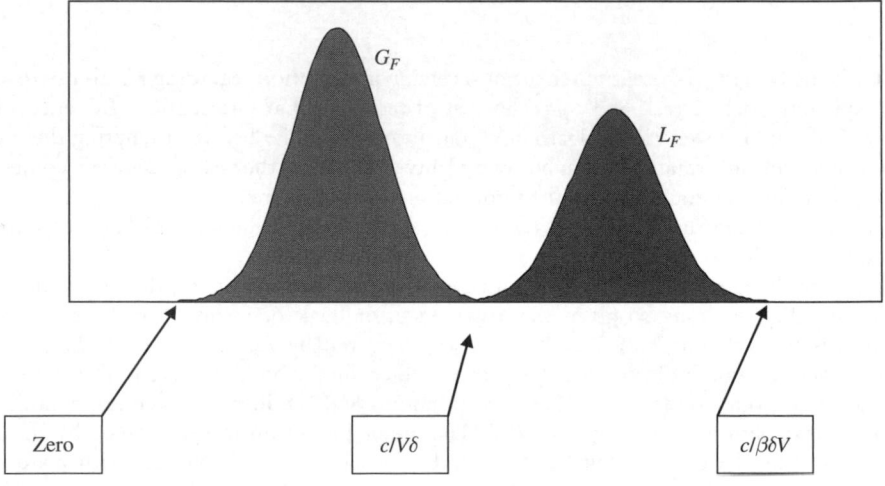

Figure 17.2   The gains or losses from correctly recollecting information in the BT model

In the world that Benabou and Tirole describe, information regarding the entrepreneur's ability to complete the task has value to the entrepreneur's Self 1 incarnation of the entrepreneur if and only if

$$\int_{0}^{c/\delta\beta V} \frac{F(\theta)}{F\left(c/\beta\delta V\right)}\, d\theta \geq \left(\frac{1-\beta}{\beta}\right)\left(\frac{c}{\delta V}\right)$$

which tells us information has value to the Self 1 entrepreneur if his ability is high, but his resolve, captured by $(1 - \beta)/\beta$, is low for a given cost/benefit of a project $(c/\delta V)$. Similarly resolve can even act as a substitute for low ability. Certainly, given the underlying attractiveness of the project $(c/\delta V)$, the more gets done the more steadfast the entrepreneur is (the closer β is to 1, i.e. perfect resolve on the part of the entrepreneur). In terms of Figure 17.2 β converges on 1 and so losses disappear and it's all gravy for the resolute entrepreneur.

17.2.2 Always Wrong but Never in Doubt

It is sometimes said of investment professionals that they are 'always wrong, but never in doubt'. How does this sad state of affairs come about?

The career of 'Captain' Bob Maxwell perhaps typifies the reckless buccaneer entrepreneur who exhibited ultimately tragic hubris. Having triumphed over personal adversity in Eastern Europe to become a Second World War hero who constructed a multi-million pound publishing empire, he brought it all down on his own head in 1991. Why do great men (or women) often 'risk it all' seemingly for no reason? The BT model can explain such behaviour as the outcome of a battle between the actor's Self 0 and the later Self 1 who must face the task/challenge he prepares for at date 0. Consider two wannabe entrepreneurs distinguished only by their level of optimism. The more optimistic of the two would-be entrepreneurs has a belief regarding his ability to succeed (and so get V), $F(\theta)$. His more timid compatriot beliefs about success are distributed as $G(\theta)$, where $\bar{\theta}_F > \bar{\theta}_G > \frac{c}{\beta\delta V}$.

So both would-be entrepreneurs are willing to undertake the task, but the more optimistic one is more likely to do so even in the face of unexpected costs or hardships. The more confident the entrepreneur is the more likely he is to undertake the challenge faced whatever the costs, c, may be. This creates a demand for self-confidence by Self 0 entrepreneur's incarnations. How that demand is satisfied is explained next.

17.2.3 The Supply of Self-Confidence in the BT Model

Benabou and Tirole consider an entrepreneur who may receive a signal, σ, about his ability to complete the task, θ, at the initial date 0. The signal, σ, states with probability $(1 - q)$ that he is not up to the job of completing the date task/challenge. A value of σ equal to H indicates that the entrepreneur has high ability to complete the task successfully (denoted θ_H), a value of σ equal to L indicates that his ability to complete the task successfully is low (hence his ability is θ_L). Alternatively, with probability q he learns nothing at date 0 about his ability to do the task at date 1. So 'no news is good news' from the Self 0 entrepreneur's viewpoint. Therefore,

$$\theta_L \equiv E[\theta|\sigma = L] < E[\theta|\sigma = \varnothing] = \theta_H$$

where $\theta_L < \theta_H$, i.e. θ is lower for low-ability entrepreneurs than for high-ability ones and $1 > q > (1 - q)$ implies that a minority of budding entrepreneurs at date 0 discover they are not up to the job of the date 1 task. For some of that minority recollection of their lack of ability may dissuade them from even trying to successfully complete the task. Denote the date 1 recollection of the date 0 signal about the entrepreneur's ability to do the task $\hat{\sigma}$ where the entrepreneur either recalls bad news about his ability to complete the task successfully or no bad news is received ($\hat{\theta} \in [L, \varnothing]$). Let the probability that Self 1 recalls his Self 0's signal correctly be λ. So

$$\lambda \equiv \Pr[\hat{\sigma}=L|\sigma=L]$$

For simplicity Benabou and Tirole assume the only 'false memories' at date 1 concern the suppression of bad news about the entrepreneur's ability to do the task. The 'natural' rate of recall of the signal, θ, is given by λ_N which maximizes date 0 utility, u_0. Entrepreneurs at date 0, deciding as Self 0, can suppress memory of the signal at date 1 below this 'natural' level at some cost M, where $M = 0$ at the 'natural' accuracy of the recollection.

Since it is impossible to 'choose to forget' (no matter how much we might try), the suppression of memories brings its own problems. In particular, the entrepreneur's Self 1 incarnation, being aware of Self 0's tricks in strategically suppressing negative signals concerning his ability to complete the task successfully, i.e. $\sigma = L$, must make an assessment of the credibility of his recollection. Even good news (which is no news in this context) becomes tainted with the fear that it is a false memory. That is bad news has been received and its memory strategically suppressed by Self 0.

So the entrepreneur in his Self 1 incarnation faces two conflicting forces:

- A desire for immediate gratification through abandonment of the project and the costs it brings, which we might call his lack of 'resolve' to complete the task because of its current cost, c.
- A possible over-optimism embedded in Self 1 about his ability, because of the manipulation by Self 0 of what Self 1 recollects of the signal σ, recalled at date 1 (denoted $\hat{\sigma}$).

The resulting equilibrium reflects the balancing of these two pressures.

This conflict is the curse of a boss too tyrannical to be presented with bad news by his subordinates: 'It's the courtiers who kill the King' and they do so with kind words designed to avoid conflict. So to guard against this the Self 1 entrepreneur must judge the reliability, r^*, of his date 1 recollection of the date 0 signal, $\hat{\sigma}$ (given to his Self 0 incarnation). These initial beliefs have some probability λ^* of correctly recalling a signal he has low ability, i.e. $\sigma = L$. Benabou and Tirole assume the Self 1 entrepreneur infers the reliability of the recalled signal, $\hat{\sigma}$, rationally using Bayes' rule as follows.

$$r^* = \Pr[\sigma = \varnothing | \sigma = \varnothing, \lambda^*] = \frac{q}{q + (1 - q)(1 - \lambda^*)}$$

where the date 1, Self 1, entrepreneur's inferred confidence becomes a weighted average of the signal about ability implied by receiving a signal L, θ_L or 'no news', θ_H (which is good news) where the weights reflect Self 1's confidence in his recollection

$$\theta(r^*) \equiv r^*\theta_H + (1 - r^*)\theta_L$$

So if Self 1 is perfectly confident, $\theta(r^*) = \theta_H = 1$. For the more timid even good recollections are diluted by fear of false memories of Self 1's true ability to successfully complete the task.

To simplify the structure, Benabou and Tirole assume the payoff to successfully facing the date 1 task/challenge is equal to one, $V = 1$. Further, the cost to Self 1 of facing the challenge is given by c, drawn from an interval $[\underline{c}, \bar{c}]$ with a uniform distribution $\Phi(c)$ and density $\varphi(c)$. To make the decision of the Self 0 entrepreneur non-trivial, Benabou and Tirole assume costs are in the range $\bar{c}$ to $\underline{c}$ and $\bar{c} < \beta\delta\theta_H > \beta\delta\theta_L > \underline{c}$. This implies that the expected gain from undertaking the task always lies between the bounds of possible gains given by complete confidence by Self 1 that he can successfully perform the task and complete certainty he cannot (recall $V = 1$ and so is already implicitly present in the expected payoffs under high and low ability $\theta_H\beta\delta$ and $\theta_L\beta\delta$ respectively). Given the problem he faces the Self 1 entrepreneur only attempts all tasks for which $c < \beta\delta E[\theta|\sigma]$, which means his Self 0 incarnation has a prospective payoff of:

$$\beta\delta \int_0^{\beta\delta E[\theta|\hat{\sigma}]} (\delta E[\theta|\sigma] - c)d\Phi(c)$$

which is the net payoff, after allowing for the cost of effort spent on the task, over the range of costs he finds acceptable. Note that the range of tasks attempted only goes as far as the limiting payoff $\beta\delta E[\theta|\sigma]$, whereas the entrepreneur in his Self 0 incarnation would prefer to attempt all tasks with net benefits to successful completion of up to $\delta E[\theta|\sigma]$. So the decrement in tasks attempted by Self 1 from Self 0's viewpoint is simply the additional discounting of the payoff V (here set equal to 1) reflected in β, a measure of Self 1's impatience to get V.

To address this impatience in Self 1, or his lack of 'resolve' β, Self 0 simply responds by increasing the recollected ability of Self 1 by an amount equal to the impatience to be rewarded he expects that Self 1 will display. So Self 0 presets the recollected ability of Self 1 to $E[\theta|\sigma]/\beta$. Hence

$$E[\theta|\hat{\sigma}] = \frac{E[\theta|\sigma]}{\beta}$$

where the recollection of the signal $\hat{\sigma}$ is simply the true signal regarding the entrepreneur's Self 1 ability to do the task. This is simply equated to the signal received by his Self 0 incarnation but grossed up by a factor (β) reflecting his impatience or 'lack of resolve'.

In a later paper Benabou and Tirole (2004) rework many of these issues of self-control, time inconsistency and optimism, but the utility of imposing personal rules (like only drinking in company, or always arriving early for meetings) is interpreted as a way of developing will-power and thus self-control. One of the insights they offer is that too much control exercised too early can weaken an individual's ability to effectively manage their lives later. So having overbearing parents, institutionalized life in a prison, entering a religious cult, can serve to undermine the individual's ability to effectively monitor their own behaviour. By setting the cost of deviating from externally imposed rules too high, the desire or need to exercise self-control is stunted. Thus we might expect entrepreneurs to emerge from relatively relaxed, creative environments where development of personalized objectives and techniques of accomplishing them are likely to flourish.

17.2.4 Numerical Illustration of the BT Model

Using the initializing values in Table 17.1, Figure 17.3 evaluates the condition for the value to the entrepreneur of receiving information about his ability to effectively complete the date 1 task. Recall the benefits of getting information about his ability rather depends on how able the entrepreneur is to complete the task. Bad news might undermine his steely resolve. Figure 17.3 results from letting the entrepreneur's ability be drawn from a normal distribution with a mean 1 (the same as that assumed in evaluating the loss-function L_F) and standard deviation 1. Recall that given the assumptions of the normal distribution two-thirds of the distribution (of mean 1) lies within the bounds 2 and 0 and 95% within 3 and −1 (the famous 'reverse Midas touch'). Figure 17.3 results from evaluating

Table 17.1 Initial values for the evaluation of the value of information condition in the BT model (Equation (17.4))

Parameter	Value
δ – the normal discount rate	$0.9 = 1/1.1$
Ability (generate on unit normal here) (mean is zero, standard deviation is 1)	Θ
Average inferred ability by self = zero	$\bar{\theta}_F = 1$
C – the cost of undertaking the task	0.8
V – the value of the project	1

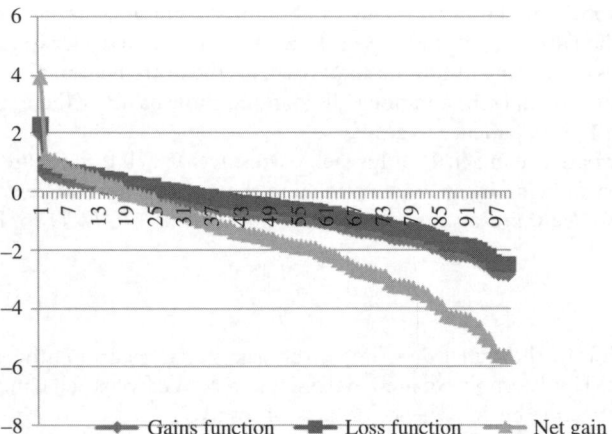

Figure 17.3 Numerical illustration of Benabou and Tirole model

Equation (17.3) over 100 drawings of the normal distribution of mean 1 and standard deviation 1 and ranking the results in terms of the resultant net gain to acquiring information. For the initial values provided in Table 17.1 only 13 of the 100 draws from a normal distribution allow the gains from undertaking the task to exceed its benefits. For the rest, ignorance is bliss.

17.3 Is Deluding Yourself Worth it?

Given the costs and benefits of self-deception, is the game worth the candle? Is it better just to face up to hurtful criticism and rejection – simply accepting it is information that we need to know? Shakespeare's Hamlet illustrates the dangers of being so self-aware he almost literally procrastinates himself to death. He becomes so aware of his own moral weakness that it undermines his resolve to avenge his father's death asking, 'What should such fellows as I do crawling between earth and heaven?'[1] So, getting the calculus of self-confidence versus self-deception right is clearly important for 'men of action' like entrepreneurs.

Benabou and Tirole compare two potential utility levels available to the Self 0 entrepreneur. Firstly, $U_C(\theta_L|r^*)$, which can be achieved by censoring the recollection of Self 1 regarding the signal about his poor ability to do the task received by Self 0. Recall good news is always recollected clearly. Alternatively, Self 0 can simply let Self 1 face the unpleasant truth, giving him utility $U_T(\theta_L)$. Which course he follows depends on the comparative net benefits on offer from either undertaking or passing up on the project. This net benefit is given by the expression

$$U_C(\theta_L|r^*) - U_T(\theta_L) = \beta\delta\left(\int_{\beta\theta_L}^{\delta\theta_L} ((\delta\theta_L - c)d\Phi(c)) - \int_{\delta\theta_L}^{\beta\delta\theta(r^*)} (c - \delta\theta_L)d\Phi(c)\right)$$

where the first integral on the right-hand side is the distribution of net benefits to undertaking the task, given Self 1's ability and the distribution of costs ($\Phi(c)$) faced. Note the first integral goes to zero if Self 1 has perfect 'resolve' ($\beta = 1$). If Self 1 is of solid resolve there is never any benefit to self-deception, but as resolve ebbs, or weak will grows, the first term increases in falling β and censoring of information passed to Self 1 by Self 0 becomes valuable. The second integral on the right-hand side captures the potential loss from overconfidence if the Self 1 entrepreneur takes on projects whose costs exceed their benefits (so $(c - \delta\theta_L) > 0$). In the case of worthwhile projects for which benefits exceed their costs, i.e. when $(c - \delta\theta_L) < 0$, recall there are no costs only benefits of Self 0 induced optimism in his Self 1 incarnation.

Given this calculus we might expect firm resolve, tenacity, if not just sheer bloody-mindedness to feature large in the psychology of successful entrepreneurs.

17.3.1 Optimism, Self-Control and Society

From the BT model one could form the impression that some non-delusional level of self-induced optimism is a good thing, but Brocas and Carillo (2004), in a model with some similarities to the BT framework, point out that this may not be the case from a macroeconomic viewpoint. In their model, agents are also optimistic and discount gains in the far future more than those in the near future, that is to say they are more 'impatient' than consideration of the market interest rate would suggest. The difference here is that wannabe entrepreneurs with the best prospects forgo seeking advice on the likelihood of success of their business plan in order to avoid inefficient procrastination. While this 'strategic ignorance' (Carillo & Marriotti 2000) may make sense from an individual entrepreneur's viewpoint, it may have large social/macroeconomic costs. So there arises a 'fallacy of aggregation' where what is good for each of us is not good for all of us. This arises because of excess investment in market niches for which there can only be limited demand. Think of broadband, Wi-Fi, or mobile ring-tone suppliers as examples here. Each product has a discernible demand, but the response to that demand quickly passed saturation point. Seizing the moment, even at the risk of misplaced effort, may make individuals' action socially harmful, thus suggesting a role for corrective education to ensure self-awareness.

This danger of overinvestment in niche markets by strategically ignorant entrepreneurs poses a further threat to the adoption of active macroeconomic management by the state.[2] A policy-maker, using monetary policy to suppress interest rates and encourage investment, needs to be aware of the danger of inducing excessive investment as well. Hence intervention to facilitate greater self-awareness amongst wannabe entrepreneurs can reduce wasteful investment. Only by doing so can such entrepreneurs avoid the danger of displacing productive investment with speculative bubbles in narrow niche markets.

17.3.2 The Social Benefits of the Maverick Entrepreneur

We are beneficiaries of those who dared to think differently from the crowd, having the temerity to believe women could be allowed to vote, the earth goes round the sun, or man could walk on the moon. 'Thinking outside the box' is almost the new mantra of conformism it seems, but in reality it is often easier to conform to social mores in our views and behaviour. This very pattern of conformity can lead to 'informational cascades' in which we sheepishly follow the crowd, almost regardless of our social preferences.

Becker (1991) illustrated this trend with the example of two restaurants facing each other in a quiet town a long way from the next competitor. Imagine the first hungry customer to arrive on the scene. He must decide on the basis of some rational criteria which restaurant to enter. He can look at the menu, read a review or just randomly dive into one of them. Now suppose a married couple follow along some time later. They too can choose the restaurant on the basis of the menu, a review or some other sensible criterion. But they have one additional piece of information: one restaurant is empty. Meanwhile in the other restaurant a man is tucking into his main course. On balance, if both restaurants seem similar, they might avoid the empty restaurant. If they do so the next potential diner is more likely to go to the restaurant where it's hip to be seen rather than its shunned competitor. Of course the problem is the fourth diner just following the crowd rather than making an objective judgement. This is fine if the choice made by the crowd is sensible, but if the crowd decide to smoke, inject heroin or speed on the motorway, this may not be so good. A role emerges for those who will buck the trend to blaze a new path. This is where the entrepreneur comes in.

Bernardo and Welch (2001) point to the maverick role of entrepreneurs introducing dispersion into accepted beliefs and behaviour. In their framework the social benefit of the entrepreneur derives from his ability to introduce dispersion into beliefs and behaviour, modes of production, marketing, etc. It is the very overconfidence or insularity of the entrepreneur that allows him to choose the restaurant he likes, even if everyone else chose the one across the road. In doing so he breaks the 'informational cascade', clearing the way for others to make a less pressurized decision between following the crowd and joining in a new approach. The effect of the maverick decisions by 'preference entrepreneurs' is to broadcast their information regarding a possible new production technique or lifestyle.

17.4   Conclusion and Summary

In Chapter 7 I discussed optimism as a bias or flaw that we are all victims of. Accepting I will never be a film star or win a Nobel Prize is just too painful. But perhaps the negative costs of optimism contain their own positive. Optimism strengthens our resolve and makes us undertake ambiguous tasks where the chances of success are objectively low. To abolish slavery, uncover the role of DNA, or fly to the moon is very hard, but I am very glad that my forebears had the glint of madness to undertake these liberating projects. So maybe biases like optimism and impatience, or lack of resolve, need to be optimally traded off rather than be simply repressed. Like many seemingly useless, or even harmful things, for example my appendix (the organ not the section of this chapter), there is a reason for its existence. If so we may need to embrace biases into the construction of models of financial behaviour rather than simply try to deny their presence and/or effect.

Appendix: Entrepreneurs and the BT Model – Some Case Studies

This section attempts to apply the BT model to some of the most charismatic entrepreneurs of the new economy. The late 1990s' boom is often remembered for the hubris of those at its helm, but it is often forgotten that, along with the surface dross, many credible businesses which are still thriving (although sometimes in a transformed state) were formed during the last frantic years of the last millennium. In this section I discuss the emergence and success of such iconic figures in light of the BT model and the central place it gives to optimism, self-control and their interaction as a basis for success as an entrepreneur.

Jim Clark, Silicon Graphics, Netscape and Healtheon

The Netscape IPO in 1997 is often seen as the starting gun of the 'greatest legal creation of wealth in the history of the planet'.[3] On the first day of trading Netscape's stock price rose from $28 to $58.25. Three months after the IPO Netscape's stock traded at $140. Its founder, an ex-professor of electrical engineering at Stanford, Jim Clark, became an instant billionaire in the process. Clark had retained a fifth of Netscape's stock and remained its largest shareholder.

Clark had previously founded Silicon Graphics, a computer hardware venture, but had been frozen out of control by professional managers brought in to run the firm by venture capitalists who funded its foundation. Later he would use his great wealth to found, but not run, Healtheon, a health care coordination site.

Clark was nothing if not self-aware. Michael Lewis in his description of a road journey with Jim Clark, *The New New Thing: A Silicon Valley Story* (Lewis 2000), describes the foundation of Healtheon:

> If he was going to found the most valuable company in America, the company would need a name. He might as well call it Jim Clark Enterprises, for that is what it amounted to. Instead he wrote Healthscape'[4]

(Lewis, 2000, p.90).

Indeed by this stage Clark had no plan to be involved in the execution of his project, preferring to remain at the conceptualization stage. Again Lewis (2000, p.91) describes it thus, 'He had ceased to be a businessman and become a conceptual artist'.

Clark's prior involvement in Silicon Graphics and Netscape had taught him that the compromise politics of everyday management were not for him. Recalling a batch of psychological tests, performed at an away-day to try to ease disputes within Silicon Graphics, Clark recalls, 'The psychologists determined that everyone else on the Executive Committee was passive aggressive and I was just aggressive' (Lewis 2000, p.45). Elsewhere Lewis points out the benefits that Clark extracted from his aggression by pointing out, 'He was the guy who always won the game of chicken, because his opponents suspected he might actually enjoy a head on collision' (Lewis 2000, p.181).

This aggression led to intense conflict with the management team brought in by venture capitalists to run Silicon Graphics after Clark had founded it. The aggression was clearly motivated, as a close colleague recalled:

> Jim Clark has a clarity of vision that is prompted by the purest form of greed.... Nothing clouds it

(Lewis 2000, p.109).

Clark in his own history of Netscape, *Netscape Time* (Clark & Edwards 2000), tackles the same issue in the following way:

Although a personal financial obsession will lead to problems, the ultimate goal of a business is to become self-sustaining, which means that it must make sufficient money to keep its employees paid and remain competitive. The entrepreneur without a financial motive will not be successful

(Clark & Edwards 2000, p.13).

Clark's greed would be pretty well sated by his subsequent achievements. On the day Healtheon finally floated in early 1999 Clark had a net worth of $1.5 billion and many of his newly recruited engineers were made instantaneous multi-millionaires (Lewis 2000, pp.235–9). Adding in all his other new-economy equity stakes (in @Home, Netscape, etc.), Clark was worth over $3 billion after tax by the end of the millennium. He clearly did something right.

Specifically Clark had a real taste for creative destruction, leading Michael Lewis to call him 'Disorganisation man'. Clark argued for Silicon Graphics 'cannibalizing itself' by driving costs down to a point where they could access the domestic, or at least serious amateur, user market. Clark feared the emergence of the personal computer as an emerging threat to high-specification dedicated machines like the ones made by Silicon Graphics.

But giving up is hard as Michael Jensen pointed out in his presidential address (Jensen 1993). Facing failure or technical obsolescence is never easy as it requires change and redirection. While conventional businesspeople struggled with this Clark saw such self-reinvention as an essential part of his nature.

In doing this his contagious optimism was consciously used. Discussing the process of recruiting key technical staff Clark comments:

Like a circuit preacher, I can be evangelical when I'm selling my own optimism – anyone who lacks that tendency tends to have a hard time as an entrepreneur in high-tech'

(Clark & Edwards 2000, p.53).

This innate drive allowed him to attract other key talents to his new ventures. On hearing that Marc Andreessen had quit the University of Illinois National Center for Supercomputer Applications after developing and distributing a path-breaking Internet browser called Mosaic only to be taken off the project by university management, Clark decided to seize the moment of opportunity left by the University of Illinois's misjudgement. He moved swiftly to gather the team that had developed Mosaic, adding in a few of his most talented ex-colleagues from Silicon Graphics. Clark comments, 'It's the ability to recruit, inspire and hold onto smart people that offers the key to ongoing success' (Clark & Edwards 2000, p.42).

Not being the creator of the technology that produced the Netscape browser himself prevented Clark from becoming over attached to the company. At the initial public offering he was content to hand over control to his newly recruited CEO, Jim Barksdale. Clark seemed able to prevent great ambition spilling over into self-delusion regarding his own powers.

In his role, Clark, as a new-economy big fish, was happy to define his territory as a compliment to the biggest fish in the market: Bill Gates's Microsoft. He had huge ambition, but managed to avoid letting this tip him into self-delusion. Chastened by the Netscape experience before founding Healtheon (initially called Healthscape), he asked: 'How can I make myself another billion dollars before Microsoft notices what I am up to?' (Lewis 2000, p.88).

Clark's pitch to the Silicon Graphics board of directors for funding Netscape asked 'How can we be to entertainment computing what Microsoft is to productivity computing?' (Lewis 2000, p.62). Once Microsoft began to encroach on Netscape's monopoly the game was up in his view. Clark did not stick around for the 'browser wars' in the courts, but simply moved on to a new enterprise. Similarly, Healtheon would eventually be merged into WebMD, a Microsoft-supported site, to avoid a head-on conflict with Gates.

This willingness to accommodate Microsoft, combined with Clark's inner conviction that he knew best, posed real problems during the 'browser war' trials of the mid-1990s. Following a complaint initiated by Clark, the US Department of Justice, headed by Joe Klein, commenced antitrust proceedings against Microsoft, arguing that it was in breach of a prior agreement not to 'bundle' its Internet software into its operating system. E-mails from Bill Gates to AOL asking 'How much do we have to pay you to screw Netscape?' (Lewis 2000, p.190) didn't help Microsoft's case.

At the subsequent court case it emerged that prior to making the complaint Clark had actually invited Microsoft to take an equity stake in Netscape. Clark closed off the e-mail by making the offer 'No one in my organization knows about this message' (Lewis 2000, p.196). This was true and unfortunate because Netscape would devote much of the next two years trying to prove that Microsoft was forcing its intentions of merging upon Netscape.

With this much apparent contradiction within his own life and his relationship with others Clark needed a brutal ability to structure his own thoughts and emotions. In a passage almost eerily reminiscent of the BT model discussed earlier, Lewis sums up Clark's unique personality thus:

> Above all, one thing was clear: his pursuits of the new new thing depended on a curious amnesia. His ability to forget what he said he would do next, or he'd thought would make him happy, was the mortar on which he laid his endless tiers of self-renewal. He'd make a kind of religion of keeping only those parts of his past he needed for fuel on his journey into the future

> (Lewis 2000, p.259).

Larry Page and Sergey Brin

The inception of strong businesses by effective pairings seems pretty common in the new economy. Bill Gates and Paul Allen at Microsoft are an archetype followed later by Steve Jobs and Steve Wozniak at Apple and Jerry Yang and David Filo at Yahoo!. A similar pairing gave rise to the well-known Google search engine.

Larry Page and Sergey Brin met in the PhD student accommodation of the Gates Building of Stanford's computer science department. From their meeting in 1996 and arguing and working all hours as graduate students, the pair went on to form Google and entered the Forbes 400 rich list at joint 43rd position having an estimated personal wealth in excess of $10 billion each (Vise 2005, p.323). Like Jim Clark both men combined strong mathematical-scientific backgrounds with a good sense of optimism and self-worth. Addressing college students at his old high school Page stated:

> Optimism is important. You have to be a bit silly in the goals you are going to set. There is a phrase I learned in college called 'Having a healthy disregard for the impossible'.

> (Vise 2005, p.11).

In a similar vein an ex-teacher commented upon the pair's non-conformist streak as follows:

> They have a somewhat skeptical view of authority. If they see the world going one way and they believe it should be going the other way they are more likely to say 'The rest of the world is wrong' rather than 'Maybe we should reconsider'. They were confident in their approach and would tell you everyone else was wrong

> (Vise 2005, p.42).

Such attitudes seem consistent with the BT framework in which optimism enables an intense focus on the job at hand. Such focus would be much needed as the business concept took form in Room 360 of the Gates Building in Stanford. from Brin's original PageRank[5] search algorithm. Initial attempts to sell the PageRank algorithm to Excite and Yahoo! were unsuccessful. The quality of the search product was then seen as less important than its ability to generate cash-flow from advertising.

Brin and Page had many things in common: the academic nature of their parents; their attendance at Montessori schools which emphasize the self-expression and self-motivation of pupils as the basis of learning; as well as their mathematical skill. These family backgrounds may have helped to induce a well-calibrated sense of self-control in the pair. Indeed, it was the combination of their dissertation projects that informed the Google search engine. Page was seeking to download the whole contents of the Web onto his personal computer. Brin was developing an algorithm to rank webpages, initially by the number of citations. So if the course webpage for this book is an important source of information on behavioural finance it will have many teachers directing students to it via hyperlinks from their own website. For PageRank to work effectively it needed to swallow as many webpages as possible. So Google's search power comes from the combination of the discriminatory power of Brin's algorithm combined with the voracious appetite of Page's acquisition of material for it to search. This combination of comprehensiveness with relevance required vast amounts of computing power as Google's use spread beyond the confines of the Stanford campus. This would force Brin and Page into hardware as well as software development at an early stage. But it was their complementary strengths that seem to have made them a winning team. A friend from their Stanford graduate days commented:

> They were brilliant in different ways. Sergey was practical, a problem solver, an engineer. If something worked it worked. He was also mathematical, lightning fast and outgoing. He was the brash young man, but he was so smart it just oozed out of him. Page on the other hand was a deep thinker. He wanted to know why things worked. Possessed of boundless ambition, Page had a more reserved demeanour

> (Vise 2005, p.34).

Another contemporary of theirs in the Gates Building said, 'As well as forming a coherent team Brin and Page were able to motivate others to share their vision for the development of an enabling new technology'. Vise (2005, p.34) comments:

> Strip away all the technical knowledge and what you found were two young guys with character. That would translate well into the work they did, especially in a field where people needed to trust you in order to trust your products.

It is difficult to overestimate the audacity, if not arrogance, of the project that Brin and Page developed. In 1996 the Web was estimated to have 10 million documents available. The number of documents on-line was estimated to be growing at 2000% a year. In terms of the BT framework a little misplaced optimism may not have gone amiss in undertaking so daunting a task.

Part of the way in which this was achieved was by giving key technical staff lots of freedom and mimicking a university department's ethos of creating space for new ideas to flourish. Central to this was the practice of empowering key technical workers to allocate 20% of their time to topics of interest to them (rather than a senior colleague at Google). This allowed them to pre-commit resources to unstructured innovation that might otherwise get squeezed out by pressure for immediate results. They were simultaneously ruthlessly ambitious, while recognizing the long-term benefits of allowing 'blue-sky' curiosity driven research to thrive within the company. Page argued:

> We are trying to be ruthlessly efficient about how we run our business and we are in this to make a lot of money. But we are not necessarily going to make money from all the things we have

> (Vise 2005, p.267).

As Google moved outside the boundaries of being a search engine, Page and Brin sought mechanisms which allowed them to retain the coalition of human capital necessary to launch a challenge to Microsoft as the world's premier technology brand. To facilitate this they created 'founders' awards', which are multi-million dollar stock option offerings to those who produced valuable products. Page was well aware of the frustration felt by innovators like Nikola Tesla, whose inventions led to X-rays and solar cells, on seeing the glory and wealth produced by those products largely taken by his overbearing employer Thomas Edison (Battelle 2005, pp.65–6).

The very concept of a search-based venture was somewhat against the grain of the prevailing wisdom of Internet commerce. Yahoo!, Excite and HotBot, all formed originally as search engines, were by this point busily engaged in diversifying into more general-purpose portals, with sections for finance, dating, news, chat, etc. In fact the motivation for Michael Moritz, of Sequoia Capital, was to allow a prior investment of his in Yahoo! to keep an option on licensing Google's search technology as its own efforts went increasingly elsewhere.

The IPO process crystallized many of the strengths and weaknesses of the founding duo. The IPO prospectus filed with the SEC included an 'Owner's Manual for Google's Shareholders' (S1 filing), written by Larry Page. Adopting an uncompromising tone it opened with the sentence 'Google is not a conventional company. We do not intend to become one' (Battelle 2005, p.217). The IPO initiated the dual class voting structure within Google which granted Page and Brin 10 votes at shareholders' meetings for every one share they held. Given that they retained joint ownership of 30% of the company, this ensured their control of Google for the foreseeable future. The S1 filing document justified the dominating presence of the founders by analogy to large media companies, such as the *Wall Street Journal* or the *Washington Post*. The fact that the founders drew an analogy to an old economy content supplier might itself be seen as indicative of the future direction they had set for the company.

The announcement in the S1 filing that Google would not be providing 'earnings guidance' to analysts did not go down well with those following the new company's fortunes with Mitch Kapor (founder of Lotus), a venture capital investor, stating:

> Google says: Give us your money and we'll sell you a lottery ticket. We know what we're doing and it would be counter-productive for you to have any control over what we do. Sit in the backseat, enjoy the ride and don't think too much about the odds

> (Battelle 2005, p.219).

The problem with such an attitude is that it could be interpreted as arrogance. This may have contributed to the great volatility of Google's share price in the run-up to the IPO.

The very tenacity and focus of the pair on maintaining a high-quality search-engine-only site was in many ways the key to their success. Indeed the basic business model of getting businesses to bid in an auction for keywords (like 'books' or 'theatre tickets'), which subsequently influenced their position in search results presented to the consumer, had already been developed by Bill Gross at GoTo. Gross only charged for links clicked on, rather than having an advert appear on the GoTo.com site per se. It was Gross's decision to abandon GoTo's own site in 2000 in favour of a licensing-only business model that cleared the field for Google's expansion. Google took the same auction model and allowed it to influence only search results listed on the right-hand side of the search results screen. This allowed a compromise between developing a credible profit-making strategy and keeping faith with the integrity of an unbiased search engine.

Questions

1. Return to Equations (17.3) and (17.4) of the BT model and consider the impact on the benefit to the entrepreneur of information about his ability to undertake the date 1 task of a rise in the payoff to undertaking it (V). Most entrepreneurs set up simple, low-risk, businesses – a take-away, a cleaning company or an antique shop. Frontier, 'blue-sky' creativity ventures like Google or Netscape are rare. How well does the BT model fit these low-risk, low-payoff ventures (V), as opposed to the 'monster' entrepreneurs?
2. Return to Table 17.1 and the numerical illustration of the condition for value of information about his ability to the entrepreneur. Keep all the initializing assumptions as given in Table 17.1 apart from one. In my original illustration I drew 100 values for the entrepreneur from a normal distribution of mean 1 and standard deviation of 1. Let ability be drawn from a distribution of mean 1 and a standard deviation of 2. Now two-thirds of the values drawn will lie between -1 and 3 and 95% between -3 (yes some entrepreneurs can be that stupid) and 5. What is the impact on the value of this, more diffuse, signal about his ability on the entrepreneur's evaluation of its value (according to the condition in Equation (17.4))?
3. Read through the appendix. Do you find any support for the practical relevance of the BT model? Are there any aspects of the model that you find difficult to square with a sensible model of entrepreneurship?

Notes

1. Indeed Brocas and Carillo (2004) start their paper with a quotation from *Hamlet*, Act 3, Scene 1:

   And thus the native hue of resolution,
   Is sicklied o'er with the pale cast of thought,
   And enterprises of great pitch and moment
   With this regard their currents turn awry
   And lose the name of action.

2. Such an interventionist stance has not really flourished since the influence of the 'new classical macroeconomics' of Robert Lucas, Thomas Sargent and others.
3. A quotation attributed to John Doerr of Kleiner Peabody venture capitalists. Doerr became instantly rich as a result of the Netscape IPO.
4. Sadly for the poetry of the story someone had already grabbed Healthscape as a web address, so Clark changed it to Healtheon.
5. PageRank's original version was called BackRub and asked which sites reference forward to other sites. If I reference Shefrin's (2002) behavioural finance textbook site, then that is clear from the face of my website, but if Shefrin referenced my site I may not even know he had done so. To work all these links out is a pretty data/search-intensive job.

References

Battelle, J. (2005). *The Search: How Google and its Rivals Rewrote the Rules of Business and Transformed Our Culture*. London: Penguin.

Becker, G. (1991). A note on restaurant pricing and other examples of social influences on price. *Journal of Political Economy*, **99**(5): 1109–16.

Benabou, R. & J. Tirole (2002). Self-confidence and personal motivation. *Quarterly Journal of Economics*, **117**(3): 871–913.

Benabou, R. & J. Tirole (2004). Willpower and personal rules. *Journal of Political Economy*, **112**(4): 848–86.

Bernardo, A. & I. Welch (2001). On the evolution of overconfidence and entrepreneurs. *Journal of Economics and Management Strategy*, **10**: 301–30.

Brocas, I. & J. Carillo (2004). Entrepreneurial boldness and excessive investment. *Journal of Economics and Management Strategy*, **13**: 321–50.

Carillo, J. & T. Marriotti (2000). Strategic ignorance as a self-disciplining device. *Review of Economic Studies*, **67**: 529–44.

Clark, J. & O. Edwards (2000). *Netscape Time: The Making of the Billion-Dollar Start-up that Took on Microsoft*. New York: St Martin's Griffin.

Fisher, I. (1930). *The Theory of Interest*. London: Macmillan.

Huarta de Soto, J. (2008). *The Austrian School: Market Order and Entrepreneurial Activity*. Cheltenham: Edward Elgar.

Jensen, M. (1993). The modern industrial revolution, exit, and the failure of internal control systems. *Journal of Finance,* **48**: 831–80.

Jensen, M. (1998). *Self-Interest, Altruism, Incentives and Agency Theory Foundations of Organizational Strategy*. Boston, MA: Harvard University Press.

Lewis, M. (2000). *The New New Thing: A Silicon Valley Story*. New York: W.W. Norton.

Parker, S. (2004). *The Economics of Self-Employment and Entrepreneurship*. Cambridge: Cambridge University Press.

Schumpeter, J. (1947). The creative response to economic history. *Journal of Economic History*, **7**: 149–59.

Shefrin, H. (2002). *Beyond Greed and Fear: Understanding Behavioral Finance and the Psychology of Investing*. Oxford: Oxford University Press.

Thaler, R. & H. Shefrin (1981). An economic theory of self-control. *Journal of Political Economy*, **89**: 392–406.

Vise, D. (2005). *The Google Story: Inside the Hottest Business, Media and Technology Stock of Our Time*. London: Pan.

Part IV
The Professions

Chapter 18

Analysts' Conflicts of Interest

‘ Wall Street is about allocating capital. Great companies can get money easily – bad ones
have to pay more of it. Wall Street gets paid by controlling access to that capital, and
charging fees to get it. . . . The dirty little secret is that people on Wall Street keep half of all
the revenue they generate ,

(Kessler 2003, p.81).

Financial analysts often wear two hats: a marketing hat for drumming up trade and hence
commissions and a research hat for giving 'independent' investment advice to clients regarding
how best to invest their money. If the analysts' employer, a merchant bank, is affiliated in some
way to the company being followed then such 'conflicts of interest' between selling the stock and
impartially reporting its prospects can become intense. Mehran and Stultz (2007) define a conflict
of interest to be 'a situation in which a party to a transaction can potentially gain by taking actions
that adversely affect the counterparty'. Such conflicts of interest between the duty of an analyst to
his employer and client have become the focus of major litigation in both the United States and the
United Kingdom, but, as the above quote from Anson Beard (given in Kessler 2003), a senior
banker at Morgan Stanley in the late 1990s, makes clear, it is almost a universal characteristic of
the worldwide investment banking industry. A recent special issue of the *Journal of Financial
Economics* confirms the renewed academic interest in this important area of professional practice'
(Mehran & Stultz 2007).

The most famous illustration of this conflict was the 2004 Global Analyst Settlement by 10 US
investment banks who gave poor advice about the prospects of dot.com companies. These
investment banks agreed to pay $1.4 billion in settlement of threatened litigation arising from
their clients' losses. This included particular penalties for two star analysts of the dot.com (and
especially broadband) boom, Jack Grubman and Henry Blodget. As part of the settlement the
banks paid out $845 million in disgorged profits, $432.5 million to fund investment research,
and $80 million to fund education for investors. The perceived failings of analysts were
addressed by Title 5, Section 501, of the Sarbanes–Oxley Act. This attempts to outlaw conflicts
of interest for analysts and enforces a declaration of independence from the firms they cover
upon them. In 2002 the UK Financial Services Authority (FSA) issued guidelines about how to
handle such conflicts of interest and a recently completed study by the FSA has evaluated the
efficacy of these guidelines.

Much of the response of regulatory agencies and the courts to the manifestation of these conflicts
appears grounded in a belief in a somewhat standard version of the efficient markets hypothesis and
the perspective it suggests regarding conflicts faced the investing public. The presence of noise-
traders, sentiment-based trade and overreaction to short-term trends suggests existing policy may
have an inadequate/unrealistic foundation.

Louis Brandeis speaking of the US Supreme Court ruling is supposed to have claimed 'Sunlight is
the best disinfectant and electric light the most efficient policemen' in a 1933 book entitled *Other*

People's Money and How Bankers Use It. But in noisy financial markets is this the case? Can foreknowledge be enough to forearm investors against analysts' conflicts of interest?

Discussion of the conflicts of interests that analysts face has really focused on two issues which are outlined below:

- Are such conflicts actually a problem for the clients of investment banks at all? This reasoning challenges the prohibition or legal penalization of such conflicts.
- If these conflicts are a problem for investors how are they best prohibited or monitored?

18.1   Illustration and Structure

Increasingly during the dot.com boom, analysts felt the pressure to cross such Chinese walls to support their investment banking colleagues who accounted for the lion's share of their common employer's revenue. On being asked about the objectivity of his research in 1997, given his position on the board of directors of WorldCom, Global Crossing and other companies he recommended for purchase, Jack Grubman of Salomon Smith Barney stated

> What used to be called conflict is now synergy. Objective research? The other word for it is uninformed research

> (Gasparino 2005, p.146).

While some chafed at Grubman's candour this quote was most probably a stark expression of the underlying reality analysts faced at that time. Indeed the *Wall Street Journal* praised Grubman in 1997 for how deftly he negotiated the conflicts of interest between being a good stock-picker and helping drive corporate banking revenue for his employer in an article entitled 'The jack of all trades: for Salomon, Grubman is a big telecom rainmaker', stating that what separated

> Grubman from the pack is how skilfully he manages to walk the divide between banking and research with his credibility intact

> (Gasparino 2005, p.87).

With such praise it is easy to see why few analysts saw the problem in their conflicted position. The US Congressional hearings in 2001 may have displayed a certain amount of selective memory in damning analysts for their conflicted investment advice offered to their clients. Mary Meeker, the 'Internet Queen' of Morgan Stanley, has asked 'Whatever happened to personal responsibility?' Meeker had started out as the protégé of Frank Quattrone at Morgan Stanley. Quattrone was nothing if not enthusiastic (and possibly delusional) in his support for Morgan Stanley's Internet-based investment banking clients.

Meeker's grave doubts about the stocks she was asked to take public by her employer led her to veto many proposed floatation deals touted by Morgan Stanley's investment banking arm. Conveniently for later struggles Meeker kept a tally of the 50% of deals she rejected after 1995. As early as 1991 Meeker in advancing her 'Ten Commandments of investing in Tech stocks' in a circular to clients advised on adopting a contrarian strategy. In particular she advised:

> Buy stocks when no one is interested in them as investments .... But sell them when everyone is interested in technology

> (Gasparino 2005, p.53).

Specifically Meeker advised clients to 'not fall in love with technology companies' and 'Remember to treat them as investments' (Gasparino 2005, p.53).

If this advice had been followed many of the Congressional Committee's concerns would have been addressed. Even as late as early 2000, but before the crash, Meeker in the *Wall Street Journal* warned investors, 'You never want to catch a falling knife' (Gasparino 2005, p.129).

But in the post-boom depression as President Bush lambasted the 'Dark side of Capitalism', such truths were conveniently forgotten. At some distance from those events, perhaps a more considered appraisal of the market impact of analysts' conflicts of interest is now possible. Montier (2006) discusses some of the dangers of a naive believe in what analysts tell us to do with our money in Sections 1.2.7 and 1.2.8 of his book.

Section 18.2 explains the origin and nature of the conflicts of interests faced by analysts. I consider broader empirical studies of the market impact of analysts' conflicts of interests on financial market returns and how such market distortions have been addressed by regulatory authorities like the FSA. Section 18.3 looks in greater detail at the regulatory regime in place in the United Kingdom, Europe and the United States to give redress to investors who believe they have suffered at the hands of conflicted analysts. This includes the US common law position as well as the statutory regime which predominates in the United Kingdom and Europe. Section 18.4 summarizes and concludes the chapter.

After reading this chapter the reader should:

* Understand the evidence regarding the damaged caused by analysts' conflicts of interest in terms of diminished returns to following their advice.
* Understand the policy response of the US, UK and EU authorities to these conflicts.
* Be able to model the impact of noise traders' presence in the market on the investment value of conflicted analysts' advice.

18.2 Evidence of Conflicts of Interest from Empirical Studies

Even prior to the excesses of the dot.com boom a number of studies were undertaken of analysts' conflicts of interest. These include Lin and McNichols (1998), Dugar and Nathan (1995) and Michaely and Womack (1999). A related study by Gompers and Lerner (1999) examines the market performance of initial public offerings (IPOs) brought to market in years 1970–92 by venture US capital firms that are subsidiaries of investment banks. In such circumstances the investment bank underwriter has a clear incentive to overprice the IPO since it stands to receive a large part of the deal's proceeds. But these authors find the market recognizes this conflict and discount the price of venture capital offerings by affiliated investment banks accordingly. These early studies formed the backdrop that informed the inception of the Sarbanes–Oxley Title 5 legislation. Their results suggest that analysts exhibited an additional 'reporting' bias due to their need to mollify their employers' investment banking clients, which is separable from and incremental to the many previously documented 'cognitive' biases they exhibit (optimism, overreaction, herding, etc., see Francis & Philbrick 1993).

A study by Barber *et al.* (2007) in a study of over 300,000 recommendations issued by 409 securities firms concerning the fortunes of over 11,000 separate companies in the years 1996–2003 concludes that it is during market downturns that the most damage is done to the informational role of prices by analysts' conflicts of interest. Specifically they report that after the stock-market downturn in early 2000 a large gap appeared between the investment value offered by recommendations issued by independent as against conflicted financial institutions. Specifically, after the downturn a 3.1 basis point daily abnormal return appeared to open up following independent research from institutions without an investment banking arm, as against recommendations issued by compromised investment banks. For companies issuing equity during the test period covered the mark-up to following independent advice was even bigger. Oddly, prior to the downturn there was a small insignificant benefit to following the conflicted analysts' advice (viz., 'just keep buying'). This implies the extent of damage done by analysts' conflicts of interest depends on the sentiment of the market at the point in time of the test. In market booms conflicts of interest may work to investors' advantage because biased forecasts provide a more efficient signal regarding company value. Conflicted analysts are indeed more optimistic than their independent peers, but their optimism is largely borne out by subsequent events, even if the background against which they forecast is objectively bleak.

A more recent study of the impact of analysts' conflicts of interest suggests that while such conflicts manifestly exist, their impact on traded prices may not be particularly great (Agrawal & Chen 2008). Conflicted analysts are indeed more optimistic in their recommendations, and were especially so in the 1990s' boom era, but investors recognize this and discount the value of their recommendations accordingly. The one-year-ahead forecast performance of conflicted and truly independent analysts showed little statistical difference on average. This suggests there may be little potential public harm to investors for public policy to be concerned with. The law is not typically concerned with the 'average', or 'representative', agent, but with individual plaintiffs and their perceived, or actual, losses. So the results of market-based studies do not resolve the question of the need for regulatory intervention to protect investors.

At the end of the dot.com/con (Cassidy 2002) boom the search for sacrificial lambs began and it was not long before the names of leading technology analysts, Henry Blodget, Jack Grubman, Frank Quattrone and Mary Meeker started to come up as the usual suspects for inciting a bubble psychology to the market. These analysts were seen to typify a new style of investment advisor, who assumed the role of advisor to the firms whose fortunes they predicted for clients, in order to achieve greater insight into their corporate lives and possible futures.

As the Internet boom continued analysts straddled, and even crossed, the 'Chinese walls' separating investment banking (preparing companies for floatation and giving advice on mergers and acquisitions) from providing investment advice to buy, sell or hold particular shares. These walls were erected to prevent analysts' advice being compromised by a perceived need to support their colleagues in investment banking. So a company stumbling after an IPO underwritten by the analyst's employer would be condemned to a sell recommendation by the bank's analysts offering objective advice to their clients. Analysts had historically been expected to 'Call them like they see them' regardless of what their employer had done for the company in the past, or hoped to do in the future.

18.2.1   No Conflict, No Interest

John Doerr of Kleiner Peabody commented on his involvement in both the start-up financing and management of various new-economy firms – Netscape, Google, etc. – that where there was no conflict of interest he had no interest in investing (Clark & Edwards 2000, p.8). The motivation to earn money as an individual can drive an analyst or investment bank to pick winners. In short the opportunity for personal profit, via an underwriting commission related bonus, can motivate more accurate and profitable coverage of a stock.

Spindler (2006a) has argued for the decriminalization, if not encouragement, of conflicts of interest in investment research. He has advanced three primary arguments to support this case:

- Independent research is research based on public sources with little more value than an article in *The Economist* or *Investors Chronicle*. Conflicted research is value-added research benefiting from in-depth, behind the scenes and legally required public filings (recall the Grubman quote above).

- Company management bears a duty of strict liability for claims and representations in an initial public offering, or acquisition, prospectus. For example, if a claim is made to a piece of intellectual property and this is subsequently successfully legally challenged, management are legally liable for its investors' subsequent losses at common law. The fact that this was a reasonable claim and one the management truly believed cannot protect them in the court leads to hedging, legalese and banal claims in prospectus documents. Often the only way to convey the good prospects of the firm without incurring strict liability is perhaps via a buoyant investment analyst's report, or forthright claim in the pre-deal 'road-show' to prospective investors.
- Underwriters seem to display little inclination to compete on price with 7% of the IPO proceeds being a fairly well-established 'going rate' for the job of taking firms public (Chen & Ritter 2000). Price competition has little to offer merchant banks as a way of selling their services. Competition in 'pitching' for a spot as an investment advisor to a major corporation is largely based upon the quality of the representation to potential investors on offer. So, conflicts of interest, while potentially damaging to investors as analysts' clients, can serve to raise the quality of investment banking representation, even if the cost remains fixed at 7%.

This is a fairly compelling set of arguments if disclosure is sufficient protection for investors. Much existing public policy suggests that this is the prevailing political orthodoxy, but this orthodoxy is now being questioned.

18.2.2   Is Disclosure of a Conflict of Interest Sufficient Protection for Investors?

The light touch regulatory response to many conflicts of interest in professional life is to ensure disclosure and allow the market to work its magic. Recent studies of the investment value of stock recommendations imply that this may indeed work in the average case. Conflicting objectives may lead some analysts to make exaggerated claims on behalf of the companies they follow, but the market recognizes both the presence and the approximate scale of this 'reporting' bias and adjusts prices accordingly.

Brown, Hugson and Lui (2006) report on the efficacy of one such attempt at self-regulation. They studied a programme of public disclosure of past misdemeanours by analysts organized by the National Association of Security Dealers (NASD), including criminal actions, civil suits, dismissals for misconduct and SEC investigations into their conduct. They find such infringements of the Association's rules are not that rare, with 11% of their sample companies attracting forecasts from analysts who have disclosures in the NASD database. The forecasts of disclosed analysts are less accurate and recognized to be so by the market than a control group of analysts with similar characteristics but no NASD disclosures. The impression given by the study is that disclosure can indeed ameliorate the corrosive impact of professional misconduct on the market value of investment advice. Again these conclusions hold for the average firm. The implication being self-regulation can at least partially mitigate any losses that investors accrue due to exposure to the 'reporting' bias exhibited by conflicted analysts.

18.2.3   Conflicts in the Laboratory

Experimental evidence concerning the impact of conflicts of interest on forecasting performance has been provided by Cain, Lowenstein and Moore (2005). They enrolled 147 Carnegie Mellon students to undertake a task of determining the value of a jar full of pennies. The students were randomly assigned to one of two groups: a team of advisors or a team of estimators. Advisors were allowed to examine the jar of pennies and were given a range of values within which the true value of the coins contained within lay. Advisors issued a report on the value of the jar's contents to estimators. The estimator was also shown the jar briefly for 10 seconds at a distance of three feet away. Based on their own guesses and the advice received from their advisor, estimators were asked to state the value of the contents of the jar full of pennies. Their reward was based on how accurate their statement of value was. Some advisors were told they would be rewarded for giving advice that led to accurate valuations by estimators (call them the 'accurate' advisors). Another group of advisors were told they would be rewarded for making the estimators' valuations as high as possible (call them 'high' advisors).

Advice was given and estimates supplied six times during each experimental session. During the first three evaluations estimators had no idea that 'high advisors' might be present, or what was the motivation behind the advice they were being presented with. But in the last three sessions those receiving advice from 'high advisors' were warned that their advisor had an incentive to make his evaluation as high as possible.

The results of the experiment showed that advisors rewarded for going high did so and were able to raise estimators' valuations by doing so. Estimators receiving advice from 'high' advisors did not raise their valuations by as much as the biased advice they received implied, but they did raise it significantly. The impact of disclosure of the high/accurate status of the advisor in the last three rounds was simply to exacerbate these trends. 'High' advisors raised their valuations even further and this fed through to induce even greater overvaluations by estimators.

Cain *et al*. (2005) explain their results in three ways:

- Firstly, it is possible that disclosure makes the advisors feel it is morally acceptable to give poor advice. They may think 'well, they do know!'. This can induce even poorer standards regarding the quality of advice provided to assessors.
- Secondly, the 'availability' heuristic suggests that the estimators' guesses might become anchored on the 'high' advisors' estimate of value, even though they realized its value is compromised.
- Finally, backward induction of the 'they know I know' type may deceive the estimator into failing to fully control for the bias the 'high' advisors impart to their suggested valuations.

These factors combine to cast doubt on the efficacy of disclosure as a cure-all solution to the presence of conflicts of interests amongst analysts from an investor's viewpoint. The addition of noise traders who do not trade on fundamental value raises further reasons for having doubt regarding the efficacy of disclosure as a complete source of amelioration to the economic damage imposed by conflicts of interest.

18.3 Regulating Conflicts of Interest

18.3.1 UK Policy on Conflicts of Interest

UK policy on conflicts of interest has largely evolved via successive interventions by the FSA and responses to the European Union's Market Abuse Directive of 2004. A particular concern emphasized in the FSA's Discussion Paper 171 of February 2003 (FSA 2003a) was the growth of two worrying investment practices:

- 'Laddering',[1] or the attempt to access part of the profits from a floatation by channelling shares to favourite clients and employees.
- 'Spinning', using IPO allocations to give incentives to other companies, or individuals, to reciprocate with subsequent investment banking contracts or reciprocal allocation arrangements.

In order to address these abuses the FSA's consultation paper (FSA 2003a) makes recommendations in a wide range of areas, including:

- the supervision and management of analysts;
- analysts' involvement in investment banking and equity sales;
- analysts' compensation and reward structures;
- exposure by analysts to pressure by their employer's investment banking clients.

The emphasis here is on the Code of Business and guidance rather than formal sanctions. As such these guidelines can be seen to form part of 'meta regulation' of financial services providers by the FSA, which uses the company's own internal governance procedures to detect and remedy threats to the FSA's statutory objectives. Gray and Hamilton (2006, p.39) describe this trend as follows:

> Rather than directly imposing detailed procedural requirements on firms as to the design of their internal risk management the framework seeks to leverage off firms' own systems and expertise in aid of reducing the risk to the FSA's objectives.

These conflicts of interest and other bad practices were addressed in an FSA consultation paper of February 2003 (FSA 2003a). This document formed tentative policy views partially based on written responses to an earlier discussion paper of mid-2002 (FSA 2002). The discussion paper on conflicts of interest in investment advice generated three primary responses from market participants:

- A preference for the current UK 'principles' based regime, as opposed to the more heavy-handed legalistic approach preferred by the Securities and Exchange Commission in the United States.
- A perceived need for greater clarity on what the boundaries are between the marketing of shares and giving impartial investment advice.
- A desire for the UK, US and EU regulatory regimes to be consistent, while recognizing those regional differences which still persist.

The FSA accepted this preference for broad principles, where most intervention is in the form of guidance and a published Code of Business, rather than new laws and statutory instruments, etc.

The outcome of the consultation process is reported in Consultation Paper 171 (FSA 2003a) and is outlined in Consultation Paper 205 (FSA 2003b). This consultation makes a number of changes to FSA policy in relation to conflicts of interest.

- Foremost amongst these is the move to require the writing and publication of a 'management of conflict' policy by institutions offering investment research. This constitutes part of a general trend of FSA policy implementation away from rules-based regulation towards the provision of models for effective internal governance (Gray & Hamilton 2006).
- The requirement to publish a management of conflict policy relates only to those who claim to produce 'independent' research, as opposed to marketing stocks, or summarizing/commenting upon the analysis of others. The scope of the policy includes non-equity investments, corporate bonds and hedge funds, if their advice is likely to be published to clients outside the firm.
- Initial proposals to introduce a US style of 'quiet' periods around IPOs were abandoned because they seemed to offer little in the way of abating the underlying conflicts of interest between advisors and their clients.

Of particular relevance to James Spindler's arguments in favour of encouraging, or at least not penalizing, conflicts of interests is the FSA's reluctance to allow conflicted analysts to issue documents or recommendations which supplement or enhance information given in the IPO prospectus. Overall the FSA's response contains a strong theme of 'buyer beware' advice. As Gray and Hamilton (2006, p.47) state the case:

> The FSA is attempting to recast citizens as proactive risk-aware consumers of financial services products, who seek the opportunity to secure their financial future through participation in financial markets and who accept responsibility for the results of the choices made.

In this latter part of the chapter I ask what happens if one of the types of risk that consumers face is noise-trader risk. How does this type of risk impact upon the costs and benefits of accepting investment advice from conflicted analysts?

18.3.2   EU Policy on Conflicts of Interest

As a member of the European Union (EU), the UK's policy on analysts' conflicts of interest must reflect and embody that of the EU. The relevant EU legislation is the Insider Dealing and Market Manipulation Directive or more commonly the Market Abuse Directive (perhaps somewhat mischievously abbreviated to MAD). The Directive was enacted in January 2003 but must still pass into law in each state, via the 'Lamfalussy process'. The MAD has a number of requirements relevant to analysts' behaviour, including (see Dubois & Dumontier 2008):

- A prohibition on selective disclosure to a cosy club of friendly analysts or fund managers, mirroring Regulation FD in the United States. Price-sensitive information must be available to all market participants publicly at the same time. If an inadvertent release occurs, in discussion with an individual enquirer for example, that information also must promptly be revealed.
- Ensure the 'fair, clear and accurate presentation of information and disclosure of interests and conflicts of interest'. This requires that recommendations be attributed to named individuals, as opposed to teams, and applicable to stated horizons, applying from a given date. The valuation technology used to derive the forecast or recommendation must be reasonably described. Investment banks must indicate their overall stance by reporting the proportion of buy, sell and hold recommendations made in each quarter.
- Conflicts of interest must be addressed by disclosure of participation in mergers and acquisition work, initial public or seasoned equity offerings within the last year. Similarly any cross-shareholding between the house issuing the recommendation/forecast and the corporate entity being advised upon must be disclosed.

Where the existing UK regime was more extensive than the MAD provisions, then the more intrusive legislation was left in force. The UK FSA issued a consultative document on how to complete the enabling legislation most effectively in June 2004.

The UK implemented the MAD on 17 March 2005 via a statutory instrument pursuant of the Financial Markets and Services Act 2000 (FMSA 2000, see SI 2005 Number 381 of 23 February 2005). These rules allow the FSA to suspend trading in a share in the event that its issue has been in breach of the insider trading restrictions of the MAD.

These regulations define a range of abusive behaviours in financial markets which might lead to the statutory instruments' invocation (see amendments to FMSA 2000, p.118). These include:

- insider dealing, or attempt to so deal;
- the company officer discloses price-sensitive information other than in the proper course of his employment;

- where the individual abuses information not known to those involved in a transaction with the company or fails to act in a way reasonably expected of a company officer holding his position;
- the officer misleads investors regarding the supply, demand or price of the company's shares;
- the company officer uses a 'contrivance or fictitious device', like false rumours, to deceive the market.

Here as elsewhere the assumption is that disclosure, as opposed to prohibition or fines, is sufficient to combat the evils that conflicts induce. The FSA currently recognizes 2900 separate financial institutions for the purposes of advising investors, so policing the whole community of analysts is unlikely to be effective. In this sort of diffuse market heavy reliance on self-regulation is almost inevitable. Both the UK and EU legislation places considerable reliance in disclosure of conflicts to 'allow sunlight to be the best disinfectant', as against a more prohibitive regime.

18.3.3   US Policy on Conflicts of Interest

In the United States legislative policy on the conflicts of interest faced by analysts is now enshrined in Title V of the Sarbanes–Oxley Act entitled 'Treatment Of Securities Analysts By Registered Securities Associations'. The Securities and Exchange Commission issued Regulation Analyst Certification ('Regulation AC') in February 2003. This requires that brokers and dealers certify that the views expressed in their reports accurately reflect his or her true personal views. Further, these agents must disclose whether or not the analyst received compensation, or other payments, in connection with their recommendations. Once again this is a disclosure-based solution to the conflict of interest problem, which behavioural research leads us to doubt. Any solution to these problems may be rendered far more difficult in the presence of 'noisy' prices whose variance is not entirely driven by news about the economic fundamentals determining future cash-flows to holding assets. Broker-dealers are required to obtain periodic certifications for the research analysts they employ in connection with their public appearances to support clients on 'road-shows' etc. Regulation AC became effective in the United States as of April 2003, but the impact of this legislation now extends to overseas subsidiaries of US institutions and those servicing them via the Sarbox compliance regime.

18.3.4   The Common Law of Conflicts of Interest

While it is uniformly the case that representations made at the date of IPOs are held to standards of strict liability, Yadlin (2001) points to a divergence between US and UK common law practice regarding the punishment of unreliable statements made with respect to issues into the secondary market. Yadlin (2001) distinguishes three conceivable common law regimes:

- The traditional common law model, which requires plaintiffs show the issuance of representation by the firm to that particular investor, that they did rely on the representation identified once it was made and that doing so caused the loss for which they claim damages. Therefore successful claimants are required to show all three elements of the claim – proximity, reliance and causation – before their claim can succeed at common law. This is the current position in the UK courts in relation to representations regarding securities traded in secondary markets.
- An intermediate reliance regime in which the claimant is not required to show any personal relationship with the company which made the representation or even knowledge on the part of company officials that he had in fact relied on their representation in trading.

- The current US common law position, based on the 'fraud on the market' doctrine, which simply requires that the claimant show he held the security whose value fell due to a false representation subsequently being unmasked, even if he never knew of its prior contribution to the value of the security he held.

Yadlin (2001) points out the US common law position currently greatly favours the position of noise-liquidity traders, as opposed to active investors who take an active role in monitoring the company's management. The US 'fraud on the market' doctrine facilitates free-riding of active investors' efforts to restrain managerial abuses of power. Here I focus on the role of liquidity traders also, but I do so to expose a common weakness of the legal regime on both sides of the Atlantic. This is the reliance of both the common law and regulatory responses to analysts' conflicts of interest on disclosure as a suitable, and possibly sufficient, remedy.

18.3.5   The Dura Pharmaceuticals Case

It is the judicial response to analysts' conflicts of interest that is by far the most controversial aspect of US public policy on this issue. As in the case of Spindler's advocacy of the benign nature of conflicts of interest, many of these decisions reflect a strong degree of confidence in traditional notions of an 'efficient market'. A particularly contentious example of this is the recent *Broudo v. Dura Pharmaceuticals* decision of the Supreme Court (339 F.3rd 993 936-7 (9th Circuit 2003)). The *Dura* case changes the basis for the award of damages in conflicts of interest claims. While a stock price change has always been required to prove reliance of investors on the company's claims in conflicts of interest cases, until *Dura* stock price movements had not been the focus in awarding damages.

Broudo and a group of investors purchased equity in Dura Pharmaceuticals (Dura) after a series of claims by Dura regarding its new respiratory delivery/inhaler device. Dura later revealed that the Federal Drug Administration (FDA) would not approve the device because of concern about its safety/reliability. Upon release of the FDA decision, Broudo alleged Dura and its officials had made misleading statements about the inhaler's fitness for purpose and invoked a Securities Acts 1934 Section 10(b) – 5 'fraud on the market' claim. This interpretation of what Congress intended when 10(b) was enacted was established within the US Supreme Court in the prior case of *Basic Inc. v. Levinson*. Under this doctrine an investor does not have to show he personally acted upon the damaging representation of the firm. He must merely show that the market as a whole was influenced by it and hence it was reasonable for the plaintiff to do so. Since the market presumably accurately prices the stock to reflect value it is reasonable to buy at the market price. This is the statutory version of the common law doctrine: that a market test can be used to establish reliance on the company representation.

Specifically, Broudo alleged that Dura had falsely exaggerated the progress the respiratory device had made towards being a licensed product. The loss-causation element of a plaintiff's case, as opposed to the reliance part, normally requires the plaintiff to prove a causal connection between the alleged fraud and a subsequent decline in stock price. Since Broudo had failed to establish a connection, the district court dismissed the plea.

The 9th Circuit Court of Appeals held the loss-causation element of damages does not require proof of a causal connection between the alleged fraud and the fall in the share price. According to the court, 'plaintiffs establish loss causation if they have shown that the price on the date of the purchase was inflated because of the misrepresentation'. The court determined Broudo had presented enough support for his allegation that Dura's stock price was inflated due to fraud to survive a motion to dismiss. Broudo may not have been aware of the specific reasons for Dura's price being inflated, but at common law all he needed to show was that he accepted the prevailing price as a fair indication of Dura's true value. Any gap between what he paid and what Dura was subsequently shown to be worth (after the deception was revealed) was a financial loss for which Dura was potentially liable in the Court of Appeal's view.

The *Dura* decision can be seen as leading to some dysfunctional, and perhaps unexpected, consequences. Spindler (2006b) points out that one possible effect of *Dura* is to give company management an incentive to bundle announcements to disguise their stock-market impact; or shift the timing of announcements to a day when the company's stock price is especially 'noisy' – so true fundamental value is hard to discern. By doing so the company may hope to disrupt the alleged causal chain upon which the plaintiff seeks to rely. Even more worryingly Spindler (2006b) argues the *Dura* decision may give incentives for company management to lie 'big' if they need to lie at all. The ex-post damages award rule is based on the scale of the share price decline, after the truth is revealed, rather than the scale of the deception initially perpetrated. This means if you are going to lie about your business prospects you may as well make it a whopper. The stock market's frequent overreaction to relatively trivial disclosures might encourage such distortion of truthful representation by company managers.

The very extension of the 'fraud on the market' doctrine from use in proving reliance on a representation to the estimation of damages arising from that misrepresentation is fraught with danger. In pointing out the danger in this transition Cornell and Rutten (2006) remind us that the basis of the 'reliance on the market' theory in the court's judgement is:

> based on the hypothesis that, in open and developed securities market, the price of a company's stock is determined by the available material information regarding the company and its business . . . . Misleading statements will therefore defraud purchasers even if they do not directly rely on the misstatements.[2]

In dissenting comments Justice White in the *Basic Inc.* case warned of the dangers of any extension of the 'fraud on the market' principle to assessing damages. For while rough and ready market efficiency implies company representations will influence price, the assessment of damages requires not only that the stock market responds to new information but also that the magnitude of its response reflects information disclosed about underlying asset value in that information. Numerous well-documented stock-market biases – overreaction, underreaction and investor herding – suggest this may not be a sound basis for public policy.

18.3.6   Market Efficiency, Conflicts of Interest and the Courts

As seen above both judicial and legislative responses to the problem of analysts' conflicts of interest place considerable reliance on the efficiency of financial markets. This is done both in the assessment of damages in the US courts and the assumed sufficiency of disclosure as a cure to damage caused by analysts' conflicts of interest by the UK regulatory authority, the FSA. This has underpinned the FSA's response to conflicts of interest by means of guidance regarding best practice forms of internal governance and compliance procedures with investment banking firms.

18.4   Conclusion and Summary

This chapter has focused on the regulation of analyst conflicts of interest that arise from the fact that they serve their clients, and their employer – an investment bank. In nearly every case both judges and regulatory authorities see disclosure and the 'buyer beware' principle as being a sufficient response to presence of conflicts of interests faced by analysts. There is also no clear evidence that, on average, investors suffer from the presence of such conflicts. Knowing of their presence they simply discount advice given appropriately according to the source from which it derives.

This chapter has presented empirical evidence that disclosing a conflict of interest may not in fact entirely ameliorate its impact. Noisy financial markets might allow optimism bias deriving from conflicts of interest to be exacerbated, not corrected, in competitive, noisy, financial markets.

Questions

1. The FSA is required to undertake a regulatory assessment of the MAD implementation according to the stated criteria that the regulations be proportionate to perceived abuse, effective and consistent with the MAD's requirements. If the FSA asked you to appear as an 'expert witness' with regard to the regulatory impact of the UK's implementation of the MAD, what would you say?
2. The FSA's implementation of the MAD provides certain 'safe harbours' for people who disclose information in the best interest of the shareholders whom they serve. Under what sort of circumstances can insiders disclose price-sensitive interest without breaching their fiduciary duty to shareholders?
3. Your reputation as an 'expert witness' is growing apace. Dura Pharmaceuticals has now contacted you. They want to appeal the decision of the Supreme Court. What's your advice? How convincing do you find the 'fraud on the market' doctrine on which that judgement was based? Do you think the share price drop at the time the alleged fraud was unmasked is a fair measure of investors' economic loss?

Notes

1. Bernie Ebbers of WorldCom was a well-known recipient of IPO share grants by Salomon Smith Barney (Gasparino 2005).
2. *Basic Inc v. Levenson* 485 US at 241-242, quoted in Cornell and Rutten (2006).

References

Agrawal, A. & M. Chen (2008). Do analysts' conflicts matter? Evidence from stock recommendations. *Journal of Law and Economics*, 51(August): 503–38.

Barber, B., R. Levahy *et al.* (2007). Comparing the stock market recommendation performance of investment banks and independent research firms. *Journal of Financial Economics*, 85: 490–515.

Brown, L., A. Hugson & H. Lui (2006). *Broker Industry Self-Regulation: The Case of Analysts' Background Disclosures*. SSRN volume, DOI: http://papers.ssrn.com/sol3/papers.cfm?abstract_id=9307448high=%20Lawrence%20Brown.

Cain, D., G. Lowenstein & D. Moore (2005). The dirt on coming clean: perverse effects of disclosing conflicts of interest. *Journal of Legal Studies*, 34: 1–25.

Cassidy, J. (2002). *Dot.Con: The Greatest Story Ever Sold*. London: Penguin.

Chen, H.-C. & J. Ritter (2000). The 7% solution. *Journal of Finance*, 55: 1105–131.

Clark, J. & O. Edwards (2000). *Netscape Time: The Making of the Billion-Dollar Start-Up that Took on Microsoft*. New York: St Martin's Griffin.

Cornell, B. & J. Rutten (2006). Market efficiency, crashes and security litigation. *Tulane Law Review*, 81: 443–71.

Dubois, M. & P. Dumontier (2008). *Regulating the Financial Analyst Industry: is the European Directive effective?* Switzerland: University of Neuchatel.

Dugar, A. & S. Nathan (1995). The effect of investment banking relationships on financial analysts' earnings forecasts and investment recommendations. *Contemporary Accounting Research*, 12: 131–60.

Francis, J. & D. Philbrick (1993). Analysts' decisions as products of a multi-task environment. *Journal of Accounting Research*, 31: 216–30.

FSA (2002). *Discussion Paper 15: Investment Research: Conflicts and Other Issues.* London: HMSO.

FSA (2003a). *Consultation Paper 171: Conflicts of Interest: Investment Research and Issues of Securities.* London: HMSO.

FSA (2003b). *Consultation Paper 205: Conflicts of Interest: Investment Research and Issues of Securities – Feedback on CP 171.* London: HMSO.

Gasparino, C. (2005). *Blood on the Street: The Sensational Inside Story of How Wall Street Analysts Duped a Generation of Investors.* New York: Free Press.

Gompers, P. & J. Lerner (1999). Conflicts of interest in the issuance of public securities: evidence from venture capital. *Journal of Law and Economics*, 62: 28.

Gray, J. & J. Hamilton (2006). *Implementing Financial Regulation: Theory and Practice.* Chichester: John Wiley & Sons, Ltd.

Kessler, A. (2003). *Wall Street Meat: Jack Grubman, Frank Quattrone, Mary Meeker, Henry Blodget and Me.* Escape Velocity Press.

Lin, H.-W. & M. McNichols (1998). Underwriting relationships, analysts' earnings forecasts and investment recommendations. *Journal of Accounting and Economics*, 25: 101–27.

Mehran, H. & R. Stulz (2007). The economics of conflicts of interest in financial institutions. *Journal of Financial Economics*, 85: 267–96.

Michaely, R. & K. Womack (1999). Conflict of interest and credibility of underwriter analyst recommendations. *Review of Financial Studies*, 12: 653–86.

Montier, J. (2006). *Behavioural Finance: Insights into Irrational Minds and Markets.* Chichester: John Wiley & Sons, Ltd.

Spindler, J. (2006a). Conflict or credibility: research analyst conflicts of interest and the market or underwriting business. *Journal of Legal Studies*, 35: 303–25.

Spindler, J. (2006b). *Why Shareholders Want their Shareholders to Lie More after Dura Pharmaceuticals.* University of Southern California Law School.

Yadlin, O. (2001). Fraud on the market: a relational investment approach. *International Review of Law and Economics*, 21: 69–85.

Chapter 19

Accounting Reform

The global diffusion of International Accounting Standards and the rise to hegemony of the International Accounting Standards Committee (IASC) as an accounting regulator heralds a small revolution in accounting practice. The IASC has a clearly stated agenda for accounting reform. A prominent feature of that reforming zeal is the move from historic cost to a 'fair' valuation of assets based on either the observed, or implied, market values for assets reported on the company's balance sheet. For a mutual fund this may be fairly simple to apply because the stocks it holds are 'marked to market' in stock markets with prices being easily observable each day. However, for a construction firm specializing in building bridges this may be more difficult since dumper trucks, cranes or bridges are not commonly traded in transparent markets. It is in the second type of firm that the use of implied prices for fair values is required and the use of 'fair'/market values becomes more problematic.

Opposition to fair-value accounting has been most intense in the banking industry, especially in France. This has led the European Union (EU) to only partially enforce International Accounting Standard 39 on Financial Instruments: Recognition and Measurement despite full adoption of international standards within the EU's borders since 2005. Of course the use of mark-to-market accounting runs the risk of perverse outcomes if the decline in market value of liabilities (due to increased perceived default risk, for example) increases the net asset value of a toppling bank or other enterprise. Some see such perversities as contributing to the financial crisis unfolding in 2008–9 as I complete this book.

19.1 Illustration and Structure

On 16 September 2008 the end came for Lehman Brothers, the fourth-largest bank in the United States. The bank sought Chapter 11 bankruptcy protection from creditors wishing to be repaid on outstanding funding arrangements originally backed by securitized debt instruments secured upon US residential loans (the so-called 'toxic debt' of the 'credit crunch'). A UK newspaper report commented,

> On page 62 of last year's accounts, under the heading 'off balance sheet arrangements' you will find a staggering figure. Lehman had derivative contracts with a face value of $738 billion. The notes fairly make the point that the fair value is smaller than the notional amount – Lehman believed the figure was $36.8 billion

> (*The Guardian*, 16 September 2008, p.2).

The reported 'fair values' of the Lehman Brothers' instruments weren't looking so fair anymore. This chapter examines the issue of accounting-based valuation, financial analysis and the role of 'fair values', and the mark-to-market accounting that gave rise to those values. Section 19.2 reviews the conflict between historic cost and 'fair-value' approaches to balance-sheet valuations. Section 19.3

examines a standard accounting-based valuation model and looks at the role that book values and earnings play in that model. Section 19.4 examines how behavioural biases and especially the undervaluation of balance-sheet assets affects the accounting-based valuation. It shows financial markets make systematic mistakes in judging the value of companies as implied by accounting-based performance metrics like earnings and book value. The ability of mark-to-market, or 'fair-value', accounting to serve as a widespread solution to these problems is cast in some doubt. Section 19.5 summarizes and concludes the chapter. An appendix considers the role of fair-value accounting in Enron's spectacular collapse in 2001.

After reading this chapter the reader should:

- Understand how accounting numbers are used in reaching corporate valuations.
- Realize how the shift from historical cost to mark-to-market accounting may affect valuation exercises based on accounting valuation metrics, notably earnings and the book value of assets.

19.2 The Onward March of 'Fair-Value' Accounting

For more than 20 years there has been policy concern about companies that implode from huge stock-market values to worthless liquidation in a matter days, leaving investors empty handed. How could these investors have paid so much for so little? These huge discrepancies between stock-market values and true worth seemed particularly hard to understand in the case of bank collapses like Johnson Matthey (in 1984) or BCCI (1991) and the recent fragility of the UK's Northern Rock, where much of the bank's assets were financial assets in the form of securitized debt. In 1989 the IASC began a project to improve the recognition, and disclosure of financial instruments (Jackson & Lodge 2000). In 1992 the Financial Accounting Standards Board (FASB) in the United States went further when Statement of Financial Accounting 107 (SFAS107) required disclosure of fair value of all financial instruments on a company's balance sheet. For banks this meant constructing and reporting fair-value estimates of their loan portfolios, deposits, other borrowings and off-balance-sheet financial instruments such as interest-rate swaps and derivative contracts. Fair value is defined by the FASB in a statement endorsed by the IASB as follows (see FAS157 Fair Value Measurements and quoted in Penman 2006, p.4):

> Fair value is the price that would be received to sell an asset or transfer a liability in an orderly transaction between market participants at the measurement date.

This shift towards fair value was pushed further in 1993 by SFAS115, which required inclusion of fair-value estimates for some securities in the primary accounts, the balance sheet, profit and loss (income statement in the United States) and the cash-flow statement. The last piece of the fair-value trend in the United States was SFAS133 Accounting for Derivative Instruments and Hedging Activities, which required comprehensive fair-value accounting of all debt and equity finance instruments including derivatives.

19.2.1 Historic Cost versus Fair Value

To evaluate the benefits and costs of fair value one needs some idea of what each seeks to do and how that objective can be used in valuing the firm (see Penman 2006). Currently financial reports are largely constructed under a historic cost convention, which aggregates the set of transactions that occurred in the accounting period and attempts to 'match' them using a well-defined accruals technology. For example, a depreciation schedule tries to allocate capital expenditure on machines and new premises, etc., to the stream of revenues generated by that investment. Similarly, bad debts on credit-card defaulters can be netted off against the sales that generated them. The accruals technology means earnings are reported as a stream of value generated by the assets in place within the company, so earnings are simply a 'rent' earned upon the book value of assets – earnings$_t = r \times$ bookvalue$_{t-1}$, where r is some appropriate market interest rate. This is not inconsistent with Modigliani and Miller's original statement of corporate value as being given by a perpetuity in the company's present reported net income plus a term to reflect how well the firm can add value over and above the risk-free rate of capital on funds borrowed (Modigliani & Miller 1961). The Ohlson–Feltham framework ignores this second term, which captures value-added to investments earning a 'supernormal' return, i.e. a return above that offered on a similar investment in the same risk class. Both the residual income valuation metric and the Modigliani–Miller valuation framework stress the importance of value addition over growth for growth's sake. As Modigliani and Miller (1961, p.417) state:

> The essence of 'growth' in short is not expansion but the existence of opportunities to invest significant amounts of funds at higher than 'normal' rates of return.

Which of these two models works best in a particular application will depend on the company involved. The Modigliani and Miller framework makes the assumption about the 'supernormal' return, which is assumed to be present, far more visible. This focus on the implicit 'yield curve' for assets assumed may be useful as mark-to-market accounting has greater impact on reported value.

The cost of mark to market may be borne by the first term in Modigliani and Miller's valuation equation, the perpetuity in current earnings. In the limit if book values are simply set to the market value of the firm, changes in book values (assuming an efficient market) are just random unpredictable 'noise'.

One of the problems of mark-to-market/fair value is that it emphasizes valuation on the balance sheet at the expense of earnings, but traditional valuation models have tried to use both for different purposes.

In some ways the very suggestion that accounting be reformed to include fair-market values beats a retreat from an earlier belief that accounting could provide an independent guide to the value of a share without any recourse to observed price. Benjamin Graham, the father of 'value' investing, preached an investment philosophy based on an asset's 'worth', which could become markedly uncoupled from its price in frothy speculative markets. For Graham:

> The single most important factor determining a stock's value is held to be the indicated average future earnings power, i.e. the estimated average earnings for a future span of years. Intrinsic value would then be found by first forecasting this earnings power and then multiplying that prediction by an appropriate discount factor
>
> (Graham, Dodd & Cotterhill 1962, p.28, quoted in Penman 1992).

More recently Professor Stephen Penman of Columbia University in New York has made a similar call for a 'return to fundamentals' in asset valuation (Penman 1992). As well as pointing to a need for fundamental analysis, Penman indicates some progress in the development of tools to undertake such an analysis. I begin by reviewing Professor Penman's manifesto for a new fundamental analysis, before venturing into more detail concerning how fundamental analysis might be conducted.

19.2.2   *A Return to Fundamental Valuation*

A brief backward glance into recent history warns of the danger of equating the price and worth of an asset, but such an equation underlies the very notion that financial markets allocate capital to its most effective use. The role of fundamental analysis, as outlined by Penman (1992), is to seek 'the discovery of price without reference to price'. This, of course, is the very converse of what the IASC is aiming at by its promotion of fair/market valuation of balance-sheet assets.

In the case of equities it is fairly straightforward to see that their 'fundamental', or 'intrinsic', value is simply the value of the discounted stream of future dividends payable to those who own them, ($P = d/(r - g)$). Therefore, inferring fundamental value has two parts:

- Forecasting the stream of future dividends (d) payable, and their long-term growth rate (g).
- Applying an appropriate, risk-adjusted, discount rate (r) to that stream of dividend payments.

The belief that current dividends are a good guide to the future prospects of a share seems somewhat naive. Indeed the most successful firms, like Google and Amazon, seem to disdain the payment of dividends regarding themselves as 'growth stocks' which are above such concessions to investors. A corporate history of Amazon opens with Jeff Bezos, the founder, being questioned at an annual shareholder meeting about the high and increasing losses of Amazon. He argues in reply:

> There's so much Internet opportunity that now is the time to invest. We're trying to make all of our decisions in a long-term context

> (Spector 2000).

Neither dividends nor profits were given priority in this 'Get Big Fast' business model. More generally, current dividends seem to bear little relation to observed price. So we have what is sometimes termed the 'dividend conundrum' by which prices are determined by the future stream of dividends, but appear to exhibit no close correspondence to dividends paid in the short run.

Accounting by contrast has at least some characteristics that make it attractive for fundamental analysis:

- It is a measurement system based on compiling and tracking 'net worth' or the book value of assets.
- It is a measurement system with rules for which violation is increasingly costly since the establishment of the Financial Reporting Council in the United Kingdom and the Sarbanes–Oxley legislation in the United States.
- It is independent of dividends because both earnings and book values are calculated net of their payment.

These attractions have led to the development of valuation models reliant on accounting inputs, specifically earnings and book values and we discuss one such model in the next section.

19.3   An Accounting-Based Valuation Model

The most commonly employed accounting-based valuation model currently in use is the residual income valuation model. While this model has a very long history going back at least to Edwards and Bell (1961), more recent discussion has been associated with the work of James Ohlson of Arizona University and his co-authors (see Feltham & Ohlson 1995, Ohlson 1995, 2005, Ohlson & Jeuttner-Nauroth 2005). Here

I adopt a simplified version of the model used in some empirical tests of it by Dechow, Hutton and Sloan (1999) for example. This is based upon the Ohlson (1995) version, which I also focus on in a theoretical discussion of the model. The model begins by returning to the standard dividend discount model (DDM) that sees price evolving as a function of the discounted value of future dividends (d_t)

$$P_t = \sum_{\tau = 1}^{T} \frac{E[d_{t+\tau}]}{(1 + r)^\tau} \quad DDM \tag{19.1}$$

where r is some appropriate, fixed, risk-adjusted, interest rate (as before don't worry about declining interest rate for now).

The Ohlson model values assets under a particular idealized form of accounting. This is called a 'clean-surplus' relationship (CSR), which assumes balance-sheet book values (b_t) cumulate earnings (x_t), recorded in the profit and loss account net of dividends paid/owner's withdrawals (d_t). So book values evolve as follows

$$b_t = b_{t-1} + x_t - d_t \quad CSR \tag{19.2}$$

While this stylized ideal, which envisages full 'articulation' of the accounts, turns out to be very useful, it has to be recalled it is just an ideal. In reality companies' financial reports are littered with off-balance sheet assets and often losses are 'written off' straight to reserves avoiding the need to reduce net worth recorded on the balance sheet.

Companies are often thought to try to understate book values in order to make their return on equity (the ratio of earnings to prior book values), a key market performance indicator in stock markets, look better. The reason for this is that companies are often judged by fund managers and others on their return on capital equity. This practice of understating book value is known as conservatism in accounting and complicates the application of models based on clean-surplus accounting.

Once the clean-surplus assumption is made we can immediately harness it to convert the dividend discount model (DDM or Equation (19.1)) using the CSR (Equation (19.2)). Noting

$$b_t = b_{t-1} + x_t - d_t$$
$$\Rightarrow \Delta b_t - x_t = -d_t$$
$$\Rightarrow x_t - \Delta b_t = d_t$$

This solution for dividends can then be plugged straight into the standard dividend valuation model to iteratively drive out future price and results in a valuation model that captures fundamental value 'without reference to price'

$$P_t = \frac{P_{t+1} + d_t}{(1 + t)}$$

$$\Rightarrow P_t = \frac{[P_{t+1} + (x_{t+1} - \Delta b_{t+1})]}{(1 + r)}$$

$$\Rightarrow P_t = \frac{\frac{[P_{t+2} + (x_t - \Delta b_{t+2})]}{(1 + r)}}{(1 + r)} + \frac{[(x_{t+1} - \Delta b_{t+1})]}{(1 + r)}$$

$$\Rightarrow P_t = \frac{[(x_{t+1} - \Delta b_{t+1})]}{(1 + r)} + \frac{[P_{t+2} + (x_{t+2} - \Delta b_{t+2})]}{(1 + r)^2}$$

$$\Rightarrow P_t = \frac{[(x_{t+1} - \Delta b_{t+1})]}{(1+r)} + \frac{[(x_{t+2} - \Delta b_{t+2})] + \dfrac{[P_{t+3} + (x_{t+3} - \Delta b_{t+3})]}{(1+r)}}{(1+r)^2}$$

$$\Rightarrow P_t = \frac{[(x_{t+1} - \Delta b_{t+1})]}{(1+r)} + \frac{[(x_{t+2} - \Delta b_{t+2})]}{(1+r)^2} + \frac{[P_{t+3} + (x_{t+3} - \Delta b_{t+3})]}{(1+r)^3} \qquad (19.3)$$

So price can be seen as being composed of a discounted aggregation of future reported earnings net of the changes in book values plus a terminal value in future price.

19.3.1   Are All Reported Earnings Additions to Shareholder Value?

A building company could just sell its dumper trucks, cranes and shovels and stick the money in a building society. Or an investor could save a company the trouble, not invest and put the money in the building society himself. If you did this you might at least expect a risk-free rate of return, r. This is the opportunity cost of having your investment tied up in this company rather than tucked up safe in the bank. But the same idea applies to investing in another company facing the same risks. Here r might be set to equal the same value as that used in discounting cash-flows for a company in the same 'risk class'.

So why should I be pleased that Tesco, a UK supermarket, is growing my investment in the book value of its assets at the same rate as its competitors Sainsbury, Waitrose and Asda? Tesco only adds value in my portfolio if it grows the book value of its assets at a rate exceeding that of its rivals in the industry which are alternative stock picks for my portfolio. This benchmark forces Tesco to 'value-add' relative to its competitors if it wishes to attract limited shareholder investment funds. So we can now revisit Equation (19.3) replacing earnings with 'abnormal' earnings. I define 'abnormal' earnings to be earnings in excess of a capital charge to reflect the opportunity cost of using the assets the company has in production recorded on its balance sheet

$$x_t^a = x_t - rb_{t-1}$$

And plugging this value metric into Equation (19.3) yields:

$$P_t = \frac{[P_{t+1} + x_{t+1} - rb_t - (b_{t+1} - b_t)]}{(1+r)}$$

$$\Rightarrow P_t = \frac{[P_{t+1} + x_{t+1} - (1+r)b_t - b_{t+1}]}{(1+r)}$$

$$\Rightarrow P_t = b_t + \left[\frac{(P_{t+1} - b_{t+1}) + x_{t+1}}{(1+r)} \right]$$

$$P_t = b_t + \frac{\left[\dfrac{P_{t+2} + x_{t+2} - rb_{t+1} + (b_{t+2} - b_{t+1})}{(1+r)} \right]}{(1+r)} + \left[\frac{x_{t+1} - r.b_t}{(1+r)} \right]$$

$$P_t = b_t + \left[\frac{x_{t+1} - rb_t}{(1+r)}\right] + \left[\frac{x_{t+2} - r.b_{t+2}}{(1+r)^2}\right] + \left[\frac{P_{t+2} - b_{t+2}}{(1+r)^2}\right]$$

$$P_t = b_t + \left[\frac{x_{t+1} - rb_t}{(1+r)}\right] + \left[\frac{x_{t+2} - r.b_{t+2}}{(1+r)^2}\right] + \frac{\left[\frac{P_{t+3} - x_{t+3} - rb_{t+2} + (b_{t+3} - b_{t+2})}{(1+r)^2}\right]}{(1+r)}$$

$$P_t = b_t + \left[\frac{x_{t+1} - rb_t}{(1+r)}\right] + \left[\frac{x_{t+2} - r.b_{t+1}}{(1+r)^2}\right] + \left[\frac{x_{t+3} - r.b_{t+2}}{(1+r)^3}\right] + \left[\frac{P_{t+3} - b_{t+3}}{(1+r)^2}\right] \tag{19.4}$$

This is the basic structure of the residual income valuation model where value is modelled as a function of the opening book value of assets and a time-discount weighted average of future earnings, plus a terminal value to reflect 'goodwill' (the difference between the book value per share value of the assets and the price at which they sell in market). After enough forward iterations I can drive the terminal value to a sufficiently small proportion of total price so as to be able to safely ignore it. I have then succeeded in Penman's quest for a statement of value 'without reference to price' of the form

$$P_t = y_t + \sum_{\tau=1}^{T} R^{-\tau} E\left[x_{t+\tau} - (R_f - 1)y_{t+\tau-1}\right] \tag{19.5}$$

This is, of course, a hollow victory. The final line of Equation (19.4) is just a restatement of the dividend growth model in Equation (19.1), the price given in both equations must be the same, and there is really nothing new in Equation (19.4) compared to the DDM of Equation (19.1). What we need is more structure to our thoughts and much of Professor James Ohlson's work has been an attempt to impose that structure.

The vacuity of Equation (19.4) should not be overstated. One of its great benefits is that it is stated in terms of a future variable for which we have many observable market forecasts – earnings. Indeed a whole industry of financial analysis, earnings-per-share forecasting and stock recommendations exists and forecasts of earnings are readily and freely available from sources such as Yahoo! Finance. This contrasts with the situation for dividends where market forecasts are rare and forecasts by company management almost unheard of. So a great benefit of the Equation (19.4) restatement of the DDM is its ease of use in practical valuation tasks. It may contain no new insights, but it makes old insights easier to use.

19.3.2 The Dynamics of Abnormal Earnings Valuation

The residual income valuation model had been a mainstay of the management accounting literature at least since the 1930s and, while its use in valuing stocks was an innovation, its superiority over the discounted dividend valuation model was very limited. The real value-added of the Ohlson valuation model largely lies in providing additional structure regarding how the central valuation model in that framework evolves. Ohlson (1995) specifies some 'linear information dynamics' (or LID) of how abnormal earnings evolve over time. These specify that abnormal earnings follow a process.

$$\tilde{x}^a_{t+1} = \omega x^a_t + v_t + \tilde{\varepsilon}_{1t+1}$$
$$\tilde{v}_{t+1} = \gamma v_t + \tilde{\varepsilon}_{2t+1} \qquad LID \tag{19.6}$$

where $0 < \omega, \gamma < 1$ and v is 'other non-accounting information' regarding value (e.g. announcements about changes in corporate strategy, senior management changes, etc.) and $\varepsilon_1, \varepsilon_2 \sim N(0, \sigma)$ are pure random, unpredictable, 'noisy' elements of value. A '$\sim$' over a variable here denotes an expected, as opposed to actual, value. Recalling the definition of abnormal earnings as

$$x_t^a = x - (R_f - 1)y_{t-1}$$

we can equate terms with Equation (19.6) of the LID above to obtain

$$x_{t+1} - (R_f - 1)y_t = x_t^a + v_t + \varepsilon_{1t+1}$$

Note that since dividends are paid straight out of net assets, or book value, every penny paid out as dividends to investors diminishes future earnings by its assumed 'normal' rate of growth at $(1 - R_f)$. Thus the LID imposes additional useful structure on the valuation problem. The payment of dividends is no longer value relevant and the pattern of abnormal earnings accretion is rendered central to the valuation exercise. This is still, of course, just a restatement of the dividend discount model of Equation (19.1), but it is a restatement that throws the weight of explaining valuation changes firmly on to the future path of earnings rather than dividends.

19.3.3 Some Examples of the Ohlson Model in Action

To illustrate the additional structure that the LID brings to valuation Lundholm (1995) has provided some neat examples of the valuation model in action and I review some of those here. I do this to give some traction on how the basic model works in practice before continuing with any refinement of it. The first simple example is of a company that has an opening book value y at date 0 of 100, which it invests for an uncertain return z at date 2. No dividend d is paid, apart from the liquidating dividend z at date 2. So we have a payoff structure as given in Table 19.1.

We can consider the same investment opportunity but now make a specific assumption about the expected growth rate of earnings. In particular let us now assume some 'normal' rate of earnings growth at the risk-free rate of interest, so book value b grows each period by an amount yR_f where $R_f = 1 + r_f$ and r_f is the risk-free rate of interest. The resulting payoff structure is as shown in the reworked Table 19.2.

Table 19.1 Example of valuation exercise with Ohlson model

Time period	Book value	Earnings	Dividend
0	100	0	-100
1	$100 - d_1$	0	d_1
2	0	z	$100 - d_1 + z$

Table 19.2 Example of valuation exercise with Ohlson model when abnormal earnings grow at the risk-free rate

Time period	Book value	Earnings	Dividend
0	100	0	-100
1	$R_f(100 - d_1)$	$(R_f - 1)100$	d_1
2	0	$(R_f - 1)(R_f 100 - d_1) + z$	$R_f(R_f 100 - d_1) + z$

Note here abnormal earnings bear no relation to their own past values, so $\omega = 0$ in Equation (19.6) above. Nor is there any role for non-accounting information, so $v = 0$ in the LID of Equation (19.6). All that has changed in moving from the two examples is the implied growth rate of earnings is specified in the latter example to be given by the risk-free discount factor $R_f = 1 + r_f$. So price declines by the full amount of dividends paid out $\delta P_t / \delta d_t = -1$. This throws the focus of valuation firmly on abnormal earnings as the valuation metric. If dividends can be conclusively ruled out as a source of value changes in this restated version of the residual income model, what determines value? The answer is abnormal earnings and how you account for their accretion.

Aggressive revenue recognition

The rate at which earnings are recognized depends on the accounting practices applied and prominent amongst these are those concerning the recognition of revenue. See Table 19.3 for an example. Revenue is a very big number, often one of the biggest numbers in the financial reports, and how you construct it matters a lot. Suppose, for example, that company management has a pretty good idea that the company will earn an amount z on its date 0 investment of 100 and so recognize its present value on their books at date 1. This would make sense if the company was a mutual fund and it simply 'marked to market' the value of its portfolio. Its current value is a pretty good guess of the value in one period's time. So this case is just an application of the general valuation rule.

$$P_1 = b_1 + E[x_2^a]$$
$$P_1 = R_f \cdot 100 - d_1 + \frac{z}{R_f}$$

If the expected value of next period's abnormal earnings are included in 'mark-to-market' book value at date 1, b_1 fully reflects value and future abnormal earnings, $E[xa^t{}_2]$, can be ignored. The book-value term already captures the value of future abnormal earnings. Conversely, if no recognition of future asset value on the balance sheet is allowed then current book value is diminished by the expected value of z, z/R_f, but this value then reappears as reported abnormal earnings in period 2. So in this case the effect of booking the future value of abnormal earnings is to reduce the volatility of firm value. In the final period 2 no new value appears and firm value remains unchanged, but if future abnormal profits are not booked then firm value increases in the final period.

Therefore, company management may have to choose between the stable and growing firm values offered by alternative accounting treatments. Of course if the date 1 estimate of date 2's future earnings z is imperfect the decision calculus regarding the most favourable accounting treatment is made even more problematic.

Table 19.3 Example of valuation exercise with Ohlson model when future abnormal earnings are included in recognized book value

Time period	Book value	Earnings	Dividend
0	100	0	−100
1	$(R_f 100 - d_1) + (1/R_f)z$	$(R_f - 1)100 + (1/R_f)z$	d_1
2	0	$(R_f - 1)[(R_f 100 - d_1) + (1/R_f)z]$	$R_f(R_f 100 - d_1) + z$

Conservatism in accounting valuations

One of the common rules for the recognition of asset values is to record them at the lower of their cost or market value. In the above illustration this can be thought of as recognizing z if it is a liability ($z < 0$) but not if it is an asset ($z > 0$). Table 19.4 captures the revised position. This sort of asymmetric asset recognition underlines a basic principle of conservatism to 'anticipate no gains, but recognize all losses'. So we can consider reworking the above example for the case of recognizing a liability (lower panel of table) as well as an asset (in the upper panel). The upper panel simply follows the previous example of anticipation of the liability z/R_f at date 1. Here z denotes a necessary reduction in asset value, but otherwise the mechanics of the valuation exercise remain unchanged. In the case of an anticipated gain z/R_f has no place in date 1 book value, only appearing later at date 2.

An important point to note is that while the recognition of asset value as the lower of cost and market value is widespread in accounting practice, it is not adequately captured within the Ohlson valuation framework. This suggests that the model may inadequately capture some of the realities of accounting-based valuation. This needs to be borne in mind in the usage of the model to inform the policy debate over the rise of fair-value accounting.

This contingent recognition of future asset value implies a solution for date 1 'goodwill', as the difference between date 1 book value and price as follows

$$E_0(P_1 - b_1) = Pr(z < 0).0 + \frac{Pr(z > 0)E(z|z > 0)}{R_f}$$

Since this expression is always positive the rule to recognize an asset's value at the lower of cost and market value understates date 1 book value.

19.3.4 Implications for Price

Given our basic valuation Equation (19.1), the clean-syurplus accounting of Equation (19.2) and the linear information dynamics of Equation (19.6) we can derive a fairly simple solution for implied price as a function of abnormal earnings x^a, and the non-accounting information, not yet included in the financial statements, v. This takes the form

$$P_t = b_t + \alpha_1 x_t^a + \alpha_2 v_t$$

Table 19.4 Example of valuation exercise with Ohlson model when future abnormal earnings are included in recognized book value and conservative accounting is practised

Time period	Book value	Earnings	Dividend
Recognizing a loss, $z < 0$			
0	100	0	-100
1	$(R_f 100 - d_1) + (1/R_f)z$	$(R_f - 1)100 + (1/R_f)z$	d_1
2	0	$(R_f - 1)[(R_f 100 - d_1) + (1/R_f)z]$	$R_f(R_f 100 - d_1) + z$
Recognizing a loss, $z > 0$			
1	$R_f 100 - d_1$	$(R_f - 1)100$	d_1
2	0	$(R_f - 1)[(R_f 100 - d_1) + z]$	$(R_f 100 - d_1) + z$

where

$$\alpha_1 = \frac{\omega}{(R_f - \omega)} \geq 0$$

$$\alpha_2 = \frac{R_f}{(R_f - \omega)(R_f - \gamma)} > 0 \qquad (19.7)$$

Ohlson (1995) gives the derivation of this result in an appendix to his 1995 paper, but since it draws on a recollection of some basic techniques in linear algebra I follow his lead and discuss the proof in an appendix to this chapter. Not all readers will wish to revisit such details and are free to skip over them. The Ohlson model's implication for returns is quickly seen from remembering what drives fundamental value and hence price movements in the model. Price changes occur because of movements in book value and expectations of future abnormal return. So we have

$$E[P_{t+1} + d_{t+1} - R_f P_t] = E[(b_{t+1} + d_{t+1} + \alpha_1 x_{t+1}^a + \alpha_2 v_{t+1}) - R_f(b_t + \alpha_1 x_t^a + \alpha_2 v_t)]$$

This equation reminds us of the information about fundamentals that moves price in the Ohlson world. We call to mind the clean surplus equation (Equation (19.2)) to recall that $d_t + 1 = (b_t + 1 - b_t) + x_t$ and the definition of abnormal returns themselves, $x_t - (R_f - 1)b_t$. This allows us to restate the determinants of share price returns above as

$$E[P_{t+1} + d_{t+1} - R_f P_t] =$$
$$E[(b_{t+1} + (b_{t+1} - b_t) + x_{t+1}) + \alpha_1(x_{t+1} - (R_f - 1)b_t) + \alpha_2 v_{t+1} - R_f(b_t + \alpha_1 x_t^a + \alpha_2 v_{t+1})]$$
$$E[P_{t+1} + d_{t+1} - R_f P_t] = E[(\alpha_1 + 1) + \alpha_2 v_{t+1} - R_f(\alpha_1 x_t^a - \alpha_2 v_t)]$$

Recall the dynamics for abnormal returns (x^a) and non-accounting information (v) given by the LID of Equation (19.6) states

$$x_{t+1}^a = \omega x_t^a + v_t + \tilde{\varepsilon}_{1t+1}$$
$$v_{t+1} = \gamma v_t + \tilde{\varepsilon}_{2t+1}$$

which can be used to rearrange the expression for share price returns as follows:

$$E[P_{t+1} + d_{t+1} - R_f P_t] = E[(\alpha_1 + 1)\{\omega x_t^a + \gamma v_t + \tilde{\varepsilon}_{1t+1}\} + \alpha_2\{\gamma v_t + \tilde{\varepsilon}_{2t+1}\}$$
$$+ R_f \alpha_1 x_t^a + R_f \alpha_2 v_t]$$

which simplifies to

$$E[P_{t+1} + d_{t+1} - R_f P_t] = E[(\alpha_1 + 1)\varepsilon_{1t+1} + \alpha_2\varepsilon_{2t+1} + [(\alpha_1 + 1)\omega - \alpha_1 R_f].x_t^a$$
$$+ [(\alpha_1 + 1) + \alpha_2\gamma v_t - R_f \alpha_2]v_t]$$

At this point we call to mind our prior solution for the coefficients on price

$$\alpha_1 = \frac{\omega}{(R_f - \omega)}$$

$$\alpha_2 = \frac{R_f}{(R_f - \gamma)(R_f - \omega)}$$

This allows us to further simplify the expression for share price returns given above as follows:

$$E[P_{t+1} + d_{t+1} + R_f] = E\left[(\alpha_1 + 1)\tilde{\varepsilon}_{1t+1} + \alpha_2\tilde{\varepsilon}_{2t+1} + \left[\left(\frac{\omega}{(R_f - \omega)} + 1 \right)\omega - \left(\frac{R_f\omega}{(R_f - \omega)} \right) \right].x_t^a \right.$$

$$\left. + R_f\left[\frac{R_f\gamma + R_f}{(R_f - \gamma)(R_f - \omega)} \right].v_t \right]$$

$$E[P_{t+1} + d_{t+1} + R_f] = E\left[(\alpha_1 + 1)\tilde{\varepsilon}_{1t+1} + \alpha_2\tilde{\varepsilon}_{2t+1} + \left[\frac{\omega}{(R_f - \omega)} + 1 - \frac{R_f}{(R_f - \omega)} \right]\omega.x_t^a \right.$$

$$\left. + \left[\frac{\gamma - R_f}{(R_f - \gamma)(R_f - \omega)} \right].R_f.v_t \right]$$

From this it is clear that the coefficients on abnormal returns and non-accounting information are expressed solely in terms of coefficients already known at t and the risk-free discount factor, R_f. Given the realization of abnormal earnings and non-accounting information are also known at t they are not likely to drive future share price returns.

19.3.5   *Implications for Returns*

The expected change in the underlying valuation fundamentals, both abnormal share price returns and other non-accounting valuation relevant information, is zero. So innovations in price, or returns, are driven solely by innovations in the process driving fundamentals. So the share price returns process reduces to

$$\left[\frac{P_{t+1} + d_{t+1} - R_f P_t}{P_t} \right] = \left[\frac{(\alpha_1 + 1)\varepsilon_{1t+1} + \alpha_2\varepsilon_{2t+1}}{P_t} \right]$$

$$\left[\frac{P_{t+1} + d_{t+1}}{P_t} \right] = R_f + \left[\frac{(\alpha_1 + 1)\varepsilon_{1t+1} + \alpha_2\varepsilon_{2t+1}}{P_t} \right]$$

Returns are driven by unpredictable shocks to abnormal earnings, ε_1, and other non-accounting valuation relevant news, ε_2, with these shocks adding a value premium to equity values. The first term in this solution for share returns captures the pure rate of time preference of equity investors for consumption today as against consumption tomorrow and is assumed constant here. The second term is the risk premium associated with innovations in value from both abnormal earnings and non-accounting information sources. This term is time varying and may explain the observed spike in both trading volume and price volatility around earnings announcements.

This may occur if 'news' is clustered around earnings announcements and the cycle of meetings between company management and fund managers that follows on from the announcement of earnings. This term may also capture some 'noisy' elements of investors' expectations.

19.3.6   *Does the Ohlson Model Work?*

Yes, it appears to work. The huge interest in Professor Ohlson's work is very largely motivated by how well the model does work. In an era of declining relationships between share price returns and numerous other value metrics the correlation between returns and value measures implied by the Ohlson model has been consistently strong. The basic concept of efficient markets requires that prices move to eliminate any short-term discrepancy between price and value in terms of future cash-flows/ earnings. This idea is often captured at the level of statistical testing by the requirement that prices 'mean-revert' to the fundamental value. For example, if the market-to-book ratio is to be a helpful guide to price we might expect its average value to be one and any deviation from that value to be swiftly reversed.

Lee, Myers and Swaminathan

Lee and his colleagues ran a 'truth race' between the price–earnings ratio, the dividend yield (dividend/price), the book-to-market ratio and the implied value under Ohlson's model (see Lee, Myers & Swaminathan 1999 and Lee & Swaminathan 1999). In an examination of the US Dow index for the years 1963–96 Lee and co-authors modelled the ratio of the implied value from the Ohlson model to price, which they denote V/P, the value to price valuation metric (where V is something like Equation (19.4) above), which has strong explanatory and predictive power. In such a 'truth race' to determine what explains the movement and dispersion of share price returns the Ohlson model appears to win hands down over many fundamental value ratios. In particular Lee and co-authors evaluate the model on:

- Its ability to track the observed value of the Dow and to predict its future value. A good intrinsic value estimator has a low standard deviation in its deviations from observed price and deviations that erode at a faster rate, its ability to predict future market returns. If price tends to return to value then movements below the metric imply prices will rise and movements above imply prices will fall in the future.

In their results Lee *et al.* find large tracking error generally which is indicative of a specification's inability to predict future returns. So perhaps these criteria are best seen as complements rather than substitutes in the evaluation of any proposed valuation proxy.

Movements away from a V/P ratio of one can have two sources. Firstly, the Ohlson model may not really capture fundamental value that well. Secondly, the stock market may deviate from fundamental values: that is the stock market is inefficient in constraining price to reflect fundamental values. Lee and colleagues make clear the importance of including earnings forecasts and the use of a time-varying discount rate. Lee *et al.* use consensus forecasts of earnings from the Institutional Brokers Estimation Service (marketed by First Call, a part of the Thompson Financial group) to capture earnings expectations. Using these 'market' expectations significantly enhances the predictability of the model, but these consensus forecasts are only published on a regular basis from 1979. Lee *et al.* also experiment with monthly and longer term discount rates. In their study using a model incorporating short-term discount rates, based on monthly data, induces the highest predictability of the value-to-price (V/P) measure for predicting future share price returns.

Dechow, Hutton and Sloan

A very closely related study by Patricia Dechow of UCLA Berkley and co-authors uses a fixed discount rate of 12% to evaluate variant specifications of the Ohlson model (Dechow, Hutton & Sloan 1999). In particular Dechow *et al.* focus on the comparative advantage in explaining, or predicting, price of differing specifications of the LID (Equation (19.6)). Remember before the LID is introduced the residual income valuation model (Equation (19.5)) is just a neat restatement of the dividend discount model of Equation (19.1). The LID is the real 'value-added' in the Ohlson valuation framework. So it is important to get the LID specification right. This is what Dechow *et al.* aim to help us do. Recalling the Ohlson (1995) specification of the linear dynamic evolution of abnormal earnings in Equation (19.6)

$$\tilde{x}\,^a_{t+1} = \omega x^a_t + v_t + \tilde{\varepsilon}_{1t+1}$$

$$\tilde{v}_{t+1} = \gamma v_t + \tilde{\varepsilon}_{2t+1} \qquad LID$$

Dechow *et al.* consider different ways of modelling this pair of equations when estimating the Ohlson model on actual market data. Some specifications simply ignore other information entirely, i.e. always set v_t equal to zero or assume it never persists in its effect on company value, $\gamma = 0$. Others assume abnormal earnings are competed away immediately, or simply never competed away, $\omega = 0$ or $\omega = 1$. Finally, some specifications, rather than imposing estimates of the persistence of abnormal earnings, or the impact of non-accounting information, that is ω and γ, try to estimate them based on historic data. Dechow *et al.* perform their tests on US annual accounting data, earnings and book values in the years 1976–95, a sample period that yields over 50,000 firm year observations.

Table 19.5 summarizes the various alternative settings of the LID. In the first column valuations which ignore non-accounting information, so $v_t = 0$, are considered. The first model assumes abnormal earnings are immediately competed away and so sets $\omega = 0$ in the LID. One can imagine this specification fitting a perfectly competitive, 'hit-and-run' market where profits entice a host of competitors to immediately rise up to grab any profits left on the table. This specification of the

Table 19.5 Dechow *et al.* typology of the LID

Abnormal earnings persistence	'Other information' persistence parameter (γ)			
	Ignore other information	$\gamma = 0$	$\gamma = 1$	$\gamma = \gamma\omega$
$\omega = 0$	$E[x^a_{t+1}] = 0$ $P_t = b_t$	$E[x^a_{t+1}] = f^a_t$ $P_t = b_t + \dfrac{f_t}{(1+r)}$	$E[x^a_{t+1}] = f^t_t$ $P_t = \dfrac{f^a_t}{r}$	$E[x^a_{t+1}] = f^a_t$ $P_t = b_t + \dfrac{1}{(1+r+\gamma^\omega)}f^t_t$
$\omega = 1$	$E[x^a_{t+1}] = x^a_t$ $P_t = \dfrac{x_t}{r} + x_t - d_t$	$E[x^a_{t+1}] = f^a_t$ $P_t = \dfrac{f_t}{r}$	Not considered	Not considered
$\omega = \omega u$	$E[x^a_{t+1}] = \omega^u x^a_t$ $P_t = b_t + \dfrac{\omega^u}{(1+r-\omega^u)}x^a_t$	$E[x^a_{t+1}] = f^a_t$ $P_t = b_t + \dfrac{\omega^c}{(1+r-\omega^c)}f^a_t$	Not considered	$E[x^a_{t+1}] = f^a_t$ $P_t = b_t + \dfrac{1}{(1+r-\omega^u)}x^a_t$ $+ \dfrac{(1+r)}{(1+r-\omega^u)(1+r+\gamma^\omega)}v_t$
$\omega = \omega c$	$E[x^a_{t+1}] = \omega^c x^a_t$ $P_t = b_t + \dfrac{\omega^c}{(1+r-\omega^c)}x^a_t$	Not considered	Not considered	Not considered

LID results in price equalling current book value since no future value addition arises from growing the book value of assets in place at a rate in excess of the 12% rate of return.

The next model goes to the other extreme. While still ignoring non-accounting information (I am just discussing the first column in the Table 19.5 at the moment), in this specification abnormal returns last forever, so $\omega = 1$. We might think of this as capturing the case of perfect monopoly, where you cannot just set up your own nuclear fuel company to get a bit of the action, even if it is very profitable to do so. Here the company's price is given as perpetuity in earnings net of current dividend pay-outs.

We can think of abnormal earnings dying out immediately or lasting forever, $\omega = 0$ or $\omega = 1$, as special cases which illustrate idealized extremes of the industrial spectrum. Most firms lie in the thick middle having some market power yet still facing competition. Dechow *et al.* capture this scenario by considering two ways of estimating the persistence of abnormal earnings denoted ω in Equation (19.6). The first is to set it to its value last year in a cross-sectional regression across all firms in the sample: this captures the average persistence of abnormal earnings across the whole sample. This is termed the unconditional estimate of persistence of abnormal earnings and is denoted ω^u. Ignoring other information (and so staying in that first column of Table 19.5), this specification, using the unconditional mean of persistence of abnormal returns across the sample, produces a valuation which is the sum of book value and a term to reflect future earnings. This is more like the standard residual income valuation model of Equation (19.5).

19.3.7 Earnings Persistence in the Ohlson Model

Dechow *et al.* consider an alternative, more sensitive, way of estimating how much we might expect earnings to persist. This takes into account five factors which determine the competitive pressures that erode the abnormal earnings a company currently captures. These are:

- The current level of abnormal earnings, the more loot you are running away with the more attractive your market is for firm entry.
- 'Special' or extraordinary items which by their one-off nature tend not to last.
- The level of operating accruals – accrual accounting is by its design self-reversing in its impact on cash-flow since its principal objective is 'match' revenues and expenditures to the same accounting period. So if income is brought forward this quarter, or year, it must diminish income in later accounting periods.
- Dividends – remember dividends tend to be pretty sticky and investors don't like dividend cuts, or even worse non-payment (dividend omissions) once a dividend has been initiated.
- An industry dummy – some industries are just very competitive by their nature, for example computer hardware manufacture. Others, like water supply or nuclear fuel manufacture, are natural monopolies where one firm per district, or even country, is the norm.

While this conditional estimate of abnormal earnings persistence, denoted ω^c by Dechow *et al.*, is potentially far more sensitive to variations in persistence of abnormal returns, it again yields a solution for price very much like Equation (19.5), the standard residual-income valuation model.

19.3.8 Other Information in the Ohlson Model

So far I have considered specifications estimated by Dechow *et al.* which ignore other information (those in the first column of the Table 19.5). Introducing other information into the valuation complicates the valuation, but it is essentially another route to inducing persistence in abnormal earnings. So in the first column of the Table 19.1, where other information is not allowed to enter the valuation, zero persistence in abnormal earnings, $\omega = 0$, drives price to equal book value. Once other information is introduced abnormal earnings will nevertheless persist despite ω being set to zero, by means of the other information term, v_t: either assuming perfectly persistent abnormal earnings x^a, or perfect persistence in other information v; that is setting either ω or γ to equal one results in identical valuations. To see this compare the valuation under $\omega = 0$ and $\gamma = 1$ (second row and second column of Table 19.5) to that given by $\omega = 1$ and $\gamma = 0$ (first row and second column of table). Both these pairs of assumptions result in the price of the stock being set equal to a perpetuity in the consensus forecast of next year's earnings.

This means that the two persistence effects tend to double up producing highly volatile predictions of future earnings streams. For this reason Dechow *et al.* keep it simple and do not estimate models that allow both abnormal earnings and news about non-accounting information to persist over time, i.e. where $\omega > 0$ and $\gamma > 0$. This accounts for the various 'Not considered' entries in Table 19.5. This has the danger of ignoring some very credible combinations of weak persistence in both abnormal earnings and news about non-accounting information regarding value, but it has the strength of making the model easy to estimate and avoids discussion of models with possibly 'explosive' abnormal earnings paths.

Dechow *et al.* find that the extra effort in estimating a conditional estimate of abnormal earnings persistence, using the five predictive variables outlined, is worth it to improve predictions of future abnormal earnings outcomes. Models incorporating conditioned estimates of persistence of abnormal earnings predict future abnormal earnings streams best (the bottom line of the table).

19.4   Behavioural Bias in Estimates of the Ohlson Model

Frustratingly, despite the incremental power of conditional estimates of abnormal earnings persistence in predicting future abnormal earnings, this does not convert into a better ability to explain price. It would appear that expectations of earnings embedded in observed stock-market prices underestimate the extent to which abnormal earnings fade away in response to the five factors discussed. Prices seem capable of temporarily swinging away from 'fundamental value', at least as that construct is captured by Ohlson's (1995) model. Indeed the overestimation of abnormal earnings persistence is so great that Dechow *et al.* find that, while assuming perfectly abnormal earnings, that is $\omega = 1$, predicts current price best this assumption is the worst for predicting returns or future price movements.

Hence it appears that the stock market creates a cult of 'good' companies for which they have unrealistically high expectations regarding future value creation and 'bad' firms for which investors have unrealistically poor expectations regarding future value destruction. In reality most companies are drawn from the thick middle where good and bad news broadly average out. Abnormal earnings revert to the industry average pretty quickly for most companies truncating extremes of the share price return distribution. The failure to recognize how transitory abnormal earnings are for most companies appears to be a predictable mistake by investors capable of exploitation by appropriately formed arbitrage strategies.

A further finding of the Dechow *et al.* paper is that stock prices seem to underweight book values in forming price. Observed prices for the Dechow sample, over the years 1976–95 are consistent with a weighting of 0.95 on last year's abnormal earnings in the LID Equation (19.6) above and the exclusion of any persistence in past non-earnings information, i.e. a combination of the form $(\omega, \gamma) = (0.95, 0)$. As Table 19.5 shows, a very similar model for implied price is obtained when the LID assumes perfect correlation between this period's and last period's abnormal earnings while ignoring other information, that is the LID pairing $(\omega,\gamma) = (1,0)$ reduces the valuation equation to a perpetuity in the next year's forecasted earnings. This is the valuation model in the second column and second row of our LID comparison in Table 19.5, but we hardly need to estimate the full-blown Ohlson model to use the forecast of next year's earnings as a valuation metric. Elsewhere Dechow *et al.* show that abnormal earnings are far from being perfectly persistent, being more consistent with a value of ω of roughly 0.62 – but prices fail to reflect this. Nor does the market seem to impound the statistical dependence of price on book values. This means those advancing the efficacy of fair-value accounting have a job ahead of them to educate the investing public. As the book value becomes the central valuation metric investors will need a better understanding of how book values evolve over time.

19.4.1   Inferring Value from Accounting Data: Fair Values versus Historic Costs

The Ohlson model captures implied fundamental value as a function of two performance metrics:

- The book value of assets, or 'net worth', a store of value.
- Earnings or profit, a flow of value yielded by working the book value of assets in place within the firm.

This division accords with a general distinction between valuation of the firm on a balance sheet or an 'income' perspective. Obviously if we were going to break up a firm and sell off the assets we would be principally interested in the book value of the assets. How much can we get for the dumper trucks, the cranes and that half-finished bridge from the latest contract? The assets in the balance sheet could have been valued in two ways:

- Historical cost: how much we paid for them when they were bought.
- 'Fair'/market value: how much they sell for in the market now.

The second method probably works fine for the dumper trucks and the crane (just going to stalls in the nearest agricultural show should do the job), but half-finished bridges on an approach road to Totnes most probably don't trade that much, so getting a 'market' price in that case is more tricky.

A very similar distinction to that outlined above is that between 'entry values' – how much we pay to get an asset either now or when we first got it, or if we wished to purchase it now in the open market – and 'exit' values – how much we could get for the asset if we sold it or would pay to get it back if it was taken.

Recently the IASC and other regulatory agencies have been encouraging a move towards the use of real, or implied, market values in the valuation of assets, the so-called 'fair' value treatment of such assets in the balance sheet. Indeed this does seems wise given the value of an asset is often reported as the cost of replacing it tomorrow, if it was stolen or destroyed by a natural disaster for example. But recalling Penman's call for a measure of fundamental/intrinsic value 'without recourse to price' the IASC seems to be sending us the other way. Fair-value accounting encourages us to measure business worth by 'marking to market' the assets used by the firm. In this process a market price for the assets used like cranes and dumper trucks enters our reported value of the firm. Indeed the reality may be worse than this, as traded prices are not always used to infer market values.

19.4.2   The Three Levels of Fair Value

The FASB guidelines (in FAS157) on fair-value implementation suggest three descending 'levels' of mark-to-market assets on the balance sheet:

1. using quoted prices in actively traded markets;
2. using accepted valuation models, like the Black–Scholes model of option pricing or the cost-of-carry model for valuing futures;
3. using the company's own valuation model and assumptions for valuation.

The use of level 3 fair-value estimates gives considerable scope for subjectivity if not outright deception in fair-value estimates of asset value. The example of Enron's optimism in pricing the value of the natural gas derivative contracts it held is explored in an appendix to the chapter.

19.4.3   Some Implicit Trade-Offs in Fair-Value Accounting

Recently Plantin, Sapra and Shin (2007) have advanced a theoretical framework for debating the comparative advantages of historic and fair-value accounting. They state the problem thus:

> The fundamental trade-off can be described as follows. The historical cost regime relies on past values and so accounting values are insensitive to price signals. This leads to one type of inefficiency arising from excessive conservatism. Marking to market overcomes this conservatism by relying on current market prices, but it also distorts this information. When the decision horizons are shortened due to agency problems, the anticipation of future prices affects firm's decisions which, in turn, injects artificial volatility into prices. Knowing this the firms become more sensitive to price movements.[1]

Modelling these trade-offs generates three primary implications regarding the impact of the introduction of fair-value accounting:

- The longer the maturity of the asset the more sensitive it is to artificial, noise-induced volatility. Beyond some point a historical cost regime dominates a mark-to-market accounting regime.
- The more illiquid the asset the more sensitive it is to artificial, noise-induced volatility. For illiquid assets it is better to adopt historic cost; for assets with deep liquid markets the move to marking to market is unproblematic.
- Claims with little upside but lots of downside risk, like senior debt, are more sensitive to artificial, noise-induced volatility. Claims with little downside and a lot of upside potential, like junior debt, are not best handled by historic cost.

Under historic cost the firm has every incentive to sell assets it has held a long time to realize profits on holding them. Marking to market solves this problem at the expense of introducing another. This arises if asset value appreciation causes attempts to sell off the asset, in order to realize holding gains, to become widespread in the industry. Then the prices for assets, which have recently appreciated, consequently decline sharply as price pressure from holding gain-motivated sales spreads across the economy.

A false volatility, unrelated to underlying cash-flows from holding the asset, appears. Noise trading and speculative sentiment is free to affect the firm's decisions. In general marking to market will amplify the transmission mechanism from price changes to asset redistribution across the productive economy and the welfare effect of this is hard to predict. The choice between marking to market and historic cost asset valuation regimes depends on the trade-off between shareholder losses due to forgone holding gains-motivated asset sales and the stock-market propagation of those losses through mark-to-market accounting. A switch to mark-to-market accounting for asset values removes the need for holding gains-motivated sales, but the asset revaluations that are now reported can propagate 'bubble' psychology; with asset redistributions unrelated to underlying productive values of productive assets in place resulting.

19.5 Conclusion and Summary

This chapter has discussed the proliferation of mark-to-market accounting. This trend is to be welcomed insofar as market efficiency ensures that the 'the price is right' and fairly reflects asset value, but as we have seen this may be an unreasonable demand to make of financial markets. In reality stock prices appear to embed systematic mistakes in forming expectations about earnings and book-value outcomes.

The benefits to be obtained from a shift to mark-to-market depend on the extent of these biases in prices relative to the intrinsic balance-sheet conservatism that characterizes historical cost accounting. As in the case of entrepreneurs the best of possible worlds derives from optimally trading off implicit biases in financial markets as opposed to hoping to simply eliminate the presence of bias. The appendix discusses one case of a catastrophic abuse of mark-to-market accounting. However, such cases must be weighed against the informational value of market prices and the intrinsic conservatism of historic cost valuations.

This chapter considered accounting-based valuation models and the light they shed on the current debate about the use of 'fair value' to value assets recorded on the corporate balance sheet. It has illustrated the important role that behavioural bias and the impact of the presence of 'noise traders' have on how the fair-value debate is resolved. Once again one is struck by the important policy implications of a proper understanding of behavioural bias and how it impacts upon pricing and ultimately asset allocation. While existing biases reappear in new guises – underreaction to book values, extrapolation of abnormal earnings and 'noise' in asset revaluations – the underlying texture remains the same. Enron shows how these biases and the perverse incentives they imbue in the management team can have a terminal effect. Behavioural bias is widespread, predictable in nature and significant in its market impact. Policy-makers need to consider these impacts before changing existing accounting policy.

Appendix A: Mark-to-Market Accounting at Enron – A Case Study

The enthusiasm amongst accounting regulators for mark-to-market accounting is surprising given the part it played in the downfall of Enron, the corporate scandal that so besmirched the authority of the accounting profession and wiped out a major auditing partnership. Yet that scandal was almost a textbook case in the application and subsequent perversion of mark-to-market accounting.

On 16 October 2001 Enron Corporation, an icon of the new economy and a pioneer of the 'hollow' corporation, asset-light and thriving on informational arbitrage, announced a $544 million write-off against income and a reduction in the book value of shareholders' equity of $1.2 billion. Subsequently on 8 November Enron announced earnings restatements (downwards) for the years 1997–2000.

Reported earnings for 1997 were reduced by \$28 million (a 27% reduction in the previously reported figure), 1998 earnings were reduced by \$133 million (a 19% reduction), 1999 earnings were reduced by \$248 million (a 28% reduction) and reported earnings for the year 2000 were reduced by \$99 million (a 10% reduction) (see Benston & Hargraves 2002, pp.105–6). These developments followed on from a period of meteoric rise in Enron's stock price. Enron's stock price rose 56% in 1999 and 87% in 2000. This occurred against the background of a 20% rise in the S&P500 index in 1999 and a 10% decline in that index in 2000 (Healy & Palepu 2003, p.3).

While Enron is a pathological case of the perverse use of a set of accounting techniques, which can be very informative in responsible hands, it is in many ways an informative warning of a more general problem for as Healy and Palepu (2003, p.4) point out:

> While Enron presents an extreme example, it is also a useful test case for potential weaknesses in U.S. capital market systems. We believe that the problems of governance and incentives that emerged at Enron can also surface at many other firms and may potentially affect the entire capital market.

The Role of Accounting in the Collapse of Enron

The collapse of Enron reflects a failure of business judgement, political control, good governance, regulatory oversight and morality. Often in reading its story one feels sadness that so much human talent was wasted on such a house of cards. Here we focus largely on those parts of the collapse which could reasonably have been expected to be investigated and prevented by accounting professionals. Benston and Hargraves (2002) list at least six such issues:

- accounting for investments in special-purpose entity subsidiaries;
- changes in accounting practice motivated by Enron's stock-price decline;
- sales of failing venture capital purchases on to SPEs that were not in reality independent of Enron, although they were accounted for as if they were;
- fair-value estimates based on heroic level 3 estimates;
- treating capital gains on Enron stock as increases in earnings, i.e. earnings go up because the stock price rose and the stock price rising in response to announced increases in earnings;
- disclosure of conflicts of interest in the accounts and the prevention of such conflicts arising.

Humble Origins

The origin of Enron was in the sleepy, heavily regulated, grime of the mid-west natural gas market (McLean & Elkind 2003 give a very readable discussion of these issues).[2] Founded by Ken Lay, a PhD in economics who had worked in Washington as a lobbyist, Enron was formed from the merger of Houston Natural Gas and InterNorth, a far larger company, in 1985. Part of the merger process was the rise to chairman and CEO's position of Ken Lay. But by the early 1990s falling natural gas prices and previous unsuccessful gambling in financial speculation had left Enron in poor financial shape.

The structure of the natural gas industry was such that gas suppliers like Enron were bound to take the gas provided to them under long-term contracts, whether they could sell it on to consumers at a profit or not. This is because of an industry practice of issuing 'take-or-pay' contracts, which locked both parties into a price set at the start of the contract for the supply of gas. The problem by 1991 was that the prices set in the 1980s, when prices shot up, were now far too high for suppliers like Enron, who could buy far more cheaply in the spot market, if it were not for their pre-commitment to earlier high-price, take-or-pay contracts.

The most damaging of the take-or-pay contracts written by Enron occurred well after their virtual disappearance from the market for natural gas in the United States. In 1993 Enron wrote a take-or-pay contract for the provision of gas from the J-Block field in the North Sea, off the English shoreline, by a consortium led by Phillips Petroleum. Once again betting on sharp rises in gas prices, as the UK market was deregulated by the Thatcher government and the 'dash-for-gas' proceeded, proved to be a disaster for Enron. As prices rose Enron hoped to sell on the gas it had contracted to buy at a cheap price from the consortium.

In reality these contracts were to lose a staggering amount of money. By 1995 Enron's total exposure to losses was approaching $2 billion at a time when its total market capitalization was around $5 million. Ultimately once Jeff Skilling assumed the CEO position, following Rich Kinder's departure, he took a $675 million charge against earnings to extricate Enron from the J-Block morass. This was an expensive lesson in the dangers of take-or-pay contracts.

The rapid metamorphosis occurring in Enron's business model may help explain why auditors and regulators were later found sleeping on the job as Enron careered off the rails. They were used to dealing with oil and gas manufacturers and were poorly trained to assess dealings in a complex financial institution (Benston & Hargraves 2002, p.127).

Jeff Skilling and the Adoption of Mark-To-Market Accounting

Enter Jeff Skilling, the man with a plan from McKinsey Consulting. Skilling's idea was to create a virtual 'gas bank'. Gas producers would continue to offer gas at some fixed price for a fixed period. Simultaneously gas suppliers to consumers and producers could contract to buy gas at a fixed price for a fixed term. At the centre stood the 'gas bank', which profited by arbitraging between what producers would supply for and suppliers were willing to pay. Since supply and demand was in effect fixed at the contract date this constituted a form of riskless arbitrage that is the holy grail of finance. Of course the tricky point here is that without assuming risk it is hard to earn any profit in a highly liquid, reasonably efficient, market like that for natural gas provision. So it was more common to only partially hedge the risk by various 'dirty hedge' strategies (e.g., by 'stacking and rolling' the contract, i.e. only fully hedging the contracts in early years and simply hoping for the best at expiration). Even the slim pickings that arbitrage offered were soon to be eroded by clone competitors like Dynegy, El Paso and Mirant.

Once this type of arbitrage was possible it only remained to standardize the contract terms and devise a trading platform capable of allowing a myriad of would-be speculators to enter. These need not be oil, or energy, companies at all. Indeed in establishing the market Skilling entered a partnership with Bankers Trust of America because of their well-established reputation in innovative trading strategies in trading derivatives.

Marking to Market and the Growth of Gas Contract Trading

A very important part of implementing this vision for rebuilding Enron was the adoption of mark-to-market accounting, more commonly used in banks, to this part of Enron's business (which was to be named Enron Finance with Skilling as CEO). Skilling had described this as 'a lay-my-body-across-the-tracks issue'. The reason was that he wanted to obtain recognition for the value his trading team created at the point of buying or selling contracts they traded. To bring forward recognition of the future value creation or destruction associated with each day's trading position required the analytical modelling of expected future cash-flows deriving from Enron Finance's current trading stance in the market. In formulating an implied value for the contract Enron needed to make assumptions regarding future interest rates, gas prices and the demand and supply of natural gas.

This sort of calculation is allowed under level 3 asset recognition as envisaged by FASB157. If the model is sound then this system should broadly work as a scheme of value recognition and accounting for company value, but if subjectivity, optimism, if not delusional hype, enter valuations then a problem can be created.

One example of this is the treatment of a 20-year contract with Blockbuster video to introduce entertainment on demand to a number of US cities. Pilot implementations of such an entertainment system in Portland, Seattle and Salt Lake City cast doubt on whether the system could ever work or at least prove economic to provide. Nevertheless Enron recognized future profits of $110 million in July 2000 on the deal with Blockbuster (Healy & Palepu 2003, p.10).

Whatever the integrity of the accounting process for mark-to-market gas contracts their effects were particularly pernicious for a company talking such a big game as Enron. Lay and Skilling were in the habit of promising 15% growth in annual earnings in meetings with fund managers and analysts. This was most probably acceptable in the early stages as Enron Finance established the market and tapped new sources of value. But the problem was that the future value of successful contracts last quarter are already fully capitalized and reported in that quarter's earnings, so further growth had to be achieved from a higher base each quarter – you have to climb the 15% growth rate each quarter anew. Under historic cost recognition the value created by profitable contracts in the past slowly accrues over successive periods, so one good, profitable, contract could benefit the company's earnings for a long time. Under mark-to-market every quarter traders face a brutal struggle to reach the requisite growth in earnings in each quarter. As the market for natural gas contracts grew the marginal contract traded rarely met the requisite 15% return the market had been encouraged to expect.

In reality the 15% growth-rate target for earnings was not enforced vigilantly anyway. When Lay had his contract of employment as chairman and CEO renewed in late 1996 earnings growth was only 11.6%. No problem. The board, packed with tame non-executives, simply reworded the performance contract to read 'earnings in double digits'. Despite the decline in earnings growth Lay was granted an annual salary of $990,000 plus 1.25 million options to buy Enron's stock. The options alone were valued at $90 million in the market at that time. A gap between stated performance objectives and that being enforced at the most senior figure of the corporation had clearly emerged.

Enron finally received permission from the Securities and Exchange Commission to apply mark-to-market accounting to Enron Finance's gas trading contracts on 30 January 1992. Champagne corks popped in Skilling's office and the stage for the subsequent demise of Enron was set.

Lou Pai and ECT

The supreme architect of the emerging trading culture within Enron was Lou Pai, the head of the Enron Capital and Trade Resources (ECT). Skilling described Pai as 'my ICBM' (intercontinental ballistic missile) and he was to have a devastating effect on Enron's development. ECT made a market between Enron's gas bankers, the children of Skilling's original brainwave, and the marketers within

Enron who wrote long-term contracts for the provision of gas to industrial producers. Under mark-to-market accounting ECT could fully recognize any profits from arbitraging across these two groups within Enron immediately. One might imagine collegiality would ensure ECT offered a price to those writing industrial contracts within Enron that was very keen, or at least price quotes as good as that on offer to those outside Enron. Not with Lou Pai at the head of ECT. Pai aimed to maximize ECT's profits regardless of its effect on other Enron divisions.

The awesome power of ECT's trading ability was first demonstrated in 1992 when Enron contracted to supply the entire gas needs of a 1000-megawatt energy plant in upstate New York. Enron had convinced the plant's developer Sithe Energy to use gas, rather than coal the traditional fuel, to power the plant. The contract required Enron to provide 195 million cubic metres of gas every day for 20 years, worth nearly $4 billion over the life of the contract, a pretty serious level of commitment. Under mark-to-market accounting Enron booked profit from the deal even before the plant produced a single watt of electricity. In 1992 alone the contract brought in $122 million in income for ECT, making it the second-biggest profit centre in Enron. The deal made Jeff Skilling pretty happy too after he sold back 30% of his equity stake to Enron for $4.7 million.

While the accounts of Enron showed Sithe to be hugely profitable, much of this was due to level 3 type guesswork in the calculation of market values within ECT. Futures contracts for a duration of a year or so were easily marked to market using the liquid New York Mercantile Exchange's prices quoted for similar standardized contracts. But beyond an 18-month horizon there are no organized trading markets for gas futures, so the value of energy contracts, such as that for Sithe, were calculated by constructing implicit yield curves (based on future gas price projections) within ECT. When Enron needed to show a bit more quarterly earnings the temptation was to simply ramp up the implied yield curve a little. ECT under Lou Pai certainly fell victim to this temptation.

Unleashing the Balance Sheet by Securitization

Enron with the help of Pai and ECT seemed to have found the magic fleece for generating profits for Wall Street. As wonderful as this was Enron still needed some hard cash to pay the bills. If Enron went to the banks, especially the major investment banks, they were likely to quickly spot the flaws in its business model. So Enron needed a new trick to generate ready cash and not just paper profits.

The solution Skilling found to this problem set the stage for the final implosion of Enron. This was the concept of securitizing the contracts for gas provision that Enron had originally made. Securitization revolutionized Enron's business model as it revolutionized most major financial markets. An early advocate of securitization, Lowell Bryan one of Skilling's fellow McKinsey consultants, stated 'securitization's potential is great because it removes capital and balance sheets as constraints on growth'. This was the very problem Enron faced, a lack of capital to grow the ECT business model, and securitization held the key to unlocking that potential for rapid growth.

The securitization of the mark-to-market contracts for gas provision on Enron's balance sheet was facilitated in 1991 by means of a special-purpose entity (or SPE) created by Skilling called Cactus. This initial deal was completely transparent and business-like. Enron bundled some $900 million of the money it had promised to gas producers into Cactus and sold shares in the loans to institutions such as General Electric. An SPE could be created fairly easily under US GAAP with the provision of no more than 3% of independent equity from outside the company. Their use was widespread in major corporations, it being common for joint company ventures to give charitable help to the local community for example. But Andrew Fastow, a finance executive reporting to Skilling, had other ideas for the use of SPEs.

A final imprimatur of the uprightness of this securitization of gas contract debt via SPEs was given by the California Public Employees Retirement Schemes (CALPERS) investment of $250 million of retirees' cash in one such vehicle in 1993. Since CALPERS was one of the largest and most respected institutional investors in the whole of the United States, SPEs had by now truly moved out of the basement as a vehicle for trading within Enron. The new partnership for the CALPERS deal had been given the moniker JEDI by Fastow. His rise within Enron was soon to be a major cause of its downfall.

With this financial architecture in place ECT was all set to transform Enron. The basic 'asset-lite', but ideas-intensive, business model of Enron was set. By 1996 ECT was producing $280 million in earnings over the year and accounted for 20% of Enron's total earnings. Skilling and Pai were seen as untouchable and Enron's fate was now firmly tied to the success of their trading strategies.

From Pumping Gas to Trading Gas: The Emergence of the Asset-Lite Strategy

Soon the transformation of Enron was to follow a pattern driven by Skilling's desire to shed heavy fixed assets in favour of an asset-light trading-based culture where innovation in trading strategies and the exploitation of regulatory loopholes for profit was all. As stated by McLean and Elkind (2003, p.110):

> Skilling believed Enron's strength lay in what became known as his asset-lite strategy, driven by brainpower not physical infrastructure ... Skilling thought he had it down to a formula: Enron would buy the infrastructure needed to crack the code; build a new trading business – and then unload the assets as everyone else started to pile in.

Much of Enron's proliferation of its natural gas trading model in the electricity, water and Internet broadband sectors can be interpreted as particular applications of this broad rubric. Skilling had started to dematerialize Enron but without a secure trading profit stream to fall back on. The fixed (non-current) section of the balance sheet was being emaciated to be replaced by 'intangible' trading skills – an intellectual property right later shown to be of questionable worth.

For Skilling 'the Stock Price was his Report Card'

A disturbing aspect of the Enron collapse was not that its accounting was a misrepresentation about its true value but that this delusion was so consciously and wilfully undertaken by the senior management team. While at the subsequent Powers' investigation (Powers 2002) and various Senate hearings into Enron's demise, senior managers, principally Lay and Skilling, seemed to know remarkably little about the company's financial position, the basic objective of financial reporting was clear to all. McLean and Elkind (2003, p.125) observe for Skilling that 'the stock price was his report card'. They state,

> In the Skilling era, the stock price became something else entirely: it became an obsession. A stock ticker in the headquarters lobby offered a constant update on the value of Enron shares. Employees were repeatedly encouraged to buy Enron shares; on average they kept more than half their 401(k) retirement holdings in Enron shares. In 1998 when the stock price hit $50, Skilling and Lay treated it as a major corporate milestone, handing out $50

bills to every Enron employee. Later Lay announced a new personnel initiative: if the company hit performance targets over several years, every employee would get twice his annual salary in Enron shares.

While such ostentation and displays of greed are almost inherently repellent they do display the sort of behaviour a complete internationalization of mark-to-market accounting can induce. The stock price is company value and the objective of financial reporting is simply to maximize that value at all cost. A trader quoted by McLean and Elkind (2003, p.288) had clearly understood the company line:

> People did not know the difference between mark-to-market earnings and cash. It wasn't on our annual review or included in our targets. It had nothing to do with how they measured our bonus. It was nothing we were paid for so who cares? I knew that we had no cash and that our earnings were subject to manipulation. *This is a game.* I know that, everyone knows that, but it was a game we were winning.

Mark-to-market accounting featured heavily in the finessing of earnings-per-share figures towards the consensus forecast and so kept the analysts happy. Originally in 1991 the SEC gave Enron permission to use mark-to-market accounting to value ECT's natural gas contracts on its balance sheet, but by 1997 mark-to-market's usage had proliferated unchecked to a wide range of trading platforms housed within Enron – contracts for electricity provision and profits from Enron's 50% stake in the JEDI joint venture with CALPERS were all now marked to market (the appendix to Healy & Palepu 2003 describes this deal). This was not unproblematic. Electricity, unlike gas, cannot be stored away for sale later, so its price tends to be far more volatile than natural gas. This made pricing derivatives based on electricity supply even bigger guesswork than the original natural gas deals. Mark-to-market's application became so widespread as to reach a form of open abuse in its application to venture-capital acquisitions undertaken by Enron.

This monomaniacal focus on Wall Street and its envoys, financial analysts, was most intense in the days leading up to the release of quarterly earnings announcements as 10 q filings by the Securities and Exchange Commission. In mounting this ramp Skilling frequently made use of repricing (upwards) the large number of energy provision contracts in Enron's portfolio. This was a get-out-of-jail-free card so frequently played by Skilling that he called the energy contract portfolio his 'gold mine'. Skilling certainly mined Enron's energy provision contract portfolios for considerably more than they were worth in constructing quarterly earnings in the late 1990s.

Even before the final calamity this sort of reckless recognition of valueless 'assets' had clearly gone wildly wrong. One group of venture-capital acquisitions, called the Industrial Group, under the leadership of Kevin McConnell, induced a potential earnings write-off of $400 million in 1999. The cumulative impact of aggressive future earnings recognition followed by disappointing performance soon stimulated intense pressure to mask the consequences of poor trading results.

Early Warnings

While politicians expressed horror at the sudden implosion of Enron some early warnings were in fact present. In *Fortune* magazine in 1993 Toni Mack wrote an article entitled 'Hidden Risks' questioning the appropriateness and mode of implementation of mark-to-market accounting within Enron. Mack stated 'If you accelerate your income then you have to do more and more deals to show the same or rising income' (McLean & Elkind 2003, p.94).

In 1995 a rather similar article in *Fortune* by Harry Hunt III alleged the use of 'byzantine accounting methods of managing earnings within Enron'. Hunt noted that once you stripped out one-time exceptional, or 'special', items Enron was far from the huge success it had claimed to analysts. So going forward you could not be confident in Enron's business model as a means of adding value for shareholders. And indeed there was much smoke and many mirrors in operation even before Enron entered into the recognizably fraudulent activity that led to its collapse.

In 1994 Enron span off a subsidiary called Enron Power and Pipelines (EPP). EPP was a vehicle to acquire resources from Enron's troubled subsidiary Enron International (about which more below). This allowed Enron International to show profits simply by selling off assets piecemeal. This Enron International did, offloading 50% of its stake in a huge $20 billion Dabhol plant.

Under US generally accepted accounting practice (GAAP) this was fine (and in fact not uncommon amongst major corporations) as long as EPP was 'independent' of both Enron International and Enron itself. This was hard to show as Enron owned a majority of EPP's equity and its CEO Jim Alexander was appointed and paid by Enron to run EPP. Rich Kinder (Enron's chief operating officer and president) was also chairman of EPP. Nevertheless, by means of the establishment of an independently manned 'Oversight Committee', Arthur Andersen, Enron's auditors, and Vincent and Elkins their corporate lawyers found a way to get a majority-owned subsidiary regarded as 'independent' for the purposes of accounting treatments of Enron's performance. This established the base camp for the further blurring of the 'entity principle' concerning whose performance Enron's accounts actually reported on. This confusion was to grow into a cloak for many serious problems under the stewardship of Andrew Fastow as CFO.

EOG and the Asset-Lite Strategy

Another asset sale inspired by Skilling's asset-lite philosophy was the disposal of Enron Oil and Gas (or EOG) despite its capable and profitable performance under its CEO since 1987, Forrest Hoglund. EOG traded as a separate company, although it was in reality just another subsidiary of Enron. Hogland had made both Enron and himself a fortune, netting $19 million in option sales in 1994 alone, but for Skilling holding on to gas and oil plants was just too mundane. If Enron wished to go long in gas it could do so on the trading floor with no need to keep valuable capital tied up or get its hands dirty.

When Occidental made an approach in 1998 to acquire EOG during a temporary lull in gas prices Skilling jumped at the chance. Occidental's cash and shares offer valued EOG at $22 per share, while it currently traded in the market at $14. The $600 million in cash going to Enron was too much for Skilling to resist. He sold despite Hogland's protests and a rare minority rebellion on Enron's board of directors. Sure enough by the end of 2000 EOG was trading at $54 per share and Skilling was seen to have waved goodbye to $1 billion worth of shareholder value.

Creating a 'Market Operating System'

A central core of Enron's business strategy which won great praise at the time of its implementation was the introduction of competition into sleepy inefficient basic commodity and energy markets. Lay and Skilling had used basic economic theory to revolutionize natural gas markets and now their chosen disciples. As Gary Hempel, the London Business School Professor and leading business book author, commented 'Like Microsoft has created DOS, Enron is creating MOS; the market operating system: and they can apply it everywhere' (McLean & Elkind 2003, p.226).

The most dramatic development in this way of thinking came with the development of Enron Online by a self-selected group of pioneers headed by Louise Kitchen and her boss Greg Whalley, head of Enron's European trading operations at that time. Whalley was soon trusted to run all Enron's wholesale businesses, giving his trading instinct a broader span of control.

The idea for Enron Online was fairly simple. This was to create a Web-based trading system for trading commodities, with Enron as the clearing house, a sort of eBay for wholesale commodity trading. Skilling or Lay were never consulted until the business was up and running. By the time trading commenced 350 Enron employees had agreed to use the trading platform being offered. When Skilling was informed he was excited and soon rewarded those who spearheaded the development. Greg Whalley's boldness in building the Enron Online trading platform was celebrated in a Harvard Business School case on the 'Intrapreneur'. Sherif, one of the founding members of Enron Online, told the Harvard researcher, 'The overriding philosophy at Enron is if you are going to do something, don't dabble. Do it in a big way and do it fast' (McLean & Elkind 2003, p.222).

With this success traders saw it as the time to go generic. Soon steel, pulp, paper, lumber, freight and metal markets were being considered for the Enron Online treatment. This proliferation brought at least two problems:

- As Enron left behind energy markets it strayed into markets in which it had no informational advantage, often to face incumbents who certainly did know the market.
- Expansion in these markets stretched Enron's already threadbare capital base.

Enron International

If the rot began in ECT's trading of natural gas derivative contracts it was soon exported through all the business segments of Enron. If Skilling was promoting an 'asset-lite' business model for Enron his *bête noire*, Rebecca Mark, had a very different vision of where the company should go from her base in Enron International. Following the apparent success of the Teesside project, Mark was charged to replicate that success in emerging markets, especially South America, China and India.

As if the meteorological, technological and regulatory risks of the US natural gas markets were not bad enough, emerging markets in the mid-1990s were truly the final frontier. Despotic governments, inbred corruption and political instability made most companies wary of entering such markets unless aid agencies fully underwrote potential losses. Despite these concerns Mark marched Enron into a deal to construct an 1800-mile pipeline for $2 billion to pump gas from Santa Cruz, Bolivia to Porto Alegre, Brazil. As in the case of ECT executives within Enron International, Mark was rewarded on the basis of completed deals and their projected, not actual, cash-flows. Mark told a researcher from Harvard Business School:

> We are in the business of doing deals . . . this deal mentality is central to what we do

> (McLean & Elkind 2003, p.77)

The problem was that once the deal was done execution was deemed almost irrelevant and actual cash-flows often fell far below projections with little remedial action being taken. One example of how deal quality was allowed to slip became known as the 'snowball' within Enron.

Originally it was intended that spending resources on fruitless negotiations would be discouraged by insisting costs incurred on deals that were never signed were written off against the reported profits of Enron International. This gave Mark and her team a strong incentive to focus on doable deals, which would not damage their profits. Following the expenditure of $18 million on trying to build a power plant in Vietnam the project was cancelled, nevertheless the $18 million was booked as an asset in Enron International's accounts. Rich Kinder, the president and chief operating officer of Enron, who shared Skilling's dim view of Mark's abilities, insisted this 'snowball' of false assets stay below $90 million. Mark's status as one of Ken Lay's favourites meant nothing was done as the 'snowball' exceeded $200 million by the late 1990s.

Mark and the Dabhol Gas Plant Project

Mark's canonization was to occur in India, however, with the development of a gas plant in Dabhol besides the Arabian Sea, about 100 miles south of Mumbai in the Maharashtra province. This $20 billion project for a 2,015 megawatt gas plant, essentially in the middle of nowhere, required the provincial power company, the Maharashtra State Energy Board (MSEB), to buy 90% of the plant's power. From the start locals, including the novelist Arundhati Roy, strongly opposed the project seeing it as the rapacious intervention of an American multinational to rob poor Indian natives with government encouragement. Mark fought in the Indian courts for two years and by 1995 the project was cleared to go forward with $643 million in finance from a banking consortium headed by Bank of America. This was just in time to greet the incoming Hindu Nationalist Party who had been elected on a mandate to 'push Enron into the Arabian Sea'. In August 1995 the new government ordered building of the plant to cease causing Mark to exclaim, 'What we are experiencing here is every investor's worst nightmare...I am in grief'.

Amazingly Mark was able to rescue the project. While Rich Kinder called daily 8am crisis meetings in Houston to oversee the meltdown, Mark flew to India for six weeks. By February 1996 she had renegotiated the deal at a 20% reduction in the price Enron would receive for electricity supplied and (almost incredibly) a modest increase in the size of the already gargantuan project from a 2,015 to a 2,184 megawatt production capacity. This second condition seemed odd since no one seemed to be able to work out who would use all the electricity that Enron was generating in Dabhol.

Once again the way in which the executive compensation scheme was based on deal-flow and forecasts, rather than actual cash-flow, covered a multitude of Enron International's sins. In negotiating a $20 million bonus for the project team (a fairly decent slice for herself) for securing the Dabhol deal, Mark relied on estimates of 20% earnings growth. Today the Dabhol plant lies idle: a testimony to the misplaced optimism of those cash-flow projections.

Mark's Nemesis at Azurix

By July 1998 Rebecca Mark felt ready for a big challenge. She was still widely perceived as a possible successor to Lay, who it was thought might join the Bush administration (as Minister of Energy) any day. In stark contrast to Skilling's 'asset-lite' gospel for Enron's reconstruction, Mark targeted the water industry, one of the most heavily capitalized, government-regulated industries in existence. Enron entered the UK water industry with a £2.4 billion all-cash purchase of Wessex Water. This deal had two particularly unfortunate aspects. Firstly, it denied Enron the cash it so badly needed – so many of its activities produced only 'paper profits' that $2.4 billion was a punishing reduction in its cash-flow. Secondly, because Azurix was formed as a separate public company, its failure could not be hidden and it was the first open crack in the facade of Enron's never-ending success.

Because of the cash crisis within Enron the Azurix deal could only be funded via a little help from Fastow's Global Finance operation. For the Azurix purchase of Wessex Water Fastow created an SPE called Marlin. Marlin issued $1 billion in debt and $125 million in equity certificates[3] to institutional investors amongst Fastow's favourites. Once again the attraction of each of these instruments was the fact that they were underwritten against yielding losses by Enron itself. So it was clear to all investors if Azurix went down it was a problem for Enron, but they still got paid.

Some within Enron even believed Skilling had somewhat perversely set up his ex-lover Mark to fail in a very public way in order to pave the way for her removal. Skilling did not exactly crush this rumour by stating after Azurix's collapse:

> Azurix was in some ways – and I know this is going to sound terrible – probably good because it resolved discussion. It was absolutely clear it was not the way to go

> (McLean & Elkind 2003, p.246)

By this comment Skilling meant holding heavy assets was just pointless unless holding them gave you an informational advantage for trading purposes. This was the essence of his 'asset-lite' trading strategy.

The basic pitch used to launch Azurix was a re-run of Lay's rationalization for Enron's trading of natural gas. Privatization would deliver massive cost reductions. Certainly water was a huge $300 billion business worldwide and if Mark could crack it open the sky was the limit. Mark told reporters in March 1999, 'The only way to bring capital to solve the problem is to place it in private hands and increase accountability' (McLean & Elkind 2003, p.247). There certainly was a major social problem of water provision with the World Bank estimating over a billion people worldwide were denied easy access to clean, drinkable water.

Unfortunately for Mark the water industry already had two large well-capitalized French competitors present in the market: Vivenda and Suez Lyonnaise des Eaux. These companies were one part of Napoleon III's contribution to French civic life in the late nineteenth century. Mark's basic strategy was to 'Get Big Fast' and use cash-flow from acquired assets to fund further growth, but on every deal she had to compete head on with two French incumbents with a deeper capital base and well-established track records. Her competitors ran their acquisitions in a low-cost penny-pinching style that Mark was not known for and positively disliked. In the year before Enron's acquisition, Wessex Water's overhead was $29 million. In its first year under Mark this grew to $118 million. The reason for this was the truckload of MBA Enron clones she imported into the business, which had traditionally been run by dour experienced water industry men. This was going to be tricky to handle in an industry facing the introduction of rate regulation, given its history of very profitable monopoly provision.

In order to fund her ambitions Mark developed the idea of taking Azurix public as a separate company. This exposed Azurix to full public gaze and potentially humiliating exposure and collapse. The IPO was scheduled for 9 June 1999 and soon Mark was pounding the 'road-show' beat trying to convince fund managers to bid for shares in Azurix. Doing so was not easy because despite talking a big game Mark had not actually completed any deals for water provision since her acquisition of Wessex Water the year before.

During the pre-IPO road-show tour an opportunity emerged to bid for water provision directly to customers in the Buenos Aires province of Argentina. This was to be a 30-year contract to provide water to the whole of Buenos Aires containing over two million inhabitants and wastewater to part of it. By bidding $439 million Azurix won the contract just in time to boast about it at the IPO's close. The Azurix bid was three times more generous than the next competing offer, implying it may have been a bit hasty. The extent to which this was true soon became apparent when the Buenos Aires operation recorded a $11.6 million loss during the first six months of Azurix's ownership.

Amazingly, and in a strong testimony to Rebecca Mark's marketing skills, the IPO went well. Azurix floated on 9 June raising $700 million, while stock opened at $19 per share rising towards $25 within the month. This, despite a secret internal McKinsey report that Azurix was worth half that.

As further deals proved elusive and rate regulation was imposed on Wessex Water in the UK, Azurix's stock tumbled down towards $13 by late October 1999.

In a cruel twist of fate in April 2000 there was a bad case of water pollution and customer poisoning (from living algae in the water) in the city of Bahia Blanca, Buenos Aires. Although responsibility was hard to determine, Azurix certainly got the blame. On 8 August Azurix warned it would not be able to meet the third-quarter consensus forecast of its earnings. By mid-August Mark resigned and the Azurix escapade was over.

Rebecca Mark stepped out smelling of roses as usual. During the late 1990s she had sold over $80 million in Enron and Azurix stock. Her primary opponent Skilling was not to fare as well.

Turning Off the Lights in California

Surrounded by so much failure and loss it may appear amazing that Enron's implosion did not occur far earlier. That it did not may largely be explained by the huge profits made by Tim Belden and his Portland, Oregon, based trading team, from the deregulation of the Californian electricity market in the late 1990s. According to a Moody's presentation on the topic Belden's trading desk in Oregon generated more than $2 billion in cash from arbitrage trade during the California energy crisis (McLean & Elkind 2003, p.282). While this revelation was not designed to make Enron popular it is not clear whether Enron did anything illegal or simply ruthlessly exploited a fundamentally flawed system of supervisory re-regulation introduced in response to the deregulation of electricity prices in April 1998.

This deregulation process required the state's three main electricity providers – Pacific Gas & Electric, San Diego Gas & Electric and Southern California Edison – to sell off their electricity production capacity and buy electricity in the open market each day. The daily spot market was to operate under the watchful eye of two regulatory bodies. First, the California Power Exchange (Cal PX), which set hourly spot prices for electricity by means of organized auctions between suppliers and the three utility companies. Once the price was set, the second regulatory body, the Independent System Operator (ISO), ensured the reliability of supply to customers across the state. If electricity supply became 'congested', due to too much power flooding into a specific part of the state grid, then the ISO was empowered to pay any power company willing to relieve the blockage.

This latter rule turned out to be unfortunate because it simply led Tim Belden and his Oregon trading group to spend months reworking configurations of power supply that would overload the grid enough to bring it down. Belden's search finally converged on the Silverpeak terminal in the middle of the California desert. So it was on 24 May 1999 at 6am that Belden and his team delivered 2,900 megawatts of electricity to the remote Silverpeak terminal. Transmission out of Silverpeak could occur at a rate of only 15 megawatts and Belden's provision of electricity completely overwhelmed the station. The ISO in panic let spot prices of electricity rise by 70% to ease the congestion. This, the first of Belden's excursions into blackmailing the ISO, cost California $7 million and there was more to come.

Andrew Fastow and the Special-Purpose Entities

There is little doubt that Andrew Fastow became a convenient whipping-boy for those wishing to deny their own culpability in Enron's collapse. Skilling, for example, claimed in an amazing statement for a CEO, 'I'm not particularly interested in the balance-sheet. It seemed to be doing well. We always had money' (McLean & Elkind 2003, p.164). But it is equally true that Fastow was central to the conceit of Enron's 'walk-on-water' survival of the stock-market crash of early 2000.

Fastow arrived at Enron in 1990 having built expertise in securitization of debt, and especially clever financial structures to house them at Continental Bank. He had worked on the original Cactus and JEDI deals with Skilling to securitize ECT's trading contracts, but this type of job limited Fastow's personal income because finance and treasury management, as internal service functions, had no deal-flow and hence no bonuses associated with them.

When Fastow became CFO of Enron in 1998 he was determined to reap his true worth as he saw it. Fastow took charge of financial affairs at Enron just as some of the losses from previous speculative escapades were starting to bite. Enron needed cash and not just paper profits. Fastow pestered Skilling to go to the equity markets, which he finally agreed to, but Skilling was worried about the dilutive effect of issuing more equity for the share price. Issuing more debt was problematic too given the existing levels of leverage that were attracting critical press comment.

Fastow established the Global Finance group whose special mission was largely the creation of off-balance-sheet investment vehicles capable of bridging the funding gap in Enron's operations. By 2000 Global Finance was providing $20 billion a year in working capital to fund Enron's faltering operations. Indeed, Fastow himself often described his role within Enron as to 'feed the beast' (McLean & Elkind 2003, p.151). An internal memo by Joe Deffner, produced at the Special Investigation, noted that over the years 1995–2000 SPE transactions accounted for 56% of Enron's operating cash-flow.

Far from being clandestine about his basic strategy, Fastow both publicly boasted about it and was rewarded for doing so. On winning the 1999 CFO of the year award from *CFO Magazine*, he was lauded for 'thinking outside the box' and 'inventing a new ground-breaking strategy' for treasury management. Skilling commented (in slight tension with his view at the Senate Investigation): 'We needed someone to rethink the entire financial structure ....[Fastow] deserves every accolade tossed his way'.

Credit rating agencies knew about much of Enron's off-balance sheet debt, but Fastow made sure he kept some deals, especially those in which he had personally invested, only for the information of close associates. Two of the closest were Michael Kopper and Ben Glisan, his lieutenants in Global Finance.

A very important method of feeding the beast used by Fastow was the use of so-called 'prepays' to boost quarterly earnings. Here Enron agreed to deliver gas, oil or electricity to what was, at least for accounting purposes, an independent firm and Enron was paid for this up front (just in time for the announcement of quarterly earnings). In reality of course the sale was to a purpose-built, off-shore SPE set up by one of Enron's many lenders, so the money added to quarterly earnings was just increased debt, but it never appeared in the accounts! According to the Senate Investigations Committee Enron injected $8.6 billion in prepays from Chase Manhattan bank alone, for which Chase was paid $100 million in fees. Of course ultimately these prepay contracts had to honoured, which created more pressure to show cash rather than paper profits. Standard & Poor analysts were to later claim that they did not know about the prepays and if they did they would have certainly downgraded Enron's bonds from their BBB rating to junk status (McLean & Elkind 2003, p.237).

The highly lucrative nature of investment banking services to Enron meant few financial institutions wished to rock the boat. Fastow understood this well and always played off financial institutions against each other for Enron's and his own well-being. While investment banking and investment research are in theory separated by 'Chinese walls', in reality these walls can be pretty thin. I study analysts' conflicts of interest in a separate chapter, but with this much money on offer few analysts took the time or effort to raise awkward questions and any that did were heavily leant on. Fastow even ranked Global Finance's stable of banking partners Tier 1 through 3. Tier 1 banks got the best deals, but had to be willing to underwrite loans of up to $1 billion at short notice.

A key element of every deal Global Finance did was how much Fastow himself and his most intimate team got out of it. He even approached Ron Astin at Enron's lawyers Vinson and Elkins about setting up a separate partnership for him and his wife Lea to invest in Enron deals. Both Astin and Skilling were nervous and Fastow backed off. As an alternative from the early 1990s Fastow used a rosta called the Friends of Enron (mainly Fastow cronies) to provide the 3% independent equity stake in the dizzying array of SPEs he was in the process of setting up. Since Enron underwrote investments made in the 'independent' SPEs this was a no downside investment risk (until the game was up and Enron folded).

The ultimate impact of all of this on Enron's viability as a going concern was well understood, at least by Fastow himself. On being quizzed by a colleague about what would happen to his escalating pyramid of SPEs if Enron ceased to grow and could no longer settle past pre-payment bills as they matured by issuing new pre-payment contracts, Fastow answered, 'It implodes' (McLean & Elkind 2003, p.151) and this it duly did in 2001.

Gambling for Resurrection in Electricity and Broadband Markets

It is in the nature of equity investment that when the prospect of liquidation looms large projects with big upside risk, even at the cost of a terminal downside, start to look attractive. Financial theorists term such strategies as 'gambling for resurrection' in a potentially critical situation or 'going for broke'.

Jeff Skilling now adopted such strategies with relish. For a long time Enron's diversification strategy had been taking them out of the oil and natural gas markets into the wholesale electricity market. Enron became a 'market-maker' arbitraging between what electricity providers would sell at and the retail supply chain would buy at. Skilling's next move was potentially a masterstroke. He would simply remove one element in the chain. Enron would now present itself as a complete 'energy solution' to end-users. He planned to do this by forming a new Enron subsidiary, Enron Energy Services (EES), headed by none other than Lou Pai. Just as many major corporations contract out management of their information system, or catering needs, to concentrate on their own 'core competences' they could now let Enron keep the lights on while they focused on their principal line of business. EES's pitch was 'You go focus on building your widgets, and we'll worry about the energy side of the business. We're the energy experts' (McLean & Elkind 2003, p.177). Owens Corning, the University of California, Chase Manhattan Bank and many others soon answered the call. The problem once again was execution. Enron simply knew nothing about changing light-bulbs, energy conservation and a host of other essentials such a business requires. They could not even get the billing right. The University of California delayed reimbursement to Enron of its electricity bill for 18 months until they claimed a credible amount. This meant Enron was giving interest-free loans to a public body. Having signed off deals at a 5% to 15% discount on the company's prior energy bill, Enron did little to conserve energy or otherwise recoup cost.

The main reason why nobody bothered about performing on the contracts signed is that once again marking to market meant the cash-flow from the contract could appear in earnings the day it was signed. But this time aggressive recognition of earnings would not be enough for Pai. He wanted to be able to recognize revenue, without costs entering the performance metric at all. To do this Tom White, his deputy, devised a new performance metric to parade to analysts each quarter, the 'total contract value'. Total contract value was the discounted value of all cash-flows that EES expected to receive on the contracts signed. It bore no resemblance to earnings, net present value, or any other accepted corporate valuation method.

But total contract values certainly gave EES the impression of a highly successful new enterprise. In 1998 Enron announced it had contracts with a 'total value' of $3.8 billion and by the end of 1999 this claimed value grew to $8.5 billion. Of course, many analysts preferred the earning metric they knew and loved and remained unmoved by an essentially discounted revenue measure of performance. For such diehards Skilling promised that EES would become profitable by the turn of 2000. Further, to make sure the EES contract team understood the score he issued a memo to EES staff in February 1999, 'Q4 EBIT Positive is Nonnegotiable. We have a gap – and it must be filled... We must change the way we operate NOW' (McLean & Elkind 2003, p.182).

This created incredible pressure to do deals at any cost and be creative with pricing the contracts. EES was not even constrained to use the same pricing assumptions regarding future electricity and gas prices as those trading in the wholesale market within Enron. Few checks and intense pressure to deliver profits meant modelling contract value ceased to be guess and became little more than an expression of hope. Both Skilling and Pai held large phantom equity stakes in EES and far from questioning the illusion of value creation they had every incentive to encourage its growth.

Meanwhile life was sweet aboard the doomed ship Enron. According to a study by the Joint Committee on Taxation, the top 200 Enron executives together cleared $193 million in salaries and bonuses in 1998, this rose to $402 million, finally in 2000 every one of the top 200 Enron officers earned more than $1 million each (McLean & Elkind 2003, p.241). Failure had never tasted so good.

LJM1 and Fastow's Compromised Position

The Power's report on the demise of Enron lists the proximate cause of Enron's collapse as being undisclosed transactions with SPEs created by Andrew Fastow, in particular Chewco, named after a *Star Wars*' character, and LJM1 and 2 named after Fastow's wife Lea and their two sons Jeffrey and Matthew.

As stated before Fastow had long desired to put his own money into the SPEs that Enron was founding and earn himself a tidy profit. Up to now even Enron's weak internal controls had frustrated him in this desire, but in May 1999 the profit on an Enron venture-capital investment, Rhythms NetConnections, gave him a new opportunity to justify his investment. During the Internet bubble the $10 million investment had yielded a stake worth $300 million at Rhythm's IPO. In fact Enron still needed to wait out the 'quiet period' after the IPO to sell its shares, given that it was represented on Rhythm's board of directors. In mid-1999 Internet stocks were clearly very frothy and prone to sudden decline if not implosion. Skilling was concerned about getting his $300 million payoff up front before the bubble burst. He called meetings to solicit solutions to the jam Enron found itself in.

Fastow's road to the rescue was with LJM1 (or LJM Cayman), an SPE he founded with $1 million of his own cash plus $15 million from two outside investors. These were drawn from the ranks of its Tier 1 trusted banks, with Chase Manhattan and a British bank, NatWest, bringing the opportunity to invest in Fastow's pet project. A subsidiary of LJM1 entitled Swap Sub would provide a put option to Enron to unload its holding at a price of $56 per share. Given that Rhythm's stock traded at $69 at the close of the day of its IPO, this covered at least the worst part of any of Enron's losses due to the Internet bubble bursting. In return for this service Enron was to issue LJM1 with 3.4 million of its own shares, worth about $276 million at the date of issue. The stock was actually issued in a restricted form (restricting to whom it could be sold) and so was sold at a 40% discount on the market price. The underlying economic risk of the capital gain it held in Rhythm declining was now hedged against its own stock price. Since its own price would decline if Rhythm tanked, this was in reality a hedge with no economic purpose or effect. The sole purpose of the transaction was to allow Enron to realize that part of its capital gain locked into by the put option (the difference between its stake sold at $56 per share and the $10 million purchase price) immediately.

The head of Enron's research group, Vince Kaminski, immediately saw through to the heart of the transaction and the conflict of interest it entailed for Fastow. The deal's terms required it to be 'heads the partnership wins, tails Enron loses' (McLean & Elkind 2003, p.192). If the put went out of the money LJM1 swallowed $260 million for nothing, if Rhythm's price fell Enron's share price would collapse anyway since it had already booked the profit and diluted its shareholding by issuing 3.4 million shares to LJM1.

Enron even had the foresight to put controls in place to prevent this sort of abuse of power by its employees. Enron's Code of Ethics forbade employees from profiting from other companies engaged in business dealings with Enron. Fastow brought the LJM1 SPE vehicle and its role in hedging the Rhythm shareholding to the board of directors for approval. He assured the board that the requisite hedge would be provided by LJM1 'at no cost to Enron' beyond a payment to him of a half-million dollars a year management fee. Amazingly, the Enron board authorized the transaction and gave Fastow exemption from Enron's Code of Ethics to undertake it. Fortunately the Internet bubble kept swelling during 1999 and soon LJM1 sat on large capital gains on its 3.4 million shares in Enron. Despite the assurances given to the board, Fastow swiftly set about setting up yet further SPEs to distribute profits to those involved in setting up LJM1. In July 2000 a trust created for the benefit of Fastow's family received a distribution of $18 million from LJM1. Fastow was now sitting on both sides of the transaction with Enron shareholders raking in millions in profits and fees. Fastow found this position a nice place to be and soon set about replicating LJM1 activities on an enormous scale.

LJM2: the Final Chapter

LJM1 was to be a training exercise for Fastow before getting started on some serious looting of Enron via LJM2. LJM2 opened up the SPE to a far wider range of investors to create a more powerful investment vehicle. Now Fastow sought permission to establish a fund of $200 million, but which actually attracted funding of nearly $400 million from 51 separate investment institutions. In attracting investors Fastow openly boasted how they could expect to benefit from his 'familiarity with Enron's assets and understanding of Enron's objectives' (McLean & Elkind 2003, p.198). The implication was that Fastow would cherry-pick Enron's portfolio pushing the best deals LJM2's way.

In reality the principal purpose of LJM2 was earnings management for Enron. The worst dogs in the Enron portfolio, surplus-to-requirements power plant turbines off the Nigerian coast and other dross, were all sold on LJM2. Indeed this was clearly understood by LJM2 participants. A Citigroup executive representing his bank within the SPE explained to a colleague:

> LJM2 principals argue that Enron would make the fund whole should it suffer losses because the vehicles the fund invests in are critically important to Enron's earnings management

> (McLean & Elkind 2003, p.205).

Even then it promised participants a 30% rate of return, with 2% of the fund's value going to Fastow. He even hinted that LJM2 could be a lead into a completely separate investment vehicle headed by Fastow after he left Enron.

In a similar vein the court-appointed bankruptcy examiner for Enron concluded many of LJM2's business dealings 'had no valid business purpose from Enron's perspective other than to achieve desired financial statement reporting targets'. And indeed the pressure to deliver was intense. Enron's stock rose 55% in 1999 alone. Under a long-term incentive plan (LTIP) if Enron's share-price performance, averaged over the years 1997–2001, was amongst the top six performers in the S&P500 this triggered payment of a substantial bonus to all the senior management team at Enron. If failure had ever been an option that option was unthinkable to Enron insiders now. True enough LJM2's deals did turn up trumps for its participants. Of LJM2's 23 deals by the date of liquidation 21 were with Enron itself. All 21 made profits for LJM2's partners, $85.3 million in all. If there was any downside risk borne by LJM2 in these deals it never manifested itself until the Enron stock, in which it was often paid, was rendered worthless.

Case Study Overview

Enron shows how accounting practice can massively impact on corporate valuations. Finance texts often guide us that smart investors 'see through' accounting manipulations to true discounted cash-flow or 'true value'. Even if they do so their personal motivations may be more aligned with their own compensation contract which is often based on earnings, not cash-flow targets. In reality few, if any, investors or commentators could honestly claim to have 'seen through' the labyrinth of SPEs Fastow constructed to hide away Enron's debt burden. Despite standard finance assumptions it appears we are just not that smart. Looking at the tree diagrams of interlocking SPE structures Fastow constructed I cannot honestly claim to personally understand how the scheme worked even now. If the key drivers of the deception realized ultimate implosion was inevitable, they may have relied on the 'greater fool' theory to believe they could jump ship before the iceberg hit. After all Skilling and Pai did abandon ship and Pai walked away a free and very wealthy man. So 'accounting matters' and radical reform, like the shift to mark-to-market accounting proposed by the IASC, should be judged in light of the human frailties in decision making that the collapse of Enron exposed.

Appendix B: Solving for Price in Terms of Abnormal Earnings and Non-Accounting Information only (Equation (19.7))

My treatment is based on Appendix 1 to Ohlson (1995, p. 682). We begin with Equations (19.5), (19.2) and (19.6)

$$P_t = y_t + \sum_{\tau=1}^{T} R^{-\tau} E\left[x_{t+\tau} - (R_f - 1)y_{t+\tau-1}\right]$$

$$b_t = b_{t-1} + x_t - d_t \quad CSR$$

$$x_{t+1}^a = \omega x_t^a + v_t + \varepsilon_{1t+1}$$

$$v_{t+1} = \gamma v_t + \varepsilon_{2t+1} \quad LID$$

Let **P** be defined as a two-by-two matrix of the form

$$\mathbf{P} = \frac{1}{R_f}\begin{bmatrix} \omega & 1 \\ 0 & \gamma \end{bmatrix}$$

which allows us to more concisely express the LID of equation (1.6) to read

$$\left(\tilde{x}^a_{t+1}, \tilde{v}_t\right) = R_f \mathbf{P}\left(x^a_t, v_t\right) + \left(\tilde{\varepsilon}_{1t+1}, \tilde{\varepsilon}_{2t+1}\right)$$

and the basic valuation equation of Equation (1.5) to read

$$R_f^{-\tau} E\left[\tilde{x}^a_{t+\tau}\right] = (1,0)\mathbf{P}^\tau \left(x^a_t, v_t\right)$$

which implies a solution for goodwill, the difference between current price and reported book value per share, of the form

$$P_t - b_t = \sum_{\tau=1}^{\infty} R_f^{-\tau} E_t\left[\tilde{x}^a_{t+\tau}\right] = (1,0)\left[\mathbf{P} + \mathbf{P}^2 + \ldots\right]\left(x^a_t, v_t\right) \equiv (\alpha_1, \alpha_2)\left(x^a_t, v_t\right)$$

Note that the sum of the infinite series $[\mathbf{P} + \mathbf{P}^2 + \ldots]$ sums to $\mathbf{P}[\mathbf{I} - \mathbf{P}] - 1$. This is the result of its characteristic root being less than unity. Recall the characteristic root of the matrix $\mathbf{P}$ is defined by the condition

$$(\mathbf{P} - r\mathbf{I}) = 0$$

This matrix expression generalizes the scalar solution to a polynomial expansion of a number less than one in value. To see this, consider a polynomial expression for the value of a third. We have

$$x + x^2 + x^3 + x^4 + x^5 + \ldots$$

For a value of a third is

$$0.333 + 0.111 + 0.0347 + 0.012 + 0.004 + 0.001 + \ldots \approx 0.5$$

and

$$0.333/(1 - 0.333) = 0.333/0.666 = 0.5.$$

Applying this rule to the matrix $\mathbf{P}$ reduces to the condition

$$\frac{(1-\omega)-r}{R_f} \cdot \frac{(1-\gamma)-r}{R_f}$$

$$\frac{r^2 + (1-\omega)r + (1-\gamma)r + (1-\omega)(1-\gamma)}{R_f^2} = 0$$

where this expression must have two roots, one or both of which may be imaginary but all of which are less than one given the value of $\omega\gamma$.

We have the expression $(\alpha_1, \alpha_2) = (1,0)\mathbf{P}.[\mathbf{I} - \mathbf{P}]^{-1}$ where $[\mathbf{I} - P]$ is given by

$$[\mathbf{I} - \mathbf{P}] = \frac{1}{R_f}\left[\begin{bmatrix} 1 & 0 \\ 0 & 1 \end{bmatrix} - \begin{bmatrix} \omega & 1 \\ 0 & \gamma \end{bmatrix}\right] = \begin{bmatrix} \dfrac{(1-\omega)}{R_f} & \dfrac{-1}{R_f} \\ 0 & \dfrac{(1-\gamma)}{R_f} \end{bmatrix}$$

and we need to remember the procedure for matrix inversion at this point from some long-lost quantitative methods class lecture notes. Lipschutz and Lipson (2001. p.36) outline the procedure as three stages as follows:

1. Interchange the two elements of the principal diagonal of the matrix to be inverted.
2. Take the negatives of the off-diagonal elements of the matrix to be inverted.
3. Multiply the resulting matrix by the inverse of its determinant (the sum of the products of the principal and off-diagonal elements) $1/|A|$

If the determinant of the matrix P is equal to zero, $|A| = 0$, then P has no inverse and is said to be a 'singular' matrix.

Applying this reasoning we obtain

$$|P| = \frac{1}{R_f}[(1 - \omega)(1 - \gamma) + 1.0] = \frac{1}{R_f}(1 - \omega)(1 - \gamma)$$

$$\frac{1}{\frac{1}{R_f}(1 - \omega)(1 - \gamma)} \begin{bmatrix} \frac{(1 - \gamma)}{R_f} & 1 \\ 0 & \frac{(1 - \omega)}{R_f} \end{bmatrix}$$

Questions

1. Return to the illustration of the Ohlson model and the workings of the LID provided by Lundholm (1995). Now assume you invest £10 at an expected risk-free rate of return of 15%. The company will pay a dividend at date 1 of £2 and a liquidating dividend at date 2 of £3. Value your investment at date 0, 1 and 2 under historic cost and mark-to-market, fair-value accounting.
2. Return to the Ohlson residual income valuation model of Equations (19.1) to (19.5) above. The following data is for Google Inc:

	2003	2004	2005	2006	2007
Earnings per share	0.77	2.07	1	0.49	1.2
Dividends per share	0	0	0	0	0

Assume an opening book value of $10 per share in 2003 and a discount rate of 12.5%. What price would you expect Google to trade at in 2003 if the Ohlson–Feltham residual income valuation model (as described by Equations (19.1) to (19.5)) holds? Hint: begin by calculating clean-surplus book values in 2004 to 2007 (so you can make the capital changes to construct measures of future residual income).
3. Read Appendix A. What was the role of mark-to-market accounting in Enron's downfall?

Notes

1. From Plantin, G., H. Sapra & H. Song Shin (2007). Reproduced by permission of Blackwell Publishing.
2. Unless otherwise stated the material in this section comes from McLean and Elkind (2003).
3. Equity paying a fixed return.

References

Benston, G. & A. Hargraves (2002). Enron: what happened and what can we learn from it? *Journal of Accounting and Public Policy*, **21**: 105–27.

Dechow, P., A. Hutton & R. Sloan (1999). An empirical assessment of the residual income valuation model. *Journal of Accounting and Economics*, **26**: 1–34.

Edwards, E. & P. Bell (1961). *The Theory and Measurement of Business Income*. Berkeley: University of California Press.

Feltham, G. & J. Ohlson (1995). Valuation and clean-surplus accounting for operating and financial activities. *Contemporary Accounting Review*, **11**: 689–711.

Graham, B., D. Dodd & S. Cotterhill (1962). *Security Analysis: Principles and Techniques*. New York: McGraw-Hill.

Healy, P. & K. Palepu (2003). The fall of Enron. *Journal of Economic Perspectives*, **17**: 3–26.

Jackson, P. & D. Lodge (2000). Fair value accounting: capital standards, expected loss provisioning and financial stability. *Bank of England Financial Stability Review*, **8**: 105–25.

Lee, C. & B. Swaminathan (1999). Valuing the Dow: a bottom-up approach, *Financial Analysts Journal*, **55**: 4–23.

Lee, C., J. Myers & B. Swaminathan (1999). What is the intrinsic value of the Dow? *Journal of Finance*, **54**: 1693–741.

Lipschutz, S. & M. Lipson (2001). *Schaum's Outline of the Theory and Problems of Linear Algebra*. New York: McGraw-Hill.

Lundholm, R. (1995). A tutorial on the Feltham–Ohlson valuation models: answers to some frequently asked questions. *Contemporary Accounting Review*, **11**: 749–61.

McLean, B. & P. Elkind (2003). *The Smartest Guys in the Room: The Amazing Rise and Scandalous Fall of Enron*. New York: Portfolio.

Modigliani, F. & M. Miller (1961). Dividend policy, growth and the valuation of shares. *Journal of Business*, **34**: 411–33.

Ohlson, J. (1995). Earnings, book values and dividends in equity. *Contemporary Accounting Review*, **11**: 661–87.

Ohlson, J. (2005). On accounting-based valuation formula. *Review of Accounting Studies*, **10**: 323–47.

Ohlson, J. & B. Jeuttner-Nauroth (2005). Expected EPS and EPS growth as determinants of value. *Review of Accounting Studies*, **10**: 349–65.

Penman, S. (1992). Return to fundamentals. *Journal of Accounting, Auditing and Finance*, **7**: 465–83.

Penman, S. (2006). *Financial Reporting Quality: Is Fair Value a Plus or a Minus? Information for Better Markets*. London: Institute of Chartered Accountants of England and Wales.

Plantin, G., H. Sapra & H. Song Shin (2007). Marking to market: panacea or Pandora's box? *Journal of Accounting Research*, **46**(2): 435–60.

Powers, W. (2002). Report of Investigation by the Special Investigative Committee of the Board of Directors, Enron.

Spector, R. (2000). *Amazon.com: Get Big Fast*. New York: HarperBusiness.

Chapter 20

Conclusion

I began Chapter 1 by quoting Richard Thaler as saying behavioural finance would have succeeded when it was just an ordinary part of finance, taking its place alongside corporate, personal, market microstructure financial models, etc. All finance invokes behavioural assumptions, so the only question is, Which assumptions are best?

I write this conclusion as the financial markets of the world implode with $700 billion and £50 billion 'bailout' plans in the United States and the United Kingdom, respectively. It has never been a better time to rethink the fundamentals of our understanding of how financial markets work. The most credible path to work towards such a rebuild is by enhancing and enriching the existing corpus of theory. The road ahead is evolutionary not revolutionary and we should be inspired, rather than frustrated, by that.

This text has identified at least two central elements to the evolution of standard theory:

- A renewed interest in those who trade for reasons unrelated to changes in the fundamental value of the asset, that is 'noise', or liquidity traders. We cannot simply assume such investors die out, but equally conditions need to be laid down and tested for their survival. If they survive, how do they survive and how could they win converts to their cause?
- The investor's divided nature as he struggles for self-command of his future self today. The most obvious manifestation of this phenomenon is setting the appropriate discount rate for future payoffs, but it may also explain commitment to heroic, but very worthwhile, projects, for example, going to the moon or unravelling the sequence of DNA. Perhaps only those foolish enough to underestimate the scale of the task can perform such amazing feats.

My book has largely followed the usual textbook format of considering a bias or heuristic in each chapter, so Chapter 9 is about overreaction, but Chapter 7 is about optimism. In reality financial decisions are most probably the product of multiple, possibly conflicting, biases and heuristics, for example, the equity premium puzzle reflects a 'prospect theory' utility function, but also a short-term investment evaluation horizon; entrepreneurs exhibit optimism to offset the hyperbolic discounting of future rewards (as discussed in Chapter 17).

This latter example illustrates an important point. The presence of biases or the use of heuristics is not necessarily a bad or 'irrational' thing. The same impulsive 'fight-or-flight' response that saves me from the opportunistic mugger underlies my overreaction to changes in financial circumstances. I perceive the need to 'do something' which is hardwired into me by my ancestors hunting game on the plains of the savannah. Fortunately, I 'don't need to think' before reaching out to support a child falling from its mother's arms or to remove my hand from a hot surface.

Recognizing the role of bias and heuristics in financial decision making should not be seen as an irritating concession to a dreary need to be 'relevant' in our teaching or research. An interest in the quirks of human nature, characterized by work of the subject's founding fathers – Adam Smith, William Stanley Jevons – has only fairly recently been jettisoned in favour of a possible 'rigour' in theorizing financial decision making. But Adam Smith, if he knew what we know about the function-ing of our minds, and the close relation between emotion and reason in decision making, may not have started off as he did. Finance, like us, is a product of childhood for better or worse. As we learn more about our own cognitive processes we need to set aside childish things in favour of an understanding of financial decision making based on a more informed view about how our minds actually work.

Such a new understanding needs to be incorporated into the current research programme of building explicit models, with testable and potentially refutable hypotheses. It is not enough to claim that investors may be loss averse or short term in their evaluation of future payoffs without ever being able to determine whether they are or not. To do so is to yield to the temptation to invoke behavioural aspects of decision making as a 'get out of jail free card'. When all else fails just throw your hands up and say investors are stupid or merely bad people. Our choice should not be between rigour and recognition of the messy realities of human cognition; it should rather be the development of coherent theories of how investors handle the cognitive processes required of them.

I hope that this textbook in emphasizing theory over illustrative 'stories' has gone some way to facilitating this task. Part I gives some building blocks from which this new theory appears to be now emerging. Parts II, III and IV illustrate how this theory is being applied to various areas of finance.

In one sense the behavioural approach has been an understandable response to the crisis in the legitimacy of academic perspectives on finance. Those brave enough to appear before television during the recent financial meltdown (of October 2008) looked almost as agog as the 'common man' who now seemed to be rendered wiser by an awareness of his own ignorance. Hong and Stein (1999, p.2143)* explain the genesis of the behavioural approach in these terms:

> As an alternative to these traditional models, many are turning to behavioural theories, where behavioural assumptions can be broadly construed as involving some departure from the classical assumptions of strict rationality and unlimited computational capacity on the part of investors. But the difficulty with this approach is that there is a potentially huge number of such departures that one might entertain, so it is hard to know where to start.

My book has been very largely concerned with this ameliorative/sticking plaster role for beha-vioural finance as it plugs various gaps in standard theory. Why is the return to equity so high? Why do winners become losers and losers become winners? Why are people crazy enough to manufacture products for which there is unknown demand, and which may simply never work anyway?

Behavioural finance will ultimately have to leave behind the role of being a patch-up job on standard theory if it is to gain true respectability for itself. The ultimate aim of a behavioural approach is to create new knowledge and not simply critique existing knowledge. Daniel *et al.* (1998) pick up on this point when they state:

> To deserve consideration a theory should be parsimonious, explain a range of anomalous patterns in different contexts, and generate new empirical implications.

The future of behavioural finance is to raise new issues that might not even be considered issues by standard theory. Indeed this process of mapping out a specifically behavioural set of economic issues has already begun. Perhaps this trend is best exemplified by the policy prescriptions offered by behavioural researchers like Professor Cass Sunstein of Harvard Law School and Professor Richard Thaler of Chicago Business School (see Sunstein 2007 and Thaler & Sunstein 2008).

Sunstein has pointed out the difference in response across two catastrophic 'worse-case scenarios' that the government must face on the electorate's behalf. In the case of terrorism the state has introduced radical changes in law, including permitting the use of investigative methods (at the least) bordering on torture and prolonged periods of unaccountable detention. The motivation for this has been the fear of another terrorist outrage and further mass murder of the innocent. Conversely, despite the equally horrendous prospect of catastrophic climate change, with London disappearing under water, it appears the government has done remarkably little. Given that terrorism and climate change involve similar low probabilities of horrific loss of life we might expect similar responses to both these threats. But while the problems might be similar, the way in which the political process frames them might be very different. Thaler and Sunstein (2008) point out that if framing can affect social choices maybe the role of a 'liberal paternalist' is to frame our choices appropriately when we choose whether to smoke, invest for our retirement, etc. In this way a distinctively behavioural approach to economic and social policy is now being forged.

When I wrote Chapter 5 of this book it was 'just history', a few interesting stories about those foolish enough to pay a fortune for a tulip bulb, or to be seduced by the dot.com gold rush. I write this conclusion as we 'live the history' of the bank bailouts and nationalizations of late 2008. In this tumultuous age the behavioural approach may find a sympathetic audience. If it does I hope this book encourages those inspired to undertake a study of this new area of research.

Note

* Hong, H. and J. Stein (1999). Quote from p. 2143. Reproduced by permission of Blackwell Publishing.

References

Daniel, K., D. Hirshleifer *et al.* (1998). Investor psychology and security market under- and overreaction. *Journal of Finance*, 52(3): 1–33.

Hong, H. & J. Stein (1999). A unified theory of underreaction, momentum, trading and overreaction in assets markets. *Journal of Finance*, 54: 2143–84.

Sunstein, C. (2007). *Worse-Case Scenarios*. Cambridge, MA: Harvard University Press.

Thaler, R. & C. Sunstein (2008). *Nudge: Improving Decisions about Health, Wealth and Happiness*. Michigan: Caravan Books.

Index

This index was prepared by Neil Manley.